KT-371-013

Marketing Plans
Seventh Edition

WITHDRAWN
FROM THE LIBRARY OF
UNIVERSITY OF ULSTER

100578398

Marketing Plans

How to Prepare Them, How to Use Them

Seventh Edition

Malcolm McDonald
Hugh Wilson

WILEY

A John Wiley and Sons, Ltd, Publication

100578398

658.
802
MAC

This edition first published 2011
© 2011 Malcolm McDonald and Hugh Wilson

Registered office

John Wiley & Sons Ltd, The Atrium, Southern Gate, Chichester, West Sussex, PO19 8SQ, United
Kingdom

For details of our global editorial offices, for customer services and for information about how to
apply for permission to reuse the copyright material in this book please see our website at
www.wiley.com.

The right of the author to be identified as the author of this work has been asserted in accordance
with the Copyright, Designs and Patents Act 1988.

All rights reserved. No part of this publication may be reproduced, stored in a retrieval system, or
transmitted, in any form or by any means, electronic, mechanical, photocopying, recording or
otherwise, except as permitted by the UK Copyright, Designs and Patents Act 1988, without the
prior permission of the publisher.

Wiley also publishes its books in a variety of electronic formats. Some content that appears in print
may not be available in electronic books.

Designations used by companies to distinguish their products are often claimed as trademarks. All
brand names and product names used in this book are trade names, service marks, trademarks or
registered trademarks of their respective owners. The publisher is not associated with any product
or vendor mentioned in this book. This publication is designed to provide accurate and authorita-
tive information in regard to the subject matter covered. It is sold on the understanding that the
publisher is not engaged in rendering professional services. If professional advice or other expert
assistance is required, the services of a competent professional should be sought.

Library of Congress Cataloging-in-Publication Data

McDonald, Malcolm.
    Marketing plans : how to prepare them, how to use them / Malcolm McDonald, Hugh
Wilson.   —7th ed.
     p. cm.
    Includes bibliographical references and index.
     ISBN 978-0-470-66997-6 (pbk.)
     1. Marketing—Management.   2. Marketing—Planning.   I. Wilson, Hugh, 1962-   II. Title.
  HF5415.13.M255 2011
  658.8′02—dc22

                     2010050393

A catalogue record for this book is available from the British Library.

ISBN 978-0-470-66997-6 (paperback), ISBN 978-0-470-67016-3 (ebk),
ISBN 978-0-470-67012-5 (ebk), ISBN 978-0-470-67011-8 (ebk)

Set in 9/11pt ITC Garamond by MPS Limited, a Macmillan Company, Chennai, India
Printed in Italy by Printer Trento, Italy

Contents

Preface and acknowledgements

Please read this as it contains important information about this book.

The importance of marketing planning is demonstrated by the half million copies of this book which have been sold in English and many other languages since it was first published in 1984.

Since the book's launch, it has helped and encouraged hundreds of thousands of practising managers with the difficult task of marketing planning. Many of them have been kind enough to write expressing their thanks for the book's practical, no-nonsense style and approach to the subject. This has encouraged the first author, Malcolm McDonald, to update the book continually in previous editions, and in this edition to ask his esteemed colleague Professor Hugh Wilson to join him as co-author. Originally a computer scientist, Hugh brings to the book deep experience in the latest thinking on marketing in a digital world, including integrated marketing communications, e-commerce, multichannel strategy and CRM. The authors have been working together on how to evolve marketing planning in a digital world for over 20 years.

The purpose of this book is quite simply to explain and demonstrate how to prepare and use a marketing plan. It is equally relevant for consumer, service and industrial goods companies, as well as not-for-profit organizations, since the process is universal.

It is based on our research into the marketing planning practices of industrial, service and retail companies, which has revealed marketing planning as an area of major weakness. Almost without exception, companies that thought they were planning were in fact only forecasting and budgeting, and suffered grave operational difficulties as a result. The problem, as companies face up to the opportunities and challenges of the twenty-first century is not that the *philosophy* of marketing is not believed; rather it is that most companies, particularly industrial goods companies and many service organizations, have difficulty in making it work.

This is largely because of ignorance about the process of planning their marketing activities, for which little help is provided in the extant body of literature. Books or articles often turn out to be about the management of the several elements of the marketing mix rather than about how the process of combining them into a coherent plan can be managed. Others treat marketing planning in such a generalized way that it is difficult to distil from them any guidance of operational significance. Finally, there are many excellent papers about individual aspects of the marketing planning process.

The truth is, of course, that the actual *process* of marketing planning is simple in outline. Any book will tell us that it consists of: a situation review; assumptions; objectives; strategies; programmes; and measurement and review. What other books *do not* tell us is that there are a number of contextual issues that have to be considered that make marketing planning one of the most baffling of all management problems.

Here are some of those issues:

- *When* should it be done, *how often*, by *whom*, and *how*?
- Is it different in a *large* and a *small* company?
- Is it different in a *diversified* and an *undiversified* company?
- Is it different in an *international* and a *domestic* company?

- What is the role of the *chief executive*?
- What is the role of the *planning department*?
- Should marketing planning be *top-down* or *bottom-up*?
- What is the relationship between *operational* (one year) and *strategic* (longer term) planning?

Since effective marketing planning lies at the heart of a company's revenue-earning activities, it is not surprising that there is a great demand for a guide which strips away the confusion and mystery surrounding this subject and helps firms to get to grips with it in a practical and down-to-earth manner.

This book explains what marketing is, how the marketing planning process works, how to carry out a marketing audit, how to set marketing objectives and strategies, how to schedule and cost out what has to be done to achieve the objectives, and how to design and implement a simple marketing planning system.

Our approach is both logical and practical. This view has been confirmed by the hundreds of letters referred to above, and by the fact that this book is now a standard text on many marketing courses in universities, and in-company training programmes around the world.

This book includes:

- Application questions, to help you personalise the learning
- Exercises at the end of every chapter to enable practising managers to translate the theory into practice
- Mini case studies to exemplify the points being made
- A step-by-step process, with templates, for producing marketing plans

Additionally, a comprehensive online Tutors' Guide is available for those who wish to teach the subject to others. This Tutors' Guide contains lecture plans, PowerPoint masters, case studies, tutors' discussion points and additional assignments for use by tutors. Please visit www.marketingplansbook.com.

We should like to thank our friends and colleagues for the advice they have given us and material they have generously allowed us to use during the life of this book. To the following we are especially grateful: Dr Chris Bailey, Dr Krista Bondy, Lindsay Bruce, Professor Martin Christopher, Professor Moira Clark, Professor Elizabeth Daniel, Dr Iain Davies, Matt Hobbs, Professor Aamir Khan, Ardi Kolch, John Leppard, Dr Emma Macdonald, Professor Simon Majaro, Dr Stan Maklan, Anne Mollen, Aly Moore, Peter Mouncey, Professor Adrian Payne, Beth Rogers, Professor Lynette Ryals, Dr Brian Smith, Rod Street and Diana Woodburn. To them and the many other scholars and practitioners who have contributed invaluable ideas in specific sections we will always be grateful. Rather than updating the flow of the text by providing complete individual references, we restrict ourselves to a few references at the end of each chapter. For fuller bibliographies, please see the PhD research on which this book is primarily based: details are available from m.mcdonald@cranfield.ac.uk or hugh.wilson@cranfield.ac.uk.

Professor Malcolm McDonald
Professor Hugh Wilson
Cranfield University School of Management
February 2011

How to use this book to achieve the best results

At the end of each chapter, you will find a number of application questions. More importantly, there are also a number of exercises designed to help you translate the theory into practice in the context of your own organization.

As you work through this book, you will find that some of the exercises are diagnostic and enable you to 'plot' where your company is. Some will help you to understand what might be happening to your organization. Other exercises are more concerned with generating factual information about your organization, its products, its markets or its planning processes. We find this combination of exercises not only provides you with insights and learning about many aspects of marketing planning, but it also helps you to assemble information which can contribute to a marketing plan for your organization.

Whenever scoring and interpretation are required for an exercise, you will find the answers are provided at the end of each chapter.

This book is written to fulfil three principal needs. The first relates to the *process* of marketing planning, which, while theoretically simple, is in practice extraordinarily complex, involving, as it does, people, systems and organizational structures. One purpose, then, is to ensure that readers fully understand the process, what the pitfalls are and how to negotiate them.

The second purpose is to ensure that readers know which are the appropriate marketing diagnostic tools, structures and frameworks to use at each stage of the process.

The third and most important purpose, however, is to give both students and managers a no-nonsense, practical, step-by-step guide on how to prepare a really good, strategic marketing plan that will help their organizations to create sustainable competitive advantage for themselves and for their customers.

KEY AREAS FOR IMPROVEMENTS IN STRATEGIC MARKETING PLANNING: WHERE TO LOOK IN THIS TEXT FOR PRACTICAL GUIDANCE

This help section is based on the analysis of over 700 strategic marketing plans from over fifty multi-nationals during a period of twenty five years. A fee was charged for each analysis, so these comments are based on considerably more than just opinions.

Summary of the book

A strategic marketing plan should be a clear and simple summary of key market trends, key target segments, the value required by each of them, how we intend to create superior value (to competitors), with a clear prioritization of marketing objectives and strategies, together with the financial consequences.

Alas, frequently, they come across as diffuse, confusing compilations of unconnected sections, masquerading as marketing plans.

Specific problems encountered and where to look for guidance

* Market overviews contain substantially more information than is necessary, with no hint of the implications for marketing activity. See Chapters 2 and 3.
* Key segments are rarely identified. 'Segments' are often sectors or products, rather than groups of customers with similar needs. See Chapter 4.
* The competitive situation is not well analysed and plans appear to assume no activity or reaction by competitors. See Chapter 6.
* SWOT analyses rarely pin down convincingly the value that is required by segments. They are frequently too general to lead to any actionable propositions. See Chapter 5.
* Our own distinctive competences are rarely isolated and built on. See Chapters 5.
* SWOTs are rarely summarized clearly and logically in a portfolio which provides a categorization of the relative potential of each and our relative strengths in each. See Chapter 5.
* Marketing objectives are frequently confused with marketing strategies and do not follow logically from the portfolio summary. See Chapter 6.
* The resource implications of effecting the marketing plans are not always clear. See Chapter 13.
* Communications such as advertising are fragmented and based on habit, rather than being integrated with each other and targeted on the value required by attractive segments. See Chapter 7.
* The sales plan is developed in isolation from the marketing plan. See Chapter 8.
* There is no particular logic behind pricing. See Chapter 9.
* Channels are taken for granted, rather than used as a key source of innovation and differentiation. See Chapter 10.
* CRM is delegated to IT or operations. See Chapter 11.

Main differences between the Sixth Edition and this Seventh Edition

While all chapters have been extensively updated, the most dramatic changes in this edition are as follows.

Chapter 7 on *integrated marketing communications* (previously 'advertising and sales promotion') has significant new material on how to decide what communications tools to use and how to fit them together – the key problem in IMC planning which every other book we've looked at skirts around rather than actually solving! This is based on recent research at Cranfield and elsewhere which we've successfully road-tested with practitioners and in our teaching. The chapter also has rewritten and considerably expanded sections on *digital communications* which draw on the latest developments in this fast-moving field.

Chapter 8 on *sales* (now 'sales and key account management') now reflects the considerable attention given to key account management, as solution/adaptive selling, co-creation and global accounts change the world of selling totally. New material outlines what key account management is, what constitute key accounts, who you need as key account managers, how different relationship stages require different KAM, and how to develop a key account portfolio. Cranfield School of Management is a global force in sales and key account management research, teaching and consulting, so this material is world leading.

Chapter 9 on *pricing* now includes considerably expanded material on *value-in-use*: the art of increasing the value obtained by the client as a means of accessing larger profit pools and maintaining, if not raising, prices. Any fool can plot a response curve and reduce prices to increase demand, often at the cost of profits; our approach is all about increasing demand while maintaining prices. This material draws on the latest research by the authors, other Cranfield faculty and scholars worldwide on service-dominant logic, co-creation and value, and reflects our work with many leading blue-chips in recent years.

Chapter 10 on *The multichannel plan: the route to market* (formerly 'The distribution plan and customer service plan') summarises key lessons from the authors' influential publications on multichannel strategy over the last decade. It reflects the significant shift from channels operating in isolation to multiple channels combining in the customer journey. This is a hot topic in tough times, as companies struggle to make the best use of low-cost channels without damaging their customer experience or market coverage. This chapter has world-class, thoroughly proven tools to square this circle, road-tested with the blue-chip members of Cranfield's best practice clubs, whose strategy reviews have resulted in multi-million dollar and on two occasions multi-billion dollar contributions to profit. The chapter also includes up-to-the-minute material on *customer experience*.

Chapter 11 on the *CRM* plan draws on 5 years of work of our Customer Management Forum. Through tens of top management case study presentations in Cranfield, as well as two surveys of 800 companies, we have synthesized a definitive update on what works in crafting long-term profitable relationships through retention, cross-sell and upsell processes. The chapter is structured around 10 key success factors for CRM which delivers sector-leading customer lifetime value.

Chapter 13 on *marketing effectiveness* addresses one of the key demands of chief executives from their marketing directors: greater accountability for spending. A proper metrics set enables continuous improvement in results and forms a crucial complement to any marketing plan. This new chapter explains how to develop metrics aligned with the plan which will drive the organization in the right direction. It is based on several years of research work in this domain with a group of leading companies.

Learning features

Marketing Plans Seventh Edition has full pedagogical features as follows:

Summary

Each chapter begins with bullet points which highlight the main features and learning to be covered in the chapter.

Key Concepts

Principal marketing ideas and themes are highlighted as snapshots throughout the text.

Crucial Terms

Concise definitions of important terms and vocabulary are provided in the margin to allow for a smoother, easier reading of the text.

Examples

Provide additional illustrative marketing accounts to contextualize learning.

Marketing Insights

Real-life marketing anecdotes contextualize learning.

Headlines

Highlights taken from the text as marginalized notes bring important points to the attention of the reader.

Case Studies

In-depth studies of marketing experiences show how the theories work in real world companies.

Application Questions

These appear at the end of each chapter and relate the theory to practice by asking the reader to apply the theory to real-life situations.

Chapter Review

Condenses the main themes of the chapter and directs the reader to relevant exercises for each topic for them to try.

Exercises

These appear at the end of each chapter and are preceded by a brief introduction which informs the reader of the issues and concepts they will find within each exercise. Each exercise helps the reader to translate the theory into practice and reinforces the learning gained from each chapter. Many exercises also end with an 'interpretation' to guide the reader in their workings.

Tutor's guide

Tutor and student support sites for using Marketing Plans Seventh Edition for teaching and learning can be found at www.marketingplansbook.com.

This will include:

* Introduction to the Tutor's Guide and Use of the Text
* PowerPoint slides
* Case studies and detailed Tutor's Guides
* Examples of Marketing Plans
* Exercises
* Tutor's Notes

1 Understanding the marketing process
2 The marketing planning process: The main steps
3 The marketing planning process: Removing the myths
4 Completing the marketing audit: The customer and market audit
5 Completing the marketing audit: the product audit
6 Setting marketing objectives and strategies
7 The integrated marketing communications plan
8 Sales and key account management plan
9 The pricing plan
10 The multichannel plan: The route to market
11 The customer relationship management plan
12 Implementation and organizational issues in marketing planning
13 Measuring the effectiveness of marketing planning
14 A step-by-step marketing planning system

* Working with Case Studies/Case Studies

Case 1: Eindhoven Containers
Case 2: Multi-electronique et Cie
Case 3: Property Services International
Case 4: International Electrical Supplies
Case 5: Rentlow Cars SA
Case 6: The Dynamic Manager
Case 7: Cranchem marketing plan
Case 8: Lockwell Company Ltd
Case 9: Hydraulic Industries Ltd: Acquisition in West Germany

An important note to the reader from the authors

STOP

Producing an effective marketing plan that will give your organization competitive advantage is not easy. It takes knowledge, skills, intellect, creativity and, above all, time.

Everything you need to succeed is in this book, but you must be prepared to devote time to it. It is most definitely not a quick read!

FAST TRACK

However, for those who need a fast track to producing a marketing plan, Chapter 14 will help you. Be careful, however:

A little learning is a dangerous thing. Drink deep, or taste not the Pierian Spring.

(Alexander Pope)

INTERMEDIATE TRACK

For those interested principally in how to tie all marketing initiative together in a strategic marketing plan, it is possible to omit Chapters 7–11, as these contain a level of detail on specific area of the marketing mix. Again, however, be careful and only omit these chapters if you feel that you already know enough about promotion, pricing, sales, channels, CRM and customer service to be able to outline appropriate strategies in your strategic marketing plan. Also, particularly in Chapters 7, 10 and 11 there are some crucially important state-of-the-art developments in digital marketing described in some detail, each of which is substantially changing the face of marketing.

An important test to help you decide which track you need

It is important that you complete the questionnaire which follows before you start Chapter 1. This test was developed by the authors for the President of a global IT company, who asked what he should be looking for in a world class strategic marketing plan.

Interpretation

In our experience, it is unlikely that many readers will score above five on many of these questions. This is not the point, however. The purpose of the questionnaire is to focus your attention at the beginning of the book on what essential deliverables a marketing plan should produce. If you work carefully through this book and implement it in your organization, you will be able to give yourself high scores in all boxes. Then, you will be a truly market-driven organization!

We have just one more suggestion for readers of this book, which is that they should also complete the very last questionnaire in this book, at the end of Chapter 14. This will most certainly alert readers to the need to focus on the contents of this research-based book.

Professor Malcolm McDonald
Professor Hugh Wilson

ARE YOU GETTING THESE ESSENTIAL DELIVERABLES FROM YOUR STRATEGIC MARKETING PLAN

Market structure and segmentation   Score out of 10

- Is there a clear and unambiguous definition of the market you are interested in serving?
- Is it clearly mapped, showing product/service flows, volumes/values in total, your shares and critical conclusions for your organization?
- Are the segments clearly described and quantified? These must be groups of customers with the same or similar needs, **not** sectors.
- Are the real needs of these segments properly quantified, with the relative importance of these needs clearly identified?

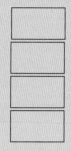

Differentiation

- Is there a clear and quantified analysis of how well your company satisfies these needs compared to competitors?
- Are the opportunities and threats clearly identified by segment?

Scope

- Are all the segments classified according to their relative potential for growth in profits over the next three years and according to your company's relative competitive position in each?
- Are the objectives consistent with their position in the portfolio (volume, value, market share, profit)?
- Are the strategies (including products, price, place and service) consistent with these objectives?
- Are the key issues for action for all departments clearly spelled out as key issues to be addressed?

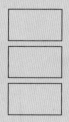

Value capture

- Do the objectives and strategies add up to the profit goals required by your company?
- Does the budget follow on logically from all of the above, or is it merely an add on?

Total score

Chapter

UNDERSTANDING THE MARKETING PROCESS

SUMMARY

- What marketing is
- Its role in getting the best out of an organization's asset base
- The link between the external environment, customers and their needs and the marketing mix
- Clearing up the confusion surrounding marketing's role
- Clarification of what customers look for in their suppliers
- The differences and similarities between consumer, service and industrial marketing
- Whether a marketing department is essential
- Exercises to turn the theory into actionable propositions
- Readers who are already wholly familiar with the role of marketing in organizations may wish to go straight to Chapter 2, which begins to explain the marketing planning process

THE MARKETING CONCEPT*

In 1776, when Adam Smith said that consumption is the sole end and purpose of production, he was in fact describing what in recent years has become known as the marketing concept.

> The central idea of marketing is of a matching between a company's capabilities and the wants of customers in order to achieve the objectives of both parties.

It is important at this stage to understand the difference between the marketing concept (often referred to as 'market orientation') and the marketing function, which is concerned with the management of the marketing mix. The management of the marketing mix involves using the various tools and techniques available to managers in order to implement the marketing concept.

---

* The authors would like to remind the reader that they will use the word 'product' throughout the text to avoid unnecessary references to 'services', 'not-for-profit services', 'capital goods' and 'retail'. The text is equally relevant to all of these.

> The marketing concept implies that all the activities of an organization are driven by a desire to satisfy customer needs

For the sake of simplicity, these are often written about and referred to as the four Ps, these being Product, Price, Promotion and Place although today many scholars include a number of additional Ps, such as People and Process.

However, before any meaningful discussion can take place about how the marketing function should be managed, it is vital to have a full understanding about the idea of marketing itself, and it is this issue that we principally address in this chapter.

For readers who are interested in a history of marketing and the role of key players like Levitt, Kotler, Hunt, Alderson, Holbrook and others, please refer to Jones (1999) in the bibliography at the end of the chapter.[1]

THE MARKETING FUNCTION

There are many definitions of marketing and much confusion about what it is. The following definition should clarify this for readers.

Marketing is a process for:

- defining markets
- quantifying the needs of the customer groups (segments) within these markets
- determining the value propositions to meet these needs
- communicating these value propositions to all those people in the organization responsible for delivering them and getting their buy-in to their role
- playing an appropriate part in delivering these value propositions (usually only communications)
- monitoring the value actually delivered.

For this process to be effective, organizations need to be consumer/customer driven.

This definition is represented as a 'map' in Figure 1.1. This definition and map are important because we will refer to them throughout the remainder of this book.

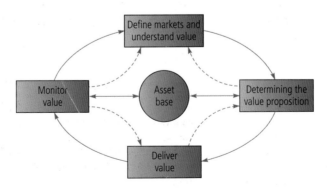

Figure 1.1: A map of marketing.

Starting at the top and moving clockwise, it should be pointed out that the first two boxes are concerned with strategies for markets, whereas the bottom box and the box on the left are concerned with implementing the strategies, once formulated. The fundamental difference between strategies and tactics will be expanded on in Chapter 2.

COMPANY CAPABILITIES

For now, let us return to the notion of bringing about a matching between a company's capabilities and the wants of its customers. In Chapter 4 we will explain what we mean when we talk about customer wants. But for now it is important to understand what we mean when we talk about a company's capabilities. To explain this more fully, let us imagine that we have been made redundant and have decided to set ourselves up in our own business.

The first thing we would have to do is to decide what it is that we can actually do. In answering this question we would quickly realize that our actual knowledge and skills restrict us very severely to certain obvious areas. For example, it would be difficult for a former sales manager to set himself up in business as an estate agent, or for an estate agent to start a marketing consultancy, unless, of course, both had the necessary skills and knowledge. A little thought will confirm that it is exactly the same for a company.

Many commercial disasters have resulted from companies diversifying into activities for which they were basically unsuited.

One such case concerns a firm making connectors for the military and aviation markets. When these traditional markets went into decline, the company diversified into making connectors for several industrial markets such as consumer durables, automobiles and so on. Unfortunately these markets were so completely different from the ones that the company had been used to that they quickly went into a loss-making situation. Whereas the connector which the company had previously manufactured had been a highly engineered product made to the specifications of a few high technology customers, the company now had to mass produce simple connectors for broad markets. This meant making for stock and carrying field inventory. It also meant low competitive prices. The sales force did not know how to cope with the demands of their new markets. They had been used to making one or two calls a day and to having detailed technical discussions with buyers, whereas now they were expected to make eight or nine calls a day and to sell against many competitive products. Furthermore, the company just did not have the right image to succeed in the market. The results of all this were very serious financial losses.

The lesson simply is that all firms have a unique set of capabilities in the form of resources and management skills which are not necessarily capable of taking advantage of all market opportunities as effectively, hence as competitively, as other firms. To summarize, the matching process between a company's capabilities and customer wants is fundamental to commercial success. That this is so will become clearer as we get further into the task of explaining the role and the nature of marketing.

THE ROLE OF MARKETING IN BUSINESS

What causes success in the long run, by which we mean a continuous growth in earnings per share and in the capital value of the shares, has been shown by research[2] to depend on four elements as shown in Figure 1.2.

1. An excellent core product or service and all the associated R and D, which closely matches the wants of the organization's target segments. Clearly, marketing will have a heavy input into this process. All this is showing is that companies with average products deserve average success.
2. Excellent, world class, state-of-the-art operations. All this is saying is that inefficiency today is likely to be punished. Marketing should, of course, have an input to defining operational efficiency in customer satisfaction terms. Where it is not allowed to, because of corporate culture, quality often becomes a sterile token.
3. A culture which encourages and produces an infrastructure within which employees can be creative and entrepreneurial within the prescribed company procedures. Bored and boring people, for whom subservience and compliance is the norm, cause average or below-average performance. This is particularly important because it is the organization's people who deliver value to customers.
4. Professional marketing departments, staffed by qualified professionals (not failures from other functions). All this means is that companies who recruit professionally qualified marketers with appropriate experience have a far greater chance of success than those whose marketing departments are staffed by just about anybody who fancies themselves as marketers.
5. Finally, observe that everything in Figure 1.2 is organized around customers.

(ISO is a set of international quality standards)

Given these ingredients and, above all else, a corporate culture which is not dominated (because of its history) by production, operations or financial orientation, all the evidence shows that marketing as a function makes a major contribution to the achievement of corporate objectives. Its principal role is to spell out the several value propositions demanded by different customer groups so that everyone in the organization knows what their contribution is in creating this value.

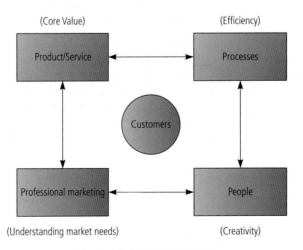

Figure 1.2: Business success.

THE MARKETING ENVIRONMENT

The matching process referred to earlier takes place in what we can call the *marketing environment*, which is the milieu in which the firm is operating. Perhaps the most obvious constituent of the marketing environment is our competitors, for what they do vitally affects our own behaviour as a company.

The point is that, since what our competitors do so vitally affects our own decisions, it is necessary to find some way of monitoring this and other elements of the environment and of building this into our decision-making process. In Chapter 11 we show how this can be done.

The *political, fiscal, economic, social* and *legal* policies of the governments of the countries where we sell our goods also determine what we can do. For example, inflation reduces the discretionary spending power of consumers, and this can result in market decline. Legislation concerning such things as labelling, packaging, advertising, environmentalism, and so on, all affect the way we run our business, and all these things have to be taken account of when we make our plans.

Technology is constantly changing, and we can no longer assume that our current range of products will continue to be demanded by our customers. Perhaps one of the saddest examples of this is the demise of the once-mighty Kodak, a company that for just too long thought it was a chemical company in the photographic paper and film making business. It lost an early dominance in 35 mm cameras to Canon and Nikon, then made a disastrous excursion into Instant Print, infringing on the patents held by Polaroid. Having burnt its fingers expensively there, it seemed to hold back on being at the forefront of the well-predicted move to digital because of its vested manufacturing interests worldwide. Volumes of 35mm film hit a peak as late as 2000 and, of course, with the switch to digital the traditional film processing market has since collapsed very rapidly indeed. Kodak no longer dominates the photography market in the way that it once did, and observationally seems to have allowed Hewlett Packard and Canon to muscle in with the new technology. Photography itself, the 'memory' and 'time capture' business, shows no sign of diminishing. Is Kodak another Gestetner or IBM, caught in the headlights at the wrong end of changing technology?

Likewise, the advent of the microprocessor revolutionized the computer industry, with a devastating effect on companies such as IBM, who remained dependent for too long on their supremacy in mainframes. It is interesting to note that IBM is now mainly a service company, with little involvement in hardware, but it took many years of declining profits and a chairman from outside the industry to help them make the transition.

Merging technologies have also revolutionized traditional industries such as telecommunications, printing, publishing, IT and many others.

The point is that the environment in which we operate is not controlled by us, and it is dynamic. Hence, it must be constantly monitored and we must be prepared to adapt our asset base and our approach to markets. An approach for doing this is outlined in subsequent chapters.

So far, we have talked about the three constituent parts of what we have described as a matching process:

1. The capabilities of a firm
2. The wants of customers
3. The marketing environment.

Diagrammatically, it is shown in Figure 1.3.

Figure 1.3: The matching process.

CUSTOMER WANTS

Although we shall be dealing with this subject in Chapter 4, let us briefly turn our attention to the subject of customer wants, so that we can complete our understanding of what marketing is.

Perhaps one of the greatest areas for misunderstanding in marketing concerns this question of customer wants. Companies are accused of manipulating innocent consumers by making them want things they do not really need.

If this were so, we would not have a situation in which a very high proportion of all new products launched actually fail! The fact is people have always had needs, such as, say, for home entertainment. What changes in the course of time is the way people satisfy these needs. For example, television was only commercially viable because people needed home entertainment, and this was yet another way of fulfilling that need.

But let us not be fooled into believing that the customer, in the end, does not have the final say. All customer needs have many different ways of being satisfied, and wherever people have choice they will choose that product which they perceive as offering the greatest benefits to them at whatever price they are prepared to pay.

Colgate, Nestlé, Johnson & Johnson, Procter and Gamble, Tesco and other longstanding great companies create shareholder value by applying the following values: an inspiring vision; clear strategies; rigorous segment and brand positioning; consistent innovation; superior customer value; high employee morale; tight cost control; and concern for *all* stakeholders, not just customer groups. Having said this, unless customer needs are satisfied in ways which lead to superior market performance, nothing else is possible.

What this means, in effect, since all commercial organizations incur costs in taking goods or services to the market, is that profit, through customer satisfaction, is the principal measure of efficacy or worth of what the company is doing.

Cheapness, efficiency, quality (in the sense of international standards such as ISO) or, indeed, any other measure, are not criteria of effectiveness, since there is little point in producing anything cheaply, efficiently or perfectly if people don't actually want it and don't buy it.

Since costs are incurred in producing products, it is necessary to find customers to buy those products at a sufficiently high price and in sufficient volume (margin turnover) to enable the company to cover its costs and to make a surplus (or profit). This is an economic necessity to enable the company to stay in business and means that, unless what is being offered is seen by customers as satisfying their wants, they will not buy it. Hence, all other stakeholder groups will be disappointed.

In the commercial sector, research has shown that there is a direct link between long-run profitability and the ability of a firm to understand its customers' needs and provide value for them.[4] For industries previously protected from competition, such as the airline industry and telecommunications, many now know that sustainable profitability can only come in the long run through continuous customer satisfaction.

In the not-for-profit sector, customer satisfaction is obviously a proxy for profitability. We shall say more about this important point in Chapter 4 on market segmentation.

To summarize, any organization that continues to offer something for which there is a long-term fundamental decline in demand, unless it is prepared to change so as to be more in tune with what the market wants, in the end will go out of business. Even less sensible would be for a government, or a parent company, to subsidize such an operation, since we know that to go on producing what people do not want is economically inefficient, especially when people will get what they want from abroad if they cannot buy it in their home country.

The same line of reasoning must also apply to those who continually counsel increased productivity as the only answer to our economic problems. Unfortunately, any additional production would more than likely end up in stock unless people actually wanted what was being produced.

It would be different, of course, if there was only a temporary hiccup in demand, but, unfortunately, this is rarely the case, because markets are dynamic and we must learn to adapt and change as our markets mutate.

Central to this question of customer wants is an understanding that there is rarely such a thing as 'a market'. To start with, it is clear that it is customers who buy products, not markets. A market is merely an aggregation of customers sharing similar needs for which they want the products and services that best meet these needs. In reality, most markets consist of a number of submarkets, each of which is different. For example, the airline market consists of freight and passenger transport. The passenger side can be subdivided further into VFR (visiting friends and relatives), holidays, business travel, and so on. Failure to understand the needs of these very different customer groups would result in failure to provide the desired services at an acceptable price.

Of course, it is not quite as easy as this, which is why we devote the whole of Chapter 4 to this very important aspect of what we call 'market segmentation'. But for now it is only necessary to understand that it is our ability to identify groups of customer wants which our particular company capabilities are able to satisfy profitably that is central to marketing management.

THE MARKETING MIX

As we have already said, managing the marketing mix involves the use of the tools and techniques of marketing. Thus, in order for the matching process to take place, we need *information*. External and internal marketing information flows (marketing research) and database management are discussed further in Chapter 11.

Having found out what customers want, we must develop products or services to satisfy those wants. This is known as 'product management' and is discussed in Chapter 5. Obviously we must charge a price for our products, and this is discussed in Chapter 9.

We must also tell our customers about our products, for we can be certain that customers will not beat a path to our door to buy whatever it is we are making. Here we must consider all forms of communication, especially advertising, personal selling and sales promotion. These are discussed in Chapters 7 and 8.

All that remains now is to get our products into our customers' hands, thus giving a time and a place utility to our product. Distribution and customer service are discussed in Chapter 10.

Finally we must consider how to tie it all together in the form of a marketing plan. This latter point is so important that the next two chapters are devoted to a discussion of the marketing planning process.

CONFUSION ABOUT WHAT MARKETING IS – VENEER OR SUBSTANCE?

It is a sad reflection on the state of marketing that in spite of almost 50 years of marketing education, ignorance still abounds concerning what marketing is.

The marketing function (or department) never has been, nor ever will be, effective in an organization whose history to date is one of technical, production, operations or financial orientation. Such enterprises have long since adopted the vocabulary of marketing and applied a veneer of marketing terminology.

MARKETING INSIGHT

Thus, some of the high street banks have spent fortunes on hiring marketing people, often from the fast moving consumer goods sector (FMCG), producing expensive TV commercials and creating a multiplicity of products, brochures and leaflets. Yet still most customers would have difficulty in distinguishing between the major players – so where's the competitive advantage?

Is this marketing in the sense of understanding and meeting customers' needs better than the competition or is it old-fashioned selling with the name changed, where we try to persuade customers to buy what we want to sell them, how, when and where we want to sell it?

The computer industry provides perhaps even clearer examples. For years they have used the word 'marketing' quite indiscriminately as they tried to persuade customers to buy the ever more complex outpourings of their technology. At least one major hardware manufacturer used to call its branch sales managers 'marketing managers' to create the illusion of a local process of understanding and responding to customer needs. Racked by recession, decline and huge losses, this is an industry in which most of the major players have either gone bankrupt or have changed fundamentally their business model.

The following are the major areas of confusion about marketing:

1. *Confusion with sales.* One managing director aggressively announced to everyone at the beginning of a seminar in Sydney, Australia: 'There's no time for marketing in my company until sales improve!' Confusion with sales is still one of the biggest barriers to be overcome.
2. *Confusion with product management.* The belief that all a company has to do to succeed is to produce a good product also still abounds, and neither Concorde, Sinclair's C5, the EMI Scanner, nor the many thousands of brilliant products that have seen their owners or inventors go bankrupt during the past 30 years will convince such people otherwise.
3. *Confusion with advertising.* This is another popular misconception and the annals of business are replete with examples such as British Airways who won awards with their brilliant advertising campaigns, while failing to deliver what the advertising promised. Throwing advertising expenditure at the public is still a very popular way of tackling deep-rooted marketing problems.
4. *Confusion with customer service.* The 'Have a nice day' syndrome is still having its heyday in many countries of the world, originally popularized, of course, by Peters and Waterman's book *In Search of Excellence* (Warner Books, 1982). Many organizations now know, of course, that training staff to be nice to customers does not help a lot if the basic offer is fundamentally wrong. For example, in many railway companies around the world, while it helps to be treated nicely, it is actually much more important to get there on time! 'Stop sending me birthday cards and answer your damned phone!' is a *cri de cœur* many customers will sympathize with.

It should by now be obvious that those people who talk about 'the sharp end' – by which they usually mean personal selling – as being the only thing that matters in marketing, have probably got it wrong.

Selling is just one aspect of communication with customers, and to say that it is the only thing that matters is to ignore the importance of product management, pricing, distribution and other forms of communication in achieving profitable sales. Selling is just one part of this process, in which the transaction is actually clinched. It is the culmination of the marketing process, and success will only be possible if all the other elements of the marketing mix have been properly managed. Imagine trying to sell a horse that didn't have four legs! The more attention that is paid to finding out what customers want, to developing products to satisfy these wants, to pricing at a level consistent with the benefits offered, to gaining distribution, and to communicating effectively with our target market, the more likely we are to be able to exchange contracts through the personal selling process.

Likewise, it is naive to assume that marketing is all about advertising, since it is by now clear that advertising is only one aspect of communication. Many firms waste their advertising expenditure because they have not properly identified what their target market is.

> For example, one public transport company spent half a million euros advertising how reliable their bus service was when, in reality, utilization of buses by the public was declining because they somehow felt that buses were working class! This was a classic case of believing that advertising will increase sales irrespective of what the message is. Had this company done its research, it could have decided to what extent and how advertising could be used to overcome this prejudice. As it was, the company spent a small fortune telling people something that was largely irrelevant!

In reality, many companies spend more on advertising when times are good and less on advertising when times are bad. Cutting the advertising budget is often seen as an easy way of boosting the profit and loss account when a firm is below its budgeted level of profit. This tendency is encouraged by the fact that this can be done without any apparent immediate adverse effect on sales. Unfortunately, this is just another classic piece of misunderstanding about marketing and about the role of advertising in particular. The belief here is that advertising is caused by sales! Also, it is naive in the extreme to assume that advertising effectiveness can be measured in terms of sales when it is only a part of the total marketing process.

For a discussion, with evidence, that cutting promotional expenditure during a recession is precisely the wrong thing to do, see a report by the Institute of Practitioners in Advertising.[5]

The same, of course, applies to any form of communications, including all modern media, which we discuss in Chapter 10.

WHAT DOES THE CUSTOMER WANT?

Finally, we have to beware of what the words 'finding out what the customer wants', which appear in most definitions of marketing, really mean. The reality, of course, is that most advances in customer satisfaction are technology driven. For example, the fabulous technological breakthroughs that occurred as a result of the Houston space programme, when the Americans put two men on the Moon, have provided thousands of opportunities for commercial exploitation. The role of marketing has been to find commercial applications for the technology.

The truth, of course, is that there are two kinds of research and development:

1. Technology driven
2. Market driven.

From the kinds of technology-driven programmes that take place on science parks and in laboratories around the world come opportunities for commercial exploitation.

MARKETING INSIGHT

From the kinds of market-driven programmes that most companies engage in come incremental, and sometimes discontinuous, improvements to product performance. Both are legitimate activities. The former has been glamorized and popularized by companies such as 3M, who claim to encourage and institutionalize unfocused scientific research. This has led to the formation of a number of new businesses and product launches, the most famous of which is Post-it.

The main point to remember, however, is that customers do not really know what they want! All they really want are better ways of solving their problems, so one of the main tasks of marketing is to understand the customers and their problems in depth so that we can continuously work on ways of making life easier for them. Whether this happens as a result of serendipity or focused research and development is less important than the end result.

ARE BUSINESS-TO-BUSINESS, CONSUMER AND SERVICE MARKETING DIFFERENT?[6]

The central ideas of marketing are universal and it makes no difference whether we are marketing furnaces, insurance policies or margarine. Yet problems sometimes arise when we try to implement marketing ideas in service companies and industrial goods companies.

A service does not lend itself to being specified in the same way as a product, as it does not have the same reproducible physical dimensions that can be measured. Thus, with the purchase of any service, there is a large element of trust on the part of the buyer, who can only be sure of the quality and performance of the service after it has been completed. Largely because of this, the salesperson actually selling the service obviously becomes part of the service, since this is one of the principal ways in which the potential efficacy of the service can be assessed. Additionally, a service product cannot be made in advance and stored for selling 'off the shelf' at some later stage. Nonetheless, apart from some differences in emphasis, the principles of marketing apply to services in exactly the same way.

Business-to-business goods are simply those goods sold to other businesses, institutional or government buyers for incorporation into their own products, to be resold, or to be used by them within their own business. Principal types of business-to-business goods are raw materials, components, capital goods and maintenance, repair and operating goods and equipment, although even service companies sell direct to other companies rather than to consumers.

The fact that the share of world trade enjoyed by some manufacturing countries has slumped so dramatically over the past 50 years is not generally because their products were not as good as those produced by other countries, but because they failed to monitor and understand the environmental changes taking place and stuck doggedly to what had worked in the past, whereas organizations that continued to thrive did, including, where necessary, the sourcing of manufacturing in countries with lower costs.

One reason for this is that many manufacturing companies naively believe that the name of the game is making well-engineered products. Making well-engineered products is all some companies are concerned about, in spite of the fact that all the evidence points to the conclusion that more often

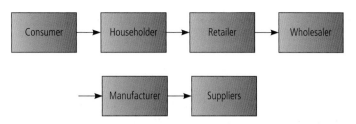

Figure 1.4: Supply chain.

than not it is for other reasons that the final choice is actually made. Failure to understand the importance of market segmentation (to be discussed in Chapter 4), market share, service and reputation, among other things, is the principal reason why such companies fail to compete successfully in so many world markets. Making what they consider to be good products and then giving them to the sales force to get rid of is just not enough.

> Failure to understand the importance of market segmentation is the principal reason for failure to compete effectively in world markets

But, quite apart from the fact that there appears to be a sort of status about being on the technical side of business, which sometimes acts as a barrier to the consideration of marketing issues, it is also a fact that marketing is difficult in many business-to-business markets. This makes it inevitable that managers will resort to doing things they can understand. For example, demand for all industrial products is derived from the demand for consumer products, which adds greater uncertainty to decision making and makes forecasting extremely difficult.

It can be readily appreciated from Figure 1.4 that the further a company gets from the eventual consumer, the less control it has over demand. Take the example of brewers. They can communicate direct with their consumers, whereas the company making their plant and the suppliers in turn to the plant company are, in the final analysis, also dependent on ultimate consumers.

Also, information about business-to-business markets is not so readily available as in consumer goods markets, which makes it more difficult to measure changes in market share. There are other difficulties besides these, which make marketing in the business-to-business area more difficult.

Unfortunately, the answer to this problem by many companies has been to recruit a 'marketing person' and leave them to get on with the job of marketing. But it will now be obvious that such a solution can never work, because the marketing concept, if it is to work at all, has to be understood and practised by all executives in a firm, not just by the marketing manager. Otherwise everyone goes on behaving just as they did before and the marketing person quickly becomes ineffective.

Again, however, the conclusion must be that, apart from differences in emphasis, the principles of marketing apply in exactly the same way.

DO YOU NEED A MARKETING DEPARTMENT?

This brings us finally to the question of whether it is necessary for a company to have a marketing department.

It is not essential to have a formalized marketing department for the analysis, planning and control of the matching process. This is particularly so in small, undiversified companies where the chief executive has an in-depth understanding of customers' needs. Even in large companies it is not necessary to have a marketing department, because the management of products can be left to the engineers, pricing can be managed by the accountants, distribution can be managed by distribution specialists, and selling and advertising can be managed by the sales manager.

The dangers in this approach, however, are obvious. Technicians often place too much emphasis on the physical aspects of the products, accountants can be too concerned with costs rather than with market values, distribution people can often succeed in optimizing their own objectives for stock, yet at the same time suboptimizing other more important aspects of the business, such as customer service, and selling and promotion can often be carried out in a way that may not be in the best interests of the firm's overall goals.

However, as a company's product range and customer types grow, and as competitive pressures and environmental turbulence increase, so it often becomes necessary to organize the management of marketing under one central control function, otherwise there is a danger of ending up with the kind of product which is brilliant technically, but disastrous commercially.

In professional organizations, great care is necessary in thinking about the appropriate organizational form for marketing. For example, in a postgraduate business school the major role of the marketing department has traditionally been in the domain of promotion and information coordination. While it does obviously act as a facilitator for strategy development, it is intellectually simplistic to imagine that it could be the originator of strategy. In some other service organizations, the central marketing function might also provide the systems to enable others to carry out effective marketing, but in such organizations marketing departments never have actually *done* marketing, nor ever will.

The reasons are obvious. If the term 'marketing' is intended to embrace all those activities related to demand creation and satisfaction and the associated intelligence, then it is clear that most marketing takes place during the service delivery and customer contact process, in all its forms. Marketing, then, reflects this process and it is absurd to believe that it is the sole domain of those people in the organization who happen to belong to the marketing department.

In the best professional firms, a 'Marketing Partner' is often appointed. Such a person is usually a qualified professional, such as a lawyer or an accountant, and they take the qualified marketers in the marketing department under their wing so that marketing has a voice in the boardroom.

> It is absurd to believe that marketing is the sole domain of those people in the organization who happen to belong to the marketing department.

As Alan Mitchell, a freelance journalist for *Marketing Business*, said: 'To say the Marketing Department is responsible for marketing is like saying love is the responsibility of one family member.'

It is equally absurd to suggest that the personnel department should actually emphasize personnel management, with all other managers in the organization having nothing to do with people. The same could be said for finance and information systems. Indeed, it is such myopic functional separation that got most struggling organizations into the mess they are in today.

Much more important, however, than who is responsible for marketing in an organization is the question of its marketing orientation, i.e. the degree to which the company as a whole understands the importance of finding out what customer groups want and of organizing all the company's resources to satisfy those wants at a profit.

Nonetheless, given the definition of marketing supplied earlier, we repeat Figure 1.1 (as Figure 1.5) as a diagram of this definition, which we shall return to later.

We should like to make one final important point in this introductory chapter. It has always been tempting to give in to that strident minority who criticize the whole topic of marketing and marketing planning in particular. So, to conclude this chapter on a positive note we include a quotation from *Management Today*.[7]

Diageo's well-deserved win as Britain's most admired company is a tale of meticulously planned strategy, consistently executed over many years, with little regard to the whims of corporate fashion.

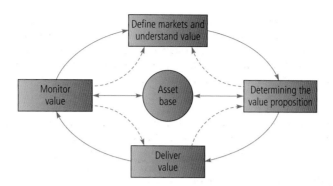

Figure 1.5: A map of marketing.

APPLICATION QUESTIONS

1. Describe as best you can what you think marketing means in your company.
2. Describe the role of your marketing department, if you have one.
3. If you do not have a marketing department, describe how decisions are made in respect of the following:
   * the product itself
   * price
   * customer service levels
   * physical distribution
   * advertising
   * sales promotion
   * the sales force
   * information about markets.
4. How do you distinguish between marketing, promotion and selling in your organization?
5. Would you say your products are what the market wants, or what you prefer to produce?
6. Do you start your planning process with a sales forecast and then work out a budget, or do you start by setting marketing objectives, which are based on a thorough review of the previous year's performance? If the former, describe why you think this is better than the latter.

CHAPTER 1 REVIEW

The marketing concept

Providing goods or services for which there is a known customer demand, as opposed to selling what the company likes to produce. By focusing on customers and their wants the company is better positioned to make a profit. The company is then said to be market led, or to have a 'market orientation'.

The marketing function

There are many definitions of marketing and much confusion about what it is. The following definition should clarify this for readers:

Marketing is a process for:

* defining markets
* quantifying the needs of the customer groups (segments) within these markets

- determining the value propositions to meet these needs
- communicating these value propositions to all those people in the organization responsible for delivering them and getting their buy-in to their role
- playing an appropriate part in delivering these value propositions (usually only communications)
- monitoring the value actually delivered.

For this process to be effective, organizations need to be consumer/customer driven.

This definition is represented as a 'map' in Figure 1.1, repeated here as Figure 1.6.

Starting at the top and moving clockwise, it should be pointed out that the first two boxes are concerned with *strategies* for markets, whereas the bottom box and the box on the left are concerned with implementing the strategies, once formulated. The fundamental difference between strategies and tactics will be expanded on in Chapter 2.

Try Exercise 1.1

Company capabilities

The company will not be equally good at all things. It will have strengths and weaknesses. The astute company tries to identify customer wants that best match its own strengths, be they its product range, relations with customers, technical expertise, flexibility, or whatever. Inevitably there is an element of compromise in the matching process, but successful companies strive to build on their strengths and reduce their weaknesses.

Try Exercise 1.2

The marketing environment

No business operates in a vacuum; it has an environment which not only contains all its existing and potential customers and its competitors, but many factors outside its control. Changes in the environment in terms of

- customer wants
- fashions
- technology
- environmental concerns
- legislation
- economic climate
- competition, etc.

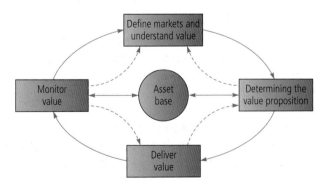

Figure 1.6: Map of the marketing process.

present the company with both opportunities and threats. Keeping a finger on the pulse of the environment is essential for the successful company.

Try Exercise 1.3

Questions raised for the company

1. Q: Is it different marketing a product or a service?
   A: The central ideas of marketing are universal.
2. Q: What do customers want?
   A: They don't always know, but dialogue with them and intelligent research can help to answer this question.
3. Q: Do we need to bother with marketing?
   A: Some companies are very successful by chance. They happen to be in the right place at the right time. Most other companies need to plan their marketing.

Try Exercise 1.4

4. Q: Do we need a marketing department?
   A: Not necessarily. It will depend upon the size and complexity of the company's range of products and services. The higher the complexity, the more difficult it is to coordinate activities and achieve the 'matching' of a company to its customers.

EXERCISES

The exercises are intended to give you an opportunity to explore ways of looking at marketing. Exercise 1.1 enables you to make an assessment of your own beliefs about marketing; the remaining exercises can be applied to your organization.

Exercise 1.1 Marketing orientation

Below are a number of definitions of marketing that have appeared in books and journals over the last 20 or so years. Read through them carefully and note on a piece of paper the numbers of those which most accurately reflect your own views.

While there is no upper limit to the number of definitions you can choose, try, if you can, to limit your choice to a maximum of nine or 10 definitions.

1. 'The planning and execution of all aspects and activities of a product so as to exert optimum influence on the consumer, to result in maximum consumption at the optimum price and thereby producing the maximum long-term profit.'
2. 'Deciding what the customer wants; arranging to make it; distributing and selling it at a profit.'
3. 'Marketing perceives consumption as a democratic process in which consumers have the right to select preferred candidates. They elect them by casting their money votes to those who supply the goods or services that satisfy their needs.'

(Continued)

4. 'The planning, executing and evaluating of the external factors related to a company's profit objectives.'

5. 'Adjusting the whole activity of a business to the needs of the customer or potential customer.'

6. '. . . marketing is concerned with the idea of satisfying the needs of customers by means of the product and a whole cluster of things associated with creating, delivering and, finally, consuming it.'

7. 'The total system of interacting business activities designed to plan, price, promote and distribute products and services to present and potential customers.'

8. '(Marketing is) the world of business seen from the point of view of its final result, that is from the customer's viewpoint. Concern and responsibility for marketing must therefore permeate all areas of the enterprise.'

9. 'The activity that can keep in constant touch with an organization's consumers, read their needs and build a programme of communications to express the organization's purposes.'

10. 'The management function which organizes and directs all those business activities involved in assessing and converting customer purchasing power into effective demand for a specific product or service and moving the product or service to the final customer or user so as to achieve the profit target or other objectives set by the company.'

11. 'The marketing concept emphasizes the vital importance to effective corporate planning and control, of monitoring both the environment in which the offering is made and the needs of the customers, in order that the process may operate as effectively as is humanly possible.'

12. 'The organization and performance of those business activities that facilitate the exchange of goods and services between maker and user.'

13. 'The process of: (1) Identifying customer needs, (2) Conceptualizing these needs in terms of the organization's capacity to produce, (3) Communicating that conceptualization to the appropriate locus of power in the organization, (4) Conceptualizing the consequent output in terms of the customer needs earlier identified, (5) Communicating that conceptualization to the customer.

14. '(In a marketing company) all activities – from finance to production to marketing – should be geared to profitable consumer satisfaction.'

15. 'The performance of those business activities that direct the flow of goods from producer to consumer or user.'

16. 'The skill of selecting and fulfilling consumer wants so as to maximize the profitability per unit of capital employed in the enterprise.'

17. 'The economic process by means of which goods and services are exchanged and their values determined in terms of money prices.'

18. 'The performance of business activities that direct the flow of goods and services from producer to consumer in order to accomplish the firm's objectives.'

19. 'Marketing is concerned with preventing the accumulation of non-moving stocks.'

20. 'The process of understanding markets and the present and future value required by the different groups within these markets, of communicating it to all customer-impacting functions within the organization and of measuring the value actually delivered.'

Scoring for Exercise 1.1

You should have selected a number of definitions that you identify with. To work out your score, tick the boxes in the table below which equate to your chosen statements. Now add the number of ticks in each group and enter the total in the boxes at the end of each row.

For example, if you selected definitions 1, 3, 5, 6, 10 and 14, then 1 and 10 would score a total of 2 in Group A and 3, 5, 6 and 14 would score a total of 4 in Group B.

Group A	1	2	4	7	10	12	15	17	18	19	
Group B	3	5	6	8	9	11	13	14	16	20	

Interpretation of Exercise 1.1

If you study the various definitions, you will find that the essential difference between those in Group A and those in Group B is that *Group B definitions make an unambiguous reference about identifying and satisfying customer needs and building systems around this principle.* This is generally accepted as true marketing orientation, and is the stance taken throughout this book about marketing.

Group A definitions tend to focus far less on the customer (unless it is to decide what customers want, or to *exert influence* on the customer – i.e. to do things to the customer – and more on the company's own systems and profit motives. Thus Group A definitions could be described as being more traditional views about managing a business. Therefore the more Group B and the fewer Group A answers you have, the higher your marketing orientation and the less at odds you should be with the ideas put forward in this book.

Please note that this is your personal orientation towards marketing and nothing to do with your company.

Exercise 1.2 Company capabilities and the matching process

1. Reflect on your company's recent history, say the last five years. Over that period, what would you say have been the key strengths that have carried the company to its present position?

    (a) Make a list of these below. *Note*: In a small company, among the strengths might be listed key people. Where this happens, expand on what the person actually brings to the organization, e.g. sales director – his/her contacts in the industry.

    (i) _____

    (ii) _____

    (iii) _____

    (b) What would you say are the three main weaknesses at present?

    (i) _____

    (ii) _____

    (iii) _____

(Continued)

2. Again, considering the last five-year period, has the company got better at matching its strengths to customers and to its business environment, or worse? Often there are both positive and negative forces at work.

    (a) Make a note of the factors which led to improvements in the space below.

    (b) Make a note of the factors which led to a deterioration in the space below.

At this stage you do not need to draw any specific conclusions from this exercise, although you will probably find it useful to return to this information as you progress through the book.

Exercise 1.3 The marketing environment

You will be asked to consider the marketing environment in more detail later. For now, think back over the last five years of the company's history and answer these questions:

1. Which were the three most significant opportunities in the environment which contributed to the company's success/present situation?

    (a) _____ ( )
    (b) _____ ( )
    (c) _____ ( )

    Put a score against each factor listed, in the brackets, using a 1–10 scale (where 10 is extremely significant).

2. Which were the three most significant threats which operated against the company over this period and which inhibited its success?

    (a) _____ ( )
    (b) _____ ( )
    (c) _____ ( )

    Again, score these threats on a 1–10 scale as above.

3. Reflect on what you have written above and consider whether or not these opportunities and threats are increasing or decreasing in significance, or if new ones are on the horizon. Make notes below, looking ahead for, say, the next three years.

    Opportunities → _____
    Threats   → _____

Again, at this stage, you do not need to draw any specific conclusions from this exercise, although you will probably find it useful to return to this information as you progress through the book.

Exercise 1.4 Marketing quiz*

Place a tick after each statement in the column which most accurately describes your company situation.

	Very true	True	Don't know	Untrue	Very untrue
1. (a) Our return on invested capital is satisfactory.					
(b) There is good evidence it will stay that way for the next five years.					
(c) Detailed analysis indicates that it is probably incapable of being materially improved.					
2. (a) Our market share is not declining.					
(b) This is a fact, based on objective evidence.					
(c) There is objective evidence that it will stay that way.					
3. (a) Our turnover is increasing.					
(b) At a rate faster than inflation.					
(c) But not at the expense of profitability.					
4. I know for sure that our sales organization is only allowed to push less profitable lines at the expense of more profitable ones if there are rational reasons for doing so.					
5. (a) I understand why the company has performed the way it has during the past five years.					
(b) I know (apart from hoping) where it is heading during the next five years.					
6. (a) I am wholly satisfied that we make what the market wants, not what we prefer to produce.					
(b) Our functional strategies (such as production, finance, IT, HR, operations, R and D, etc.) are based on a clear understanding of the required customer value, rather than for self-serving functional reasons.					

*Adapted by Professor Malcolm McDonald from a questionnaire devised by Harry Henry Associates in 1971.

(Continued)

	Very true	True	Don't know	Untrue	Very untrue
(c) I am satisfied that we do not use short-term tactics which are injurious to our long-term interests.					
7. (a) I know that sales and profit forecasts presented by operating management are realistic.					
(b) I know they are as exacting as they can reasonably be.					
(c) If anyone insists that they are raised, it is because a higher level is attainable not just because a better-looking budget is required.					
8. (a) The detailed data generated internally are analysed to provide timely information about what is happening in the key areas of the business.					
(b) Marketing research data which operating management acquire are synthesized into plain English and are actually needed and used in the key decision-making process.					
9. (a) We do not sell unprofitably to any customer.					
(b) We analyse our figures to be sure of this.					
(c) If we do, it is for rational reasons known to us all.					
10. Our marketing policies are based on market-centred opportunities which we have fully researched, not on vague hopes of doing better.					

Join up the ticks down the page and count how many are to the left of the *Don't know* position, and how many are at the *Don't know* position or to the right of it.

Interpretation of Exercise 1.4

If you have 11 or more answers in the *Don't know* position or to the right of it, then the chances are that your company isn't very marketing orientated. It needs to take a closer look at itself in the ways suggested by this book.

Scores between 12 and 20 to the left of the *Don't know* position indicate an organization that appears to have reasonable control of many of the significant ingredients of commercial success. Nonetheless, there is clearly still room for improvement, and this book should be useful in bringing about such an improvement.

Scores above 20 to the left of the *Don't know* position indicate an organization completely in command of the key success variables. Are you certain that this is a true reflection of your organization's situation? If you are, then the chances are that its marketing skills are already highly developed. However, this book will still be useful for newcomers to the marketing function who wish to learn about the marketing process, and it will certainly help to maintain your high standards.

REFERENCES

1. Jones, D.G.B. (1999) Historical research in marketing. In *The IEBM Encyclopedia of Marketing*. International Thomson Business Press, 18–35.
2. Wong, V. and Saunders, J. (1993) Business orientations and corporate success. *Journal of Strategic Marketing* 1, 1.
3. Davidson, H. (2009) Shareholder value is bad for marketing. *Market Leader*, November, 22–27.
4. Buzzell R.D. and Gale B.T. (1987) *The PIMS Principles: Linking Strategy to Performance*. Free Press, New York, 1987.
5. Binet, L. and Field, P. (2007) *Marketing in an Age of Accountability*. IPA Data Mine.
6. McDonald, M. and Payne, A. (2006) *Marketing Plans for Service Businesses*. Butterworth-Heinemann, Oxford.
7. *Management Today*, December 2008, p. 32.

Chapter

THE MARKETING PLANNING PROCESS: 1 THE MAIN STEPS

SUMMARY

- What marketing planning is
- Why it is essential
- The difference and the connection between a strategic and a tactical marketing plan
- Budgets and associated problems
- The marketing planning process
- What a marketing audit is
- Why marketing audits are essential
- Their place in organizational planning
- Who should carry out marketing audits
- What should be done with the audit results
- What the relationship is between strategic marketing planning and corporate planning
- Positioning marketing planning within marketing
- What the key components of the strategic marketing plan are
- How strategic marketing plans should be used
- What the link is to the budget
- Exercises to turn the theory into actionable propositions

INTRODUCTION

Although marketing planning would appear to be a simple, step-by-step process, in reality it is a multifaceted, complex, cross-functional activity that touches every aspect of organizational life. This chapter explains and explores some of these pan-company issues by focusing on the process of marketing planning. It is not an attempt to suggest that the model outlined here is the only one that can be implemented. Indeed, other models are discussed. However, the one we select to concentrate on is the one most widely used and accepted by both academics and practitioners.

WHAT IS MARKETING PLANNING?

Any manager will readily agree that a sensible way to manage the sales and marketing function is to find a systematic way of identifying a range of options, to choose one or more of them, then to schedule and cost out what has to be done to achieve the objectives.

This process can be defined as marketing planning, which is the planned application of resources to achieve marketing objectives.

Marketing planning, then, is simply a logical sequence and a series of activities leading to the setting of marketing objectives and the formulation of plans for achieving them. Companies generally go through some kind of management process in developing marketing plans. In small, undiversified companies, this process is usually informal. In larger, more diversified organizations, the process is often systematized. Conceptually, this process is very simple and involves a situation review, the formulation of some basic assumptions, setting objectives for what is being sold and to whom, deciding on how the objectives are to be achieved, and scheduling and costing out the actions necessary for implementation.

The problem is that, while as a process it is intellectually simple to understand, in practice it is the most difficult of all marketing tasks.

> Revenue is the monetary value received by a company for its goods or services. It is the net price received, i.e. the price less any discounts

The reason is that it involves bringing together into one coherent plan all the elements of marketing, and in order to do this at least some degree of institutionalized procedures is necessary. It is this which seems to cause so much difficulty for companies.

Another difficulty concerns the cultural, organizational and political problems that surround the process itself. This will be dealt with in Chapter 3.

> Profit cannot be simply defined, as different organizations define it in different ways and use different terminology. It can, for example, be trading profit, return on sales, return on investment, shareholder value added (SVA) and many other measures. In this book the term is used as a measure of shareholder satisfaction with the financial return made by a commercial organization in which they have an interest

WHY IS MARKETING PLANNING ESSENTIAL?

There can be little doubt that marketing planning is essential when we consider the increasingly hostile and complex environment in which companies operate. Hundreds of external and internal factors interact in a bafflingly complex way to affect our ability to achieve profitable sales. Also, let us consider for a moment the four typical objectives which companies set: maximizing ▶ revenue; maximizing ▶ profits; maximizing return on investment; and minimizing ▶ costs. Each one of these has its own special appeal to different managers within the company, depending on the nature of their particular function. In reality, the best that can ever be achieved is a kind of 'optimum compromise', because each of these objectives could be considered to be in conflict in terms of equivalences.

Managers of a company have to have some understanding or view about how all these variables interact and managers must try to be rational about their business decisions, no matter how important intuition, feel and experience are as contributory factors in this process of rationality.

Most managers accept that some kind of formalized procedure for marketing planning helps sharpen this rationality so as to reduce the complexity of business operations and add a dimension of realism to the company's hopes for the future. Because it is so difficult, however, most companies rely only on sales forecasting and budgeting systems. It is a well-known fact that any fool can write figures down! All too frequently, however, they bear little relationship to the real opportunities and problems facing a company. It is far more difficult to write down marketing objectives and strategies that relate to known opportunities in the market. Take the following hypothetical example, shown in Figure 2.1.

> Costs are charges incurred in running an enterprise. They can take many forms including overhead, direct, indirect, attributable, avoidable and others. In this book the type of costs will be defined when the term is used

From Figure 2.1 it can be seen that in the current year, this company achieved a 15 per cent increase in sales revenue over the previous year. But, being optimistic, the chief marketing officer set a so-called 'stretch' target of plus 20 per cent for next year, giving a target of 9.6 million which, if achieved, would satisfy the budget holder.

However, consider for a moment a different and more professional way of setting an objective for next year. If the market addressed were a growing market, a strategic objective might be 'To be market leader in three years' time'. In order to achieve such an objective, the chief marketing officer would need an assessment of market size in three years' time – say 100 million. Market leadership in this particular market would be, say, 25 per cent. So, representing this in Figure 2.2 and extrapolating backwards from this target would give a target of 15 million next year, not the backwards-looking historical target of 20 per cent (9.6 million).

Were the target to be set at 15 million as opposed to 9.6 million, everything the company planned to do for the following year in order to achieve 15 million as opposed to 9.6 million would be different, including R and D, operations, IT, HR, etc.

Also, consider for a moment the possibility that the trend in the previous year had occurred in a growth market, with little effort on the part of the sales force. In such circumstances, it is not uncommon to find complacent sales forces selling the products that are easiest to sell to those customers who treat them nicest, with the resultant sales going into the company's database. Also, it is not

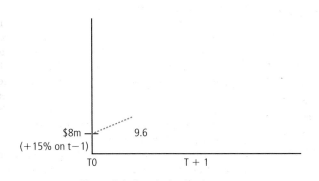

Figure 2.1: A typical sales forecast.

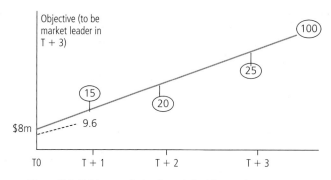

Figure 2.2: Evidence of why the original forecast was wrong.

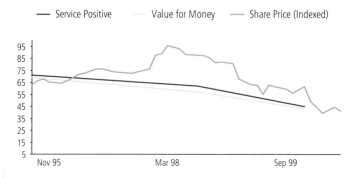

Figure 2.3: A major retailer's trends.

uncommon to find senior managers setting challenging targets such as a reduction in working capital, which often find their way down to logistics managers. Such managers, in a desperate attempt to achieve their reduced inventory goal, may well find themselves having to turn away legitimate demand in order to achieve their budget target. The result is, of course, the company's database and, in such a system, it is clear that to use it as a basis for forecasting is tantamount to extrapolating its own inefficiencies and has little to do with market reality.

Here, it is worth pointing out why forecasts and budgets can never be a substitute for the kind of planning which is the subject of this book.

> The information appearing in the majority of boardrooms remains predominantly financial in nature. Without (additional) information on value-creating activities management are typically flying blind – when financials tell them there is a problem management have already missed the optimal point for taking appropriate corrective action.
>
> (Transparency in Corporate Reporting,
> *PricewaterhouseCoopers' Value Reporting Review 2003, p. 25)*

Figure 2.3 shows that, in the case of a major retailer, while share prices were rising for a number of years, underlying customer service and perceived value for money were declining until eventually the shares, together with company confidence, collapsed. For a number of years, this retailer has been struggling to recover.

Performance (£million)	Base year	1	2	3	4	5
Sales revenue	£254	£293	£318	£387	£431	£454
- Cost of goods sold	135	152	167	201	224	236
Gross contribution	£119	£141	£151	£186	£207	£218
- Manufacturing overhead	48	58	63	82	90	95
- Marketing & sales	18	23	24	26	27	28
- Research & development	22	23	23	25	24	24
Net profit	£16	£22	£26	£37	£50	£55
Return on sales (%)	6.3%	7.5%	8.2%	9.6%	11.6%	12.1%
Assets	£141	£162	£167	£194	£205	£206
Assets (% of sales)	56%	55%	53%	50%	48%	45%
Return on assets (%)	11.3%	13.5%	15.6%	19.1%	24.4%	26.7%

Table 2.1: InterTech's five-year performance

Performance (£million)	Base year	1	2	3	4	5
Market growth	18.3%	23.4%	17.6%	34.4%	24.0%	17.9%
InterTech sales growth (%)	12.8%	17.4%	11.2%	27.1%	16.5%	10.9%
Market share (%)	20.3%	19.1%	18.4%	17.1%	16.3%	14.9%
Customer retention (%)	88.2%	87.1%	85.0%	82.2%	80.9%	80.0%
New customers (%)	11.7%	12.9%	14.9%	24.1%	22.5%	29.2%
% Dissatisfied customers	13.6%	14.3%	16.1%	17.3%	18.9%	19.6%
Relative product quality	+10%	+8%	+5%	+3%	+1%	0%
Relative service quality	+0%	+0%	−20%	−3%	−5%	−8%
Relative new product sales	+8%	+8%	+7%	+5%	+1%	−4%

Table 2.2: InterTech's five-year market-based performance

Table 2.1 shows a real company (whose identity has been disguised), which appears to be doing extremely well financially. Again, it is important to stress that this is the kind of financial information typically discussed at board meetings, most of which is based on forecasts and budgets.

A glance at Table 2.2, however, shows that on every market-based dimension, the company is losing ground dramatically and is likely to suffer serious consequences the moment the market stops growing.

Here are some quotes from well-known sources:

Improvements in a short-term financial measure such as economic profit can be achieved through postponing capital investments, reducing marketing and training expenditures, or by divesting assets, each of which may have a positive effect on near term performance but could adversely affect long term value creation performance. Nevertheless, when incentivised with bonuses to 'manage for the measure' this is exactly what many managers will do irrespective of the consequences on shareholder value.

(Why Value Based Management Goes Wrong,
Simon Court, Market Leader, 2002)

- 90% of USA and European firms think budgets are cumbersome and unreliable, providing neither predictability nor control.
- They are backward-looking and inflexible. Instead of focussing managers' time on the customers, the real source of income, they focus their attention on satisfying the boss, i.e. The budget becomes the purpose.
- Cheating is endemic in all budget regimes. The result is fear, inefficiency, suboptimisation and waste.
- In companies like Enron, the pressure to make the numbers was so great that managers didn't just doctor a few numbers, they broke the law.
- People with targets and jobs dependent on meeting them will probably meet the targets, even if they have to destroy the enterprise to do it.

(S. Caulkin (2005) 'Escape from the budget straitjacket',
Management Today, *January, pp. 47–49)*

Well before the banking crisis of 2008, a major bank was criticized for its contribution to personal debt of £1 trillion in the UK:

Employees are set tough targets for selling loans and double their low salaries, which encourages customer abuse and leaves many borrowers facing ruin.
Banks are no longer there to help customers find the most suitable solution.

('We have a target-driven culture that staff must hit targets',
a major bank, 10 May 2005)

Many economic commentators and politicians remark on the destructive nature of targets set by government for public services. The common thread running through countless examples is that members of the public have ceased to be the focus of the organization. The majority of police, doctors, nurses, teachers and government officers now complain about the way their skills and time are being subverted by the culture of targets. They long to put the 'customer' back in the centre of their working lives.

To summarize, the good thing about not having a strategic plan is that failure comes as a complete surprise and is not preceded by a long period of worry and depression.

Apart from the need to cope with increasing turbulence, environmental complexity, more intense competitive pressures, and the sheer speed of technological change, a marketing plan is useful:

- for the marketer
- for superiors
- for non-marketing functions
- for subordinates
- to help identify sources of competitive advantage
- to force an organized approach
- to develop specificity
- to ensure consistent relationships
- to inform
- to get resources
- to get support
- to gain commitment
- to set objectives and strategies.

Finally, there are some other pragmatic, profit-related reasons for needing to prepare a strategic marketing plan.

All organizations have a mix of different types of market. Figure 2.4 shows a version of Michael Porter's generic strategies matrix.[1]

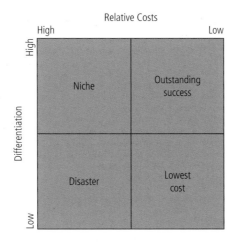

Figure 2.4: Porter's generic strategies.

The matrix shows that some markets are inherently more prone to lack of differentiation in products and services (bottom right box). It is obvious that products such as flat glass, chlorine, car insurance policies and the like are harder to differentiate than, say, perfume, beer, clothes, and so on. In such cases, the attainment of low costs must be a corporate goal, otherwise lack of adequate margins may result. Equally, if an organization's products or services are substantially different from another's, costs are rarely the principal driving force (top left box).

In reality, in their different ways, most organizations have a mix of products or services that could be classified in all four boxes. All organizations have some 'disaster' products, some 'lowest cost' products, some 'niche' products and some 'outstanding success' products.

MARKETING INSIGHT

For example, Canada Dry used to have to sell 'pop' products such as large bottles of lemonade in order to have a full line of soft drinks, even though they made their profits on 'mixer' drinks such as tonic water and ginger ale. It was a requirement to have a full line in order to be a serious player in the market.

Likewise, while it is tempting for accountants to want to delete products like this, it is essential to understand the role they play in making profits. Consequently, it is the role of the strategic marketing plan to spell out at least three years in advance what the mix will be between products and services in each of the four boxes in Figure 2.4.

Also, all organizations have products and services that produce different levels of sales and profit margins. Figure 2.5 shows the make-up of RONA and it is clear from this that profit occurs because of a mix of different margin products and different levels of turnover for each of these products. It is the purpose of the marketing plan to spell out at least three years in advance what the desired mix is of low turnover, high margin/high turnover products and all variations in between. It isn't enough just to do the accounts at the end of the fiscal year and hope the right net profit occurs. How the plan should do this is explained clearly in Chapter 6.

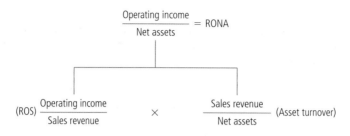

Figure 2.5: Return on net assets.

ARE WE TALKING ABOUT A TACTICAL OR A STRATEGIC MARKETING PLAN?

The authors' own research has shown that, in peering into the murky depths of organizational behaviour in relation to marketing planning, confusion reigns supreme, and nowhere more than over the terminology of marketing.

> Few practising marketers understand the real significance of a ▶ strategic marketing plan as opposed to a ▶ tactical, or operational marketing plan.

> A strategic plan is a plan which covers a period beyond the next fiscal year. Usually this is for between three and five years

Why should this be so? For an answer, we need to look at some of the changes that have taken place during the past three decades. For example, the simple environment of the 1970s and early 1980s, characterized by growth and the easy marketability of products and services, has now been replaced by an increasingly complex and abrasive environment, often made worse by static or declining markets. For most, the days have gone when it was only necessary to ride the tidal wave of growth. There wasn't the same need for a disciplined, systematic approach to the market. A tactical, short-term approach to marketing planning seemed to work perfectly well in such conditions. But, by failing to grasp the nettle of strategic orientation in plans that identify and develop their distinctive competence, companies became casualties in the 1990s and continued to become so in the first decade of the twenty-first century (for evidence of this, see McDonald[2]).

> A tactical plan covers in quite a lot of detail the actions to be taken, by whom, during a short-term planning period. This is usually for one year or less

The problem is really quite simple.

> Most managers prefer to sell the products they find easiest to sell to those customers who offer the least line of resistance. By developing short-term, tactical marketing plans first and then extrapolating them, managers merely succeed in extrapolating their own shortcomings, as was illustrated in Figures 2.1 and 2.2.

It is a bit like steering from the wake – all right in calm, clear waters, but not so sensible in busy and choppy waters! Preoccupation with preparing a detailed one-year plan first is typical of those many companies who confuse sales forecasting and budgeting with strategic marketing planning – in our experience the most common mistake of all.

MARKETING INSIGHT

It is interesting to note that, of Tom Peters' original 43 so-called 'excellent companies' in 1982, very few would be classed as excellent today, while many have disappeared altogether because of a fixation with excellent tactics at the expense of strategy (Richard T. Pascale, *Managing on the Edge*, Simon and Schuster, 1990).

This brings us to the starting point in marketing planning – an understanding of the difference between strategy and tactics and the association with the relevant adjectives 'effective' and 'efficient'. This point is expanded on in Figure 2.6, which shows a matrix in which the horizontal axis represents strategy as a continuum from ineffective to effective. The vertical axis represents tactics on a continuum from inefficient to efficient. Those firms with an effective strategy (Box 1) continue to thrive. Those with an effective strategy but inefficient tactics (Box 2) have merely survived. Those firms to the left of the matrix are destined to die, as too much emphasis is placed on tactics, so avoiding the underlying strategic issues surrounding changing market needs. Any organization doing the wrong things more efficiently (Box 3) is destined to die more quickly than their less efficient counterparts. It is a bit like making a stupid manager work harder, thus doubling the chaos and probably offending twice as many customers!

MARKETING INSIGHT

Already, companies led by chief executives with a proactive orientation that stretches beyond the end of the current fiscal year have begun to show results visibly better than the old reactive companies with only a short-term vision.

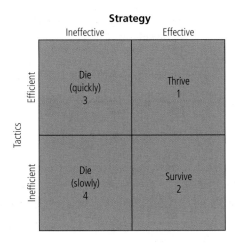

Figure 2.6: Strategy/tactics matrix.

One Scandinavian capital goods manufacturer was devoting its energies to stock control, headcount reduction, cash flow and the like. The problem, however, was one of falling demand. Had it not been pointed out to the board that this underlying marketing issue had to be addressed, it is easy to imagine how anorexia industrialosa could have resulted (an excessive desire to be leaner and fitter, leading to emaciation and, eventually, death).

Figure 2.7 shows the old style of company in which very little attention is paid to strategy by any level of management. It will be seen that lower levels of management do not get involved at all, while the directors spend most of their time on operational/tactical issues.

Figure 2.8 is a representation of those companies that recognize the importance of strategy and who manage to involve all levels of management in strategy formulation.

The rule, then, is simple:

* Develop the *strategic* marketing plan first. This entails greater emphasis on scanning the external environment, the early identification of forces emanating from it, and developing appropriate strategic responses, involving all levels of management in the process.
* A strategic plan should cover a period of between three and five years, and only when this has been developed and agreed should the one-year operational marketing plan be developed. Never write the one-year plan first and extrapolate it.

The emphasis throughout this book is on the preparation of a *strategic* marketing plan. The format for an operational or tactical plan is exactly the same, except for the amount of detail. This will be dealt with in Chapter 14.

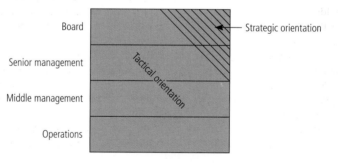

Figure 2.7: Managerial/tactical orientation.

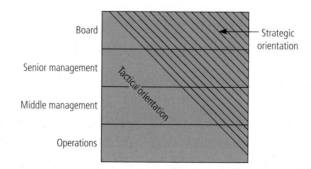

Figure 2.8: Managerial strategic/tactical orientation.

THE EFFECTIVENESS OF MARKETING PLANNING

Research into the efficacy of formalized marketing planning[3-10] has shown that marketing planning can make a significant contribution to commercial success. The main effects within organizations are:

* the systematic identification of emerging opportunities and threats
* preparedness to meet change
* the specification of sustainable competitive advantage
* improved communication among executives
* reduction of conflicts between individuals and departments
* the involvement of all levels of management in the planning process
* more appropriate allocation of scarce resources
* consistency of approach across the organization
* a more market-focused orientation across the organization.

However, although it can bring many benefits, a strategic marketing plan is mainly concerned with competitive advantage – that is to say, establishing, building, defending and maintaining it.

In order to be realistic, it must take into account the organization's existing competitive position, where it wants to be in the future, its capabilities and the competitive environment it faces. This means that the marketing planner must learn to use the various available processes and techniques which help to make sense of external trends, and to understand the organization's traditional ways of responding to these.

However, this poses the problem regarding which are the most relevant and useful tools and techniques, for each has strengths and weaknesses and no individual concept or technique can satisfactorily describe and illuminate the whole picture. As with a jigsaw puzzle, a sense of unity only emerges as the various pieces are connected together.

The links between strategy and performance (referred to in Chapter 1) have been the subject of detailed statistical analysis by the Strategic Planning Institute. The PIMS (Profit Impact of Market Strategy) project identified six major links from 2,600 businesses.[11] From this analysis, principles have been derived for the selection of different strategies according to industry type, market conditions and the competitive position of the company.

However, not all observers are prepared to take these conclusions at face value. Like strategy consultants Lubatkin and Pitts,[12] who believe that all businesses are unique, they are suspicious that something as critical as competitive advantage can be the outcome of a few specific formulae. For them, the PIMS perspective is too mechanistic and glosses over the complex managerial and organizational problems which beset most businesses.

What is agreed, however, is that strategic marketing planning presents a useful process by which an organization formulates its strategies, *providing it is adapted* to the organization and its environment.

HOW MARKETING PLANNING FITS IN WITH CORPORATE PLANNING AND OTHER FUNCTIONS

First of all, it is necessary to position marketing planning firmly within the context of strategic planning generally. Strategic decisions are concerned with:

* the long-term direction of the organization, as opposed to day-to-day management issues
* defining the scope of the organization's activities in terms of what it will and will not do
* matching the activities of the organization to the environment in which it operates, so that it optimizes opportunities and minimizes threats
* matching the organization's activities to its resource capacity, be it finance, workforce, technology or skill levels.

Strategic management characteristically deals with an uncertain future and new initiatives. As a result of this, it is often the harbinger of change. Organizations build their business strategies in a number of different ways.

There are six accepted strategy-forming models:

1. *A Planning Model*. Strategic decisions are reached by use of a sequential, planned search for optimum solutions to defined problems. This process is highly rational and is fuelled by concrete data.
2. *An Interpretative Model*. The organization is regarded as a collection of associations, sharing similar values, beliefs and perceptions. These 'frames of reference' enable the stakeholders to interpret the organization and the environment in which it operates, cultivating the emergence of an organizational culture particular to that company. Strategy thus becomes the product, not of defined aims and objectives, but of the prevailing values, attitudes and ideas in the organization.
3. *A Political Model*. Strategy is not chosen directly, but emerges through compromise, conflict and consensus-seeking among interested stakeholders. Since the strategy is the outcome of negotiation, bargaining and confrontation, those with the most power have the greatest influence.
4. *A Logical Incremental Model*. Strategies emerge from 'strategic sub-systems', each concerned with a different type of strategic issue. Strategic goals are based on an awareness of needs, rather than the highly structured analytical process of the planning model. Often, due to a lack of necessary information, such goals can be vague, general and non-rigid in nature until such a time when events unfold and more information becomes known.
5. *An Ecological Model*. In this perspective, the environment impinges on the organization in such a way that strategies are virtually prescribed and there is little or no free choice. In this model, the organization which adapts most successfully to its environment will survive in a way which mirrors Darwin's theory of natural selection.
6. *A Visionary Leadership Model*. Strategy emerges as the result of the leader's vision, enforced by their commitment to it, their personal credibility, and how they articulate it to others.

(Based on research by A. Bailey and J. Johnson[13].)

It is unlikely that an organization will use a pure version of any of these models. In all probability, its strategic decision-making model will be a hybrid of some of them. However, it is possible that one or two of these will predominate and thereby give strategic decision making a distinct 'flavour'.

While academics cannot seem to agree on a single, best approach, company executives have to get on with strategy formulation as best they can, using a combination of experience, intuition and hope. One of the earliest PhDs in the domain of marketing planning (the author's[8]) came to the conclusion that the process they go through is some sort of a logical sequence leading to the set-ting of objectives and the formulation of strategies and tactics for achieving them, together with the associated financial consequences. The formality of this process will be a function of the degree of product/market complexity, organizational size and the degree of environmental turbulence. In other words, the degree of formality will be driven in part by the dominant decision-making model in the organization.

Strategic marketing planning obviously cannot be discussed in isolation from the above strategic planning models and it is likely that the way in which an organization's marketing planning is carried out will be a microcosm of the principal mode used by a company for its corporate planning.

For the purpose of this book, however, the Planning Model will be used, as elements of this will underpin all marketing planning processes.

While marketing planning is based on markets, customers and products, business planning involves other corporate resources, which will have a bearing on the identified markets. Corporate planning usually involves applying business planning to several different units of the business aggregate.

Before turning our attention to the steps in the marketing planning process, it would be useful to discuss how marketing planning relates to the corporate planning process.

There are five steps in the corporate planning process. As can be seen from Table 2.3, the start-ing point is usually a statement of *corporate financial objectives* for the long-range planning period of the company, which are often expressed in terms of turnover, profit before tax, and return on investment.

This long-range planning horizon used to be five years although, more recently, three years is becoming increasingly the norm. However, the precise period should be determined by the nature of the markets in which the company operates. For example, five years would not be a long enough period for a glass manufacturer, since it takes that period of time to commission new capital plant, whereas in some fashion industries five years would be too long. A useful guideline in determining the planning horizon is that there should be a market for the compa-ny's products for long enough at least to amortize any new capital investment associated with those products.

Nonetheless, for the purpose of putting in sufficient detail for a strategic plan to be of any practical use, it is advisable to keep the period down to three years if possible, since beyond this period detail of any kind is likely to become pointless. There can certainly be scenarios for five to ten years, but not a plan in the sense intended by this book.

The next step is the *management audit*, to be discussed in more detail later in this chap-ter. This is an obvious activity to follow on with, since a thorough situation review, particularly in the area of marketing, should enable the company to determine whether it will be able to meet the long-range financial targets with its current range of products in its current markets. Any projected gap can be filled by the various methods of product development or market extension.

Step 1 Corporate financial objectives	2 Management audit	3 Objective and strategy setting	4 Plans	5 Corporate plans
	Marketing audit: Marketing	Marketing objectives, strategies	Marketing plan	
	Distribution audit: Stocks and control; transportation; warehousing	Distribution objectives, strategies	Distribution plan	
Corporate financial objectives	*Operations audit:* Value analysis; engineering development; work study; quality control; labour; materials, plant and space utilization; production planning; factories; R and D; information technology, etc.	Operations objectives, strategies	Operations plan	Issue of corporate plan, to include corporate objectives and strategies; operations objectives and strategies, etc.; long-range profit and loss accounts; balance sheets
	Financial audit: Credit, debt, cash flow and budgetary control; resource allocation; capital expenditure; long-term finance	Financial objectives, strategies	Financial plan	
	Personnel audit: Management, technical and administrative ability, etc.	Personnel objectives, strategies	Personnel plan	

Table 2.3: Marketing planning and its place in the corporate cycle

Undoubtedly the most important and difficult of all stages in the corporate planning process is the third step, *objective and strategy setting*, since if this is not done properly everything that follows is of little value.

Later on, we will discuss marketing objectives and strategies in more detail. For now, the important point to make is that this is the time in the planning cycle when a compromise has to be reached between what is wanted by the several functional departments and what is practicable, given all the constraints that any company has. For example, it is no good setting a marketing objective of penetrating a new market if the company does not have the production capacity to cope with the new business, and if capital is not available for whatever investment is necessary in additional capacity. At this stage, objectives and strategies will be set for three years, or for whatever the planning horizon is.

Step 4 involves producing detailed *plans* for one year, containing the responsibilities, timing and costs of carrying out the first year's objectives, and broad plans for the following years.

These plans can then be incorporated into the *corporate plan*, which will contain long-range corporate objectives, strategies, plans, profit and loss accounts, and balance sheets.

At this point it is worth noting that one of the main purposes of a corporate plan is to provide a long-term vision of what the company is or is striving to become, taking account of shareholder expectations, environmental trends, resource market trends, consumption market trends, and the distinctive competence of the company as revealed by the management audit.

What this means in practice is that the corporate plan will usually contain at least the following elements:

1. The desired level of profitability
2. Business boundaries
   - what kinds of products will be sold to what kinds of markets
   - (marketing)
   - what kinds of facilities will be developed (operations, R and D, information systems, distribution, etc.)
   - the size and character of the labour force (personnel)
   - funding (finance)
3. Other corporate objectives, such as social responsibility, corporate image, stock market image, employer image, etc.

Such a corporate plan, containing projected profit and loss accounts and balance sheets, being the result of the process described above, is more likely to provide long-term stability for a company than plans based on a more intuitive process and containing forecasts which tend to be little more than extrapolations of previous trends. This process is further summarized in Figure 2.9.

One of the main purposes of a corporate plan is to provide a long-term vision of what the company is or is striving to become.

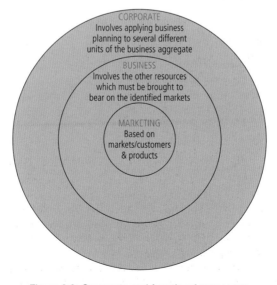

Figure 2.9: Corporate and functional processes.

MARKETING INSIGHT

The headquarters of one major multinational company with a sophisticated budgeting system used to receive 'plans' from all over the world and coordinate them in quantitative and cross-functional terms such as numbers of employees, units of sales, items of plant, square feet of production area, and so on, together with the associated financial implications. The trouble was that the whole complicated edifice was built on the initial sales forecasts, which were themselves little more than a time-consuming numbers game. The really key strategic issues relating to products and markets were lost in all the financial activity, which eventually resulted in grave operational and profitability problems.

Positioning Marketing Planning Within Marketing

Smith's PhD thesis[10] proved a direct link between organizational success and marketing strategies that conform to what previous scholars have agreed constitutes strategy quality, which was shown to be independent of variables such as size, sector, market conditions, and so on.

This thesis linked superior performance to strategies with the following qualities:

1. Homogeneous market segment definition
2. Segment-specific propositions
3. Strategy uniqueness
4. Strength leverage and weakness minimization
5. Creation of internal and external synergies
6. Provision of tactical guidance
7. Alignment to objectives
8. Alignment to market trends
9. Appropriate resourcing
10. Clear basis of competition.

Let us first, however, position strategic marketing planning firmly within the context of marketing itself.

As can be deduced from Chapter 1, marketing is a process for:

- defining markets
- quantifying the needs of the customer groups (segments) within these markets
- determining the value propositions to meet these needs
- communicating these value propositions to all those people in the organization responsible for delivering them and getting their buy-in to their role
- playing an appropriate part in delivering these value propositions to the chosen market segments
- monitoring the value actually delivered.

For this process to be effective, we have also seen that organizations need to be consumer/customer driven.

The map of this process is repeated in Figure 2.10. This process is clearly cyclical, in that monitoring the value delivered will update the organization's understanding of the value that is required by its customers. The cycle is predominantly an annual one, with a marketing plan documenting the output from the 'understand value' and 'determine value proposition' processes, but equally changes throughout the year may involve fast iterations around the cycle to respond to particular opportunities or problems.

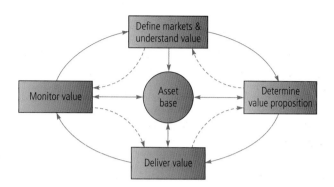

Figure 2.10: Map of the marketing process.

It is well known that not all of the value proposition delivering processes will be under the control of the marketing department, whose role varies considerably between organizations.

The marketing department is likely to be responsible for the first two processes, 'Understand value' and 'Determine value proposition', although even these need to involve numerous functions, albeit coordinated by specialist marketing personnel. The 'Deliver value' process is the role of the whole company, including, for example, product development, manufacturing, purchasing, sales promotion, direct mail, distribution, sales and customer service. The marketing department will also be responsible for monitoring the effectiveness of the value delivered.

The various choices made during this marketing process are constrained and informed not just by the outside world, but also by the organization's asset base. Whereas an efficient new factory with much spare capacity might underpin a growth strategy in a particular market, a factory running at full capacity would cause more reflection on whether price should be used to control demand, unless the potential demand warranted further capital investment. As well as physical assets, choices may be influenced by financial, human resources, brand and information technology assets, to name just a few.

Thus, it can be seen that the first two boxes are concerned with strategic marketing planning processes (in other words, developing market strategies), while the third and fourth boxes are concerned with the actual delivery in the market of what was planned and then measuring the effect.

Input to this process will commonly include:

- the corporate mission and objectives, which will determine which particular markets are of interest
- external data such as market research
- internal data which flow from ongoing operations.

Also, it is necessary to define the markets the organization is in, or wishes to be in, and how these divide into segments of customers with similar needs. The importance of doing this correctly was emphasized earlier in the reference to Smith's 2003 PhD. The choice of markets will be influenced by the corporate objectives as well as the asset base. Information will be collected about the markets, such as the market's size and growth, with estimates for the future.

The map is inherently cross-functional. 'Deliver value proposition', for example, involves every aspect of the organization, from new product development through inbound logistics and production to outbound logistics and customer service.

The map represents best practice, not common practice. Many aspects of the map are not explicitly addressed by well-embedded processes, even in sophisticated companies.

Also, the map is changing. One-to-one communications and principles of relationship marketing demand a radically different sales process from that traditionally practised. Hence exploiting new media such as the Internet requires a substantial shift in thinking, not just changes to IT and hard processes. An example is illuminating. Marketing managers at one company related to us their early experience with a website which was enabling them to reach new customers considerably more cost-effectively than their traditional sales force. When the website was first launched, potential customers were finding the company on the Web, deciding the products were appropriate on the basis of the website, and sending an e-mail to ask to buy. So far so good. But stuck in a traditional model of the sales process, the company would allocate the 'lead' to a salesperson, who would phone up and make an appointment perhaps three weeks hence. The customer would by now probably have moved on to another online supplier who could sell the product today, but those that remained were subjected to a sales pitch which was totally unnecessary, the customer having already decided to buy. Those that were not put off would proceed to be registered as able to buy over the Web, but the company had lost the opportunity to improve its margins by using the sales force more judiciously. In time the company realized its mistake: unlike those prospects which the company identified and contacted, which might indeed need 'selling' to, many new Web customers were initiating the dialogue themselves, and simply required the company to respond effectively and rapidly. The sales force was increasingly freed up to concentrate on major clients and on relationship building.

Having put marketing planning into the context of marketing and other corporate functions, we can now turn specifically to the marketing planning process, how it should be done and what the barriers are to doing it effectively. We are, of course, referring specifically to the second box in Figure 2.10. See Chapter 4 for more detail on market segmentation.

THE MARKETING PLANNING PROCESS

Figure 2.11 illustrates the several stages that have to be gone through in order to arrive at a marketing plan. This illustrates the difference between the process of marketing planning and the actual plan itself, which is the output of the process, which is discussed later in this chapter.

Each of the process stages illustrated in Figure 2.11 will be discussed in more detail in this chapter. Stages 5–8 will usually have to be gone through more than once before final programmes can be written.

How Formal Should This Process Be?

Although research has shown these marketing planning steps to be universally applicable, the degree to which each of the separate steps in the diagram needs to be formalized depends to a large extent on the size and nature of the company. For example, an undiversified company generally uses less formalized procedures, since top management tends to have greater functional knowledge and expertise than subordinates, and because the lack of diversity of operations enables direct control to be exercised over most of the key determinants of success. Thus, situation reviews, the setting of marketing objectives, and so on, are not always made explicit in writing, although these steps have to be gone through.

In contrast, in a diversified company, it is usually not possible for top management to have greater functional knowledge and expertise than subordinate management, hence planning tends to be more formalized in order to provide a consistent discipline for those who have to make the decisions throughout the organization.

Either way, there is now a substantial body of evidence to show that formalized planning procedures generally result in greater profitability and stability in the long term and also help to reduce friction and operational difficulties within organizations.

Bailey *et al.*'s typology of the different styles of planning went some way to throwing light on the actual degree of formalization of marketing planning processes, although Smith's 2003 thesis reduced these to three – visionary processes, rational processes and incremental processes, with most successful companies using some combination of all three.

Where marketing planning has failed, it has generally been because companies have placed too much emphasis on the procedures themselves and the resulting forecasts, rather than on

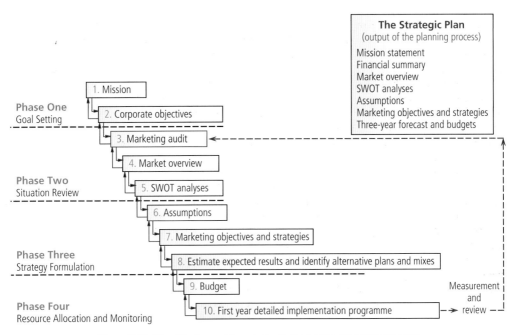

Figure 2.11: The 10 steps of the strategic marketing planning process.

generating information useful to and consumable by management. But more about reasons for failure in Chapter 3. For now, let us look at the marketing planning process, starting with the mission statement. At this stage, our purpose is merely to outline the steps in the process, as each stage will be spelled out in more detail in later chapters.

Step 1 Mission Statement

Figure 2.11 shows that a strategic marketing plan should begin with a mission or purpose statement. This is perhaps the most difficult aspect of marketing planning for managers to master, because it is largely philosophical and qualitative in nature. Many organizations find their different departments, and sometimes even different groups in the same department, pulling in different directions, often with disastrous results, simply because the organization hasn't defined the boundaries of the business and the way it wishes to do business.

Here, we can see two levels of mission. One is a corporate mission statement; the other is a lower level, or purpose statement. But there is yet another level, as shown in the following summary:

Type 1 'Motherhood' – usually found inside annual reports designed to 'stroke' shareholders; otherwise of no practical use

Type 2 The real thing – a meaningful statement, unique to the organization concerned, which 'impacts' on the behaviour of the executives at all levels

Type 3 This is a 'purpose' statement (or lower level mission statement). It is appropriate at the strategic business unit, departmental or product group level of the organization

The following is an example of a meaningless, vapid, motherhood-type mission statement, which most companies seem to have. They achieve nothing and it is difficult to understand why these pointless statements are so popular. Employees mock them and they rarely say anything likely to give direction to the organization. We have entitled this example 'The Generic Mission Statement' and they are to be avoided.

THE GENERIC MISSION STATEMENT

Our organization's primary mission is to protect and increase the value of its owners' investments while efficiently and fairly serving the needs of its customers. [. . . insert organization name . . .] seeks to accomplish this in a manner that contributes to the development and growth of its employees, and to the goals of countries and communities in which it operates.

Another example of a meaningless mission statement was recorded in *HBR*[14] in 2008 and is included here:

PLATITUDINOUS, GENERIC MISSION STATEMENT

To maximise shareholder wealth by exceeding customer expectation and providing opportunities for our employees to lead fulfilling lives while respecting the environment and the communities within which we operate.

The following should appear in a mission or purpose statement, which should normally run to no more than one page:

1. *Role or contribution*
   * profit (specify), or
   * service, or
   * opportunity seeker.
2. *Business definition* – define the business, preferably in terms of the *benefits* you provide or the *needs* you satisfy, rather than in terms of what you make.
3. *Distinctive competences* – these are the essential skills/capabilities resources that underpin whatever success has been achieved to date. Competence can consist of one particular item or the possession of a number of skills compared with competitors. If, however, you could equally well put a competitor's name to these distinctive competences, then they are not distinctive competences.
4. *Indications for the future*
   * what the firm will do
   * what the firm might do
   * what the firm will never do.

Step 2 Setting Corporate Objectives

What corporate objectives are, and where they fit in the total process, was discussed in the previous section.

Step 3 The Marketing Audit

Any plan will only be as good as the information on which it is based, and the marketing audit is the means by which information for planning is organized. There is no reason why marketing cannot be audited in the same way as accounts, in spite of its more innovative, subjective nature. A marketing audit is a systematic appraisal of all the external and internal factors that have affected a company's commercial performance over a defined period.

Given the growing turbulence of the business environment and the shorter product lifecycles that have resulted, no one would deny the need to stop at least once a year at a particular point in the planning cycle to try to form a reasoned view of how all the many external and internal factors have influenced performance.

Sometimes, of course, a company will conduct a marketing audit because it is in financial trouble. At times like these, management often attempts to treat the wrong symptoms, most frequently by reorganizing the company. But such measures are unlikely to be effective if there are more fundamental problems which have not been identified. Of course, if the company survived for long enough, it might eventually solve its problems through a process of elimination. Essentially, though, the argument is that the problems have first to be properly defined. The audit is a means of helping to define them.

Two kinds of variable

Any company carrying out an audit will be faced with two kinds of variable. First, there is the kind over which the company has no direct control, for example economic and market factors. Second, there are those over which the company has complete control, the operational variables, which are usually the firm's internal resources. This division suggests that the best way to structure an audit is in two parts, external and internal. Table 2.4 shows areas which should be investigated under both headings. Each should be examined with a view to building up an information base relevant to the company's performance.

Many people mistakenly believe that the marketing audit should be some kind of final attempt to define a company's marketing problems, or, at best, something done by an independent body from time to time to ensure that a company is on the right track. However, many highly successful companies, as well as using normal information and control procedures and marketing research throughout the year, start their planning cycle each year with a formal, audit-type process, of everything that has had an important influence on marketing activities. Certainly, in many leading consumer goods companies, the annual self-audit approach is a tried and tested discipline.

Objections to line managers doing their own audits usually centre on the problem of time and objectivity. In practice, a disciplined approach and thorough training will help. But the discipline must be applied from the highest to the lowest levels of management if the tunnel vision that often results from a lack of critical appraisal is to be avoided.

Where relevant, the marketing audit should contain lifecycles for major products and for market segments, for which the future shape will be predicted using the audit information. Also, major products and markets should be plotted on some kind of matrix to show their current competitive position.

The next question is: what happens to the results of the audit? Some companies consume valuable resources carrying out audits that produce very little in the way of results. The audit is simply a database, and the task remains of turning it into intelligence, that is, information essential to decision making.

Step 4 Market Overview

This step, which appears prominently in the actual strategic marketing plan, should spell out clearly:

- what the market is
- how it works
- what the key decision-making points are
- what the segments are.

External audit	Internal audit
Business and economic environment Economic, political, fiscal, legal, social, cultural Technological Intra-company	Own company Sales (total, by geographical location, by industrial type, by customer, by product) Market shares
The market	Profit margins, costs
Total market, size, growth and trends (value/volume)	Marketing information/research
Market characteristics, developments and trends: products, prices, physical distribution, channels, customers, consumers, communication, industry practices	Marketing mix variables: product management, price, distribution, promotion, operations and resources
Competition Major competitors Size Market share/coverage Market standing and reputation Production capabilities Distribution policies Marketing methods Extent of diversification Personnel issues International links Profitability Key strengths and weaknesses	

Table 2.4: Conducting an audit

Market definition is fundamental to success and must be made in terms of need sets rather than in product/service terms. Thus, Gestetner failed by defining its markets as 'duplicators' and IBM almost failed by defining its market as 'mainframes'. Accordingly, a pension is a product, not a market, as many other products can satisfy the same or similar needs. Having done this, a 'market map' should be drawn, which plots the flow of goods or services from supplier through to user, with quantities through the chain which add up to the market size.

In the sense that if five million radiators are made or imported, five million radiators must be distributed, five million radiators must be installed and the decision about which radiators are to be installed must be made by someone. It is the purpose of the market map to spell all this out quantitatively.

It is at key decision points that market segmentation should take place. A segment is a group of customers or consumers that share the same (or approximately the same) needs; this is discussed in detail in Chapter 4. This step is crucial, for it is upon the key segments from the market map that SWOT analyses should be completed.

Step 5 SWOT Analyses

The only remaining question is what happens to the results of the audit? Some companies consume valuable resources carrying out audits that bring very little by way of actionable results.

Indeed, there is always the danger that, at the audit stage, insufficient attention is paid to the need to concentrate on analysis that determines which trends and developments will actually affect the company. While the checklist demonstrates the completeness of logic and analysis, the people carrying out the audit should discipline themselves to omit from their audits all the information that is not central to the company's marketing problems. Thus, inclusion of research reports, or overdetailed sales performance histories by product which lead to no logical actions whatever, only serve to rob the audit of focus and reduce its relevance.

Since the objective of the audit is to indicate what a company's marketing objectives and strategies should be, it follows that it would be helpful if some format could be found for organizing the major findings.

One useful way of doing this is in the form of a number of SWOT analyses. A SWOT is a summary of the audit under the headings, internal strengths and weaknesses as they relate to external opportunities and threats.

A SWOT should be conducted for each segment that is considered to be important in the company's future. These SWOT analyses should, if possible, contain just a few paragraphs of commentary focusing on *key* factors only. They should highlight internal *differential* strengths and weaknesses *vis-à-vis* competitors and key external opportunities and threats. A summary of reasons for good or bad performance should be included. They should be interesting to read, contain concise statements, include only relevant and important data, and give greater emphasis to creative analysis.

How to conduct SWOT analyses is discussed in detail in Chapter 5.

Step 6 Assumptions

Let us now return to the preparation of the marketing plan. If we refer again to the marketing planning process, and have completed our marketing audit and SWOT analyses, assumptions now have to be written.

There are certain key determinants of the marketing plan. If we refer again to the marketing planning process, and have completed our marketing audit and SWOT analyses, assumptions now have to be written.

It is really a question of standardizing the planning environment. For example, it would be no good receiving plans from two product managers, one of whom believed the market was going to increase by 10 per cent, while the other believed the market was going to decline by 10 per cent.

Examples of assumptions might be:

With respect to the company's industrial climate, it is assumed that:

1. Industrial overcapacity will increase from 105 per cent to 115 per cent as new industrial plants come into operation.
2. Price competition will force price levels down by 10 per cent across the board.
3. A new product in the field of *x* will be introduced by our major competitor before the end of the second quarter.

Assumptions should be few in number, and if a plan is possible irrespective of the assumptions made, then the assumptions are unnecessary.

Step 7 Marketing Objectives and Strategies

The next step in marketing planning is the writing of marketing objectives and strategies, the key to the whole process.

An *objective* is what you want to achieve. A *strategy* is how you plan to achieve your objectives.

Thus, there can be objectives and strategies at all levels in marketing. For example, there can be advertising objectives and strategies, and pricing objectives and strategies.

However, the important point to remember about marketing objectives is that they are about *products* and *markets* only. Common sense will confirm that it is only by selling something to someone that the company's financial goals can be achieved, and that advertising, pricing, service levels, and so on are the means (or strategies) by which we might succeed in doing this. Thus, pricing objectives, sales promotion objectives, advertising objectives and the like should not be confused with marketing objectives. Marketing objectives are simply about one (or more) of the following:

* Existing products for existing markets
* New products for existing markets
* Existing products for new markets
* New products for new markets.

They should be capable of measurement, otherwise they are not objectives. Directional terms such as 'maximize', 'minimize', 'penetrate', 'increase', etc. are only acceptable if quantitative measurement can be attached to them. Measurement should be in terms of some, or all, of the following: sales volume; sales value; market share; profit; percentage penetration of outlets (for example, to have 30 per cent of all retail outlets stocking our product by year 3).

Marketing strategies are the means by which marketing objectives will be achieved and generally are concerned with the four Ps, as follows:

Product – The general policies for product deletions, modifications, addition, design, branding, positioning, packaging, etc.

Price – The general pricing policies to be followed by product groups in market segments

Place – The general policies for channels and customer service levels

Promotion – The general policies for communicating with customers under the relevant headings, such as advertising, sales force, sales promotion, public relations, exhibitions, direct mail, etc.

Step 8 Estimate Expected Results and Identify Alternative Plans and Mixes

Having completed this major planning task, it is normal at this stage to employ judgement, analogous experience, field tests, and so on, to test out the feasibility of the objectives and strategies in terms of market share, costs, profits, and so on. It is also normally at this stage that alternative plans and mixes are considered, if necessary.

Step 9 The Budget

In a strategic marketing plan, these strategies would normally be costed out approximately and, if not practicable, alternative strategies would be proposed and costed out until a satisfactory solution could be reached. This would then become the budget. In most cases, there would be a budget for the full three years of the strategic marketing plan, but there would also be a very detailed budget for the first year of the plan which would be included in the one-year operational plan.

It will be obvious from all of this that the setting of budgets becomes not only much easier, but the resulting budgets are more likely to be realistic and related to what the *whole* company wants to achieve, rather than just one functional department.

The problem of designing a dynamic system for budget setting, rather than the 'tablets of stone' approach, which is more common, is a major challenge to the marketing and financial directors of all companies.

The most satisfactory approach would be for a marketing director to justify all marketing expenditure from a zero base each year against the tasks he or she wishes to accomplish. A little thought will confirm that this is exactly the approach recommended in this chapter. If these procedures are followed, a hierarchy of objectives is built up in such a way that every item of budgeted expenditure can be related directly back to the initial corporate financial objectives. For example, if sales promotion is a major means of achieving an objective in a particular market, when sales promotional items appear in the programme, each one has a specific purpose which can be related back to a major objective.

Doing it this way not only ensures that every item of expenditure is fully accounted for as part of a rational, objective and task approach, but also that when changes have to be made during the period to which the plan relates, these changes can be made in such a way that the least damage is caused to the company's long-term objectives.

The incremental marketing expense can be considered to be all costs that are incurred after the product leaves the factory, *other than* costs involved in physical distribution, the costs of which usually represent a discrete subset.

There is, of course, no textbook answer to problems relating to questions such as whether packaging should be a marketing or a production expense, and whether some distribution costs could be considered to be marketing costs. For example, insistence on high service levels results in high inventory carrying costs. Only common sense will reveal workable solutions to issues such as these.

Under *price*, however, any form of discounting that reduces the expected gross income, such as promotional discounts, quantity discounts, royalty rebates, and so on, as well as sales commission and unpaid invoices, should be given the most careful attention as incremental marketing expenses.

Most obvious incremental marketing expenses will occur, however, under the heading 'promotion', in the form of advertising, sales, salaries and expenses, sales promotional expenditure, direct mail costs, and so on. The important point about the measurable effects of marketing activity is that anticipated levels should be the result of the most careful analysis of what is required to take the company towards its goals, while the most careful attention should be paid to gathering all items of expenditure under appropriate headings. The healthiest way of treating these issues is a zero-bases budgeting approach.

Step 10 First Year Detailed Implementation Programme

In a one-year tactical plan, the general marketing strategies would be developed into specific subobjectives, each supported by more detailed strategy and action statements.

A company organized according to functions might have an advertising plan, a sales promotion plan, a pricing plan, and so on.

A product-based company might have a product plan, with objectives, strategies and tactics for price, place and promotion as necessary.

A market or geographically based company might have a market plan, with objectives, strategies and tactics for the four Ps as necessary.

Likewise, a company with a few major customers might have customer plans.

Any combination of the above might be suitable, depending on circumstances.

WHAT SHOULD APPEAR IN A STRATEGIC MARKETING PLAN?

A written marketing plan is the backdrop against which operational decisions are taken. Consequently, too much detail should be avoided. Its major function is to determine where the company is, where it wants to go and how it can get there. It lies at the heart of a company's revenue-generating activities, such as the timing of the cash flow and the size and character of the labour force. What should actually appear in a written strategic marketing plan is shown in Table 2.5. This strategic marketing plan should be distributed only to those who need it, but it can only be an aid to effective management. It cannot be a substitute for it.

1. Start with a mission statement.
2. Here, include a financial summary which illustrates graphically revenue and profit for the full planning period.
3. Now do a market overview: Has the market declined or grown? How does it break down into segments? What is your share of each? Keep it simple. If you do not have the facts, make estimates. Use lifecycles, bar charts and pie charts to make it all crystal clear.
4. Now identify the key segments and do a SWOT analysis for each one: Outline the major external influences and their impact on each segment. List the key factors for success. These should be less than five. Give an assessment of the company's differential strengths and weaknesses compared with those of it competitors. Score yourself and your competitors out of 10 and then multiply each score by a weighting factor for each critical success factor (e.g. CSF 1 = 60, CSF 2 = 25, CSF 3 = 10, CSF 4 = 5).
5. Make a brief statement about the key issues that have to be addressed in the planning period.
6. Summarize the SWOTs using a portfolio matrix in order to illustrate the important relationships between your key products and markets.
7. List your assumptions.
8. Set objectives and strategies.
9. Summarize your resource requirements for the planning period in the form of a budget.

Table 2.5: What should appear in a strategic marketing plan

It will be obvious from Table 2.5 that not only does budget setting become much easier and more realistic, but the resulting budgets are more likely to reflect what the whole company wants to achieve, rather than just one department.

We have just described the strategic marketing plan and what it should contain. The tactical marketing plan layout and content should be similar, but the detail is much greater, as it is for one year only.

MARKETING PLANNING SYSTEMS DESIGN AND IMPLEMENTATION

While the actual process of marketing planning is simple in outline, a number of contextual issues have to be considered that make marketing planning one of the most baffling of all management problems. The following are some of those issues:

- When should it be done, how often, by whom, and how?
- Is it different in a large and a small company? Is it different in a diversified and an undiversified company?
- What is the role of the chief executive?
- What is the role of the planning department?
- Should marketing planning be top-down or bottom-up?
- What is the relationship between operational (one year) and strategic (longer-term) planning?

REQUISITE STRATEGIC MARKETING PLANNING

Many companies with financial difficulties have recognized the need for a more structured approach to planning their marketing and have opted for the kind of standardized, formalized procedures written about so much in textbooks. Yet these rarely bring any benefits and often bring marketing planning itself into disrepute.

It is quite clear that any attempt at the introduction of formalized marketing planning requires a change in a company's approach to managing its business. It is also clear that unless a company recognizes these implications, and plans to seek ways of coping with them, formalized strategic planning will be ineffective.

Research[8] has shown that the implications are principally as follows:

1. Any closed-loop planning system (but especially one that is essentially a forecasting and budgeting system) will lead to dull and ineffective marketing. Therefore, there has to be some mechanism for preventing inertia from setting in through the over-bureaucratization of the system.
2. Planning undertaken at the functional level of marketing, in the absence of a means of integration with other functional areas of the business at general management level, will be largely ineffective.
3. The separation of responsibility for operational and strategic planning will lead to a divergence of the short-term thrust of a business at the operational level from the long-term objectives of the enterprise as a whole. This will encourage preoccupation with short-term results at operational level, which normally makes the firm less effective in the longer term.
4. Unless the chief executive understands and takes an active role in strategic marketing planning, it will never be an effective system.
5. A period of up to three years is necessary (especially in large firms) for the successful introduction of an effective strategic marketing planning system.

A key account is a major customer considered by the supplying company to be of strategic importance to the achievement of its own objectives. Hence, such a customer is singled out for special treatment

The same PhD thesis also found that the principal barriers to implementing marketing planning are those listed in Table 2.6.

Let us be dogmatic about requisite planning levels. First, in a large diversified group, irrespective of such organizational issues, anything other than a systematic approach approximating to a formalized marketing planning system is unlikely to enable the necessary control to be exercised over the corporate identity. Second, unnecessary planning, or overplanning, could easily result from an inadequate or indiscriminate consideration of the real planning needs at the different levels in the hierarchical chain.

This process and its relationship to the other issues discussed in this chapter are summarized in Figure 2.12.

1. Weak support from the chief executive and top management.
2. Lack of a plan for planning.
3. Lack of line management support due to any of the following, either singly or in combination:
   • hostility
   • lack of skills
   • lack of information
   • lack of resources
   • inadequate organizational structure.
4. Confusion over planning terms.
5. Numbers in lieu of written objectives and strategies.
6. Too much detail, too far ahead.
7. Once-a-year ritual.
8. Separation of operational planning from strategic planning.
9. Failure to integrate marketing planning into total corporate planning system.
10. Delegation of planning to a planner.

Table 2.6: Barriers to the integration of strategic marketing planning

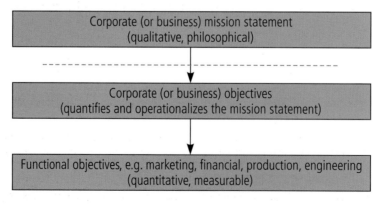

Figure 2.12: Heirarchy of planning.

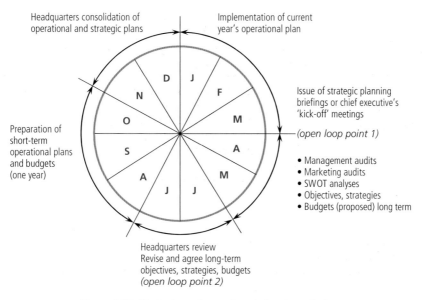

Figure 2.13: Strategic and operational planning – timing.

Figure 2.13 is another way of illustrating the total corporate strategic and marketing planning process. This time, however, a time element is added, and the relationship between strategic planning briefing, long-term strategic plans and short-term operational plans is clarified.

THE POSITION OF KEY ACCOUNT PLANNING IN THE CYCLE

There is much debate about this, but it will be clear from looking at the planning cycle in Figure 2.13 that ▶ key account planning must take place at the same time as, or even before, draft plans are prepared for a strategic business unit.

If this is not clear, let us give an example of a supplies company servicing the needs of a national health service shown in Figure 2.14. It will be seen that there are four 'markets' within hospitals to be served. These are:

* Medical
* Administration
* Catering
* Energy.

There will be a number of key accounts, or hospital groups, referred to here as Hospital Groups A, B, C, D, etc. Each of these hospital groups may well have their own key account manager who has to plan for them. Figure 2.14 illustrates this.

Thus, for example, the key account manager for Hospital A has to prepare a draft plan across all four 'markets' and this would clearly be a key input to the planning process shown in Figure 2.15.

University of Ulster LIBRARY

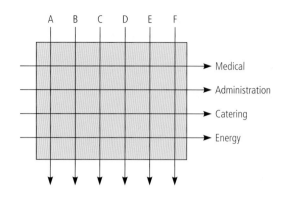

Figure 2.14: Markets and customers within markets.

Corporate plan					
Marketing plan					
Segment plan		Segment plan		Segment plan	
Account plan 1	Account plan 2	Account plan 3	Account plan 4	Account plan 5	Account plan 6

Figure 2.15: A hierarchy of the plan.

THE POSITION OF KEY ACCOUNT PLANNING IN STRATEGIC MARKETING PLANNING

As a general principle, planning should start in the market where the customers are. Indeed, in anything other than small organizations, it is clearly absurd to think that any kind of meaningful planning can take place without the committed inputs of those who operate where the customers are.

Figure 2.15 shows a hierarchy of strategic planning starting with key account planning. Every principle outlined in this chapter applies right down to the individual key account. Thus, the planning process shown in Figure 2.10 would start with key accounts. This book, however, does not deal specifically with key account planning, which is dealt with in detail in another book by one of the authors.[15]

APPLICATION QUESTIONS

1. Describe your company's marketing planning system in detail.
2. List the good things and the bad things about it.
3. Say how you think it could be improved.

CHAPTER 2 REVIEW

What is marketing planning?

Marketing planning is a logical sequence of events leading to the setting of marketing objectives and the formulation of plans for achieving them.

The sequence is:

1. Mission statement
2. Set corporate objectives
3. Conduct marketing audit
4. Conduct SWOT analyses
5. Make assumptions
6. Set marketing objectives and strategies
7. Estimate expected results
8. Identify alternative plans and mixes
9. Set the budget
10. Establish first year implementation programmes.

Try Exercise 2.1

The plan itself contains:
1. Mission statement
2. Financial summary
3. Market overview
4. SWOT analyses
5. Portfolio summary
6. Assumptions
7. Marketing objectives and strategies
8. Forecasts and budgets.

Try Exercise 2.2

Why do it?

As business becomes increasingly complex and competition increases, a marketing plan is essential.

The benefits are as follows:

1. It allows better coordination of activities.
2. It identifies expected developments.
3. It increases organizational preparedness to change.
4. It minimizes non-rational responses to the unexpected.
5. It reduces conflicts about where the company should be going.
6. It improves communications.
7. Management is forced to think ahead systematically.
8. Available resources can be better matched to opportunities.
9. The plan provides a framework for the continuing review of operations.
10. A systematic approach to strategy formulation leads to a higher return on investment.

Try Exercise 2.3

Will it help us to survive?

All companies need to have a longer-term (strategic) marketing view as well as a short- term (tactical) marketing operation. Often the most potent short-term tactic is the use of the sales force. These can combine thus:

From this it can be seen that being good at implementing the wrong strategy can lead to a very quick death!

Try Exercise 2.4

Questions raised for the company

1. Q: Can we 'buy' an 'off-the-peg' planning system?
   A: Since all companies are different, the process has to be 'tailored' to fit individual requirements.
2. Q: Are we talking about tactics or strategy?
   A: A strategic marketing plan takes a long-term look (say three years) and is therefore strategic. A tactical, or operational, marketing plan is a detailed scheduling and costing out of the *first* year of the strategic marketing plan.
3. Q: How is the marketing plan used?
   A: The plan determines where the company is now, where it wants to go and how to get there. It therefore should be the backdrop against which all organizational decisions are made.
4. Q: Does the plan have to be written?
   A: The planning sequence is really a thinking process. However, key pieces of information are worth writing down because they reduce confusion and aid communication. The degree of formality depends on the size of the company and the complexity of its business.
5. Q: How detailed should it be?
   A: Enough to be useful.

EXERCISES

The first exercise enables you to make an objective analysis of your company's marketing planning process. If you choose, you can then take matters further by working out in what ways the planning process might be improved.

The second exercise helps to clarify an often misunderstood issue, that of the company's mission statement.

The third exercise explores the extent to which your company is receiving the benefits that are usually attributed to a marketing planning process.

The final exercise will enable you to plot your company's position on the 'survival matrix'. There are several benefits to be derived from knowing this:

1. It infers the relation between your company's focus on long-term versus short-term issues.
2. It can be a powerful means of communicating to your colleagues that all might not be well in the company.
3. It provides an unambiguous message about what the company needs to address for future survival.

Exercise 2.1 The marketing planning process questionnaire

This questionnaire enables you to make an objective assessment about the marketing planning process in your company. It is designed to enable you to take a 'helicopter view' of the way your company does its planning and then to home in on the areas where improvements can be made. This approach will also enable you to identify information gaps that might be unknown to you at present.

Although care has been taken to use generally accepted terminology in the wording of this questionnaire, there will always be the company that uses different words. For example, when we talk about return on investment (ROI), other companies might well use other expressions or measures, such as return on capital employed, etc.

With this caveat in mind, please respond to the questionnaire by putting a tick against each question in one of the four columns provided.

	Yes	No	Don't know	Not appli- cable
Section 1 Corporate issues				
1. Is there a corporate statement about:				
(i) The nature of the company's current business mission?				
(ii) Its vision of the future?				
2. Is there a target figure for ROI?				
3. Is there a corporate plan to channel the company resources to this end?				
4. Are there defined business boundaries in terms of:				
(a) Products or services (that will be offered)?				
(b) Customers or markets (to deal with)?				

(Continued)

	Yes	No	Don't know	Not applicable
(c) Operations facilities?				
(d) Distribution facilities?				
(e) Size and character of the workforce?				
(f) Sources and levels of funding?				
5. Are there objectives for promoting the corporate image with:				
(a) The stock market?				
(b) Customers?				
(c) The local community?				
(d) The employees?				
(e) Environmentalist/conservationist lobby?				
(f) Government departments?				
(g) Trade associations, etc.?				
Section 2 Strategic issues				
1. Is there a marketing plan?				
2. Is it compatible with the corporate plan?				
3. Does it cover the same period?				
4. Is the marketing plan regularly reviewed?				
5. Is the plan based on an assessment of market potential and past performance?				
6. Will the plan close the 'gap' if carried out?				
7. Is there a marketing plan by product/service?				
8. Do relevant managers have a copy of the marketing plan?				
9. Are the following factors monitored in a regular and conscious way, in terms of how they affect the company's business prospects?				
(a) Business environment				
(i) Economic factors?				
(ii) Political/legal factors?				
(iii) Fiscal factors				
(iv) Technological developments?				
(v) Social/cultural factors?				
(vi) Intra-company issues?				
(b) The market				
(i) Trends in market size/growth in volume and in value				

	Yes	No	Don't know	Not applicable
(ii) Developments/trends in product use, product demand, product presentation, accessories and substitutes				
(iii) Developments/trends in prices, terms and conditions and trade practices				
(iv) Developments/trends in physical distribution, channels of distribution, purchasing patterns, stockholding and turnover				
(v) Developments/trends in communications, use of sales force, advertising, promotions, exhibitions, the internet				
(c) Competition Developments/trends of competitors, their marketing strategies, their strengths, their weaknesses, new entrants, mergers/acquisitions and their reputation				
(d) The industry				
(i) Activities of trade association(s)				
(ii) Inter-firm comparisons				
(iii) Industry profitability				
(iv) Investment levels of competitors				
(v) Changes in cost structure				
(vi) Investment prospects				
(vii) Technological developments				
(viii) Sources of raw materials				
(ix) Energy utilization				
Section 3 SWOT analyses				
1. Is there someone (individual or group) responsible for converting the analysis of factors in Section 2 into a summary which highlights: (a) The company's principal strengths? (b) The company's principal weaknesses (in terms of relating to external opportunities/threats)?				
2. Does this person(s) have access to the necessary information?				
3. Is this person(s) sufficiently senior for his or her analysis to make an impact?				

(Continued)

	Yes	No	Don't know	Not appli-cable
4. Is the organizational climate such that a full and accurate analysis is seen as a striving for improvement rather than an attack on specific departments or vested interests?				

Section 4 Assumptions

1. Is there a set of assumptions around which the marketing plan is formulated?
2. Are these assumptions made explicit to senior company personnel?
3. Do they cover:
   (a) The business environment?
   (b) The market?
   (c) The competitors?
   (d) The industry?
4. Are the assumptions valid in the light of current and predicted trading situations?

Section 5 Marketing objectives/strategies

1. Are the marketing objectives clearly stated and consistent with the corporate objectives?
2. Are there clear strategies for achieving the stated marketing objectives?
3. Are sufficient resources made available?
4. Are all responsibilities and authority clearly made known?
5. Are there agreed objectives about:
   (a) The product range?
   (b) The value of sales?
   (c) The volume of sales?
   (d) Profits?
   (e) Market share?
   (f) Market penetration?
   (g) Number of customers and retention levels?
   (h) Introducing new products/services?
   (i) Divesting of old products/services?
   (j) Organization changes to:
       (i) Develop company strengths?
       (ii) Reduce company weaknesses?

	Yes	No	Don't know	Not applicable
Section 6 Monitoring evaluation				
1. Is the planning system well conceived and effective?				
2. Do control mechanisms exist to ensure planned objectives are met?				
3. Do internal communications function effectively?				
4. Are there any problems between marketing and other corporate functions?				
5. Are people clear about their role in the planning process?				
6. Is there a procedure for dealing with non-achievement of objectives?				
7. Is there evidence that this reduces the chance of subsequent failure?				
8. Are there still unexploited opportunities?				
9. Are there still organizational weaknesses?				
10. Are the assumptions upon which the plan was based valid?				
11. Are there contingency plans in the event of objectives not being met/conditions changing?				

Scoring and interpretation for Exercise 2.1

1. Add up how many ticks were listed under 'not applicable'. It is our experience that if there are more than eight ticks, then some aspects of planning that are covered by most companies are being avoided. Reappraise those items you initially ticked as 'not applicable'. Try getting a second opinion by checking your findings with colleagues.

2. Look at those items you ticked as 'don't know'. Find out if those activities are covered in your company's planning process.

3. Having ascertained what is and what isn't done in your company, list:
   (a) the *good* things in your company's planning process
   (b) the *bad* things about it.

4. Make a note, in the space on page 60, or on a separate sheet of paper, of ways in which you think the planning process in your company could be improved.

(Continued)

Personal notes

Exercise 2.2 The mission statement

The following should appear in a mission statement:

1. *Role or contribution*: 'Profit' (specify), or 'Service', or 'Opportunity-seeker'.
2. *Business definition*: this should be defined in terms of the benefits you provide or the needs you satisfy, rather than in terms of what you do or what you make.
3. *Distinctive competence:* what essential skills/capabilities/resources underpin whatever success has been achieved to date? (Note: These factors should not apply equally to a competitor, otherwise there is no distinctive quality about them.)
4. Indications for the future: what the company *will* do. What the company *might* do. What the company will *never* do.

Questions

1. To what extent does your company's mission statement meet the criteria listed above?
2. If you do not have a mission statement, try writing one, following the guidelines provided here. Try it out on your colleagues and see if they agree with you or if they can find ways to improve on what you have written.

Scoring and interpretation for Exercise 2.2

Use the following to gauge whether you feel you and your colleagues have developed a mission statement that is of real value:

- What values are true priorities for the next few years?
- What would make me professionally commit my mind and heart to this vision over the next five to 10 years?
- What is unique about us?
- What does the world really need that our company can and should provide?
- What do I want our company to accomplish so that I will be committed, aligned, and proud of my association with the institution?

Exercise 2.3 The benefits of marketing planning

What follows is a list of the benefits of marketing planning. With your company in mind, score each benefit by means of the scale given below.

0	1 2 3	4 5 6	7 8 9	10
Never	Sometimes	Frequently	Most of the time	Always

1. Our approach to marketing planning ensures that we get a high level of coordination of our various marketing activities ....

2. Our marketing planning process enables us to identify unexpected developments in advance ....

3. Because of the way we approach marketing planning, there is an increased readiness for the organization to change in response to the issues 'flagged up' ....

4. When we are faced with the unexpected, our marketing planning process minimizes the risk of non-rational responses ....

5. Having a marketing plan reduces the conflicts between managers regarding 'where the company should be going' ....

6. Our marketing plan improves communications about market-related issues ....

7. Because of our marketing planning process, management is forced to think ahead systematically ....

8. Having a marketing plan enables us to match our resources to opportunities in an effective way ....

9. Our marketing plan provides us with a useful framework for a continuing review of progress ....

10. Our marketing planning has led us to develop more profitable marketing strategies ....

TOTAL _____

Scoring and interpretation for Exercise 2.3

The maximum score for the exercise is 100. Check your scores below.

81–100: Marketing planning is really paying off in your company

61–80: You are not receiving the benefits you should be receiving. What's getting in the way? (Exercise 2.1 might give some clues.)

(Continued)

41–60: You appear to be moving along the right lines, but there is still a long way to go.

0–40: Either your marketing planning process is inadequate, or your company is not really trying to make marketing planning work.

Before you tackle this exercise, it is important to remember that profitability and high market growth are nearly always correlated. In other words, the higher the market growth, the higher the profitability.

This phenomenon can sometimes obscure the fact that a company that appears to be doing well can still be losing ground in comparison with its competitors. While apparently thriving, it is in fact dying slowly. The crunch comes when the erstwhile buoyant market growth slows down, and the other companies demonstrate quite clearly their superior performance.

Exercise 2.4 Survival matrix
Instructions

Before coming to the matrix, please respond to the following statements by scoring them as follows:

0	1 2 3	4 5 6	7 8 9	10
Never	*Sometimes*	*Frequently*	*Most of the time*	*Always*

1. When it comes to recruiting salespeople, we seem able to pick the best candidates in the job market · · · · · · · · ·

2. The training we provide for salespeople is second to none · · · · · · · · ·

3. Our salespeople consistently meet or exceed their sales targets · · · · · · · · ·

4. Compared with our competitors, our salespeople have a better image · · · · · · · · ·

5. We actually have the most appropriate number of salespeople employed · · · · · · · · ·

6. Our sales staff are clear about the role they are expected to play · · · · · · · · ·

7. Our sales managers are very good motivators · · · · · · · · ·

8. Territory planning is a strong point of our sales force · · · · · · · · ·

9. The sales force has a good conversion rate in terms of number of visits per order · · · · · · · · ·

10. Our sales force is reasonably stable, i.e. there is not a labour turnover problem · · · · · · · · ·

TOTAL _____

Scoring and interpretation for Exercise 2.4

Enter the sales force effectiveness score on the vertical axis on the matrix (Figure 2.16) and then draw a horizontal dotted line across the matrix. Take the marketing benefits score from Exercise 2.3 and enter this on the horizontal axis of the matrix. Draw a vertical dotted line up from this point. Where the two dotted lines meet is where you position your company on the survival matrix.

This book, however, does not deal specifically with key account planning, which is spelled out specifically in another book by one of the authors.[15]

Questions

1. What are the implications for your company?
2. What actions might be required if improvements are needed?

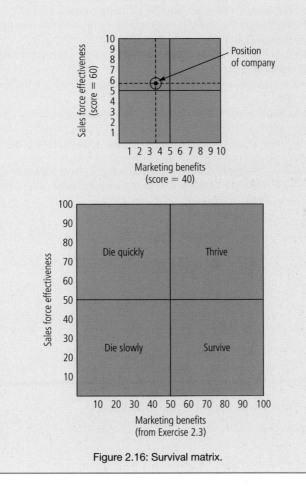

Figure 2.16: Survival matrix.

REFERENCES

1. Porter, M.E. (1980) *Competitive Strategies*. Free Press, New York.
2. MacDonald, M. (2009) The future of marketing: brightest star in the firmament or a fading meteor? Some hypotheses and a research agenda. *Journal of Marketing Management* 25, 5–6, 431–450.
3. Thompson, S. (1962) How companies plan. AMA Research Study No. 54, Chicago.
4. Leighton, D.S.R. (1966) *International Marketing Texts and Cases*. McGraw Hill, New York.
5. Kollatt, D.J., Blackwell, R.D. and Robeson, J.F. (1972) *Strategic Marketing*. Holt, Rinehart and Winston, New York.
6. Ansoff, H.I. (1977) The state and practice of planning systems. *Sloan Management Review*, 18(20), 1–24.
7. Greenley, G. (1984) An exposition into empirical research into marketing planning. *Journal of Marketing Management* 3(1), 83–102.
8. McDonald, M. (1982) The theory and practice of marketing planning for industrial goods in internal markets. PhD thesis, Cranfield Institute of Technology.
9. Piercy, N.F. (2000) *Market-led Strategic Change – Transforming the Process of Going to Market*, 3rd edn. Butterworth-Heinemann, Oxford.
10. Smith, B.D. (2003) The effectiveness of marketing strategy making in medical markets. PhD thesis. Cranfield University School of Management.
11. Buzzell, R.D. and Gales, B.T. (1987) *The PIMS Principles: Linking Strategy to Performance*. Free Press, New York.
12. Lubatkin, M. and Pitts, M. (1985) The PIMS and the policy perspectives: a rebuttal. *Journal of Business Strategy*, Summer, 85–92.
13. Bailey, A. and Johnson, G. (1994) A framework for understanding strategy development. Cranfield University School of Management, unpublished research paper.
14. Collis, D. and Rukstad, M. (2008) Can you say what your strategy is? *HBR*, April, 80–92.
15. McDonald, M. and Woodburn, D. (2011) *Key Account Management: The Definitive Guide Second Edition*. John Wiley, Chichester.

Chapter

THE MARKETING PLANNING PROCESS: 2 REMOVING THE MYTHS

SUMMARY

- Problems and barriers that have to be overcome to make marketing planning work
- Ignorance about the process of marketing planning and associated operational problems
- The main barriers are described and include:
  - weak support from the board of directors
  - lack of a plan for planning
  - confusion over planning terms
  - numbers in lieu of written marketing objectives and strategies
  - too much detail, too far ahead
  - once-a-year ritual
  - separation of strategic and operational planning
  - failure to integrate strategic marketing planning into corporate planning
  - delegation of planning to a planner
- These problems can be overcome by requisite systems, which are outlined
- Exercises to turn the theory into practice
- Readers who are sure these barriers do not exist in their organization may go straight to Chapter 4

Note to readers: While this is an extremely important chapter, in that many excellent marketing plans fail because of the barriers and problems explained here, those readers who wish to cut to the chase, as it were, may choose to go straight to Chapter 4, although it is strongly recommended by the authors that this chapter should be read before attempting to prepare a plan.

INTRODUCTION

In spite of the apparent simplicity and logic of the process described in the last chapter, marketing planning remains one of the most baffling subjects, both for academics and practitioners alike.

The purpose of this chapter is to remove some of the myths which surround this very complex area of marketing management and to explain why much of what passes for marketing planning is largely ineffective. These conclusions are based on a four-year study by this author into how 200 British companies carried out their marketing planning. Four hundred directors were interviewed, the companies being broadly representative of the complete spectrum of type and size of a business to business company. These results have been confirmed by many other studies carried out at universities in America, Europe and Australia.

Marketing's contribution to business success in manufacturing, distribution or merchanting activities lies in its commitment to detailed analysis of future opportunities to meet customer needs and a wholly professional approach to selling to well-defined market segments those products or services that deliver the sought-after benefits. While prices and discounts are important, as are advertising and promotion, the link with operations through the product is paramount.

Such a commitment and such activities must not be mistaken for budgets and forecasts. Those, of course, we need and have already got. Our accounting colleagues have long since seen to that.

> The process of marketing planning is concerned with identifying what and to whom sales are going to be made in the longer term.

No – put quite bluntly, the process of marketing planning is concerned with identifying what and to whom sales are going to be made in the longer term to give revenue budgets and sales forecasts any chance of achievement. Furthermore, chances of achievement are a function of how good our intelligence services are; how well suited our strategies are; and how well we are led.

MARKETING INSIGHT

Einstein wrote: 'The formulation of a problem is far more essential than its solution, which may be merely a matter of mathematical or experimental skill. To raise new questions, new possibilities, to regard old problems from a new angle, requires creative imagination.'

Unfortunately, such creativity is rare, especially when most managers are totally absorbed in managing today's business. Accordingly, they need some system which will help them to think in a structured way about problem formulation.

It is the provision of such a rational framework to help them to make explicit their intuitive economic models of the business that is almost totally lacking from the forecasting and budgeting systems of most companies.

Let us stress at this point that we are not recommending convoluted planning processes using impenetrable jargon. Indeed, as Jeremy Bullmore said: 'Today's most successful business leaders insist on

* brevity
* clarity
* simplicity
* transparency.

The use of impenetrable business jargon marks an executive out as a second-rater' (Jeremy Bullmore, *Management Today*, February 2008, p. 71).

NAIVETY ABOUT MARKETING PLANNING

There are, of course, many studies which identify a number of benefits to be obtained from marketing planning. But there is little explanation for the commercial success of those companies that do not engage in formalized planning. Nor is there much exploration of the circumstances of those commercially unsuccessful companies that also have formalized marketing planning systems; and where the dysfunctional consequences are recognized, there is a failure to link this back to any kind of theory.

'Success' is, of course, influenced by many factors apart from just planning procedures. For example:

1. Financial performance at any one point in time is not necessarily a reflection of the adequacy or otherwise of planning procedures (cf. the hotel industry, location, tourism, etc.).
2. Some companies just happen to be in the right place at the right time(s).
3. Companies have many and varied objectives, such as, for example, stylistic objectives.
4. There is a proven relationship between management style and commercial success, as is the case, for example, with Virgin.
5. Some industries still have a quasi-monopolistic environment.
6. Some industries with few competitors happen to be in growth and in such circumstances it is difficult not to be successful.

There are, however, many problems that occur in companies that do not bother much with markets and customers. For example, the authors usually begin board level workshops by asking the directors to write down their key target markets in order of importance (without consulting with each other). Most frequently, they can only write down their products! Confusion is then complete when they are asked to write down their company's sources of differential advantage against each key target market. Since it is only by selling something to someone that any organization can make money, surely the board should be aware of their key target markets and at least have some idea why customers should buy their products rather than those of any competitor who happens to offer something similar.

One would think so, but in a *Harvard Business Review* article in 2008, Collis[1] said: 'It is a dirty little secret that most directors don't know what the elements of a strategy are, which makes it impossible to develop one. The result? An astonishing number of executives, front line employees and all between are frustrated and confused because no strategy exists.'

Collis goes on to explain: 'Any strategy statement that cannot explain why your customers should buy your product or service is doomed to failure.'

Let us briefly explain one workshop run for the 65 managing directors of a construction group which had just posted a 65 per cent increase in net profits. One of them had posted a 185 per cent increase in net profits, yet when the authors asked him some questions, the responses were a little on the disappointing side.

'Did your market grow last year and, if so, how much of your growth in profts came from this?' He didn't know.

'Did you grow your market share last year? If so, by how much and how much of your growth in profits came from this?' It is obvious that if he couldn't answer the first question, he couldn't answer the second!

'Did you have any net-of-inflation price increases? If so, how much of your profit growth came from this?' He didn't know.

There were other questions, but we are sure you get the message that this company was profitable only because it was in a growth market in which demand exceeded supply.

Since then, of course, we have all witnessed what has happened to the construction industry during the recession!

In other words, marketing planning procedures *alone* are not enough for success.

> Marketing planning procedures alone are not enough for success.

So it is by no means essential for any company not suffering from hostile and unstable competitive and environmental conditions to have an effective marketing planning system, but there are some negative consequences.

Without exception, all those companies in one of this author's studies[2] which did not have an effective marketing planning system, and which were profitable, were also operating in buoyant or high-growth markets. Such companies, though, were less successful than comparable companies with effective marketing planning systems.

Success was considered to be not only a company's financial performance over a number of years, but also the way it coped with its environment.

What this means is that, apart from profitability, a company with an effective marketing planning system is likely to have:

* widely understood objectives
* highly motivated employees
* high levels of actionable market information
* greater interfunctional coordination
* minimum waste and duplication of resources
* acceptance of the need for continuous change and a clear understanding of priorities
* greater control over the business and less vulnerability from the unexpected.

In the case of companies without effective marketing planning systems, while it is possible to be profitable over a number of years, especially in high-growth markets, such companies will tend to be less profitable over time and to suffer problems which are the very opposite of the benefits referred to above.

Furthermore, companies without effective marketing planning systems tend to suffer more serious commercial organizational consequences when environmental and competitive conditions become hostile and unstable.

None of these points are new, in the sense that most of these benefits and problems are discernible to the careful observer. They are, however, actionable propositions for marketers.

One further comment by Jeremy Bullmore will help to round off this section. 'Tough times make people think more. Those companies which have confused customer habit with customer loyalty quickly discover they are not the same. Unless underpinned by intrinsic quality, "added value" begins to seem little more than fancy packaging' (Jeremy Bullmore, *Market Leader*, Quarter 3, 2009, p. 15).

MARKETING PLANNING SYSTEMS: DESIGN AND IMPLEMENTATION PROBLEMS

Many companies currently under siege have recognized the need for a more structured approach to planning their marketing and have opted for the kind of standardized, formalized procedures written about so much in textbooks. These, however, rarely bring the claimed benefits and often bring marketing planning itself into disrepute.

It is clear that any attempt at the introduction of formalized marketing planning systems has serious organizational and behavioural implications for a company, as it requires a change in its approach to managing its business.

It is also clear that unless a company recognizes these implications, and plans to seek ways of coping with them, formalized marketing planning will be ineffective.

Marketing planning is in practice a complex process, proceeding as it does from reviews to objectives, strategies, programmes, budgets and back again, until some kind of acceptable compromise is reached between what is desirable and what is practicable, given all the constraints that any company has.

It has been stated that what has been written about this topic underestimates the operational difficulties of designing and implementing systems and procedures for marketing planning, and that the task becomes progressively more complex as the size and diversity of a company increases. Also, the literature is inadequate in the extent to which it provides practical guidance on design and implementation.

The authors' research included a number of examples of companies that had been forced by market pressures to initiate procedures to help top management gain better control over the business. In all such cases, those responsible for designing the system found very little of practical help, either in the literature or in management courses. Enormous difficulties in system design and implementation were encountered in every instance.

The purpose of this section is to discuss these design and implementation problems. The most frequently encountered problems are summarized in Table 3.1.

Weak Support From Chief Executive and Top Management

There can be no doubt that unless the chief executive sees the need for a formalized marketing planning system, understands it, and shows an active interest in it, it is virtually impossible for a senior functional marketing executive to initiate procedures that will be used in a meaningful way.

This is particularly so in companies that are organized on the basis of divisional management, for which the marketing executive has no profit responsibility and in which he or she has no line management authority. In such cases, it is comparatively easy for senior operational managers to create 'political' difficulties, the most serious of which is just to ignore the new procedures entirely. Usually,

1. Weak support from chief executive and top management
2. Lack of a plan for planning
3. Lack of line management support
   - hostility
   - lack of skills
   - lack of information
   - lack of resources, inadequate organization structure
4. Confusion over planning terms
5. Numbers in lieu of written objectives and strategies
6. Too much detail, too far ahead
7. Once-a-year ritual
8. Separation of operational planning from strategic planning
9. Failure to integrate marketing planning into a total corporate planning system
10. Delegation of planning to a planner

Table 3.1: Marketing planning systems: design and implementation problems

however, the reasons for not participating in procedures, or for only partially following instructions, centre on the issues summarized in Table 3.1.

The vital role that the chief executive and top management must play in marketing planning underlines one of the key points in this section.

MARKETING INSIGHT

A multinational oil company struggled for four years to make its new marketing planning system work. It was only after the board took an interest and the new European chief executive started to drive the process that any tangible results were achieved.

This key point is that it is *people* who make systems work, and that system design and implementation have to take account of the 'personality' of both the organization and the people involved, and that these are different in all organizations.

One of the most striking features we have observed is the difference in 'personalities' between companies, and the fact that within any one company there is a marked similarity between the attitudes of executives. These attitudes vary from the impersonal, autocratic kind at one extreme to the highly personal, participative kind at the other. This is discussed further in Chapter 11.

Any system, therefore, has to be designed around the people who have to make it work, and has to take account of the prevailing traditions, attitudes, skills, resource availability and organizational constraints. Since the chief executive and top management are the key influencers of these factors, without their active support and participation any formalized marketing planning system is unlikely to work. This fact emerged very clearly from research by one of the authors, the worst possible manifestation of which was the way in which chief executives and top managers ignored plans which emerged from the planning system and continued to make key decisions which appeared illogical to those who had participated in the production of the plans. This very quickly destroyed any credibility that the emerging plans might have had, and led to the demise of the procedures and to serious levels of frustration throughout the organization.

Indeed, there is some evidence leading to the belief that chief executives who fail, first, to understand the essential role of marketing in generating profitable revenue in a business, and, second, to understand how marketing can be integrated into the other functional areas of the business through marketing planning procedures are a key contributory factor in poor economic performance.

> There is a depressing preponderance of executives who live by the rule of 'the bottom line' and who apply universal financial criteria indiscriminately to all products and markets, irrespective of the long-term consequences.

There is a similar preponderance of technical managers who see marketing as an unworthy activity that is something to do with activities such as television advertising; and who think of their products only in terms of their technical features and functional characteristics, in spite of the evidence that exists that these are only a part of what a customer buys.

Not surprisingly, in companies headed by people like this, marketing planning is either non-existent, or where it is tried, it fails. This is the most frequently encountered barrier to effective marketing planning.

> The active interest of the chief executive and top management is vital if a formalized marketing planning system is to be successful.

Lack of a Plan for Planning

The next most common cause of the failure or partial failure of marketing planning systems is the belief that, once a system is designed, it can be implemented immediately.

MARKETING INSIGHT

One company achieved virtually no improvement in the quality of the plans coming into headquarters from the operating companies over a year after the introduction of a very sophisticated system.

The evidence indicates that a period of around three years is required in a major company before a complete marketing planning system can be implemented according to its design.

Failure, or partial failure, then, is often the result of not developing a timetable for introducing a new system, to take account of the following:

1. The need to communicate why a marketing planning system is necessary.
2. The need to recruit top management support and participation.
3. The need to test the system out on a limited basis to demonstrate its effectiveness and value.

4. The need for training programmes, or workshops, to train line management in its use.
5. Lack of data and information in some parts of the world.
6. Shortage of resources in some parts of the world.

Above all, a resolute sense of purpose and dedication is required, tempered by patience and a willingness to appreciate the inevitable problems that will be encountered in its implementation.

This problem is closely linked with the third major reason for planning system failure, which is lack of line management support.

Lack of Line Management Support

Hostility, lack of skills, lack of data and information, lack of resources, and an inadequate organizational structure all add up to a failure to obtain the willing participation of operational managers.

Hostility on the part of line managers is by far the most common reaction to the introduction of new marketing planning systems. The reasons for this are not hard to find, and are related to the system initiators' lack of a plan for planning.

New systems inevitably require considerable explanation of the procedures involved and are usually accompanied by pro formas, flow charts and the like. Often these devices are most conveniently presented in the form of a manual. When such a document arrives on the desk of busy line managers, unheralded by previous explanation or discussion, the immediate reaction often appears to be fear of their possible inability to understand it and to comply with it, followed by anger, and finally rejection. They begin to picture headquarters as a remote 'ivory tower', totally divorced from the reality of the marketplace.

This is often exacerbated by their absorption in the current operating and reward system, which is geared to the achievement of current results, while the new system is geared to the future. Also, because of the trend in recent years towards the frequent movement of executives around organizations, there is less interest in planning for future business gains from which someone else is likely to benefit.

Allied to this is the fact that many line managers are ignorant of basic marketing principles, have never been used to breaking up their markets into strategically relevant segments, nor of collecting meaningful information about them.

This lack of skill is compounded by the fact that there are many countries in the world that cannot match the wealth of useful information and data available in the USA and Europe. This applies particularly to rapidly growing economies, where the limited aggregate statistics are not only unreliable and incomplete, but also quickly out of date. The seriousness of this problem is highlighted by the often rigid list of corporate headquarters' informational requirements, which is based totally on the home market.

The solution to this particular problem requires a good deal of patience, common sense, ingenuity and flexibility on the part of both headquarters and operating management. This is closely connected with the need to consider resource availability and the prevailing organization structure. The problem of lack of reliable data and information can only be solved by devoting time and money to its solution, and where available resources are scarce it is unlikely that the information demands of headquarters can be met.

It is for this reason that some kind of appropriate headquarters organization has to be found for the collection and dissemination of valuable information, and that training has to be provided on ways of solving this problem.

Again, these issues are complicated by the varying degrees of size and complexity of companies. It is surprising to see the extent to which organizational structures cater inadequately for marketing as a function. In small companies, there is often no one other than the sales manager, who spends all his or her time engaged either in personal selling or in managing the sales force. Unless the chief executive is marketing orientated, marketing planning is just not done.

In medium sized and large companies, particularly those that are divisionalized, there is rarely any provision at board level for marketing as a discipline. Sometimes there is a commercial director, with line management responsibility for the operating divisions, but apart from sales managers at divisional level, or a marketing manager at head office level, marketing as a function is not particularly well catered for. Where there is a marketing manager, he or she tends to be somewhat isolated from the mainstream activities.

The most successful organizations are those with a fully integrated marketing function, whether it is line management responsible for sales, or a staff function, with operating units being a microcosm of the head office organization.

However, it is clear that without a suitable organizational structure, any attempt to implement a marketing planning system which requires the collection, analysis and synthesis of market-related information is unlikely to be successful.

> Igor Ansoff is a famous American planning guru who constructed a matrix known as the Ansoff Matrix, which had two dimensions and four boxes – existing products, new products, existing markets, new markets

> Lack of a suitable organizational structure for an integrated marketing function, compounded by lack of meaningful information about market segments, means that marketing planning is unlikely to be successful.

A classic example of this was a large diversified multinational, where no provision was made at headquarters for marketing, other than through the divisional directors, and where divisions also generally had no marketing function other than sales management. Their first attempt at writing a strategic plan as a result of market pressures was a complete failure.

The problem of organizing for marketing planning is discussed further in Chapter 11.

Confusion Over Planning Terms

Confusion over planning terms is another reason for the failure of marketing planning systems. The initiators of these systems, often highly qualified, frequently use a form of planning terminology that is perceived by operational managers as meaningless jargon. One company even referred to the ▶ Ansoff Matrix,[3] and made frequent references to other forms of matrices, missions, dimensions, quadrants, and so on.

Those companies with successful planning systems try to use terminology which will be familiar to operational management, and, where terms such as 'objectives' and 'strategies' are used, these are clearly defined, with examples given of their practical use.

Numbers in Lieu of Written Objectives and Strategies

Most managers in operating units are accustomed to completing sales forecasts, together with the associated financial implications. They are not accustomed to considering underlying causal factors for past performance or expected results, nor of highlighting opportunities, emphasizing key issues, and so on. Their outlook is essentially parochial and short term, with a marked tendency to extrapolate numbers and to project the current business unchanged into the next fiscal year.

Thus, when a marketing planning system suddenly requires that they should make explicit their implicit economic model of the business, they cannot do it. So, instead of finding words to express the logic of their objectives and strategies, they repeat their past behaviour and fill in the data sheets provided without any narrative.

It is the provision of data sheets, and the emphasis which the system places on the physical counting of things, that encourages the questionnaire-completion mentality and hinders the development of the creative analysis so essential to effective strategic planning.

Those companies with successful marketing planning systems ask only for essential data and place greater emphasis on narrative to explain the underlying thinking behind the objectives and strategies.

Too Much Detail, Too Far Ahead

Connected with this is the problem of overplanning, usually caused by elaborate systems that demand information and data that headquarters do not need and can never use. Systems that generate vast quantities of information are generally demotivating for all concerned.

The biggest problem in this connection is undoubtedly the insistence on a detailed and thorough marketing audit. In itself this is not a bad discipline to impose on managers, but to do so without also providing some guidance on how it should be summarized to point up the key issues merely leads to the production of vast quantities of useless information. Its uselessness stems from the fact that it robs the ensuing plans of focus and confuses those who read it by the amount of detail provided.

The trouble is that few managers have the creative or analytical ability to isolate the really key issues, with the result that far more problems and opportunities are identified than the company can ever cope with. Consequently, the truly key strategic issues are buried deep in the detail and do not receive the attention they deserve until it is too late.

In a number of companies with highly detailed and institutionalized marketing planning systems, the resulting plans contain so much detail that it is impossible to identify what the major objectives and strategies are.

Also, the managers in these companies are rarely able to express a simplified view of the business or of the essential things that have to be done today to ensure success. Such companies are often overextended, trying to do too many things at once. Overdiversity, and being extended in too many directions, makes control over a confusingly heterogeneous portfolio of products and markets extremely difficult.

In an overdetailed and institution-alized planning system, the key strategic issues may be buried so deep in the detail that they get overlooked until it is too late.

In companies with successful planning systems, there is at all levels a widespread understanding of the key objectives that have to be achieved, and of the means of achieving them.

In such companies, the rationale of each layer of the business is clear, and actions and decisions are disciplined by clear objectives that hang logically together as part of a rational, overall purpose.

The clarity and cohesiveness is achieved by means of a system of 'layering'. At each successive level of management throughout the organization, lower-level analyses are synthesized into a form that ensures that only the essential information needed for decision making and control purposes reaches the next level of management. Thus, there are hierarchies of audits, SWOT analyses, assumptions, objectives, strategies and plans. This means, for example, that at conglomerate headquarters, top management have a clear understanding of the really key macro issues of company-wide significance, while at the lower level of profit responsibility, management also have a clear understanding of the really key micro issues of significance to the unit.

It can be concluded that a good measure of the effectiveness of a company's marketing planning system is the extent to which different managers in the organization can make a clear, lucid and logical statement about the major problems and opportunities they face, how they intend to deal with these, and how what they are doing fits in with some greater overall purpose.

Once-a-Year Ritual

One of the commonest weaknesses in the marketing planning systems of those companies whose planning systems fail to bring the expected benefits is the ritualistic nature of the activity. In such cases, operating managers treat the writing of the marketing plan as a thoroughly irksome and unpleasant duty.

The pro formas are completed, not always very diligently, and the resulting plans are quickly filed away, never to be referred to again. They are seen as something which is required by headquarters rather than as an essential tool of management.

In other words, the production of the marketing plan is seen as a once-a-year ritual, a sort of game of management bluff. It is not surprising that the resulting plans are not used.

While this is obviously closely related to the explanations already given as to why some planning systems are ineffective, a common feature of companies that treat marketing planning as a once-a-year ritual is the short lead time given for the completion of the process. The problem with this approach is that, in the minds of managers, it tends to be relegated to a position of secondary importance.

In companies with effective systems, the planning cycle will start in month 3 or 4 and run through to month 8 or 10, with the total 12-month period being used to evaluate the ongoing progress of existing plans by means of the company's marketing intelligence system. Thus, by spreading the planning activity over a longer period, and by means of the active participation of all levels of management at the appropriate moment, planning becomes an accepted and integral part of management behaviour rather than an addition to it which calls for unusual behaviour. There is a much better chance that plans resulting from such a system will be formulated in the sort of form that can be converted into things that people are actually going to do.

Separation of Operational Planning From Strategic Planning

This subsection must be seen against the background of the difficulty which the majority of companies experience in carrying out any meaningful strategic planning. In the majority of cases, the figures that appear in the long-term corporate plan are little more than statistical extrapolations that satisfy boards of directors. If they are not satisfactory, the numbers are just altered, and frequently the gap between where a company gets to, compared with where it had planned to be in real terms, grows wider over time.

> Nevertheless most companies make long-term projections. Unfortunately, in the majority of cases these are totally separate from the short-term planning activity that takes place largely in the form of forecasting and budgeting.

The view that they should be separate is supported by many of the writers in this field, who describe strategic planning as very different, and therefore divorced, from operational planning. Indeed, many stress that failure to understand the essential difference between the two leads to confusion and prevents planning from becoming an integrated part of the company's overall management system. Yet it is precisely this separation between short- and long-term plans which this author's research revealed as being the major cause of the problems experienced today by many of the respondents.

> It is the failure of long-term plans to determine the difficult choices between the emphasis to be placed on current operations and the development of new business that leads to the failure of operating management to consider any alternatives to what they are currently doing.

The almost total separation of operational or short-term planning from strategic or long-term planning is a feature of many companies whose systems are not very effective.

The almost total separation of operational planning is a feature of many companies with ineffective systems.

More often than not, the long-term strategic plans tend to be straight-line extrapolations of past trends, and because different people are often involved, such as corporate planners, to the exclusion of some levels of operating management, the resulting plans bear virtually no relationship to the more detailed and immediate short-term plans.

This separation positively discourages operational managers from thinking strategically, with the result that detailed operational plans are completed in a vacuum. The so-called strategic plans do not provide the much-needed cohesion and logic, because they are seen as an ivory tower exercise which contains figures in which no one really believes.

Unless strategic plans are built up from sound strategic analysis at grass-roots level by successive layers of operational management, they have little realism as a basis for corporate decisions.

At the same time, operational plans will become increasingly parochial in their outlook and will fail to incorporate the decisions that have to be taken today to safeguard the future.

Operational planning, then, should very much be part of the strategic planning process, and vice versa. Indeed, wherever possible, they should be completed at the same time, using the same managers and the same informational inputs.

The detailed operational plan should be the first year of the long-term plan, and operational managers should be encouraged to complete their long-term projections at the same time as their short-term projections. The advantage is that it encourages managers to think about what decisions have to be made in the current planning year, in order to achieve the long-term projections.

Failure to Integrate Marketing Planning Into a Total Corporate Planning System

It is difficult to initiate an effective marketing planning system in the absence of a parallel corporate planning system. This is yet another facet of the separation of operational planning from strategic planning. For, unless similar processes and timescales to those being used in the marketing planning system are also being used by other major functions such as distribution, operations, finance and personnel, the sort of tradeoffs and compromises that have to be made in any company between what is wanted and what is practicable and affordable will not take place in a rational way. These tradeoffs have to be made on the basis of the fullest possible understanding of the reality of the company's multifunctional strengths and weaknesses, and opportunities and threats.

One of the problems of systems in which there is either a separation of the strategic corporate planning process, or in which marketing planning is the only formalized system, is the lack of participation of key functions of the company, such as research and development (R and D), information technology (IT) or production. Where these are key determinants of success, as is frequently the case, a separate marketing planning system is virtually ineffective.

How this problem can be overcome is spelled out in Chapter 11.

However, where marketing is a major activity, as in fast-moving industrial goods companies, it is possible to initiate a separate marketing planning system. The indications are that when this happens successfully, similar systems for other functional areas of the business quickly follow suit because of the benefits which are observed by the chief executive.

Delegation of Planning to a Planner

The incidence of this is higher with corporate planning than with marketing planning, although where there is some kind of corporate planning function at headquarters, and no organizational function for marketing, whatever strategic marketing planning takes place is done by the corporate planners as part of a system which is divorced from the operational planning mechanism. Not surprisingly, this exacerbates the separation of operational planning from strategic planning and encourages short-term thinking in the operational units.

Very often, corporate planners are young, highly qualified people, attached to the office of the chairman or group chief executive. They appear to be widely resented and are largely ignored by the mainstream of the business. There is not much evidence that they succeed in clarifying the company's overall strategy and there appears to be very little account taken of such strategies in the planning and thinking of operational units.

The literature sees the planner basically as a coordinator of the planning, not as an initiator of goals and strategies. It is clear that without the ability and the willingness of operational management to cooperate, a planner becomes little more than a kind of headquarters administrative assistant. In many large companies, where there is a person at headquarters with the specific title of marketing planning manager, he or she has usually been appointed as a result of the difficulty of controlling businesses that have grown rapidly in size and diversity, and which present a baffling array of new problems to deal with.

The marketing planning manager's tasks are essentially those of system design and coordination of inputs, although he or she is also expected to formulate overall objectives and strategies for the board.

> In all cases, it is lack of line management skills and inadequate organizational structures that frustrates the company's marketing efforts, rather than inadequacies on the part of the planner. This puts the onus on the planner alone to do a lot of the planning, which is, not surprisingly, largely ineffective.

Two particularly interesting facts emerged from the authors' research. First, the marketing planning manager, as the designer and initiator of systems for marketing planning, is often in an impossibly delicate political position *vis-à-vis* both superior line managers and more junior operational managers. It is clear that not too many chief executives understand the role of planning and have unrealistic expectations of the planner, whereas the planner cannot operate effectively without the full understanding, cooperation and participation of top management, and this rarely happens. Often, the appointment of a marketing planning manager, and sometimes of a senior marketing executive, seems to be an easier step for the chief executive and the board to take than giving serious consideration themselves to the implications of the new forces affecting the business and reformulating an overall strategy.

| Without the cooperation of operational management, a planner becomes little more than a headquarters administrative assistant. |

This leads on naturally to a second point. The inevitable consequence of employing a marketing planning manager is that he or she will need to initiate changes in management behaviour in order to become effective. Usually these are far-reaching in their implications, affecting training, resource allocation, and organizational structures. As the catalyst for such changes, the planner, not surprisingly, comes up against enormous political barriers, the result of which is that he or she often becomes frustrated and, eventually, ineffective. This is without doubt a major problem, particularly for big companies. The problems which are raised by a marketing planning manager occur directly as a result of the failure of top management to give thought to the formulation of overall strategies. They have not done this in the past because they have not felt the need. However, when market pressures force the emerging problems of diversity and control to the surface, without a total willingness on their part to participate in far-reaching changes, there really is not much that a planner can do.

| The inevitable consequence of employing a marketing planning manager is the need for change in management behaviour, the implications of which may be far-reaching. |

This raises the question again of the key role of the chief executive in the whole business of marketing planning. Without his or her support and understanding of the very serious implications of initiating effective marketing planning procedures, whatever efforts are made, whether by a planner or a line manager, they will be largely ineffective.

REQUISITE MARKETING PLANNING SYSTEMS

The implications of all this are principally as follows:

1. Any ▶ closed loop marketing planning system (but especially one that is essentially a forecasting and budgeting system) will lead to a gradual decline of marketing and creativity. Therefore, there has to be some mechanism for preventing inertia from setting in through the overbureaucratization of the system.
2. Marketing planning undertaken at the functional level of marketing, in the absence of a means of integration with other functional areas of the business at general management level, will be largely ineffective.
3. The separation of responsibility for operational and strategic marketing planning will lead to a divergence of the short-term thrust of a business at the operational level from the long-term objectives of the enterprise as a whole. This will encourage a preoccupation with short-term results at operational level, which normally makes the firm less effective in the long term.
4. Unless the chief executive understands and takes an active role in marketing planning, it will never be an effective system.
5. A period of up to three years is necessary (especially in large firms) for the successful introduction of an effective marketing planning system.

> A closed loop system is a bureaucratic planning system that consists mainly of pro formas for completion by managers according to predetermined headings and formats. Such systems frequently degenerate into stale form-filling exercises and there is little opportunity for adding creative insights

In Chapter 12 of this book we will explore in detail what is meant by the term 'requisite marketing planning' when we explain how to design and implement an effective marketing planning system.

For now, we believe we have given sufficient background information about the *process* of marketing planning and why this apparently simple process requires much more perception and attention than is typically accorded it. We can now go on to explore in more detail each of the elements of this process before putting all the pieces together again in the final chapter.

One Final Point

It is now widely accepted by academics and leading practitioners that marketing plans should above all be *market driven*, as stated in the following quotation:

> The Traditional Inside Out Model
>
> We have some well-defined products and services that may be of interest to you. But, we also have some non-negotiable rules and procedures and if you consent to jump through these hoops, then we may be able to do business with you.
>
> The business is concerned to match customers to its range of products, rather than being concerned with finding the products that are required by the customer. Those inside the business entity define how the relationship will function and the customer is invited to take it or leave it.
>
> Customers are the spoils of commercial war. They are not the object of strategy.
>
> *(Sean Kelly,* The Customer Information Wars,
> *John Wiley and Sons Ltd, 2005)*

APPLICATION QUESTIONS

Taking each of the issues listed in Table 3.1:

1. In what ways do they apply to your company?
2. In what ways do you deal successfully with them?

CHAPTER 3 REVIEW

Ignorance

Most companies plan, using a combination of forecasting and budgeting systems. These tend to project current business into the future, which can work if the future is going to be the same as the present or the past. As a result of using such systems, the following problems often occur:

1. Lost opportunities for profit
2. Meaningless numbers in long-term plans
3. Unrealistic objectives
4. Lack of actionable market information
5. Interfunctional strife
6. Management frustration
7. Proliferation of products and markets
8. Wasted promotional expenditure
9. Confusion over pricing
10. Growing vulnerability to changes in the business environment
11. Loss of control over the business.

Try Exercise 3.1

Common implementation problems

1. Weak support from the chief executive and top management
2. Lack of a plan for planning
3. Lack of line management support due to:
   * hostility
   * lack of skills
   * lack of resources
   * lack of information. Inadequate organization structure
4. Confusion over planning terms
5. Numbers in lieu of written objectives and strategies
6. Too much detail, too far ahead
7. Once-a-year ritual
8. Separation of operational marketing planning from strategic marketing planning
9. Failure to integrate marketing planning into the total corporate planning system
10. Delegation of planning to a planner.

Try Exercise 3.2

Questions raised for the company

1. Q: If we introduce marketing planning, will we automatically become more successful?
   A: No. Many other factors come into play.
2. Q: What are these factors?
   A: Here are three common factors:

(a) Companies who by chance are in high growth markets often don't plan. They are just dragged along by the general momentum.

(b) If the company's culture and management style are not really supportive of marketing planning (i.e. there is no real belief in it), no improvements will occur.

(c) If the business is highly competitive, no improvement will necessarily be seen. But the company might fare much worse without a marketing plan.

3. Q: Is all the time and effort put into marketing planning going to be worthwhile?
    A: Only you can say. Weigh up the costs of planning against the costs of not planning.

EXERCISES

Introduction to Chapter 3 exercises

The first exercise focuses on the types of problem that your company might be experiencing because of inefficiencies in the marketing planning system. In this sense it is providing an additional diagnosis about whether or not you need to improve your system. At the same time it helps to uncover some of the areas on which any new planning process needs to make an impact.

The second exercise attempts to be quite specific in pinpointing which aspects of the company need to be addressed in order to bring about the biggest improvements in marketing planning.

Exercise 3.1 Symptoms of a lack of marketing planning

Put an 'X' at the point you feel is appropriate as being descriptive of your company against each of the statements below:

	Mainly true	Mainly untrue
1. We seem to be missing opportunities for making profit		
2. Our long-term planning seems to be nothing more than lots of meaningless numbers		
3. Looked at rationally, our marketing objectives are unreasonable		
4. We lack actionable marketing information		
5. Managers are frustrated by the interfunctional strife and rivalry which seem to exist		
6. There seems to be a steady proliferation of products and/or markets		
7. Much of our promotional expenditure is wasted		
8. There is confusion over pricing		
9. We are becoming increasingly vulnerable to changes in our business environment		
10. There is a feeling that we are not running the business, but instead it and outside forces are running us		

(Continued)

If you find it difficult to put an 'X' against any statement, you should confer with some colleagues rather than making guesses.

Join the 'X' for statement 1 to the 'X' of statement 2 with a straight line. Then join 2 to 3, 3 to 4, etc. in a similar way down to 10.

Interpretation of Exercise 3.1

You have just drawn a 'profile' of 'marketing planning' in your company.

If your 'profile line' tends to be positioned to the right-hand side of the spectrum, then it appears that you are not experiencing many of the problems which stem from a lack of marketing planning. In other words, you appear to be doing things fairly well. If, on the other hand, your profile line tends towards the left-hand side, you are much less fortunate, and should consider reviewing your current marketing planning process, paying particular attention to the problems you wish to overcome.

Exercise 3.2 Marketing planning questionnaire – organizational issues

You are asked to answer a series of statements about your organization's approach to marketing planning. Since this quest is for useful and genuine data, please try to be as accurate and objective as you can as you complete this document.

You score the questionnaire by entering a number, 1–5, *only in the position indicated by the line next to each statement*. Choose your scores, using these criteria:

1. If you strongly disagree with statement
2. If you tend to disagree with statement
3. If you don't know if you agree or disagree
4. If you tend to agree with statement
5. If you strongly agree with statement.

	A	B	C	D	E
1. The chief executive and directors show an active interest in marketing planning					-
2. The chief executive and directors demonstrate their understanding of marketing planning	-				
3. The chief executive and directors use the marketing plan as the basis for making key marketing decisions				-	
4. The chief executive and directors allocate adequate resources to ensure the marketing plan is completed satisfactorily		-			
5. The need for a marketing plan is clearly explained to all managers	-				
6. There is adequate information/data upon which to base a marketing plan		-			

	A	B	C	D	E
7. Our marketing plan has a good balance between short-term and long-term objectives			-		
8. People are clear about their role in the marketing planning process					-
9. Line managers are trained to understand how the marketing planning process operates	-				
10. Line operational managers believe the marketing plan is a useful document				-	
11. Enough time is allowed for the planning process		-			
12. It is made easy for line managers to understand the plan	-				
13. Marketing planning is never starved for lack of resources		-			
14. It is reasonable for a company like ours to have a well-thought-out marketing plan				-	
15. Reasons for past successes or failures are analysed			-		
16. In our organization we don't leave planning just to the planners; other managers have a valuable contribution to make					-
17. Our organizational style encourages a sound marketing planning process				-	
18. There is a clear understanding of the marketing terminology we use in our organization	-				
19. Market opportunities are highlighted by the planning process			-		
20. Functional specialists contribute to the marketing planning process					-
21. We limit our activities so that we are not faced with trying to do too many things at one time		-			
22. Taking part in marketing planning in our organization holds a high prospect of being rewarded, either financially or in career terms				-	
23. Only essential data appear in our plans			-		
24. Marketing does not operate in an 'ivory tower'				-	
25. From the wealth of information available to use, we are good at picking out the key issues	-				
26. There is a balance between narrative explanation and numerical data in our plans			-		
27. Our field sales force operates in a way which is supportive to our marketing plan					-

(Continued)

	A	B	C	D	E
28. Our plan demonstrates a high level of awareness of the 'macro' issues facing us	-				
29. Inputs to the planning process are on the whole as accurate as we can make them		-			
30. Marketing planning is always tackled in a meaningful and serious way			-		
31. Our plan doesn't duck the major problems and opportunities faced by the organization				-	
32. There is a high awareness of 'micro' issues in our plan	-				
33. Our plans recognize that in the short term we have to match our current capabilities to the market opportunities		-			
34. Inputs to the marketing planning process are an integral part of the job of all line managers					-
35. Marketing planning is a priority issue in our organization				-	
36. Our planning inputs are not 'massaged' to satisfy senior executives		-			
37. People understand and are reasonably happy that our marketing planning process is logical and appropriate	-				
38. We use the same timescale for our marketing plans as we do for finance, distribution, production and personnel		-			
39. We view our operational plan as the first year of our long-term plan, not as a separate entity			-		
40. Senior executives do not see themselves as operating beyond the confines of the marketing plan				-	
41. The advocates of 'correct' marketing planning are senior enough in the company to make sure it happens			-		
42. People are always given clear instructions about the nature of their expected contribution to the marketing plan		-			
43. We try to make data collection and retrieval as simple as possible	-				
44. Our marketing plans do not go into great detail, but usually give enough information to make any necessary point			-		

	A	B	C	D	E
45. The role of specialists is made quite clear in our planning process					-
46. We are always prepared to learn any new techniques that will make our marketing planning process more effective	-				
47. The role of marketing planning is clearly understood in the organization					-
48. Marketing research studies (by internal staff or agencies) are often used as inputs to our marketing planning process		-			-
49. Our marketing planning is regularly evaluated in an attempt to improve the process			-		
50. The chief executive and directors receive information which enables them to assess whether or not the marketing plan is coming to fruition as expected					-
TOTAL SCORES					

Add up the total scores in each column.

The Rationale behind the questionnaire

There are many ways of looking at organizations and establishing 'models' of how they operate. One very common model is the organization chart, which attempts to show how responsibility is distributed throughout the company and to clarify the chains of command.

Other models are derived from the inputs and outputs of the company. For example, a financial model is built up by analysing all the necessary financial inputs required to conduct the business and monitoring the efficiency by which these are converted into sales revenue.

The questionnaire in Exercise 3.2 is based on a particularly useful model, one which helps us to understand the relationship between different facets of the organization. By understanding the nature of these relationships, we are better placed to introduce organizational change – in this case, an improved marketing planning system.

There are three main assumptions behind this model:

1. *That the organization today is to some extent often very strongly conditioned by its historical background.* For example, if historically there has never been a pressing need for a comprehensive marketing planning system because of favourable trading conditions, then this will be reflected in the current planning system and the attitudes of the company's staff.
2. *That the organization today is to some extent sometimes strongly conditioned and directed by its future goals.* For example, the company that senses its marketing planning processes need to improve will take steps to introduce changes. That these

(Continued)

changes will make an impact on organizational life is self-evident. Furthermore, much of the resistance to be overcome will stem from the 'historical' forces mentioned above.

3. *What actually happens in an organization is determined by the skills, knowledge, experience and beliefs of the organization's personnel*. Thus at the heart of any organization is the collective expertise or 'knowledge' at its disposal. This will ultimately determine the success it has in any work it undertakes, whether it is making goods or providing services.

Clearly, then, the level of 'knowledge' will also be a determining factor in the quality and scope of the company's marketing planning process. These assumptions provide the 'skeleton' of our organizational model (Figure 3.1).

There are still important elements missing from this model. Irrespective of the company's corporate sum of available skills and knowledge, nothing can be produced without physical resources being made available. The key resources required for marketing planning will be accurate data, means of storing and retrieving the data, adequate staff and time to analyse the data.

There are still important elements missing from this model. Irrespective of the company's corporate sum of available skills and knowledge, nothing can be produced without physical *resources* being made available. The key resources required for marketing planning will be accurate data, means of storing and retrieving the data, adequate staff and time to analyse the data.

However, having the right resources isn't the whole solution; the company must also develop the best systems or *routines* to optimize the use of these resources. In marketing planning terms, concern is likely to focus on routines associated with collecting data, evaluating past performance, spotting marketing opportunities, sifting essential information from non-essential information, etc.

Routines, however, do not necessarily look after themselves. As soon as any system is set up, roles and relationships need to be defined. Who is going to do what to ensure that things happen?

Again, in marketing planning terms this will call into question the role of various members of staff from the chief executive downwards. How clear are people about their role in the planning process? Should planning just be left to the planning department? What is the role of functional specialists? Who actually collects marketing data? Whom do they present it to? Many questions have to be answered if the subsequent routines are going to function smoothly.

Even this isn't the end of the story, because once roles are defined, there is still the problem of setting up the right *organizational structure and climate*, one that will enable people to fulfil their roles in a productive way.

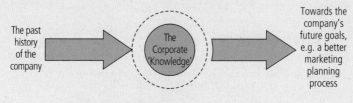

The past history of the company → The Corporate 'Knowledge' → Towards the company's future goals, e.g. a better marketing planning process

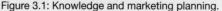

Figure 3.1: Knowledge and marketing planning.

From a marketing planning viewpoint, structure and climate issues surface in several ways. For example, the level of commitment to the planning process, the degree to which functional specialists are integrated into the planning process, the degree to which long- and short-term issues are accommodated, the extent to which the company is prepared to tackle the real and important issues it faces, the openness of communications, etc.

It is now possible to see how the completed model looks (Figure 3.2).

From the foregoing explanation, it is possible to see how the different facets of the organization all interrelate.

A the 'corporate knowledge', about marketing planning
B the resources allocated to planning
C the routines or systems that are used
D the roles and relationships of those engaged in marketing planning
E the organizational structure and climate, and the extent to which it supports marketing planning

Thus, to introduce an improved marketing planning system might call for changes in all these areas. Some personnel might need training, more or different resources might be required, routines or systems might need improving, roles and relationships perhaps need to be reappraised, and the structure and climate of the organization re-examined.

Conversely, only one or two of these areas might need tackling. The questionnaire is designed to provide a 'snapshot' of the company and to help you identify which areas might be the starting point for introducing improvements.

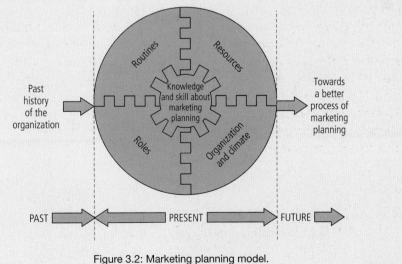

Figure 3.2: Marketing planning model.

(Continued)

Interpretation of Exercise 3.2

Add up the scores for columns A, B, C, D and E and write them in the boxes provided. Each of the letters represents a potential barrier to marketing planning, namely:

A Cognitive barrier, i.e. knowledge and skills
B Resource barrier, i.e. lack of time, people, data
C Systems/routine barrier, i.e. lack of procedures
D Organizational climate barrier, i.e. belief and interest in marketing planning
E Behaviour barrier, i.e. the roles people play

The maximum score for each of these areas is 50 points. The higher the score, the less that potential barrier to marketing is likely to be making an impact. In other words, the areas with low scores (below 30) will probably be the areas worth investigating initially in the search for improvement.

Personal notes

List what actions need to be taken.

REFERENCES

1. Collis, D. and Rukstad, M. (2008) Can you say what your strategy is? *HBR*, April, 82–91.
2. McDonald, M. (1982) The theory and practice of industrial marketing planning. PhD thesis, Cranfield University.
3. Ansoff, I. (1957) Strategies for diversification. *HBR*, September/October.

Chapter

COMPLETING THE MARKETING AUDIT: 1 THE CUSTOMER AND MARKET AUDIT

SUMMARY

- A discussion of whom we sell to
- The difference between consumers and customers
- Why market share is important and why the term 'market' must be carefully defined
- Pareto analysis (the 80/20 rule) and its implications
- The market segmentation process is outlined. The steps are:
  - defining the market
  - market mapping
  - listing decision makers and their purchases
  - noting why these decision makers buy what they buy
  - combining like-minded decision makers into segments by means of cluster analysis
- Methodologies are outlined and explained throughout
- A quick market segmentation method is provided
- Examples of market segmentation are provided
- Exercises to turn the theory into actionable propositions
- The next chapter focuses on what we sell to these identified markets

INTRODUCTION

This chapter contains some extracts from *Market Segmentation: How to do it; How to profit from it* by Malcolm McDonald and Ian Dunbar (Goodfellow Publishers, Oxford, 2010)[1]. These are reproduced with the permission of the authors.

Now that we understand the process of marketing planning, we can begin to look in more detail at its principal components. We have, as it were, seen the picture on the front of the jigsaw puzzle; we can now examine the individual pieces with a better understanding of where they fit.

The next two chapters are designed to help us to carry out a meaningful marketing audit. We have already looked at the issues that need to be considered; what we need now are the means to help us to undertake such an analysis.

It should be stressed that, while the following two chapters deal specifically with how to carry out a customer, market, and product audit, it should not be assumed that, in carrying out a marketing audit, price, promotion, place, information and organization are unimportant. Indeed, Chapters 7–11 are devoted to these important determinants of commercial success and will provide the marketing auditor with the necessary confidence to carry out these specific parts of the audit.

> It is also important to stress that we are still dealing with steps in the marketing planning process, rather than with the all-important output of the process, the strategic marketing plan itself.

This chapter continues to explain the process of marketing planning, rather that the plan itself.

It will be recalled that the contents of the strategic marketing plan, outlined in Chapter 2, represent the summarized conclusions emanating from the marketing audit and will only be as good as the audit allows. The marketing audit itself should be a separate step in the process and under no circumstances should voluminous data and analysis appear in the plan itself. All of this rightly belongs in the marketing audit document.

Thus, the marketing audit is a crucial stage in the marketing plan itself, the actual contents of which are set out in detail in Chapter 13.

At this point, let us revisit our earlier definition of marketing and the accompanying diagram, shown here as Figure 4.1.

The actual contents of the marketing plan itself are set out in detail in Chapter 14.

Marketing is a process for:

- defining markets
- quantifying the needs of the customer groups (segments) within these markets
- determining the value propositions to meet these needs
- communicating these value propositions to all those people in the organization responsible for delivering them and getting their buy-in to their role
- playing an appropriate part in delivering these value propositions (usually only communications)
- monitoring the value actually delivered.

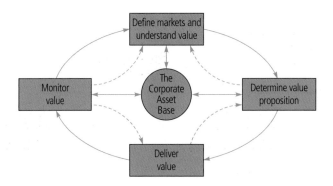

Figure 4.1: Overview of marketing map.

For this process to be effective, organizations need to be consumer/customer driven.

This process is clearly cyclical, in that monitoring the value delivered will update the organization's understanding of the value that is required by its customers. The cycle may be predominantly an annual one, with a marketing plan documenting the output from the 'understand value' and 'create value proposition' processes, but equally changes throughout the year may involve fast iterations around the cycle to respond to particular opportunities or problems.

This chapter and Chapter 5 describe the process involved in this first box under the headings 'The customer and market audit' and 'The product audit', both being integral to defining markets and understanding and quantifying the value required by the customer groups (segments) within these markets.

Input to this process will commonly include:

- The corporate mission and objectives, which will determine which markets are of interest
- External data such as market research
- Internal data which flows from the *deliver value* activities.

The process in the first box in Figure 4.1 involves four major subprocesses, shown in Figure 4.2.

First, it is necessary to define the markets the organization is in, or wishes to be in, and how these divide into segments of customers with similar needs. The choice of markets will be influenced by the corporate objectives as well as the asset base. Information will be collected about the markets, such as the markets' size and growth, with estimates for the future.

Once each market or segment has been defined, it is necessary to understand what value the customers within the segment want or need. This value is most simply thought of as the benefits gained from the product or service, but it can also encompass the value to the customer of surrounding services such as maintenance or information. This step also encompasses what the customer is prepared to give in exchange, in terms of price and other criteria, such as lifetime running cost or convenience of purchase. One way of expressing customer value requirements is via a critical success factor analysis which might list such criteria as product specification, quality or reliability, the quality and range of services, price and the ease of purchase,  and which might also include weights to illustrate their relative importance to the customer in the buying decision.

This step of 'Understand value required' also includes predicting the value which will be required in the future.

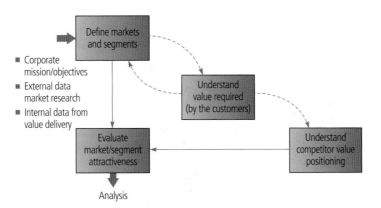

Figure 4.2: Define markets and understand value.

In performing this step, it may emerge that subsets of the customers within a market have very different requirements. In this case, the market may need to be further segmented to represent these subsets. Hence there is an important feedback loop from this step to the 'Define markets' step. How markets are defined and segmented will be spelled out later in this chapter.

'Understand competitor value positioning' refers to the process of establishing how well the organization and its competitors currently deliver the value that the customers seek. To illustrate in terms of critical success factors, this process would correspond to scoring the organization and its competitors on each of the customers' critical success factors. Again it involves looking into the future to predict how competitors might improve, clearly a factor in planning how the organization is to respond. SWOT analysis is one tool used here and will be explained in detail in Chapter 5.

From these three processes, the relative attractiveness of the different markets or segments can be evaluated.

> The consumer is the final consumer of goods or services. Customers are people or organizations who buy directly from us

The output will be some form of analysis, such as a 'marketing audit'. One way of summing up much of the key information is a portfolio matrix such as a Boston Matrix or a Directional Policy Matrix. These are explained in detail in Chapter 5.

We now turn our attention to one of the key determinants of successful marketing planning – *market segmentation*. This is fundamental to the matching process described in Chapter 1. But, in order to understand market segmentation, it is first necessary to appreciate the difference between ▶ customers and ▶ consumers, the meaning of *market share* and the phenomenon known as the *Pareto effect*.

THE DIFFERENCE BETWEEN CUSTOMERS AND CONSUMERS

Let us start with the difference between customers and consumers. The term 'consumer' is interpreted by most to mean the final consumer, who is not necessarily the customer. Take the example of a mother or father who is buying breakfast cereals. The chances are that they are intermediate customers, acting as agents on behalf of the eventual consumers (their family) and, in order to market cereals effectively, it is clearly necessary to understand what the end-consumer wants, as well as what the parents want.

> The term 'customers' in the definition refers to the final users of the product or service being bought.

This is only relevant in that it is always necessary to be aware of the needs of eventual consumers down the buying chain.

Consider the case of the industrial purchasing officer buying raw materials such as wool tops for conversion into semi-finished cloths, which are then sold to other companies for incorporation into the final product, say a suit, or a dress, for sale in consumer markets. Here, we can see that the requirements of those various intermediaries and the end-user are eventually translated into the specifications of the purchasing officer to the raw materials manufacturer. Consequently, the market needs that this manufacturing company is attempting to satisfy must in the last analysis be defined in terms of the requirements of the ultimate users – the consumer – even though the direct customer is quite clearly the purchasing officer.

Given that we can appreciate the distinction between customers and consumers and the need constantly to be alert to any changes in the ultimate consumption patterns of the products to which our own contributes, the next question to be faced is: who are our customers?

Direct customers are those people or organizations who actually buy direct from us. They could, therefore, be distributors, retailers and the like. However, as intimated in the previous paragraph, there is a tendency for organizations to confine their interest, hence their marketing, only to those who actually place orders. This can be a major mistake, as can be seen from the following case history.

A fertilizer company that had grown and prospered during the 1970s and 1980s, because of the superior nature of its products, reached its farmer consumers via merchants (wholesalers). However, as other companies copied the technology, the merchants began to stock competitive products and drove prices and margins down. Had the fertilizer company paid more attention to the needs of its different farmer groups and developed products especially for them, based on farmer segmentation, it would have continued to create demand pull through differentiation.

This company recovered its position by understanding the needs of its different farmer groups and targeting them with specific propositions, resulting in it becoming the most profitable company in its sector.

A fuller explanation of how it did this is provided later in this chapter.

MARKETING INSIGHT

There are countless other examples of companies which, because they did not pay sufficient attention to the needs of users further down the value chain, gradually ceased to provide any real value to their direct customers and eventually went out of business.

An excellent example of good practice is Procter & Gamble in the USA supplying Wal-Mart, the giant food retailer. As can be seen from the simple diagram below, P&G create demand pull (hence high turnover and high margins) by paying detailed attention to the needs of consumers. But they also pay detailed attention to the needs of their direct customer, Wal-Mart. Wal-Mart are able to operate on very low margins because, as the bar code goes across the till, this is when P&G invoice them, produce another and activate the distribution chain, all of this being done by means of integrated IT processes. This way, they have reduced Wal-Mart's costs by hundreds of millions of dollars.

Closely related to the question of the difference between customers and consumers is the question of what our market share is.

MARKET SHARE

Most business people already understand that there is a direct relationship between relatively high share of any market and high returns on investment, as shown in Figure 4.3.

Clearly, however, since BMW are not in the same market as Ford, for example, it is important to be most careful about how 'market' is defined. Correct market definition is crucial for: measuring market share and market growth; the specification of target customers; recognition of relevant competitors; and, most importantly of all, the formulation of marketing strategy, for it is this, above all else, that delivers differential advantage.

The general rule for 'market' definition is that it should be described in terms of a customer need in a way which covers the aggregation of all the products or services which customers regard as being capable of satisfying the same need. For example, we would regard the in-company caterer as only one option when it came to satisfying lunch-time hunger. This particular need could also be satisfied at external restaurants, public houses, fast food specialists and sandwich bars. The emphasis in the definition, therefore, is clearly on the word 'need'.

> A market is the aggregation of all the products or services which customers regard as being capable of satisfying the same need

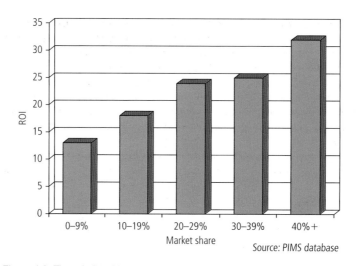

Figure 4.3: The relationship between market share and return on investment.

Aggregating currently available products/services is, however, simply an aid to arriving at the definition, as it is important to recognize that new products, yet to be developed, could better satisfy the users' need. For example, the button manufacturer who believed their market was the 'button market' would have been very disappointed when zips and Velcro began to satisfy the need for fastenings! A needs-based definition for this company would have enabled the management to recognize the fickleness of current products, and to accept that one of their principal tasks was to seek out better ways of satisfying their market's needs and to evolve their product offer accordingly.

The following example may help in defining the market your business is in.

A company manufacturing nylon carpet for the commercial sector wanted to check that it had a realistic definition of the market it was in. The first step was to map out the total available market for all floor covering:

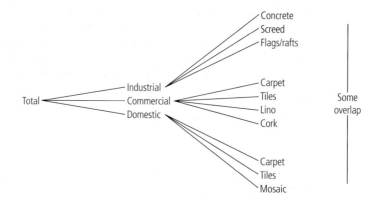

Clearly, it would be wrong to include the three types of floor covering used in the industrial sector in the company's market definition. The qualities required from such flooring cannot hope to be matched in a carpet made from any currently known type of fibre. Similarly, in both the commercial and domestic sectors, nylon carpet is not a competitor for the luxury end of the market. This luxury part of the market buys carpet made from natural fibres, particularly wool.

This leaves the non-luxury commercial and domestic sectors which, in total, represented the company's potential available market. It was potentially available because the company could, for example, produce nylon carpet for the domestic sector and extend its market this way. Similarly, the company could move into manufacturing nylon carpet tiles and extend its operation into this product for both the domestic and commercial sectors. There was also no reason why the company should not look at replacing lino, cork or mosaic flooring with nylon carpet.

Many of the opportunities in the potentially available market, however, represent possible strategies for the future. They would be considered during the marketing planning process when the future plans for the current business activity did not achieve the required financial targets. The question now, therefore, is, what is the company's realistically available market?

To assist the company in this final stage of arriving at a market definition the 'needs' being met by the current products, as highlighted by the current customers, were first listed. This revealed that the company's nylon carpet was bought because:

- It fell into a particular price range
- It was quiet underfoot
- It had a life expectancy of 15 years
- It was available in pleasant colours and textures
- The market was within a 60-mile radius of the manufacturing plant.

In addition to the obvious, this list removed lino, cork and mosaic from the company's available market.

Finally, the company looked at the applicability of its current distribution and selling methods to the potentially available market, ruling out those sections of the market which required different selling and distribution approaches. This meant that it was unrealistic to include the domestic sector in the market definition.

> It is necessary to arrive at a meaningful balance between a wide market definition and a manageable market definition.

Products and manufacturers which met all the criteria were then listed, along with their end-users. The company had now arrived at both a market definition and a current market size, while still keeping open the option of extending it, should the need arise.

This example also illustrates the need to arrive at a meaningful balance between a wide market definition and a manageable market definition. Too narrow a definition has the pitfall of restricting the range of new opportunities segmentation could open up for your business.

On the other hand, too wide a definition may make marketing planning meaningless. For example, the television broadcasting companies are in the 'entertainment' market, which also consists of theatres, cinemas and theme parks, to name but a few. This is a fairly wide definition. It may, therefore, be more manageable for the television broadcasters, when looking at segmenting their market, to define their market as being the 'home entertainment' market. This could then be further refined into the pre-school, child, teenager, family, or adult home entertainment market.

To help with calculating market share the following definitions are useful:

- Product class, e.g. cigarettes, computers, fertilizers, carpets
- Product subclass, e.g. filter, personal computers, nitrogen, carpet tiles
- Product brand, e.g. Silk Cut, IBM, Intel, Heuga.

Silk Cut as a brand, for the purpose of measuring market share, is only concerned with *the aggregate of all other brands that satisfy the same group of customer wants*. Nevertheless, the manufacturer of Silk Cut also needs to be aware of the sales trends of filter cigarettes and the cigarette market in total.

One of the most frequent mistakes that is made by people who do not understand what market share really means is to assume that their company has only a small share of some market, whereas if the company is commercially successful, it probably has a much larger share of a smaller market.

While it is tempting to think that the examples given above amount to 'rigging' the definition of market and that there is the danger of fooling ourselves, we must never lose sight of the purpose of market segmentation, which is to enable us to create competitive advantage for ourselves by creating greater value for our customers.

MARKETING INSIGHT

Thus, for the carpet manufacturer, or for a London orchestra that defines its market as the aggregation of all London classical orchestras rather than as all entertainment, as long as its market definition enables it to outperform its competitors and grow profitably, this is the key. Obviously, however, the definition needs to be kept under review and revised, if necessary.

To summarize, correct market definition is crucial for the purpose of:

* Share measurement
* Growth measurement
* The specification of target customers
* The recognition of relevant competitors
* The formulation of marketing objectives and strategies.

This brings us to another useful and fascinating observation about markets.

PARETO EFFECT

It is a phenomenon commonly observed by most companies that a small proportion of their customers account for a large proportion of their business. This is often referred to as the 80/20 rule, or the ▶ Pareto effect, whereby about 20 per cent of customers account for about 80 per cent of business.

> Pareto's law indicates that approximately 20 per cent of any activity will result in approximately 80 per cent of the output

If we graph the proportion of customers that account for a certain proportion of sales, then we might expect to find a relationship similar to that shown in Figure 4.4. Here, customers have been categorized simply as A, B or C according to the proportion of sales they account for. The A customers, perhaps 25 per cent of the total, account for about 70 per cent of sales; B customers, say 55 per cent of the total, account for 20 per cent of total sales; and C customers, 20 per cent of the total, account for the remaining 10 per cent of sales.

The Pareto effect is found in almost all markets, from capital industrial goods to banking and consumer goods. What is the significance of this? What is certain is that it does not mean that a company should drop 80 per cent of its customers! For one thing, the sales volume bought by these customers makes a valuable contribution to overheads. For another, it is almost certain that the 80/20 rule would still apply to the remaining 20 per cent. One could go on forever, until there was only a single customer left! However, in carrying out this kind of analysis, it should become obvious where the company should be placing its greatest effort.

There are, however, two serious dangers. The first is that this form of analysis is static. In other words, the best potential customers may well be in the 80 per cent, or even in the larger group of

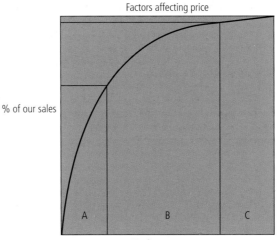

Figure 4.4: The '80/20' effect.

non-customers. The second is that the same analysis needs to be done for profitability, preferably using activity-based costing (ABC) to establish whether the top 20 per cent of customers are also contributing to the largest proportion of profits.

It is obvious, then, that while such analysis is vital, great care is necessary over how it is used. This is something we can now begin to discuss.

One manufacturer in the soft drinks industry did an analysis of its trade in the south-east of England and found that almost 85 per cent of its trade was coming from 20 per cent of its customers. Yet exactly the same service was being given to them all. All were receiving fortnightly calls from the sales force, all received a fortnightly delivery, and all paid the same price for the product. Not surprisingly, this led to an enormous investment in depots and vehicles, while the associated operating expenses were out of all proportion to the margins enjoyed by the company. In this case, there was a simple answer. Most of the small accounts were handed over to a grateful wholesaler, which freed valuable capital and management time to concentrate on the really important areas of the business. Meanwhile, the company's pricing policy was revised to reward those customers who bought more, and the sales force was now free to concentrate on developing its existing business and on opening new profitable outlets.

MARKETING INSIGHT

The chairman of one European airline, alas now bankrupt, told his assembled general managers that his ambition was for his airline to be the best in the world and to provide customer service to the point of obsession. The problem was that his airline didn't compete in many markets, while their unfocused customer obsession policy led them to give service they just couldn't afford. Heroic and unfocused statements such as this chairman's do more harm than good!

One of the most important aspects of marketing planning is being able to choose the best 20 per cent of your market to focus on, the 'best' being the most profitable now and in the future. A method of doing this will be provided in Chapter 5.

MARKET DEFINITION AND SEGMENTATION

Introduction

It has become clear after at least 70 years of formalized marketing that market definition and segmentation are the very core of the discipline.

> A market segment consists of a group of customers within a market who share a similar level of interest in the same, or comparable, set of needs.

How to measure market share has always been at the centre of controversy in discussions of success or failure. As stated earlier, defining a market too widely or too narrowly can both lead to meaningless statistics.

The remainder of this chapter deals in detail with these problems.

While this is not the place to spell out the academic history of market segmentation, it is so crucial to the success of marketing planning that at least a brief commentary is called for. One of the authors of this chapter did a catholic review of scholarly research into the history of market segmentation (Jenkins and McDonald, 1997)[3] in which 36 references were cited. However, due to scale constraints here is a very brief summary of this research.

The father of market segmentation is widely considered to be Wendell Smith (1956)[4], who proposed market segmentation as an alternative to product differentiation. Yet it wasn't until Wind's (1978)[5] review of the state of market segmentation that the topic went to the top of the agenda of researchers and practitioners. His plea was for new segmentation bases, data analysis techniques and for generally putting market segmentation at the heart of strategic decision making.

In 2009, a whole issue of the *Journal of Marketing Management* was devoted to market segmentation and for those readers wanting an updated literature review, see Bailey (2009)[6] in that issue. They confirm that most of the work over the intervening years has been primarily around what segmentation bases to use, such as size of purchase, customer characteristics, product attributes, benefits sought, service quality, buying behaviour and, more recently, propensity to switch suppliers, with much of this work being biased towards fast-moving consumer goods rather than to business to business and services.

In 2002, Coviello[7] and a host of others, with the advent of relationship marketing and customer relationship management, proposed one-to-one as a successor to market segmentation, although Wilson et al. (2002)[8] found that most CRM projects fail because of poor segmentation. Rigby (2002)[9] summed this up succinctly by saying that trying to implement CRM without segmentation is like 'trying to build a house without engineering measures or an architect's plan'.

Given the amount of academic scholarships and attempts at implementation in the world of practice over the 54 years since Wendell Smith first raised the consciousness of the community to the importance of market segmentation, it is surprising that so little progress has been made. In 2006, Christensen[10], in the *Harvard Business Review* found that of 30,000 new products launched in the USA, 85 per cent failed because of poor market segmentation. Yankelovich's paper in 2006[11] also reported the widespread failure of segmentation initiatives. This matches the author's own research over a 35-year period. Their analysis of 3,000 marketing plans revealed that only 300 contained proper needs-based segmentation – i.e. 90 per cent didn't.

One of the the authors of this chapter, having been marketing director of a major fast-moving consumer goods company and having worked on practical segmentation with senior teams from leading global multinationals down to SMEs for 35 years, finds much of the academic debate referred to above somewhat arrogant and inward-looking.

The justification for saying this is that anyone who says 'we segment markets by...' is totally missing the point. Any market, once correctly defined in terms of needs rather than products, consists of 100 per cent of what is bought, how it is used and why it is bought and used in these ways. The role of any supplier is to understand these behavioural patterns and to discover their rationale, rather than trying to impose some predetermined segmentation methodology onto the market.

Excellent strategies	Weak strategies
Target needs-based segments	Target product categories
Make a specific offer to each segment	Make similar offers to all segments
Leverage their strengths and minimize their weaknesses	Have little understanding of their strengths and weaknesses
Anticipate the future	Plan using historical data

Table 4.1: The link between shareholder value added and excellent strategies.

Readers who wish to are referred to the *Journal of Marketing Management*, Volume 25, Nos 3–4, 2009, which is devoted to bridging the segmentation theory/practice divide.

The purpose here is to spell out proven methodologies for market definition and market segmentation developed over a 20-year period of research at Cranfield School of Management. During this period, a link between shareholder value creation and excellent marketing is shown in the left hand column of Table 4.1.

Essential Background

'A market is the aggregation of all the products or services which customers regard as being capable of satisfying the same need' (Malcolm McDonald and Ian Dunbar, *Market Segmentation*, Goodfellow Publishing, Oxford, 2010).

Companies frequently confuse target markets with products – pensions or mainframe computers, for example; this, coupled with a lack of knowledge about the sources of differential advantage against each segment, signals trouble. Figure 4.5 shows the first attempt at a market map by a publisher of marketing books. Figure 4.6 shows their second attempt when, instead of defining their market as 'books', they defined their market as the promulgation of marketing knowledge in order to reflect the customers' need. This led to a whole new corporate strategy.

Many companies pride themselves on their market segmentation even though these so-called 'segments' are in fact 'sectors', which is a common misconception. Everyone with a marketing qualification knows that a segment is a group of customers with the same or similar needs and that there are many different purchase combinations within and across sectors.

But the gravest mistake of all is *a priori* segmentation. Most books incorrectly state that there are several bases for segmentation, such as socio-economics, demographics, geo-demographics and the like. But this misses the point totally. For example, Boy George and the Archbishop of Canterbury are both socio-economic group A, but they don't behave the same! Nor do all 18- to 24-year-old women (demographics) behave the same! Nor does everyone in one street (geo-demographics) behave the same!

All goods and services are made, distributed and used and the purchase combinations that result make up an *actual* market, so the task is to understand market structure, how the market works and what these different purchase combinations (segments) are.

First, let us examine the factors that cause markets to break into smaller groups (see Figure 4.7).

When something new is invented such as television, computers, microwaves, the Internet and the like, not everyone adopts them at the same time. Many years ago an American researcher, called Everett Rogers, studied how new products are defused across markets over time. Imagine that television has just been invented. Let us take any market, Germany will do, and let us imagine that there are only 100 households in Germany. Let us further imagine that there is a law limiting each household in Germany to only one television. Clearly, the potential market for televisions in Germany is 100, but not everyone buys one at the same time. Someone has to be the first to adopt new products. Normally, about 2.5 per cent of any population will be the first to adopt new products. These people are known as 'Innovators'. They are very unusual people who enjoy being different.

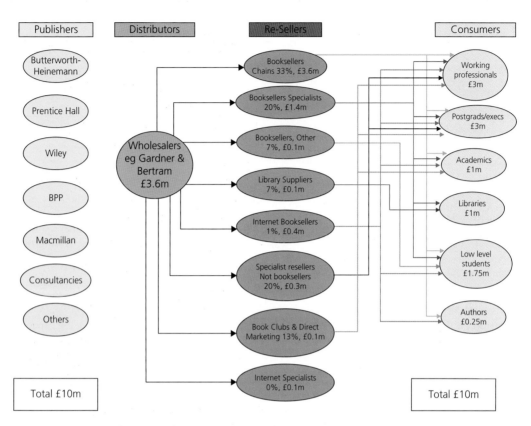

Figure 4.5: Original market map of the marketing books market.

These people are followed by another group, known as 'Opinion Leaders'. These people tend to be affluent, are well educated, very privileged, and they are independent thinkers, who do not care much what other people think of them. They are, however, crucial in getting any new product or service adopted. We can think of them as the Joneses, in the sense of the expression: 'Keeping up with the Joneses'.

This group is followed by a much larger group known as the 'Early Majority'. These people admire the opinion leaders and can be thought of as the Smiths, in the sense of the expression: 'The Smiths try to keep up with the Joneses'. When these people start to enter a market, there is a rapid growth in sales.

By now, approximately 50 per cent of all those who could adopt the new product have done so, and it is now that the 'Late Majority' begin to enter the market. Generally, these people are less privileged and less affluent, and price often becomes important at this stage in the market.

Finally, the remaining 16 per cent of the population adopt the new technology. Rogers referred to these people as 'Laggards'. By now, everyone who could have one has got one. For example, in the United Kingdom, almost everyone has a mobile phone, they are very cheap, and the market can now be considered to be a replacement market, in which growth will be dependent on population size, demographics and the like. Clearly, in mature markets, getting growth will be much more difficult.

Although this is not the purpose of this chapter, it is useful to note, before we leave the diffusion of innovation curve, that when launching a new product or service, it is advantageous to know who the opinion leaders are in a market, as these people should be targeted first by the sales force, and by other promotional media, as they will be the most likely to respond. For example, certain doctors will

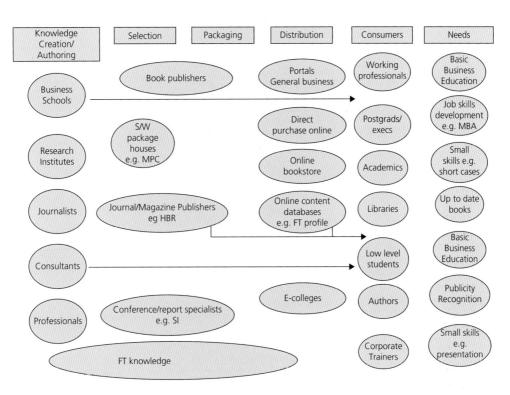

Figure 4.6: Market map of the market for the acquisition of marketing knowledge.

Adapted from Everett Rogers

Figure 4.7: Non-cumulative diffusion pattern.

be more open-minded about new drugs, whereas other doctors will not risk prescribing a new drug until it has been on the market for a number of years.

The diffusion of innovation curve also explains the phenomenon known as the product lifecycle, and why, after the 50 per cent point on the diffusion of innovation curve is reached, the market continues to grow, but the rate of growth begins to decline until maturity is reached (see Figure 4.8)

At the beginning of any market, TECHNOLOGY tends to be the driving business force, largely because new products tend to be at the cutting edge. As the new technology begins to take hold, as explained in the earlier references to the research of Everett Rogers[13], PRODUCTION tends to be

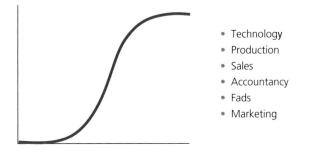

- Technology
- Production
- Sales
- Accountancy
- Fads
- Marketing

Figure 4.8: The diffusion of innovation curve.

very important, because at this stage it is not unusual for demand to be greater than supply. However, as the market grows and new entrants begin to introduce competitive products, SALES as a function becomes increasingly important, as the new competition entails a growing consumer choice. A problem frequently occurs at the next stage of the market lifecycle, as there is now more supply than demand, so frequently organizations attempt to cut costs, so ACCOUNTANCY tends to come to the fore. This is often followed by implementing the latest management consultancy FADS, such as those promulgated by gurus such as Tom Peters in works like *In Search of Excellence*. Finally, however, all organizations come to the same conclusion, which is that they need to understand their consumers and customers better in order to meet their needs and this, of course, is where market segmentation, the subject of this section of this chapter, becomes crucial.

All this has been explained in order to introduce the key concept of market segmentation and why it happens. Clearly, in the early days, markets will tend to be homogeneous. But, as demand grows rapidly with the entry of the early majority, it is common for new entrants to offer variations on the early models, as we have just explained, and consumers now have a choice. In order to explain this more clearly, let us illustrate the approximate shape of markets. If we were to plot the car market in terms of speed and price, we would see very small, inexpensive cars in the bottom left hand corner of Figure 4.9. In the top right, we would see very fast, expensive cars. Most cars, however, would cluster in the middle; what we might call: 'The Mr and Mrs average market'.

In the same way, the lawn mower market would look very similar (see Figure 4.10). With lawn size on the vertical axis and price on the horizontal axis, at the bottom left would be small, inexpensive, hand-pushed mowers, with expensive sit-on machines for large estates in the right hand corner.

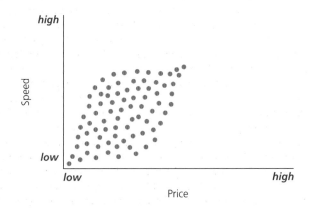

Figure 4.9: Illustration of the shape of the car market.

Figure 4.10: Illustration of the shape of the lawn mower market.

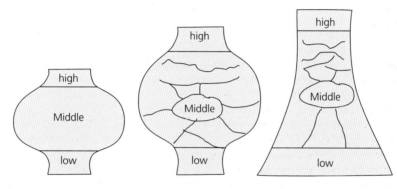

Figure 4.11: The shape of markets from birth to maturity.

That leaves the majority of the market with average size lawns, and average-sized lawn mowers, which is where the mass market is.

We can now redraw this to represent the shape of any market, particularly at the early growth stage (the shape on the left in Figure 4.11). But when rapid growth begins, new entrants join the market and offer variations on standard products in order to attract sales, and it is at this stage that markets begin to break into smaller groups, while still growing overall. (This is represented by the shape in the middle.) Eventually, when markets mature, and there is more supply than demand, any market growth tends to come in the lower price end of the market, while the top end of the market tends to be immune. (This is represented by the shape on the right.) It is usually the middle market that suffers at this stage, with many competitors vying with each other on price. This, however, is the whole point of market segmentation, for competing only on price is to assume that this is the main requirement of customers, whereas the truth is that this is rarely the case. It is just that a general lack of understanding about market segmentation on the part of suppliers about the real needs of customers in mature markets forces them to trade on price, so encouraging the market to become a commodity market.

It is not widely known that price is rarely the decisive factor in most buying situations. It is certainly the experience of the authors over many years of working on every continent of the world that price accounts for less than 10 per cent of all decisions. The following is a quote from an IPA report ('Advertising in a downturn', March 2008, page 5). 'The average proportion of consumers who were motivated by price was around ten per cent and even if this increased during a downturn, the proportion would remain small.'

Figure 4.12: Examples of segments for the fertilizer case study.

The segmentation project for the fertilizer case study referred to earlier revealed that there were seven distinct types of farmer, each with a different set of needs. Three of which are illustrated in Figure 4.12. To give just a few examples of these segments: first, there was a segment they called Arthur, a television character known for his deals. He bought on price alone but represented only 7 per cent of the market, not the 100 per cent put about by everyone in the industry, especially the sales force. Another type of farmer they called Oliver. Oliver, an arable farmer, would drive around his fields on his tractor with an aerial linked to a satellite and an on-board computer. He did this in order to analyse the soil type and would then mix P, N and K, which are the principal ingredients of fertilizer, solely to get the maximum yield out of his farm. In other words, Oliver was a scientific farmer, but the supply industry believed he was buying on price because he bought his own ingredients as cheaply as possible. He did this, however, only because none of the suppliers bothered to understand his needs. Another type of farmer they called Martin. Martin, a dairy farmer, was a show-off and liked his grass to look nice and healthy. He also liked his cows to look nice and healthy. Clearly, if a sales representative had talked in a technical way to Martin, he would quickly switch off. Equally, to talk about the appearance of crops would have switched Oliver off, but this is the whole point. Every single supplier in the industry totally ignored the real needs of these farmers, and the only thing anyone ever talked about was price. The result: a market driven by price discounts, accompanied by substantial losses to the suppliers. ICI, however, armed with this new-found information, launched new products and new promotional approaches aimed at these different farmer types, and got immediate results, becoming the most profitable subsidiary of ICI and the only profitable fertilizer company in the country.

Let us now return to market dynamics and what happens to markets at the rapid growth stage. At this stage, new entrants come into the market, attracted by the high sales and high profits enjoyed by the industry. Let us illustrate this with another case history. In the early 1970s, a photocopier company had 80 per cent market share and massive profit margins. This is represented by the big circle in the middle of Figure 4.13. When a Japanese newcomer entered the market with small photocopiers, the giant ignored them. The Japanese product grew in popularity, however, forcing the giant to reduce its prices. Within three years, the giant's share was down to 10 per cent, and the battle was lost. They had failed to recognize that the market was segmented and tried to compete in all segments with their main product, a mistake made by hundreds of erstwhile market leaders. The main point about this case history is that companies should not attempt to compete in all segments with the same product, but should recognize that different segments or need groups develop as the market grows, and that they should develop appropriate products and services, and position and brand them accordingly.

Let us summarize all of this by showing a product lifecycle representation with some generalizations about how marketing strategies change over time (see Figure 4.14 – product lifecycles are

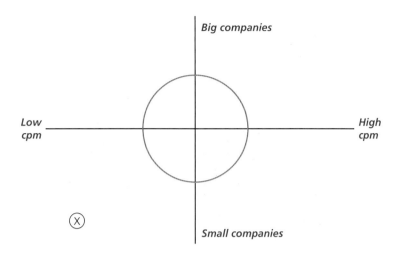

Figure 4.13: The photocopier market in the 1970s.

Key Characteristics	Unique	Product Differentiation	Service Differentiation	"Commodity"
Marketing Message	Explain	Competitive	Brand Values	Corporate
Sales	Pioneering	Relative Benefits Distribution Support	Relationship Based	Availability Based
Distribution	Direct Selling	Exclusive Distribution	Mass Distribution	80 : 20
Price	Very High	High	Medium	Low (Consumer Controlled)
Competitive Intensity	None	Few	Many	Fewer, bigger International
Costs	Very High	Medium	Medium/Low	Very low
Profit	Medium/High	High	Medium/High	Medium/low
Management Style	Visionary	Strategic	Operational	Cost Management

Figure 4.14: The product/market lifecycle and market characteristics.

explained in more detail in the next chapter). From this, which we suggest you study carefully, you will see at least four major changes that occur over the lifecycle. At the top of the far right hand column, you will see the word 'commodity', but the point we want to make is that this is by no means inevitable, and only occurs in markets where the suppliers do not understand the power of market segmentation, as illustrated in the fertilizer case history. There are other options, of course, including the option to get out of mature markets. Another is to move the goalposts as it were, somewhat in the manner of First Direct, Direct Line, Michael Dell, Virgin, Amazon.com, and countless others. The strategy we want to concentrate on here, however, is market segmentation, which in our view should be the very first consideration as markets begin to mature.

MARKET SEGMENTATION – HOW TO DO IT

We can now begin to concentrate on a methodology for making market segmentation a reality, market segmentation being the means by which any company seeks to gain a differential advantage over its competitors.

Markets usually fall into natural groups, or segments, which contain customers who exhibit a similar level of interest in the same, or comparable, set of needs.

These segments can be regarded as forming separate markets in themselves and can often be of considerable size. Taken to its extreme, each individual consumer is a unique market segment, for all people are different in their requirements. While CRM systems have made it possible to engage in one-to-one communications, this is not viable in most organizations unless the appropriate organizational economies of scale have been obtained at a higher level of aggregation such as at segment level. Consequently, products are made to appeal to groups of customers who share approximately the same needs.

It is not surprising, then, to hear that there are certain universally accepted criteria concerning what constitutes a viable market segment:

* Segments should be of an adequate size to provide the company with the desired return for its effort.
* Members of each segment should have a high degree of similarity in their requirements, yet be distinct from the rest of the market.
* Criteria for describing segments must enable the company to communicate effectively with them.

While many of these criteria are obvious when we consider them, in practice market segmentation is one of the most difficult of marketing concepts to turn into a reality. Yet we must succeed, otherwise we become just another company selling what are called 'me too' products. In other words, what we offer the potential customer is very much the same as what any other company offers and, in such circumstances, it is likely to be the lowest priced article that is bought. This can be ruinous to our profits, unless we happen to have lower costs, hence higher margins, than our competitors.

There are basically three stages to developing segments, all of which have to be completed (see Figure 4.15).

The first establishes the scope of the project by specifying the geographic area to be covered and defining the 'market' which is to be segmented, followed by taking a detailed look at the way this market operates and identifying where decisions are made about the competing products or services. Successful segmentation is based on a detailed understanding of decision makers and their requirements.

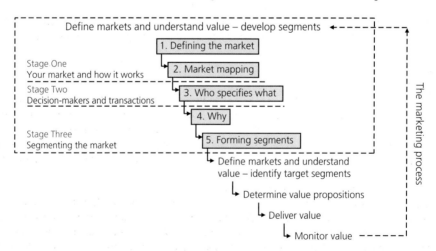

Figure 4.15: The process of developing segments and its position in the marketing process.

The second is essentially a manifestation of the way customers actually behave in the marketplace and consists of answering the question 'Who is specifying what?'

The third stage looks at the reasons behind the behaviour of customers in the marketplace and answers the question 'Why?' and then searches for market segments based on this analysis of needs.

The following sections provide an overview of the steps required to complete these three stages and is presented in a format for conducting a segmentation project using internal resources.

Stage 1 – Your Market and How it Works

Defining the market

The first step in market segmentation establishes the scope of the segmentation project by specifying the geographic area covered by the project and by clearly understanding from a customer's perspective the 'market' in which your products or services are competing with those of your competitors. Where necessary, the scope is modified to take into account the realistic capabilities of your organization.

A clear geographic boundary enables you to size the market, to identify the localities in which the dynamics of the market have to be understood and, once the segments have been identified, to develop the appropriate marketing objectives and strategies for those localities.

Keeping the project within the borders of a single country is a manageable starting point because the stage of market development, the available routes to market and the pattern of marketing activity will probably be the same throughout the country. Even this, however, may be too broad for some companies, simply because their geographic reach is limited by physical and/or economic considerations, or even because their appeal has a strong local sentiment attached to it.

For companies trading in numerous countries around the world, there is clearly an enormous attraction in finding a single global segmentation model that can be applied to every country. However, the experience of 'globalization' has highlighted for many of these companies that they have to 'act local' in order to succeed in their market. This doesn't mean that every country is completely unique in respect of the segments found within it. For the international company, a useful guide to predetermining which countries can be included in a single segmentation project is to ensure that in each of these countries the stage of market development, the available routes to market and the pattern of marketing activity are the same, or at least very similar.

As a reminder, the general rule for 'market' definition is that it should be described in a way which covers the aggregation of all the alternative products or services which *customers* regard as being capable of satisfying that same need.

Table 4.2 is an example from financial services.

Having established changes/developments in products and channels by defining markets in terms of needs, it is still necessary to draw a market map for your major products and services. A method for doing this is now explained.

Market mapping

A useful way of identifying where decisions are made about competing products and services and, therefore, those who then proceed to the next stages of segmentation is to start by drawing a 'market map'.

A ▶ market map defines the distribution and value added chain between final users and suppliers of the products or services included within the scope of your segmentation project. This should take into account the various buying mechanisms found in your market, including the part played by 'influencers'.

An example of a market map is given in Figure 4.16.

It is useful to start your market map by plotting the various stages (referred to as 'junctions') that occur along the distribution and value added chain between the final users and all the suppliers of products or services competing with each other in the defined market. At the same time, indicate the particular routes to market the products are sourced through, as not all of them will necessarily involve all of these stages.

Market	Need
Car insurance	Financial protection to cover the unexpected costs of accidents and losses associated with a motor vehicle
Retirement income	The ability to maintain a desired standard of living (for self and/or dependants) from the date of retirement
Future event planning	Schemes to protect and grow money for anticipated cash calling events (e.g. car replacement/repairs, education, weddings, etc.)
Day-to-day transactions	The ability to store, access and move money as and when required
Income protection	The ability to maintain a desired standard of living (for self and/or dependants) in times of an unplanned loss of salary.

Table 4.2: Some market definitions (personal market)

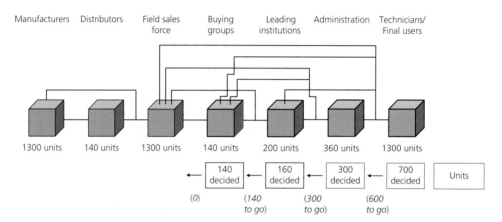

Figure 4.16: Market map – specialized technical equipment – including where decisions are made.

Note at each junction on your market map, if applicable, all the different types of companies/customers that are found there, as illustrated in Figure 4.17.

It is useful at this point to split the volume or value quantity dealt with by each junction between the junction types. Make the most informed estimates you can for these figures if they are not known and note this as a requirement for any follow-up work.

This is shown in Figure 4.18.

What we are particularly interested in is where decisions are made in the market (referred to as 'market leverage points') as this identifies the customer group(s) who we will take through to the next stage of the segmentation process.

The easiest junction at which to start this stage of market mapping is at the final users' junction, noting at each junction with leverage the volume/value (or percentage of the total market) that is decided there. Once again make the most informed estimates you can; approximate percentages or actuals are acceptable and note this as a further requirement for any follow-up work generated by this first pass at segmenting your market.

This is illustrated in Figure 4.19.

In Figure 4.19 we see a market in which 30 per cent of annual sales are decided at junctions other than the final user junction.

An example of a pharmaceutical market map for lipids in South Africa is shown in Figure 4.20. Without providing a detailed case history – as there isn't space here – only a brief comment is called

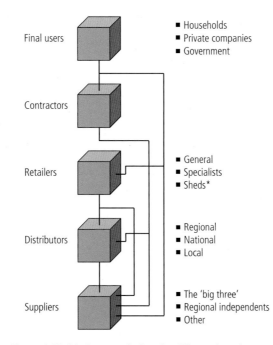

Figure 4.17: Market map listing the different junction types.

Note: * 'Sheds' is the name sometimes used to refer to hardware superstores.

Final users 300k	Households	30k	(10%)
	Private companies	150k	(50%)
	Government	120k	(40%)
		300k	(100%)

Figure 4.18: Quantities split between junction types.

for. The company (ABC) just wasn't putting its marketing effort into where the decisions were being made as the percentages clearly show.

A second market map (Figure 4.21) is for a type of office equipment. Once again, this map shows a disparity between where the company was putting resources and where decisions were actually being made.

The whole point of market mapping is to answer the question 'Who is the customer?' Without this knowledge of where the 80/20 rule applies in terms of where real decisions are made, market segmentation just isn't possible.

So far, we have built a market map by tracking the distribution and value added chain found between final users and suppliers, and shown the various routes that are taken through the map to link the two together. We then quantified the map. This was followed by expanding the detail to show the different types of companies/customers found at each junction on the map and these were also quantified.

We now need to take each major junction on the market map where decisions are made (i.e. 'Final users' in Figure 4.19) and apply the market segmentation process to them.

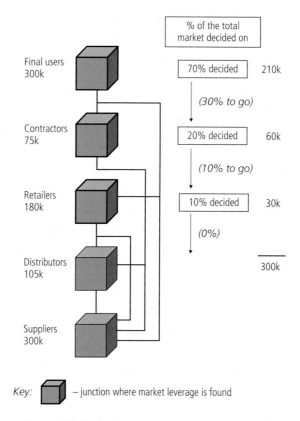

Key: ▨ – junction where market leverage is found

Figure 4.19: Market leverage points on a market map.

Stage 2 – Decision Makers and Transactions

Who specifies what where, when and how?

In this step we are developing a representative sample of different decision makers which identifies the characteristics and properties of a purchase on which decisions are made along with the customer attributes that will be used to describe the decision makers. Each constituent of this sample is called a ▶ 'micro-segment'.

The uniqueness of a micro-segment is that when determining which of the alternative offers are to be bought, the decision makers it represents demonstrate a similar level of interest in a specific set of features, with the features being the characteristics and properties of 'what' is bought, 'where' it is bought, 'when' it is bought and 'how' it is bought as appropriate to the micro-segment. To this is added the descriptors that explain who the micro-segment represents along with an estimate of the volume or value they account for in the defined market.

The principle behind this step is that by observing the purchase behaviour of decision makers and understanding the key constituents of this behaviour, we have a platform for developing a detailed understanding of their motivations. It is, therefore, a critical link with the next step of the segmentation process, which looks at why decision makers select the particular products and services they specify. This, in turn, becomes the basis on which the segments are formed.

Essentially, this step involves identifying all the different purchase combinations that take place in a market made up of the features different customers see as key to making their decision between competing offers. A simple format for capturing this information appears in Figure 4.22.

Key features could include such principal forms as size, colour, specific type of product/service, add-ons, supporting services, branded, unbranded, etc. along with the channels used, the preferred

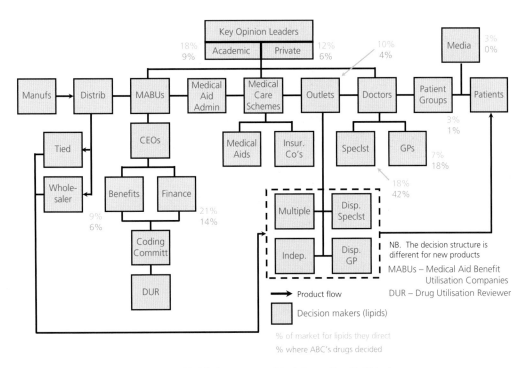

Figure 4.20: Market map – ethical drugs (South Africa).

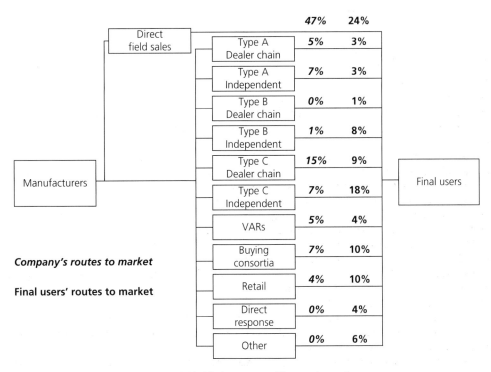

Figure 4.21: Market map – office equipment.

Micro-segment	1	2	3	4	5	6	7	8	9	10
What is bought										
Where										
When										
How										
Who										

Figure 4.22: Micro-segments.

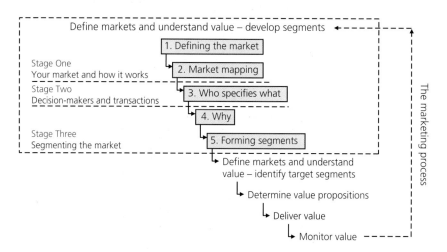

Figure 4.23: The process of developing segments and its position in the marketing process.

timing of purchases (when) and how it is bought such as cash or credit. Next, it is important to describe who behaves in each particular way using relevant descriptors such as demographics. For industrial purchases this might be standard industrial classifications, size of firm, etc., whereas for consumer purchases this might be socio-economic groups such as A, B, C1, C2, D and E or stage in the lifecycle, or age, sex, or geography. Although in Figure 4.22 there are only 10 micro-segments, it is normal in most markets for companies to identify around 20 to 30 micro-segments, occasionally more. Remember, these micro-segments are actual decision makers and purchase combinations that take place in a market.

With Stage 2 complete we can now progress to the final stage of developing segments. This can be seen in Figure 4.23, a repeat of the process summary presented in Figure 4.15.

Before continuing with the process, it must be pointed out that segmentation can and should be carried out at all major leverage points on the market map, not just at the final user junction as in the example referred to earlier (Figure 4.19).

Stage 3 – Segmenting the Market
Why?
For this penultimate, and most difficult, step each purchase combination has to have a brief explanation of the reason for this particular type of behaviour. In other words, we need to list the benefits sought, and it is often at this stage that an organization needs to pause and either commission market research or refer to its extant database of previous market research studies.

But one with many
different purchase
combinations

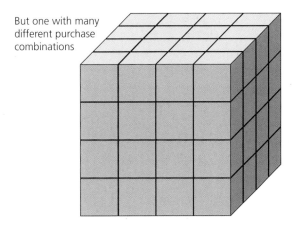

Figure 4.24: An undifferentiated market.

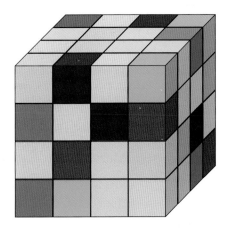

Figure 4.25: Different needs in a market.

Forming segments

To summarize, it is clear that no market is totally homogeneous and consists of a number of different purchase combinations (see Figure 4.24).

To form meaningful segments we first have to understand these different purchase combinations by the needs that they are satisfying (see Figure 4.25).

However, as it is impracticable to deal with more than between seven and 10 market segments, a process has to be found to bring together or cluster all those micro-segments that share similar or approximately similar needs (see Figure 4.26).

Once the basic work has been done in describing micro-segments, that is steps 3 and 4, any good statistical computer program can carry out cluster analysis to arrive at a smaller number of segments. The final step also consists of checking whether the resulting segments are big enough to justify separate treatment, are indeed sufficiently different from other segments, whether they have been described sufficiently well to enable the customers in them to be reached by means of the organization's communication methods, and, finally, whether the company is prepared to make the necessary changes to meet the needs of the identified segments.

Before summarizing the process of market segmentation, it will by now be clear that market segmentation is fundamental to corporate strategy. It is also clear that, since market segmentation affects

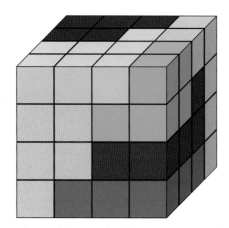

Figure 4.26: Segments in a market.

Understand market segmentation
• Not all customers in a broadly-defined market have the same needs
• Positionings is easy. Market segmentation is difficult. Positioning problems stem from poor segmentation.
• Select a segment and serve it. Do not straddle segments and sit between them.
1. Define the market to be segmented and size it (market scope)
2. Determine how the market works and identify who makes the decisions (market mapping)
3. Develop a representative sample of decision-markers based on differences they see as key (including what, where, when and how), note who they are (demographics) and size them
4. Understand their real needs (why they buy, the benefits sought)
5. Search for groups with similar needs

Table 4.3: Understand market segmentation

every single corporate activity, it should not be just an exercise that takes place within the marketing department, and has to involve other functions. Finally, the most senior levels of management must lead this initiative if their organization is to be truly market or customer need driven.

Table 4.3 is a summary of what we have discussed so far. It is obvious that there will be very few markets in the world where all customers have the same needs. Also, once market segmentation has been carried out, positioning products and services to meet the different needs of the different segments is comparatively easy. The difficult bit is segmenting markets. The third point is that it is vital to focus on serving the needs of the identified segments, while it is dangerous to straddle different segments with the same offer. The photocopier example was only one example of thousands of well-known companies that have suffered from this mistake as markets began to break into segments. The computer industry during the 1980s and 1990s is also replete with examples of this mistake.

The process of developing segments itself consists of five steps. One, be clear about your market and understand how it works. This involves defining the market, drawing a market map and identifying the decision makers. Two, for these decision makers list the different purchase combinations that occur covering what is bought, where, when, and how, and who these decision makers are using descriptors such as demographics and location. Three, list who the customers are for each of these different purchase combinations. Four, list why they buy, especially the benefits sought. Five, finally, search for groups with similar needs. These will be the final market segments.

Market structure and market segmentation are the heart and soul of marketing (see Figure 4.27). Unless an organization spends time on market segmentation driven from the board downwards, it

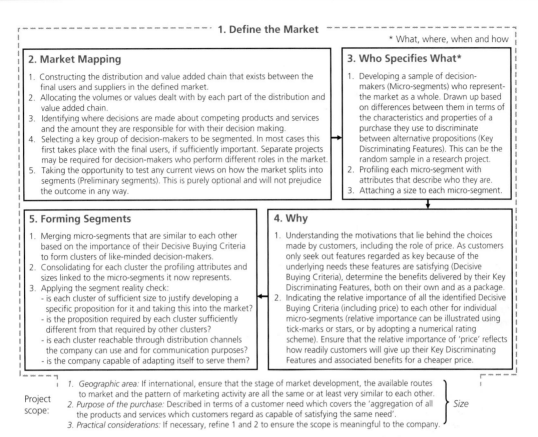

Figure 4.27: The market segmentation process summary – developing segments.

is virtually impossible for it to be market driven, and in any organization that isn't market driven the marketing function will be ineffective, or at best will spend its time trying to promote and sell products or services that are inappropriate for the market. The figure describes in more detail each of the important steps for developing segments in the market segmentation process and it would be beneficial to study it in some detail.

To see the details behind each stage, read *Market Segmentation; How to Do It; How to Profit from It* (McDonald and Dunbar, 2010)[1].

Professional market segmentation is hard work and time-consuming, but it is also hugely rewarding and is pivotal to a succesful marketing strategy.

There follows a quick segmentation exercise (thanks to Dr Brian Smith[12] of Pragmedic and a Visiting Fellow at the Open University Business School). This will quickly produce a very rough segmentation of your market, but it is no substitute for the proper, more detailed and accurate process described above, as the results will only ever be approximate.

Quick market segmentation solution

- Write down *the main* benefits sought by customers
- Hygiene factors are benefits that any product or service must have to be acceptable in the market. Try to ignore these.
- Motivators are those benefits that contribute towards the customer's decision about which product to buy
- Take the 'motivators' and choose the 2 main ones

- Draw two straight horizontal lines and make an estimate of the percentage of customers at each end. So for example, if service level is a key motivator of what is bought, see below:

60% _____ 40%

Low service   High service

- Likewise, if the breadth of the product range is a key motivator of what is bought, see below:

60% _____ 40%

Small product range   Large product range

- Take the left hand point of the first horizontal line and drag it over the second horizontal line to make a cross as shown

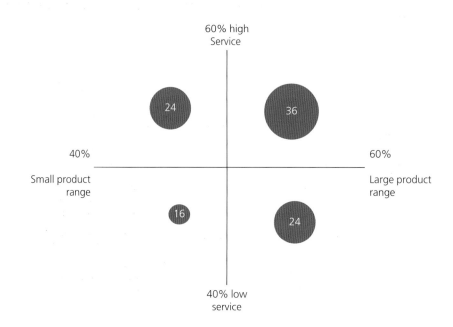

- Starting at the top, and moving in a clockwise direction, multiply 60% by 60% to give 36% (see 1st circle).
- Then multiply 60% by 40% to give 24% (see second circle)
- Then multiply 40% (the bottom of the vertical axis) by 40% to give 16% (see third circle).
- Lastly, multiply 40% by 40% to give 16% (see fourth circle).
- The circles represent segments in the market.

Interpretation
- The 1st segment (36%), the biggest segment, requires both high service and a large product range.
- The second segment (24%) prefers a large product range and is less interested in service.
- The third segment (16%), doesn't care much about either a large product range or service.
- The fourth segment (24%) prefers good service and is less interested in a large product range.
- Although not essential, you might consider giving each segment a name.

Action
- Ensure your 'offer', including the product, price, service and promotion reflect the differing needs of each segment.

Example

- An example of segmentation of the A4 paper market follows. Please note that if, as in the case of the A4 paper market, there is one very large segment (in this case 56%), the exercise can be repeated for just this large segment, resulting in seven segments in total.

Example = Copier Paper

- *Service* delivery – (Fast, paper always 'there' – point of delivery availability of products; service levels)
- *Product fit for purpose* – (Hi quality print finish for colour copiers; consistency of quality; paper that doesn't screw up in the machine; print definition; no waste)
- *Environmental factors* – *(Recyclable)*
- *Level of support* – (Delivered in small lots; consignment stock; easy ordering {on-line]; delivered to difficult locations)

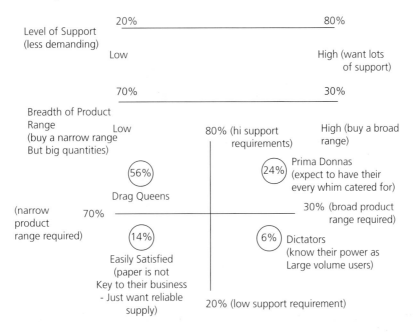

LOOKING TO THE FUTURE

One final, but crucial, step remains in this part of the marketing audit.

The essence of this stage is to revisit the market map, and consider in what ways it might be affected by e-commerce. Reconfiguring the market map involves examining the current market map, and redrawing it to take account of various anticipated effects of e-commerce.

The resulting vision of how the industry could change as a result of e-commerce presents the organization with choices as to how to position itself in the future industry structure and how to manage the transition period. Here is a list of options based on our research of how the market map might be reconfigured.

1. *Disintermediation.* As with other IT-enabled channels such as call centres, e-commerce can enable a link to be removed from the market map, by removing intermediaries whose primary function of information transfer can be more effectively performed using the internet. An example is the direct sales of greetings cards to the public being trialled by a card publisher, thereby bypassing the retailer.

2. *Partial channel substitution.* This forms a halfway house towards disintermediation, in which an intermediary's role is reduced but not eliminated, through some of its value being provided remotely by the supplier to the intermediary's customer. This is the model adopted by a card manufacturer in its relationship with retailers, where its website is supplementing its agent network rather than replacing it. Similarly, a drinks manufacturer is using data gleaned from its information exchange with distributors to promote directly to retailers, providing 'pull-through' demand which the distributors perceive as of mutual benefit.

3. *Reintermediation.* In some cases, a previous intermediary is replaced by a new online intermediary, rather than bypassed, or an intermediary appears between two types of organization which previously dealt with each other directly. At the time of writing, a groceries' manufacturer is having to define its strategy with respect to the various business-to-business exchanges, or e-hubs, which are appearing in its industry to link retailers to manufacturers. Similarly, the health portals such as Healtheon are forming influential intermediaries between manufacturers of drinks products with a health claim and the consumer.

Predicting what reintermediation will occur is particularly difficult, as the possibilities are numerous. Will a given relationship – say, between CTN (confectioners, tobacconists and newsagents) stores and their suppliers – be a direct one? If so, will the shops buy from a range of suppliers' websites, or will the suppliers respond to tender requests provided electronically by shops? Or will there be a new intermediary acting as a marketplace between the two? Possibilities can be placed in an approximate order, from a supplier's website (such as Japan Airlines, which puts out open invitations to tender to suppliers) at one extreme, to a vendor's website (such as *Harvard Business Review*, which provides an online version at a cost) at the other. Neutral marketplaces are midway between the two. An example is an auction site, which is tied neither to the buyer nor to the seller. Somewhat closer to the vendors are intermediaries such as Broadspeed, which passes on leads to a local car dealer. A more buyer-oriented intermediary is General Electric's TPN Register, a prototypical e-hub which has achieved considerable scale: set up by a consortium of buyers, it acts to ensure that they gain low prices as well as transaction-cost efficiencies through economies of scale.

Our research suggests that which of these possibilities becomes the dominant trading mechanism in a given relationship appears to depend on the number of vendors and buyers, and the relative power of suppliers and buyers. Where there are few buyers and many suppliers, or buyer power is great, the market will tend towards either individual buyer websites or buyer-oriented intermediaries such as the Covisint trading platform being set up by Ford, General Motors and Daimler Chrysler. Conversely, a small number of suppliers selling to large numbers of customers will have the power to control the market through their own websites or through supplier-oriented consortia. Large numbers of both suppliers and buyers will tend to use a neutral marketplace to reduce the search costs of both parties, though a supplier with a particularly strong brand and/or product differentiation, such as *Harvard Business Review*, may choose not to participate in such marketplaces.

To illustrate this thinking about reintermediation, consider Figure 4.23, a simplified value map from the groceries market.

The current market structure, shown in black, involves manufacturers reaching consumers via a combination of the major multiple supermarkets, independent stores and CTN stores. Our analysis suggests that because the major multiples are few in number and hold considerable buying power, their relationship with manufacturers will either continue to be a direct one, using purchasing systems dictated by the multiples, or will be mediated by a buyer-oriented intermediary, as indicated in the potential future structure shown in blue. However, the many-to-many relationship between manufacturers and independents or CTNs needs a more neutral intermediary, such as is provided currently by warehouses and wholesalers. We predict a similarly neutral online intermediary succeeding here, either through a new entrant start-up or through media addition by a wholesaler. Likewise, the relationship between manufacturers and suppliers is likely to include a neutral spot market for commodity ingredients. These predictions appear consistent with industry developments to date.

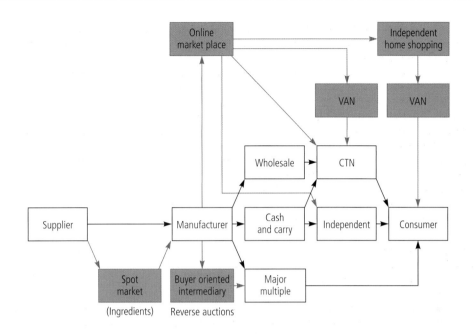

To reconfigure the market map, therefore, one needs to consider the potential effect of each of our three broad changes in turn. In each case, one needs to:

* Sketch the effect of the possible change on the market map
* If the effect is positive for some segments, incorporate the transformation in a revised market map (say, for three years hence).

WHY MARKET SEGMENTATION IS VITAL IN MARKETING PLANNING

In today's highly competitive world, few companies can afford to compete only on price, for a product has not yet been sold that someone, somewhere, cannot sell cheaper – apart from which, in many markets it is rarely the cheapest product that succeeds anyway. This is an issue we will return to in Chapter 9 dealing with the pricing plan. What this means is that we have to find some way of differentiating ourselves from the competition, and the answer lies in market segmentation.

The truth is that very few companies can afford to be 'all things to all people'. The main aim of market segmentation as part of the planning process is to enable a firm to target its effort on the most promising opportunities. But what is an opportunity for firm A is not necessarily an opportunity for firm B, depending on its strengths and weaknesses. The whole point of segmentation is that a company must either:

* Define its markets widely enough to ensure that its costs for key activities are competitive; or
* Define its markets in such a way that it can develop specialized skills in serving them to overcome a relative cost disadvantage.

Both have to be related to a firm's *distinctive competence* and to that of its competitors.

All of this should come to the fore as a result of the marketing audit referred to previously and should be summarized in SWOT analyses. In particular, the differential benefits of a firm's product or service should be beyond doubt to all key members of the company.

Even more important than this, however, is the issue of marketing planning and all that follows in this book. It is worth repeating why market segmentation is so important. Correct market definition is crucial for:

* Share measurement
* Growth measurement
* The specification of target customers
* The recognition of relevant competitors
* The formulation of marketing objectives and strategies.

To summarize, the objectives of market segmentation are:

* To help determine marketing direction through the analysis and understanding of trends and buyer behaviour
* To help determine realistic and obtainable marketing and sales objectives
* To help improve decision making by forcing managers to consider in depth the options ahead.

SEGMENTATION CASE HISTORIES

This chapter concludes with two case histories to illustrate how superior profitability results from successful market segmentation.

CASE STUDY

CASE STUDY 1 – SODIUM TRI-POLY PHOSPHATE!

Sodium Tri-Poly Phosphate (STPP) was once a simple, unexciting, white chemical cleaning agent. Today, one of its uses is as the major ingredient of a sophisticated and profitable operation, appearing under many different brand names, all competing for a share of what has become a cleverly segmented market.

Have you ever wondered how the toothpaste marketers classify you in their segmentation of the market? The following chart, adapted from R. Haley's 'Benefit segmentation: a decision-oriented research tool' (*Journal of Marketing*, Vol. 32, July 1968), which presents the main segments, may assist you.

	Segment name	Worrier	Sociable	Sensory	Independent
Profile	Demographic	C1 C2	B C1 C2	C1 C2 D	A B
		25–40	Teens	Children	35–40
		Large families	Young smokers		Male
	Psychographic	conserva-tive: hypo-chondriacs	high sociability: active	high self-involvement: hedonists	high auton-omy: value orientated
What is bought, where, when and how	Product examples	Signal	Macleans	Colgate	Own label

	Segment name	Worrier	Sociable	Sensory	Independent
	Product features	Mentadent P	Ultrabrite	Aquafresh	small tubes
	Outlet	large canisters	large tubes	medium tubes	independent
	Purchase frequency	health properties	whitening properties	flavouring	quarterly
		supermarket	supermarket	supermarket	
		weekly	monthly	monthly	
Why it is bought	Benefits sought	stop decay	attract attention	taste	functionality
Price paid		medium	high	medium	low
Percentage of market		50%	30%	15%	5%
Potential for growth		low	high	medium	nil

Note: 'C1', 'C2' and so on appearing in the demographic profiles of each segment represent socio-economic groups which were in use in the UK until 2001, now replaced in official statistics by eight analytic classes numbered from 1 through to 8. 'Signal' and 'Mentadent P' are trade marks of Lever Fabergé; 'Macleans' and 'Aquafresh' are trade marks of GlaxoSmithKline; 'Ultra brite' and 'Colgate' are trade marks of Colgate-Palmolive.

CASE STUDY

CASE 2 – GLOBALTECH (SERVICE SEGMENTATION)
SUMMARY

This case history describes the use of market segmentation to assist in the development of a service product. Customer requirements were captured via qualitative research. The segmentation was completed through the use of quantitative research. The result was a set of segments that enabled the development of a new approach to delivering service while improving customer satisfaction. *GlobalTech* is the fictitious name of a real company marketing high-tech and service products globally. Customers are counted in hundreds of thousands. The markets are mainly business-to-business with a few very large customers buying thousands of items. Service is a major revenue stream measured in billions of dollars. The lessons learnt could be of interest to any organization having to care for large numbers of customers.

BACKGROUND
A Failed Segmentation

An internal GlobalTech team tried to complete a marketing audit early in 2000. This included market definition, market segmentation and quantification. Each product division conducted

(Continued)

their audit separately. They used mainly brainstorming techniques to define their markets and to produce the data required.

LESSON 1

Markets transcend your internally defined product divisions. Therefore it is best to understand the markets and monitor your overall performance in those markets. To reshape market information to meet the needs of internal reporting will lead to misinformation.

On completion, the results were compared across the divisions. It rapidly became apparent that each division addressed almost all the markets. However, the market definitions they produced were different, with significant bias towards just the products they offered. Similarly, the segments each division identified were in conflict with the outputs from the other divisions.

On reflection, it was agreed that the results were unreliable. They could not be used to help shape future strategies or marketing investments.

GlobalTech was now in the uncomfortable situation of being in a market information vacuum. Any confidence they had had in their understanding of the market had been destroyed. Consequently the decision was taken that all future market analysis and understanding tasks would be supported by appropriate investments in market research.

LESSON 2

Do not rely on the internally gathered opinions of your sales and marketing staffs to define markets and identify customer requirements and attitudes. Do invest in the necessary market research to provide a reliable segmentation and support for strategy and product development.

First market segmentation. The following year the segmentation was redone, supported by extensive qualitative and quantitative market research. The objective was to understand and group into segments the product buyers in the overall market.

The qualitative study produced a very clear picture and definition of the markets addressed by GlobalTech. It also provided the customers' view of the benefits they sought from the products and the differences in their attitudes towards their suppliers. The questionnaire for the quantitative study was based on the results of the qualitative study. The result was seven clearly defined segments.

This enhanced understanding of the market assisted with hardware and software products but did not address service products or customer satisfaction and loyalty issues.

The Internal Need

At the dawn of the twenty-first century, the market lifecycle had matured. All but the more sophisticated products were perceived as commodities. Consequentially, the opportunities for effective product differentiation had diminished. GlobalTech, in common with its competitors, was finding that customers were becoming increasingly disloyal.

For many years, product churns and upgrades from existing customers had accounted for some 70 per cent of GlobalTech's product revenues. Service and exhaust revenues* almost equalled total product revenues. Service was perceived to be a key influencer of loyalty. But

---

* Exhaust revenues are those revenues that follow on, almost automatically, from an initial product sale. These would normally include service plus training, consultancy, consumables, supplies and add-ons, etc.

the costs of delivering service were becoming unacceptable to customers. Concurrently, service pricing was coming under increasing competitive pressures.

The challenge was to increase loyalty while achieving a step function improvement in margins. Thus it was decided to invest in a better understanding of the service market as an enabler to delivering cost-effective differentiation and loyalty. This case history covers the project from inception to implementation.

The Segmentation Project

Buy-in

The GlobalTech main board director responsible for customer service sponsored the project. This was a critical prerequisite, as the outcome would have a significant impact on the organization, its processes and behaviours.

Similarly the project team included key members of service, marketing and finance to ensure buy-in. However, at that time, it was deemed inappropriate to include representatives from all but two of the countries due to travel implications, costs, and resource impacts. In retrospect this was not a good decision.

LESSON 3

Try to anticipate the scale of organizational change that may result from a major segmentation project. Then ensure the buy-in planned from the start of the project embraces all those who will eventually have a say in the final implementation.

Business Objectives

The project team agreed the overall business objectives as:

- To develop strategies for profitable increase in market share and sustainable competitive advantage in the service markets for GlobalTech's products.
- To identify opportunities for new service products and for improving customer satisfaction within the context of a robust customer needs segmentation, which can be readily applied in the marketplace.
- To identify the key drivers of loyalty so that GlobalTech may take actions to increase customer loyalty significantly.
- To provide the information required to help develop a new and innovative set of service products designed and tailored to meet differing customer requirements while significantly reducing internal business process costs.

Results from the qualitative study. The output from the qualitative study was a 93-page report documenting the results, in line with the desired research objectives. Some of the more surprising aspects were supported by verbatims. A key output was the polarization of very different attitudes towards service requirements that some buyers had in comparison with others. For example:

- Some wanted a response within a few hours, whereas many others would be equally happy with next day.
- Some wanted their staff thoroughly trained to take remedial actions supported by a specialist on the phone.
- Others did not want to know and would just wait for the service provider to fix the problem.
- Some wanted regular proactive communications and being kept up to date.
- Others wanted to be left alone.
- Some would willingly pay for a premium service, under a regular contract, while others would prefer to take the risk.

(Continued)

The attitudes of professional buyers, procuring on behalf of user departments, were consistently different from those of the user departments.

Results from the quantitative study. The output from the quantitative study was extensive. Much of the output was detailed demographic data, opportunities information and competitive positioning comparisons. However, the focus was on a fairly extensive executive summary for internal communications within GlobalTech. What follows are summarized extracts from those outputs.

The segments. Six market segments were identified as a result of iterative computer clusterings. Initially the clustering routines had identified more segments but by careful analysis these were reduced to what was decided to be the most manageable level. Some previously very small segments were merged with very similar larger segments. A summary of the six concluding segments follows.

Koala Bears

28% of Market

Preserve their assets (however small) and use, say, an extended warranty to give them cover. Won't do anything themselves, prefer to curl up and wait for someone to come and fix it.

Small offices (in small and big companies)

Teddy Bears

17% of Market

Lots of account management and love required from a single preferred supplier. Will pay a premium for training and attention. If multi-site, will require supplier to effectively cover these sites. (Protect me.)

Larger companies

Polar Bears

29% of Market

Like Teddy Bears except colder! Will shop around for cheapest service supplier, whoever that may be. Full third party approach. Train me but don't expect to be paid. Will review annually (seriously). If multi-site will require supplier to effectively cover these sites.

Larger companies

Yogi Bears

11% of Market

A 'wise' Teddy or Polar Bear working long hours. Will use trained staff to fix if possible. Needs skilled product specialist at end of phone, not a bookings clerk. Wants different service levels to match the criticality of the product to their business process.

Large and small companies

Grizzly Bears

6% of Market

Trash them! Cheaper to replace than maintain. Besides, they're so reliable that they are probably obsolete when they bust. Expensive items will be fixed on a pay-as-when basis – if worth it. Won't pay for training.

Not small companies

Andropov Big Bears

9% of Market

My business is totally dependent on your products. I know more about your products than you do! You will do as you are told. You will be here now! I will pay for the extra cover but you will...!

Not small or very large companies

Polarizations in Attitude

The computer clustering generated the segments by grouping customers with similar attitudes and requirements. This resulted in some marked differences in attitude between segments. As illustrated below, the Koalas really did not want to know about being trained and having a go. But the Teddies, Yogis and Polars had an almost opposite attitude.

Satisfaction and loyalty. GlobalTech was measuring customer satisfaction for use both locally, as a business process diagnostic tool, and globally, as a management performance metric. These satisfaction metrics were averaged across all customers, both by geographic business unit and by product division to meet internal management reporting requirements.

However, the outputs from the quantitative study clearly showed that these traditionally well-accepted metrics were, in fact, almost meaningless. What delighted customers in one market segment would annoy customers in another, and vice versa. To make the metrics meaningful, they had to be split by key criteria and the market segments.

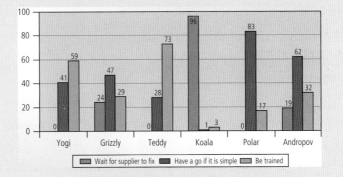

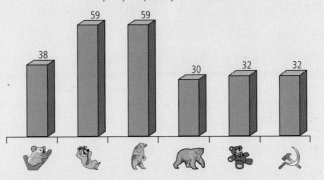

% very likely to repeat buy from GlobalTech

Loyalty was obviously highest where GlobalTech's 'one size fits all' service deliverable coincidently best matched a segment's requirement, as illustrated.

(Continued)

Correlation between loyalty and customer satisfaction. The market lifecycle for many of GlobalTech's products was moving into the commodity phase. Therefore, not surprisingly, customers were becoming less loyal.

Each percentage point increase in loyalty translated into almost the same increase in market share. Each percentage point in market share added many millions of dollars of gross revenues. The cost of reselling to a loyal customer was about one-sixth the cost of winning a new customer. Consequentially, each percentage point increase in loyalty had a significant impact on the bottom line.

Because of this, the quantitative study included correlating the key drivers of satisfaction and loyalty within each market segment. The qualitative study identified some 28 key customer requirements of their service provider. The quantitative study prioritized these to provide a shorter list of 17 common requirements. The correlation exercise reduced this to only two requirements that drew a significant correlation between satisfaction and loyalty:

- Providing service levels that meet your needs
- Providing consistent performance over time.

Although GlobalTech was achieving the second, it was really only delivering the first in two of the market segments.

Segment Attractiveness

As an aid to deciding where best to invest, a chart of segment attractiveness was produced using attractiveness factors determined by GlobalTech. Demographic data from the quantitative study was combined with internal GlobalTech financial data.

Each factor was weighted to reflect the relative importance to GlobalTech. This highlighted quite a few issues and some opportunities. For instance, the highest margins where coming from some of the least loyal segments.

Market Attractiveness Factors

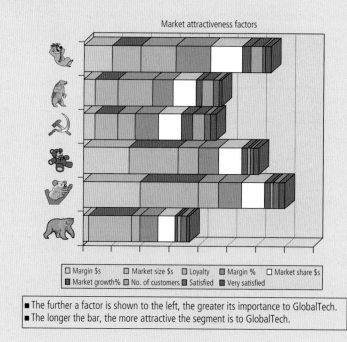

Market attractiveness factors

☐ Margin $s   ☐ Market size $s   ☐ Loyalty   ■ Margin %   ☐ Market share $s
■ Market growth%   ☐ No. of customers   ■ Satisfied   ■ Very satisfied

- The further a factor is shown to the left, the greater its importance to GlobalTech.
- The longer the bar, the more attractive the segment is to GlobalTech.

Competitive positioning. Fortunately for GlobalTech, its competitors did not appear to have an appreciation of the market segments or the differing requirements of their customers. They were also mainly delivering a 'one size fits all' service offering. However, there were some noticeable differences in their offerings. These resulted in each major competitor being significantly stronger in just one or two market segments where their deliverable best matched the segment needs.

The quantitative study provided detailed rankings of the decisive buying criteria (DBCs) and critical success factors (CSFs) for each market segment. These were to prove invaluable during the phase of designing the service products and developing the strategy to achieve competitive advantage.

- *DBCs* (decisive buying criteria) are the needs (benefits) buyers are seeking to have satisfied by their choice of product or service.
- *CSFs* (critical success factors) are the constituents of the other required to deliver each benefit (DBC).

Reachability. Key to GlobalTech successfully implementing any strategies or communications that were to be market segment based would be being able to identify each customer by segment. As part of the quantitative study, two statistical reachability tasks were completed.

A sampling of internal GlobalTech databases showed that there was sufficient relevant data to achieve better than 70 per cent accuracy, using statistical imputation methods, to code each customer record with its market segment. This was considered to be good enough to enhance marketing communications measurably, but might not be sufficiently accurate to ensure always making the most appropriate offer. Statistical analysis identified four questions that would provide acceptable accuracy in segment identification. These questions could then be used during both inbound and outbound call centre conversations until such time as all customers had been coded.

The recommendation was to use both methods in parallel so that accuracy would improve over time. Also, the coding of larger customers should be given a priority.

LESSON 4

Understanding the different market segments helps in designing the required offers. But do not get hung up on reachability. It is not essential to code every customer to the right segment from day one. Where you are not really sure, let them see different offers and so position themselves.

Similarly, be willing to accept that within a large organization some buyers may fall into different market segments, though the difference will only be on one or perhaps two buying criteria rather than across all the buying criteria.

Strategy Development and Implementation

Market understanding and strategy development. The challenge now was for the project team to absorb and understand all the findings from the two research studies. The team then had to turn that understanding into realizable strategies. To achieve this, a workshop process covering opportunities, threats and issues (OTIs) was used.

Briefly, the process involved an extensive, but controlled, brainstorming session followed by a series of innovative strategy development workshops.

A facilitator took the team systematically through every piece of relevant information available. Using brainstorming, the team tried to identify every conceivable opportunity, threat or

(Continued)

internal issue associated with each item of information. The information was also then tested against a predetermined list of business behaviours and processes in an endeavour to entice additional and creative ideas out of the brainstorming. Using the decisive buying criteria and critical success factors from the market model, strengths and weaknesses were added, thus turning the process into a SWOT. Like ideas were merged and de-duplicated.

Each idea was given two scores in the range of 1–9. The first ranked the probable financial impact, the second ranked the probability of success. The ideas were then grouped by like activity and where they had the same or an overlapping financial impact. This ensured that double counting was eliminated and that opportunities and threats were offset as appropriate. Any one group of ideas would take on the highest single financial impact score and a reassessed probability of success score. If the resolution of an internal issue was a prerequisite for capturing an opportunity or overcoming a threat, then the issue plus associated costs and resources was included in the same group as the opportunity or threat. The norm was for a single issue to be attached to many groups. The groups were named and then ranked both by financial impact and probability of success. This provided a prioritized shortlist of imperatives that should deliver the maximum realizable benefits to both GlobalTech and its customers. Iterative discussions developed this into an overall strategy with a number of prioritized substrategies. Each substrategy was supported by a documented description of the opportunity. At this stage encouragement was given to creating innovative, yet simple, implementation options that would maximize the chances of success. Each implementation option was supported by market, revenue and organizational impact data, associated issues, resources, costs, and required control metrics. Board members were involved in an option selections and investment approvals process. Finally, the implementation programmes and project plans were created.

The strategy. The overall recommendation was to create a set of service deliverables tailored to the individual needs of each segment. These would be complemented by a set of premium addons that could be offered to the appropriate segments. By focusing on business process simplification, during the design of the offering for each segment, redundancy was eliminated.

The objective of each offering was to increase customer satisfaction significantly, with an emphasis on those items that would most positively impact loyalty. Some offerings were quite different from others, both in terms of the deliverable and the internal processes that made it possible. This differentiation was also intended to create a measurable competitive advantage in a number of the market segments.

A key to the implementation of the project was a recommended change to the customer satisfaction metrics, so that they became an effective diagnostic tool for tuning the ongoing deliverables for each market segment.

Implementation. Throughout the project, the same core team had been intimately involved with each stage of the project. They guided the work and took on board the results. They delved deeply into the analysis and did their best to understand the markets, their customer requirements and likely competitive impacts. Finally they worked hard at developing the proposed strategies. They thought buy-in had been achieved by being sponsored by a main board director.

The implementation rollout across country boundaries became difficult. Each country wanted their say. They had different views of their customer needs and how things should be done in their country. They did not easily understand or even accept the findings of the research and the meaning of the outputs.

The majority of these internal barriers were eventually overcome. Inevitably there were compromises. These led the project team into believing that not all the market segments would be fully satisfied with the new offerings in all countries.

APPLICATION QUESTIONS

1. Choose a major product or service. What are its features? Identify the benefits (to the customer) of each feature. Identify which of these are differential benefits.
2. If you cannot identify any differential benefits, in what ways could you develop some?
3. For those you have identified, how can they be improved on?
4. Identify your key market segments. How do you describe them?
5. If you cannot identify any distinct segments, how can you begin to identify one or more?

CHAPTER 4 REVIEW

Customers or consumers?

Customers are people who buy from you. Consumers are the users of your products or services – for example, a husband (customer) buys perfume for his wife (consumer). Sometimes the customer is also the consumer. Marketers need to know about the characteristics of both if they are to develop the best 'package' to meet their needs.

Market share

Market share is a key concept in marketing. It is the proportion of actual sales (either volume or value) within a defined market. How the company defines its market is extremely critical.

Try Exercise 4.1

Research shows that there is a direct correlation between market share and profitability.

Critical success factors

Within any given market segment there are critical success factors (CSFs) for winning the business, e.g. reliable delivery, acceptable design, low running costs, and so on. It will be essential for the company to establish what these are and how well it compares with its closest competitors, when measured against these factors.

Try Exercise 4.2

Market segmentation

A market segment consists of a group of customers within a market who share a similar level of interest in the same, or comparable, set of needs which can be satisfied by a distinct marketing proposition.

Each segment is sufficiently large to give the company a return for its effort. Members of each segment have a high degree of similarity. The criteria for describing segments must enable the company to communicate effectively with them.

Segmentation can be based on a combination of:

1. Analysis of customer behaviour:
   * What do they buy?
     - value/volume
     - price
     - frequency

— where they buy/outlet
— products/services, etc.

Try Exercise 4.3

* Why do they buy?
  — benefits
  — lifestyle
  — fashion/novelty
  — personality types
  — peer-group pressure preferences, etc.

Try Exercise 4.4

2. Analysis of customer characteristics (who they are):
   * customer size
   * socio-economic groups
   * demographic considerations
   * industrial classification
   * cultural/geographic factors.

Try Exercise 4.5

Questions raised for the company

1. Q: Why is market segmentation so important?
   A: Few companies can be 'all things to all people'. Segmentation allows the firm to target its effort on the most promising opportunities.
2. Q: How can we be expected to know our market share?
   A: The more accurately you can define your market segments, the more accurately you will find you can measure your market share. Correct market definition is also critical for:
   * growth measurement
   * specifying target customers
   * recognizing relevant competitors
   * setting marketing objectives and strategies.
3. Q: How can we keep tabs on all our competitors?
   A: You don't have to – just concentrate on your closest competitors and try to ensure that you maintain some differential advantage over them.

EXERCISES

Introduction to Chapter 4 exercises

Exercise 4.1 looks at the most crucial and complex issue in marketing, i.e. how a market is defined. Until this is clearly understood, issues such as market share, the identification of target customers and their needs, and even the recognition of competitors, will continuously cause difficulty.

Exercise 4.2 examines critical success factors. Exercise 4.3 provides a technique for auditing industrial goods and services.

Exercise 4.4 introduces another technique, benefit analysis, and this is extended and put into practice in Exercise 4.5, which provides a case study for analysis.

Exercise 4.1 Market definition

Often there is confusion regarding what constitutes a market. Unless such confusion is dispelled from the outset, the whole marketing edifice will be built on sand. However, as so often is the case, what on the surface appears to be a relatively simple task can prove to be extremely testing. Take the example shown in Figure 4.28, which vastly simplifies the problem.

Figure 4.28: Example of market definition.

XYZ Ltd has five major products, A, B, C, D and E, which are sold to five different markets, as represented in Figure 4.28. Virtually all sales are achieved in the shaded areas.

Is this company's market:

(a) The shaded areas?
(b) The intersection of products A, B and C and markets 2, 3 and 4?
(c) Products A, B and C for all markets?
(d) Markets 2, 3 and 4 for all products?
(e) The entire matrix?

Scoring and Interpretation for Exercise 4.1

1. It would be possible to define our market as the shaded areas ((a) in the exercise), i.e. the product/market area currently served. The problem with this is that it might tend to close our eyes to other potential opportunities for profitable growth and expansion, especially if there is a danger that our current markets may become mature.
2. It is also possible to define our market as the intersection of products A, B and C and markets 2, 3 and 4 ((b) in the exercise). The problem with this is that while we now have a broader vision, there may be developments in product areas D and E and markets 1 and 5 that we should be aware of.
3. To a large extent, this problem would be overcome by defining our market as products A, B and C for all markets ((c) in the exercise). The problem here is that markets 1 and 5 may not require products A, B and C, so perhaps we need to consider product development (products D and E).
4. It is certainly possible to consider our market as all products for markets 2, 3 and 4 ((d) in the exercise). The potential problem here is that we still do not have any interest in markets 1 and 3.

(Continued)

5. Finally, it is clearly possible to call the entire matrix our market ((e) in the exercise), with markets 1 to 5 on the vertical axis and each of products A to E on the horizontal axis. The problem with this is that we would almost certainly have too many markets, or segments, and this could lead to a costly dissipation of effort.

The answer to the conundrum therefore is that it is purely a matter of management judgement. Any combinations of (a)–(e) above could be used, as long as there is a sensible rationale to justify the choice.

In addition, remember the following definition of 'market':

A market is the aggregation of all the products or services which customers regard as being capable of satisfying the same need.

Remember also the following useful definition of market segmentation:

An identifiable group of customers with requirements in common that are, or may become, significant in terms of developing a separate strategy.

Often, the way a market was selected in the first instance can provide clues regarding how it can be defined. Generally, either consciously or intuitively, a screening process is used to eliminate unsuitable markets and to arrive at those with potential. This screening process often works something like that shown in Figure 4.29.

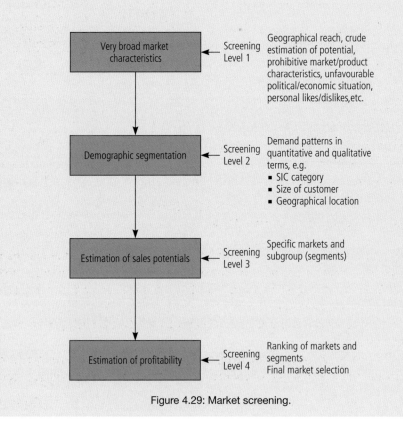

Figure 4.29: Market screening.

Consider one of your current markets and explain:

1. How it came to be chosen
2. How you would define it, so that it is clearly distinct from any other market.

Remember that the crude method outlined above, while working at a very general level, rarely leads to the development of differential advantage, and it is suggested that the other exercises in this chapter should be completed in order to get a better understanding of the central significance of market segmentation in marketing success.

Exercise 4.2 Critical success factors (CSFs)

Critical success factors can vary from one type of business to another, or indeed from one market segment to another. Therefore it is impossible to be prescriptive about your CSFs, and you will have to draw on the expertise you have about your business and establish which ones are correct for you.

Remember, a CSF is something which helps you to clinch the business. Thus, by definition, if it were absent, your success rate would plummet.

Normally there would only be a few CSFs – probably not more than five – although there might be many other factors which contribute to success.

Table 4.4 is an example of the way a firm of quantity surveyors analysed their business.

CSF	Weighting	Score out of 10 (10 = very high standard)	Adjusted score*
1 Reputation for on-time completion	0.5	6	30
2 Track record of quality	0.3	6	18
3 Quality of sales staff	0.2	8	16
Total	1.0		64%

Table 4.4: Critical success factors (1).

*Adjusted score = score out of 10 × weighting factor.

Weighting factors are distributed to each CSF according to their relative importance. In Table 4.4, CSF1 is the most important, but the company only scores 6, just over average. In contrast, on CSF3 the company scores high, but this factor is the least critical of those listed and so the net result is diminished.

The company now repeats this process (Table 4.5), this time focusing on its nearest competitors.

On the evidence in Table 4.5, our company can see that Competitor A, even with a lower quality sales force and a slightly poorer track record, has a competitive advantage because

(Continued)

of its ability to complete contracts on time. Similarly, Competitor C is a force to be reckoned with. In contrast, Competitor B has a lot of ground to make up in all areas.

CSF	Weighting	Comp. A score		Comp. B score		Comp. C score	
		Raw	Adjusted	Raw	Adjusted	Raw	Adjusted
1	0.5	9	45	5	25	7	35
2	0.3	5	15	5	15	7	21
3	0.2	6	12	5	10	5	10
Total			72%		50%		66%

Table 4.5: Critical success factors (2).

This technique can be applied to all companies and provides three useful outcomes:

1. It forces people to think about their critical success factors.
2. It provides an overview of relative competitiveness when measured against their main competitors.
3. It highlights the areas where the most effective improvements might be made.

Now try it on your company. See Tables 4.6 and 4.7.

CSF	Weighting	Score out of 10 (10 = very high standard)	Adjusted score*
CSF1			
CSF2			
CSF3			
CSF4			
CSF5			

Table 4.6: Critical success factors (3).

CSF	Weighting	Comp. A score		Comp. B score		Comp. C score	
		Raw	Adjusted	Raw	Adjusted	Raw	Adjusted
CSF1							
CSF2							
CSF3							
CSF4							
CSF5							

Table 4.7: Critical success factors (4).

Exercise 4.3 Market audit – industrial goods and services

Using your own company as the study vehicle, complete the market audit form (Table 4.8) by following these instructions:

Step 1   In column 1, list all those industries that are consumers of your goods or services. Note that there is no need to structure this list, just write them down as they occur to you.

Step 2   In column 2, write the actual turnover figure.

Step 3   In column 3, write down the percentage value of turnover that results from each of the industries.

Step 4   In column 4, indicate whether or not this, when considered from the point of view of profitability, is high or low, by scoring 10 for high, 5 for good, and 1 for low (here, 'profitability' means whatever your company considers it to mean).

Step 5   Using column 5, consider what capacity and skills you have at your disposal to continue supplying each industry – a score of 10 would show that you have considerable capacity, with minimal interference to other products or services; 1 would indicate severe limitations.

Step 6   Using a similar scoring procedure, complete column 6. Ask yourself how confident your company is that it can supply each industry with the right quality and design of goods/services, delivered on time. Are you more confident about some than others?

Step 7   Now consider the market potential (demand) for your output in each of the listed industries. Using column 7, score 10 for high potential and 1 for low.

Step 8   Add the scores you have allocated in columns 4, 5, 6 and 7, and enter them in column 8.

Step 9   Using the information you have put together, identify your key market segments. They ought to be those industries which collected the highest aggregate scores, but for your type of business you might identify other factors that would influence your choice of market. Make a note of these in column 9. In addition, use column 9 to record any particular opportunities or threats presented in each market.

Step 10 Balancing the notes you made in column 9 against the arithmetic calculations (column 8), study the information you have assembled, and select what you regard as the best industrial market. Enter 1 against this in column 10. Continue ranking each industry, using 2 for the next best, 3 for the third, etc. until column 10 is filled.

Information from this market audit could be used at a later stage, when marketing objectives and strategies are examined (Exercises 6.6 and 6.7).

Exercise 4.4 Benefit analysis

Customers buy products and services because they seek to acquire a range of benefits which go with them. In this sense, all products and services are problem-solvers. Thus, customers buy aspirin to solve the problem of headaches, they buy drills because they need holes, they buy convenience foods because they solve the problem of there not being enough hours in the day.

It is essential for providers of products or services to be aware that their output is only saleable for as long as it provides the benefits the customer requires, and for as long as it

(Continued)

1	2	3	4	5	6	7	8	9	10
Industry	Actual T/O	% T/O	Profitability, L_1 $_{10}H$	Capacity, L_1 $_{10}H$	Confidence, L_1 $_{10}H$	Potential, L_1 $_{10}H$	Total (Cols 4, 5, 6, 7)	Additional factors, opportunities/ threats	Rank

Table 4.8: Market audit industrial goods and services

is seen by the customer to be good value when compared with other possible methods of solving their problems. Once there is a better, cheaper, quicker, tidier, more enjoyable way of putting holes in walls, the drill manufacturer will go the way of the buggy-whip maker. Therefore it is vitally important to know just as much about the benefits they supply as it is to know about the products or services themselves.

Standard benefits

These are provided by the product but are not in any way unique – for example, 'the propellant in our aerosol does not damage the ozone layer'. Although in this respect your product might be like all others, not to make customers aware of this standard benefit could imply that you still use environmentally unfriendly materials. Clearly this would be to your disadvantage.

Company benefits

The business transaction links the customer to the company. In turn, this means that there ought to be some benefits to that customer for making that choice. Customers will prefer to deal with companies that provide better customer service, inspire confidence, have a reputation for fair trading policies, and so on. Company benefits are a means of differentiating your products or services from competing ones, if to all intents and purposes they are similar. For example, some banks are trying to establish specific identities to the benefits they supply. Hence there is 'the listening bank' and 'the bank that likes to say yes'. Perhaps eventually there will be 'the bank that is open when its customers want it to be'!

Differential benefits

These are the benefits that only your products or services provide. It is these that give the company its competitive advantage. It is these that must be identified, developed and exploited if the company is to win success. Here are some examples:

- 'We are the only company that provides a genuine 24-hour breakdown service. Therefore, any time you need us, we are there to get you moving again.'
- 'This is the only product on the market with this self-cleaning facility, so you can install it and have no maintenance worries.'

Not every benefit will have equal appeal to all customers, or groups of customers. However, by talking to them, or carrying out research, it ought to be possible to establish which are the important benefits in their eyes.

It is now possible to prepare a systematic benefit analysis along the lines shown in these examples. See Table 4.9.

Note:

1. To get from a feature to an advantage, and then to a benefit, the phrase 'which means that' can be helpful – for example, 'It's coated in new formula paint (feature), which means that the colour will never fade (advantage).' If you know this is what the customer needs, then you have also arrived at a benefit.

(Continued)

Customer(s) _____				
Service/product _____				
Customer appeal	**Features**	**Advantages**	**Benefits**	**Proof**
What issues are of particular concern to the customer, e.g. cost, reliability, safety, simplicity, etc.?	What features of the product/ service best illustrate these issues? How do they work?	What advantages do these features provide, i.e. what do they do for the customer?	How can tangible benefits be expressed to give maximum customer appeal, i.e. what does the customer get that he/she needs?	What evidence can be provided to back up the benefit and show it can be attained?
Example – *saucepans*				
Ease of use, ease of washing-up	Teflon-coated	This is a non-stick material	Trouble-free cooking, quicker washing-up	Results of tests
Example – *office services bureau*				
Accuracy and speedy turn-round of work	We use the latest equipment and very skilled staff	We are extremely versatile	Minimum of errors, cost-saving	What customers say

Table 4.9: Features, Advantages, Benefits (1).

2. To check whether you have arrived at a benefit and not just an advantage, apply the 'so what?' test. Ask this question after the benefit. If the 'so what?' prompts you to go further, the chances are you have not yet reached the real benefit – for example, 'Our products are handmade (feature), which means they are better quality than machine-made ones (benefit?)' – so what? – 'which means they last longer (the real benefit)'.

Now try producing a benefit analysis for one of your own products or services, as it impacts on a specific customer or customer group. Use Table 4.10.

The customer audit applied to your own company

Working alone, and using your own company as the study vehicle:

1. Choose a major product or service, and identify:
   (a) The main customers
   (b) The features with maximum customer appeal
   (c) The benefits to the customer of each feature
   (d) Which of these benefits are differential benefits (i.e. benefits not recognized or stressed by your major competitors).

Customer(s) _____

Service/product _____

Customer appeal	Features	Advantages	Benefits	Proof

Table 4.10: Features, Advantages, Benefits (2).

2. If you cannot identify any differential benefits, in what ways could you develop them?
3. For those you have identified, how could they be improved upon?
4. Identify your key market segments. How do you describe them?
5. If you cannot readily identify any distinct segments, what would be a sensible way to segment your markets?

Personal notes

Exercise 4.5 Micro-segments

Use the form provided to work out the micro-segments found in your market. For instructions on doing this, please refer to pages 140–142.

Micro-segment	1	2	3	4	5	6	7	8	9	10	
Application (if applicable)											
What is bought											
Where,											
When,											
and How											
Who											
Why (benefits sought)											

(Continued)

A selection of standard approaches to profiling benefits

1. *Demographic characteristics*
   - Standard Industrial Classification (SIC) – the latest details are available from the appropriate statistical office. Summaries of both the UK/European and North American SIC systems appear below.

     United Kingdom and Europe

     Agriculture, Hunting and Forestry (01–02)

     Fishing (05)

     Mining and Quarrying (10–14)

     Manufacturing (15–37)

     Electricity, Gas and Water Supply (40–41)

     Construction (45)

     Wholesale and Retail Trade; Certain Repairs (50–52)

     Hotels and Restaurants (55)

     Transport, Storage and Communication (60–64)

     Financial Intermediation (65–67)

     Real Estate, Renting and Other Business Activities (70–74)

     Public Administration and Defence; Compulsory Social Security (75)

     Education (80)

     Health and Social Work (85)

     Other Community, Social and Personal Service Activities (90–93)

     Private Households with Employed Persons and Miscellaneous (95–97)

     Extra-territorial Organizations and Bodies (99)

     North America (USA, Canada and Mexico)

     Agriculture, Forestry, Fishing and Hunting (11)

     Mining (21)

     Utilities (22)

     Construction (23)

     Manufacturing (31–33)

     Wholesale Trade (42)

     Retail Trade (44–45)

     Transportation and Warehousing (48–49)

     Information (51)

     Finance and Insurance (52)

     Real Estate and Retail and Leasing (53)

     Professional, Scientific and Technical Services (54)

     Management of Companies and Enterprises (55)

     Administrative and Support and Waste Management and Remediation Services (56)

     Education Services (61)

     Health Care and Social Assistance (62)

     Arts, Entertainment and Recreation (71)

     Accommodation and Food Services (72)

  Other Services (except Public Administration) (81)
  Public Administration (92)

- Size of company – Very small, Small, Small–Medium, Medium, Medium–Large, Large, Very large, Very large+
- Department/Section – Manufacturing, Distribution, Customer Service, Sales, Marketing, Commercial, Financial, Bought Ledger, Sales Ledger, Personnel Estates, Office Services, Planning Contracts, IT
- Multidemographic – combining a selection of demographic criteria, such as size of company with job title, along with whether the company is public or private.

2. *Geographic*
   - Postcode
   - City, town, village, rural
   - Country
   - Region – frequently defined in the UK by TV region
   - Country
   - Economic/Political union or association (e.g. ASEAN)
   - Continent.

3. *Psychographics* – buyer characteristics
   - Personality – stage in its business life-cycle (start-up, growth, maturity, decline, turn-round); style/age of staff (formal, authoritarian, bureaucratic, disorganized, positive, indifferent, negative, cautious, conservative, old-fashioned, youthful)
   - Attitude – risk takers or risk avoiders; innovative or cautious, and many of the adjectives used to describe different types of personality can also express a company's attitude towards your product line (as opposed to their distinctive personal character)
   - Lifestyle – environmentally concerned; involved with the community; sponsor of sports/arts.

A selection of standard approaches to profiling individuals

1. *Demographic characteristics*
   - Age – <3, 3–5, 6–11, 12–19, 20–34, 35–49, 50–64, 65+
   - Sex – male, female
   - Family life-cycle – Bachelor (young, single), split into dependants (living at home or full-time student) and those with their own household; Newly married (no children); Full nest (graded according to the number and age of children); Single parent; Empty nesters (children left home or a childless couple); Elderly single
   - Family size – 1–2, 3–4, 5+
   - Type of residence – Flat/house, terraced/semi-detached/detached, private/rented/council, number of rooms/bedrooms
   - Income (£k) – <10, 10–15, 16–20, 21–30, 31–50, >50
   - Occupation – operatives; craftsmen, foremen; managers, officials, proprietors; professional, technical; clerical, sales; farmers; retired, students; housewife; unemployed. White-collar (professional, managerial, supervisory, clerical); Blue-collar (manual)

(Continued)

- Education (highest level) – secondary, no qualifications; GCSE; graduate; postgraduate
- Religion – Christian, Jewish, Muslim, Buddhist, Other
- Ethnic origin – African, Asian, Caribbean, UK, Irish, Other European
- Nationality
- Socio-economic – the eight-class version of the socio-economic classification (SEC) introduced by the Office for National Statistics (UK) 2001 and the former Registrar General's 'Social Class' can be found on pages 140 to 142.
- Multidemographic – combining a selection of demographic criteria, such as life-cycle stages and occupation groupings, on the basis that these are indicative of different aspirations and behaviour patterns.

2. *Geographic*
   - Postcode
   - City, town, village, rural
   - Coastal, inland
   - County
   - Region (frequently defined in the UK by TV areas – Anglia, Border, Carlton London, Carlton Central, Carlton West Country, Channel, Grampian, Granada, HTV, LWT, Meridian, Scottish, Tyne Tees, UTV, Yorkshire)
   - Country
   - Economic/Political union or association (e.g. NAFTA)
   - Continent
   - Population density
   - Climate.

3. *Geodemographics*. A Classification of Residential Neighbourhoods (ACORN) produced by CACI Ltd* is one of the longer established geodemographic classifications in the UK, updated with Census information and lifestyle data. ACORN covers every street in Great Britain and classifies the whole population into fifty-six types, summarized into seventeen groups, which in turn are condensed into five broad categories. These five broad categories act as a simplified reference to the overall household classification structure and are as follows:
   1. 'Affluent Achievers'
   2. 'Urban Prosperity'
   3. 'Comfortably Off'
   4. 'Modest Means'
   5. 'Hard Pressed'

Geodemographic data are also combined with financial data to provide detailed information on financial product ownership. For example, Financial ACORN combines Census and financial research data into fifty-one types, twelve groups and four categories.

4. *Psychographic characteristics*
   - Personality – compulsive, extrovert, gregarious, adventurous, formal, authoritarian, ambitious, enthusiastic, positive, indifferent, negative, hostile; specific ones by sex have also been developed.

---

* 'ACORN' and 'CACI' are trademarks of CACI Ltd. Further details can be found at www.caci.co.uk

- Attitude – degree of loyalty (none, total, moderate), risk takers or risk avoiders, likelihood of purchasing a new product (innovator, early adopter, early majority, late majority, laggard), and many of the adjectives used to describe different types of personality can also express an individual's attitude towards your product line (as opposed to their distinctive personal character).
- Customer status – purchase stage (aware, interested, desirous, ready for sale), user classification (non-user, lapsed user, first time, potential).
- Lifestyle – consists of three main dimensions:

Activities	Work, hobbies, social events, vacation, entertainment, club membership, community, shopping, sports
Interests	Family, home, job, community, recreation, fashion, food, media, achievements
Opinions	Selves, social issues, politics, business, economics, education, products, future, culture

Because the data are based on individuals, variations in the attributes to be used can result in different people in the same household being selected.

- Multidimensional – combining psychographic profiles with selected demographic data and identifying geographic areas where the resulting 'behavioural' types are found. For example, Experían's MOSAIC* classifies all the households and neighbourhoods (postcodes) in Great Britain into fifty-two distinct types which describe their socio-economic and socio-cultural behaviour. These fifty-two types are aggregated into twelve broad groups:

A	High Income Families	E	Council Flats	I	Independent Elders
B	Suburban Semis	F	Victorian Low Status	J	Mortgaged Families
C	Blue Collar Owners	G	Town House and Flats	K	Country Dwellers
D	Low Rise Council	H	Stylish Singles	L	Institutional Areas

In addition to MOSAIC for Great Britain as a whole, there are separate MOSAICs for Scotland, Northern Ireland and London which identify differences only found in those areas. Experían has also extended MOSAIC to areas outside Great Britain.

---

*'Experían' and 'MOSAIC' are trademarks of Experían Ltd. Further details can be found at www.micromarketing-online.com and www.experian.co.uk

REFERENCES

1. McDonald, M. and Dunbar, I. (2010) *Market Segmentation: How to Do It; How to Profit from It*. Goodfellow Publishing, Oxford.
2. Buzzell, R.D. and Gale, B.T. (1987) *The PIMS Principles: Linking Strategy to Performance*. The Free Press, New York.
3. Jenkins, M. and McDonald, M. (1997) Market segmentation: organisational archetypes and a research agenda. *European Journal of Marketing*, 31(1), 17-30.
4. Smith, W. (1956) Product differentiation and market segmentation as alternative marketing strategies. *Journal of Marketing*, 21, July, 3-8.
5. Wind, Y. (1978) Issues and advances in segmentation research. *Journal of Marketing Research*, 15, 317-337.
6. Bailey, C., Baines, P., Wilson, H. and Clark, M. (2009) Segmentation and customer insight in contemporary services marketing practice: why grouping customers is no longer enough. *Journal of Marketing Management*, 25(3-4), 228-251.
7. Coviello, N., Brodie, R., Danacher, P. and Johnston, W. (2002) How firms relate to their markets: an empirical examination of contemporary marketing practice. *Journal of Marketing*, 66(3), 33-46.
8. Wilson, H., Daniel, E. and McDonald, M. (2002) Factors for success in relationship marketing. *Journal of Marketing Management*, 18(1-2), 199-218.
9. Rigby, D., Reicheld, F. and Scheffer, P. (2002) Avoid the four pitfalls of CRM. *Harvard Business Review*, 80(2), 101-109.
10. Christensen, C., Cook, S. and Hall, T. (2005) Marketing malpractice: the cause and the cure. *Harvard Business Review*, 83(12), December, 74-83.
11. Yankelovitch, D. (2006) Rediscovering market segmentation. *Harvard Business Review*, 84(6), February, 122-131.
12. Smith, B. (2003) The effectiveness of marketing strategy: making processes in medical markets. April. Cranfield Doctoral Thesis.
13. Rogers, E.M. (1976) New product conception and diffusion. *Journal of Consumer Research*, 2, March, 220-230.
14. McDonald, H. and Alpert, F. (2007) Who are innovators and do they matter? *Marketing Intelligence and Planning*, 25(5), 421-435.

Chapter

COMPLETING THE MARKETING AUDIT: 2 THE PRODUCT AUDIT

SUMMARY

- What we sell to the segments identified in the last chapter
- What a 'product' is – throughout the chapter the word 'product' is used, but the guidelines provided apply equally to services
- What a brand is
- What the difference is between a successful and an unsuccessful brand
- Key diagnostic tools, specifically
  - lifecycle analysis
  - the Boston Matrix
  - the directional policy matrix
- The growing importance of category management
- Examples of all these tools in practice are provided in the form of mini case histories
- Exercises to turn the theory into actionable propositions

INTRODUCTION

It will be recalled that, at the beginning of the last chapter, the diagram of the marketing process – repeated here as Figure 5.1 – indicated that Chapters 4 and 5 would be concerned with Box 1, for clearly a marketing audit is concerned not just with whom we sell to but also with what we sell to them. Consequently, this chapter is concerned with this aspect of the audit.

What is a Product?

Throughout this chapter we refer to the term 'product'. However, everything we say is equally applicable to a service.

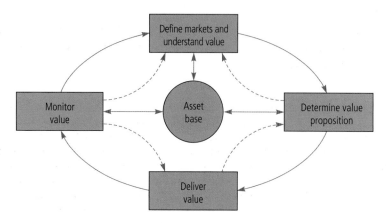

Figure 5.1: Overview of marketing map.

Figure 5.2: What we sell to meet customers needs.

The central role that the ▶ product plays in marketing management makes it such an important subject that mismanagement in this area is unlikely to be compensated for by good management in other areas.

The vital aspects of product management we shall discuss in this chapter are concerned with the nature of products, product lifecycles, how products make profits, the concept of the product portfolio, and new product development. The purpose of this discussion is to help us to carry out a product audit in order that we can set meaningful marketing objectives. But before we can begin a proper discussion about product management, it is necessary first to understand what a product is, since this is the root of whatever misunderstanding there is about product management.

We have already looked at customers; now we begin to look at what we sell to them (see Figure 5.2). Let us begin by explaining that a product is a problem-solver, in the sense that it solves the customer's problems, and is also the means by which the company achieves its objectives. And since it is what the customer actually gets for what they pay, it is clearly a subject of great importance.

> A product (or service) is the total experience of the customer or consumer when dealing with an organization

The clue to what constitutes a product can be found in an examination of what it is that customers appear to buy. Customers have needs and they buy products to satisfy them. This was made clear in the last chapter on market segmentation. At its simplest level, someone who needs a hole may buy a drill. But if a better way of making a hole is invented – say a pocket laser – demand for drills may fall.

MARKETING INSIGHT

Some years ago, Gestetner got into serious difficulties because they thought they were in the duplicator market, when it was clear that other solutions to the duplication problem had become available.

The important point about this is that a company which fails to think of its business in terms of customer benefits rather than in terms of physical products or services is in danger of losing its competitive position in the market.

But while this is important at the highest level of a company, it is also extremely relevant even at the level of the salesperson. A salesperson announcing that the quench tank on their furnace is three times bigger than a competitor's quench tank must not be surprised if this news is met with complete indifference, especially if this feature requires a hole to be dug in the ground three times bigger than the one the customer currently has! Much more relevant would be the fact that this larger quench tank would enable the customer to save a large amount of money each year on operating costs, which is a benefit and which is the main aspect the customer is interested in.

So far, we have not said much about service products, such as consulting, banking, insurance, and so on. The reason for this is simply that, as we said in Chapter 1, the marketing of services is not very different from the marketing of goods. The greatest difference is that a service product has benefits that cannot be stored. Thus, an airline seat, for example, if not utilized at the time of the flight, is gone forever, whereas a physical product may be stored and used at a later date.

In practice, this disadvantage makes very little difference in marketing terms. The major problem seems to lie in the difficulty many service product companies have in actually perceiving and presenting their offerings as 'products'. Consider the example of the consultant. This country is full of a constantly changing army of people who set themselves up as consultants, and it is not unusual to see people presenting themselves, for example, as marketing consultants. It would be difficult for any prospective client to glean from such a description exactly what benefits this person is offering. Yet the market for consulting is no different from any other market, and it is a simple matter to segment the market and develop 'products' that will deliver the particular package of benefits desired.

We can now begin to see that, when a customer buys a product, even as an industrial buyer purchasing a piece of equipment for a company, he or she is still buying a particular bundle of benefits perceived as satisfying their own particular needs and wants.

We can now appreciate the danger of leaving product decisions entirely to technical experts. If we do, they will often assume that the only point in product management is the actual technical performance, or the functional features of the product itself.

These ideas are incorporated in Figure 5.3.

The two outer circles are depicted as 'product surround'. This product surround can account for as much as 80 per cent of the added values and impact of a product. Often, these only account for about 20 per cent of costs, whereas the reverse is often true of the core product. This is shown in Figure 5.4.

THE IMPORTANCE OF THE BRAND

It will be clear that here we are talking about not just a physical product, but a *relationship* with the customer, a relationship that is personified either by the company's name or by the ▶ brand name on the product itself. IBM, BMW and Shell are excellent examples of company brand names. Persil, Coca-Cola, Foster's Lager, Dulux Paint and Castrol GTX are excellent examples of product brand names.

A brand is a name or symbol which identifies a product. A successful brand identifies a product as having sustainable, competitive advantage

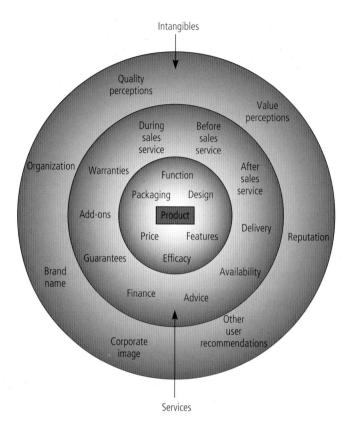

Figure 5.3: What is a product?

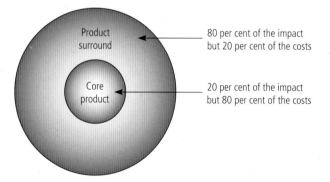

Figure 5.4: Product costs.

Most people are aware of the Coca-Cola/Pepsi-Cola blind taste tests, in which little difference was perceived when the colas were drunk 'blind'. On revealing the labels, however, 65 per cent of consumers claimed to prefer Coca-Cola. This is one of the best indications of the value of what we have referred to as the 'product surround'. That it is a major determinant of commercial success there can be little doubt. When one company buys another, as in the case of Nestlé and Rowntree, it is abundantly clear that the purpose of the acquisition is not to buy the tangible assets which appear

Gillette brand	**£4.0 billion**
Duracell brand	£2.5 billion
Oral B	£2.0 billion
Braun	£1.5 billion
Retail and supplier network	£10.0 billion
Gillette innovative capability	£7.0 billion
TOTAL	£27.0 billion

Table 5.1: P and G have paid £31 billion for Gillette, but have bought only £4 billion of tangible assets

(David Haigh, Brand finance, *Marketing Magazine*, 1 April 2005)

on the balance sheet, such as factories, plant, vehicles, and so on, but the brand names owned by the company to be acquired.

In 2006, Procter & Gamble paid £31 billion for Gillette yet, as can be seen from Table 5.1, they acquired only £4 billion of tangible assets.

In 2010, Kraft bought Cadbury for over £10 billion, most of which was for the brand names rather than the tangible assets.

This is because it is not factories that make profits, but relationships with customers, and it is company and brand names that secure these relationships.

It is also a fact that, whenever brand names are neglected, what is known as 'the commodity slide' begins. This is because the physical characteristics of products are becoming increasingly difficult to differentiate and easy to emulate. In situations like these, one finds that purchasing decisions tend to be made on the basis of price or availability in the absence of strong brands.

Business history is replete with examples of strong brand names which have been allowed to decay through lack of attention, often because of a lack of both promotion and continuous product improvement programmes.

MARKETING INSIGHT

The fruit squash drink market is typical of this. The reverse can be seen in the case of Intel, which is a fantastic branding success story in a highly competitive global market.

Figure 5.5 depicts the process of decay from brand to commodity as the distinctive values of the brand are eroded over time, with a consequent reduction in the ability to command a premium price.

The difference between a brand and a commodity can be summed up in the term 'added values', which are the additional attributes, or intangibles, that the consumer perceives as being embodied in the product. Thus, a product with a strong brand name is more than just the sum of its component parts. The Coca-Cola example is only one of thousands of examples of the phenomenon.

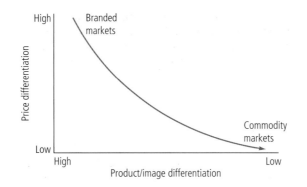

Figure 5.5: The commodity slide.

MARKETING INSIGHT

In the same way, Glaxo's Zantac in the ulcer market communicates an aura of quality and reliability that enables it to protect its advantage over lesser known brands.

Research has shown that perceived product quality, as explained above, is a major determinant of profitability. This issue is further discussed in Chapter 6 under the heading 'Competitive strategies'.

The Difference Between Successful and Unsuccessful Brands

Successful brand building helps profitability by adding values that entice customers to buy. They also provide a firm base for expansion into product improvements, variants, added services, new countries, and so on. They also protect companies against the growing power of intermediaries. And last, but not least, they help transform organizations from being faceless bureaucracies to ones that are attractive to work for and deal with.

We must not, however, make the mistake of confusing successful and unsuccessful 'brands'. The world is full of products and services that have brand names, but which are not successful brands. They fall down on other important criteria.

A successful brand has a name, symbol or design (or some combination) that identifies the 'product' of an organization as having a sustainable competitive advantage – for example, Coca-Cola, IBM, Tesco. A successful brand invariably results in superior profit and market performance. An IPA report in March 2008[1] stated: 'The average proportion of consumers across all categories who were motivated by price was 10 per cent. There was, therefore, good reason in continuing to build brand preference during a downturn.' ROCE and market share were considerably enhanced by increased brand expenditure during a downturn. Brands are only assets if they have sustainable competitive advantage. Like other assets, brands depreciate without further investment – for example, Hoover, Singer, MG, Marks & Spencer, and so on.

MARKETING INSIGHT

There are many 'products' that pretend to be brands, but are not the genuine article. As the Director of Marketing at Tesco said, 'Pseudo brands are not brands. They are manufacturer's labels. They are "me-toos" and have poor positioning, poor quality and poor support. Such manufacturers no longer understand the consumer and see retailers solely as a channel for distribution' (Marketing Director, Tesco, reported in *Marketing Globe*, Vol. 2, No. 10, 1992).

In the vast majority of buying decisions, brands simply provide a short cut, because whether we buy Brand A or Brand B isn't a matter of life or death so we buy on a whim or habitual choice[2].

Seen in this light, pseudo brands can never be mistaken for the real thing, because the genuine brand provides added brand values. Customers believe that the product:

* will be reliable
* is the best
* is something that will suit them better than product X
* is designed with them in mind.

These beliefs are based not only on perceptions of the brand itself relative to others, but also on customers' perceptions of the supplying company and beliefs about its reputation and integrity.

As Mark Ritson said: 'Great stars shine brightest when the sky is darkest. In austere times, great brands bestow pleasure, maintain their premium and take a long view.'[3]

The title 'successful brand' has to be earned. The company has to invest in everything it does so that the product meets the physical needs of customers, as well as having an image to match their emotional needs. Thus it must provide concrete and rational benefits that are sustained by a marketing mix that is compatible, believable and relevant.

IBM, despite all its recent trials and tribulations, still has a substantial world market share and that three-lettered logo is still very powerful.

The Components of a Brand

There are three principal components: brand strategy; brand positioning; and brand personality.

The first of these, *brand strategy*, stems from the position of the brand in the portfolio of the organization that owns the brand. Later in this chapter we will see that some poor brands are competing in high-growth markets, while others are competing in mature or declining markets. Thus the objectives for the brand could well call for different levels and types of investment (invest or harvest), innovation (relaunch, augment, cut costs), sales and distribution patterns (extension, reduction, broad, narrow), market share, usage aims (new, existing behaviour), and so on.

The first point to be made, then, is that an organization must be clear what the appropriate objectives are for a brand.

The second component, *brand positioning*, is concerned with what the brand actually does and with what it competes. In other words, brand positioning starts with the physical or functional aspects of the brand (the centre circle in Figure 5.3). For instance, Canada Dry is positioned in the UK as a mixer for brandies and whiskies, rather than as a soft drink competing with Coca-Cola, Pepsi-Cola and 7-Up. Tide is a tough, general-purpose detergent, rather than a powder for woollens. Tesco is a high-quality grocer rather than a low-price supermarket. SAS is positioned as the business person's airline.

There are usually several main motivators in any market, only one or two of which are of real importance. These dimensions are best seen as bipolar scales along which brands can be positioned – for example:

* expensive/inexpensive
* strong/mild
* big/small
* hot/cold
* fast/slow
* male/female
* etc.

Because they are so obvious, they are easy to research in order to establish which are those that people regard as the most fundamental basis for buying. It will be obvious that not all consumers look for the same functional performance, so market segmentation becomes important at this stage. A useful starting point in this kind of primary market interpretation is to draw a bipolar map, as shown in Figure 5.6. Figure 5.7 shows an actual bipolar map for detergents.

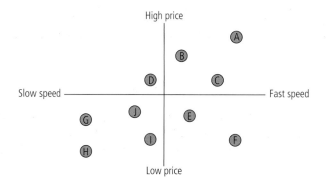

Figure 5.6: A brand position map.

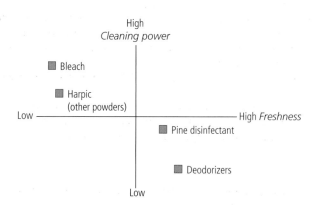

Figure 5.7: Bipolar map for detergents.

Clearly the physical dimensions of any market will change over time, so this kind of basic research should be conducted on a regular basis to establish, first, what the main dimensions are and, second, whether the position of any competing product has changed.

In highly mature markets, brands are likely to be positioned close to one another, thus indicating that the basic functional or physical characteristics are less likely to be the sole basis on which a product or service is selected.

MARKETING INSIGHT

This brings us to the final component, *brand personality*. The late Stephen King said that a product is something that is made in a factory; a brand is something that is bought by a consumer. A product can be copied, but a successful brand is unique and, particularly in mature markets, is a key discriminator in the marketplace.

Brand personality is a useful descriptor for the total impression that consumers have of brands, and in many ways brands are like people, with their own physical, emotional and personality characteristics. Brands are very similar, in that they are a complex blend of physical, emotional and personality characteristics. Thus two brands can be very similar in terms of their functions, but have very different personalities.

MARKETING INSIGHT

For example, small Fords, Peugeots, VWs and Fiats all perform about the same along the functional dimensions of size, speed and price. Yet each one has a totally different personality, which is the result of a blend of three sorts of appeal: sensual, rational and emotional.

Sensual appeal, that is, how the product or service looks, feels, sounds, and so on, can have an important influence on buying behaviour. It is easy to imagine how this appeal can differ in the case of, say, cigarettes or cars.

Rational appeal, that is, how the product or service performs, what they contain, and so on, can also have an important influence on buying behaviour.

Emotional appeal, however, is perhaps the most important and has a lot to do with the psychological rewards the products or services offer, the moods they conjure up, the associations they evoke, and so on. It is easy to imagine the overt appeal of certain products as being particularly masculine, or feminine, or chic, or workmanlike, or flashy.

BMW cars are noted for their hard, sporty personalities, while Mercedes is noted for its solid, reliable engineering prowess.

The point is that, for any brand to be successful, all these elements have to be consistent, as they will all affect the brand's personality and it is this personality, above all else, that represents the brand's totality and makes one brand more desirable, or appealing, than another.

Put at its simplest, it is a brand's personality that converts a commodity into something unique and enables a higher price to be charged for it.

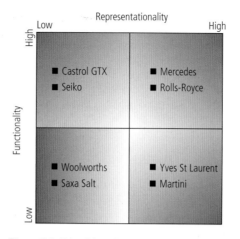

Figure 5.8: Brand functionality and personality.[4]

Figure 5.8 combines brand functionality and personality in a matrix. The vertical axis refers to a brand's ability to satisfy utilitarian needs, such as quality, reliability, effectiveness, and so on, where the consumer's need for such benefits is high. The horizontal axis represents the brand's ability to help consumers express something about themselves, be it, for example, their mood, their membership of a particular social group, their status, and so on. Brands are chosen on this dimension because they have values that exist over and above their physical values. We call this dimension representationality. For example, products such as Yves St Laurent neckties are effective brands for expressing particular personality types and roles, with functional attributes being secondary.

It is possible, by means of ▶ market research, to identify the degree to which consumers perceive a brand as reflecting functionality and representationality. Having done this, it is then possible for the marketer to consider how best to use the available resources to support the brand.

For products and services in the top right hand box (that is, ones that both provide functional excellence and are good vehicles for non-verbal communication about themselves), a creative strategy that reinforces consumers' lifestyle requirements should be adopted and communicated through appropriate media channels. Additionally, the quality of the brand needs to be maintained through high standards of quality control and continuous product development. Also, strict control over channels of distribution should be exercised.

Market research is the collection, organization, analysis and dissemination of facts and opinions from existing or potential customers and consumers about an organization or its products

For products and services in the top left hand box (that is, ones bought by consumers because of a high utilitarian need rather than because of a need to say something about themselves), product superiority needs to be continuously maintained, as 'me-tooism' is a continuous threat to such brands. Also, heavy promotional support is important in communicating the functional benefits of the brand.

For products and services in the bottom right hand box (that is, ones that are less important for their functional attributes, but which are high as symbolic devices), it is clearly important to reinforce continuously the cultural and lifestyle aspects of the brand and a heavy promotional presence is almost certainly more important than product-development issues.

For products and services in the bottom left hand box (that is, those that are bought by consumers who are not particularly concerned about either functional differences or self-image), successful branding is more difficult, because it is likely that they must have wide distribution and be very price competitive. Cost leadership, then, becomes important to the brand owner, which entails being an efficient producer. Brands in this sector are obviously vulnerable and, to succeed, an attractive price proposition is usually necessary.

The Company as a Brand

It will, by now, be obvious that it is frequently the case that a company's name is the brand used on different products or services, as opposed to an individual brand name for each product, as in the case of, say, Persil.

To present themselves in the most favourable way, firms develop a corporate identity programme, ensuring that all forms of external communication are coordinated and presented in the same way. Corporate identity can be a valuable asset, which if effectively managed, can make a major contribution to brand success.

MARKETING INSIGHT

In this respect it is easy to see why Ford has been unable to compete effectively in the high-class car market. Ford wasn't even effective in managing the Jaguar brand, which it bought to enter the up-market segment. Equally, it can be seen why Mars was able to enter the ice-cream market using the Mars corporate brand name, but why it uses a totally different brand name, Pedigree, in the animal foodstuffs market.

Classic examples of this include IBM, Shell, Mercedes, Sony, Yamaha, JCB, Virgin and countless others. It works well as a policy, given the prohibitive costs of building individual brands *ab initio*, providing the product or service in question is consistent with the corporate image.

While there is a 'halo' effect of using a famous corporate name on a new product or service, there are also risks to the total portfolio, should any one new product prove to be disastrous.

For a quantitative financial technique for calculating what is known as the capital at risk concept, see McDonald.[5]

For products with high representationality, a strong creative strategy needs to be pursued. For products with high functionality, product performance strategy is very important. For example, Levi Strauss was known and respected for jeans. Their extension into Levi tailored classic suits failed because of wrong association. Adding the name Pierre Cardin to bathroom tiles in Spain did little for the value of this core brand!

The late Peter Doyle developed a useful matrix for considering what an appropriate strategy might be towards corporate, as opposed to individual, product branding. This is given in Figure 5.9.

Global Versus Local Brands

So, if we can now distinguish between a brand and a pseudo brand, what is a ▶ global brand? Here is a definition: *a global brand is a product that bears the same name and logo and presents the same or similar message all over the world*. Usually the product is aimed at the same target market and is promoted and presented in much the same way.

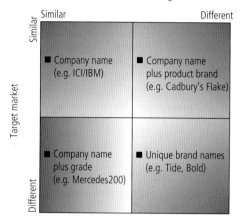

Figure 5.9: Corporate brand positioning. (Source: Professor Peter Doyle, reproduced with his kind permission)

Most of the brand valuation companies such as Brand Finance concur on which are the world's most popular and valuable brands and the top 10 usually include names like Google, Wal-Mart and Microsoft, but Coca-Cola, Sony, Mercedes, Disney, McDonald's, Toyota, IBM and Pepsi are always in such lists. Probably there are few surprises here, but what are the alternative options to having a mass global brand?

There are only two broad options:

* develop a global brand, such as American Express, or Coca-Cola
* or have a local or regional brand in each country or region of operation.

> A global brand is a product that bears the same name and logo and presents the same or similar message all over the world

What fuels the decision making regarding which choice? Clearly, it depends mainly upon the types of customer. However, there are some other practical considerations to take into account, such as the cost of production, the distribution costs, promotion, competitive market structure, channels, legal constraints and operational structures.

Procter & Gamble experienced major problems trying to get washing powders and liquids established under one brand name across Europe. For one thing, they had to try to accommodate different types of washing machines, different types of water, different washing habits, and different cultures. Then there was the business of getting to grips with market structures and competition, and, last but not least (because it can be the greatest barrier of all), getting its own operating structure right.

Clearly, then, the benefits to be derived from economies of scale have to be weighed very carefully against the difficulty of setting up a global brand, as the matrix in Figure 5.10 shows.

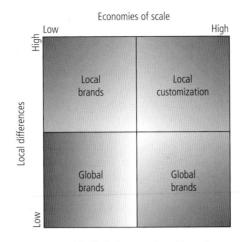

Figure 5.10: Global versus local brands.

Although three of the boxes reduce to fairly obvious choices, the top right hand box is still something of a poser. Our own inclination is that, when faced with high difficulty, but high economies of scale, we would endeavour to establish global brands.

Of course, while the matrix only represents a concept, it is possible to develop concrete data for it in much the same way as the directional policy matrix, which is described later in this chapter. For example, all the savings attributable to economies of scale could be calculated, such as manufacturing, R and D, purchasing, logistics, better management control, and so on. Equally, local differences could be assessed taking into account the infrastructure of markets, demand homogeneity, culture, political/legal framework, market structure, competition, and the like.

By looking at international markets in this way, the odds come out very much higher in favour of global brands as against local ones. Predictions about future trends only serve to reinforce this hypothesis. For example, in the European single market it has been predicted that:

- prices will tend to harmonize towards the lowest levels across Europe
- purchasers will tend to buy on a pan-European basis to gain maximum price advantage
- major distributors (especially importers) will operate transnationally and take advantage of remaining price differentials and low-cost suppliers.

MARKETING INSIGHT

Donald Casey of Lauder Associates asserts, 'The growth in global branding is a direct result of the explosion of media consumption amongst the young. In every country the data show that the younger consumers are significantly more aware of international brands, particularly in fields like TV, music, video and sports.' Further support is provided by Alan Woofe who says, 'The most fundamental point of all this is that one day there will eventually be a Euro-market, and there may one day be Euro-consumers in the foreseeable future.'

There is much evidence to confirm that these trends are already happening. The portents are clear. Already, large pan-European retailing groups are appearing and if an organization does not have a European brand, especially if it is in fast-moving consumer goods, it does not appear to have very good prospects. It is brand names that win customers, make a profit and create customer loyalty. As stated earlier, Nestlé wanted to buy Rowntree purely for its brands, not for its factories. A good brand, at the end of the day, is the company's best marketing asset. For that reason it is short-sighted not to invest in the brand. To allow it to slip and become a 'me-too' commodity is tantamount to commercial vandalism.

To summarize, a successful brand is an identifiable product, service, person or place augmented in such a way that the buyer or user perceives relevant, unique added values which match their needs most closely. Its success results from being able to sustain these added values against competitors. Being able to do this on a global basis will bring great rewards, but it will not be easy.

CATEGORY MANAGEMENT

Next a few words about category management are necessary.

Category management (CM) is a concept that has developed as a radical alternative to brand management in retail marketing since the mid-1990s. The process of CM can be summarized as:

The strategic management of a group of products clustered around a specific customer need. This group, or category, is managed as a strategic business unit with clearly defined profitability goals.

The impact of CM is that it shifts attention from individual brands to the management of overall categories as defined by local customer needs.

CM emerged from the development of ideas within the concept of Efficient Customer Response (ECR) that was initiated industry-wide in the USA from the mid-1980s onwards. The emphasis of ECR is on sales profitability rather than sales volume and spans the entire business process from the purchase of raw materials to manufacturing, distribution and sale. It is founded on the recent improvements in technology that have allowed suppliers and buyers to reduce waste and stockholding as well as reduced discounts as a means of generating sales. The focus of the concept is the business processes to be found in retail organizations.

Growth of Category Management

Brand management focuses on individual brands from the manufacturer's perspective, grouping all functions that affect a brand's profitability under one manager. Retailers, however, will often group brands together by product (e.g. soap powder) because that is more convenient for their customers and reflects the way in which customers shop.

The resultant categories are therefore defined by customers, but this can lead to problems of definition. For instance, when a customer wants a cleaner for the bathroom, does he or she categorize it as a bathroom product, a cleaner, or a home safety product? In addition, categories tend to vary regionally and according to customer types, rather than on a broader cross-cultural basis. In response some manufacturers have had to recast their brands for categories, but this in turn raises the question of whether some products should appear in more than one category – for instance, should herbs be categorized with fresh produce, baking goods or both?

In the final analysis, what is important to retailers is that their shelf space sells more than it would if managed another way. Retailers' expertise lies in providing space to sell products and services to facilitate this. Sometimes, an external supplier is appointed as category manager, who is then made responsible for optimizing sales from that space. By doing so, retailers are exploiting manufacturer skills in such areas as display, sales promotion and merchandising.

The retailer will normally set minimum standards for the category such as demanding that there must be at least one major brand name and one 'own label' product displayed. After that, the category managers make their own stocking and communications decisions on behalf of their assigned category. For example, if SmithKlineBeecham were to identify opportunities for increased toothbrush sales within the oral hygiene category for which they acted as category manager, they could spend their own budget on promoting them.

Contrary to traditional practices, CM obliges manufacturers to consider the profitability of an entire product segment rather than that of just their own brands. The fact that retailers have forced this change is another example of the evolution of retailers from passive distributors to proactive marketers and the shift of power from manufacturer to retailer.

> CM reflects the shift of power from manufacturer to retailer.

Where category managers are appointed internally, they usually have a similar role – i.e. the management of a partnership between a supplier or a number of suppliers with the objective of sales and profit enhancement.

The trend towards CM has also required a shift from the traditionally narrow focus of brand management. Looked at from a category perspective, it is possible to see that the consumer choice is not just about selecting from competing brands such as Coca-Cola or Pepsi, but involves an entire drinks portfolio of soft drinks, juices, beverages and alcohol. Heinz began realigning its business along category management principles in 1997 and now has eight global categories: ketchups, condiments and sauces, infant feeding, seafood (tuna), organic and nutritional food, pet food, frozen food, and convenience food (H.J. Heinz Company Corporate Profile, 2000).

Rather than relying on the power of their brand names, organizations need to ensure that all of their support systems demonstrate to retailers that they are capable of managing categories to advantage. This might mean a review of all of the organization's systems for retail supply such as the logistics of keeping the shelves fully supplied or maintaining efficient electronic data interchange systems for stocks.

Limitations of Category Management

Viewed purely as a strategy to reduce waste and therefore costs, CM loses its focus on the end customer as the absolute priority. Concentrating on the maximization of shelf space profitability may not improve customer satisfaction levels and this, in the long run, may reduce profits.

One recent report concluded that the availability of a wide selection of goods is a major determinant in customers' decisions about where to shop. CM limits the choice of products to those which are most profitable for the retailer and this can have a negative impact on the customers' shopping experience. If customers feel hindered in their purchase decisions by the inability to compare prices of different brands, the CM process will ultimately rebound.

Further difficulties arise from the issue of positioning different product categories. Should paper tissues, for instance, be categorized with bathroom products or health and beauty? And, should the two categories be set next to each other or apart? In addition, different retailers and manufacturers could well work to different category definitions.

> CM's emphasis on the manufacturer/retailer relationship can demote a customer focus.

These limitations reflect the fact that much of the emphasis of CM has been on the manufacturer/retailer relationship. As far back

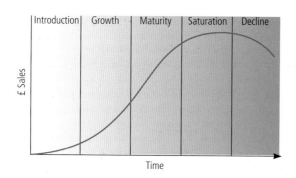

Figure 5.11: Category management evolution.

as 1994, a *Financial Times* survey found that consumers have effectively been demoted as the focus of marketing strategy as retailers have grown in importance, with consumers attracting 30 per cent of marketing expenditure against retailers at 54 per cent.

Challenges for the Future

One of the most difficult challenges facing CM is reducing the number of superfluous items on the shelves. This is in opposition to traditional brand marketing which aims to prolong the life of the brand by extending the product range. Possible ways of evolution are demonstrated by Figure 5.11.

Mass customization has been made possible by the increased sophistication in consumer information which has allowed marketers to provide variations on the central product to suit each customer. The growth of retailers' own label products (e.g. Tesco's 'finest' and 'value') reflects this, but further limits the available shelf space for branded supplies. The difficulty for retailers is ensuring that limiting consumers' brand choice is not perceived as limiting their category choice just because they cannot find their favourite products.

The future of CM must necessarily take account of the distribution systems for an increasingly 'global village' market. Many mass retailers are unable to market so many products properly, even when redefined as categories. Providing marketing expertise is therefore one way in which manufacturers can hope to retain some kind of balance in the relationship with such international retailers.

In order to sustain a customer focus, manufacturers need free access to customer information. This can be obtained through large panel companies such as Nielsen or Taylor Nelson Sofres (TNS), or through the development of a manufacturer's own database, such as Heinz. Manufacturers can also try to establish a reputation for themselves as leaders in ECR.

> CM can help deliver customer satisfaction by focusing retailers on customer preferences.

Future emphasis will probably be on targeting customer satisfaction more effectively in order to maximize long-term profit. CM can help by focusing on the retail audience and the way in which category sales are driven. This is turn helps retailers build an effective vehicle for appealing to the variety of customers' product decisions and needs. The challenge is to make this happen on a store-by-store basis, at an affordable cost.

PRODUCT LIFECYCLE

Having discussed the vital factor of benefits as a part of product management, we must now ask ourselves whether one product is enough.

There are many examples of entrepreneurs who set themselves up in business to manufacture, say, toys such as clackers, who make their fortune and who then just as quickly lose it when this fashion-conscious market changes to its latest fad. Such examples are merely the extreme manifestation of what is known as the ▶ product lifecycle. This, too, is such a vital and fundamental concept that it is worth devoting some time to a discussion of the subject.

Historians of technology have observed that all technical functions grow exponentially until they come up against some natural limiting factor which causes growth to slow down and, eventually, to decline as one technology is replaced by another. There is universal agreement that the same phenomenon applies to products, so giving rise to the concept of the product lifecycle, much written about in marketing literature during the past six decades.

The product lifecycle postulates that if a new product is successful at the introductory stage (and many fail at this point), then gradually repeat purchase grows and spreads and the rate of sales growth increases. At this stage, competitors often enter the market and their additional promotional expenditures further expand the market. But no market is infinitely expandable, and eventually the rate of growth slows as the product moves into its maturity stage. Eventually, a point is reached where there are too many firms in the market, price wars break out, and some firms drop out of the market, until finally the market itself falls into decline. Figure 5.11 illustrates these apparently universal phenomena.

Nevertheless, while the product lifecycle may well be a useful practical generalization, it can also be argued that particular product lifecycles are determined more by the activities of the company than by any underlying 'law'.

MARKETING INSIGHT

For example, Bailey's liqueur, while exhibiting all the characteristics of the classic product lifecycle, went on to new record sales heights following the appointment of a new brand manager.

Nevertheless, while this example illustrates the dangers inherent in incorrect interpretation of lifecycle analysis, even in this case, sales will eventually mature.

From a management point of view, the product lifecycle concept is useful in that it focuses our attention on the likely future sales pattern if we take no corrective action. There are several courses of action open to us in our attempts to maintain the profitable sales of a product over its lifecycle.

> A product lifecycle plots the volume or value of sales of a product from its launch to its decline and withdrawal

Figure 5.12 illustrates the actual courses taken by an American company in the management of one of its leading industrial market products. As sales growth began to slow down, the company initiated a programme of product range extensions and market development which successfully took the brand into additional stages of growth. At the same time the company was aggressively seeking new products and even considering potential areas for diversification.

Even more important are the implications of the product lifecycle concept on every element of the marketing mix. Figure 5.13 gives some guide as to how the product has to change over its lifecycle. In addition to this, however, every other element also has to change. For example, if a company

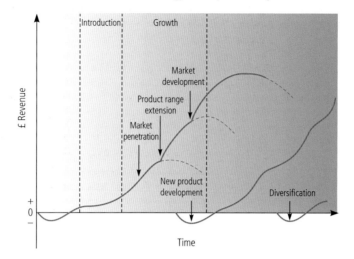

Figure 5.12: Extending the product life cycle.

The product/market life-cycle and market characteristics

Key characteristics	Unique	Product differentiation	Service differentiation	'Commodity'
Marketing message	Explain	Competitive	Brand values	Corporate
Sales	Pioneering	Relative benefits Distribution support	Relationship based	Availability based
Distribution	Direct selling	Exclusive distribution	Mass distribution	80:20
Price	Very high	High	Medium	Low (consumer controlled)
Competitive intensity	None	Few	Many	Fewer, bigger, international
Costs	Very high	Medium	Medium/low	Very low
Profit	Medium/high	High	Medium/high	Medium/low
Management style	Visionary	Strategic	Operational	Cost management

Figure 5.13: Strategy changes over the product life cycle.

rigidly adhered to a premium pricing policy at the mature stage of the product lifecycle, when markets are often overcrowded and price wars begin, it could well lose market share. It could be regretted later on when the market has settled down, for it is often at this stage that products provide extremely profitable revenue for the company. It will become clearer later in this chapter why market share is important.

The same applies to promotion. During the early phase of product introduction, the task for advertising is often one of creating awareness, whereas during the growth phase the task may need to change to one of creating a favourable attitude towards the product. Neither should the policy towards channels be fixed. At first we are concerned with getting distribution for the product in the most important channels, whereas during the growth phase we have to consider ways of reaching the new channels that want our product. All of these points will become clearer in those chapters specifically concerned with the management of price, place and promotion.

MARKETING INSIGHT

The famous 3M Post-it notes are representative of the changes which have to take place over the life of a product. At first, prices and margins were high, there were no competitors and the route to market was via direct selling. Sooner or later, new competitors entered the market. When the market reached maturity, 3M added clearer branding to the product and the route to market changed. Today, consumers have a choice of own label, coloured, lined, and small or large versions of the Post-it note. Faced with such a change in market circumstances, it is obvious that the key characteristics of management also had to change to ensure continued success.

MARKETING INSIGHT

Another example is an American multinational that, in 1972, had 80 per cent share of the photocopier market and gross margins of 40 per cent. Five years later, they had 10 per cent share and a 10 per cent margin. This was because they failed to recognize that markets tend to segment as they entered the growth phase. In this case, the Japanese entered with small photocopiers.

Drawing a product lifecycle, however, can be extremely difficult, even given the availability of some form of time series analysis. This is connected with the complex question of market share measurement.

First, let us remind ourselves that a firm needs to be concerned with its share (or its proportion of volume or value) of an actual market, rather than with a potential market. The example of the carpet manufacturer given in Chapter 4 emphasized the importance of measuring the right things when determining what a company's market is.

For the purpose of helping us to draw lifecycles, it is worth repeating the definitions given in Chapter 4:

- Product class, e.g. carpets
- Product subclass, e.g. nylon rolls
- Product brand, e.g. 'X'.

'X' as a brand, for the purpose of measuring market share, is concerned only with the aggregate of all other brands that satisfy the same group of customer wants.

Nevertheless, the manufacturer of 'X' also needs to be aware of the sales trends of other kinds of carpets and floor covering in the institutional market, as well as of carpet sales overall.

One of the most frequent mistakes made by companies that do not understand what market share really means is to assume that their company has only a small share of some market, whereas if the company is commercially successful, it probably has a much larger share of a smaller market segment.

The important point to remember at this stage is that the concept of the product lifecycle is not an academic figment of the imagination, but a hard reality which is ignored at great risk.

It is interesting to see how many commercial failures can be traced back to a naive assumption on the part of managements that what was successful as a policy at one time will continue to be successful in the future.

MARKETING INSIGHT

A reference back to Figure 5.13 will immediately explain the demise of many companies, particularly in the information technology industry, who continued to pursue policies more appropriate to the second column, when, in reality, the markets for some of their products had moved to the fourth column.

> Diffusion is the adoption of new products or services over time by consumers within social systems, as encouraged by marketing. Diffusion refers to the cumulative percentage of potential adopters of a new product or service over time

Table 5.2 shows a checklist used by one major company to help it determine where its markets are on the lifecycle.

DIFFUSION OF INNOVATION

In Chapter 4 we briefly referred to Everett Rogers' Diffusion of Innovation curve to explain why markets eventually fragment into market segments.

We make no apologies for reintroducing this important concept once again in the context of product management, as it is fundamental to commercial success.

A useful explanation and extension of the product lifecycle is what is known as the 'diffusion of innovation'. This will be referred to again in Chapter 6. ▶ Diffusion is the adoption of new products or services over time by consumers within social systems, as encouraged by marketing. Diffusion refers to the cumulative percentage of potential adopters of a new product or service over time.

Everett Rogers[6] examined some of the social forces that explain the product lifecycle. The body of knowledge often referred to as 'reference theory' (which incorporates work on group norms, group pressures, etc.) helps explain the snowball effect of diffusion. Rogers found that the actual rate of diffusion is a function of a product's:

* relative advantage (over existing products)
* compatibility (with lifestyles, values, etc.)
* communicability (is it easy to communicate?)
* complexity (is it complicated?)
* divisibility (can it be tried out on a small scale before commitment?).

Maturity stage factor	Embryonic	Growth	Mature	Declining
1. *Growth rate*	Normally much greater than GNP (on small base).	Sustained growth above GNP. New customers. New suppliers. Rate decelerates toward end of stage.	Approximately equals GNP.	Declining demand. Market shrinks as users' needs change.
2. *Predictability of growth potential*	Hard to define accurately. Small portion of demand being satisfied. Market forecasts differ widely.	Greater percentage of demand is met and upper limits of demand becoming clearer. Discontinuities, such as price reductions based on economies of scale, may occur.	Potential well defined. Competition specialized to satisfy needs of specific segments.	Known and limited.
3. *Product line proliferation*	Specialized lines to meet needs of early customers.	Rapid expansion.	Proliferation slows or ceases.	Lines narrow as unprofitable products dropped.
4. *Number of competitors*	Unpredictable.	Reaches maximum. New entrants attracted by growth and high margins. Some consolidation begins toward end of stage.	Entrenched positions established. Further shakeout of marginal competitors.	New entrants unlikely. Competitors continue to decline.
5. *Market share distribution*	Unstable. Shares react unpredictably to entrepreneurial insights and timing.	Increasing stability. Typically, a few competitors emerging as strong.	Stable with a few companies often controlling much of industry.	Highly concentrated or fragmented as industry segments and/or is localized.
6. *Customer stability*	Trial usage with little customer loyalty.	Some loyalty. Repeat usage with many seeking alternative suppliers.	Well-developed buying patterns with customer loyalty. Competitors understand purchase dynamics and it is difficult for a new supplier to win over accounts.	Extremely stable. Suppliers dwindle and customers less motivated to seek alternatives.
7. *Ease of entry*	Normally easy. No one dominates. Customers' expectations uncertain. If barriers exist, they are usually technology, capital or fear of the unknown.	More difficult. Market franchises and/or economies of scale may exist, yet new business is still available without directly confronting competition.	Difficult. Market leaders established. New business must be 'won' from others.	Little or no incentive to enter.
8. *Technology*	Plays an important role in matching product characteristics to market needs. Frequent product changes.	Product technology vital early, while process technology more important later in this stage.	Process and material substitution focus. Product requirements well known and relatively undemanding. May be a thrust to renew the industry via new technology.	Technological content is known, stable and accessible.

Table 5.2: Guide to market maturity

Diffusion is also a function of the newness of the product itself, which can be classified broadly under three headings:

1. Continuous innovation (e.g. the new miracle ingredient)
2. Dynamically continuous innovation (e.g. disposable lighter)
3. Discontinuous (e.g. microwave oven).

However, Rogers found that, for all new products, not everyone adopts new products at the same time, and that a universal pattern emerges as shown in Figure 5.14.

In general, the innovators think for themselves and try new things (where relevant); the early adopters, who have status in society, are opinion leaders and they adopt successful products, making them acceptable and respectable; the early majority, who are more conservative and who have slightly above-average status, are more deliberate and only adopt products that have social approbation; the late majority, who are below average status and sceptical, adopt products much later; the laggards, with low status, income, etc. view life 'through the rear mirror' and are the last to adopt products.

This particular piece of research can be very useful, particularly for advertising and personal selling. For example, if we can develop a typology for opinion leaders, we can target our early advertising and sales effort specifically at them. Once the first 7–8 per cent of opinion leaders have adopted our product, there is a good chance that the early majority will try it. Hence, once the 10–12 per cent point is reached, the champagne can be opened, because there is a good chance that the rest will adopt our product.

We know, for example, that the general characteristics of opinion leaders are that they are: venturesome; socially integrated; cosmopolitan; socially mobile; and privileged. So we need to ask ourselves what the specific characteristics of these customers are in our particular industry. We can then tailor our advertising and selling message specifically for them.

It can, however, also be both a practical diagnostic and a forecasting tool. There follows a worked example of how forecasts, and eventually strategic marketing plans, were developed from the intelligent use of the diffusion of innovation curve in respect of computerized business systems for the construction industry in the UK.

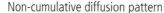

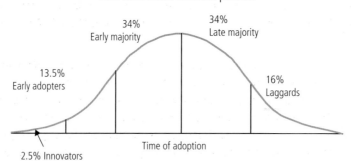

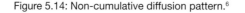

Figure 5.14: Non-cumulative diffusion pattern.[6]

1ST ESTIMATE OF MARKET SIZE

1. Number of contracting firms   160,596
   (Department of Environment,
   Housing and Construction)
2. Number of firms employing 4–79   43,400
   direct employees
3. Exclude painters, plasterers, etc.   6,100
4. Conservative estimate of main target   37,300 (1)
   area or 23% of total

2ND ESTIMATE OF MARKET SIZE

5. Using the Pareto (80/20 rule)
   likelihood that 20 per cent will be
   main target area, i.e. 160,596 20%   32,000 (2)

3RD ESTIMATE OF MARKET SIZE

6. Total number of firms in construction   217,785
   industry (Business Statistics Office)
7. Number of firms classified by
   turnover from £100,000 to £1,000,000
   (£K) 100–249   26,698
   (£K) 250–499   10,651
   (£K) 500–999   5,872
   (£K) 43,221 (3)
8. Company's best estimate of size of   37,300
   target market
9. Company's estimate of the number of   3,500   (9.4%)
   micro installations in this segment
   Plotting this on the diffusion of innovation curve shows:

- Penetration of innovators and early adopters has taken four years. Adoption rate will now accelerate. It will probably be complete within one year.
- *One-year* balance of early adopters = 6.6 per cent = 2,462 firms = installed base of 5,968. Sales objective = 360 installations plus present base of 400 = 760 = 12.7 per cent market share.

It will be seen from this that three independent estimates were made of the market size in order to establish the current position on the diffusion of innovation curve.

In contrast, a Dutch computer supplier attempted to launch hardware and software into the motor trade using an undifferentiated product at a high sales price. An elementary study would have indicated that this market is already well into the late majority phase, when price and product features become more important. Not surprisingly, the product launch failed.

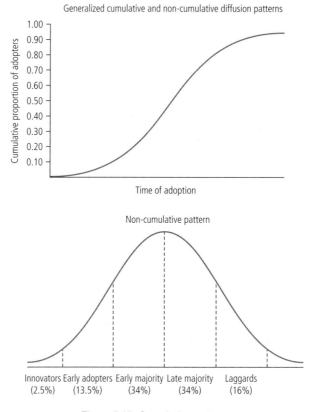

Figure 5.15: Cumulative pattern.

The diffusion of innovation curve, when seen in conjunction with the product lifecycle, helps to explain the dynamics of markets. Figure 5.15 illustrates this relationship. It shows that, when all potential users of a product are using it, the market is a replacement market.

MARKETING INSIGHT

For example, virtually everyone in Western Europe has fridges, washing machines, dishwashers, televisions and cars. The market is dependent on population growth or decline, so most of these are replacement markets and most competitors wishing to grow their sales would probably have to take it from competitors.

PRODUCT PORTFOLIO

We might well imagine that, at any point in time, a review of a company's different products would reveal different stages of growth, maturity and decline.

In Figure 5.16, the dotted line represents the time of our analysis, and this shows one product in severe decline, one product in its introductory stage, and one in the saturation stage.

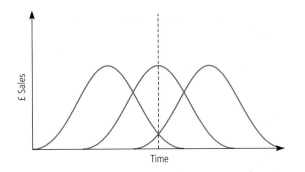

Figure 5.16: Product life cycle for three products.

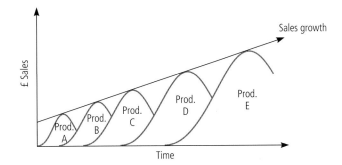

Figure 5.17: New product introductions over time.

If our objective is to grow in profitability over a long period of time, our analysis of our product portfolio should reveal a situation like the one in Figure 5.17, in which new product introductions are timed so as to ensure continuous sales growth.

The idea of a ▶ portfolio is for a company to meet its objectives by balancing sales growth, cash flow and risk. As individual products progress or decline and as markets grow or shrink, then the overall nature of the company's product portfolio will change. It is, therefore, essential that the whole portfolio is reviewed regularly and that an active policy towards new product development and divestment of old products is pursued. In this respect, the work of the Boston Consulting Group, begun in the early 1960s, had a profound effect on the way managements think about this subject and about their product/market strategy.

> A portfolio plots either products or markets using at least a two-dimensional matrix in order to balance growth, cash flow and risk

UNIT COSTS AND MARKET SHARE

There are basically two parts to the thinking behind the work of the Boston Consulting Group (BCG). One is concerned with *market share*; the other with market growth.

It is a well-known fact that we become better at doing things the more we do them. This phenomenon is known as the *learning curve*. It manifests itself especially with items such as labour efficiency, work specialization and methods improvement.

> The experience effect reflects the improvements (usually resulting in lower costs) that result from economies of scale, learning and improved productivity over time

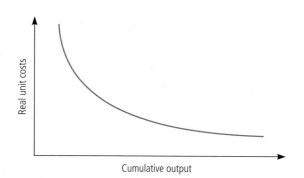

Figure 5.18: Unit cost decline over cumulative output.

Cost decline applies more to the value-added elements of cost than to bought-in supplies.

Such benefits are themselves a part of what we can call the ▶ experience effect, which includes such items as process innovations, better productivity from plant and equipment, product design improvements, and so on. In addition to the experience effect, and not necessarily mutually exclusive, are economies of scale that come with growth. For example, capital costs do not increase in direct proportion to capacity, which results in lower depreciation charges per unit of output, lower operating costs in the form of the number of operatives, lower marketing, sales, administration, and research and development costs, and lower raw materials and shipping costs. It is generally recognized, however, that cost decline applies more to the value-added elements of cost than to bought-in supplies.

In fact, the Boston Consulting Group discovered that costs decline by up to 30 per cent for every cumulative doubling of output. This phenomenon is shown in Figure 5.18. Imagine a factory producing 100 units a year for eight years. It will be seen from the following simple calculation that it becomes more difficult each year cumulatively to double output.

Year	Cumulative	Total
1	100	100
2	100	200 D
3	100	300
4	100	400 D
5	100	500
6	100	600
7	100	700
8	100	800 D

It is this phenomenon which explains the shape of the curve in Figure 5.18. The BCG used logarithmic scales on the data to enable them to make predictions about future costs at forecast output levels, a method favoured for many years by the Japanese as a way of capturing markets in America and Western Europe.

While there are many implications from this for marketing strategy, particularly in relation to pricing policy, we will confine ourselves here to a discussion of the product/market implications.

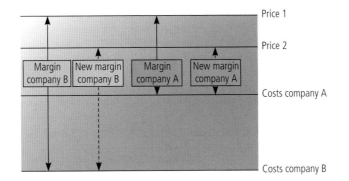

Figure 5.19: The relationship between costs and margin.

There is sufficient evidence to show that this real cost reduction actually occurs, in which case it follows that the greater your volume, the lower your unit costs should be. Thus, irrespective of what happens to the price of your product, providing you have the highest market share (hence the biggest volume), you should always be relatively more profitable than your competitors. This is illustrated in Figure 5.19.

Thus, as a general rule, it can be said that market share *per se* is a desirable goal.

Indeed, the Strategic Planning Institute's Profit Impact of Market Strategies research has confirmed that market share and profitability are linearly related. However, as we made clear in Chapter 4, we have to be certain that we have carefully defined our market, or segment.

This explains why it is apparently possible for many small firms to be profitable in large markets. The reason is, of course, that, in reality, they have a large share of a smaller market segment. This is another reason why understanding market segmentation is the key to successful marketing.

It would be unusual if there were not many caveats to the above 'law', and, although what these might be are fairly obvious, nevertheless it should be noted that the evidence provided by the Boston Consulting Group shows overwhelmingly that, in general, these 'laws' apply universally, whether for consumer, industrial or service markets.

Turning now to *market growth*, we observe that, in markets which are growing at a very low rate per annum, it is extremely difficult and also very costly to increase your market share. This is usually because the market is in the steady state (possibly in the saturation phase of the product lifecycle) and is dominated by a few major firms who have probably reached a stage of equilibrium, which it is very difficult to upset.

In markets which are going through a period of high growth, it is fairly obvious that the most sensible policy would be to gain market share by taking a bigger proportion of the market growth than your competitors. However, such a policy is very costly in promotional terms. So, many companies prefer to sit tight and enjoy rates of growth lower than the market rate. The major problem with this approach is that they are, in fact, losing market share, which gives cost advantages (hence margin advantages) to competitors.

Since we know from previous experience of product lifecycles that the market growth rate will fall, when this stage is reached and the market inevitably becomes price sensitive, the product will begin to lose money and we will probably be forced out of the market. Indeed, seen in this light, it becomes easier to understand the reasons for the demise of many industries in those countries of the world where the Japanese have entered the market.

It is interesting to note, however, that even the Japanese have suffered in recent years from lower cost suppliers entering the markets using lower prices than they can offer. These suppliers include the Koreans, the Chinese and, more recently, the Indians and South Americans. It is unlikely that high-cost 'Western' companies can compete on price alone in most of these markets, which is why segmentation is so important in strategy development today.

MARKETING INSIGHT

Typical of this is the motorcycle industry in the UK in which the output of the Japanese increased from thousands of units to millions of units during a period of market growth, while the output of the British remained steady during the same period. When the market growth rate started to decline, the inevitable happened. Even worse, it is virtually impossible to recover from such a situation, while the Japanese, with their advantageous cost position, have now dominated practically every market segment, including big bikes.

THE BOSTON MATRIX

The Boston Consulting Group combined these ideas in the form of a simple matrix, which has profound implications for the firm, especially in respect of cash flow. Profits are not always an appropriate indicator of portfolio performance, as they will often reflect changes in the liquid assets of the company, such as inventories, capital equipment, or receivables, and thus do not indicate the true scope for future development. Cash flow, on the other hand, is a key determinant of a company's ability to develop its product portfolio.

> The Boston Matrix classifies a firm's products according to their cash usage and their cash generation using market growth and relative market share to categorize them in the form of a box matrix

The ▶ Boston Matrix classifies a firm's products according to their cash usage and their cash generation along the two dimensions described above, i.e. relative market share and market growth rate. Market share is used because it is an indicator of the product's ability to generate cash; market growth is used because it is an indicator of the product's cash requirements. The measure of market share used is the product's share relative to the firm's largest competitor. This is important because it reflects the degree of dominance enjoyed by the product in the market. For example, if company A has 20 per cent market share and its biggest competitor also has 20 per cent market share, this position is usually less favourable than if company A had 20 per cent market share and its biggest competitor had only 10 per cent market share. The relative ratios would be 1:1 compared with 2:1. It is this ratio, or measure of market dominance, that the horizontal axis measures. This is summarized in Figure 5.20.

The definition of high relative market share is taken to be a ratio of one or greater than one. The cut-off point for high, as opposed to low, market growth should be defined according to the prevailing circumstances in the industry, but this is often taken as 10 per cent. There is, however, no reason why the dividing line on the vertical axis cannot be zero, or even a minus figure. It depends entirely on the industry, or segment, growth or decline. Sometimes, in very general markets, gross domestic product (GDP) can be used.

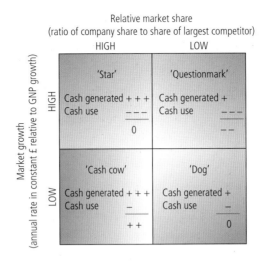

Figure 5.20: BCG and cash flows implications.

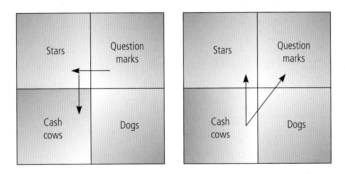

Figure 5.21: Using cash from 'cash cows' to invest in 'stars' and 'question marks'.

The somewhat picturesque labels attached to each of the four categories of products give some indication of the prospects for products in each quadrant. Thus, the 'question mark' is a product which has not yet achieved a dominant market position and thus a high cash flow, or perhaps it once had such a position but has slipped back. It will be a high user of cash because it is in a growth market. This is also sometimes referred to as a 'wildcat'.

The 'star' is probably a newish product that has achieved a high market share and which is probably more or less self-financing in cash terms.

> The picturesque labels given to the four categories in the Boston Matrix give some indication of the prospects for products in each quadrant.

The 'cash cows' are leaders in markets where there is little additional growth, but a lot of stability. These are excellent generators of cash and tend to use little because of the state of the market.

'Dogs' often have little future and can be a cash drain on the company. While it is possible that such products are necessary to support more successful products, they are probably candidates for divestment, although often such products fall into a category aptly described by Peter Drucker as 'investments in managerial ego'.

The art of product portfolio management now becomes a lot clearer. What we should be seeking to do is to use the surplus cash generated by the 'cash cows' to invest in our 'stars' and to invest in a selected number of 'question marks'. This is indicated in Figure 5.21.

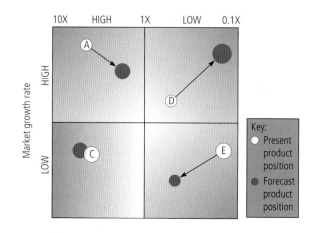

Figure 5.22: An unbalanced portfolio forecast.

The Boston Matrix can be used to forecast the market position of our products, say three years from now, if we continue to pursue our current policies.

Figure 5.22 illustrates this process for a manufacturer of plastic valves. The area of each circle is proportional to each product's contribution to total company sales volume. In the case of this particular company, it can be seen that they are following what could well prove to be disastrous policies in respect of their principal products. Product A, although growing, is losing market share in a high-growth market. Product D is also losing market share in a high-growth market. Products E and C are gaining market share in declining markets.

Such a framework also easily helps to explain the impracticability of marketing objectives such as 'to achieve a 10 per cent growth and a 20 per cent return on investment'. Such an objective, while fine as an overall policy, if applied to individual products in the portfolio, clearly becomes a nonsense and totally self-defeating. For example, to accept a 10 per cent growth rate in a market which is growing at, say, 15 per cent per annum, is likely to prove disastrous in the long run. Likewise, to go for a much higher than market growth rate in a low-growth market is certain to lead to unnecessary price wars and market disruption.

This type of framework is particularly useful to demonstrate to senior management the implications of different product/market strategies. It is also useful in formulating policies towards new product development.

Weaknesses in the Boston Matrix Approach

Unfortunately, many companies started using the Boston Matrix indiscriminately during the 1970s and, as a result, it gradually lost its universal appeal. The reason, however, had more to do with lack of real understanding on the part of management than with any major defects in the methodology.

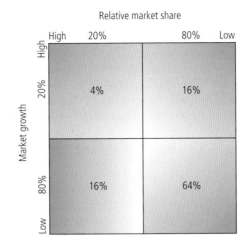

Figure 5.23: Avoid rituals such as 'divest the dogs'.

Nonetheless, there are circumstances where great caution is required in its use. Imagine for a moment a company with 80 per cent of its products in low-growth markets, and only 20 per cent of its products as market leaders. Their matrix would look as depicted in Figure 5.23. As can be seen, almost 65 per cent of the company's products are 'dogs'. To divest these may well be tantamount to throwing the baby out with the bath water!

Consider, also, those industries in which market share for any single product in the range has little to do with its 'profitability'. Often a low market share product enjoys the same production, distribution and marketing economies of scale as other products in the portfolio, as, for example, in the case of beers and chemical products.

MARKETING INSIGHT

Let us take the case of a product which is manufactured using basically the same components as other large market share products, is manufactured in the same plant as part of a similar process, and is distributed on the same vehicles and via the same outlets. In such a case it is easy to see how this low market share product can indeed be extremely profitable.

None of this, however, invalidates the work of the Boston Consulting Group, the principles of which can be applied to companies, divisions, subsidiaries, strategic business units, product groups, products, and so on. Providing great care is taken over the 'market share' axis, it is an extremely valuable planning tool.

Further Developments of the Boston Matrix

It is complications such as those outlined above that make the Boston Matrix less relevant to certain situations. While it is impossible to give absolute rules on what these situations are, suffice it to say that great caution is necessary when dealing with such matters. In any case, two principles should always be adhered to.

> First, a business should define its markets in such a way that it can ensure that its costs for key activities will be competitive. Second, it should define the markets it serves in such a way that it can develop specialized skills in servicing those markets and hence overcome a relative cost disadvantage. Both, of course, have to be related to a company's *distinctive competence.*

However, the approach of the Boston Consulting Group is fairly criticized in such circumstances as those described above as relying on two single factors, i.e. relative market share and market growth. Many readers will be aware of companies with high market share in a growing market that are not profitable.

To overcome this difficulty, and to provide a more flexible approach, General Electric and McKinsey jointly developed a multi-factor approach using the same fundamental ideas as the Boston Consulting Group. They used industry attractiveness and business strengths as the two main axes and built up these dimensions from a number of variables. Using these variables, and some scheme for weighting them according to their importance, products (or businesses) are classified into one of nine cells in a 3 × 3 matrix. Thus, the same purpose is served as in the Boston Matrix (i.e. comparing investment opportunities among products or businesses) but with the difference that multiple criteria are used. These criteria vary according to circumstances, but often include at least some of those shown in Figure 5.24.

It is not necessary, however, to use a nine-box matrix, and many managers prefer to use a four-box matrix similar to the Boston box. Indeed this is the author's preferred methodology, as it seems to be more easily understood by, and useful to, practising managers.

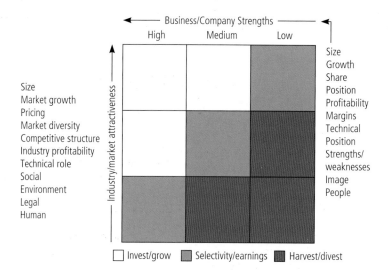

Figure 5.24: The 9 box directional policy matrix.

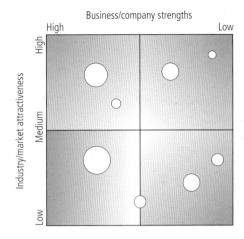

Figure 5.25: The McDonald four-box DPM.

The four-box directional policy matrix (DPM) is shown in Figure 5.25. Here, the circles represent sales into an industry, market or segment and in the same way as in the Boston Matrix, each is proportional to that segment's contribution to turnover.

The difference in this case is that, rather than using only two variables, the criteria which are used for each axis are totally relevant and specific to each company using the matrix. It shows:

- markets categorized on a scale of attractiveness to the firm
- the firm's relative strengths in each of these markets
- the relative importance of each market.

The specific criteria to be used should be decided by key executives using the device, but a generalized list for the vertical axis is given in Table 5.3. It is advisable to use no more than five or six factors, otherwise the exercise becomes too complex and loses its focus. Read on, however, before selecting these factors, as essential methodological instructions on the construction of a portfolio matrix follow.

> It is advisable to use no more than five or six factors for the vertical axis of the DPM, otherwise the calculations become too complex and lose focus.

A DETAILED, STEP-BY-STEP APPROACH TO CREATING A PORTFOLIO

The Strategic Business Unit (SBU)

Although the DPM, like other models of 'portfolio analysis', attempts to define a firm's strategic position and strategy alternatives, this objective cannot be met without considering what is meant by the term 'firm'. The accepted level at which a firm can be analysed using the DPM is that of the 'strategic business unit'.

The most common definition of an SBU is as follows:

1. It will have common segments and competitors for most of the products.
2. It will be a competitor in an external market.
3. It is a discrete, separate and identifiable 'unit'.
4. Its manager will have control over most of the areas critical to success.

Market factors	Financial and economic factors

Size (money, units, or both)
Size of key segments
Growth rate per year:
    total
    segments
Diversity of market
Sensitivity to price, service features and
  external factors
Cyclicality
Seasonality
Bargaining power of upstream suppliers
Bargaining power of downstream suppliers
	Contribution margins
	Leveraging factors, such as economies of
	  scale and experience
	Barriers to entry or exit (both financial and
	  non-financial)
	Capacity utilization

	Technological factors Maturity and volatility Complexity Differentiation Patents and copyrights Manufacturing process technology required

Competition
Types of competitors
Degree of concentration
Changes in type and mix
Entries and exits
Changes in share
Substitution by new technology
Degrees and types of integration
	Socio-political factors in your environment
	Social attitudes and trends
	Laws and government agency regulations
	Influence with pressure groups and
	  government representatives
	Human factors, such as unionization and
	  community acceptance

Table 5.3: Factors contributing to market attractiveness

The process of defining an SBU can be applied all the way down to product or department level.

It is possible, however, to use the DPM for any unit that has in it a number of different variables that could be usefully plotted using a two-dimensional matrix.

What Should be Plotted on the Matrix?

This is also comparatively simple to deal with, but confusion can arise because the options are rarely spelled out.

The DPM can be used on:

- countries (not all countries are equally attractive)
- sectors (such as agriculture, steel, etc.)
- markets
- regions
- distributors
- segments
- major customers.

Here we will use the 'market' level to explain the DPM.

The DPM is useful where there is more than one (at least three, and a maximum of 10 are suggested) 'markets' or segments between which the planner wishes to distinguish. These can be either existing or potential markets.

In order to implement the DPM, the following simple definition of 'market' and 'market segment' is offered:

An identifiable group of customers with requirements in common that are, or may become, *significant* in determining a separate strategy.

The results from Exercise 4.1 from the previous chapter should be plotted on the matrix.

The principal unit of analysis for the purpose of entering data will be the user's definition of 'product for market'.

Preparation

Prior to commencing analysis, the following preparation is recommended:

1. Product profiles should be available for all products/services to be scored.
2. The markets in which the products/services compete should be clearly defined.
3. Define the time period being scored. Three years are recommended.
4. Define the competitors against which the products/services will be scored.
5. Ensure sufficient data is available to score the factors (where no data is available, this is no problem as long as a sensible approximation can be made for the factors).
6. Ensure up-to-date sales forecasts are available for all products/services, plus any new products/ services.

Analysis Team

In order to improve the quality of scoring, it is recommended that a group of people from a number of different functions takes part, as this encourages the challenging of traditional views through discussion. It is recommended that there should be no more than six people involved in the analysis.

Ten Steps to Producing the DPM

Step 1   Define the products/services for markets that are to be used during the analysis.

Step 2   Define the criteria for market attractiveness, set the parameters and define weights for the market attractiveness criteria.

Step 3   Score the relevant products/services for market. Multiply the scores by the weights.

Step 4   Define the organization's relative strengths for each product/service for market.

Step 5   Analyse and draw conclusions from the relative position of each product/service for market.

Step 6   Draw conclusions from the analysis with a view to generating objectives and strategies.

Step 7   (Optional) Position the circles on the box assuming no change to current policies – that is to say, a *forecast* should be made of the future position of the circles.

Step 8   Redraw the portfolio to position the circles where the organization wants them to be – that is to say, the objectives they wish to achieve for each product/service for market.

Step 9   Detail the strategies to be implemented to achieve the objectives.

Step 10   Detail the appropriate financial consequences in terms of growth rate by product/service for market and return on sales.

Two Key Definitions

▶ Market attractiveness is a measure of the *potential* of the marketplace to yield growth in sales and profits. It is important to stress that this should be an objective assessment of market attractiveness using data *external* to the organization. The criteria themselves will, of course, be determined by the organization carrying out the exercise and will be relevant to the objectives the organization is trying to achieve, but it should be independent of the organization's position in its markets.

▶ Business strengths/position is a measure of an organization's *actual* strengths in the marketplace (i.e. the degree to which it can take advantage of a market opportunity). Thus, it is an objective assessment of an organization's ability to satisfy market needs relative to competitors.

> Market attractiveness is a measure of the potential of the marketplace to yield growth in sales and profits

The Process

There follows a more detailed step-by-step explanation of the process for constructing a DPM.

Step 1 List the population of products/services for markets that you intend to include in the matrix

The list can consist of: countries; companies; subsidiaries; regions; products; markets; segments; customers; distributors; or any other unit of analysis that is important.

The DPM can be used at any level in an organization and for any kind of SBU.

> Business strengths/position is a measure of an organization's actual strengths in the marketplace (i.e. the degree to which it can take advantage of a market opportunity)

Step 2 Define market attractiveness factors (MAFs)

In this step, you should list the factors you wish to consider in comparing the attractiveness of your markets.

It is also important to list the markets that you intend to apply the criteria to before deciding on the criteria themselves, since the purpose of the vertical axis is to discriminate between more and less attractive markets. The criteria themselves must be specific to the population and must not be changed for different markets in the same population.

Factors	Example weight
Growth rate	40
Accessible market size	20
Profit potential	40
Total	**100**

Note: As profit = market size × margin × growth, it would be reasonable to expect a *weighting* against each of these to be at *least* as shown, although an even higher weight on *growth* would be understandable in some circumstances (in which case, the corresponding weight for the others should be reduced).

The above represent a combination of a number of factors. These factors, however, can usually be summarized under three headings.

1. *Growth rate.* Average annual growth rate of revenue spent by that segment (2011 over 2010 plus % growth 2012 over 2011, plus % growth 2013 over 2012, all divided by 3). If preferred, compound average growth rate could be used.

2. *Accessible market size.* An attractive market is not only large – it can also be accessed. One way of calculating this is to estimate the *total* revenue of the segment in $t + 3$, less revenue impossible to access, *regardless of investment made.* Alternatively, total market size can be used, which is the most frequent method, as it does not involve any managerial judgement to be made that could distort the truth. *This latter method is the preferred method.* A market size factor score is simply the score multiplied by the weight (20 as in the example above).

3. *Profit potential.* This is much more difficult to deal with and will vary considerably, according to industry. For example, Porter's Five Forces model could be used to estimate the profit potential of a segment, as in the following example:

Sub-factors	10 = Low × 0 = High	Weight	Weighted factor score
1. Intensity of competition		50	
2. Threat of substitutes		5	
3. Threat of new entrants		5	
4. Power of suppliers		10	
5. Power of customer		30	
Profit potential factor score			

Alternatively, a combination of these and industry-specific factors could be used. In the case of the pharmaceutical industry, for example, the factors could be:

Sub-factors	High	Medium	Low ×Weight	Weighted factor score
Unmet medical needs (efficacy)			30	
Unmet medical needs (safety)			25	
Unmet medical needs (convenience)			15	
Price potential			10	
Competitive intensity			10	
Cost of market entry			10	
Profit potential factor score				

These are clearly a proxy for profit potential. Each is weighted according to its importance. The weights add up to 100 in order to give a *profit potential factor score,* as in the Porter's Five Forces example above.

The most usual and simplest measure to use, however, is the weighted average % return on sales (ROS) that *any* competitor could expect to achieve in this market.

Note that, following this calculation, the *profit potential factor score* is simply multiplied by the weight (40 as in the example above).

Variations Naturally, growth, size and profit will not encapsulate the requirements of all organizations. For example, in the case of an orchestra, artistic satisfaction may be an important consideration. In another case, social considerations could be important. In yet another, cyclicality may be a factor.

> It is possible, then, to add another heading, such as 'Risk' or 'Other' to the three factors listed at the beginning of Step 2. In general, however, it should be possible to reduce it to just the three main ones, with subfactors incorporated into these, as shown.

Now set the parameters for each MAF. For example, a growth rate greater than 10% merits a high score, whereas a growth rate less than 1% merits a low score.

Step 3 Score the relevant products/services for markets
In this step you should score the products/services for markets against the criteria defined in Step 2.

Can market attractiveness factors change while constructing the DPM? The answer to this is no. Once agreed, under no circumstances should market attractiveness factors be changed, otherwise the attractiveness of our markets is not being evaluated against common criteria and the matrix becomes meaningless. Scores, however, will be specific to each market.

Can the circles move vertically? No is the obvious answer, although yes is also possible, providing the matrix shows the current level of attractiveness at the present time. This implies carrying out one set of calculations for the present time according to market attractiveness factors, in order to locate markets on the vertical axis, then carrying out another set of calculations for a future period (say, in three years' time), based on our forecasts according to the same factors. In practice, it is easier to carry out only the latter calculation, in which case the circles can only move horizontally.

Step 4

(i) Define business strengths/position This is a measure of an organization's *actual* strengths in the marketplace and will differ by market/segment opportunity.
These factors will usually be a combination of an organization's relative strengths versus competitors in connection with *customer-facing* needs, i.e. those things that are required by the customer.
These can often be summarized under:

* product requirements
* price requirements
* service requirements
* promotion requirements.

The weightings given to each should be specific to each market/segment. In the same way that 'profit' on the market attractiveness axis can be broken down into subheadings, so can each of the above be broken down further and analysed. Indeed, this is to be strongly recommended. These subfactors should be dealt with in the same way as the subfactors described under 'market attractiveness'.

For example, in the case of pharmaceuticals, product strengths could be represented by:

- relative product strengths
- relative product safety
- relative product convenience
- relative cost-effectiveness.

(ii) Broadening the analysis
It will be clear that an organization's relative strengths in meeting customer-facing needs will be a function of its *capabilities* in connection with *industry-wide success factors*. For example, if a depot is necessary in each major town/city for any organization to succeed in an industry and the organization carrying out the analysis doesn't have this, then it is likely that this will account for its poor performance under 'customer service', which is, of course, a customer requirement. Likewise, if it is necessary to have low feedstock costs for any organization to succeed in an industry and the organization carrying out the analysis doesn't have this, then it is likely that this will account for its poor performance under 'price', which is, of course, a customer requirement.

Thus, in the same way that subfactors should be estimated in order to arrive at 'market attractiveness' factors, so an assessment of an organization's capabilities in respect of *industry-wide success factors* could be made in order to understand what needs to be done in the organization in order to satisfy customer needs better. This assessment, however, is quite separate from the quantification of the business strengths/position axis and its purpose is to translate the analysis into actionable propositions for other functions within the organization, such as purchasing, production, distribution, and so on.

In the case of pharmaceuticals, for example, factors such as 'patent life' are simply an indication of an organization's capability to provide product differentiation. They are irrelevant to the doctor, but need to be taken account of by the organization carrying out the analysis.

(iii) How to deal with business strengths/position
The first of these concerns the quantification of business strengths within a 'market'.

Many books for the manager are not particularly useful when used to construct a marketing plan. Few of the factors they mention take account of the need for a company to make an 'offer' to a particular 'market' that has a sustainable competitive advantage over the 'offers' of relevant competitors.

The only way a company can do this is to understand the real needs and wants of the chosen customer group, find out by means of market research how well these needs are being met by the products on offer, and then seek to satisfy these needs better than their competitors.

The worked example given in the table below shows how to assess the strength of a company in a market. The following three questions are used to plot the firm's (SBU's) position on the horizontal axis (competitive position/business strengths):

1. What are the few key things that any competitor has to do right to succeed (i.e. what are the critical success factors, also known as CSFs, in this industry sector)? In this example, we have shown product, price, service and image as critical success factors, but it is clear that each of these needs to be decomposed into much greater detail, as explained above.
2. How important is each of these critical success factors (measured comparatively using a score out of 100)?
3. How do you and each of your competitors score (out of 10) on each of the critical success factors?

These questions yield the information necessary to make an overall assessment of an SBU's competitive strengths (shown in the table below). From this it will be seen that:

- this organization is not market leader
- all competitors score more than 5.0.

Critical success factors (What are the few key things that any competition has to do right to succeed?)	Weighting (How important is each of these CSFs? Score out of 100)		Strengths/weaknesses analysis (Score yourself and each of your main competitors out of 10 on each of the CSFs, then multiply the score by the weight)			
			You	Comp A	Comp B	Comp C
1. Product	20		9 = 1.8	6 = 1.2	5 = 1.0	4 = 0.8
2. Price	10		8 = 0.8	5 = 0.5	6 = 0.6	10 = 0.1
3. Service	50		5 = 2.5	9 = 4.5	7 = 3.5	6 = 3.0
4. Image	20		8 = 1.6	8 = 1.6	5 = 1.0	3 = 0.6
These should normally be viewed from the customer's point of view	Total 100	Total score × weight	6.7	7.8	6.1	5.5

The problem with this and many similar calculations is that rarely will this method discriminate sufficiently well to indicate the relative strengths of a number of products in a particular company's product/market portfolio, and many of the SBU's products would appear on the left of the matrix if a scale of 1 to 10 is used.

Some method is required to prevent all products appearing on the left of the matrix. This can be achieved by using a ratio, as in the Boston Matrix. This will indicate a company's position relative to the best in the market.

In the example provided, Competitor A has most strengths in the market, so our organization needs to make some improvements. To reflect this, our weighted score should be compared with that of Competitor A (the highest weighted score). Thus 6.7:7.8 = 0.86:1.

If we were to plot this on a logarithmic scale on the horizontal axis, this would place our organization to the right of the dividing line as follows:

3 ×   1   0.3

(We should make the left hand extreme point 3 and start the scale on the right at 0.3.*)

Step 5 Produce the DPM

Finally, circles should be drawn on a four-box matrix, using market size (as defined in Step 2 above) to determine the area of the circle. An organization's market share can be put in as a 'cheese' in each circle. Alternatively, an organization's own sales into each market can be used. This will usually produce a smaller circle to superimpose on the larger market size circle.

In practice, however, it is advisable to do both and compare them in order to see how closely actual sales match the opportunities.

Step 6 Analysis and generation of marketing objectives and strategies

The objective of producing the DPM is to see the portfolio of products/services for markets relative to each other in the context of the criteria used. This analysis should indicate whether the portfolio is well balanced or not and should give a clear indication of any problems.

---

*A scale of 3 to 0.3 has been chosen because such a band is likely to encapsulate most extremes of competitive advantage. If it doesn't, just change it to suit your own circumstances.

Step 7 (Optional) Forecasting

The forecast position of the circles should now be made. This is simply done by re-scoring the products/services for markets in three years' time, assuming the organization doesn't change its strategies (see Step 3). This will indicate whether the position is getting worse or better.

It is not necessary to change the scores on the vertical axis (see Step 3).

Step 8 Setting marketing objectives

This involves changing the volumes/values and/or market share (marketing objectives) and the scores on the horizontal axis (relative strength in market) in order to achieve the desired volumes/values. Conceptually, one is picking up the circle and moving it/revising it without specifying how this is to be achieved. Strategies are then defined, which involve words and changes to individual CSF scores (Step 9).

Step 9 Spell out strategies

This involves making specific statements about the marketing strategies to be employed to achieve the desired volumes/values.

Step 10 Sales and profit forecasts

Once this is done, organizations should be asked to do the following:

1. Plot average % growth in sales revenue by segment ($t - 3$ to $t0$); plot average % ROS by segment ($t - 3$ to $t0$)
2. Plot forecast average % growth in sales revenue by segment ($t0$ to $t + 3$); plot forecast average % ROS by segment ($t0$ to $t + 3$)

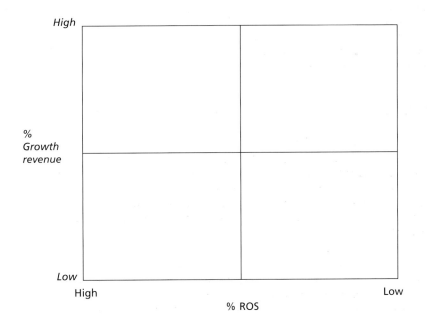

This will show clearly whether past performance and, more importantly, forecasts match the market rating exercise above. *This should preferably be done by someone else (e.g. accountants).*

One major chemical company used the directional policy matrix to select 50 distributors out of the 450 they were dealing with. They needed to do this because the market was in decline and the distributors began buying for customers rather than selling for the supplier. This led to a dramatic fall in prices. The only way the chemical company could begin to tackle the problem was by appointing a number of exclusive distributorships. The issue of which distributorships to choose was tackled using the directional policy matrix, as clearly some were more attractive than others, while the company had varying strengths in their dealings with each distributor.

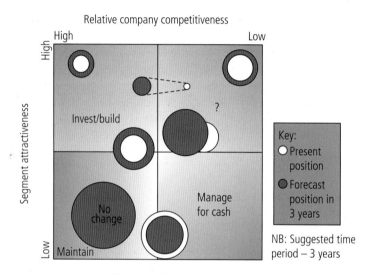

Figure 5.26: A completed DPM.

Portfolio Summary

The resulting portfolio summary pulls together the information from the SWOT analyses, demonstrates the overall competitive position and indicates the relative importance of each product/market segment. The four-box matrix, as in Figure 5.26, illustrates the position most effectively.

Table 5.4 shows how market attractiveness was calculated for three of the segments. Table 5.5 shows how the strengths and weaknesses for one segment were calculated. These were transferred to the directional policy matrix, which shows how the circles are positioned.

The horizontal axis in Figure 5.26 reflects the scores in the strengths and weaknesses analysis and the vertical axis quantifies the attractiveness, to the organization, of each of the important segments contained in the plan. The circle sizes are relative to the current turnover in each. The darker circles indicate forecast sales in three years' time. From this graphical representation of a portfolio of products or range of segments, a number of marketing options present themselves:

1. In the top left box, where strengths are high and markets are attractive, the probable option would be to invest heavily in these markets and increase market share.
2. In the bottom left box, where strengths are high, but markets are less attractive, a likely aim would be to maintain market share and manage for sustained earnings.

Attractiveness	Weight	Segment 1		Segment 2		Segment 3	
		score	total	score	total	score	total
Growth	25	6	1.5	5	1.25	10	2.5
Profitability	25	9	2.25	8	2.0	7	1.75
Size	15	6	0.9	5	0.75	8	1.2
Vulnerability	15	5	0.75	6	0.9	6	0.9
Competition	10	8	0.8	8	0.8	4	0.4
Cyclicality	10	2.5	0.25	3	0.3	2.5	0.25
Total	100	6.45	6.0	7.0			

Table 5.4: Establishing how attractive each segment is to your business

Note: This could be calculated for Year 0 and Year 3, though it is easier and quicker to carry out only the calculations for the final year

CSFs	Weight	Your company		Competitor A		Competitor B	
		score	total	score	total	score	total
1. Price	50	5	2.5	6	3.0	4	2.0
2. Product	25	6	1.5	8	2.0	10	2.5
3. Service	15	8	1.2	4	0.6	6	0.9
4. Image	10	6	0.6	5	0.5	3	0.3
Total	100	5.8	6.1	5.7			

Table 5.5: Scoring your company and your competitors

Note: Calculations are first made for Year 0 as this enables you to establish a fixed position on the portfolio matrix for your company in each segment against which the forecast outcome of alternative strategies and assumptions for the planning period can be seen when plotted onto the DPM.

3. In the top right box, low strengths, combined with an attractive market, indicate a probable policy of selective investment, to improve competitive position.
4. Finally, in the bottom right box, low strengths allied to poor market attractiveness, point to a management for profits strategy, or even withdrawal.

This matrix gives a clear indication of the marketing objectives for each product for market shown; strategies will be set separately. This is the subject of more detailed treatment in Chapter 6.

COMBINING PRODUCT LIFECYCLES AND PORTFOLIO MANAGEMENT

Figure 5.27 illustrates the consequences of failing to appreciate the implications of both the product lifecycle concept and the dual combination of market share and market growth.

Companies A and B both start out with question marks (wildcats) in years 5 and 6 in a growing market. Company A invests in building market share and quickly turns into a star. Company B, meanwhile, manages its product for profit over a four-year period so that, while still growing, it steadily

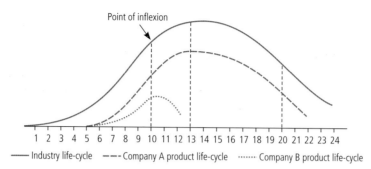

Figure 5.27: Short-term profit maximization versus market share and long-term profit maximization.

loses market share (i.e. it remains a question mark or wildcat). In year 10, when the market becomes saturated (when typically competitive pressures intensify), Company B with its low market share (hence typically higher costs and lower margins) cannot compete and quickly drops out of the market. Company A, on the other hand, aggressively defends its market share and goes on to enjoy a period of approximately 10 years with a product which has become a cash cow. Thus, company B, by pursuing a policy of short-term profit maximization, lost at least 10 years' profit potential.

RELEVANCE OF LIFECYCLE ANALYSIS AND PORTFOLIO MANAGEMENT TO THE MARKETING AUDIT

It will be recalled that this discussion took place against the background of the need to complete a full and detailed marketing audit prior to setting marketing objectives. Such analyses as those described in this chapter should be an integral part of the marketing audit.

The audit should contain a product lifecycle for each major product and an attempt should be made (using other audit information) to predict the future shape of the lifecycle. It should also contain a product portfolio matrix showing the present position of the products.

CASE STUDY

This section concludes with some case histories showing the use and misuse of the DPM.

CASE STUDY 1 – A BLUE-CHIP COMPANY

The first concerns a senior marketing manager of a blue-chip company who dismissed the DPM as irrelevant because he had only four principal products, each one of which was sold to the same customer (or market). Clearly we are talking about major capital sales in this instance.

The manager had plotted products A, B, C and D on the horizontal axis with only one 'market' on the vertical axis. The resulting matrix obviously had four circles in a straight line. Since the purpose of a matrix is to develop a relationship between two or more variables judged by the planner to be of significance in a given planning context, this matrix was clearly absurd and served no useful purpose whatever.

If this manager really wished to use the DPM, he would have to put products A, B, C and D on the vertical axis and look at their respective size and strengths on the horizontal axis. In such a case, all we have done is to change the nomenclature, making a product equivalent to a market, which is clearly acceptable. The main point is that the purpose of the DPM is to display clearly and visibly the relationship between product/market variables.

CASE STUDY

CASE STUDY 2 – A BUSINESS SCHOOL PORTFOLIO

This is certainly the case for a business school portfolio. Here, the 'product' (for example, the MBA programme) equals 'market'. This is shown in Figure 5.28. (By astute management, some of these circles have since been moved to the left of the matrix, surely the purpose of using the DPM in the first place!)

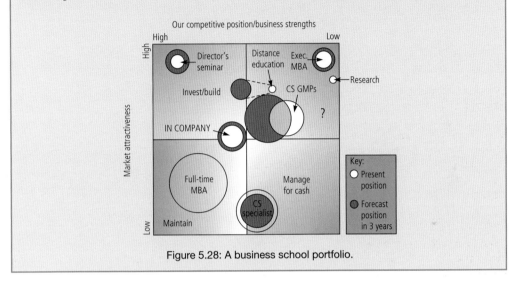

Figure 5.28: A business school portfolio.

Let us now look at two companies whose revenue and profits were static for two consecutive years, and both of which kept their shareholders at bay by selling off part of their assets. The boards of both companies attempted to use the DPM to help clarify the options. In both cases, the resulting matrix was not a reflection of the reality.

CASE STUDY

CASE STUDY 3 – AN INTERNATIONAL ENGINEERING COMPANY

Here, the Shipping, Food, Thermal and Separation Divisions were all operating in no-growth markets; only the Biotechnology Division was in a growth market. Using market growth as a factor obviously caused all divisions to appear in the bottom half of the matrix, except the Biotechnology Division. The other factor used, however, was profitability, which in the case of Shipping and Separation was high. The weighting of 60 per cent on the profit factor pulled both of these divisions into the upper part of the matrix. Strengths in each case were different, and the resulting matrix looked as shown in Figure 5.29.

However, since both the Shipping and Separation Divisions had little (if any) potential to increase their volume and profitability in mature markets, and since the Food and Biotechnology Divisions did, the circles were clearly in the wrong place. The reality facing the company was as shown in Figure 5.30.

(Continued)

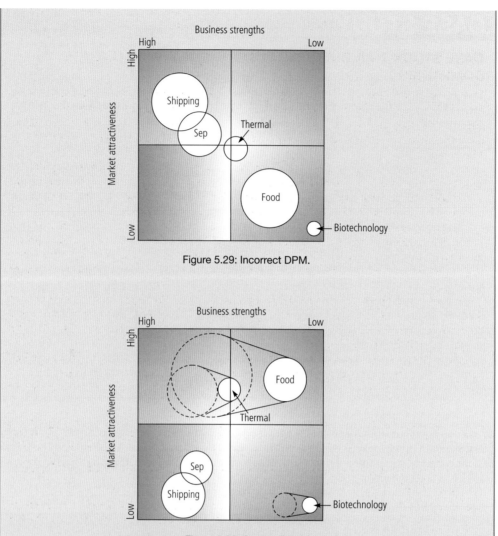

Figure 5.29: Incorrect DPM.

Figure 5.30: Correct DPM.

The opportunity was clearly there for this company to invest in the Food Division, where it was comparatively weak, and also in the Thermal Division. Both of these markets provided ample opportunity for the company to improve its market share and strengths (especially if it also used productivity measures at the same time), in spite of the fact that both markets were relatively mature.

In other words, all we are really interested in is the potential for us to increase our volume and profits, and, in some instances, externally derived factors of market growth and profitability, however accurate, are not particularly useful.

Having reached the conclusion above, obviously this company then took each division in turn and completed the DPM for each of their component parts in order to decide how best to allocate resources.

CASE STUDY

CASE STUDY 4 – A CONGLOMERATE WITH 12 SEPARATE COMPANIES

This group, although enjoying very high return on capital employed (ROCE), was also under extreme pressure from the financial institutions because its turnover and profits were static. At a directors' meeting, the DPM was used as one of the basic tools of analysis. ROCE of the companies varied between 500 per cent and 5 per cent, with seven about 50 per cent and five below 15 per cent.

Again, using market growth and industry return-on-sales (ROS) as the factors, weighted 30 and 70, not surprisingly all the high-profit companies appeared in the top left of the matrix and all the low-profit companies appeared in the bottom half of the matrix. All this did was to confirm the group's existing position, but was of little value when considering the future.

The directors were advised by the authors of this book to change the factors to encapsulate potential for growth in volume and profits rather than the existing profitability of the markets themselves. The resulting DPM then showed most of the high-profit companies in the lower half of the matrix, since few of them were in growth markets and most already had high market shares.

It also demonstrated clearly another point of policy. One company enjoying a 500 per cent ROCE could grow, providing the chief executive officer was prepared to allow them to redefine their market more broadly and move into lower ROS segments. Such a policy move would have put this particular company back into the top part of the matrix!

But this, of course, is the whole point of using the DPM in the first place. It should raise key issues and force senior executives into thinking about the future in a structured way.

CASE STUDY

CASE STUDY 5 – AN AUSTRALIAN DIVISION OF AN INTERNATIONAL AGROCHEMICAL COMPANY

This Australian division of an international agrochemical company was under extreme pressure to grow the revenue and profits in a declining market. At first glance, the marketing plans looked to be extremely sophisticated. The plans themselves were also well presented.

The problem was that they did not succeed in spelling out a clear strategy to achieve the corporate objectives, the individual product/market objectives appearing to be little more than 'wish lists'. On closer examination, it became clear that the underlying diagnosis was at fault.

The SWOT analysis shown in Table 5.6 is a typical example of the format used. Even a cursory glance at this shows that none of these factors are discriminators in the choice of supply. On discovering, however, that the SWOT had been done on the merchants (or channel) and that merchants were motivated mainly by price, it was easy to conclude that the three main brands were really commodities in the eyes of the merchant, albeit they were major brand names.

The real bottom line on all of this was that the merchants were calling the shots, a situation that was bound to get worse and that would continue to drive the price down.

The next obvious conclusion was that this company needed to go down the value chain to the farmer and to segment them according to need in order to enable the company to create

(Continued)

Critical success factors	Success factor scores			
	Weight	Us	Comp A	Comp B
Product efficacy	30	9	8	8
Product price	25	9	9	9
Product image	20	9	8	9
Profitability	20	8	9	6
Formulation	5	8	8	7
		8.8	8.4	8.0

Table 5.6: Critical success factors scores.

demand pull, thus reducing the power of the channel. SWOTing at the next link in the chain quickly revealed two things:

1. There was ample opportunity for this company to create value for the farmer
2. Not enough was known about farmers' needs to enable proper SWOTs to be done on them.

The marketing plan of this company contained what looked to be quite sophisticated DPMs. Again, however, on closer examination of the underlying data, one circle that appeared at the top of the 'market attractiveness' axis was clearly in the wrong place, as the data in Table 5.7 illustrates.

	Product 1	Product 2
Sales in 1996	$10 million	$5 million
Profits in 1996	$1 million	$0.5 million
Projected sales in 1999	$10 million	$7 million
Projected profit in 1999	$1 million	$0.7 million

Table 5.7: Comparison of Product 1 and Product 2's scales.

From this, it can be seen that the product manager doing the analysis believed that Product 1 was more attractive than Product 2 because, even in 1999, the absolute dollar profits were going to be greater. Clearly, however, positioning Product 1 near the top of the vertical axis of the DPM implied an invest strategy, while the implied strategy for Product 2 was a maintain (or manage for sustained earnings) strategy. Both strategies would have been wholly inappropriate, thus reducing the value of the DPM as an analytical tool.

Even worse, since we have already seen that the CSF calculation (to derive the position on the horizontal axis of the DPM) was also wrong, the resulting DPM merely served to confuse, rather than to clarify and to provide valuable insights about competitive strategy.

Since then, having had the DPM properly explained to them, all of these organizations were able to develop objectives and strategies designed to grow the business and all are now thriving and prospering.

Finally, it may be useful to conclude this section with a definition of a portfolio matrix: 'The use of graphic models to develop a relationship between two or more variables judged by the planner to be of significance in the planning context.'

Whichever approach is used, it can be seen that obvious consideration should be given to marketing objectives and strategies which are appropriate to the attractiveness of a market (market growth in Boston Matrix) and the extent to which such opportunities match our capabilities (market share in Boston Matrix). What these objectives should be will be discussed in Chapter 6.

APPLICATION QUESTIONS

1. Select a major product and:
   - draw a lifecycle of: the product itself
   - draw a lifecycle of the market (segment) in which it competes
   - explain why it is the shape it is
   - predict the shape and length of the lifecycle in the future
   - say why you are making these predictions.
2. Plot your products on a Boston Matrix and:
   - explain their relative positions
   - forecast where they will be (and why), say, five years from now.
3. List your main markets or segments.
4. List criteria for attractiveness (to you).
5. List criteria for business strengths (you *vis-à-vis* competitors).
6. Devise a scoring and weighting system for each axis.
7. Put the markets or segments through the criteria.
8. Draw circles around the coordinates. The diameter of each circle should be proportional to that segment's contribution to turnover. Is this where you want the circles to be?

CHAPTER 5 REVIEW

What is a product?

A product (or service) is a problem-solver, in the sense that it provides what the customer needs or wants. A product consists of:

1. A core (functional performance)
2. A surround (a bundle of features and benefits).

Usually the core product has 20 per cent of the impact, yet leads to 80 per cent of the cost. The surround is the reverse of this.

Try Exercise 5.1

The product lifecycle

All products or services have a lifecycle which follows this pattern:

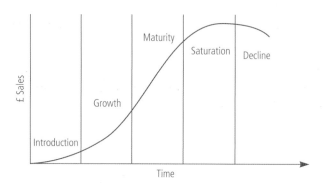

The phases of the lifecycle are:

A Introduction
B Growth
C Maturity
D Saturation
E Decline

The total lifecycle depends on the type of product or service, e.g. fashion products have short lifecycles.

There is a trend for lifecycles of most products to get shorter as changes in technology and customer expectations make greater impact. Each phase of the life cycle calls for different management responses.

Try Exercise 5.2

Diffusion of innovation

Some people/companies are always prepared to buy new products, while others wait until things are tried and tested. All products and services have customers which fall into these categories.

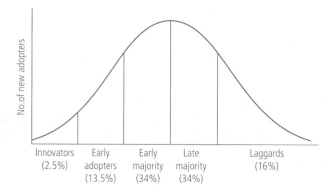

A Innovators (2.5 per cent of total)
B Early adopters (13.5 per cent of total)
C Early majority (34 per cent of total)
D Late majority (34 per cent of total)
E Laggards (16 per cent of total)

Discovering a typology for innovators and early adopters can help in the promotion of new products.

Product portfolio

Ideally, a company should have a portfolio of products whose lifecycles overlap. This guarantees continuity of income and growth potential.

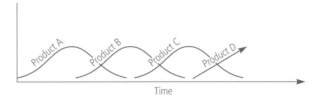

Boston matrix

The product portfolio can be analysed in terms of revenue-producing potential, using this technique.

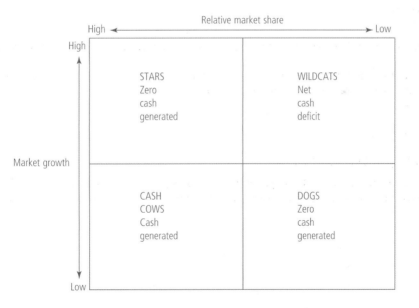

Directional policy matrix (DPM)

Not all companies possess the data required by the Boston Matrix (above). Similar results can be obtained using this technique. The axes become as shown on the figure on page 196.

Try Exercises 5.4 and 5.5

Questions raised for the company

1. Q: How useful is a brand name?

   A: Well-known brands have successfully differentiated themselves from competing products by conveying something extra. Such differentiation enables them to command a higher price than unbranded, 'commodity' products.

2. Q: How does market share relate to cash generation, as in the Boston Matrix?

   A: The higher the market share, the higher the output, and the lower the unit costs through economies of scale and the learning curve. Thus a company can command higher margins and generate more revenue.

3. Q: Should 'dogs' always be killed off?

   A: It is a question of timing. It is possible sometimes to squeeze extra earnings from a 'dog'. Sometimes a 'dog' is supportive of another product. Sometimes a 'dog' product can be profitable because it shares in the economies of scale of another product in the range.

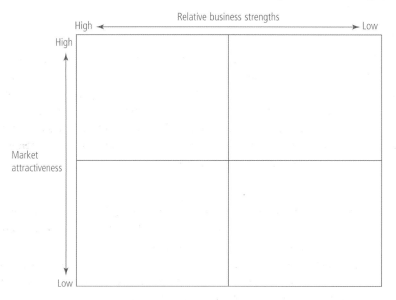

EXERCISES

The exercises are designed to help you to look at your product or service range in three different ways:

1. As a 'package' of benefits (Exercise 5.1)
2. From the point of view of their lifecycles (Exercise 5.2)
3. The final exercise in this section invites you to construct and interpret a directional policy matrix for your own company (Exercise 5.3).

Exercise 5.1 Benefit package analysis

It has been shown that customers buy products and services for many reasons. Different people look for different types of benefits from the product to satisfy their needs. Here are some typical sources of customer benefits:

1. Good comparative price
2. Well-known product/service
3. Good after-sales service
4. Reputable company image
5. Low after-sales costs
6. Prompt delivery
7. Efficient performance
8. Well-designed product
9. Fashionable
10. Ease of purchase
11. Good quality
12. Reliability
13. Safety factors.

Obviously, the better one's products/services provide benefits to customers and match their needs, the more competitive they are going to be in the marketplace. The following process is designed to help you complete a benefit analysis on your products or services.

By doing this you will discover or confirm which items of your range are the strongest on the market when compared to your competitors'. It should also provide you with insights about where attention might be paid to your products or services, either to improve existing customer benefits or to put emphasis on new ones.

Proceed as follows:

1. Study the customer benefits list above. Are these typical of the reasons why people buy your products or services? If you can think of others that are more pertinent to your particular business, write them down in the spaces provided.
2. Taking into account the market segments with which you do business, look at the customer benefits list and decide which are the three most important benefits demanded by your most important segment(s). Make a note of these.
3. Now identify the next three most important benefits demanded by these customers, and also make a note of these.
4. Finally, tick any other benefits on the list that are relevant to these customers.
5. Repeat this exercise for other important segments.
6. You are now asked to transpose this information on to Worksheet 1 (an example of a completed sheet is provided in Worksheet 2). Proceed as follows:

Step 1   In column 1 list the products or services you supply. No particular order is required.

Step 2   Take the three most important benefits that you selected above and use them as headings for columns 2, 3 and 4 on the worksheet, so that column 2 represents one benefit, column 3 another and column 4 the third.

Step 3   Fill in columns 2, 3 and 4 as follows. Starting with column 2, look at the benefit heading and work down your list of products or services scoring each one on a 1 to 10 point scale: 1 will show that the product barely supplies this particular

(Continued)

benefit to the customer and compares badly with competitors' performance, whereas a 10 score would demonstrate very high meeting of customer needs, superior to that provided by competitors. For example, if the benefit heading was 'Delivery' and, working down the list of products, the first product had a good delivery record, as good as any in the trade, then it could be allocated 9 or 10 points. If the next product on the list had a very patchy record on meeting delivery, and we knew several competitors were better, then we might only allocate 4 or 5 points, and so on. Follow the same procedure for columns 3 and 4. Note that the 1–10 scoring scale is only used on columns 2, 3 and 4 because these represent the major benefits to your customers and thus need to be weighted accordingly.

Step 4 Now take the second three most important benefits and use these as headings for columns 5, 6 and 7.

Step 5 As before rate each of your products or services against each heading, in comparison with competitor performance, but this time only use a *scoring scale of 1–6*, where again 1 point represents low provision of the benefit and 6 high. The 1–6 scoring scale is in recognition of the reduced importance these benefits have for customers.

Step 6 Finally take any other benefits you ticked above and use these as headings for column 8 and onwards as far as required.

Step 7 Again work through your list of products or services comparing them against how well they meet the benefit heading of each column, but this time only use a *1–3 points scoring scale*. The reduced scale reflects the reduced level of importance of the customer benefits in this last group.

Step 8 Aggregate the scores you have allocated to each product or service and enter the result in the Total column.

Step 9 The product or service with the highest points score is clearly that which provides most benefits to your customers and competes favourably with the competition. Therefore allocate this product with the ranking of 1 in the Ranking column. Find the next highest total score and mark that 2, and so on. You might find some total scores so close to each other that it would be helpful to rank your products or services by groups of similar scores, rather than individually, e.g. have a first 'division', second 'division', etc. of product groupings.

Step 10 On either Worksheet 1 or a separate sheet of paper, make notes about any relevant points. For example, should some scores be qualified because of recent design improvements, are some products under threat from new competition, does the ranking reflect particular strengths or weaknesses, are there any surprises?

What are the main lessons to be learned from this type of benefit analysis for your company's products/services? What steps can you recommend to improve future product development? Use the space in 'Personal notes' to record your thoughts.

Note: This analysis shows that 'containers' provide the best 'benefits package' when compared to the rest of the product range. In contrast, 'water butts' provide least benefits, falling down on price, delivery and design. This analysis enables a company to see where it needs to work at the 'product surround' to become more effective.

Worksheet 1 Benefit package analysis (Exercise 5.1)

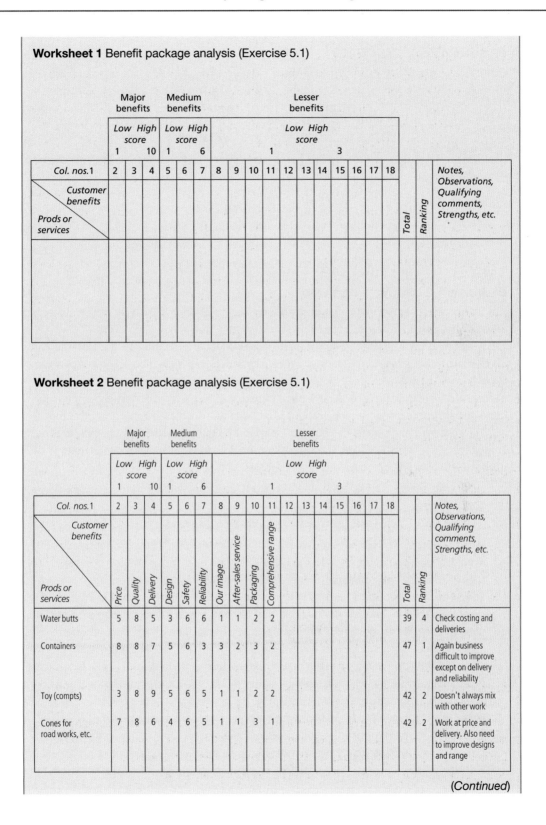

	Major benefits			Medium benefits			Lesser benefits											Total	Ranking	Notes, Observations, Qualifying comments, Strengths, etc.
	Low score 1		High 10	Low score 1		High 6			Low score 1					High 3						
Col. nos.1	2	3	4	5	6	7	8	9	10	11	12	13	14	15	16	17	18			
Customer benefits / Prods or services																				

Worksheet 2 Benefit package analysis (Exercise 5.1)

	Major benefits			Medium benefits			Lesser benefits											Total	Ranking	Notes, Observations, Qualifying comments, Strengths, etc.
	Low score 1		High 10	Low score 1		High 6			Low score 1					High 3						
Col. nos.1	2	3	4	5	6	7	8	9	10	11	12	13	14	15	16	17	18			
Customer benefits / Prods or services	Price	Quality	Delivery	Design	Safety	Reliability	Our image	After-sales service	Packaging	Comprehensive range										
Water butts	5	8	5	3	6	6	1	1	2	2								39	4	Check costing and deliveries
Containers	8	8	7	5	6	3	3	2	3	2								47	1	Again business difficult to improve except on delivery and reliability
Toy (compts)	3	8	9	5	6	5	1	1	2	2								42	2	Doesn't always mix with other work
Cones for road works, etc.	7	8	6	4	6	5	1	1	3	1								42	2	Work at price and delivery. Also need to improve designs and range

(Continued)

Personal notes

Exercise 5.2 Lifecycle analysis

It is universally accepted that all products or services go through a lifecycle of five stages – introduction, growth, maturity, saturation and, ultimately, decline.

Depending upon the nature of the particular product and its market, the lifecycle can be of short or long duration. Similarly, different products will have different levels of sales. Nevertheless, allowing for these differences in 'width' and 'height', product lifecycle curves all have a remarkably similar and consistent shape. It is because of consistency of the lifecycle curve that this aspect of the product audit becomes such a powerful analytical tool.

The following exercise is designed to help you construct a lifecycle analysis for your company's products or services. By doing this it will help to focus on information that will be used in setting marketing objectives and strategies.

1. Using Worksheet 1, invent a suitable scale for the sales volume axis, i.e. one that will encompass the sales peaks you have had or are likely to experience in your business.
2. At the position marked 'Current sales', record the levels of sales volume for your products or services. You will have to select the timescale you use. If your products are short-lived, perhaps you might have to calculate sales figures in terms of days or weeks. For longer-lived products, perhaps annual sales figures will be more appropriate.
3. Taking each product in turn, plot a lifecycle curve based upon the historical data at your disposal, e.g. if in 2 above you decided that a monthly sales analysis would be necessary to capture the movement on the lifecycle curves, then check back through your sales records and plot the sales volume for each product at monthly intervals.
4. From the lifecycle curves you have drawn, extend those into the future where extrapolation looks feasible, i.e. where a distinct pattern exists. You should finish up with a worksheet looking something like Worksheet 2.
5. Make notes about your key findings from this exercise in the space below.
6. So far you have only looked at your products in isolation. Now on a separate piece of paper (or on the same worksheet if it doesn't cause too much confusion), compare each lifecycle pattern of your major products or services with the total market lifecycle for

each one. Do your product patterns mirror the market lifecycle? Are your sales falling, while the total market sales are steady or increasing? Is the reverse happening? Many outcomes will be possible, but whatever they are, you are asked to explain them and to write in the space below what these comparisons between the total market and your sales tell you about your product/service range and its future prospects. If you find it difficult to establish total market lifecycles then refer to the 'Guide to market maturity', later in this exercise.

7. Finally, and to demonstrate that this examination of product lifecycles is not just an intellectual exercise, prepare a short presentation for one of your senior colleagues, or, better still, your boss, following the instructions given on the 'Special project brief', at the end of this exercise.

Worksheet 1 Lifecycle analysis (Exercise 5.2)

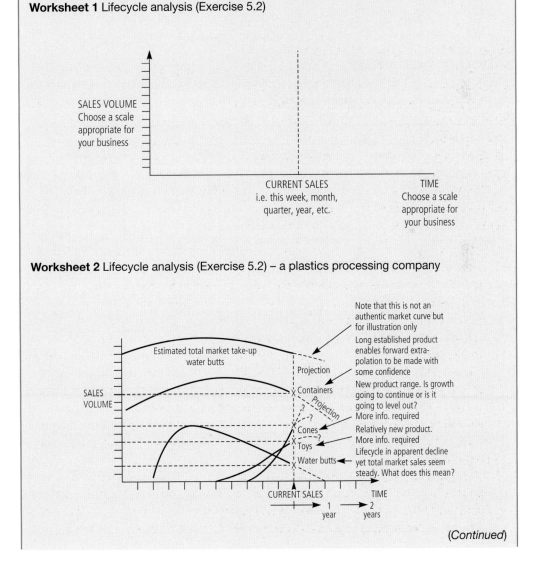

Worksheet 2 Lifecycle analysis (Exercise 5.2) – a plastics processing company

(Continued)

Personal notes

Guide to market maturity

The following checklist is used by one major company to help it determine where its markets are on the lifecycle (repeated from page 165).

Factor	Maturity stage			
	Embryonic	**Growth**	**Mature**	**Declining**
1. Growth rate	Normally much greater than GNP (on small base)	Sustained growth above GNP. New customers. New suppliers. Rate decelerates towards end of stage	Approximately equals GNP	Declining demand. Market shrinks as users' needs change
2. Predictability of growth potential	Hard to define accurately. Small portion of demand being satisfied. Market forecasts differ widely	Greater percentage of demand is met and upper limits of demand becoming clearer. Discontinuities such as price reductions based on economies of scale may occur	Potential well defined. Competition specialized to satisfy needs of specific segments	Known and limited
3. Product line proliferation	Specialized lines to meet needs of early customers	Rapid expansion	Proliferation slows or ceases	Lines narrow as unprofitable products dropped
4. Number of competitors	Unpredictable	Reaches maximum. New entrants attracted by growth and high margins. Some consolidation begins toward end of stage	Entrenched positions established. Further shakeout of marginal competitors	New entrants unlikely. Competitors continue to decline

5. Market share distribution	Unstable. Shares react unpredictably to entrepreneurial insights and timing	Increasing stability. Typically, a few competitors emerging as strong	Stable, with a few companies often controlling much of the industry	Highly concentrated or fragmented as industry segments and/or is localized
6. Customer stability	Trial usage with little customer loyalty	Some loyalty. Repeat usage with many seeking alternative suppliers	Well-developed buying patterns, with customer loyalty. Competitors understand purchase dynamics and it is difficult for a new supplier to win over accounts	Extremely stable. Suppliers dwindle and customers less motivated to seek alternatives
7. Ease of entry	Normally easy. No one dominates. Customers' expectations uncertain. If barriers exist they are usually technology, capital or fear of the unknown	More difficult. Market franchises and/or economies of scale may exist, yet new business is still available without directly confronting competition	Difficult. Market leaders established. New business must be 'won' from others	Little or no incentive to enter
8. Technology	Plays an important role in matching product characteristics to market needs. Frequent product changes	Product technology vital early, while process technology more important later in this stage	Process and material substitution focus. Product requirements well known and relatively undemanding. May be a thrust to renew the industry via new technology	Technological content is known, stable and accessible

Special project brief
Product lifecycles

Take any product you know well and prepare a short presentation (say 10 minutes) which covers the following areas/questions:

1. Brief product description – your definition of the market it serves
2. Your estimates of the product's current point in the lifecycle curve
3. Your reasons for believing it is at this point
4. Your estimate of the length and shape of this lifecycle

(Continued)

5. Your reasons for this estimate
6. Your predictions of the prospects for this product over the next three years
7. Your reasons for these predictions.

Exercise 5.3 Applying the directional policy matrix to your own organization

Follow these instructions:

1. Choose a product (or group of products) that is bought by many different markets (or segments).
2. List no more than eight of these markets (or segments).
3. Develop a set of criteria for judging:

   Market attractiveness
   Your strength in these markets.

4. Develop a scoring and weighting system for these criteria.
5. Evaluate the markets you have chosen, using these criteria.
6. Locate the point of each of these markets on a four-box directional policy matrix.
7. Using an approximate scale of your own choice, make the circle diameter proportional to your current turnover.
8. Comment on the current portfolio.
9. Indicate approximately the size and position of each circle in three years' time.
10. Outline (briefly) the strategies you would pursue to achieve these objectives.

REFERENCES

1. Binet, L. and Field, P. (2007) *Marketing in an Age of Accountability*. IPA Data Mine.
2. Clayton, R. (2009) Brand valuation: from market to boardroom. *Market Leader*, March 2009, 42–56.
3. Ritson, M. (2008) *Marketing Magazine*, Editorial Comment, 3 December, 20.
4. de Chernatony, L. and McDonald, M. (2011) *Creating Powerful Brands*. Butterworth-Heinemann, Oxford.
5. McDonald, M., Smith, B. and Ward, K. (2006) *Marketing Due Diligence*. Butterworth-Heinemann, Oxford.
6. Rogers, E. (1976) *Diffusions and Innovations*. Free Press, New York.

Chapter  6

SETTING MARKETING OBJECTIVES AND STRATEGIES

SUMMARY

- What marketing objectives are
- How marketing objectives relate to corporate objectives
- How to set marketing objectives
- What competitive strategies are
- How to use competitive strategies to gain competitive advantage
- How to start the process of marketing planning using 'gap analysis'
- New product development as a growth strategy
- What marketing strategies are
- How to set marketing strategies
- Why this step is the most crucial in the marketing planning process
- Exercises to turn the theory into actionable propositions

INTRODUCTION

From our 'map' of marketing, repeated below as Figure 6.1, we have so far dealt in detail in Chapters 4 and 5 with Box 1, 'Define markets and understand value'.

We also introduced Box 2, 'Create value proposition' in Chapter 2, when we gave an overview of the marketing planning process.

The purpose of this chapter is to expand on 'Determine the value proposition' step and to spell out how to set marketing objectives and strategies within the strategic marketing plan. We begin by expanding Box 2, 'Create value proposition' (Figure 6.2). The key input to this process is the analysis of customer needs, and the relative attractiveness of different customer segments, which were discussed in detail in Chapters 4 and 5.

The creation of the value proposition to the customer contains five subprocesses, shown in Figure 6.2.

First, using the analysis which flows from the previous process, the range of markets and segments in which the organization is to operate is chosen and prioritized, as explained in Chapters 4

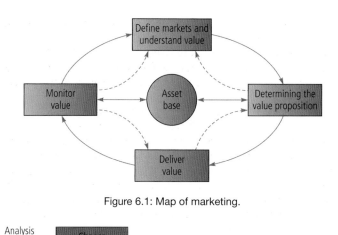

Figure 6.1: Map of marketing.

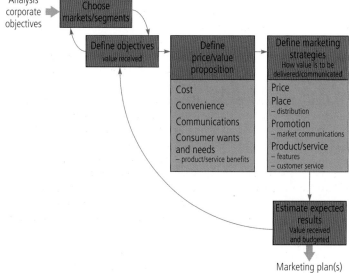

Figure 6.2: Determine value proposition.

and 5. This will take into account both the market's inherent attractiveness, and the organization's actual and potential ability to meet customer needs within the segment. It will also be shaped by the corporate objectives.

The next two processes define the core of the value proposition to the customer. While they can occur in either order, organizations typically start by defining the value they hope to receive from the segment: 'Define objectives'. This involves defining marketing objectives in terms, for example, of market share, volume, value or contribution by segment, to be discussed in more detail in this chapter.

The other half of the equation is defining the value to be delivered to the customer in return. This price/value proposition can be thought of using the four Cs: 'Cost', 'Convenience', 'Communications' and 'Consumer wants and needs'. These translate the four Ps of marketing from what the organization does to what the customer cares about. For example, the customer is concerned with 'convenience' of purchase, which influences how the organization will 'place' the product through distribution channels. Similarly, instead of 'product', we have 'consumer wants and needs' which are met by the product. The customer is interested in the total 'cost' to them, not necessarily just the upfront 'price'.

And finally, 'promotion' translates into two-way 'communications' in which customers declare their requirements and learn about the organization's offerings.

The fourth subprocess may involve iterations with the third one since, in defining the marketing strategies – how the value is to be delivered and communicated – it may be necessary to reconsider what that value can actually be. We have listed the four major aspects of this process using the four Ps. While separate plans, or plan sections, may be produced for each of these, the decisions are closely intertwined: for example, the choice of distribution channel will impact what communications are feasible, what surrounding services can be delivered, and what price can be charged.

Some reformulations of the four Ps include others such as 'Provision of customer service', 'People', and 'Processes'. We include customer service within 'Product/service', as it is often difficult to separate the core product or service from surrounding services, but clearly every aspect for the customer interaction needs to be planned for. 'People' and 'Processes' represent dimensions that certainly need to be planned, but we view them as arising from the consideration of the customer-focused four Ps by asking what changes to people or processes are necessary in order to achieve the desired product offering, price, place or promotions.

Once these issues have been resolved, an estimate of the expected results of the marketing strategies can be made, in terms of the costs to the organization and the impact of the price/value proposition on sales. This final step closes the loop from the original setting of objectives, as it may be that iteration is required if it is considered that the strategies that have been defined are not sufficient to meet the financial objectives.

The output from the 'Determine value proposition' process is typically a strategic marketing plan, or plans, covering a period of at least three years. In some cases, specific plans are produced for aspects of the four Ps, such as a pricing plan, a distribution plan, a customer service plan or a promotions plan. However, even when no plans are produced, the organization is implicitly taking decisions on the offer to the customer and how this offer is to be communicated and delivered. The content of these plans has to be communicated to and agreed with all departments or functions responsible for delivering the customer value spelled out in the plans.

We can now proceed to explain in detail how to set marketing objectives and strategies.

MARKETING OBJECTIVES: WHAT THEY ARE AND HOW THEY RELATE TO CORPORATE OBJECTIVES

There are no works on marketing which do not include at least one paragraph on the need for setting objectives. Setting objectives is a mandatory step in the planning process. The literature on the subject, though, is not very explicit, which is surprising when it is considered how vital the setting of ▶ marketing objectives is.

An objective will ensure that a company knows what its strategies are expected to accomplish and when a particular strategy has accomplished its purpose. In other words, without objectives, strategy decisions and all that follows will take place in a vacuum.

Following the identification of opportunities and the explicit statement of assumptions about conditions affecting the business, the process of setting objectives should, in theory, be comparatively easy, the actual objectives themselves being a realistic statement of what the company desires to achieve as a result of a market-centred analysis, rather than generalized statements borne of top management's desire to 'do better next year'.

> A marketing objective is the quantification of what an organization sells (its products) and to whom (its markets)

However, objective setting is more complex than at first it would appear to be.

Most experts agree that the logical approach to the difficult task of setting marketing objectives is to proceed from the broad to the specific. Thus, the starting point would be a statement of the nature of the business (the mission statement), from which would flow the broad company objectives. Next, the broad company objectives would be translated into key result areas, which would be those areas in which success is vital to the firm. Market penetration and growth rate of sales are examples of key result areas. The third step would be creation of the subobjectives necessary to accomplish the broad objectives, such as product sales volume goals, geographical expansion, product line extension, and so on.

The end result of this process should be objectives which are consistent with the strategic plan, attainable within budget limitations, and compatible with the strengths, limitations, and economics of other functions within the organization.

The logical approach to the difficult task of setting objectives is to proceed from the broad to the specific.

At the top level, management is concerned with long-run profitability; at the next level in the management hierarchy, the concern is for objectives which are defined more specifically and in greater detail, such as increasing sales and market share, penetrating new markets, and so on. These objectives are merely a part of the hierarchy of objectives, in that corporate objectives will only be accomplished if these and other objectives are achieved. At the next level, management is concerned with objectives which are defined even more tightly, such as: to create awareness among a specific target market about a new product; to change a particular customer attitude; and so on. Again, the general marketing objectives will only be accomplished if these and other subobjectives are achieved.

It is clear that subobjectives *per se*, unless they are an integral part of a broader framework of objectives, are likely to lead to a wasteful misdirection of resources.

For example, a sales increase in itself may be possible, but only at an undue cost, so that such a marketing objective is only appropriate within the framework of corporate objectives. In such a case, it may well be that an increase in sales in a particular market sector will entail additional capital expenditure ahead of the time for which it is planned. If this were the case, it may make more sense to allocate available production capacity to more profitable market sectors in the short term, allowing sales to decline in another sector. Decisions such as this are likely to be more easily made against a backcloth of explicitly stated broad company objectives relating to all the major disciplines.

Likewise, objectives should be set for advertising, for example, which are wholly consistent with wider objectives. Objectives set in this way integrate the advertising effort with the other elements in the marketing mix and this leads to a consistent, logical marketing plan.

SO WHAT IS A CORPORATE OBJECTIVE AND WHAT IS A MARKETING OBJECTIVE?

A business starts at some time with resources and wants to use those resources to achieve something. What the business wants to achieve is a ▶ corporate objective, which describes a desired destination, or result. Most often this is expressed in terms of profit, since profit is the means of satisfying shareholders or owners, and because it is the one universally accepted criterion by which efficiency can be evaluated, which will, in turn, lead to efficient resource allocation, economic and technological progressiveness and stability. How it is to be achieved is a strategy. In a sense, this means that the only true objective of a company is, by definition, what is stated in the corporate plan as being the principal purpose of its existence.

> A corporate objective describes a desired destination or result. Most often this is expressed in terms of profit

This means that stated desires, such as to expand market share, to create a new image, to achieve an x per cent increase in sales, and so on, are in fact ▶ strategies at the corporate level, since they are the means by which a company will achieve its profit objectives. In practice, however, companies tend to operate by means of functional divisions, each with a separate identity, so that what is a strategy at the corporate level becomes an objective within each division, or strategic business unit.

> The only true objective of a company is, by definition, what is stated in the corporate plan as being the principal purpose of its existence.

For example, marketing strategies within the corporate plan become marketing objectives within the marketing department and strategies at the general level within the marketing plan themselves become operating objectives at the next level down, so that an intricate web of interrelated objectives and strategies is built up at all levels within the framework of the overall company plan.

The really important point, however, apart from clarifying the difference between objectives and strategies, is that the further down the hierarchical chain one goes, the less likely it is that a stated objective will make a cost-effective contribution to company profits, unless it derives logically and directly from an objective at a higher level.

Corporate objectives and strategies can be simplified in the following way:

> Corporate strategies define how corporate objectives are to be achieved through the use of its resources

Corporate objective
- desired level of profitability

Corporate strategies
- which products and which markets (marketing)
- what kind of facilities (operations, distribution, IT, R and D, etc.)
- size and character of the staff/labour force (personnel, resource management)
- funding (finance)
- other corporate strategies such as social responsibility, sustainability, corporate image, stock market image, employee image, etc.

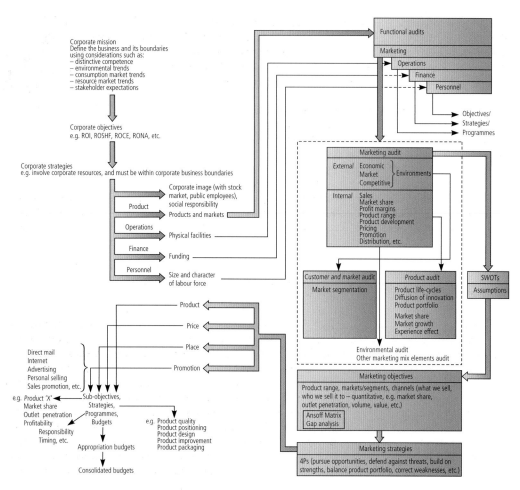

Figure 6.3: Hierarchy of objectives and strategies.

It is now clear that at the next level down in the organization, i.e. at the functional level, what products are to be sold into what markets become *marketing objectives*, while the means of achieving these objectives using the marketing mix are *marketing* strategies. At the next level down, there would be, say, advertising objectives and advertising strategies, with the subsequent *programmes* and *budgets* for achieving the objectives. In this way, a hierarchy of objectives and strategies can be traced back to the initial corporate objective. Figure 6.3 illustrates this point.

HOW TO SET MARKETING OBJECTIVES

Without doubt, the most useful starting point in setting marketing objectives is to conduct a SWOT analysis on each important product for market to be included in your strategic marketing plan. A detailed methodology for completing really useful SWOT analyses is spelled out in detail in Exercise 6.4 at the end of this chapter. So, SWOTs should be completed on each principal box in the Ansoff Matrix, which is the subject of this next section.

The Ansoff Matrix[1] can be introduced here as a useful tool for thinking about marketing objectives.

A firm's competitive situation can be simplified to two dimensions only – products and markets. To put it even more simply, Ansoff's framework is about what is sold (the 'product') and who it is sold to (the 'market'). Within this framework Ansoff identifies four possible courses of action for the firm:

> Pricing objectives, sales promotion objectives, advertising objectives, and the like, should not be confused with marketing objectives.

1. Selling existing products to existing markets
2. Extending existing products to new markets
3. Developing new products for existing markets
4. Developing new products for new markets.

The matrix in Figure 6.4 depicts these concepts.

It is clear that the range of possible marketing objectives is very wide, since there will be degrees of technological newness and degrees of market newness. Nevertheless, Ansoff's Matrix provides a logical framework in which marketing objectives can be developed under each of the four main headings above.

> In other words, marketing objectives are about products and markets only.

Common sense will confirm that it is only by selling something to someone that the company's financial goals can be achieved, and that advertising, pricing, service levels, and so on, are the means (or strategies) by which it might succeed in doing this. Thus, pricing objectives, sales promotion objectives, advertising objectives, and the like, should not be confused with marketing objectives.

Marketing objectives are generally accepted as being quantitative commitments, usually stated either in standards of performance for a given operating period, or conditions to be achieved by given dates. Performance standards are usually stated in terms of sales volume or value and various measures of profitability. The conditions to be attained are usually a percentage of market share and various other commitments, such as a percentage of the total number of a given type of distribution outlet.

There is also broad agreement that objectives must be specific enough to enable subordinates to derive from them the general character of action required and the yardstick by which performance is to be judged.

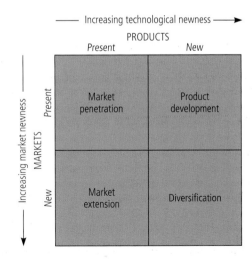

Figure 6.4: Ansoff matrix.

> Objectives are the core of managerial action, providing direction to the plans.

Objectives are the core of managerial action, providing direction to the plans. By asking where the operation should be at some future date, objectives are determined. Vague objectives, however emotionally appealing, are counterproductive to sensible planning, and are usually the result of the human propensity for wishful thinking, which often smacks more of cheerleading than serious marketing leadership. What this really means is that it is unacceptable to use directional terms such as 'improve', 'increase', 'decrease', 'optimize', 'minimize' as objectives, because it is logical that, unless there is some measure, or yardstick, against which to measure a sense of locomotion towards achieving them, then they do not serve any useful purpose.

Ansoff defines an objective as 'a measure of the efficiency of the resource-conversion process'.

An objective contains three elements: the particular attribute that is chosen as a measure of efficiency; the yardstick or scale by which the attribute is measured; and the particular value on the scale which the firm seeks to attain.

Marketing objectives then are about each of the four main categories of the Ansoff Matrix:

1. *Existing products in existing markets.* These may be many and varied and will certainly need to be set for all existing major products and customer groups (segments).
2. *New products in existing markets.*
3. *Existing products in new markets.*
4. *New products in new markets.*

Thus, in the long run, it is only by selling something (a 'product') to someone (a 'market') that any firm can succeed in staying in business profitably. Simply defined, product/market strategy means the route chosen to achieve company goals through the range of products it offers to its chosen market segments. Thus the product/market strategy represents a commitment to a future direction for the firm. Marketing objectives, then, are concerned solely with products and markets.

> Marketing objectives are concerned solely with products and markets.

The general marketing *directions* which lead to the above objectives flow, of course, from the lifecycle and portfolio analysis conducted in the audit and revolve around the following logical decisions:

1. *Maintain.* This usually refers to the 'cash cow' type of product/market and reflects the desire to maintain competitive positions.
2. *Improve.* This usually refers to the 'star' type of product/market and reflects the desire to improve the competitive position in attractive markets.
3. *Harvest.* This usually refers to the 'dog' type of product/market and reflects the desire to relinquish competitive position in favour of short-term profit and cash flow, unless there are sound reasons not to.
4. *Exit.* This also usually refers to the 'dog' type of product/market, also sometimes the 'question mark', and reflects a desire to divest because of a very weak competitive position or because the cost of staying in it is prohibitive and the risk associated with improving its position is too high.
5. *Enter.* This usually refers to a new business area.

As already stated, however, great care should be taken not to follow slavishly any set of 'rules' or guidelines related to the above. Also, the use of pejorative labels like 'dog', 'cash cow', and so on should be avoided.

A full list of marketing guidelines as a precursor to objective setting is given in Table 6.1. Figure 6.5 sets out a fuller list which includes guidelines for functions other than marketing. One word of warning, however. Such general guidelines should not be followed unquestioningly. They are included more as check-lists of questions that should be asked about each major product in each major market before setting marketing objectives and strategies.

> General guidelines should not be followed unquestioningly.

It is at this stage that the circles in the directional policy matrix (see Chapter 5) can be moved to show their relative size and position in three years' time. You can do this to show, first, where they will be if the company takes no action, and second, where you would ideally prefer them to be. These latter positions will, of course, become the marketing objectives.

> The use of pejorative labels like 'dog', 'cash cow', and so on should be avoided.

COMPETITIVE STRATEGIES

At this stage of the planning process, it would be helpful to explain developments in the field of competitive strategies, since an understanding of the subject is an essential prerequisite to setting appropriate marketing objectives.

> One of the principal purposes of marketing strategy is for you to be able to choose the customers, and hence the markets, you wish to deal with.

In this respect, the directional policy matrix discussed in Chapter 5 is particularly useful. The main components of strategy are:

* the company
* customers
* products/services
* competitors.

So far, we have said very little about competitors, although, clearly, if we are to succeed we need to work hard at developing a sustainable competitive advantage. The important word here is 'sustainable', as temporary advantages can be gained in numerous ways, such as, for example, a price reduction or a clever sales promotion.

Most business people would agree that, as markets mature, the only way to grow the business without diversifying is at the expense of competitors, which implies the need to understand in depth the characteristics of the market and of the main competitors in it. The leading thinker in this field is Michael Porter of the Harvard Business School, and any reader wishing to explore this vital subject in more depth should refer to his book.[2]

> If we are to succeed, we need to work hard at developing a sustainable competitive advantage.

Perhaps the best way to summarize this complex subject would be to tell a story.

	Business strengths		
	High		**Low**
High	*Invest for growth* Defend leadership, gain if possible Accept moderate short-term profits and, if necessary, negative cash flow Consider geographic expansion, product line expansion, product differentiation Upgrade product development effort Aggressive marketing posture, viz. selling, advertising, pricing, sales promotion service levels, as appropriate		*Opportunistic* The options are: (i) Move it to the left if resources are available to invest in it (ii) Keep a low profile until funds are available (iii) Divest to a buyer able to exploit the opportunity
Market attractiveness	*Maintain market position, manage for sustained earnings* Maintain market position in most successful product lines Prune less successful product lines, unless necessary to market success Manage for profit Differentiate products to maintain share of key segments Limit discretionary marketing expenditure Stabilize prices, except where a temporary aggressive stance is necessary to maintain market share	*Selective** Acknowledge low growth Do not view as a 'marketing' problem Identify and exploit growth segments Emphasize product quality to avoid 'commodity' competition Systematically improve productivity Assign talented managers	*Manage for profit* Prune product line aggressively Maximize cash flow Minimize marketing expenditure Maintain or raise prices at the expense of volume (all of these are on the assumption that such products are not essential to market position)
Low			

Table 6.1: Strategies suggested by portfolio matrix analysis

*Selective refers to those products or markets which fall on or near the vertical dividing line in a directional policy matrix.

Main thrust	Invest for growth	Maintain market position, manage for earnings	Selective	Manage for cash	Opportunistic development
Market share	Maintain or increase dominance	Maintain or slightly milk for earnings	Maintain selectively segment	Forgo share for profit	Invest selectively in share
Products	Differentiation – line expansion	Prune less successful Differentiate for key segments	Emphasize product quality Differentiate	Aggressively prune	Differentiation – line expansion
Price	Lead – aggressive pricing for share	Stabilize prices/raise	Maintain or raise	Raise	Aggressive – price for share
Promotion	Aggressive promotion	Limit	Maintain selectively	Minimize	Aggressive marketing
Distribution	Broaden distribution	Hold wide distribution pattern	Segment	Gradually withdraw distribution	Limited coverage
Cost control	Tight control – go for scale economies	Emphasize cost reduction, viz variable costs	Tight control	Aggressively reduce both fixed and variable	Tight – but not at expense of entrepreneurship
Production	Expand, invest (organic acquisition, joint venture)	Maximize capacity utilization	Increase productivity, e.g. specialization/automation	Free up capacity	Invest
R&D	Expand – invest	Focus on specific projects	Invest selectively	None	Invest
Personnel	Upgrade management in key functional areas	Maintain, reward efficiency, tighten organization	Allocate key managers	Cut back organization	Invest
Investment	Fund growth	Limit fixed investment	Invest selectively	Minimize and divest opportunistically	Fund growth
Working capital	Reduce in process – extend credit	Tighten credit – reduce accounts receivable, increase inventory turn	Reduce	Aggressively reduce	Invest

Figure 6.5: Guidelines suggested for different positioning on the directional policy matrix.

Imagine three tribes on a small island fighting each other because resources are scarce. One tribe decides to move to a larger adjacent island, sets up camp, and is followed eventually by the other two, who also set up their own separate camps. At first it is a struggle to establish themselves, but eventually they begin to occupy increasing parts of the island, until many years later they begin to fight again over adjacent land. The more innovative tribal chief, i.e. the one who was first to move to the new island, sits down with his senior warriors and ponders what to do, since none are very keen to move to yet another island. They decide that the only two options are:

1. Attack and go relentlessly for the enemy's territory.
2. Settle for a smaller part of the island and build in it an impregnable fortress.

These two options, i.e. terrain or impregnable fortress (or both), are in fact the same options that face business people as they contemplate competitive strategy. Let's look in turn at each of these options, continuing for a moment longer with the military analogy, and starting with terrain.

Imagine two armies facing each other on a field of battle (depicted by circles). One army has 15 soldiers in it, the other 12. Imagine also that they face each other with rifles and all fire one shot at the other at the same time, also that they don't all aim at the same soldier! Figure 6.6 depicts the progress of each side in disposing of the other. It will be seen that after only three volleys, the army on the right has only one soldier remaining, while the army on the left, with eight soldiers remaining, is still a viable fighting unit.

One interesting fact about this story is that the effect observed here is geometric rather than arithmetic, and is a perfect demonstration of the effect of size and what happens when all things are equal except size. The parallel in industry, of course, is market share.

Figure 6.6: The importance of market share.

Just look at what happened in the computer industry when in the 1970s General Electric, Rank Xerox, RCA, ICL and others attacked the giant IBM. The larger competitor was able to win the battle.

So, all things being equal, a company with a larger market share than another should win over a smaller competitor. Or *should* it? Clearly, this is not inevitable, providing the smaller companies take evasive action. Staying with the computer industry, just look at how successful NCR have been with their 'global fortress' strategy (e.g. ATMs for the financial market).

In 1992 and 1993, IBM got caught unawares, with disastrous financial results, by quicker-moving, smarter, smaller competitors. They have now recovered by regrouping and re-segmenting their market, just as Rank Xerox did in the 1970s to recover from the successful entry of the Japanese with small photocopiers. They have also used their enormous market power and reach to take advantage of the new but substantial markets for services.

MARKETING INSIGHT

In the banking market, First Direct took a commanding position by means of a differentiated product, dispensing with all the paraphernalia of expensive branches.

MARKETING INSIGHT

In the insurance market, Direct Line have completely changed the rules of warfare by dispensing with brokers, with a consequent saving in premiums for customers.

Put yet another way, look for a moment at the economists' model of supply and demand shown in Figure 6.7. Here we see that when supply is greater than demand, price will fall, and that when demand exceeds supply, the price will tend to rise. The equilibrium point is when supply matches demand. The only way a competitor can avoid the worst effects of such a situation is by taking one of the following actions:

1. Being the lowest cost supplier
2. Differentiating the product in some way so as to be able to command a higher price.

Michael Porter combined these two options into a simple matrix, as shown in Figure 6.8. It can be seen that Box 1 represents a sound strategy, particularly in commodity-type markets such as bulk chemicals, where differentiation is harder to achieve because of the identical nature of the chemical make-up of the product. In such cases, it is wise to recognize the reality and pursue a productivity drive with the aim of becoming the lowest cost producer. It is here that the experience effect described in Chapter 5 becomes especially important.

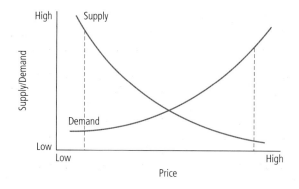

Figure 6.7: Supply/Demand/Price model.

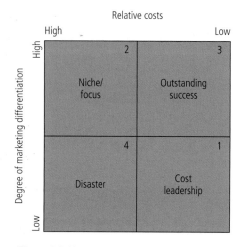

Figure 6.8: Porter's generic strategies matrix.

Many companies, however, such as Mercedes and BMW, could not hope to be the lowest cost producers. Consequently, their whole corporate philosophy is geared to differentiation and what we have called added value. Clearly, this represents a sensible strategy for any company that cannot hope to be a world cost leader and indeed many of the world's great companies succeed by means of such a focus. Many of these companies also succeed in pushing themselves into Box 3, the outstanding success box, by occupying what can be called 'global fortresses'. A good example of this is NCR, who dominate the world's banking and retail markets with their focused technological and marketing approach. American Express is another.

Companies like 3M, McDonald's, Procter & Gamble and General Electric, however, typify Box 3, where low costs, differentiation and world leadership are combined in their corporate strategies. Nothing, however, is for ever and readers will be aware of the problems encountered by McDonald's as a result of the backlash of the health lobby. They will also be aware that McDonald's successfully addressed these problems eventually.

Only Box 4 remains. Here we can see that a combination of commodity-type markets and high relative costs will result in disaster sooner or later. A position here is tenable only while demand exceeds supply. When, however, these markets mature, there is little hope for companies who find themselves in this unenviable position.

An important point to remember when thinking about differentiation as a strategy is that you must still be *cost effective*. It is a myth to assume that sloppy management and high costs are accept-able as long as the product has a good image and lots of added values. Also, in thinking about differentiation, please refer back to the section on segmentation in Chapter 4, for it is here that the route to differentiation will be found. It is also clear that there is not much point in offering ben-efits that are costly for you to provide but which are not highly regarded by customers. So consider using a matrix like the one given in Figure 6.9 to classify your benefits. Clearly, you will succeed best by providing as many benefits as possible that fall into the top right hand box.

ICI is an example of a company that proactively attempted to change its global strategy by systematically moving away from bulk chemicals in Box 1 (in Figure 6.8) towards speciality chemicals in Box 2 and then going on to occupy a 'global fortress' position in these speciali-ties (Box 3). This, however, proved extremely difficult in this mature market.

The main point here, however, is that when setting marketing objectives, it is essential for you to have a sound grasp of the position in your markets of yourself and your competitors and to adopt appropriate postures for the several elements of your business, all of which may be different. It may be necessary, for example, to accept that part of your portfolio is in the 'Disaster' box (Box 4). You may well be forced to have some products here, for example, to complete your product range to enable you to offer your more profitable products. The point is that you must adopt an appropriate stance towards these products and set your marketing objectives accordingly, using, where appropriate, the guidelines given in Table 6.1 and Figure 6.5.

Finally, here are some very general guidelines to help you think about competitive strategies.

1. Know the terrain on which you are fighting (the market).
2. Know the resources of your enemies (competitive analysis).
3. Do something with determination that the enemy isn't expecting.

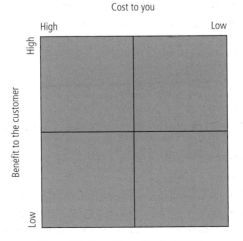

Figure 6.9: Benefits analysis matrix.

In respect of this last one, the great historian of military strategy, Lanchester, put forward the following equation when applying his findings to industry:

$$\text{Fighting strength} = \text{weapon efficiency} \times (\text{number of troops})^2$$

Let us simplify and summarize this. 'Weapon efficiency' can be elements such as advertising, the sales force, the quality of your products, and so on. '(number of troops)^2' is more difficult to explain, but is similar in concept to Einstein's theory of critical mass:

$$\text{Energy} = \text{mass (velocity of light)}^2$$
$$E = mc^2$$

Let us take as an example the use of the sales force. If your competitor's salesperson calls on an outlet, say twice a month for six months, he or she will have called 12 times. If your salesperson calls four times a month for six months, he or she will have called 24 times. What Lanchester's Square Law says, however, is that the *effect* is considerably more than twice that of your competitor.

An example of this was the Canada Dry attack on the British mixer market. By training the sales force to a high peak of effectiveness (weapon efficiency), and by focusing on specific market segments and out-calling their much larger rival, they were gradually able to occupy particular parts of the market and then move on to the next, until eventually they gained a significant market share. What would have been foolhardy would have been to tackle Schweppes, the market leader, head on in a major battle. The result would have been similar to the fate of the troops in the Charge of the Light Brigade!

STRATEGIC MARKETING PLANNING: WHERE TO START
Understanding the Variables

Figure 6.10 illustrates what is commonly referred to as 'gap analysis':

Essentially, what it says is that if the corporate sales and financial objectives are greater than the current long-range trends and forecasts, there is a gap which has to be filled. Ideally, the objective should be a 'must' objective – i.e. an objective that must be met in order to achieve your mission.

This gap can be filled in six ways:

- by improved productivity (e.g. reduce costs, improve the sales mix, increase prices, reduce discounts, improve the productivity of the sales force, and so on)
- by market penetration of existing products in existing markets (e.g. increase usage, increase market share)
- by new products in existing markets
- by existing products in new markets (e.g. new user groups, enter new segments, geographical expansion)
- by a combination of new products and markets, new strategies (e.g. acquisition, joint ventures, licensing franchising)
- by new strategies (e.g. acquisition, joint ventures, licensing franchising).

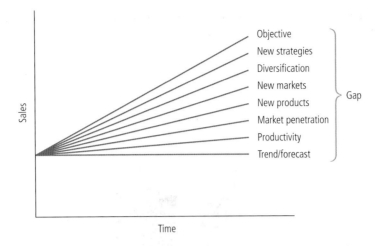

Figure 6.10: Gap analysis.

Another option, of course, is to reduce the objectives! The problem here, however, is that the objective could not have been a 'must' objective! Gap analysis is best done in two separate steps. Step 1 should be done for sales revenue only so, under the operations gap, above, reducing costs is not relevant as we are only interested in revenue growth. Step 2 should then go through the same stages, but this time looking at the profit and costs implications of achieving the sales growth.

A detailed, step-by-step methodology for completing both steps is given in the exercises at the end of this chapter.

If improved productivity is one method by which the profit gap is to be filled, care must be taken not to take measures such as 'to reduce marketing costs by 20 per cent overall'. The portfolio analysis undertaken during the marketing audit stage will indicate that this would be totally inappropriate to some product/market areas, for which increased marketing expenditure may be needed, while for others 20 per cent reduction in marketing costs may not be sufficient.

As for sales growth options, it is clear that productivity improvements and market penetration should always be a company's first option, since it makes far more sense to attempt to increase profits and cash flow from existing products and markets initially, because this is usually the least costly and the least risky.

This is so because, for its present products and markets, a company has developed knowledge and skills which it can use competitively. Associated with this is the growing interest in customer retention and there is now much evidence to show that keeping existing customers can be a source of ever-increasing profits.[3]

> As for sales growth options, it is clear that market penetration should always be a company's first option.

For the same reason, it makes more sense in many cases to move along the horizontal axis for further growth before attempting to find new markets. The reason for this is that it normally takes many years for a company to get to know its customers and markets and to build up a reputation. That reputation and trust, embodied in either the company's name or in its brands, is not so easily transferable to new markets, where other companies are already entrenched. The famous Wal-Mart's entry into Germany is an example of this. For many years they lost hundreds of millions of dollars and were consistently voted Germany's worst supermarket.

The marketing audit should ensure that the method chosen to fill the gap is consistent with the company's capabilities and builds on its strengths.

MARKETING INSIGHT

For example, it would normally prove far less profitable for a dry goods grocery manufacturer to introduce frozen foods than to add another dry foods product. Likewise, if a product could be sold to existing channels using the existing sales force, this is far less risky than introducing a new product that requires new channels and new selling skills.

New products should be consistent with the company's known strengths and capabilities. Diversification is the riskiest strategy of all.

Exactly the same applies to the company's operations, distribution, and people. Whatever new products are developed should be as consistent as possible with the company's known strengths and capabilities. Clearly, the use of existing operations capacity is generally preferable to new processes. Also, the amount of additional investment is important. Technical personnel are highly trained and specialist, and whether this competence can be transferred to a new field must be considered. A product requiring new raw materials may also require new handling and storage techniques which may prove expensive.

MARKETING INSIGHT

It can now be appreciated why going into new markets with new products (diversification) is the riskiest strategy of all, because new resources and new management skills have to be developed. This is why the history of commerce is replete with examples of companies that went bankrupt through moving into areas where they had little or no distinctive competence.

This is also why many companies that diversified through acquisition during periods of high economic growth have since divested themselves of businesses that were not basically compatible with their own distinctive competence.

The Ansoff Matrix, of course, is not a simple four-box matrix, for it will be obvious that there are degrees of technological newness as well as degrees of market newness. Figure 6.11 illustrates the point. It also demonstrates more easily why any movement should generally aim to keep a company as close as possible to its present position, rather than moving it to a totally unrelated position, except in the most unusual circumstances.

Nevertheless, the product lifecycle phenomenon will inevitably *force* companies to move along one or more of the Ansoff Matrix axes if they are to continue to increase their sales and profits. A key question to be asked, then, is how this important decision is to be taken, given the risks involved.

A full list of the possible methods involved in the process of gap analysis is given in Figure 6.12. From this it will be seen that there is nothing an executive can do to fill the gap that is not included in the list. It is worth mentioning again that the precise methodology to implement this concept is given in Exercise 6.1 at the end of this chapter.

MARKETING INSIGHT

At this point, it is important to stress that the 'objectives' point in gap analysis should not be an extrapolation, but your own view of what revenue would make this into an excellent business.

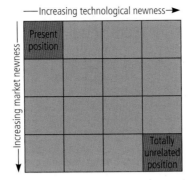

Figure 6.11: Ansoff matrix. Degrees of newness.

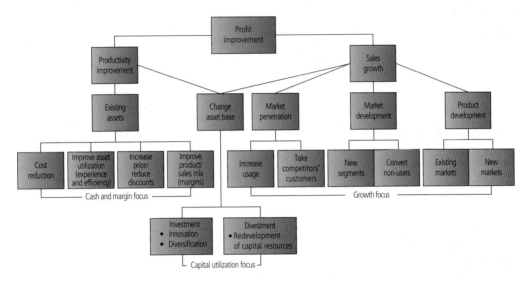

Figure 6.12: Profit/division profit improvement options. (After Professor John Saunders, Aston University, used with his kind permission.)

The word 'excellent' must, of course, be relative only to comparable businesses. If all the executives in a company responsible for SBUs were to do this, then work out what needed to be done to fill any gaps, it is easy to understand why this would result in an excellent overall business performance. Instead, what often happens is that executives wait until there is a crisis before doing any strategic planning. For many such organizations, alas, during the 1990s and the last few years of the early 2000s, it was all left too late and many went bankrupt. In the late 1990s and at the dawn of the new century, countless dotcom businesses jumped on the internet bandwagon with no properly thought-out strategies, and their demise was inevitable. We didn't even learn the lesson during the first decade of the 21st century when a record number of businesses went bankrupt.

One final point to make about gap analysis based on the Ansoff Matrix is that, when completed, the details of exactly *how* to achieve the objectives still need to be worked out. *This is the purpose of the strategic marketing plan*. So, gap analysis represents a very useful starting point in mapping out the general route, which is why we suggest you start here, rather than going to all the trouble of preparing a strategic marketing plan only to have to change it later. The point is, however, that gap analysis using the Ansoff Matrix is not a marketing plan.

NEW PRODUCT DEVELOPMENT/MARKET EXTENSION/DIVERSIFICATION

As stated earlier in this chapter, sooner or later all organizations will need to move along one or both axes of the Ansoff Matrix. How to do this should be comparatively simple if the marketing audit has been completed thoroughly.

It is not the purpose here to explore in detail subsets of marketing, such as market research, market selection, new product development, and diversification. What is important, however, in a book on marketing planning is to communicate an understanding of the framework in which these activities should take place.

What we are aiming to do is to maximize *synergy*, which could be described as the $2 + 2 = 5$ effect. The starting point is the marketing audit, leading to the SWOT (strengths, weaknesses, opportunities and threats) analyses. This is so that development of any kind will be firmly based on a company's basic *strengths* and *weaknesses*. External factors are the opportunities and threats facing the company.

Once this important analytical stage is successfully completed, the more technical process of opportunity identification, screening, business analysis, and, finally, activities such as product development, testing and entry planning can take place, depending on which option is selected (Figure 6.13 illustrates the process).

> The important point to remember is that no matter how thoroughly these subsequent activities are carried out, unless the objectives of product development/market extension are based firmly on an analysis of the company's capabilities, they are unlikely to be successful in the long term.

The criteria selected will generally be consistent with the criteria used for positioning products or businesses in the directional policy matrix described in Chapter 5. The list shown in Table 5.2 in Chapter 5, however (which is also totally consistent with the marketing audit checklist), can be used to select those criteria which are most important. A rating and weighting system can then be applied

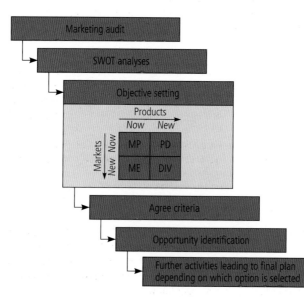

Figure 6.13: New product development in the context of the marketing planning process.

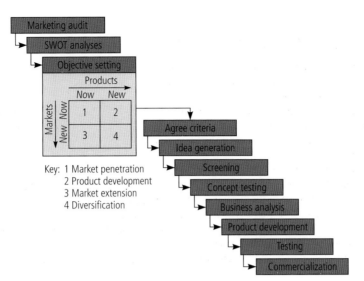

Figure 6.14: The new product development process.

to opportunities identified to assess their suitability or otherwise. Those criteria selected and the weighting system used will, of course, be consistent with the SWOT analyses.

Having said that it is not the purpose of this book to explore in detail any of the subsets of marketing such as market research, it would nonetheless be quite useful briefly to outline the process of new product development and its relationship to the gap analysis described above.

After a marketing audit and gap analysis have clarified the place of new product development in a broad company context, the organization must examine the micro considerations. These involve the range of factors that must be taken into account when a product is assessed in terms of its fit within the product portfolio and its contribution towards objectives.

Figure 6.14 depicts the relationship of the new product development process with the marketing audit and SWOT analyses. New product development can usefully be seen as a process consisting of the following seven steps:

1. *Idea generation* – the search for product ideas to meet company objectives
2. *Screening* – a quick analysis of the ideas to establish those which are relevant
3. *Concept testing* – checking with the market that the new product ideas are acceptable
4. *Business analysis* – the idea is examined in detail in terms of its commercial fit in the business
5. *Product development* – making the idea 'tangible'
6. *Testing* – market tests necessary to verify early business assessments.
7. *Commercialization* – full-scale product launch, committing the company's reputation and resources.

MARKETING STRATEGIES

What a company wants to accomplish, in terms of such things as market share and volume, is a marketing objective. How the company intends to go about achieving its objectives is strategy. Strategy is the overall route to the achievement of specific objectives and should describe the means by which objectives are to be reached, the time programme and the allocation of resources. It does not delineate the individual courses the resulting activity will follow.

There is a clear distinction between strategy and detailed implementation or tactics.

Strategy is the route to achievement of specific objectives and describes how objectives will be reached.

Marketing strategy reflects the company's best opinion as to how it can most profitably apply its skills and resources to the marketplace. It is inevitably broad in scope.

The plan which stems from it will spell out action and timings and will contain the detailed contribution expected from each department.

⎛ Marketing strategies are the means by which a company achieves its marketing objectives and are usually concerned with the four Ps ⎞

There is a similarity between strategy in business and strategic military development. One looks at the enemy, the terrain, the resources under command, and then decides whether to attack the whole front, an area of enemy weakness, to feint in one direction while attacking in another, or to attempt an encirclement of the enemy's position. The policy and mix, the general direction in which to go, and the criteria for judging success, all come under the heading of strategy. The action steps are tactics.

Similarly, in marketing, the same commitment, mix and type of resources as well as guidelines and criteria that must be met, all come under the heading of strategy.

For example, the decision to use distributors in all but the three largest market areas, in which company salespeople will be used, is a strategic decision. The selection of particular distributors is a tactical decision.

The following headings indicate the general content of strategy statements in the area of marketing which emerge from marketing literature:

1. Policies and procedures relating to the products to be offered, such as number, quality, design, branding, packaging, positioning and labelling, etc.
2. Pricing levels to be adopted, margins and discount policies.
3. Advertising, sales promotion, direct mail, call centres and the internet. The mix of these, the creative approach, the type of media, the type of displays, the amount to spend, etc.
4. What emphasis is to be placed on personal selling, the sales approach, sales training, etc.
5. The distributive channels to be used and the relative importance of each.
6. Service levels, etc. in relation to different segments.

Thus, marketing strategies are the means by which marketing objectives will be achieved and are generally concerned with the four major elements of the marketing mix.

These are:

Product. The general policies for product branding, positioning, deletions, modifications, additions, design, packaging, etc.
Price. The general pricing policies to be followed for product groups in market segments.
Place. The general policies for channels and customer service levels.
Promotion. The general policies for communicating with customers under the relevant headings, such as: advertising, sales force, sales promotion, public relations, exhibitions, direct mail, call centres, the internet, etc.

The following list of marketing strategies (in summary form) covers the majority of options open under the headings of the four Ps:

1. *Product*
   * expand the line
   * change performance, quality or features
   * consolidate the line
   * standardize design positioning change the mix branding

2. *Price*
   * change price, terms or conditions
   * skimming policies
   * penetration policies

3. *Promotion*
   * change advertising or promotion
   * change the mix between direct mail, call centres, the internet
   * change selling

4. *Place*
   * change delivery or distribution
   * change service
   * change channels
   * change the degree of forward or backward integration

Chapters 7–10 are devoted to a much more detailed consideration of promotion, pricing, service and distribution. These chapters describe what should appear in advertising and sales promotion, sales, pricing and place plans. This detail is intended for those whose principal concern is the preparation of a detailed one-year operational or tactical plan.

The relationship of these chapters to the strategic plan is in the provision of information to enable the planner to delineate broad strategies under the headings outlined above. There is no chapter specifically on product management because all the product options have been covered already, particularly in Chapter 5 in the discussion on the product audit.

There are further steps in the marketing planning process before detailed programmes are put together. These are estimating in broad terms the cost of the strategies, and delineating alternative plans. Both of these steps will be covered in more detail in Chapter 11.

At the time of writing, the world is suffering from one of the worst recessions in history.

Here are some guidelines on what to do in a recession. While not specifically concerned with marketing objectives and strategies, all economies suffer an unexpected downturn from time to time. These guidelines are intended to help managers in such difficult times.

MARKETING IN A DOWNTURN

It is pure fiction to imagine that any recession that is happening in America will not affect Western Europe.

The typical reaction to such misfortune is what Andrew Lorenz describes as 'anorexia industrialosa': an excessive desire to be leaner and fitter, leading to emaciation and eventually death. But such a pathetically inadequate response to recession today is doomed to failure largely because it results in even worse service to customers, and customers just will not stand for this any more.

The rules of competition have changed. The 'make and sell' model has been killed off by a new wave of entrepreneurial technology-enabled competitors unfettered by the baggage of legacy bureaucracy, assets, cultures and behaviours. The processing of information about products has been separated

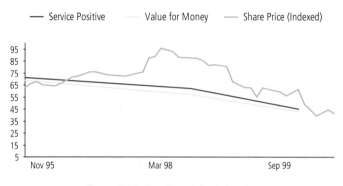

Figure 6.15: A major retailer's trends.

from the products themselves and customers can now search for and evaluate them independently of those who have a vested interest in selling them. Customers now have as much information about suppliers as suppliers have traditionally accumulated about their customers. *This new state has created a new dimension of competition based on who most effectively acts in the customers' interests.*

On top of these pressures, a new wave of business metrics such as shareholder value added and balanced scorecards, together with pressure from institutional shareholders to report meaningful facts about corporate performance rather than the traditional, high-level financial reporting that appears every year in corporate accounts, are forcing business leaders to re-examine tired corporate behaviours such as cost-cutting and downsizing as a route to profitability in recessionary times.

The differing fortunes of Tesco and Marks & Spencer in the UK tell a fascinating story: how can one get it so spectacularly right, the other so dramatically wrong?

Tesco's focus on customers is absolute. Its core purpose 'to continually increase customer value to earn their lifetime loyalty' is not just a slogan, as so many mission statements are, but actually represents the way the company thinks and acts. It strives constantly to delight its customers with innovative product and service offerings. Marks & Spencer, on the other hand, is a stark reminder of what happens when you take your eye off the customer ball. Only in recent years did it start accepting credit cards and introducing changing booths. So far did the fortunes of the once blue chip M&S fall, that there was at one stage serious doubt about its long-term future. The chart shown in Figure 6.15 clearly illustrates that, while share prices were rising, customer service was falling, until eventually disaster struck.

In a market-driven company such as Tesco, the chief executive and board instil marketing disciplines throughout its core processes and foster cross-functional working, thereby encouraging everyone to focus on the customer.

In times of recession, marketing should be even more centre stage. All that will work is a company-wide focus on market segments and customers with whom we want to work in the long term.

Nonetheless, here are some guidelines for managing in a recession, based on the above:

1. Remember that customers are attracted by promises, but are retained through satisfaction. This means that, if you can't describe the value required by customers, you certainly will not be able to deliver it. So, make a special point of understanding their needs.
2. Do not try to cover too many markets, segments and customers. Focus on the ones you want to be with in the long term.
3. Reduce your product portfolio, i.e. do you have too many products, services, pack sizes, etc.?
4. Look carefully at your distribution network. Has it grown too big?
5. Improve the productivity of all your promotional spend, but especially that of the sales force.

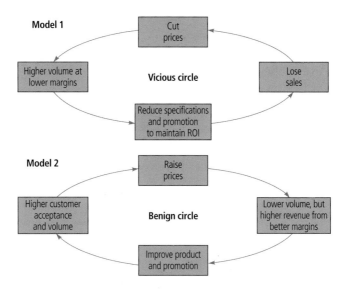

Figure 6.16: Alternative pricing models.

6. Get your costs down in unproductive areas of the business. This includes costs associated with serving unprofitable markets and customers.
7. Work out your banker (key) customers. Take them away from the sales force and give one to each of your best managers.
8. Don't let the sales force do big deals – within days everyone will have maximum discounts.
9. Selectively attack (focus) on competitors' key customers that are attractive to you. Don't worry if you lose some of your own unprofitable customers.
10. Keep the heart of the business – key products, key markets and key customers.

Above all, follow model 2 rather than model 1 in Figure 6.16.

MARKETING OBJECTIVES, STRATEGIES AND PROFITABILITY

Finally, guidelines follow on the *profitability* aspects of setting marketing objectives and strategies.

It is strongly advised, however, that you consult your accountant when considering this section, as the methodology described is quite complex and the implications are very profound for the total organization. This methodology is expanded on and explained in more detail in Chapter 13.

Valuing Key Market Segments
Background/facts
- Risk and required return are positively correlated, i.e. as risk increases, investors expect a higher return.
- Risk is measured by the volatility in expected returns, i.e. the likelihood of making a very good return or losing money. This can be described as the quality of returns.
- All assets are defined as having future value to the organization. Hence assets to be valued include not only tangible assets like plant and machinery, but intangible assets, such as key market segments.
- The present value of future cash flows is one of the most acceptable methods to value assets including key market segments.

- The present value is increased by:
  - increasing the future cash flows
  - making the future cash flows 'happen' earlier
  - reducing the risk in these cash flows, i.e. improving the certainty of these cash flows (hence the required return).

Suggested Approach

- Identify your key market segments. It is helpful if they can be classified on a vertical axis (a kind of thermometer) according to their attractiveness to your company. 'Attractiveness' usually means the potential of each for growth in your profits over a period of between three and five years and according to your relative competitive strengths in each. This will produce a Directional Policy Matrix as detailed in Chapter 5 (see Figure 6.17).
- Based on your current experience and planning horizon that you are confident with, make a projection of future net free cash in-flows from your segments. It is normal to select a period such as three or five years. These calculations will consist of three parts:
  - revenue forecasts for each year
  - cost forecasts for each year
  - net free cash flow for each segment for each year.
- Identify the key factors that are likely to either increase or decrease these future cash flows. These factors are likely to be assessed according to the following factors:
  - the riskiness of the product/market segment relative to its position on the Ansoff Matrix
  - the riskiness of the marketing strategies to achieve the revenue and market share
  - the riskiness of the forecast profitability (e.g. the cost forecast accuracy).
- Now re-calculate the revenues, costs and net free cash flows for each year, having adjusted the figures using the risks (probabilities) from the above.
- Ask your accountant to provide you with the overall SBU cost of capital and capital used in the SBU. This will not consist only of tangible assets. Thus, £1,000,000 capital at a required shareholder rate of return of 10 per cent would give £100,000 as the minimum return necessary.
- Deduct the proportional cost of capital from the free cash flow for each segment for each year.
- An aggregate positive net present value indicates that you are creating shareholder value – i.e. achieving overall returns greater than the weighted average cost of capital, having taken into account the risk associated with future cash flows.

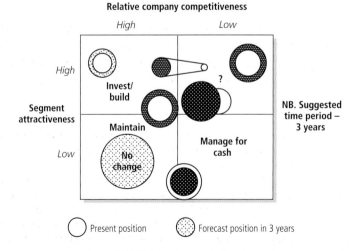

Portfolio analysis – directional policy matrix (DPM)

Figure 6.17: Valuing key market segments.

For a full explanation of the above methodology, see *Marketing Due Diligence - Reconnecting Strategy to Share Price.*[4]

CONCLUSION

Formulating marketing strategies is one of the most critical and difficult parts of the entire marketing process. It sets the limit of success. Communicated to all management levels, it indicates what strengths are to be developed, what weaknesses are to be remedied, and in what manner.

> Formulating marketing strategies is one of the most critical and difficult parts of the entire marketing process.

Marketing strategies enable operating decisions to bring the company into the right relationship with the emerging pattern of market opportunities which previous analysis has shown to offer the highest prospect of success.

Before proceeding to describe the next stage of marketing planning, i.e. the construction of actual working plans, it should be stressed that the vital phase of setting objectives and strategies is a highly complex process which, if done badly, will probably result in considerable misdirection of resources.

This chapter has confirmed the need for setting clear, definitive objectives for all aspects of marketing, and that marketing objectives themselves have to derive logically from corporate objectives. The advantages of this practice are that it allows all concerned with marketing activities to concentrate their particular contribution on achieving the overall marketing objectives, as well as facilitating meaningful and constructive evaluation of all marketing activity.

For the practical purpose of marketing planning, it will be apparent from the observations above concerning what was referred to as a hierarchy of objectives that overall marketing objectives have to be broken down into subobjectives which, taken all together, will achieve the overall objectives. By breaking down the overall objectives, the problem of strategy development becomes more manageable, hence easier.

MARKETING INSIGHT

A two-year study of 35 top industrial companies by McKinsey and Company revealed that leader companies agreed that product/market strategy is the key to the task of keeping shareholders' equity rising. Clearly, then, setting objectives and strategies in relation to products and markets is a most important step in the marketing planning process.

Once agreement has been reached on the broad marketing objectives and strategies, those responsible for programmes can now proceed to the detailed planning stage, developing the appropriate overall strategy statements into subobjectives.

Plans constitute the vehicle for getting to the destination along the chosen route, or the detailed execution of the strategy. The term 'plan' is often used synonymously in marketing literature with the terms 'programme' and 'schedule'. A plan containing detailed lists of tasks to be completed, together with responsibilities, timing and cost, is sometimes referred to as an appropriation budget, which is merely a detailing of the actions to be carried out and of the expected financial results in carrying them out. More about this in Chapters 7 to 10.

Those readers who believe they already know enough about promotion, place and pricing, and who are principally concerned with the preparation of a strategic marketing plan, can go straight to Chapter 11. Please be careful, however, as the very latest research into global best practice (spelled out in Chapters 7–10) indicates that the implications of marketing strategies will have a direct influence on the objectives from which they derive.

APPLICATION QUESTIONS

1. Critically analyse your company's corporate objectives.
2. Critically analyse your company's corporate strategies.
3. Critically analyse your company's marketing objectives.
4. Critically analyse your company's marketing strategies.
5. Has there been any product/market extension during the past 10 years which has not been compatible with your company's distinctive competence? If so, state why.
6. Draw up criteria for product/market extension which are compatible with your company's distinctive competences.

CHAPTER 6 REVIEW

Corporate objective

This is the desired level of profit the organization seeks to achieve. The *corporate strategy* for doing this covers:

1. Which products and which markets (marketing)
2. What facilities are required (e.g. operations, distribution)
3. The number and character of employees (personnel)
4. What funding is required and how (finance)
5. Social responsibility, corporate image, etc. (other corporate strategies).

Gap analysis

Gap analysis explores the shortfall between the corporate objective and what can be achieved by various strategies.

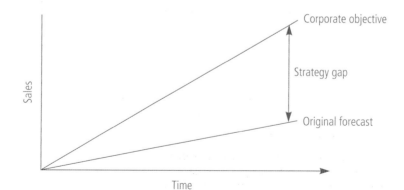

The *operations gap* can be filled by reducing costs, improving the sales mix, increasing market share.

The *strategy gap* can be filled by finding new user groups, entering new segments, geographical expansion, new product development, diversification.

Try Exercise 6.1

The marketing audit

This is the systematic collection of data and information about the external environment and about your own company's operations.

Try Exercise 6.2

The SWOT analyses

These summarize the marketing audit, which lists:

- *Internally.* The company's strengths and weaknesses.
- *Externally.* The opportunities and threats facing the company.

Each SWOT analysis should provide strong evidence about what the company should and should not try to set as marketing objectives. It should use strengths to exploit opportunities, while minimizing threats and weaknesses.

Try Exercises 6.3, 6.4 and 6.5

Marketing objectives

These are concerned with what is sold (products) and to whom it is sold (markets). There are four possible combinations of products and markets (Ansoff Matrix).

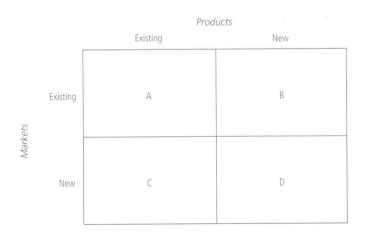

An objective contains three elements:

1. The attribute chosen for measurement, e.g. sales, market share
2. The particular value selected, e.g. 25 per cent market share
3. For a given operating period, e.g. by the end of year 3.

The matrix suggests four main categories of objectives:

A = market penetration
B = product development
C = market extension
D = diversification

Try Exercise 6.6

Marketing strategies

There are four broad strategies:

1. To invest and grow
2. To extract earnings selectively
3. To harvest
4. To divest.

There are also more specific marketing strategies concerning the four Ps:

1. *Product*
   * expand range
   * improve quality or features
   * consolidate range
   * standardize design
   * reposition product
   * change the mix
   * branding.

2. *Price*
   * change price
   * change terms and conditions
   * penetration policy
   * skimming policy.

3. *Promotion*
   * change advertising
   * change promotion
   * change the mix between call centres, direct mail and the internet
   * change selling
   * change overall communication mix.

4. *Place*
   * change channels
   * change delivery or distribution
   * change service levels
   * forward or backward integration.

Try Exercise 6.7

Questions raised for the company

1. Q: Who should set the marketing objectives and strategies?
   A: Usually they would be formulated by the marketing director, but they must be agreed at the highest level in the company so that there is genuine commitment to them.

2. Q: Is diversification really a viable objective, bearing in mind the risk in moving into the unknown?

   A: It depends how strong the *factual* evidence is for this step. Clearly it is not a decision to be taken lightly.

3. Q: How secret should marketing objectives and strategies be? Should staff at lower levels know what they are?

   A: Staff are much more committed to a company which 'knows where it is going'. Ideally subordinates should be given the necessary information to understand their job context.

4. Q: What happens if we get our marketing objectives and strategies wrong?

   A: If the process used for arriving at them was based on facts, the chances are they will not be wrong. Clearly it will be essential to monitor progress and take corrective action when required.

EXERCISES

In these exercises, the most critical part of the marketing planning process will be tackled.

Exercise 6.1 is concerned with carrying out a gap analysis.

Exercise 6.2 is concerned with collecting relevant data about your company and subjecting this to a hard-hitting examination, in summary form, of the opportunities and threats facing your organization.

Exercise 6.3 is concerned with competitor analysis, which clearly is an important part of a marketing audit.

Exercise 6.4 is concerned with carrying out a SWOT analysis.

Exercise 6.5 looks at the assumptions that are made before setting marketing objectives. Clearly, such assumptions should be kept to a minimum, but it is useful to be under no misapprehension regarding what they are, and, just as importantly, the risks attached to making such assumptions.

Exercise 6.6 gets to the heart of the matter and is concerned with setting marketing objectives, while Exercise 6.7 addresses the issue of selecting the most appropriate marketing strategies to match the chosen objectives.

Introduction to Chapter 6 exercises
Exercise 6.1 Gap analysis
Revenue

You are asked to complete this two-part exercise. The first part is concerned with revenue, the second with profit.

Objective

Start by plotting the sales position you wish to achieve at the end of the planning period, point E (Figure 6.18). Next plot the forecast position, point A.

(Continued)

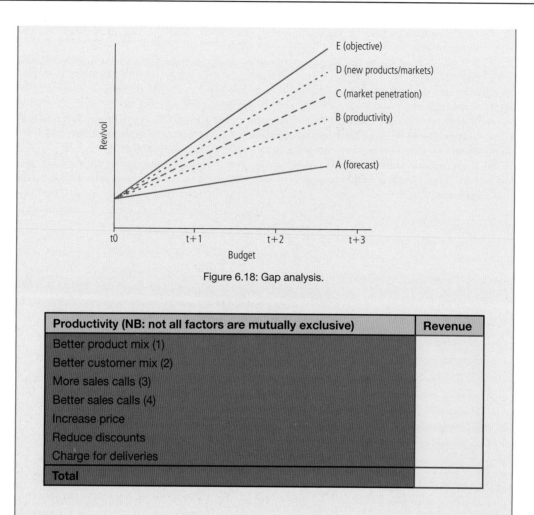

Figure 6.18: Gap analysis.

Productivity (NB: not all factors are mutually exclusive)	Revenue
Better product mix (1)	
Better customer mix (2)	
More sales calls (3)	
Better sales calls (4)	
Increase price	
Reduce discounts	
Charge for deliveries	
Total	

Table 6.2: Productivity factors (1).

Productivity

Are there any actions you can take to close the gaps under the headings in Table 6.2, point B? (These represent cash and margin focus.)

Ansoff product/market (market penetration)

List principal products on the horizontal axis (in Figure 6.19) and principal markets on the vertical axis. In each smaller square write in current sales and achievable sales during the planning period.

Next, plot the market penetration position, point C (Figure 6.20). This point will be the addition of all the values in the right hand half of the small boxes in the Ansoff Matrix. Please note, revenue from (1), (2), (3) and (4) from the productivity box should be deducted from the market penetration total before plotting point C.

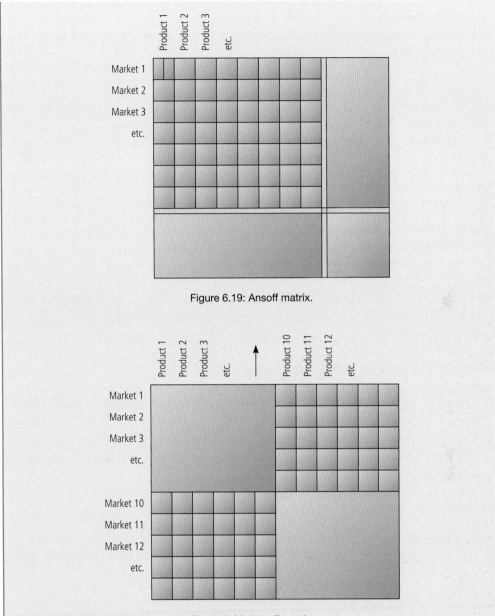

Figure 6.19: Ansoff matrix.

Figure 6.20: Ansoff matrix.

Ansoff product/market matrix (new products/new markets)

Next, list the value of any new products you might develop which you might sell to existing markets (Figure 6.20). Alternatively, or as well, if necessary, list the value of any existing products that you might sell to new markets. Plot the total value of these on Figure 6.18, point D.

(Continued)

Diversification

List the value of any new products you might develop for new markets until point E is reached. (Steps 3, 4 and 5 represent a sales growth focus.)

Capital utilization

If none of this gives the required return on investment consider changing the asset base. This could be:

(A) Acquisition

(B) Joint venture.

Profit

Objective

Start by plotting the profit position you wish to achieve at the end of the planning period, point E (Figure 6.21).

Next plot the forecast profit position, point A.

Productivity

Are there any actions you can take to close the gap under the headings in Table 6.3? Plot the total profit value of these in Figure 6.21, point B. (These represent cash and margin focus.)

Ansoff product/market (market penetration)

List principal products on the horizontal axis in Figure 6.21 and principal markets on the vertical axis. In each smaller square write in current profit and achievable profit value during the planning period.

Next plot the market penetration position, point C, Figure 6.20. This point will be the addition of all the values in the right hand half of the small boxes in the Ansoff Matrix (Figure 6.22).

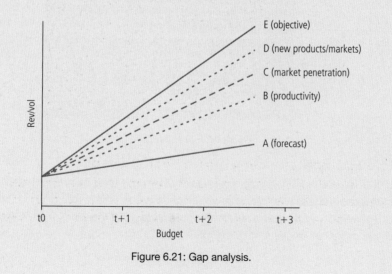

Figure 6.21: Gap analysis.

Productivity (NB: not all factors are mutually exclusive)	Profit
Better product mix	
Better customer mix	
More sales calls	
Better sales calls	
Increase price	
Reduce discounts	
Charge for deliveries	
Reduce debtor days	
Cost reduction	
Others (specify)	
Total	

Table 6.3: Productivity factors (2).

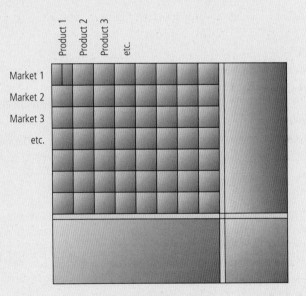

Figure 6.22: Ansoff matrix.

Ansoff product/market matrix (new products/new markets)

Next, list the value of any new products you might develop which you might sell to existing markets (Figure 6.23). Alternatively, or as well, if necessary, list the value of any existing products that you might sell to new markets. Plot the total profit value of these on Figure 6.20, point D.

(Continued)

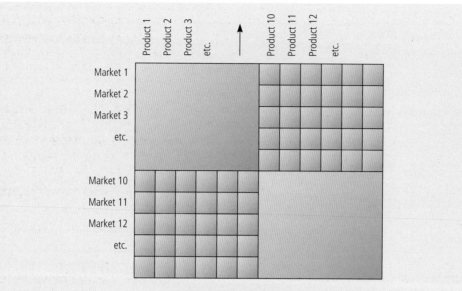

Figure 6.23: Ansoff matrix.

Diversification

List the profit value of any new products you might develop for new markets until point E is reached. (Steps 3, 4 and 5 represent a sales growth focus.)

Capital utilization

If none of this gives the required return on investment, consider changing the asset base. This could be:

(A) Acquisition

(B) Joint venture.

Exercise 6.2 The marketing audit

Stage 1 Collecting the data

All the earlier exercises in this book have been designed to improve your understanding of aspects of marketing planning and to discover information about your company and/or its key products and markets. If you completed all the preceding exercises, you should by now be in possession of a fairly comprehensive marketing audit of your organization. However, since every business is in some ways unique, there is a chance that an important piece of information might have been missed. The marketing audit checklist which follows is provided as a safeguard against this happening. (For convenience this is repeated from Chapter 2.)

Use this list to decide if there is any additional information you would want to add to that you have already collected. When you have completed assembling as much information as you can, you are in a position to progress to Stage 2 of this exercise.

The marketing audit checklist

The following is a list of factors that can affect some businesses. You should only be interested in those that will affect your particular business.

This list doesn't claim to be exhaustive but it is intended to provide fair coverage of most areas thereby acting as a guide and stimulus.

External audit

Business and economic environment
Economic
Political/fiscal/legal
Social/cultural
Technological
Intra-company

The market
Total market, size, growth and trends (value/volume)
Market characteristics, developments and trends
  Products
  Prices
  Physical distribution
  Channels
  Customers/consumers
  Communication
  Industry practices

Competition
Major competitors
Size
Market shares/coverage
Market standing/reputation
Production capabilities
Distribution policies
Marketing methods
Extent of diversification
Personnel issues
International links
Profitability
Key strengths and weaknesses

Internal audit

Marketing operational variables
Own company
Sales (total, by geographical location, by industrial
    type, by customer, by product)
Market shares
Profit margins/costs
Marketing procedures
Marketing organization

Marketing information/research
Marketing mix variables as follows:
  Product management
  Price
  Distribution
  Promotion

(Continued)

The marketing audit checklist (fuller details)
EXTERNAL (opportunities and threats)
Business and economic environment

Economic	Inflation, unemployment, energy, price, volatility, materials availability, etc.	as they affect your business
Political/fiscal/ legal	Nationalization, union legislation, human rights legislation, taxation, duty increases, regulatory constraints (e.g. labelling, product quality, packaging, trade practices, advertising, pricing, etc.)	as they affect your business
Social/cultural	Education, immigration, emigration, religion, environment, population distribution and dynamics (e.g. age distribution, regional distribution, etc.), changes in consumer lifestyle, etc.	as they affect your business
Technological	Aspects of product and/or production technology which could profoundly affect the economics of the industry (e.g. new technology, the internet, cost savings, materials, components, equipment, machinery, methods and systems, availability of substitutes, etc.)	as they affect your business
Intra-company	Capital investment, closures, strikes, etc.	as they affect your business

The market

Total market	Size, growth, and trends (value, volume).

Customers/consumers: changing demographics, psychographics and purchasing behaviour. |
| *Marketing characteristics, developments and trends* | *Products*: principal products bought; end-use of products; product characteristics (weights, measures, sizes, physical characteristics, packaging, accessories, associated products, etc.).

Prices: price levels and range; terms and conditions of sale; normal trade practices; official regulations; etc.

Physical distribution: principal method of physical distribution
Channels: principal channels; purchasing patterns (e.g. types of product bought, prices paid, etc.); purchasing ability; geographical location; stocks; turnover; profits; needs; tastes; attitudes; decision makers, bases of purchasing decision; etc.
Communication: principal methods of communication, e.g. the internet, sales force, advertising, direct response, exhibitions, public relations, etc. Industry practices: e.g. trade associations, government bodies, historical attitudes, interfirm comparisons, etc. Industry practices: e.g. trade associations, government bodies, historical attitudes, interfirm comparisons, etc. |

Competition   *Industry structure*: make-up of companies in the industry, major market standing/reputation; extent of excess capacity; production capability; distribution capability; marketing methods; competitive arrangements; extent of diversification into other areas by major companies in the industry; new entrants; mergers; acquisitions; bankruptcies; significant aspects; international links; key strengths and weaknesses.

Industry profitability: financial and non-financial barriers to entry; industry profitability and the relative performance of individual companies; structure of operating costs; investment; effect on return on investment of changes in price; volume; cost of investment; source of industry profits; etc.

INTERNAL (strengths and weaknesses)

Own company

Sales (total, by geographical location, by industrial type, by customer, by product)

Market shares

Profit margins

Marketing procedures

Marketing organization

Sales/marketing control data

Marketing mix variables as follows:

Market research	Samples
Product development	Exhibitions
Product range	Selling
Product quality	Sales aids
Unit of sale	Point of sale
Stock levels	Advertising
Distribution	Sales promotion
Dealer support	Public relations
Pricing, discounts, credit	After-sales service
Packaging	Training

Operations and resources

Marketing objectives

Are the marketing objectives clearly stated and consistent with marketing and corporate objectives?

Marketing strategy

What is the strategy for achieving the stated objectives? Are sufficient resources available to achieve these objectives? Are the available resources sufficient and optimally allocated across elements of the marketing mix?

Structure

Are the marketing responsibilities and authorities clearly structured along functional, product, end-user, and territorial lines?

(Continued)

Information system
Is the marketing intelligence system producing accurate, sufficient and timely information about developments in the marketplace? Is information gathered being used effectively in making marketing decisions?

Planning system
Is the marketing planning system well conceived and effective?

Control system
Do control mechanisms and procedures exist within the group to ensure planned objectives are achieved, e.g. meeting overall objectives, etc.?

Functional efficiency
Are internal communications within the group effective?

Interfunctional efficiency
Are there any problems between marketing and other corporate functions? Is the question of centralized versus decentralized marketing an issue in the company?

Profitability analysis
Is the profitability performance monitored by product, served markets, etc. to assess where the best profits and biggest costs of the operation are located?

Cost-effectiveness analysis
Do any current marketing activities seem to have excess costs? Are these valid or could they be reduced?

Stage 2 SWOT analyses

From the above list you will see that the *external* factors are the sources of all opportunities or threats, whereas the *internal* factors reflect the company's strengths or weaknesses.

In respect of *external factors (opportunities and threats)*, try the following exercise:

Step 1	List the principal opportunities (we suggest no more than 20).
Step 2	Allocate a code to each of these (e.g. A, B, C, etc.)
Step 3	Allocate a number between 1 and 9 to each of them. The number 1 means that in your view there is little chance of a particular opportunity occurring within the planning timescale (say three years). A 9 would mean that there is a high probability of it occurring within the planning timescale.
Step 4	Allocate a number between 1 and 9 to indicate the importance of the *impact* each of these opportunities would have on the organization, were it to occur.
Step 5	Now put each of your opportunities on the opportunities matrix (Figure 6.24).

Step 6   You will now have a number of points of intersection which should correspond to your coding system.

Step 7   All those in the top left box should be tackled in your marketing objectives
and should appear in your SWOT analysis (Exercise 6.4). All the others, while
they should not be ignored, are obviously less urgent. The whole exercise
should now be repeated for threats, using the matrix in Figure 6.25.

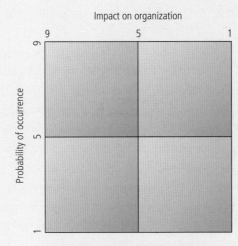

Figure 6.24: Opportunities matrix.

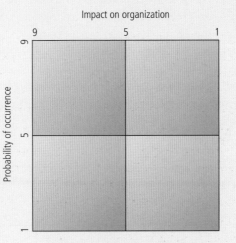

Figure 6.25: Threats matrix.

(Continued)

Exercise 6.3 Competitor analysis

Exercise 6.3 is concerned with summarizing the information gathered about your opportunities and threats in your marketing audit in a more usable format, in the SWOT analysis.

Before moving on to the SWOT analysis (Exercise 6.4), complete the competitor analysis table (Table 6.4) in order to help you to rate yourself more accurately against your competitors.

Guidelines for completing Table 6.4 are given below.

Guide to competitive position classifications

Leadership	Has major influence on performance or behaviour of others.
Strong	Has a wide choice of strategies.
	Able to adopt independent strategy without endangering short-term position. Has low vulnerability to competitors' actions.
Favourable	Exploits specific competitive strength, often in a product/market niche.
	Has more than average opportunity to improve position; several strategies available.
Tenable	Performance justifies continuation in business.
Weak	Currently unsatisfactory performance; significant competitive weakness. Inherently a short-term condition; must improve or withdraw.

The following list includes five business directions that are appropriate for almost any business. Select those that best summarize the competitor's strategy.

Business directions

1. *Enter* – allocate resources to a new business area. Consideration should include building from prevailing company or unit strengths, exploiting related opportunities and defending against perceived threats. It may mean creating a new industry.
2. *Improve* – to apply strategies that will significantly improve the competitive position of the business. Often requires thoughtful product/market segmentation.
3. *Maintain* – to maintain one's competitive position. Aggressive strategies may be required, although a defensive posture may also be assumed. Product/market position is maintained, often in a niche.

Main competitor	Products/ markets	Business direction and current objectives and strategies	Strengths	Weaknesses	Competitive position

Table 6.4: Competitor analysis

4. *Harvest* – to relinquish intentionally competitive position, emphasizing short-term profit and cash flow but not necessarily at the risk of losing the business in the short term. Often entails consolidating or reducing various aspects of the business to create higher performance for that which remains.

5. *Exit* – to divest oneself of a business because of its weak competitive position or because the cost of staying in it is prohibitive, and the risk associated with improving its position is too high.

Exercise 6.4 The SWOT analysis

Having completed the marketing audit, your task now is to summarize it into a cogent and interesting analysis of your company's particular situation in each major segment. The SWOT approach (the word SWOT incidentally being derived from the initial letters of Strengths, Weaknesses, Opportunities and Threats) will enable you to list in simple terms:

1. Your company's differential strengths and weaknesses *vis-à-vis* competitors.
2. Where the best opportunities exist, i.e. market segments.
3. The present and future threats to your business in the market segments.

The SWOT analysis for each segment should only be a few pages in length and should concern itself with key factors only, supported by relevant data.

Some of the most valuable information for the SWOT analysis will come from the life-cycle analysis and the portfolio matrix you prepared in Chapter 5. The former will give you insights about the prospects for your key products and/or services and this information can then be used on the portfolio matrix, thereby highlighting how the portfolio will change. An example of this is shown in Figure 6.26.

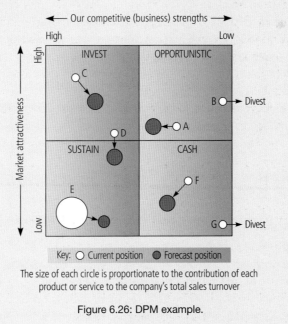

Figure 6.26: DPM example.

(Continued)

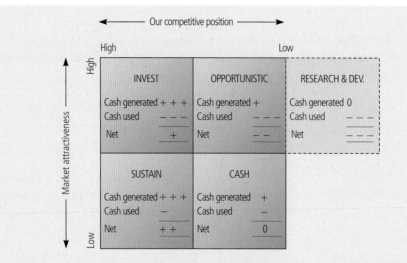

Figure 6.27: DPM guidelines.

In Figure 6.26, clearly the future portfolio is going to be significantly different from the current one. Products/segments B and G will disappear. The sales volume of A, C and D will increase, while that of E will reduce quite dramatically. All this has a tremendous bearing on how funds are generated, and, again, this is where the portfolio matrix can be helpful in letting one understand what is happening. If you recall, the text explained that different quadrants of the matrix had different characteristics when viewed as sources of funds (Figure 6.27). Although this comes from the Boston Matrix, it is just as relevant to the directional policy matrix shown in Figure 6.26.

The significance of this for any company is to have a balanced portfolio, where there are adequate 'sustains' to fund research and development and selected 'opportunistics'.

The effort and costs associated with keeping the market share for 'invests' makes them unreliable sources of funds. The benefits will be reaped later when today's 'invests' sink into the 'sustain' quadrant.

You can now proceed to complete the pro forma provided in respect of all your key market segments. Thus, if you have six key market segments, you will complete six pro formas. In this book, we have provided you with one. If you need more, just repeat the exercise using duplicate forms. See Figure 6.28.

A more detailed approach to completing the pro forma in Figure 6.28 now follows and we recommend that you read this next section most carefully.

Exercise 6.5 Assumptions

Any SWOT analysis should *not* look like the one given in Figure 6.29.

The problem with these is that they are far too generalized and tend to be conducted on what we describe here as 'the average customer/consumer' and, of course, we now understand from the segmentation section in Chapter 4 that there is no such 'person'. The result of SWOTs like this is that they end up with vapid, meaningless words and the authors have

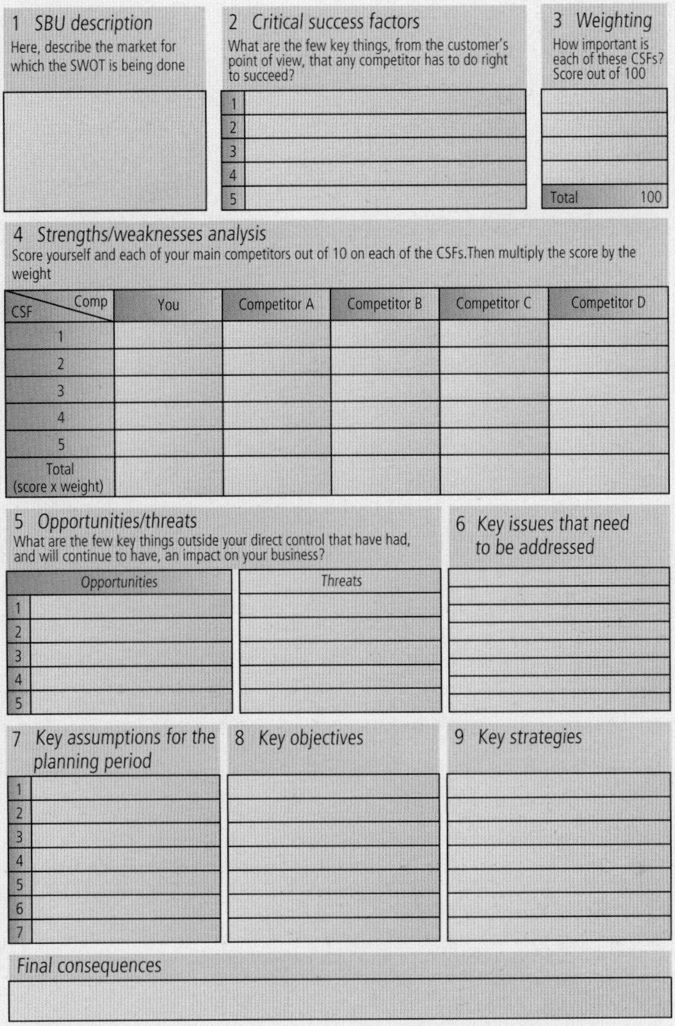

1 SBU description	2 Critical success factors	3 Weighting
Here, describe the market for which the SWOT is being done	What are the few key things, from the customer's point of view, that any competitor has to do right to succeed?	How important is each of these CSFs? Score out of 100

4 Strengths/weaknesses analysis
Score yourself and each of your main competitors out of 10 on each of the CSFs. Then multiply the score by the weight

CSF \ Comp	You	Competitor A	Competitor B	Competitor C	Competitor D
1					
2					
3					
4					
5					
Total (score x weight)					

5 Opportunities/threats
What are the few key things outside your direct control that have had, and will continue to have, an impact on your business?

Opportunities	Threats	**6 Key issues that need to be addressed**
1		
2		
3		
4		
5		

7 Key assumptions for the planning period	8 Key objectives	9 Key strategies
1		
2		
3		
4		
5		
6		
7		

Final consequences

Figure 6.28: Strategic planning exercise (SWOT analysis).

Note: This form should be completed for each product/market segment under consideration.

seen hundreds of such analyses over the years. They represent a kind of 'My head is in the oven and my feet are in the fridge, so we must be comfortable on average' sentiment. So, please avoid this at all costs and concentrate on the methodology spelled out below.

At a general level, however, there are some guidelines, which are set out in Figure 6.30. Conducting meaningful, useful SWOTs, however, is still a difficult managerial exercise. For example, on the pro forma provided in Figure 6.28, it will be seen that in Column 2 there are only five spaces. The problem here, however, is a tendency to write in words for critical

(Continued)

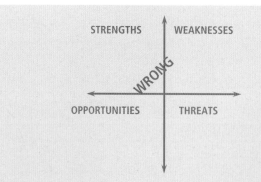

Figure 6.29: A meaningless SWOT analysis.

Strengths
It can create value for the
organisation/customer
It is unique
It is inimitable
It is lasting

Weaknesses
It is meaningful to the customer
It is unique
It is difficult to fix

Threats
It is significant
It is lasting

Opportunities
It is large
It is accessible
It is lasting

Figure 6.30: Guidelines for a meaningful SWOT analysis.

success factors (CSFs), such as 'product', 'price', 'promotion' and 'service', all of which are meaningless unless accompanied by more detailed explanation.

The following case will explain a methodology for making the summary headings in Column 2 of Figure 6.28 more meaningful.

Figure 6.31 shows five key buying principles for parents who are considering which private school to send their children to. More importantly, however, Figures 6.32 to 6.35 show the details behind each of these headings. In this example, it is in order to put in Column 2 of Figure 6.28 'Affordability', for example, but behind this summary heading, a more detailed analysis will have been completed, otherwise 'Affordability' becomes just another vapid, meaningless word.

Finally, for presentation purposes in the actual marketing plan, it is often useful to present the strengths/weaknesses data as a bar chart, as shown in Figure 6.36.

The lessons to be learned from the above example are crucial to conducting a truly powerful SWOT on each important product/market segment.

Often it is forgotten that in conducting the SWOT analysis we have had to make assumptions, or educated guesses, about some of the factors that will affect the business, e.g. about market-growth rates, about government economic policy, about the activities of our competitors, etc. Most planning assumptions tend to deal with the environment or market trends and as such are critical to the fulfilment of the planned marketing objectives and strategies.

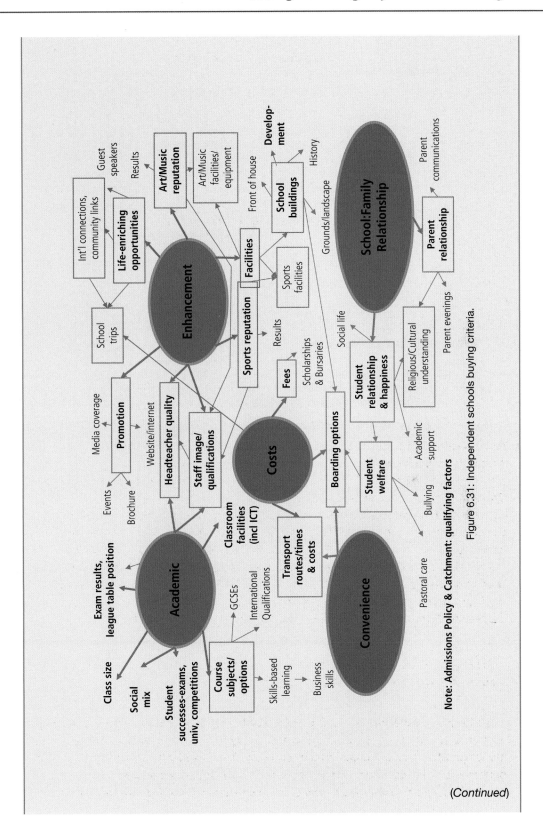

Figure 6.31: Independent schools buying criteria.

Note: Admissions Policy & Catchment: qualifying factors

(Continued)

Academic factors

Personality and vision of Head

Exam results

Class size

League table position (compared to regional competitors)

Student academic successes (Oxbridge, major universities, competitions)

Academic planning: A level, IB, pre-U; IGCSE? New subjects?

Flexibility of subject choice

Academic history (results over a number of years)

Quality/knowledge/experience of staff

Facilities for teaching and learning

Learning opportunities outside mainstream subjects (could be vocational skills)

Reporting procedures

Innovations in teaching and learning

Figure 6.32: Academic factors.

Enhancement/Attractiveness factors

Facilities
 – **Buildings and grounds**
 – **Specialist facilities** (floodlit astroturf, ICT centre, theatre)
 – **Development Planning**: plans for new/better facilities

People
 – **Quality of staff** (teaching and specialist – ie sports/music coaching)
 – Quality of staff recruitment
 – Front of House/customer focus
 – **Understanding/delivery of mission** by all staff
 – Strong **alumni association**
 – Active **parents' association**

'Preparation for Life'
 – Active **careers department**
 – Expertise in **university entrance support**
 – **Work experience, Young Enterprise**, Duke of Edinburgh's Award, Sports Leader's Award etc.

Community
 – **Links** through activities (charity fundraising, visits to elderly, working with handicapped etc.)
 – **Hire of facilities** (pool, theatre, sports, hall for weddings and parties)
 – Compliant with **Charities Act**
 – **Local reputation**

International links and opportunities
 – Language visits
 – Trips and expeditions
 – Other learning opportunities

Technology
 – Up-to-date, campus-wide access
 – Resources online to enhance study

Environmental
 – Clear **policy** and aims
 – Strong **student involvement in campaigns and issues**
 – Clear **priority status** within School – put into action

Figure 6.33: Enhancement factors.

Relationship factors

Pastoral Care
- **Welfare**: support, information, training, awareness
- Responsiveness
- **Structures**
- **Policies**: availability, clarity

Ethos
- **Mission, values**
- Tangible, delivered from top down

Parents' association

Alumni association

Communications
- Internet, intranet
- Events
- Printed communications
- Policies and procedures
- Management of problems

Figure 6.34: Relationship factors.

Cost factors

Fees
- Fee increases yr-to-yr

Scholarships
- Type? (sports, academic, all-round, music, art)
- % discount

Bursaries
- % range
- Means-testing

Sibling discounts

Transport costs

Trips, other extra costs on the bill

Price relative to regional competitors

Figure 6.35: Cost factors.

What then are the risks attached to making assumptions? Suppose we get it wrong?

To give some measure of risk assessment, a technique has been developed that looks at the assumption from the negative point of view. It leads one to ask 'What can go wrong with each assumption that would change the outcome?' For example, suppose the product was an oil derivative and was thus extremely sensitive to the price of oil. For planning purposes an assumption about the price of oil would have to be made. Using this 'Downside risk' technique we would assess to what level the price could rise before increased material costs would make our products too expensive and cause our marketing plans to be completely revised.

Now complete the following 'Downside risk assessment form' (Table 6.5) to evaluate some of the key assumptions you used in your SWOT analyses, and which you are now to use as the basis for setting marketing objectives and strategies.

(Continued)

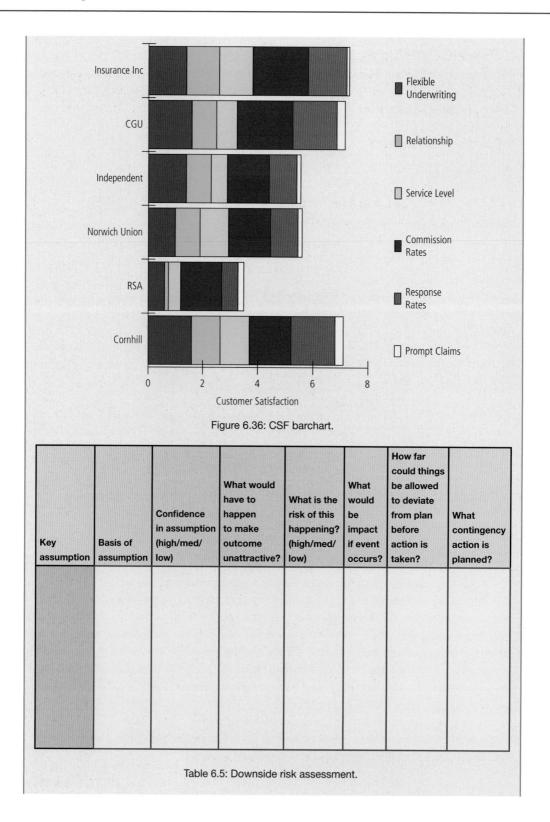

Figure 6.36: CSF barchart.

Key assumption	Basis of assumption	Confidence in assumption (high/med/low)	What would have to happen to make outcome unattractive?	What is the risk of this happening? (high/med/low)	What would be impact if event occurs?	How far could things be allowed to deviate from plan before action is taken?	What contingency action is planned?

Table 6.5: Downside risk assessment.

Exercise 6.6 Setting marketing objectives

Marketing objectives are solely concerned with which products go to which markets, and marketing strategies are concerned with how that is done. Therefore, because marketing objectives are only concerned about products and markets, an extremely useful planning aid is provided by the Ansoff Matrix, depicted in Figure 6.37.

This matrix suggests there are four types of marketing objective:

1. Selling established products into established markets (market penetration).
2. Selling established products into new markets (market extension).
3. Selling new products into established markets (product development).
4. Selling new products into new markets (diversification).

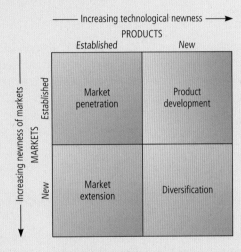

Figure 6.37: The Ansoff matrix.

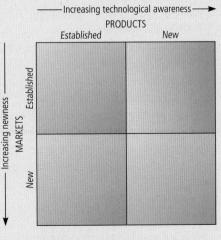

Figure 6.38: The Ansoff matrix.

(Continued)

Task 1

Using the blank Ansoff Matrix (Figure 6.38), or perhaps using a larger sheet of paper, draw the matrix for your company's products and markets.

Please note that when you consider whether or not a market is new or established, the question you must ask yourself is 'How long does it take to get one's distinctive competence known in this market?' If you have been dealing with the market for anything less than your answer to this question, then that is a new market.

Similarly, new products are those probably at the early stages of their lifecycles, where the company is still 'learning' how to make them, i.e. it hasn't solved all the operational, scheduling, quality, design and technical problems in the same way as it has for the established products.

Task 2

Combining the information on the Ansoff Matrix with that of your SWOT analyses, pick out those areas of business that offer the best prospects for your company. For each one, summarize your marketing objective for your longer-term planning horizon, i.e. 2, 3, 4 or 5 years. This must be quite explicit in terms of:

1. The product/service
2. The customer/market segment
3. The volume of sales
4. The market share.

Now repeat the exercise, stating the specific objectives for the first year of your planning horizon.

The marketing objectives should be consistent with the information from the product lifecycle analysis and portfolio matrix, completed in Chapter 5. Further guidance is provided in the notes which follow.

Guidelines for setting marketing objectives

Contained within your SWOT analyses will be key information gleaned from your marketing audit. You will know the reasons why customers want your products or services. You will know your best market segments. You will know the 'life' of your products or services and, probably most important of all, the portfolio matrix will have shown you how the various items of your range relate to each other in terms of raising funds.

Creative and intelligent interpretation of the portfolio matrix is the secret behind setting the right marketing objectives for your company. For this to happen, it is important to distinguish the essentially different characteristics of products or services falling into the four quadrants of the matrix. Let us take in turn:

Invest

Products or services in this quadrant are by implication aimed at those markets most attractive to your company. These will almost certainly be the markets with the higher growth rates.

Marketing objectives for such products should be calculated to match or exceed the market-growth rate and thereby hold or extend the company's market share. Since these markets are likely to be attractive to others, the company will have to be aggressive to achieve its objectives.

This marketing posture has to be supported by tight budgeting and control processes to ensure that all resources are used effectively. Concern for present earnings should be subordinate to the main thrust of keeping or extending market share.

The increase in sales looked for in these products or services is likely to come from:

1. Possible geographic expansion
2. Possible product line expansion
3. Possible product line differentiation.

These may be achieved by internal development, acquisition or joint ventures.

Sustain

In these less attractive markets it doesn't make sense to go for aggressive growth as with the invest quadrant – it would prove to be too costly and counterproductive. Instead, the objectives should be aimed at maintaining a profitable position with greater emphasis on present earnings.

The most successful products/services should be maintained, while less successful ones should be pruned. Marketing effort should be aimed at maintaining the market share of key market segments with minimum expenditure. Prices should be stabilized except when a temporary aggressive stance is required to maintain market share.

Sustain products must be managed to be the major source of funding for the company.

Selective

For products/services in this quadrant there are two broad choices:

1. Invest in the products for future earnings, i.e. groom them to be tomorrow's invest products and subsequent sustain products; or
2. Manage them for present earnings.

In practice it is only feasible to 'groom' a limited number of question marks and so these have to be carefully chosen for their genuine potential. Investment across the range would be prohibitive.

Cash

In effect there are two kinds of product/service in this quadrant:

1. Genuine cash products (to the right of the quadrant)
2. Select products (to the left of the quadrant, adjacent to the sustain quadrant).

The marketing objectives for *genuine cash products* should be to divest where appropriate or to manage for present earnings. Marketing expenditure should be minimized, product lines pruned and prices stabilized or raised where possible, even at the expense of sales volume.

(Continued)

The marketing objectives for *select products* should acknowledge the low growth/ attractiveness of these products and services, but still seek to identify and exploit growth segments, not by flying in the face of reason and trying to restore the product to its previous higher growth rate by costly advertising and promotion, but by emphasizing product quality and looking for improvements in productivity. Judicious marketing expenditure might be reasonable in special circumstances, but the emphasis should be on maximizing present earnings.

Exercise 6.7 Marketing strategies

Now that the marketing objectives have determined what the company must achieve, you have to decide how that might be done by your marketing strategies. Whereas there are only four types of marketing objective, there are a whole range of possible marketing strategies which can be used either singly or in combination with others. A choice of possible marketing strategies is shown in the list below.

Using this list, identify the broad marketing strategies most supportive to each of the marketing objectives you set for the company. Having done this, you will probably find it helpful to refer back to Figure 6.5. The left hand column of this figure lists the marketing variables that need to be considered, such as pricing, distribution, etc. The other columns represent the key positions on the portfolio matrix and are headed accordingly. Thus it becomes a fairly straightforward procedure to identify the best marketing strategies for your chosen objectives.

Chapters 7–10 will provide you with additional information about advertising, sales promotion, selling, pricing and distribution. Only finalize your marketing strategies after completing these later sections of this book.

Possible marketing strategies

1. Change product performance
2. Change quality or features of product
3. Change advertising
4. Change promotion
5. Change pricing
6. Change delivery arrangements
7. Change distribution channels
8. Change service levels
9. Improve operational efficiency
10. Improve marketing efficiency
11. Improve administrative procedures
12. Change the degree of forward integration
13. Change the degree of backward integration
14. Rationalize product range
15. Withdraw from selected markets
16. Standardize design
17. Specialize in certain products/markets
18. Change sourcing

19. Buy into new markets
20. Acquire new/different facilities
21.
22.
23.
24.

   Add any other strategies that occur to you in the spaces provided.

REFERENCES

1. Ansoff, I. (1957) Strategies for diversification. *Harvard Business Review*, Sept./Oct.
2. Porter, M.E. (1980) *Competitive Strategy*. The Free Press, New York.
3. Reichheld, F.F. and Sasser, W.E. (1990) Zero defections: quality comes to services. *Harvard Business Review*, Sept./Oct., 105–111.
4. McDonald, M.H., Smith, B. and Ward, K. (2006) Marketing *Due Diligence: Reconnecting Strategy to Share Price*. Butterworth-Heinemann, Oxford.

Chapter

THE INTEGRATED MARKETING COMMUNICATIONS PLAN

SUMMARY

- Defining communications objectives
- Methods for deciding on the communication mix
- Advertising
- Digital communications
- Sales promotion
- Public relations
- Sponsorship
- Exercises to turn the theory into practice

INTRODUCTION

Now that we have explored the important area of marketing objectives and strategies, let us turn our attention to the question of how we communicate with customers, both current and potential. The number of ways of communicating with customers is increasing all the time, though it is still possible to distinguish the following two main categories:

1. *Impersonal communications*, e.g. advertising, point-of-sale displays, sales promotions, search engine marketing and public relations.
2. *Personal communications*, e.g. sales meetings, personal e-mails and company moderated online forums.

Another important distinction is between *broadcast* media, such as traditional television, radio and press advertising, and *interactive* media, such as websites, social networks and call centres.

Companies have at their disposal an armoury of communication techniques, which may be used either singly or in a combination (the 'communication mix') as the particular situation demands, to achieve maximum effect within given budget constraints.

Companies with acknowledged professionalism in the area of communicating with customers are continually experimenting with the mix of communication techniques they employ in an attempt to become more cost-effective in this important, sometimes expensive, part of their business.

A number of the possible means of communicating with customers will now be examined under the two broad headings of impersonal and personal communications. This chapter will look in more detail at advertising and sales promotion with the objective of deciding how to go about preparing detailed plans for these important elements of the marketing mix. In Chapter 8, we will do the same for personal selling and the sales plan.

But while companies need expertise in this plethora of techniques, it is all too easy for companies to lose sight of what they are trying to achieve. So the aim of integrated marketing communications is to combine our communications efforts so that customers feel that they have a single, consistent conversation with the firm, helping both parties to achieve their objectives. We will therefore begin by examining how this can be achieved.

DEFINING COMMUNICATIONS OBJECTIVES

Before any decision can be made about whether to spend any money on advertising and promotions at all, let alone *how* to spend it, we need to be clear on whether communications are the right way to achieve our marketing objectives. It is all too easy for communications specialists and their budgets to become a solution looking for a problem.

A major mobile telecoms company found that the vast sums it was spending on advertising were having very little effect. Continuous experience tracking by an innovative market research firm, Mesh Planning, found that prospective customers were listening instead to negative word of mouth from current customers who were aggrieved at low service levels. The moral was clear: focus on putting service right first.

So, the first question that has to be grappled with is how to determine the communications objectives. Fortunately, the tools we covered in Chapters 4 to 6 provide an ideal basis for determining these communications objectives. Here is an example.

CASE STUDY

SETTING COMMUNICATIONS OBJECTIVES – A MAJOR TYRE COMPANY

The country director of a major tyre company felt that the company ought to be doing better in the car market, given the high quality of his premium imported product as compared with lower-quality locally manufactured competitors. He decided to construct a directional policy matrix (which we described in Chapter 5) but soon realized that he had insufficient information about how the market segmented. So he commissioned some market research which led to the four segments illustrated in Figure 7.1.

The price-sensitive segment was easily discounted. While amounting to about 20 per cent of the market, there was no way that the

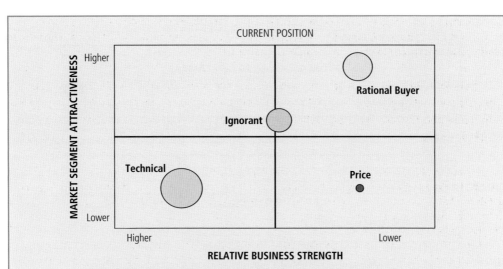

Figure 7.1: A tyre company – directional policy matrix.

company's expensive imported tyres could compete here with the locally manufactured competition. Neither would the managing director want to, as margins in this segment were wafer-thin or non-existent.

His strongest segment was the 'technical' buyers, who knew about cars, or at least thought they did. They recognized the superior quality of the company's product, and when they could afford it, they bought it. But this wasn't the most attractive segment to him. Far from being brand loyal, these customers were as likely to buy from an obscure but good-quality competitor as from his well-known brand, and they were acutely aware of market prices.

The 'ignorant' segment was at least less price sensitive. These customers would buy primarily on brand image and on the recommendation of the dealer.

But the most attractive segment was the 'rational buyers'. In the UK market we would call these 'Which? readers', after a consumer magazine. If they didn't know about tyres, they would quiz the dealer, read promotional materials or ask a friend in the trade, in an attempt to come to a reasonably informed decision. Typically in middle to high income brackets, they didn't mind paying a bit extra for a quality product. And yet they were not currently buying his product in great numbers.

How could he increase his share with this segment? The critical success factor analysis (see Chapter 5) in Figure 7.2, which compares his company's performance against a leading competitor on the segment's main buying criteria, showed what he needed to do. While he could do little about the high perceived price, the durability scores showed that customers didn't realize that the company's high quality led to a high durability and therefore just as good a price per mile. And neither had they taken in thc high safety specification.

These perceptual issues were ideal targets for advertising. The managing director cancelled his current, technology-focused advertising campaign, and a few months later launched a new campaign focused at this target segment, and in particular at their perceptions of durability and safety. Due to his market research, he was able to brief his advertising agency on the target segment: who they were, what television programmes they watched, what they read, what sports they liked, and so on.

The strategy worked: overall car tyre sales duly went up, with a doubling of his market share over three years, as he succeeded in attracting more of the profitable 'rational buyers' without losing his share of the 'technical' segment. This was achieved with no incremental spend whatsoever.

Car tyres-for-Cluster4					i

Current Critical Success Factor Scores

accept	cancel	close			done

	Factor	Weight	Score	Contribution	Competitor	Contribution
1:	Durability	18	2	0.36	3	0.54
2:	Quality	21	3	0.63	2	0.42
3:	Price	15	2	0.3	4	0.6
4:	Safety	22	3	0.66	4	0.88
5:	Track record	11	5	0.55	6	0.66
6:	Dealer support	13	5	0.65	5	0.65

Strength in Market : 3.2   Competitor: 3.8

Product-For-Market Snapshot

Figure 7.2: Measuring perceived performance against buying criteria.

Education and information	To . . . create awareness; inform; get enquiries
Branding and image building	Get company name in file Create company image Reach personnel inaccessible to salespeople
Affecting attitudes	Ease the selling task Get editorial Overcome prejudice Influence end-users
Loyalty and reminding	Reduce selling costs Achieve sales

Table 7.1: Some communication objectives

This example illustrates the point we made in Chapter 6 about how critical success factor analysis can be used as a basis for determining marketing strategies. In this case, the problem was purely a perceptual one, so the solution related solely to communication. More often than not, though, we are pulling multiple levers to increase sales, with marketing strategies that also relate to pricing, product design, distribution, and so on. The objectives of the communication part of this marketing mix are therefore more specific than increasing sales. Some common communication objectives are shown in Table 7.1.

CHOOSING THE COMMUNICATION MIX

Once we know what we are trying to communicate, based on critical success factor analysis, our next task is to decide what communications tools to use. The most common method of choosing communications tools is sheer habit! Another common method has equally little to commend it – blindly copying the competition. While communications agencies have a vested interest in persuading marketing managers that they need to achieve the same 'share of voice' as their competitors, hence ratcheting up spend across a sector, this can lead to a collective delusion that spend will necessarily lead to results. The tyre company we discussed in the previous section achieved exceptional results not by spending more, but by spending appropriately to its target segments and their buying criteria.

Fortunately, then, there are three more sensible ways of choosing the communications mix.

1. Matching Communications Tool Strengths with the Purpose of the Communication

A good place to start is to consider which of the following four tasks the communication needs to achieve:

* *Differentiate.* Positioning the company, product or brand so that it is perceived to be different from its competitors.
* *Reinforce.* Reminding or reassuring customers about a brand
* *Inform.* Making customers aware of a brand's existence or attributes
* *Persuade.* Encouraging customers to behave in particular ways.

Communication tools clearly have different strengths with respect to these four tasks. Advertising is good at informing prospective customers that the product exists and about its basic features. It is also good for differentiating, as we saw with the tyre company. Sales promotion can be useful for persuading prospective customers who already have a favourable attitude to translate this attitude into purchase, such as by offering a trial or favourable payment terms. Personal selling can also be persuasive in translating positive attitudes into a concrete forward plan, through the consultative problem-solving process which is difficult to achieve by other means. Direct marketing suits persuasive tasks which do not require such complex discussion, and can also play a role in reinforcing brand messages to existing customers.

2. Matching Communications to Segment Media Consumption

A great advantage of a good segmentation is in selecting appropriate media. It is important that segmentation projects include a profile of media usage for each segment. This is then invaluable in selecting the communications mix. An example for a house-builder is in Table 7.2. By focusing on the media within this list, which were unique to each segment, spend could be tautly focused on target segments with advertisements designed to appeal to each. Unusually for this sector, these advertisements contained pictures not of houses but of 'people like me', as research had shown that a like-minded community of neighbours was a key buying criterion. An advertisement for young single women, for example, had a picture of 'Emily' saying: 'Warm, stylish and well built. If only I could find a man like that!'

3. Combining Communications Tools in the Customer Journey

There is plenty of evidence that integrated campaigns work better than single-channel ones even when you are targeting a specific segment – provided the channels are complementing each other and not just repeating the same message. TV might be used, for example, for initial emotional engagement, followed by direct marketing for eliciting a direct response, and online for developing a dialogue and peer-to-peer advocacy, for example.

Single and young couples	20–34, no kids	Selective TV, cinema, posters, magazines
Young families	20–34, kids aged 1–4	Satellite/channel 4, radio, parenting magazines, posters
Mature families	35–54, kids aged 5–15	Weekend newspapers, home magazines, ITV, posters
Empty nesters	45+, no kids	TV, newspapers, magazines
Retired	65+, no kids	Day TV, regional press

Table 7.2: Aligning communications media to target segments: a housebuilder.

So a useful approach is to map the customer's journey from first awareness of the company or product through to purchase and repurchase. Often, communications tools work in combination at different points of this journey. For many years, people believed that advertising worked in a delightfully simple way, with the advertiser sending a message and the target receiving it and understanding it. Research, however, has shown that in a grossly overcommunicated society, the process is more complex. Figure 7.3 gives some indication of the process involved.

In business-to-business contexts, the buying process is complicated by the involvement of several people – the 'decision-making unit'. Let us consider two separate surveys on how industry buys. These are shown in Tables 7.3 and 7.4. Even a cursory glance at these will reveal the following information:

1. More than one person has an influence on what is bought.
2. Salespeople do not manage to see all the important 'influencers'.
3. Companies get the information on which they make their decisions from a variety of sources, only one of which is the salesperson.

Generally, it is possible to split the decision-making process into several distinct steps, such as the following:

1. The buyer organization recognizes it has a problem and works out a general solution. For example, the design team of a new plant, or piece of machinery, may decide that they need a specialist component which cannot be provided from within the company or from existing suppliers' stocks.

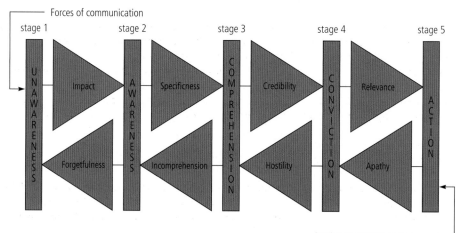

Figure 7.3: Brand loyalty ladder: the five stages of communication.

Number of employees	Average number of buying influences	Average number of contacts made by salespeople
0–200	3.42	1.72
201–400	4.85	1.75
401–1,000	5.81	1.90
1,000+	6.50	1.65

Table 7.3: Buying influences by company size

Source: McGraw-Hill

	% Small companies	% Large companies
Trade and technical press	28	60
Salesperson – calls	47	19
Exhibitions	8	12
Direct mail	19	9

Table 7.4: Sources of information

Source: Maclean Hunter

2. The characteristics and quantity of what is needed are worked out. This is the outline design process specifying performance and particular characteristics such as weight, size, operating conditions, and so on.
3. A specification is then drawn up.
4. A search is made for possible sources of supply. This may merely involve a search of suppliers' catalogues to buy a component from stock, or a complete new product may have to be designed.
5. Potential suppliers will submit plans and products for evaluation.
6. After the necessary trials, suppliers are selected.
7. An order is placed and the product eventually delivered.
8. The goods supplied are checked against specification.

Similar steps are followed for B2B *service* purchases, such as, for example, in outsourcing information technology – though the more complex the problem, the more the supplier may be involved at early stages in collaboratively developing the outline of the solution.

Clearly this process allows for variations. For example, where it is a case of simply reordering something which has been bought before, the search and even tender processes may not be necessary. The newness of the decision to the buying organization also determines which types of people and how many are involved at each stage. Newness is a function of:

* The complexity of the product
* The commercial uncertainty surrounding the outcome of the purchase.

The higher the 'newness' on both these dimensions, the more people are involved and the higher their status. If product complexity is high, but commercial uncertainty low, then the more important role is that of the design engineer and technologist. If newness is low on both dimensions, purchasing officers tend to dominate the process.

When faced with a new buy situation, the salesperson will be involved with a large number of people over a long period, helping, advising and informing, always trying to influence the decision process and to build up a growing commitment towards their product.

A typical example of this process at work can be seen in the following example of the purchase of a telecommunications system:

1. The managing director proposes to replace the company's telecommunications system.
2. Corporate purchasing and corporate telecommunications departments analyse the company's needs and recommend likely matches with potential selling organizations.
3. Corporate telecommunications department and data processing managers have an important say about which system and firm the company will deal with. Other company directors also have a key influence on this decision.
4. All employees who use the telecommunications equipment are 'consulted'.
5. The director of administration selects, with influence from others, the supplying company and the system.

The reason for going into such detail about the business-to-business buying process is simply to illustrate that it is not possible to determine the precise role of advertising versus, say, personal selling,

until a company fully understands how its potential customers buy and who are the important people that have to be contacted at the different stages in the buying process. For, clearly, financial and administrative people will be involved at a different stage from, say, the engineers, and they will also require different kinds of information. For example, price, performance characteristics, delivery, before- and after-sales service, reputation/reliability, guarantees, payment terms, and so on, are not relevant to all people at all stages in the buying process.

The first point, then, is that a firm must understand the buying process of the markets to which it addresses itself. It is important to identify the people with significant influence on the purchase decision and the specific benefits each influencer wants: this can be done simply by repeating the critical success factor exercise (from Chapter 5) for each influencer. Having done this analysis for our major customers/potential customers, it should be comparatively easy to:

1. Group them in some way (segmentation)
2. Determine the most cost-effective way of communicating these benefits to each group.

We will return to how to evaluate the cost-effectiveness of communications in the next section.

PREPARING THE ADVERTISING PLAN

Once we are clear on our communications objectives and have selected advertising as part of our communications mix, objectives for the advertising itself need to be defined. Just as for the communications activities as a whole, advertising is not the straightforward activity that many people believe it to be. It is highly unlikely, for example, that any firm will be able simply to put out an advertisement and expect their sales to increase. This brings us to perhaps the greatest misconception of all about advertising – that objectives for advertising for the purpose of measuring effectiveness

(Advertising is communication in paid-for media)

should be set in terms of sales increases. Naturally, we hope that advertising will have an important influence on sales levels, but in most circumstances advertising is only one of a whole host of important determinants of sales levels (such as product quality, prices, customer service levels, the competence of the sales force, and so on).

Generally, then, it is absurd to set sales increases as a direct objective for advertising. So, what objectives should be set for advertising? Well, we can start by agreeing that we need to *set* objectives for advertising, for the following reasons:

1. We need to set the budget for advertising.
2. We need to determine who our target audience is.
3. We need to determine the content of advertisements.
4. We need to decide on what media to use.
5. We need to decide on the frequency of advertising.
6. We need to decide how to measure the effectiveness of our advertising.

These decisions can be summarized as follows:

1. *Why* (objectives)
2. *Who* (target)
3. *What* (copy platform)
4. *Where* (media)

5. *How* (creative platform)
6. *When* (timing)
7. *How much* (budget)
8. Schedule
9. Response
10. Evaluation.

The whole edifice, however, depends on the first of these.

Advertising Objectives

Research has shown that many companies set objectives for advertising which advertising cannot achieve on its own. Apart from increasing sales, the 'annihilation of the enemy' and other such ridiculously unachievable objectives are set. For example, it is unreasonable to set as an objective 'to convince our target market that our product is best' if it is perfectly clear to the whole world that someone else's product is better. You cannot blame your advertising agency if this objective is not achieved!

MARKETING INSIGHT

Another example of inadequate thought being given to advertising expenditure was the bus company who spent vast sums advertising the reliability of their bus service, while research showed the real reason why sales were deteriorating was that many people thought buses were 'working class'. Again, this is a classic example of scoring a bull's-eye at the wrong target.

One more example should serve to prove the point.

A machine tool company could not understand why, after an expensive advertising campaign in Germany in which they emphasized the extremely high quality and reliability of their products, they made little headway in the market. Subsequent market research showed that their target customers already believed this company had the best product. What they were concerned about, and why they were not buying, was their dissatisfaction over delivery and customer service. This is yet another example of advertising wasted because of ignorance about customer beliefs.

The first step, then, is to decide on reasonable objectives for advertising. The question which must be asked is: 'Is it possible to achieve the objective through advertising alone?' If the answer is *yes*, it is an objective for advertising. If the answer is *no*, it is not an objective for advertising. Advertising through media can do the following:

- Convey information
- Alter perceptions/attitudes – provided these are consistent with word-of-mouth from current customers
- Create desires
- Establish connections (e.g. powdered cream/coffee)
- Direct actions
- Provide reassurance
- Remind

- Give reasons for buying
- Demonstrate
- Generate enquiries.

Setting reasonable, achievable objectives, then, is the first and most important step in the advertising plan. All the other steps in the process of putting together the advertising plan flow naturally from this and are summarized briefly below.

Who ... are the target audience(s)?

What do they already know, feel, believe about us and our product/service?

What do they know, feel, believe about the competition?

What sort of people are they? How do we describe/identify them?

What ... response do we wish to evoke from the target audience(s)?

...are these specific communications objectives?

...do we want to 'say', make them 'feel', 'believe', 'understand', 'know' about buying/using our product/service?

...are we offering?

...do we not want to convey?

...are the priorities of importance of our objectives?

...are the objectives which are written down and agreed by the company and advertising agency?

How ... are our objectives to be embodied in an appealing form?

What is our creative strategy/platform?

What evidence do we have that this is acceptable and appropriate to our audience(s)?

Where ... is/are the most cost-effective place(s) to expose our communications

(in cost terms *vis-à-vis* our audience)?

...is/are the most beneficial place(s) for our communications (in expected response terms *vis-à-vis* the 'quality' of the channels available)?

When ... are our communications to be displayed/conveyed to our audience?

What is the reasoning for our scheduling of advertisements/communications over time?

What constraints limit our freedom of choice?

Do we have to fit in with other promotional activity on other products/services supplied by our company, competitors' products, seasonal trends, special events in the market?

Result.   What results do we expect?

How will we measure results?

Do we intend to measure results and, if so, do we need to do anything beforehand?

If we cannot say how we would measure precise results, then maybe our objectives are not sufficiently specific or are not communications objectives?

How are we going to judge the relative success of our communications activities (good/bad/indifferent)? Should we have action standards?

Budget.   How much money do the intended activities need?

How much money is going to be made available?

How are we going to control expenditure?

Schedule. Who is to do what and when?

What is being spent on what, where and when?

The usual assumption is that advertising is deployed in an aggressive role and that all that changes over time is the creative content. But the role of advertising usually changes during the lifecycle of a product. For example, the process of persuasion itself cannot usually start until there is some level of awareness about a product or service in the marketplace. If awareness has been created, interest in learning more will usually follow. Creating awareness is, therefore, usually one of the most important objectives early on in a lifecycle.

Attitude development now begins in earnest. This might also involve reinforcing an existing attitude, or even changing previously held attitudes, in order to clear the way for a new purchase. This role obviously tends to become more important later in the product lifecycle, when competitive products are each trying to establish their own 'niche' in the market.

Diffusion of Innovation

So, also relevant in setting objectives is what is known as the 'diffusion of innovation curve', discussed in Chapter 5. To refresh our memories we will repeat the curve in Figure 7.4.

Research into any product's progress along the diffusion curve can be very useful, particularly for advertising and personal selling. For example, if we can develop a typology for opinion leaders, we can target our early advertising and sales effort specifically at them. Once the first 3 per cent of innovators have adopted our product, there is a good chance that the early adopters, or opinion leaders, will try it, and once the 8–10 per cent point is reached, the champagne can be opened, because there is a good chance that the rest will adopt our product.

We know, for example, that the *general* characteristics of opinion leaders are that they are: venturesome; socially integrated; cosmopolitan; socially mobile; and privileged. So we need to ask ourselves what are the *specific* characteristics of these customers in our particular industry. We can then tailor our advertising message specifically for them.

Finally, we should remind ourselves that advertising is not directed only at consumers. It can be directed at channels, shareholders, media, employees, suppliers and government, all of whom have an important influence on a firm's commercial success.

We now turn to decisions on what media are used for advertising. The considerations for deciding the communications mix which we discussed in the previous section apply equally for deciding on which specific advertising media to use. But often, only experience will show what media work best. So evaluating effectiveness becomes key in order to ensure value for money.

Choosing Advertising Media Through Effectiveness Metrics

Whatever the marketer's choice of advertising media, we would be foolish if we did not endeavour to refine the mix through measurement of effectiveness. This will naturally depend on the advertising objectives, but some of the possible approaches are as follows.

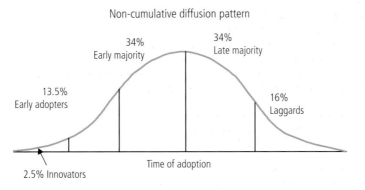

Figure 7.4: Diffusion of Innovation curve.

Individual tracking

Direct response and interactive media allow effectiveness to be directly tied to individual customers. Examples are conversion rates from direct mail or e-mail, click-through rates on banner ads and cost per click on paid search. This is clearly the ideal approach, but care is needed in two respects. First, not every lead is a good lead: where possible, customers should be tracked through to purchase and indeed to their lifetime value rather than simply measuring the cost per response. Second, where possible we should track the *advertising* impact of direct response media as well as the direct response itself. A fascinating research study showed that even the act of sending a satisfaction survey to customers can increase their loyalty as they feel listened to; similarly, a presence at a trade show or a banner ad may build engagement which contributes to a sale much later. Equally, excessive direct mail, or a clumsy cross-sale pitch in a service call centre, may actually damage the customer relationship.

Control cells

Where individuals cannot be tracked, the use of a control cell can often tease out the specific effect of different media. Control cells are groups of customers, selected at random, who are not exposed to the advertising. The random selection is important to ensure that the group does not differ in any other respect from the advertising recipients.

Figure 7.5 shows an example from an airline (with some numbers removed to protect confidentiality). A control cell was used to check on the effectiveness of a mailed magazine for loyalty card holders. The final column shows that mailed members made more transactions at a higher transaction value than the control group. From this, the airline could calculate a return on investment figure.

The airline then experimented with whether it should send e-mails along with the magazine or just mail the magazine, again by defining two random groups. Figure 7.6 shows that e-mails increased spend by a further 6 per cent.

Control cells are common in sectors making extensive use of direct mail, but this powerful tool is much underused by marketers in many other areas of practice. They can equally be used, for example, to check on whether to use sales visits, remote channels or both in the pharmaceuticals sector: one study found that the sales force cost more than it generated in incremental revenue! Or different marketing practices can be adopted in different stores or branches, again selected at random. Marketing practice is some way behind best practice in R&D in the use of experimental approaches to pilot new initiatives.

Econometric modelling

It is not always possible, however, to set aside a group who will not be exposed to a communication. In these circumstances, econometric modelling may be considered. Econometric modelling, sometimes known as marketing mix modelling, looks at the impact of several different communications tools – or other marketing mix elements – simultaneously, teasing out their relative impact statistically. This is a specialist area, requiring skills which tend to be found either in specialist agencies or in analytic divisions of the larger communications agencies, but the general idea is not hard to grasp. See Table 7.5 for an example.

In this example, a UK online retailer collected information on spend across television, radio, press and online in each week for a two-year period. For each week, the overall effectiveness of these marketing communications was measured by the number of new visitors to its website. Information was also entered on competitor activity during the week as this was thought likely to negatively impact on new visitors. A statistical analysis identified the relative effects of the communications media, as shown in the table. The retailer found that while every pound spent on television advertising provided two new visitors, a pound spent on press advertising was far more effective, generating 13 visitors. The 'half-life' of television, though, was much longer – its effects were felt long after the advertisement. Overall, the retailer rebalanced its spend to achieve greater effectiveness, while maintaining some television presence due to its significant coverage and longer-term impact.

	Performance pre-mailing		Performance post-mailing		Increase Vs pre-mailing period (%)		Out-performance of mailed members
	Mailed members	Control cell	Mailed members	Control cell	Mailed members	Control cell	
Active members							+6.8
Spend							+23.7
Visits							+7.4
Transactions							+15.1
Average transaction value							+11.8
Average spend per visit							+16.8
Average spend per member							+19.8

- The loyalty card members were split into two groups —at random: an experimental group, who were sent a magazine, and a control group, who weren't.
- This proved that the mailing increased spend by 23%.

Figure 7.5: Control cell example (1).

	Performance pre-mailing		Performance post-mailing		Increase Vs pre-mailing period (%)		Out-performance (members receiving magazine + emails)
	Magazine only	Magazine + emails	Magazine only	Magazine + emails	Magazine only	Magazine + emails	
Active members							+4.7
Spend							+5.9
Visits							+0.3
Transactions							+2.2
Spend per Active member							+1.4

- The mailed group were further divided into two – again at random. One group were also sent emails; the other group weren't
- This provided that the emails increased spend by a further 6%

Figure 7.6: Control cell example (2).

Channel	Unique users	Half-life	Unique users per £ spent
TV	12,000,000	10 wks	2
Radio	250,000	1 wk	5.5
Press	3,000,000	3.5 wks	13
Online	1,200,000	3 days	4
Competitor activity	–1,000,000	5 wks	–

Table 7.5: Econometric modelling: online retailer

Econometric modelling, then, is an excellent way to assess the relative effects of multiple influences on an objective such as sales or lead generation. It does, however, require a substantial amount of data to be available, and the need for statistical expertise means that it is not cheap. So it is generally only appropriate for products with significant promotional budgets.

DIGITAL COMMUNICATIONS

What's different about digital communications? After all, they have long left their silo in an innovation corner of the marketing function, and become in many ways simply an additional set of communications tools to use in integrated campaigns. Nonetheless, the online revolution has forced marketers to think rather differently about marketing in a digital world. Our 6 Is framework encapsulates some of these differences. The framework considers six capabilities provided by digital channels which, *when these enhance performance against the customers' buying criteria*, can be beneficial in creation of value for the customer and the firm.

The 6 Is of E-marketing

Integration: joining up the customer experience

In the early days of the internet, the talk was of pureplay business models: businesses entirely dealing with their customers online. But while some highly successful examples of this single-channel strategy clearly flourish, for the great majority of firms, the internet is part of a multichannel mix. And this is not just in the sense that different customers use different channels: rather, many individual transactions involve a multichannel customer journey from awareness through to information collection, purchase and delivery. A hotel chain found that only 8 per cent of its customers did not touch the internet at all in their purchase process. An airline found an even lower figure – around 2 per cent – despite many of the final purchases still being made by telephone or with travel agents.

So multichannel integration is as important with the internet as with any other communication medium, a fact often lost on companies who delegate the website to enthusiasts in an isolated corner of the organization, or outsource its development and operations with minimal provision for information transfer – hence repeating the mistakes often made in the early days of the call centre. Instead, Dell point customers to its website through 'e-value codes' in magazines and brochures, which direct the customer to the exact page they want. This has the crucial benefit of enabling Dell to track the

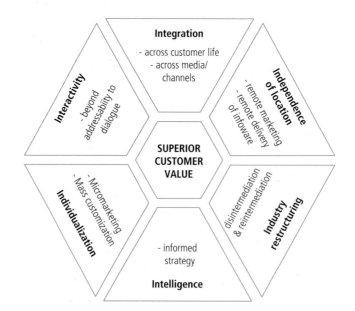

Figure 7.7: The 6 Is of E-marketing.

effectiveness of the offline communications. And once on the website, telephone numbers are prominently displayed so the customer does not give up if they need further help.

In similar vein, the dotcom director of a major retailer told us how he had been challenged by a new chief executive as to why he should keep his job. He was able to respond with proof that not only was he making a small but growing profit from online sales, but also he was generating four times as much revenue for the high-street stores as he was taking online. If a customer searches on his website for, say, a bed, the webpage offers information on the location of the nearest store with the bed in stock, so the customer can go in and try bouncing on it! And, like Dell, the retailer is careful to ensure that these cross-channel journeys can be tracked by such means as giving the customer a code to quote in the store in order to be entered for a prize draw.

A good way to think through how channels fit together in the customer journey is to draw what we call a channel chain diagram – see Figure 7.8 for an example for this retailer. The predominantly online channel chain on the left is the one followed by default when companies first go online. The middle model, starting online and ending offline, had the great advantage of exploiting the company's offline presence – providing an important differentiation compared with pureplay competitors. Furthermore, for some purchases, the customer would start in the store and complete the purchase later online – the right hand model. We will return to channel chain diagrams in Chapter 10.

The need for management of customer relationships implies the need for systems which manage data on the whole of the customer interaction, throughout the customer lifecycle, from initial contact, through configuration and sales, to delivery and post-sales service. The multiple channels by which the consumer demands to be able to reach the supplier implies that this data must also be integrated across communication mechanisms, so a telephone salesperson knows about a service request that was sent yesterday by e-mail, and a sales representative in the field can call on information about previous purchases and customer profitability to assist judgements about discount levels. We will return to this issue in our consideration of CRM in Chapter 11.

Interactivity: beyond addressability to dialogue

Knowing your customers means closing the loop between the messages sent to them and the messages they send back. It has been said that this is the age of addressability, as organizations have endeavoured to communicate with individual customers through carefully targeted direct mail, e-mail,

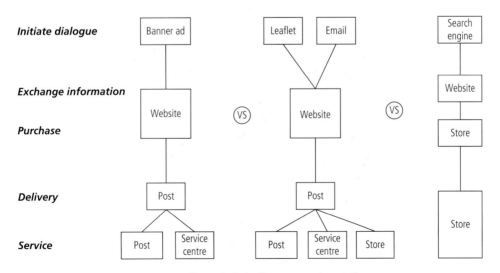

Figure 7.8: Channel chain diagram – major retailer.

Supplier perspective		Interaction perspective	Buyer perspective	
Advertising	Selling	Interaction	Decision theory	Consumer behaviour
Brand awareness		*Recognize exchange potential*	Problem recognition	Category need
			Information search	Awareness
Brand attitude	Prospecting	*Initiate dialogue*		Attitude
- info re benefits				
- brand image	Provide	*Exchange information*		Information gathering & judgement
- feelings	information		Evaluation of alternatives	
- peer influence				
	Persuade	*Negotiate/tailor*		Purchase process
			Choices/ purchase	
Trial inducement	Close sale	*Commit*		
		Exchange value	Post- purchase behaviour	Post- purchase experience
Reduce cognitive dissonance	Deliver			
	Service	*Monitor*		

Figure 7.9: An interaction perspective on communication.

paid search, and so on. Interactivity goes one step further, listening to the customer and responding appropriately, as one would in a face-to-face conversation. With so many interactive channels now available – websites, social media, call centres, mobile phone apps and so on – marketers need to think differently about the sales process, as customers rightly expect them to use interactivity to hold a true dialogue. In Figure 7.9, we contrast the traditional concept of communication as a one-way bombardment of the customer – apparent from the language of 'campaigns', 'targets', 'persuasion', and so on – with our proposed recrafting of the purchase process as an interaction between equal parties.

Traditional 'push-based' models of marketing, in which after the product is made prospects are found and persuaded to buy the product, are illustrated on the left. The delivery and service that follow are operational functions with little relationship to marketing. Traditional models of buyer behaviour, illustrated on the right of the figure, assume more rationality on the part of buyers, but underplay the importance of what the buyer says back to the seller. The seller's offer is assumed to be predetermined, rather than developed in conjunction with the buyer.

The interaction perspective replaces this one-way process as follows:

- 'Recognize exchange potential' replaces 'category need' or 'problem recognition'. Both sides need to recognize the potential for a mutual exchange of value.
- 'Initiate dialogue' replaces 'Create awareness' or 'Prospecting'. The dialogue with an individual customer may be started by either party. One feature of the web, for example, is that on many occasions, new customers will approach the supplier rather than vice versa. All too often, marketers are so busy organizing their next outbound campaign that these ad-hoc queries are not followed up.
- 'Exchange information' replaces 'Provide information'. If we are to serve the customer effectively, tailor our offerings and build a long-term relationship, we need to learn about the customer as much as the customer needs to learn about our products.
- 'Negotiate/tailor' replaces 'Persuade'. Negotiation is a two-way process which may involve us modifying our offer in order to better meet the customer's needs. Persuading the customer instead that the square peg we happen to have in stock will fit their round hole is not likely to lead to a long and profitable relationship.

- 'Commit' replaces 'Close sale'. Both sides need to commit to the transaction, or to a series of transactions forming the next stage in a relationship – a decision with implications for both sides.
- 'Exchange value' replaces 'Deliver' and 'Post-sales service'. The 'post-sales service' may be an inherent part of the value being delivered, not simply a cost centre, as it is often still managed.

One-to-one communications and principles of relationship marketing, then, demand a radically different sales process from that traditionally practised. This point is far from academic, as an example will illustrate.

MARKETING INSIGHT

The company in question provides business-to-business financial services. Its marketing managers relayed to us their early experience with a website which was enabling them to reach new customers considerably more cost-effectively than their traditional sales force. When the website was first launched, potential customers were finding the company on the web, deciding the products were appropriate on the basis of the website, and sending an e-mail to ask to buy. So far, so good.

However, stuck in a traditional model of the sales process, the company would allocate the 'lead' to a salesperson, who would phone up and make an appointment, perhaps three weeks' hence. The customer would by now probably have moved on to another online supplier who could sell the product today, but those that remained were subjected to a sales pitch, complete with glossy materials, which was totally unnecessary, the customer having already decided to buy. Those that were not put off would proceed to be registered as able to buy over the web, but the company had lost the opportunity to improve its margins by using the sales force more judiciously.

In time, the company realized its mistake, and changed its sales model and reward systems to something close to our 'interaction perspective' model. Unlike those prospects which the company proactively identified and contacted, which might indeed need 'selling' to, many new web customers were initiating the dialogue themselves, and simply required the company to respond effectively and rapidly, which was done with a small desk-based team, who only called on the sales force for complex sales where their involvement was needed and justified. The sales force was increasingly freed up to concentrate on major clients and on relationship building.

Individualization: information-enabled tailoring

Integrated information about the customer provides the basis for individualizing the product or associated services. Online newspapers from the *Wall Street Journal* to the UK's *Guardian* newspaper can be tailored to provide the topics you want, and to prompt you when material you are interested in is available. Dell Premier provides major accounts with a customized site, which allows easy ordering at individually negotiated prices, easy tracking, and easy control by the firm's central procurement of what its staff can see and order. Goods from M&M chocolates to cars can be customized online. Inhabitants of virtual world Second Life don't just spend money on virtual versions of real-world goods from apples to zoos; the traffic also flows the other way, with services such as Fabjectory 'printing' the user's online creations such as their avatar as a real-world object. In a Web 2.0 take on individualization, players of EA's Sims 2 game competed to design an H&M outfit which would be made available in 1,000 H&M stores.

The point is not that we *always* need to individualize just because the internet makes it possible; the 6Is provide e-marketing mix levers, in the same way that the 4Ps delineate the overall levers available to any marketer, to be pulled where necessary in order to achieve marketing objectives. Individualization is closely linked to independence of location, our next topic.

Independence of location: the death of distance

What is the difference between shoes made to measure by the village cobbler and customized trainers made to order by NIKEID? Both achieve individualization, but Nike combines it with post-industrial revolution economies of scale. It is able to do this because its website can serve a widely spread geographical population, using the data transport provided by the internet and the physical transport of our 21st century infrastructure, plus a database-driven manufacturing facility. Independence of location allows individualization to be achieved economically. Niche products can serve their target markets even if spread globally.

Freeing up the company from the cost of physical facilities *can* lower overall costs in sectors such as banking, travel and internet retailing: a US study calculated costs of 1 cent for a transaction conducted over the internet, as opposed to $1.07 for a branch transaction and 27 cents for an ATM. There are exceptions, however, such as the high rates of stock returns by clothes retailers – the 26 per cent returns for retailer ASOS being towards the best that can be hoped for. Another exception is the high picking and delivery costs for grocery retailers: UK retailer Ocado, loved by its customers for the high reliability that derives from its dedicated high-technology picking centre, has struggled to reach the 6 per cent gross margins which would deliver long-term profits.

MARKETING INSIGHT

The public sector has been slower to exploit independence of location in most countries, but transformations such as the UK DVLA's switch to internet ordering of tax discs show what is possible. Instead of asking car owners to go with a paper form to their local post office – a high-cost indirect channel partner from DVLA's point of view – the car owner is now encouraged to visit a website or phone an interactive voice response (IVR) service. Importantly, rather than giving away margin by lowering the price online, the DVLA instead created additional convenience benefits for the customer: the website automatically checks whether the customer has valid insurance and whether the car has an 'MOT' certificate of roadworthiness, saving much searching in drawers at home! This careful focus on the customer's buying criteria, along with a communications campaign, shifted the majority of car owners to remote channels within two years of launch.

For B2B firms, too, the cost advantages of the internet can be significant – though mostly as part of a multichannel mix. BT's Business division found that by switching simpler purchases to telephone and the web, it could reduce total sales and marketing costs from 25 per cent of revenue to 18 per cent – putting 7 per cent of revenue straight on the bottom line. Its sales force remained crucial, though, for selling more complex services to high-value customers.

For consumers, too, high-involvement products may require a face-to-face component of the mix. At the high end of the luxury goods market, Fabergé's sophisticated website cannot even be viewed without a phone conversation to a service agent based in Fabergé's head office in Switzerland. Its beautiful graphics are backed up by a chat facility with the same service centre, which may lead to the agent offering to fly over to visit the customer to show a five-figure item … an offer which one of the authors sadly decided to decline when trialling the service!

If the internet enables the firm to be independent of its location, the same can be true for the customer. Serving customers wherever *they* are can be enhanced by location-based services on mobile devices which detect their location and advise them accordingly. Location-based social network Foursquare allows users to broadcast their location to others, enabling them to meet old and new friends wherever they are in the world. Gowalla is a game variant on this theme, in which players drop off and pick up items at specified locations. In 2010, the success of such specialists led the major social networking sites such as Facebook and Twitter to launch their own location-based services.

Intelligence: informed strategy

Interactivity does not just enable individual customers to get what they want. It also provides a rich source of insight for the firm in order to inform marketing strategy. Financial services provider Egg collects information on service levels through a continuously available online questionnaire, and then displays a summary of the main concerns of customers and how it is responding on the website. Dell collates online buyer behaviour to segment its customers into segments such as 'All about price', 'Design is important', 'All about high-end products' and 'Tailored for my country', so it can ensure it has the right offer for each segment without needlessly sacrificing margin by cutting prices across the board.

In a Web 2.0 world, complaints and problems are best looked at as a source of insight rather than as a PR problem to be managed through press releases, as the famous case of Kryptonite locks showed. An online video of these bicycle locks being readily opened with a paperclip led to a defensive response from the company that sounded all too much like advertising copy: 'The world just got tougher, and so did our locks.' The response from bloggers was immediate and devastating: 'We've spent over $100 on these types of locks for our bicycles, and hearing "the world just got tougher and so did our locks", kinda got us a little miffed. The world didn't get tougher, it got Bic pens and blogs and your locks got opened.' The company never recovered.

By the time of the 'exploding laptops' problem due to faulty batteries in 2007, exacerbated by similar humorous YouTube videos, major online players such as Dell had learnt to have a more open dialogue. Its Direct2Dell and Ideastorm services provided a medium through which its customers felt listened to, not preached to. Dell staff would feel free to give in the customer's interests, with posts like: 'My advice: Don't even think about upgrading from a D420 to a D430, this is the same computer with the same flaws . . .' So when Dell recalled 4 million laptop batteries, the online buzz was predominantly positive rather than negative. Influential site imediaconnection reported: 'They actually handled it quite well. Because they already had a way to converse with customers – and their competitors who had to recall their laptop batteries did not – Dell actually may have come out ahead.'

The internet, then, provides numerous ways of gaining intelligence, ranging from traditional questionnaires to behavioural analysis. Some of the behavioural techniques available are summarized in Table 7.6.

Industry restructuring: redrawing the market map

As with all technological innovations, the effect of digital marketing is sometimes incremental but often radical, with customer needs being met in new ways by new players. Examples which would have seemed unthinkable 20 years ago are all around us. Newspapers face a torrid time as the young gain their entertainment and news from digital sources, and advertising revenues follow audiences online. High-street travel agents are 'disintermediated' by direct online sales by airlines and hotels, and 'reintermediated' by online specialists such as Expedia. Book publishers and business schools who package and disseminate knowledge face the threat of disintermediation from their customers conducting their own research online, or collaboratively creating content such as Wikipedia. Record companies were disintermediated by peer-to-peer file sharing sites and reintermediated by iTunes, allowing many musicians to self-publish with help from YouTube and other social networks.

Each of these innovations can be thought of as a redrawing of the market map which we discussed in Chapter 4. While all predictions have to be reconsidered constantly in the light of experience,

Purpose of intelligence	Example measures	Notes
Customer needs and satisfaction	Channel satisfaction (e.g. website)	e.g. American Customer Satisfaction Index (www.foreseeresults.com)
	Customer needs	Online questionnaires, focus groups
	Usability	Testing, online mystery shopping
Promotion effectiveness	Ad impressions	Number of advertisements seen
	Ad clicks	Clicks on advertisements by users
	Click-through rate	Ad clicks/ad impressions
	Cost per click	Clicks on ad (or search engine entry)/cost
	Cost per acquisition	Cost (from ad or intermediary)/acquired customer
	Unique visitors	Number of different people visiting site
Website effectiveness	Bounce rate	Proportion of single page visits
	Stickiness	Page views/visitor sessions ('PPV')
	Attrition rate	How many visitors are lost at each stage, e.g. from placing items in basket to checking out ('Basket abandonment rate')
	Conversion rate	Purchases/visitors
Performance outcomes	Channel contribution	Channel revenue – channel costs
	Multichannel contribution	Total revenue of multiple channels – sum of channel costs

Table 7.6: Gaining intelligence online: some of the available tools

these innovations are not random or fundamentally unpredictable: rather, they succeed or fail according to whether they improve the value proposition for the end customer. So a good way to do at least an initial sense-check of the plausibility of a proposed redrawing of the market map is to evaluate what its impact would be on the end customer's critical success factors, using the quantified SWOT analysis we covered in Chapter 5.

The 6 Is, then, are a way of thinking about what is different about digital communications. It is worth reflecting on a company's current position on these 6 Is: which aspects of digital media are currently being exploited well and which are not? There are numerous specific tools which can be used in support of these broad principles; while we cannot cover them in detail here, we summarize some of the main digital communications tools next.

The Digital Communications Mix

We can divide the main tools available for online communications into four categories: see Figure 7.10.

Search engine marketing

As a high proportion of customer journeys online begin with a search engine, search marketing is a crucial part of the communications mix, particularly for customer acquisition. By 2009, over 25 per cent of online ad spend was on 'paid search' – the listings on the search results pages which are reserved for paid-for entries. Figure 7.11 shows a typical first page of search results from a hotel customer. The paid search entries are the first three, shaded entries, and the results down the right hand

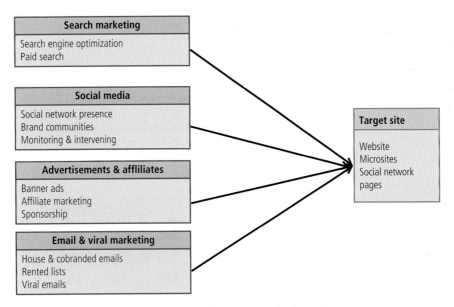

Figure 7.10: The digital communication mix.

side. The Google Adwords site (www.adwords.google.com) explains simply how to sign up for paid search, and has a keyword tool to help find out what terms customers are searching on.

However, equally important is search engine optimization (SEO): ensuring that the website naturally occurs high in the listing. And clearly, with paid search costing an average of $3 per click or $8 per 1,000 page impressions ('cost per mille' or 'CPM') in 2009, it can be cost-effective, too. A plethora of advice is available on how Google and other search engines prioritize web pages, and optimizing websites to ensure they are ranked high in the list is a specialist skillset, but the basic principles are common sense. Attractive, regularly updated content which many people appreciate, revisit and provide their own links to will find its way up the rankings.

Even if these basics are in place, it is so important to appear on the first page that it is worth going the extra mile and finding some help from a web designer with SEO skills. A 2010 study by icrossing.com found that 95 per cent of all search traffic comes from search results on page one. A luxury hotel chain found that on many commonly used search strings entered by its target customers, such as 'boutique hotel London' in Figure 7.11, it was coming on page 2 or lower. A simple analysis of its better-performing competitors showed why they were ranked higher: they included common search terms within the page title; they repeated these search words several times on the home page; and they had customer review facilities to engage repeat customers with the site, encourage traffic and provide advocacy. Some straightforward amendments brought the site onto the first page of some key search terms.

Social media

Social networks such as Facebook, MySpace and LinkedIn – along with online gaming, which is an increasingly social activity – accounted for a third of the online time of Americans by 2010, as against 12 per cent for e-mail and chat. At first glance, it therefore seems odd that advertising spend on social networks is slow to catch up, with only 4 per cent of online spend in 2009. In part, this is because the sheer pace of social network expansion has provided a surfeit of advertising space which advertisers struggle to make sense of. While this 4 per cent figure is increasing fast, though, the truth is that it is nevertheless a vast underestimate of the amount of marketing effort already going into social media. The great majority of the true cost of social media marketing is not advertising on the sidelines, but

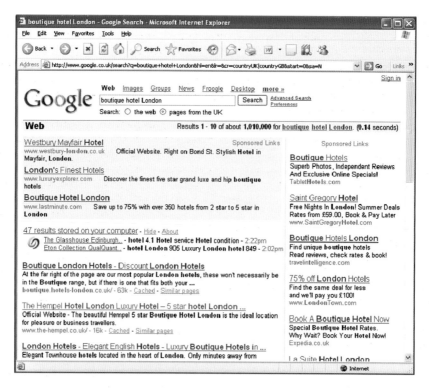

Figure 7.11: Search engine optimization and paid search: a hotel example.

joining in the conversation: blogging, hosting brand communities, and so on. Broadly there are four purposes of social media for the marketer:

1. *Customer insight.* Social media provide a vast repository of free qualitative data about how customers think about the firm's product category and its offerings. UK remote bank First Direct (www.firstdirect.com) is unusual in displaying some of this information straight back to its customers on its home page – what its customers are talking about, how much of it is positive and how much negative, what they want improved, and so on. For First Direct, this is a way of endeavouring to turn its highly enthusiastic customer base into powerful advocacy that is visible to non-customers in the notoriously sticky banking market – we are said to change our marriage partners more often than our banks!

   Some companies focus this free market insight by developing communities of innovative, enthusiastic customers – 'lead users' – who develop and evaluate new product ideas. This is the sole source of R&D in the case of clothes retailer Threadless (www.threadless.com), where the most popular ideas submitted by customers are made by the company and sold online. Other interesting examples are Nokia's Design By Community – a 2010 exercise to design a phone entirely through user community interaction (www.conversations.nokia.com/design-by-community) – and Volvo's Concept lab (conceptlabvolvo.com).

2. *Brand exposure.* The rise of social networking has been accompanied by a stream of statistics on the importance of social networks on purchase decisions, such as Gartner's 2010 claim that 74 per cent of consumers are strongly influenced by them. The default reaction of many marketers is to add community facilities to their own website, in the hope of making this the destination of choice for customers in their product category, be it soft drinks, washing powder, accounting software or electrical equipment. This can work well with high-involvement categories such as telecoms or charities. BT asked on Facebook how a storyline running through TV advertisements

about two characters, Adam and Jane, should end: it received 1.6 million responses. On a smaller scale, in May 2010 Amnesty International asked its supporters for funding for a press ad against Shell's activities in Nigeria: it collected £40,000. But there are two dangers with this thinking. The first is that not all products have 'social currency': do today's housewives, house-husbands or home workers really want to talk about washing powder? The second danger is that even if there is a relevant conversation to be had – about parenting, say, in the case of P&G – do we want to have it on a brand-owned website?

Practice is developing fast in this area, but some principles are emerging. First, not every brand can host a true destination site, any more than they can hope to host their own television channel. P&G has recognized this in its 2009 launch of supersavvyme.com, which aggregates many brands into a lifestyle site for women. At the time of writing in 2010 the jury is still out on its success: with 200,000 monthly visitors it is gaining some traffic, but also attracting less than ringing endorsements such as this blog post: 'It is full of useful bits and bobs about mothering, and along the way it has competitions featuring Procter and Gamble products, as it is P&G running the whole thing. But is this what mothers really want?'

Which raises the second principle: marketers of all but the strongest brands need to go to where the customers are. There are existing flourishing networks for many areas of professional practice (e.g. JustPlainFolks for musicians), interests (such as e-democracy.org for politics) and affinity groups (BlackPlanet for African Americans, iVillage for women, and so on), and the general networks all host these communities of interest too. Cranfield School of Management links with practitioners not just through its face-to-face courses and website but also through a presence on YouTube, Twitter (twitter.com/cranfieldki) and iTunes (e.g. www.youtube.com/user/CranfieldSoM). Coke's Facebook site had 11 million members by 2010 and has an appropriately light, playful touch for the brand, kicking off debates on such topics as 'Where is the strangest place you've ever had a Coke?' While now owned by Coca-Cola, the site was started by two Coke enthusiasts – customers showing the way to the professional marketers.

3. *Relationship building.* Where brand building ends and the sales process begins in earnest is a moot point, but social networks can play a role for customers actively involved in a current purchase. Whether online or offline, word-of-mouth often proves the most powerful communication tool of all, and it has the benefit of being free. Retailer onlineshoes.com found that customers viewing at least one product review were over twice as likely to go on to buy the product as those who don't. And products with more reviews on the retailer's site sold better, irrespective of whether the reviews were positive, negative or mixed! So the retailer positively incentivized reviews, until its customers had developed the habit of posting them regularly.

For business-to-business marketers, social networks can also be important for building personal relationships which so often act as the initial spur to a supplier being shortlisted. IBM were one of the earlier users of virtual world Second Life to build relationships that spill over into the offline world, inviting customers to a Second Life version of Wimbledon where they could watch the tennis, chat to other fans and meet their IBM hosts. A minimum for executives with a front-line role is a strong online presence on networks such as LinkedIn, so they can be found easily when prospective customers are searching for experts on a particular topic.

4. *Customer service.* The final use of social media is perhaps more mundane but no less important: the provision of customer service. Not only is online advice cheaper to provide than telephone support, as less expert time is typically needed, but also answers to common questions are available to all, providing an economy of scale. Furthermore, as compared with the call centre, a happy customer can readily tell others about their experience, as this post demonstrates:

> . . . in desperation – I turned to Twitter to try to penetrate what felt like the huge, uncaring behemoth of Carphone Warehouse. And I found Guy Stephens, the company's Knowledge and Online Help Manager, who appeared to be tackling customer rage in a passionately empathetic way on Twitter. I tweeted him at 8pm; by 8.07pm, I had a reply, rendering me unconditionally blown away. Three months of periodic call centre torture had got me nowhere, but via social media I felt listened to within minutes and my problem solved within a few days.

Even better, customers can serve each other, experienced users of a product or service advising less experienced people. This runs counter to the traditional instincts of many marketers to control the customer experience, but loss of control cannot be fought; rather, it is an inevitable part of the increasing customer empowerment which Web 2.0 exemplifies. Apple is active in supporting its user community wherever they are talking to each other: see, for example, becomingatechnician.com and scan 'The top 100 Apple /Mac blogs'. Zappos is a $1 billion online retailer which is well worth sampling as a company built on customer service, which uses social media creatively. The extensive customer reviews lower return rates and are wonderful for search engine optimization. A 'voice of customer' facility builds community and empathy. Word of mouth is facilitated by a facility to 'share' products with other customers. The site has a page aggregating all mentions of Zappos on Twitter without editing: as with First Direct, a move which would seem foolhardy were its satisfaction levels less high.

Social media, then, are perfect for customer service. Take-up is only being delayed by the tendency of many firms to delegate social media to a corner of the marketing department – typically the young, digitally literate intern!

Advertisements and affiliates

With the dramatic growth in search marketing and social media, is the traditional banner ad dead? Far from it. Yes, click-through rates have continued their long-term decline, but the same could be said for response rates to any other form of outbound advertising as we are bombarded by ever more messages in ever more media. In any case, the decline slowed from 2005 to 2010, by which time average click-through rates were around 0.1 per cent in the USA and 0.13 per cent in the UK. By 2010 around half of online advertising remained in banner ads and their variations – 'rich text' and video advertisements. Banner ads are placed in several ways, notably:

1. On individual sites
2. On the major portals such as Google, MSN, Yahoo! and AOL
3. Through ad exchanges such as Google's Doubleclick and Yahoo!'s Right Media. These provide marketplaces which match content sites with ad space to sell with advertisers.

Other formats include in-game advertising and the trends towards digital billboards and other 'digital out of home' devices. While advertisers will naturally wish to evaluate their ads on the basis of their performance, only a minority of ad space is actually bought on the basis of cost per click (about 36 per cent according to one study) or cost per acquisition (about 6 per cent), the majority still being bought on the number of impressions ('CPM').

A related technique is affiliate marketing, in which a firm places its banner ad or text link on another firm's website (the affiliate). The millions of affiliates of Amazon receive a commission of 5 per cent whenever a book sale results from a click through to Amazon's website. Affiliates drive a quarter of the online sales of UK startup Hotel Chocolat (which the authors like to follow as it was founded by Cranfield alumnus Angus Thirlwell, and the odd sample comes our way . . .). Its model is similar to that of Amazon: a 7 per cent commission, even if the customer makes the purchase up to 45 days after clicking through to the Hotel Chocolat website.

E-mail and viral marketing

Like the banner ad, the e-mail campaign no longer has the excitement of youth in the innovation-obsessed world of digital marketing, but it is nonetheless still an important part of the online communications mix. While response rates (measured by clicking on a link in the e-mail) average out at around 2.8 per cent, this masks much poor mass marketing with undifferentiated content being sent to poorly maintained lists, which can achieve considerably less than 1 per cent. Conversely, well-crafted e-mail campaigns to specific segments using a clean database will often achieve 10–15 per cent click rates. Of course, we are referring here not to unsolicited spam – which now forms three-quarters of e-mail traffic – but to customer-centric information and offers to registered customers and prospects. So, for most firms e-mail forms part of the firm's customer relationship management (CRM) strategy to grow the value of existing customers.

There are exceptions, though, where e-mail can form part of an acquisition strategy:

- Cold e-mails, using a consumer e-mail list provider such as Experian or a business e-mail list such as Corpdata, are technically opt-in as the recipient may have agreed to receive offers by e-mail, but care is needed as they can feel like spam to the recipient, and response rates are often microscopic.
- Co-branded e-mails are somewhat better. A department store, for example, teamed up with a grocery retailer to sell products which the grocer did not sell. Advertised to the grocer's e-mail list as part of a regular customer update, the e-mails generated a healthy 8 per cent response rate and a good return to both parties. Clearly the brands need to be consistent with each other, and the product lines complementary, for this to make sense.
- Finally, the customer may opt into e-mail using another medium. A campaign which has been influential within the car industry was conducted by General Motors around the launch of a new model of the Vectra. In a change from the traditional mass marketing model of this sector, this 'Dialogue' programme provided a response number and website on its advertisements. The 100,000 respondents were asked some simple questions: what car they drove, what kind of car they were interested in, when they were likely to replace their car, and whether they wished to be contacted by e-mail or post. This led to simply tailored quarterly brochures, delivered by mail or e-mail, reflecting the customer's position in the purchase cycle: soft, branding messages to begin with; harder information on model variations and pricing nearer to the customer's estimated replacement date. The end result was 7,000 more cars sold than in a control group who were not contacted – a very healthy return on some simple e-mails and mailings. The tailoring may have been simple, but it led consumers to feel that they were indeed in a relevant dialogue.

The ease of forwarding e-mails makes it an ideal vehicle for viral marketing: a promotional message which is passed from peer to peer. Most 'virals' are based on humour. Coca-Cola's Happiness Machine video, for example, a low-cost ad made specifically for viral distribution and launched on Twitter, has had 2.6 million views on YouTube at the time of writing. Successful virals can also be shocking, clever, or compulsively informative. Of course, these criteria may be met by material which is nothing to do with brands, or indeed which is created by 'economic terrorists': the telecommunications support person who fell asleep in a customer's flat is still on the first page of Google results when one searches on 'Comcast' several years after its release, at untold cost to Comcast in negative publicity, showing yet again that the most important form of promotion is to ensure that the core product or service meets the customer's buying criteria.

Finally, we should not forget the importance of *inbound* e-mails, which may be service queries, but equally may form sales leads. Many companies are so geared up to recruit customers from their outbound campaigns that no one has time to answer e-mails from prospects! These are often managed along with chat by a multimedia service centre which is also handling telephone traffic; but however they are handled, it is important in marketing plans to ensure that resources are available to react to customers when they contact a company.

SALES PROMOTION

The term *advertising* (often referred to as 'above-the-line expenditure') can be defined as all non-personal communication in measured media. This includes television, cinema, radio, print, websites, and outdoor media.

▶ Sales promotion, for which the term 'below-the-line expenditure' is often used as a synonym, is not easily defined. For example, Americans often use the term to describe all forms of communication, including advertising and personal selling. In other parts of the world, the term is used by some to describe any non-face-to-face activity concerned with the promotion of sales; some use it to describe any non-media expenditure; while others use it specifically to mean in-store merchandising.

The fact is that none of these definitions is an accurate reflection of how sales promotion works in practice, which is why there is so much confusion about many aspects of this important area of marketing activity.

In practice, sales promotion is a specific activity, which can be defined as the making of a featured offer to defined customers within a specific time limit.

> Sales promotion is non-face-to-face activity concerned with the promotion of sales. It involves the making of a featured offer to defined customers within a specific time limit

In other words, to qualify as a sales promotion, someone must be offered something which is featured, rather than just being an aspect of trade. Furthermore, the offer must include benefits not inherent in the product or service, as opposed to the intangible benefits offered in advertising, such as adding value through appeals to imagery.

Seen this way, every other element of the marketing mix, including advertising, personal selling, point-of-sale material, pricing, after-sales service, and so on, can be used as part of a structured activity in order to achieve specified objectives.

Sales Promotion in Practice

Sales promotion is essentially a problem-solving activity designed to get customers to behave more in line with the economic interests of the company.

Typical tasks for sales promotion are: slow stock movement; counteracting competitive activity; encouraging repeat purchase; securing marginal buyers; getting bills paid on time; inducing trial purchase; and so on.

From this, it will be seen that sales promotion is not necessarily concerned with volume increases. For example, it is often used to assist production and distribution scheduling by persuading customers to bring forward their peak buying from one period to another. To summarize, sales promotion seeks to influence:

- Salespeople to sell
- Customers to buy
- Customers to use more, earlier, faster, etc.
- Users to buy
- Users to use.

In recent years sales promotion activity has increased to such an extent that it now accounts for as much expenditure as above-the-line advertising.

However, it is important to realize that, on its own, sales promotion will not replace selling, change long-term trends, or build long-term customer loyalty.

Nevertheless, while sales promotion is essentially a tactical device, it also has an important strategic role to play, as we shall see later.

Different kinds of sales promotion

The many and varied types of sales promotions are listed in Table 7.7. Each of these different types is appropriate for different circumstances and each has advantages and disadvantages. For example, with a promotion that consists of a free case bonus, it is possible to measure precisely both the cost of the extra cases and the additional volume resulting from the offer; it is fast and flexible; it is effective where the customer is profit conscious; it can be made to last as long as required; and it is simple to set up, administer and sell. On the other hand, it has no cumulative value to the customer, is unimaginative, and can often be seen as a prelude to a permanent price reduction.

Target market	Type of promotion					
	Money		**Goods**		**Services**	
	Direct	**Indirect**	**Direct**	**Indirect**	**Direct**	**Indirect**
Consumer	Price reduction	Coupons Vouchers Money equivalent Competitions	Free goods Premium offers (e.g. 13 for 12) Free gifts Trade-in offers	Stamps Coupons Vouchers Money equivalent Competitions	Guarantees Group participation events Special exhibitions and displays	Cooperative advertising Stamps Coupons Vouchers for services Events admission Competitions
Trade	Dealer loaders Loyalty schemes Incentives Full-range buying	Extended credit Delayed invoicing Sale or return Coupons Vouchers Money equivalent	Free gifts Trial offers Trade-in offers	Coupons Vouchers Money equivalent Competitions	Guarantees Group participation events Free services Risk reduction schemes Training Special exhibitions Displays Demonstrations Reciprocal trading schemes	Stamps Coupons Vouchers for services Competitions
Sales force	Bonus Commission	Coupons Vouchers Points systems Money equivalent Competitions	Free gifts	Coupons Vouchers Points systems Money equivalent	Free services Group participation events	Coupons Vouchers Points systems for services Event admission Competitions

Table 7.7: Types of sales promotions

Points schemes are flexible, have wide appeal, do not involve the company in holding stocks of gifts, customers cannot easily value gifts, and they are easy to administer. On the other hand, they offer no advantages in bulk buying, are difficult to budget, and they lack the immediacy of dealer loaders. Great care is necessary, therefore, in selecting a scheme appropriate to the objective sought.

The strategic role of sales promotion

Because sales promotion is essentially used as a tactical device, it often amounts to little more than a series of spasmodic gimmicks lacking in any coherence. Yet the same management that organizes sales promotion usually believes that advertising should conform to some overall strategy. Perhaps this is because advertising has always been based on a philosophy of building long-term brand franchise in a consistent manner, whereas the basic rationale of sales promotion is to help the company retain a tactical initiative.

Even so, there is no reason why there should not be a strategy for sales promotion, so that each promotion increases the effectiveness of the next.

In this way a bond between seller and buyer is built up, so that the tactical objectives are linked in with some overall plan, and so that there is generally a better application of resources.

That this is possible can be seen from the sales promotional campaigns involving the Home Pride Flour Graders, who first appeared in the early 1960s, from the 20 million enamel brooches given out by Robertson's since the 1930s, from Mighty Ajax, Miss Pears, the Ovalteenies, and many other campaigns which have used schemes and devices that have been consistently incorporated into a product's promotional strategy.

More recent schemes, such as the Tesco Clubcard, are proof that it is possible to establish a style of promotion which, if consistently applied, will help to establish the objectives of a product over a long period of time, which are flexible, and which have staying power.

Applying sales promotion to business-to-business products

Business-to-business goods are always sold to other organizations and this has the effect of changing the emphasis placed on certain elements of the marketing mix, rather than having any fundamental effect on the relevancy of the marketing concept.

It will not be surprising, then, to learn that, suitably adapted, most consumer goods sales promotional techniques can be applied to business-to-business goods and services.

Yet in spite of this, sales promotion is comparatively rare in business-to-business markets, perhaps partly from a belief born in the engineering discipline that if a firm has to promote its products, there must be something wrong with them.

In recent years, however, business-to-business companies have begun to take note of the enormous success of sales promotion campaigns and are becoming more aware of sales promotion as a flexible and competitive tool of marketing.

One industrial goods company with divisions spanning a range of products from fast-moving industrial goods to high-priced capital goods has developed a range of special promotional schemes which include the following: trade-in allowances; competitions; reciprocal trading schemes; credit arrangements; training schemes; desk-top give-aways; custom-built guarantees – all made as featured offers.

Preparing the sales promotion plan

There is widespread acknowledgement that sales promotion is one of the most mismanaged of all marketing functions. This is mainly because of the confusion about what sales promotion is, which often results in expenditures not being properly recorded. Some companies include it with advertising, others as part of sales force expenditure, others as a general marketing expense, others as a manufacturing expense (as in the case of extra product, or special labels, or packaging), while the loss of revenue from special price reductions is often not recorded at all.

Such failures can be extremely damaging because sales promotion is such an important part of marketing strategy. Also, with increasing global competition, uncertain economic conditions, and growing pressures from channels, sales promotion is becoming more widespread and more acceptable.

This means that companies can no longer afford not to set objectives, or to evaluate results after the event, or to fail to have some company guidelines. For example, a 1 ecu case allowance on a product with a contribution rate of 3 ecu per case has to increase sales by 50 per cent just to maintain the same level of contribution.

Failure at least to realize this, or to set alternative objectives for the promotion, can easily result in loss of control and a consequent reduction in profits.

In order to manage a company's sales promotion expenditure more effectively, there is one essential step that must be taken. First, an objective for sales promotion must be established in the same way that an objective is developed for advertising, pricing, or distribution.

The objectives for each promotion should be clearly stated, such as trial, repeat purchase, distribution, display, a shift in buying peaks, combating competition, and so on. Thereafter, the following process should apply:

* Select the appropriate technique
* Pre-test
* Mount the promotion
* Evaluate in depth.

Spending must be analysed and categorized by type of activity (e.g. special packaging, special point-of-sale material, loss of revenue through price reductions, and so on).

> Sales promotion is an important part of marketing strategy, but it is one of the most mismanaged of all marketing functions.

One company manufacturing self-assembly kitchens embarked on a heavy programme of sales promotion after a dramatic reduction in consumer demand. While they managed to maintain turnover, they were worried that their sales promotional activity had been carried out in such a haphazard and piecemeal fashion that they were unable to evaluate the cost-effectiveness of what they had done. They were also very concerned about its effect on company image and their long-term consumer franchise. So, the company made a concentrated study of this area of expenditure, which now represented over half their communication budget. Next time round they had: clear objectives; a clear promotional plan properly integrated into the marketing plan; an established means of assessment.

As for the sales promotional plan itself, the objectives, strategy and brief details of timing and costs should be included. It is important that too much detail should *not* appear in the sales promotional plan. Detailed promotional instructions will follow as the marketing plan unfurls. For example, the following checklist outlines the kind of detail that should eventually be circulated. However, only an outline of this should appear in the marketing plan itself.

Checklist for promotional instruction

Heading	Content
1. *Introduction*	Briefly summarize content – what? where? when?
2. *Objectives*	Marketing and promotional objectives for new product launch.
3. *Background*	Market data. Justification for technique. Other relevant matters.
4. *Promotional offer*	Detail the offer: special pricing structure; describe premium; etc. Be brief, precise and unambiguous.
5. *Eligibility*	Who? Where?
6. *Timing*	When is the offer available? Call, delivery or invoice dates?
7. *Date plan*	Assign dates and responsibilities for all aspects of plan prior to start date.
8. *Support*	Special advertising, point of sale, presenters, leaflets, etc. public relations, samples, etc.
9. *Administration*	Invoicing activity. Free goods invoice lines. Depot stocks. Premium (re)ordering procedure. Cash drawing procedures.
10. *Sales plan*	Targets. Incentives. Effect on routing. Briefing meetings. Telephone sales.
11. *Sales presentation*	Points to be covered in call.
12. *Sales reporting*	Procedure for collection of required data not otherwise available.
13. *Assessment*	How will the promotion be evaluated?
Appendices	

Usually designed to be carried by salespeople as an aid to selling the promotion:

- Summary of presentation points
- Price structures/profit margins
- Summary of offer
- Schedules of qualifying orders
- Blank order forms for suggested orders
- Copies of leaflets

Also required by the sales force may be:

- Samples of (new) product
- Demonstration specimen of premium item
- Special report forms
- Returns of cash/premiums, etc. issued

Note: It is assumed that the broad principles of the promotion have already been agreed by other managers affected by it, such as sales managers.

Public Relations[1]

As the name suggests, 'public relations' is concerned with an organization's relationships with the various groups, or 'publics', that affect its ability to achieve its goals and objectives. The aspects of these relationships which act as a focus for public relations are the image and information a market holds about an organization. In other words, its *position* in the market. At a simple level, this is

achieved through publicity in various print and broadcast media. However, the broader views being encouraged by moves towards *relationship marketing* require public relations activities to be more specific in their targeting and objectives. Public relations, therefore, is an important support for both positioning and relationship marketing.

Public relations messages can be far more influential than advertising.

Interest in public relations is also being stimulated by the reducing power and cost-effectiveness of mass media advertising. As the volume of communications aimed at the public increases and media channels proliferate, public relations offers an alternative means of reaching the audiences which an organization would like to influence. A message received, for instance, via an editorial can be up to five times more influential than one received via an advertisement. Public relations, however, is unlikely to replace advertising or other means of communication and promotion. A more likely development is that it will increase its significance as an integral part of a communications or promotions mix.

Public Relations Communications Tools

Public relations activities cover a number of different areas

News generation

One of the most widely used is the *generation of news*. News is best structured around a story which can incorporate information about an organization or its products. Stories can be created around discoveries, achievements, personalities or changes. Often surveys or projects are commissioned to provide 'objective' reports about topics of relevance to both the sponsoring organization's products

---

[1] The sections on PR and sponsorship are indebted to Ardi Kolah.

and its position. Thus, toothpaste manufacturers might support dental health research or a financial services organization might investigate people's attitudes towards saving. News can also be used to make consumers aware of the existence of a product or service in order to stimulate enquiries from interested parties. It must also be remembered, however, that placing news where it will be accepted for publication is as important a skill as spotting and reporting newsworthy activities.

Events

Organizations can also gain people's attention through staging or sponsoring *events*. These can range from simple news conferences and seminars to exhibitions, competitive activities, anniversary dinners and stunts. All are likely to gain media coverage and draw attention to the sponsoring organization's name. They can also aid the achievement of credibility or establish images with which an organization would like to be associated. Events are also good opportunities to develop relationships with suppliers, opinion leaders and associates, as well as customers.

Publications

An organization's *publications* are another method of communication in which public relations will have an active interest. Sales support material is an obvious example, which can include brochures, manuals and presentations, usable by all personnel who have contact with the outside world. Annual reports, other public interest communiqués and special publications such as cookery books and children's stories also provide vehicles for influencing both customers and those who can affect customers' perceptions. Internal audiences and significant stakeholders are often addressed by organizational newsletters and magazines.

Support for good causes

Organizational *support for good causes* is another means of promoting an image and associating an organization with a certain set of values. This can include charity donations in return for product coupons; the sponsorship of public service activities such as festivals; and individual executives' support for local community interests such as educational establishments, hospitals or crime prevention. All these provide many opportunities for publicity elsewhere.

Expert opinion

Individuals within an organization can also act as sources of *expert opinion* for journalists, public enquiries or other forms of research and investigation. Public relations managers may seek to promote the expertise in their organization through the dissemination of contact lists and by grooming individuals' interviewing and presentational skills.

Visual identity

Organizations also often seek to establish a *visual identity* through either conformity of design or logos. While design can make it easier for customers to recognize an organization's products when they come across one, logos and other identification marks can be more important for internal markets as a means of signifying change or commonalty of purpose.

Scope of Public Relations

Public relations are a powerful support to positioning

Public relations can provide a powerful support for an organization's positioning objectives. As examples, *events* can be used to reinforce brand values, or *publications* can help to draw the public's attention to features such as the stability or innovative nature of an organization. Less directly, but still importantly, public relations can be used to establish credibility for either an organization or its technologies, on the back of which a position can be established. Similarly, public relations may be used to build awareness of new products, new processes or other changes which will enhance an organization's ability to serve its customers. Public relations can thus prepare the way for more direct positioning activities such as sales force campaigns; advertising; pricing mechanisms; and packaging.

Developing *relationships* with both customers and other markets can also benefit from public relations activities. At one level, good relationships involve sharing information, and public relations tools such as sales support materials, specialist publications and research results are useful vehicles here. At another level, relationships should involve demonstrations of commitment and, again, public relations can provide support. This can be through inviting individuals from targeted markets, be they customer markets, influencer markets, referral markets or third party intermediaries, to events. Alternatively this could be achieved by acknowledging their activities with awards, mentions in press releases or by referrals of media enquiries to them. These can be further supported by sales force and sales promotions activities.

An additional role for public relations is in dealing with special problems or disasters and *limiting the damage* such events can have on an organization. In this respect, the tobacco industry maintains a vigilant public relations campaign to limit the effects of adverse health publicity and government restrictions on advertising. An alternative example is provided by Perrier when it became known that some of their product had become contaminated with poisonous chemicals. To limit the potential damage to their brand names, they immediately embarked on a widespread public relations campaign to show that this was an isolated event and that the public were in no danger. Coca-Cola, however, were not so lucky when they launched Dosani (bottled purified water) in the UK in 2004. First, they just survived the revelation that it was simply tap water, filtered with some additives with some good defensive PR ('it goes through a sophisticated high tech filter system'). However, the death knell came a few weeks later when it was revealed that a batch of minerals had contaminated the water with a potentially carcinogenic bromate, which no amount of PR could overcome.

Public relations can be a powerful means of shaping attitudes and opinions

Public relations, then, can be a significant aspect of an organization's promotional mix and can be very influential in shaping attitudes and opinions. Relatively speaking, it is also a cheap means of gaining publicity and access to media channels. As an example, the value to Fuji of advertising on a modern airship was not the direct effect on the people it flew over, but the television coverage it gained from the novelty of the presentation. On a lesser scale, public relations are also very useful for smaller organizations with limited promotional budgets, although the exact results of public relations spending are always hard to quantify.

Sponsorship

Sponsorship has been a popular means of supporting a product or organization's position in its chosen markets since the 1980s. The impetus is to seek a wider variety of communication channels to promote a name or product derived mostly from the growing cost of media advertising. In addition, sponsoring the right kind of person or activity often gave global coverage that would have been difficult to achieve elsewhere, and sponsorship also offered tobacco companies exposure that was increasingly difficult to achieve as they were banned from TV advertising.

Sponsorship can be defined as any commercial agreement by which a sponsor, for the mutual benefit of the sponsor and sponsored party, contractually provides financing or other support in order to establish an association between the sponsor's image, brands or products and a sponsorship property in return for rights to promote this association and/or for the granting of certain agreed direct or indirect benefits.

Types of sponsorship

In general, sponsorship falls into four distinct property types: sport (83 per cent), social (5 per cent), arts and culture (7 per cent) and media (5 per cent) (Figure 7.12).

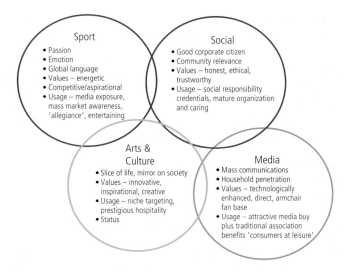

Figure 7.12: Sponsorship types.

Source: Kolah, 2006

Examples of sponsorship activities include:

The Arts – Unilever and the Tate Modern
Social and Community – Tesco's Race for Life
Educational – BT and information technology in schools
Entertainment – T in the Park
Broadcast – Nokia and X-Factor, ITV1
Sports – Emirates and Arsenal FC
Personality – Accenture and Tiger Woods

Sponsorship can be on a local, regional, national, international, and global level, ranging from as little as under £100 to over £1 billion and more. Thus, in 2002, MasterCard spent between £20 and 30 million as official sponsor of the football World Cup and several million pounds are required to sponsor a high profile football team for a year.

Growth of sponsorship

As the 21st century unfolds, sponsorship continues to be one of the fastest developing areas of marketing practice in the world today. The global sponsorship market is currently worth over £17 billion and in the UK is set to grow to over £2 billion, largely because of the sponsorship activities around the London 2012 Olympic Games.

For many organizations, sponsorship has established itself as an essential part of the marketing mix as a result of its perceived ability to make a difference, not only to brand awareness but also, more significantly, to a sponsor's 'bottom line'.

Objectives of sponsorship

To use sponsorship well, organizations have to be clear about the outcomes they desire. Simply requiring a better 'bottom line' is inappropriate since there are few occasions where increased business

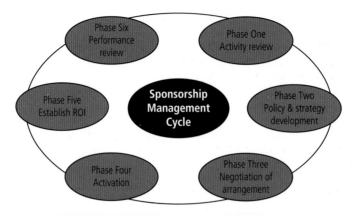

Figure 7.13: Sponsorship management cycle.

or acceptance of a price increase can be directly traced to sponsorship. More realistic and potentially more measurable objectives include:

* Competitive advantage from association or exclusivity
* Alteration or reinforcement of public perception of the sponsor
* Associating a business with particular market segments
* Involving the company's employees in the community
* Generating positive media coverage
* Building goodwill among decision makers.

Sponsorship processes

Like all positioning support activities, sponsorship needs to be carefully planned and managed as illustrated in Figure 7.13.

Phase 1: Existing activity review

The existing activity review should include all positioning support activities and how sponsorship can both complement and enhance them. It is important that any sponsorship programme is consistent with the creative aspects used in other communications and that timings of activities can be coordinated. If, for example, sponsorship is for a high profile event, other communication activities need to support the build-up to the event, and then consolidate the position as the event fades from the public's mind.

Getting the right balance of activities is particularly important if sponsorship is to be used to support brand positioning where consistency of brand values is paramount. Sponsoring a poor performing Formula One racing team, for instance, may not enhance the brand value as much as desired. Similarly, to ensure return on investment, sponsoring a televised event must take into consideration the expected audience profiles and viewing figures to be worthwhile.

Phase 2: Policy and strategy development

A sponsorship strategy needs to be focused on the positioning objectives being pursued. The core decision is what or who should be sponsored, followed by plans for leveraging the association to the maximum cost-effective extent. In the early 2000s, Vodafone's sponsorship portfolio included Manchester United, the Australian Rugby Union Team and Ferrari. The intended association was excellence on a global scale and much effort was put into gaining as many spin-off benefits as possible.

Any sponsorship policy and strategy should include:

- Measurable objectives (as far as possible)
- Audience segmentation (including employees)
- Brand essence or image being supported
- Fit with desired positioning
- Timescales and timings
- Geographical requirements
- Integration with other communications channels (spin-off opportunities)
- Desired impact on behaviour of audiences
- Contingency plans if things change.

The key issue is to ensure a good business case for any sponsorship to avoid serving personal preferences rather than positioning objectives.

Phase 3: Negotiation The objective of the negotiation phase is usually:

- An extension of a sponsorship programme
- An extension subject to certain amendments
- A new sponsorship agreement
- Termination of the old relationship.

Sponsorship negotiations vary depending on the respective bargaining strengths of the parties involved as well as the nature of the property involved. Whatever the case, however, it is important to ensure satisfactory legal arrangements, that the costs of sponsorship match the value of the intended returns, and that there is sufficient exclusivity.

Phase 4: Activation of the sponsorship programme Negotiation of the right to associate with a sponsored property is, however, only the first step in a sponsorship programme. Coca-Cola in the USA, for instance, spends upwards of four times the sponsorship rights fee in its activation of its FIFA football World Cup and Olympic Games properties. Activation activities based on Nike's sponsorship of US top basketball player Michael Jordon might include:

- Advertising (Michael Jordon wears Nike)
- New media promotions (Nike/Michael Jordon websites)
- Hospitality (come and join us at a Michael Jordon basketball match)
- Licensing (special Michael Jordon Nike shoes)
- Public relations (Michael Jordon visits Nike factory in Indonesia)
- Promotions (free entry into a 'Dinner with Michael Jordon' competition with every Nike product purchase).

Phase 5: Return on investment (ROI) Establishing an overall ROI for a sponsorship programme can be tricky since it will be hard to link sales directly with sponsorship expenditure given the more powerful impact of other marketing activities. However, if measurable objectives have been set as part of the strategy and activation processes, it is possible to ensure the expected returns in other areas are achieved. These could include:

- Expected media exposure and audience figures
- Increases in awareness, image, affinity, etc.
- Levels of association
- Attendance at sponsored events.

Phase 6: Review Following measurements of the ROI of a programme, all experiences need to be evaluated and any lessons to be learnt established. These might include seeking answers to questions such as: 'did we sponsor too many events?' and 'how did competitors respond to our sponsorships?' Sponsors may decide to withdraw sponsorship of, say, a football team if too many of its players get embroiled in violent conduct. Similarly, a retailer might withdraw from sponsorship of equipment for schools if its competitors find a better way of offering the sponsorship. In the UK in the early 2000s, supermarket giants Tesco and Sainsbury competed by offering vouchers with purchases that could be exchanged for computers and sports equipment respectively by schools. Which will lose momentum first remains to be seen.

CHAPTER 7 REVIEW

The communications mix

In order to achieve its marketing objectives, the company has to communicate with *existing* and *potential* customers. It can do this *directly*, face to face, generally using a sales force, or call centres, or *indirectly*, using advertising, promotion, electronic media and point-of-sale displays. The choice of communications mix should be determined on the basis of what is going to be most cost-effective in terms of achieving the objectives, i.e. whatever gets the best results per given cost.

Advertising objectives

There are many possible advertising objectives:

- To convey information
- To alter perceptions
- To alter attitudes
- To create desires
- To establish connections, e.g. egg and bacon
- To direct actions
- To provide reassurance
- To remind
- To give reasons for buying
- To demonstrate
- To generate enquiries.

Try Exercises 7.1 and 7.2

Acid test Is it possible to achieve this objective by advertising alone?
    No – rethink objective and/or the means of achieving it *Yes* – go ahead

The advertising plan

The advertising plan has a number of questions to ask: Who is the target audience? What do we know about them? What sort of people are they, etc.? What response do we want to achieve? What do we want to say, convey, make them feel, believe or understand, etc.? How are we going to proceed? What is our creative platform? Can we be sure this is appropriate? Where is the best place to put our communications? Will it be cost-effective? Does it generate the right image, etc.?

Try Exercise 7.3

When will our communications be displayed? Is this the best time? Does it mesh in with other activities, etc.? *Result* – what do we expect to achieve? How will we measure this? Does it mesh in with other activities, etc.? *Budget* – how much is needed? How much is going to be available? How will it be controlled, etc.? *Schedule* – who is going to do what, where and when? What is being spent on what, where and when?

Try Exercise 7.4

Sales promotion objectives

Sales promotion seeks to influence: salespeople to sell customers to buy more, customers to use earlier, users to buy faster, users to use, etc., distributors to stock. It is essentially a short-term tactic. In order to achieve these objectives the promotion can use: *money* – price reductions, coupons, competitions, etc.; *goods* – free goods, e.g. two for the price of one, trade-ins, free trials, redeemable coupons, etc.; *services* – guarantees, training, prizes for events, free services, etc.

Try Exercise 7.5

The sales promotion plan

The sales promotion plan covers the objectives of the promotion: *background* – why the method was chosen; *eligibility* – who and where?; *timing* – opening and closing dates; support in terms of materials; administration required; *the sales plan* – target, incentives; *sales presentation* – points to cover; monitoring procedure to collect data regarding progress, etc.; *assessment* – how will it be evaluated?

Try Exercise 7.6

Questions raised for the company

1. Q: Who should design the advertising?
   A: There is no golden rule and options might be limited by the available budget. Most companies use outside agencies in order to achieve the required level of professionalism. Advertising objectives, however, should *always* be set by you and *not* by an advertising agency.
2. Q: It's been said that 'half the advertising budget is wasted; the problem is to know which half'. Is this true?
   A: It might be for some companies, but, by following the notes and exercises provided here, you should be able to avoid such a problem.
3. Q: Sales promotions aren't used in our business, so would they be a viable marketing tactic for us?
   A: If, by using a promotion, a company breaks new ground, it could give it a differential advantage over competitors.
4. Q: If a sales promotion is successful, should it be kept running?
   A: Once it has achieved its objectives, there seems little point in continuing. It can always be brought back later, and thereby retain its impact and 'freshness'.

APPLICATION QUESTIONS

1. How does your company determine its communications mix (i.e. the relative emphasis given to advertising, sales promotion and personal selling)?
2. Describe the buying process in one of your major customer groups. Who are the key influencers? Critically appraise your strategy for communicating with them.
3. Critically appraise your advertising objectives.
4. Using the checklist given in the text, critically appraise your advertising plan.
5. When you launch a new product/service, do you target your communications specifically at the opinion leaders? Do you know who they are? Can you describe them in terms that are relevant to advertising?
6. Critically evaluate your sales promotional plan.
7. How do you evaluate your sales promotional activities?

EXERCISES

These exercises look at the topics in the context of a 'communications mix'.

We start with an examination of what advertising objectives are (Exercise 7.1).

We then look at how to set advertising objectives for one of your own product/market areas (Exercise 7.2), how to choose the most appropriate advertising media (Exercise 7.3) and how to build up an advertising plan (Exercise 7.4).

Sales promotion is tackled in a slightly different way. The first question that is asked is: 'Is a promotion necessary?' (Exercise 7.5). If the answer to this question is affirmative, then Exercise 7.6 demonstrates how to plan a sales promotion.

Exercise 7.1 What are advertising objectives?

There are two basic questions that advertising objectives should address. 'Who are the people we are trying to influence?' and 'What specific benefits or information are we trying to communicate to them?'

Research has shown that many companies set objectives for advertising which advertising cannot possibly achieve on its own. For example, 'to increase sales' or 'to wipe out the competition'. Equally, it is unrealistic to set an objective 'to convince the target market that our product is best', when any rational analysis would clearly show this not to be true.

Often there is an element of confusion about what advertising objectives are and what marketing objectives are. Remember, marketing objectives are concerned with what products go to which markets, whereas advertising objectives are measurable targets concerned principally with changing attitudes and creating awareness.

Here is a list of marketing or other objectives and advertising objectives mixed up together. Read through this list and write against each objective:

A – if you believe it to be an advertising objective, or
M – if you believe it to be a marketing or other objective.

Marketing (M) or advertising (A) objectives?*

1. To make attitudes more favourable to a particular product.
2. To build an image for the product.
3. To stop existing users turning to competitive products.
4. To get across the idea of a unique product.
5. To create a brand leader to help the launch of additional products at a future date.
6. To win back previous product users who have defected to a competitive product.
7. To expand the whole market.
8. To reduce existing negative attitudes.

---

* Based on a list provided by Professor David Corkindale (formerly of Cranfield University School of Management) and used with his kind permission.

9. To keep building loyalty.
10. To establish the brand and position it in a particular way, e.g. as warm and friendly.
11. To create a brand leader in a particular market.
12. To increase sales among existing users.
13. To improve the frequency of purchase.
14. To keep new entrants out of the market.
15. To convey the idea that the product is 'value for money'.
16. To say how much people like the product.
17. To improve market share compared with competitors.
18. To maintain brand distribution.

The answers to Exercise 7.1 are as follows:

Advertising objectives: numbers 1, 2, 4, 8, 9, 10, 15 and 16.

Marketing or other objectives: numbers 3, 5, 6, 7, 11, 12, 13, 14, 17 and 18.

If you made some mistakes in identifying the objectives correctly, go back and have another look at them and see if you can work out where you went wrong.

Exercise 7.2 Setting advertising objectives

Behind all effective advertising there lies a lot of careful thought and planning, and much of it goes into ensuring that the advertising objectives are the right ones. If these are wrong, everything else which follows is doomed to failure.

In this exercise you are asked to concentrate on just one key market or market segment. It should be a relatively simple matter to repeat the process for other markets at some later date.

Make a note somewhere about which market or segment you will be addressing. Remember, from the Boston Matrix or directional policy matrix, 'stars' will probably be most deserving of the advertising budget.

Now make a note about the marketing objectives which have been set for this market/segment, e.g. what products? what quantities? to whom? etc. Having assembled this information, from the list of 'Possible advertising objectives' below:

1. Select the most appropriate objectives, i.e. those that look the most promising to help the company achieve these marketing objectives (tick in the column).
2. From those you have ticked, eliminate any objectives that you believe can only be achieved by personal communication, i.e. by the sales force.
3. List your remaining objectives in rank order, the most important being at the top of the list.
4. Use only the top objective (and perhaps the second) as a basis for your advertising campaign.

(Continued)

Possible advertising objectives

	Tick here		Tick here
• To establish an immediate sale • To bring a prospect closer to a sale • To change customer perceptions • To direct customer action • To support the sales force • To reinforce attitudes of existing customers • To open up distribution • To improve company image • To demonstrate the product capabilities • To generate enquiries • To impart information • To reassure customers • To 'score points' off competitors' advertising • To enter new markets • To give reasons for buying • To create awareness • To support retailers • To convey the idea of 'value for money' • To reach new geographical areas		• To promote the idea of a unique product • To back up promotions • To develop favourable attitudes to a particular product • To counter price competition • To remind customers about our product • To reinforce the company image • To defend market position • To support the launch of a new product/service • To explain new uses for product • To emphasize range and choice • To reinforce brand recognition • To inform about product availability • To educate customers • To communicate company strengths • To build customer loyalty • To say how much people like the product	

If you think this list omits possible advertising objectives for your company, then extend the list by adding your own objectives to it.

Exercise 7.3 Choosing the advertising media

The previous exercise should have helped to identify the advertising objectives for your chosen market/segment. The next logical step would be to decide exactly what you want to communicate – your creative platform.

However, such a step does not really lend itself to an exercise. Indeed, copywriting is such a specialized form of communication that most companies engage outside specialists to deal with it. Even so, having decided upon the advertising objectives, you must switch your focus of attention now to the target population you hope to influence:

- Who are they?
- What positions do they hold?
- What is their influence on the purchasing decision?
- What personality traits do they exhibit?
- What socio-economic groupings do they belong to?
- What lifestyles do they have?
- How old are they? What sex are they? Are they married? And so on.

Please note that it is usually easier to determine the most appropriate media in the case of *business-to-business* customers, although the same logic applies.

You need to assemble as much information as you can about the target population. The more you know about them, the better your chances of selecting the best medium for your advertising platform.

The accompanying worksheet gives a list of possible advertising media. Study this list and select what would be the best choice, taking into account your objectives and the profile of the target audience.

In making your choice, you will need to take four factors into account:

1. *The character of the medium* – the geographical coverage it gives, the types of audience it reaches, its frequency of publication or showing, its physical possibilities (such as colour, sound, movement), its power or potential to reach special groups, etc.
2. *The atmosphere of the medium* – its ability to convey an image consistent with your objectives, e.g. hard and punchy, discreet, elegant, exclusive, etc.
3. *The 'size' of the medium* – the number of people exposed to the medium in terms of being aware of the contents. For example, a newspaper might be read by two or three members of a family, whereas a technical journal might be circulated to a large number of managers within a company. Alternatively, a poster might be passed by tens of thousands of people.
4. *The comparative cost* – how much will it cost to reach a specific audience.

The cost per 1,000 viewers is often used as a comparative ratio.

There is space on the accompanying worksheet to make notes about these factors, should you be required to keep a record of what influenced your choice of medium.

Worksheet Advertising media (Exercise 7.3)

	Medium	Characteristics	Atmosphere	Size	Comparative cost
Printed media	Local newspapers National newspapers Trade and technical press Magazines and periodicals Direct mail Leaflets Directories (Yellow Pages, buyers' guides, etc.)				
Others	Television Posters (static) Transport (on trains, buses, vans, etc.) Cinema Radio The internet Other (specify)				

(Continued)

Having decided what you want to communicate (your advertising objectives, Exercise 7.2), worked out the creative platform of the exact message you wish to convey, and decided on the choice of media (Exercise 7.3), you have assembled the key ingredients of an advertising plan. What remains to be done is to establish when the advertising will be used, who will be responsible for the various activities in bringing what is still an idea into life, how progress will be monitored and the criteria by which success will be judged.

The accompanying worksheet provides a simple format to record all this information. We would recommend that you try using it, and then adapt it to your particular purposes, so that you finish up with something that is genuinely tailor-made.

Exercise 7.4 The advertising plan

Worksheet Advertising plan (Exercise 7.4)

ADVERTISING PLAN FOR _____ (either product or service/
market or segment)

ADVERTISING OBJECTIVES TO _____

Selected media	Brief description of advert	Timing	Responsibility	Budget	Actual cost	Criteria by which success will be judged	Evaluation comments

Note: Now complete advertising plans for other products/services and market segments.

Exercise 7.5 Is a promotion necessary?

Sales promotions should be seen as the logical development of the company's marketing strategy. As such, they should be complementary to all other parts of the communications mix and should not be seen as an alternative, or some disconnected activity.

There are three key questions to be answered.

1. How do we decide whether or not to run a promotion?
2. What form should the promotion take?
3. How do we plan it?

The first two questions are addressed by this exercise. The planning element is covered in Exercise 7.6.

In order to give this exercise a clear focus, please select just one of the product/market areas of your portfolio and work with it. Once you have worked through this process, you will see how it can be used elsewhere, with other products/markets.

Step 1 On a separate piece of paper, write down the problems you see affecting sales of the product or service in the market/market segment you have chosen. If there are no problems, you might question why a sales promotion is being considered in this area. Your efforts might be better spent focusing on another part of your product/ service range.

Step 2 Look at the problems you have listed and rank them in order of 'seriousness', 1 being the major problem, 2 the next, and so on.

Step 3 Transfer the information you have just assembled to column 1 of the accompanying worksheet.

Step 4 Taking the major problem first, work across the page on the worksheet and consider the possible solutions to the problem listed there. You will note that there is space to add solutions of your own.

Clearly, a sales promotion is not always going to be the way to resolve a sales problem. However, the economics or convenience of one type of solution compared with another might well sway the argument. For example, the best solution to the sales problem might be to modify the product, but this might be very costly and take time to achieve. In such circumstances, a sales promotion might work in terms of both costs and immediacy.

Therefore, considered judgement has to be used in weighing up the costs and likely chances of success of each possible solution. *Only* when the sales-promotion option looks favourable should you take matters to the next stage of deciding upon the type of promotion.

Step 5 If a sales promotion will not make any impact on the major sales problem, work across the page again for the next problem down. Continue this process for other sales problems until a sales promotion is found which would appear to hold the promise of success.

Ideally, the sales promotion should make an impact on a fairly serious sales problem. If it is only going to affect a marginal issue, it raises questions about whether or not it is worth spending the time and effort on the promotion and whether another area might be more deserving of attention.

(Continued)

Worksheet Deciding if sales promotion will help (Exercise 7.5)

	PRODUCT/SERVICE/MARKET SEGMENT UNDER CONSIDERATION _____													
	Problems affecting sales	POSSIBLE SOLUTIONS												
		More advertising		More sales effort?		Change price?		Change product?		Sales promotion?		Other ideas (add your own)		
		Cost	Likely success	Cost	Likely success	Cost	Likely success	Cost	Likely success	Cost	Likely success	Cost	Likely success	Cost	Likely success
Major problem	1													
	2													
	3													
Problems listed in reducing order	4													
	5													
	6													

Having established that a sales promotion is a suitable way to have an impact on a particular sales problem you must now decide on the nature of the promotion.

In broad terms, a promotion can be aimed at three target groups:

1. Customers or consumers
2. Channels/intermediaries
3. Your own sales force.

The promotion can also take one of three forms:

1. It can involve money
2. It can involve goods
3. It can involve services.

You will have to decide first of all which target group needs to be influenced most to make impact on your sales problem. You might even decide it is more than one group.

Having made that decision, you then have to work out what type of promotion will have maximum appeal to that group. Ideally, you will be able to devise something with maximum appeal, at a modest cost. However, when considering the cost element, you must remember that the promotional costs have to be weighed up against the benefits of reducing the specific sales problem.

Table 7.4 provides a number of ideas about sales promotions and enables you to select the most appropriate type for your purposes.

Exercise 7.6 Planning a sales promotion

It is important to ensure that any sales promotion is well coordinated in terms of what happens before, during and after the promotion. At different stages, different people might be participating and special resources might be required. Therefore a plan needs to be prepared in a simple way that most people can follow. In essence, this is all you need in a plan.

Heading	Content
Introduction	Briefly summarize the problem upon which the promotion is designed to make impact
Objectives	Show how the objectives of the promotion are consistent with the marketing objectives
Background	Provide the relevant data or justification for the promotion
Promotional offer	Briefly, but precisely, provide details of the offer
Eligibility	Who is eligible? Where?
Timing	When is the offer available?
Date plan	The dates and responsibilities for all elements of the promotion
Support	Special materials, samples, etc. that are required by the sales force, retailers, etc.
Administration	Budgets, storage, invoicing, delivery, etc.
Sales plan	Briefing meetings, targets, incentives, etc.
Sales presentation	Points to be covered
Sales reporting	Any special information required
Assessment	How the promotion will be evaluated

Using these guidelines, and the accompanying worksheet, try to extend the information you assembled in Exercise 7.5 into a complete promotional plan.

Worksheet Promotion plan (Exercise 7.6)

	Heading	Content
1	Introduction	
2	Objectives	
3	Background	
4	Promotional offer	
5	Eligibility	
6	Timing	
7	Date plan	
8	Support	
9	Administration	
10	Sales plan	
11	Sales presentation	
12	Sales reporting	
13	Assessment	

Chapter

8

THE SALES PLAN

SUMMARY

- How important is personal selling?
- The role of personal selling in the marketing mix
- A method for determining the correct number of salespeople required
- How to set quantitative and qualitative sales objectives
- How to improve sales force productivity
- How sales forces should be managed
- How to manage key accounts
- How to prepare a sales plan
- Exercises to turn the theory into practice

INTRODUCTION

Personal selling has an important strategic role to play in communicating between a company and its customers. To have a chance of success, management must be able to answer the following kinds of question:

- How important is personal selling?
- What is the role of personal selling in the marketing mix?
- How many salespeople do we need?
- What do we want them to do?
- How should they be managed?
- Should we treat key accounts differently?

These and other questions will be considered in this chapter as important determinants of the sales plan. However, those readers who believe they already know enough about communications, pricing and distribution planning, and who are principally concerned with the preparation of a strategic marketing plan, can go straight to Chapter 12.

HOW IMPORTANT IS PERSONAL SELLING?

Most organizations had an organized sales force long before they introduced a formal marketing activity of the kind described throughout this text. In spite of this fact, sales force management has traditionally been a neglected area of marketing management.

> Personal selling is promotion via a person-to-person conversation, whether it be at the customer's premises, on the telephone, or elsewhere

There are several possible reasons. One is that not all marketing and product managers have had experience in a personal selling or sales management role; consequently, these managers often underestimate the importance of efficient personal selling.

Another reason for neglect of sales force management is that sales personnel themselves sometimes encourage an unhelpful distinction between sales and marketing by depicting themselves as being at 'the sharp end'. After all, isn't there something slightly daring about dealing with real live customers as opposed to sitting in an office surrounded by marketing surveys, charts and plans? Such reasoning is obviously misleading.

> Unless a good deal of careful marketing planning has taken place before salespeople make their effort to persuade the customer to place an order, the probability of a successful sale is much reduced.

The suggested distinction between marketing 'theory' and sales 'practice' is further invalidated when we consider that profitable sales depend not just on individual customers and individual products but on groups of customers (that is, market segments) and on the supportive relationship of products to each other (that is, a carefully planned product portfolio).

> Another factor to be taken into account in this context is the constant need for the organization to think in terms of where future sales will be coming from, rather than to concentrate solely on present products, customers and problems.

The authors have investigated many European sales forces over the last two decades and have found an alarming lack of planning and professionalism. Salespeople frequently have little idea about which products and which groups of customers to concentrate on, have too little knowledge about competitive activity, do not plan presentations well, rarely talk to customers in terms of benefits, make too little effort to close the sale, and make many calls without any clear objectives. Even worse, marketing management is rarely aware that this important and expensive element of the marketing mix is not being managed effectively.

The fact that many organizations have separate departments and directors for the marketing and sales activities increases the likelihood of such failures of communication. Although its importance varies according to circumstances, in many businesses the sales force is the most important element in the marketing mix.

MARKETING INSIGHT

In industrial goods companies, for example, it is not unusual to find very small amounts being spent on other forms of communication and very large sums being spent on the sales force in the form of salaries, cars and associated costs. Personal selling is also used widely in many service industries where customers are looking for very specific benefits. Insurance companies, for example, do use media advertising, but many rely for most of their sales on personal selling, whether face to face or by telephone. Customers for insurance policies in all but the simplest insurance categories almost invariably need to discuss which policy would best fit their particular needs and circumstances; it is the task of the salesperson to explain the choices available and to suggest the most appropriate policy.

Recent surveys show that more money is spent by companies on their sales forces than on advertising and sales promotion combined. Personal selling, then, is a vital and expensive element in the marketing mix.

The solution to the problem of poor sales force management can only be found in the recognition that personal selling is, indeed, a crucial part of the marketing process, but that it must be planned and considered as carefully as any other element. Indeed, it is an excellent idea for any manager responsible for marketing to go out into a territory for a few days each year and attempt to persuade customers to place orders. It is a good way of finding out what customers really think of the organization's marketing policies!

THE ROLE OF PERSONAL SELLING

Personal selling can be seen most usefully as part of the *communications mix*. (Other common elements of the communications mix, it will be remembered, are advertising, sales promotion, public relations, the internet, call centres, direct mail, exhibitions, and so on.) The surveys set out in Chapter 7 show that organizations cannot leave the communications task only to the sales force. The same question remains, however, with advertising: 'How is the organization to define the role of personal selling in its communications mix? Again, the answer lies in a clear understanding of the buying process which operates in the company's markets.

The efficiency of any element of communication depends on achieving a match between information required and information given. To achieve this match, the marketer must be aware of the different requirements of different people at different stages of the buying process. This approach highlights the importance of ensuring that the company's communications reach *all* key points in the buying chain. No company can afford to assume that the actual sale is the only important event.

> The efficiency of any element of communication depends on achieving a match between information required and information given.

In order to determine the precise role of personal selling in its communications mix, the company must identify the major influencers in each purchase decision and find out what information they are likely to need at different stages of the buying process.

Most institutional buying decisions consist of many separate phases, from the recognition of a problem through to performance evaluation and feedback on the product or service purchased. Furthermore, the importance of each of these phases varies according to whether the buying situation is a first-time purchase or a routine repurchase. A similar multi-stage process applies to more complex consumer decisions. Clearly, the information needs will differ at each stage. (This was discussed in some detail in Chapter 7 – in particular, see Figure 7.3.)

Personal selling has a number of advantages over other elements of the communications mix:

1. It is a two-way form of communication, giving the prospective purchaser the opportunity to ask questions of the salesperson about the product or service.
2. The sales message itself can be made more flexible and, therefore, can be more closely tailored to the needs of individual customers.
3. Salespeople can use in-depth product knowledge to relate their message to the perceived needs of the buyer and to deal with objections as they arise.
4. Where the product or service can be tailored to the customer, a dialogue can take place about how best to do this.
5. Most importantly, salespeople can ask for an order and, perhaps, negotiate on price, delivery or special requirements.

Once an order has been obtained from a customer and there is a high probability of a rebuy occurring, the salesperson's task changes from persuasion to reinforcement. All communications at this stage should contribute to underlining the wisdom of the purchase. The salesperson may also take the opportunity to encourage consideration of other products or services in the company's range.

Clearly, in different markets, different weighting is given to the various forms of communication available. In the grocery business, for example, advertising and sales promotion are extremely important elements in the communications process. However, the food manufacturer must maintain an active sales force which keeps in close contact with the retail buyers. This retail contact ensures vigorous promotional activity in the chain. In the wholesale hardware business frequent and regular face-to-face contact with retail outlets through a sales force is the key determinant of success. In industries where there are few customers (such as capital goods and specialized process materials) an in-depth understanding of the customers' production processes has to be built up; here, again, personal contact is of paramount importance. In contrast, many fast-moving industrial goods are sold into fragmented markets for diverse uses; in this area, forms of communication other than personal selling take on added importance.

Many companies in the IT sector use personal selling to good advantage. IT hardware and software applications vary enormously in the range of capabilities they offer. Technical details can be supplied in brochures and other promotional material, but the managers likely to be taking the purchase decision often find it difficult to evaluate the alternatives. A good salesperson can ascertain quickly the requirements of a particular client and identify to what extent these will be fulfilled by their solutions. For their part, the customer can identify quickly whether the company understands their requirements, whether it appears credible, and whether or not it is able to provide the back-up service necessary to implement the solution and establish its use in the organization. Such considerations are likely to be far more influential than the comparison of technical data sheets in a decision to purchase.[1]

DETERMINING THE REQUISITE NUMBER OF SALESPEOPLE

The organization should begin its consideration of how many salespeople it needs by finding out exactly how work is allocated at present. Start by listing all the things the current sales force actually does. These might include opening new accounts; servicing existing accounts; demonstrating new products; taking repeat orders; and collecting debts. This listing should be followed by an investigation of alternative ways of carrying out these responsibilities. For example, telephone selling has been shown to be a perfectly acceptable alternative to personal visits, particularly in respect of repeat business. The sales force can thus be freed for missionary work, which is not so susceptible to the telephone approach. Can debts be collected by mail or by telephone? Can products be demonstrated at exhibitions or showrooms? It is only by asking these kinds of question that we can be certain we have not fallen into the common trap of committing the company to a decision and then seeking data and reasons to justify the decision. At this stage, the manager should concentrate on collecting relevant, quantified data and then use judgement and experience to help in making a decision.

Basically, all sales force activities can be categorized under three headings. A field-based salesperson:

- Makes calls
- Travels
- Performs administrative functions.

These tasks constitute what can be called the *workload*. If we first decide what constitutes a reasonable workload for a salesperson, in hours per month, then we can begin to measure how long their current activities take, hence the exact extent of their current workload.

This measurement can be performed either by some independent third party or, preferably, by the salespeople themselves. All they have to do for one simple method of measurement is to record distance travelled, time in and out of calls, and the outlet type. This data can then be analysed easily to indicate the average duration of a call by outlet type, the average distance travelled in a month, and the average speed according to the nature of the territory (that is, city, suburbs or country). With the aid of a map, existing customers can be allocated on a trial-and-error basis, together with the concomitant time values for clerical activities and travel. In this way, equitable workloads can be calculated for the sales force, building in, if necessary, spare capacity for sometimes investigating potential new sales outlets.

This kind of analysis sometimes produces surprising results, as when the company's 'star' salesperson is found to have a smaller workload than the one with the worst results, who may be having to work much longer hours to achieve sales because of the nature of the territory.

There are, of course, other ways of measuring workloads. One major consumer goods company used its insight department to measure sales force effectiveness. The results of this study are summarized in Table 8.1.

The table showed the company how a salesperson's time was spent and approximately how much of their time was actually available for selling. One immediate action taken by the company was to initiate a training programme which enabled more time to be spent on selling as a result of better planning. Another was to improve the quality of the sales performance while face to face with the customers.

Armed with this kind of quantitative data, it becomes easier to determine how many salespeople are needed and how territories can be equitably allocated.

		Per cent of day		Minutes per day	
Outside call time	Drive to and from route	15.9		81	
	Drive one route	16.1		83	
	Walk	4.6		24	
	Rest and breaks	6.3		32	
	Pre-call administration	1.4		7	
	Post-call administration	5.3		27	
			49.6		254
Inside call time	Business talks	11.5		60	
	Sell	5.9		30	
	Chat	3.4		17	
	Receipts	1.2		6	
	Miscellaneous	1.1		6	
	Drink	1.7		8	
	Waiting	7.1		36	
			31.9		163
Evening work	Depot work	9.8		50	
	Entering pinks	3.9		20	
	Pre-plan route	4.8		25	
			18.5		95
			100.0		8 h 32 min

Table 8.1: Breakdown of a salesperson's total daily activity

DETERMINING THE ROLE OF SALESPEOPLE

Whatever the method used to organize the salesperson's day, there is always comparatively little time available for selling. In these circumstances, it is vital that a company should know as precisely as possible what it wants its sales force to do. Sales force objectives can be either quantitative or qualitative.

Quantitative Objectives

Principal quantitative objectives are concerned with the following measures:

* How much to sell (the value of unit sales volume)
* What to sell (the mix of product lines to sell)
* Where to sell (the markets and individual customers that will take the company towards its marketing objectives)
* Desired profit contribution (where relevant and where the company is organized to compute this)
* Selling costs (in compensation, expenses, supervision, and so on).

The first three types of objectives are derived directly from the marketing objectives, which are discussed in detail in Chapter 6, and constitute the principal components of the sales plan. There are, of course, many other kinds of quantitative objectives which can be set for the sales force, including the following:

* Number of point-of-sale displays organized
* Number of letters written to prospects
* Number of telephone calls to prospects
* Number of reports turned or not turned in
* Number of trade meetings held
* Use of sales aids in presentations
* Number of service calls made
* Number of customer complaints
* Safety record
* Collections made
* Training meetings conducted
* Competitive activity reports
* General market condition reports.

Salespeople may also be required to fulfil a coordinating role between a team of specialists and the client organization.

A company selling mining machinery, for example, employs a number of 'good general salespeople' who establish contacts and identify which ones are likely to lead to sales. Before entering into negotiations with any client organization, the company selling the machinery may feel that it needs to call in a team of highly specialized engineers and financial experts for consultation and advice. It is the task of the salesperson in this company to identify when specialist help is needed and to coordinate the people who become involved in the negotiation.

However, most objectives are subservient to the major objectives outlined above which are associated directly with what is sold and to whom.

Qualitative Objectives

Qualitative objectives can be a potential source of problems if sales managers try to assess the performance of the sales force along dimensions which include abstract terms such as 'loyalty', 'enthusiasm', 'cooperation', and so on, since such terms are difficult to measure objectively. In seeking qualitative measurements of performance, managers often resort to highly subjective interpretations, which cause resentment and frustration among those being assessed.

However, managers can set and measure qualitative objectives which actually relate to the performance of the sales force on the job. It is possible, for example, to assess the skill with which a person applies their product knowledge on the job, or the skill with which they plan their work, or the skill with which they overcome objections during a sale interview. While still qualitative in nature, these measures relate to standards of performance understood and accepted by the sales force.

Given such standards, it is not too difficult for a competent field sales manager to identify deficiencies, to get agreement on them, to coach in skills and techniques, to build attitudes of professionalism, to show how to self-train, to determine which training requirements cannot be tackled in the field, and to evaluate improvements in performance and the effect of any past training.[2]

MARKETING INSIGHT

One consumer goods company with 30 field sales managers discovered that most of them were spending much of the day in their offices engaged in administrative work, most of it self-made. The company proceeded to take the offices away and insisted that the sales managers spend most of their time in the field training their salespeople. To assist them in this task, they trained them in how to appraise and improve salespeople's performance in the field. There was a dramatic increase in sales and, consequently, in the sales managers' own earnings. This rapidly overcame their resentment at losing their offices.

IMPROVING SALES FORCE PRODUCTIVITY

Many salespeople might secretly confess to a proclivity to call more frequently on those large customers who give them a friendly reception and less frequently on those who put obstacles in their way.

If we classify customers according to their friendliness to us, as well as to their size, it is easy to see how a simple matrix can be developed to help us decide where our major effort should be directed. From Figure 8.1, it can be seen that the boxes which offer the greatest potential for increased sales productivity are Boxes 4 and 5, with Boxes 1 and 2 receiving a 'maintenance' call rate. Boxes 7 and 8 should receive an 'alternative strategy' approach to establish whether hostility can be overcome. If these alternative approaches fail, a lower call rate may be appropriate. Box 9 is the 'Don't bother' box, while Boxes 3 and 6 will receive the minimum attention consistent with our goals.

None of this is meant to indicate definitive rules about call frequencies, which will always remain a matter of management judgement. Its sole purpose is to question our assumptions about call frequencies on existing and potential accounts to check that we are not using valuable time which could be more productively used in other directions.

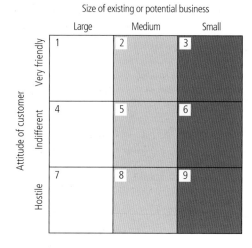

Figure 8.1: Improving sales force productivity.

MANAGING THE SALES FORCE

Sales force motivation has received a great deal of attention in recent times, largely as a result of the work done by psychologists in other fields of management. There is now widespread appreciation of the fact that it is not sufficient merely to give someone a title and an office and expect to get good results.

> Effective leadership, it is acknowledged, is as much 'follower-determined' as it is determined by management.

While for the purposes of this discussion it is not necessary to enter into a detailed discussion of sales force motivation, it is worth mentioning briefly some important factors that contribute to effective sales force management.

If a sales manager's job is to improve the performance of the sales force, and if performance is a function of incentives minus disincentives, then the more incentives can be increased and disincentives reduced, the better will be performance.

Research has shown that an important element of sales force motivation is a sense of doing a worthwhile job. In other words, desire for praise and recognition, the avoidance of boredom and monotony, the enhancement of self-image, freedom from fear and worry, and the desire to belong to something believed to be worthwhile, all contribute to enhanced performance. One well-known piece of research carried out in the USA examined the reasons for the results of the 20 highest producing sales units in one company compared with the 20 lowest producing sales units. The research showed all the above factors to be major determinants of success.

> If performance is a function of incentives minus disincentives, then the more incentives can be increased and disincentives reduced, the better will be performance.

However, remuneration will always be a most important determinant of motivation. This does not necessarily mean paying the most money, although clearly unless there are significant financial motivations within a company, it is unlikely that people will stay. In drawing up a remuneration plan, which would normally include a basic salary plus some element for special effort, such as bonus or commission, the following objectives should be considered:

- To attract and keep effective salespeople
- To remain competitive
- To reward salespeople in accordance with their individual performance
- To provide a guaranteed income plus an orderly individual growth rate
- To generate individual sales initiative
- To encourage teamwork
- To encourage the performance of essential non-selling tasks
- To ensure that management can fairly administer and adjust compensation levels as a means of achieving sales objectives.

A central concept of sales force motivation is that individual salespeople will exert more effort if managers encourage them to concentrate on:

1. Their expectations of accomplishing their sales objectives
2. The personal benefits derived from accomplishing those objectives.

This theory of sales force motivation is known as the path-goal approach because it is based on the particular path the salesperson follows to a particular sales objective and the particular goals associated with successfully travelling down that path. The salesperson estimates the probability of success of travelling down various paths or sales approaches and estimates the probability that their superiors will recognize their goal accomplishments and will reward them accordingly.

The motivational functions of the sales manager consist of increasing personal pay-offs to salespeople for work-goal attainment, making the path to these pay-offs easier to travel by clarifying it, reducing road blocks and pitfalls, and increasing the opportunities for personal satisfaction en route.

Few people would deny that sales force motivation is a difficult and highly emotive subject, and at the end of the day common sense must prevail. One of the authors once attended a sales conference which opened with girls dancing to the company song. They were followed immediately by a tawdry-looking marketing manager who spent an hour pointing to bar charts on slides. Not surprisingly, few of the sales force present remembered much about the central issues of the conference, while the few saleswomen present were offended!

Another common feature of sales conferences is the use of bellicose language, such as 'our plan is to wipe out the enemy', and so on. The use of such imagery is often in sharp contrast to the day-to-day circumstances of the average salesperson, who gets up on a rainy Monday morning, gets into their small company car, and is rejected on their first call of the week!

A bit of excitement at sales conferences is necessary, of course, but most sales directors and managers would be better occupied providing the sales force with information and tools designed to make the selling task easier, rather than providing entertainment.

Organizational support for salespeople, then, is always an issue. But in the case of key accounts, the management task in aligning sales processes with all organizational functions are far greater – so much so that some companies treat key accounts as an entirely separate channel from the regular sales force. The next section considers key account management (KAM) in detail.

HOW TO MANAGE KEY ACCOUNTS

Many firms find that a large proportion of their sales comes from just a small number of customers. These customers have always been treated differently from 'mass' customers, as the opportunities from deepening relationships with them can be very significant, and of course the risk to the business if even one is lost is far greater. So, senior management is often actively involved in these relationships, which are highly attractive for ambitious salespeople.

But the best acquirer of new customers does not necessarily make the best builder of these major relationships, which in any case cannot be simply delegated to a single salesperson, however talented. Many a 'key account manager' seems to be a fish out of water – a salesperson 'promoted' on the basis of their performance in the field in managing a territory or portfolio of smaller accounts and prospects, a very different art. So, key account management is best thought of as quite distinct from traditional field sales. In this section, we will first discuss what it is – what constitutes a key account, as well as what the job of a key account manager is.

We will then discuss how to manage KAM relationships, which vary considerably. At one extreme, what is a key account for the seller may be a minor supplier from the buyer's perspective, with no particular reason for loyalty or a deep relationship. At the other extreme, both parties may work together closely from product development through to the process of selling to the buyer's buyer – as in the case of the engine suppliers in the aerospace industry. These clearly need to be managed in a very different way. In these closer relationships, the buyers will seek to gain the benefits of vertical integration and the advantages of outsourcing simultaneously. They will be seeking to achieve advantages such as competitive pricing, additional expertise and flexibility, and avoid the disadvantages frequently encountered with internal, group suppliers: for example, high fixed cost, lack of flexibility and complacency.

MARKETING INSIGHT

A supplier of stationery products had two key accounts which were large high-street retailers. Account A viewed the supplier as a commodity provider of readily substitutable products. Account B, though, viewed the firm as a key partner in growing its stationery offering. The chief executive put two very different people in charge of these key accounts. Account A was managed by a skilled negotiator with an accountancy background, who organized highly efficient, low-cost delivery and service processes in order to hit a low price point and still maintain a margin. Account B was managed by a former retail executive, who was masterful at recrafting the customer's own category management processes to achieve the retailer's objectives – a service so valuable that the retailer would not have dreamed of delisting the supplier for fear of losing this free consultancy. When a third key account switched to a low-cost transactional strategy like Account A, though, the chief executive decided to forgo this business, to avoid an overreliance on three customers: he needed the power to lose any single customer if he was to maintain his bargaining position on price. In a tough sector, the supplier continues to grow its revenue and profits rapidly.

What is a Key Account?

We begin, then, with some definitions. A key account is a customer in a business-to-business market identified by the selling company as of strategic importance.[3] This definition immediately begs the question of how strategic importance should be defined. In practice, key accounts are effectively defined by the criteria used by selling companies to select them. While these are often implicit, it is far more sensible to have explicit criteria. These should include not just current revenue but also potential revenue, if 'strategic importance' is to mean anything; commonly, a measure of complexity is also included.

Many companies still list huge numbers of customers as key accounts. One major IT company claims to have 1,000 key accounts, compared with DHL Worldwide, who at one point claimed to have only 18. When executives genuinely embrace the idea that realisation of key account management implies development of rather intense and far-reaching relationships, they recognize the need to ration the number of candidates for this treatment. That recognition drives more rigorous selection, which finally results in a tighter definition of key accounts.

> A key account is a business-to-business customer identified by the selling company as of strategic importance

What is Key Account Management?

Key account management is the process of allocating and organizing resources to achieve optimal business with a balanced portfolio of identified accounts whose business contributes or could contribute significantly or critically to the achievement of corporate objectives, present or future.[4] There are any number of related terms, such as global account management which is a specific subset of key account management where the client is not only global but also organizes purchasing globally, at least to some extent.

It is notable that this definition does not mention selling. Indeed, in many cases where the relationship has been in existence for years, if not decades, the customer is already 'sold', and the emphasis has switched to management and development across a broad front. This change of emphasis has important implications in the definition of the role of key account managers.

> Key account management is the process of allocating and organizing resources to achieve optimal business with a balanced portfolio of identified accounts whose business contributes or could contribute significantly or critically to the achievement of corporate objectives, present or future

Note also the word 'balanced'. The reader will recall the directional policy matrix discussed in Chapter 5 as a key tool for ensuring a balanced portfolio of product-markets; this tool can also be adapted to plot not product-markets but key accounts, as we will discuss later. However, the important thing is that the company maintains balance across its entire customer portfolio, and not necessarily within its key account portfolio alone.

What is a Key Account Manager?

A key account manager is the person with overall responsibility for the commercial relationship with one or more key accounts. The key account manager typically has to work with many others within the firm to fulfil this responsibility, such as field salespeople responsible for particular countries or product lines, and technical staff involved both in sales processes and in implementation. Whether this coordinating role operates by control or persuasion is an important issue. One study of global account management found that cultural differences are such that it would be dangerous to work on a worldwide control basis, and the role should be

> A key account manager is the person with overall responsibility for the commercial relationship with one or more key accounts

one of persuasion and coordination.[5] Whether or not this is ideal, it is often inevitable in complex matrix structures, so an important part of the key account manager's skillset is influencing skills.

These influencing skills are critical not just in sales processes but also in implementation. In fact, key account management more often fails because of the selling company's organizational problems in delivery of the programme than the buying company's inability to accept it or deliver a satisfactory return to the selling company (although that is common as well).

MARKETING INSIGHT

As an example, Citibank's Global Account Management programme was highly effective with customers, but nevertheless successfully sabotaged by Country Managers (Buzzell, 1985): it was eventually revived, though some time later.[6]

It is evident that this coordinating role of key account management has important implications for how the role is remunerated. Selling has always been characterized by reward structures different from any other function in the organization. It has been widely accepted in practice that powerful financial incentives should be offered and directly linked to short-term outcomes, usually sales volume, occasionally margin. On this motivational principle has grown up a whole culture and ethos around salespeople that will not readily be changed, neither in organizations who have trusted to it for decades, nor with salespeople who have operated in this environment for their entire career. But is this appropriate for key accounts, where a large part of the job is about successful implementation, without which the lifetime value of the account could be destroyed overnight? We find that the remuneration framework is a litmus test that sets apart genuine key account managers from salespeople of all seniorities.

MARKETING INSIGHT

A major IT company remunerates key account managers on a mix of global 'share of wallet' and customer satisfaction – measured some time after each sale. The customers know it, so they know that all in the firm will work hard to ensure successful implementation. Not surprisingly, the company commands a substantial price premium over its competitors.

Having outlined what key account management *is*, we will now discuss its benefits.

Benefits of Key Account Management

Risk reduction

Clearly there are potential benefits from key account management, or companies would not be energetically engaged in pursuing this approach. Theoretically, the benefits to the selling company are business growth, risk reduction and possibly cost reduction; however, as we will see, there is a danger of uncontrolled cost increase as well. On the buying side, the impetus towards further development of supplier relationships is mainly driven by cost reduction and risk reduction (see Table 8.2 for a list of sources of benefit under each of these two headings), leading to enhanced customer satisfaction and contributing to overall competitive strategy. Benefits can include the possibility of collaboration in real mould-breaking strategies, which challenge the status quo to bypass competition, and which a buying company cannot achieve alone.

Both parties benefit from risk reduction, which must be a major driver in relationship development. 'Internal' risks are of two kinds: short-term crises such as sudden demand or supply gaps, and longer-term uncertainties which complicate planning and result in suboptimal use of resources. External risks are those originating in the market, or originating outside the market and acting through it, as in the case of government legislation, for example. A collaborative relationship has the potential to reduce external risk for both parties through market information sharing, greater flexibility in response, and leveraging market influence.

Risk reduction	Cost reduction
Sharing of assets (lower breakeven costs)	Reduced production costs
Sharing of information, informally and formally	Reduced transaction costs - better information/ reduced uncertainty - routinized transactions
Increased flexibility versus vertical Integration	
Volume commitments Future orientation with joint planning	

Table 8.2: Types of risk reduction and cost reduction for buying companies originating from partnership with selling company

Source: Ellram, 1991[7]

Financial drivers for selling companies

Building and maintaining relationships at a sophisticated level has considerable costs – a good reason to be highly selective in determining what constitute key accounts. Nevertheless, selling companies expect the direct financial benefit to outweigh the relationship costs. However, although key accounts have the potential to deliver the greatest profit, they also have the potential to generate the greatest losses. It is often a company's largest two or three customers that lose money when costs are fully attributed to them. Good, appropriate information systems and the will to use them, plus careful management, are needed in order to ensure financial benefits from key accounts. Loss situations often arise when the buyer has negotiated a price based on the cost of goods sold, but is enjoying excess value in terms of a range of additional, uncosted services. One of the major dangers in developing sophisticated relationships through key account management is the escalation of costs absorbed by and in the relationship.

There is an additional danger that sophisticated and close relationships are seen as the only formula in key account management. In fact, there are many cases of customers who should still qualify as key accounts, but who should be managed in an efficient, transactional manner. They may not want to develop the relationship further, or the business may not be able to repay investment in it. Analysis of each key account should focus on the *incremental* benefit of investing in development beyond its current status.

Nonetheless, ongoing research at Cranfield School of Management's KAM Research Club clearly indicates that this whole area is in need of further study, as they observed many companies losing substantial sums of money in their dealings with large customers. Lynette Ryals[8] (2005) has shown that this is because a majority of companies do not use activity based costing systems and consequently do not attribute major costs appropriately.

The data presented in Figure 8.2 are the result of a Cranfield survey of directors and senior managers on conferences and courses using an automated response system in order to elicit unbiased responses to a question about KAM profitability, having explained the principle of activity-based costing. In all, 500 respondents were surveyed over a five-year period ('$t - 4$' to '$t0$' in the figure), and while we do not claim that the sample is representative, the survey nevertheless provides indicative evidence that companies may still be losing money on their dealings with their top key accounts.

Cost savings for buying companies

There are 'legitimate' or mutually beneficial cost savings available to buying companies which are preferable to driving suppliers' profits below adequate levels. Better management of the flow of supplies, elimination of unnecessary or duplicated processes and tighter quality control all reduce cost.

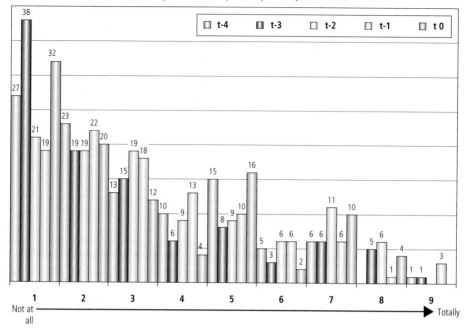

How well do you know the real profitability of the top ten accounts?

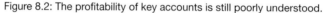

Figure 8.2: The profitability of key accounts is still poorly understood.

UK retailer Marks & Spencer is an example which predated by decades the formulation of the concept of supply chain management.

In addition to savings in current operational costs, savings through collaborative product development and R and D cost sharing are a very significant source of advantage, particularly to companies with high investment in development, long development cycles or markets with short product life-cycles. The buying company benefits from supplier expertise, leading to better and more cost-effective design, while the selling company can beta-test new products or services in real life on a larger scale than their own facilities permit.

There are potential dangers attached to close relationships for buying companies as well. The range of pitfalls may be grouped around two issues: cost increase (from duplication of effort, and/or from the substitution of cash for activity, by giving the supplier the opportunity to add some of the value that the buying company could have fulfilled itself); and concerns over control and dependence. Paradoxically, concerns about the negative aspect of dependence may be seen as an outcome derived from positive, ongoing relationship benefits, when considered together with the issue of termination costs.

All these fears are paralleled by selling companies, except that concern about price/margin erosion replaces concern about cost increase. The issue of dependence may be slightly different, but is very real if the relationship has reached a large proportion of the selling company's turnover. For both parties, then, it is important to be very clear about the strategic rationale before deepening the relationship. The relationship metaphor is an apposite one: key account relationships typically last a good deal longer than the average marriage.

However, we have observed more than once that key account relationships are not all the same, and nor should they be. We will next make this crucial idea more actionable by outlining a simple typology of stages in KAM relationship development.

The Stages of KAM Relationship Development

Research into KAM by a number of scholars shows that KAM relationships vary from highly transactional, arms-length relationships at one extreme to thoroughly integrated companies at the other. It is useful to think of KAM relationship development as proceeding through a series of stages from one to the other, though we should raise two important warnings. The first is that any stage model is an approximation. Individual firms may clearly be between stages. The second is that it should not be assumed that all KAM relationships should evolve towards the more relational, integrated end of the spectrum. Not least, if there is no desire for close relationship on the buyer's side, it is delusional and seriously expensive for the supplier to invest heavily in the relationship. Although some relationships do move steadily through these stages, others do not.

With those warnings, Figure 8.3 outlines some of the common steps which relationships move through. (This model was originally developed by Millman and Wilson[9]; their original names for each stage are shown in the figure in italics. The model was researched further by McDonald, Millman and Rogers.[10] For some recent empirical evidence and suggested refinements, see Davies and Ryals.[11]) We will describe each stage in turn.

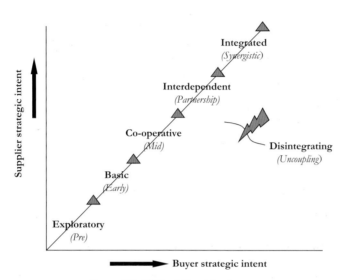

Figure 8.3: KAM relationship stages.

Exploratory KAM

This stage precedes key account management of any kind, but implies that the potential importance of the relationship will qualify the buying company to be a key account if business is secured. At this stage the selling company will be courting the buying company and exploring its needs, which of them they are required to fulfil and the size of the opportunity, as well as generally getting a feel for the organization, the people who are influential in the buying decision, their personalities and their modus operandi. At the same time, the buying company will be exploring the supplier's offer, capabilities and credentials, quite possibly with more than one supplier simultaneously. See Figure 8.4.

Figure 8.4: Exploratory KAM relationship.

Basic KAM

This stage implies a relationship with a transactional emphasis. If it is a new relationship, then it may be effectively a trial time, during which the selling company has to prove its ability to deliver its offer in an efficient manner. Buyers will obviously prefer to develop business further with suppliers who have demonstrated that they can live up to minimum operational requirements. However, trial experience of each other may not always be possible, e.g. major contracts. At this stage, the buying company may also use other suppliers of the same product/service, but not necessarily: multiple sourcing may not suit the need.

Even if the relationship is successful at this level, it may still not be appropriate to develop it for a number of good reasons, for example:

- there may be changes pending in the environment in terms of legislation, technology, market, company ownership, etc. which limit the length of life of the relationship, so that investment in relationship building is unlikely to pay back
- the buying company may be low cost focused and unresponsive to added value
- the buying company may be known for supplier switching
- in summary, the overall lifetime value of the relationship is not expected to repay investment in the relationship in terms of time, adaptation, etc.

At this stage, most contact will be one to one through the key account manager and the purchasing director or manager, as shown in Figure 8.5.

Co-operative KAM

At this stage the buying company will have been able to satisfy itself about the selling company's credentials through its own experience after a period at basic KAM level. If performance is acceptable, the selling company may then be able to work more closely with the buying company and develop the relationship. Opportunities to add value to the customer will be suggested by the supplier, and the buyer will adopt a positive and communicative attitude towards the supplier, perhaps in terms of indicating further opportunities to do business together, or helping the supplier to solve some of the operational problems which arise. If the customer uses a list of preferred suppliers, the selling company will be on it.

At this stage, contact involves a wider range of people, as illustrated in Figure 8.6. It is often at this stage that the real potential to progress the relationship from cooperative to interdependent is either grasped or not by the supplying company as, by definition, the relationship is already more complicated than at the basic stage.

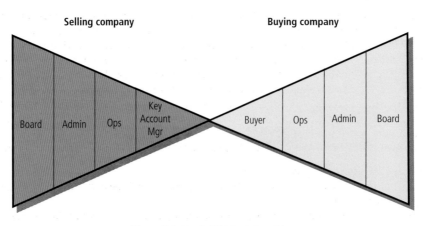

Figure 8.5: Basic KAM relationship.

Figure 8.6: Co-operative KAM relationship.

Interdependent KAM

At this stage, both buying and selling company acknowledge the importance of each to the other. They are locked into each other, not inextricably, but if the relationship were to end, retreat would be difficult and time-consuming. Inertia, as well as strategic suitability, holds the partners together. They may have set up various initiatives together, like common working practices, product specifications, joint marketing activity, and so on, which would take time and effort to undo.

Even if multiple sourcing is possible in theory, in fact the selling company has become sole or at least first option supplier. A range of functions in both organizations work closely together, orchestrated by rather than administered by or channelled through the key account manager and purchasing manager; see Figure 8.7.

One consequence of this kind of relationship is the high probability of the supplying company overserving the customer. This stage of relationship frequently results in a loss to the supply company.

Integrated KAM

This type of relationship involves working together in cross-boundary functional or project teams – see Figure 8.8. This means that the organizations become so integrated that individuals may feel more affinity with their team than with their official employer organization. The teams run the business, rather than either organization, and they make decisions about their interactions with other teams according to the strategy they are implementing. Some staff will probably be based at their partner's premises. At this stage, exit would be traumatic at both a personal and organizational level.

Disintegrating KAM

Finally, at any time, the relationship can fall apart for a number of reasons, such as a takeover of either company, a change of key people, switching to a new supplier with a sufficiently significant enhancement in the core product or service to justify the pain of switching, or the introduction of new technology. Disintegration can be sudden and exit complete, or it may be a return to a lower level of relationship at which the companies can continue to do business together, but on different terms. In any case, disintegrating KAM is not a stable state, as any of the others can be, but a transitional stage before the relationship settles down into another stage, and possibly no relationship at all. The key account manager's role may change to damage limitation, and a business developer may not be the right kind of person to fulfil this need.

In summary, then, within the sales plan it is important to be very clear for each key account on:

1. What stage the relationship is currently at
2. What a realistic target stage is, given the buyer's aspirations and the cost/benefit tradeoff of deepening the relationship
3. What actions are needed for developing the relationship and, crucially, what kind of person is best to manage a relationship of this type.

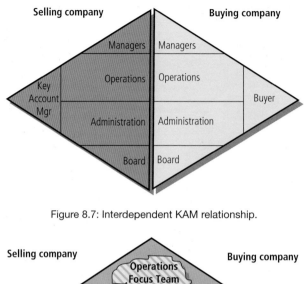

Figure 8.7: Interdependent KAM relationship.

Figure 8.8: Integrated KAM relationship.

It is also clear that key accounts need to be managed as a portfolio, reflecting their differing attractiveness and the company's different strengths of relationship. We will return to this issue in the next section on preparing the sales plan. First, however, we consider aspects of the sales plan which apply to *all* accounts, major or minor.

PREPARING THE SALES PLAN

No two sales plans will contain precisely the same headings. However, some general guidelines can be given. Table 8.3 is an example of setting objectives for an individual salesperson. Clearly, these objectives will be the logical result of breaking down the marketing objectives into actual sales targets.

All companies set themselves overall objectives, which in turn imply the development of specific marketing objectives. In this chapter, we have discussed personal selling in the context of the overall marketing activity. This approach leads us to the following hierarchy of objectives: *corporate objectives – marketing objectives – sales objectives*, as outlined in Figure 8.9.

The benefits to sales force management of following this approach can be summarized as follows:

1. Coordination of corporate and marketing objectives with actual sales effort
2. Establishment of a circular relationship between corporate objectives and customer wants
3. Improvement of sales effectiveness through an understanding of the corporate and marketing implications of sales decisions.

Task	The standard	How to set the standard	How to measure performance	What to look for
1 To achieve personal sales targets	Sales target or period of time for individual groups and/or products	Analysis of territory potential and individual customers' potential; discussion and agreement between salesperson and manager	Comparison of individual salesperson's product sales against targets	Significant shortfall between target and achievement over a meaningful period
2 To sell the required range and quantity to individual customers	Achievement of specified range and quantity of sales to a particular customer or group of customers within an agreed time period	Analysis of individual customer records of potential and present sales; discussion and agreement between manager and salesperson	Scrutiny of individual customer records; observation of selling in the field	Failure to achieve agreed objectives; complacency with range of sales made to individual customers
3 To plan journeys and call frequencies to achieve minimum practicable selling cost	To achieve appropriate call frequency on individual customers; number of live customer calls during a given time period	Analysis of individual customers' potential; analysis of order/call ratios; discussion and agreement between manager and salesperson	Scrutiny of individual customer records; analysis of order/call ratio; examination of call reports	High ratio of calls to an individual customer relative to that customer's yield; shortfall on agreed total number of calls made over an agreed time period
4 To acquire new customers	Number of prospect calls during time period; selling new products to existing customers	Identify total number of potential and actual customers who could produce results; identify opportunity areas for prospecting	Examination of call reports, records of new accounts opened and ratio of existing to potential customers	Shortfall in number of prospect calls from agreed standard; low ratio of existing to potential customers
5 To make a sales approach of the required quality	To exercise the necessary skills and techniques required to achieve the identified objective of each element of the sales approach; continuous use of sales material	Standard to be agreed in discussion between manager and salesperson related to company standards laid down	Regular observations of field selling using a systematic analysis of performance in each stage of the sales approach	Failure to identify objective of each stage of sales approach, to identify specific areas of skill, weakness, to use support material

Table 8.3: Objectives for the individual salesperson (based on the original work of Stephen P. Morse when at Urwick Orr and Partners)

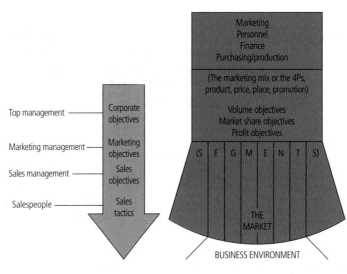

Figure 8.9: The hierarchy of objectives.

The following example illustrates the main point that a sales force cannot be managed in isolation from broad corporate and marketing objectives. The sales force of a company manufacturing stainless steel containers was selling almost any kind of container to almost anybody who could buy. This caused severe production planning and distribution problems throughout the business, down to the purchase of raw materials. Eventually, the company's profitability was seriously affected. The sales force was finally instructed to concentrate on certain kinds of products and on certain kinds of user industries. This decision eventually led to economies of scale throughout the whole organization.

In the case of key accounts, we have the additional challenge of managing the set of accounts as a portfolio. This is particularly important if limited resources are to be used on the right accounts to achieve the right objectives. If the firm has key accounts, then, a key account portfolio should be included in the plan. We discuss how this is to be done next.

PLANNING FOR A KEY ACCOUNT PORTFOLIO

Portfolio analysis is simply a means of assessing a number of different key accounts, first, according to the potential of each in terms achieving the organization's objectives and, second, according to the organization's capability for taking advantage of the opportunities identified.

Key account portfolio analysis is essentially an adapted version of the DPM which we described in Chapter 5, but plotting key accounts rather than markets or segments. It uses several indicators in measuring the dimensions of 'account attractiveness' on the one hand and 'company capabilities' (relative to competitors) on the other. These indicators can be altered by management to suit the operating conditions of particular industrial sectors. The outcome of using portfolio analysis is the diagnosis of an organization's situation and strategy options relative to its position with respect to these two composite dimensions.

The purpose of the following guidelines is to obtain the maximum value out of this methodology.

Key Definitions

We begin with two key definitions.

Key account attractiveness is a measure of the potential of the key account for yielding growth in sales and profits. It is important to stress that this should be an objective assessment of key account attractiveness using data external to the organization. The criteria themselves will, of course, be determined by the organization carrying out the exercise and will be relevant to the objectives the organization is trying to achieve.

Business strength/position is a measure of an organization's actual strengths in each key account. In other words it is the degree to which it can take advantage of a key account opportunity. Thus, it is an objective assessment of an organization's ability to satisfy key account needs relative to competitors.

> Key account attractiveness is a measure of the potential of the key account for yielding growth in sales and profits

> Business strength/position is a measure of an organization's actual strengths in each key account

Preparation

Prior to commencing portfolio analysis, the following preparation is advised:

1. Data/information profiles should be available for all key accounts to be scored.
2. Define the time period being scored. A period of three years is recommended.
3. Ensure sufficient data are available to score the factors. (Where no data are available, this is not a problem as long as a sensible approximation can be made for the factors.)
4. Ensure up-to-date sales forecasts are available for all products/services plus any new products/services.

In order to improve the quality of scoring, it is recommended that a group of people from a number of different functions take part, as this encourages the challenging of traditional views through discussion.

Twelve Steps to Producing the Key Account Management Portfolio

Step 1   Define the key accounts which are to be used during the analysis

Step 2   Define the criteria for key account attractiveness

Step 3   Allocate weights to each of the attractiveness factors

Step 4   Define scoring criteria for each attractiveness factor

Step 5   Score the relevant key accounts out of 10 on the attractiveness factors and multiply the scores by the weights to achieve a total weighted score

Step 6   Define the critical success factors (from the customer's point of view) for each key account and the weight for each

Step 7   Score your organization's performance out of 10 on each critical success factor relative to competitors

Step 8   Produce the position of key accounts on the horizontal axis in the portfolio

Step 9   Position the key accounts on the box assuming no change to current policies. That is to say a forecast should be made of the future position of the key accounts (this step is optional)

Step 10   Redraw the portfolio to position the key accounts where the organization wants them to be in, say, three years' time. That is to say the objectives they wish to achieve for each key account

Step 11   Set out the strategies to be implemented to achieve the objectives

Step 12   Check the financial outcomes resulting from the strategies.

Let us now consider each step in turn.

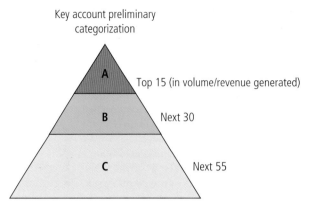

Key account preliminary
categorization

A — Top 15 (in volume/revenue generated)

B — Next 30

C — Next 55

© Professor Malcolm McDonald, Cranfield School of Management

Figure 8.10: Example of an outcome of preliminary categorization.

Step 1: List the population of key accounts which you intend to include in the matrix

As stated earlier in this chapter, the list can include key accounts with which you have no business yet or accounts which are currently small or entrepreneurial, but which have the potential to become big. To do this, it is suggested that a preliminary categorization be done according to size or potential size. Thus, if there were, say, 100 key accounts, the preliminary categorization might resemble Figure 8.10.

It is important not to use the methodology which follows on all 100 accounts at once, as the criteria for each group may need to be different. The methodology should, in the example shown, be carried out as three separate exercises: A, B and C.

Step 2: Define key account attractiveness factors

All key accounts may be attractive by definition, but with limited resources (such as people), it is important to compare their *relative* attractiveness to the firm. Key account attractiveness is a combination of a number of factors which can usually be summarized under three headings: growth rate, accessible volume or value, and profit potential.

1. *Growth* – the average annual growth rate of revenue spent on the relevant goods or services by that key account. So, this is the growth rate in the accessible spend of the customer, or 'wallet', of which we are competing for a share. All other things being equal, customers who are spending more on the product category are more attractive as there is more new business to chase.

2. *Accessible volume or value* – an attractive key account is not only large, it can also be accessed. One way of calculating this is to estimate the *total* spend of the key account on the relevant category of goods or services, *less* revenue which is impossible to access, *regardless of investment made*. Alternatively, the total spend can be used, which is the most frequent method as it does not involve any managerial judgement to be made which could distort the truth. *The former method is the preferred method.*

3. *Profit potential* – intuitively, it is clear that some key accounts offer the potential for large profits, while in the case of others, it is clear that margins will always be low. It is, however, difficult to estimate with any certainty, particularly as we are interested in the potential profit and not our current margins, which may, for example, be low due to our current investment in establishing our position with the customer. One way of assessing the profit potential is to make an estimate of the margins available to any competitor. Another is to estimate the margins achieved by the leading competitor –

that is, the competitor who currently has the greatest share of wallet with this customer. (Margin should be used rather than total profit pool, in order to avoid double-counting with accessible volume/value.)

4. *Soft factors* – naturally, growth, size and profit will not encapsulate the requirements of all organizations in what makes key accounts more or less attractive to them. It is then possible to add another heading, such as 'soft factors', 'risk', or 'other' to the aforementioned three factors (growth rate, accessible volume/value and profit potential).

> Accessible volume or value is the total spend of the key account less revenue impossible to access, regardless of investment made

The following are the factors most frequently used to determine account attractiveness.

> Profit potential is the margins available to any competitor

- Status/reference value
- Learning from customer (e.g. customer has market-leading engineering, service design, etc. from which we can learn)
- 'Focal' company in a network
- Regular flow of work – stability
- Strategy match
- Prompt payment
- Customers who see value in a broad product offering
- Ease of doing business
- Importance to a sister company
- Requirement for strategic alliances
- Willingness to abdicate (customer hands over total responsibility)
- Blue-chip customer capable of meeting your financial security requirements (e.g. top 100 company).

We find, though, that it is best to keep the total list of factors to five or less, otherwise the calculations become cumbersome and the overall logic becomes less clear.

In addition, once agreed, under no circumstances should key account attractiveness factors be changed, otherwise the attractiveness of your key accounts is not being evaluated against common criteria and the matrix becomes meaningless. However, the scores will be specific to each key account.

It is also important to list the key accounts that you intend to apply the criteria to before deciding on the criteria themselves, since the purpose of the vertical axis is to discriminate between more and less attractive key accounts. The criteria themselves must be specific to the population of key accounts and must not be changed for different key accounts in the same population.

Step 3: Allocate weights to each of the attractiveness factors

The factors should now be weighted out of 100, to indicate their relative importance to the firm in comparing the attractiveness of key accounts. For example:

Factors	Weight
Growth rate	30
Accessible volume or value	15
Profit potential	40
Reference value	15
	100

These weights will reflect the priorities of the firm. So, for example, a firm with a single factory running to full capacity might wish to weight margins more highly than accessible volume/value and growth, with perhaps 40 per cent for margins, 20 per cent for volume/value and growth, and 20 per cent for other soft factors. Conversely, a firm with aspirations to be global market leader developing

K.A. Attractiveness Factors	10-7	6-4	3-0	X weight
Volume/value	>10m	1-10m	<1m	15
Growth/potential %	>20%	5-20%	<5%	30
Profit potential %	>25%	10%-25%	<10%	40
'Soft' factors	Good	Medium	Poor	15
				100

Table 8.4: Key account attractiveness factors – weights and scoring criteria.

its plan for a relatively new country might wish to weight volume/value and growth higher – at, say, 40 per cent each – and margins/profit relatively low – at, say, 20 per cent.

Step 4: Define scoring criteria for each attractiveness factor

In the next step, each key account will be scored on each attractiveness factor out of 10. In this step, the criteria by which this will be done are defined. See Table 8.4.

Step 5: Score each key account

Score each key account on a scale of one to 10 against the attractiveness factors and multiply the score by the weight. This will place each key account in the key account attractiveness axis from low to high. This process is very similar to the comparison of market/segment attractiveness described in Chapter 5, which contains some examples, such as Table 5.3.

Step 6: Define business strength/position

This is a measure of an organization's actual strengths in each key account. Whereas we had one set of key account attractiveness criteria, for this analysis each key account will need a different set of criteria for assessing the firm's strengths, as customers differ in what they look for from suppliers. We call these criteria 'critical success factors'. For each account, therefore, in consultation with those close to the customer, it is necessary to list the few things which are most influential in determining the share of the customer's wallet in the product/service category. These will often fall under the four headings of:

- Product requirements
- Service requirements
- Price requirements
- Relationship requirements.

These should be weighted out of 100 to indicate the relative importance of the factors in the eyes of the customer. What does the customer insist on? What might the customer compromise on? This process is very similar to the critical success factor analysis for whole segments which was described in Chapter 5, which contains some examples, such as Table 5.4.

Step 7: Score critical success factors

Score the organization's *actual current* strengths in each key account on each critical success factor. These should be scored from the customer's perspective: if they think your service is unreliable, it's unreliable! By multiplying scores by weights, an overall weighted average score can be calculated for each key account. By also scoring the leading competitor, a relative score can be calculated, by subtracting the leading competitor's score from your score. Again see Table 5.4 for an example.

An alternative, easy way of doing steps 6 and 7 is simply to decide what stage the relationship is currently at, from *basic* to *integrated*, in order to find the position on the horizontal axis in step 8:

1. *Exploratory* (you do not currently do business with this account)
2. *Basic* (you have some transactional business with this account)
3. *Cooperative* (you have regular business with this account and may well be a preferred supplier, but you are only one of many suppliers and pricing is still important)
4. *Interdependent* (you have multifunctional, multilevel relationships, but the customer could still exit if necessary)
5. *Integrated* (you have multifunctional, multilevel relationships, your systems are interlinked, and exit for both parties would be difficult).

This simplified method is useful for gaining an overview of the portfolio when time is short, but the full critical success factor analysis is important for developing detailed strategies for each account.

Step 8: Produce the portfolio matrix

Now a matrix can be plotted as illustrated by Figure 8.11:

* The circle size is proportional to the firm's current revenue from the key account. A cross can be used in the case of an account that has been identified as key to the future but where revenue is currently negligible.
* The vertical position is determined by the attractiveness analysis (step 5). *Note*: it is sensible to spread out the circles, as what matters is their relative attractiveness. So if the least attractive account, for example, is scored at 5.8 out of 10, and the most attractive at 7.5 out of 10, it might make sense to put 5 at the bottom of the vertical axis and at 8 at the top.
* The horizontal position is determined by the critical success factor analysis (step 7). So, for example, if we score 7/10 and the leading competitor scores the same, our relative score is 0 and the circle would appear on the mid-line. If we score 7/10 and the leading competitor scores 6/10, our relative score is +1, so the circle would appear to the left of the line. If we score 7/10 and the leading competitor scores 8/10, our relative score is -1 and we would appear to the right of the line. Generally, it works well to label this axis from +2 at the left to -2 at the right.

Figure 8.12 provides some further guidance as to how each quadrant should be treated; but this guidance should always be subject to management judgement. It is, however, a good prompt for a senior management conversation.

Figure 8.13 is a real example from an insurance company, with the figures disguised to protect anonymity.

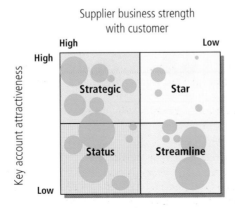

Figure 8.11: The key account portfolio.

Business strength/position

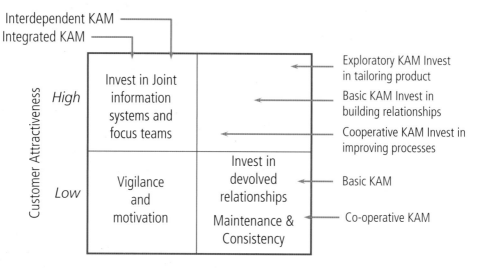

Figure 8.12: Further guidance on key account matrix.

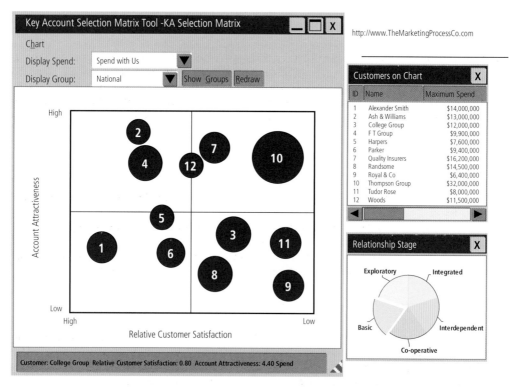

Figure 8.13: Key account matrix – insurance example.

Step 9: Produce a forecast matrix (optional)

This optional further analysis should position the key accounts on the horizontal axis where they are projected to be three years from now, *assuming no change to your current policies*. This is calculated by re-scoring your competitors on the critical success factors (step 7), while leaving your scores the same (or perhaps adjusting them to reflect improvements which are already thoroughly in hand). The key accounts can only move *horizontally*, either to the left or to the right, because you have already taken account of potential future growth on the vertical axis.

Now enter a new figure for your *forecast* sales for each account, assuming no change in your current polices. This should take into account your new position on the horizontal axis: if with no change in policies you are to the right of the mid-line, for example, it is likely that much of the new business will go to the competition.

The first time you complete this analysis, it is unlikely that the forecast position will be satisfactory.

Step 10: Produce a matrix showing the objective position

This analysis should position each key account on the horizontal axis showing the *objective* position at the end of the planning period (e.g. three years ahead). This is done by revisiting the critical success factor scores, amending our score but also remembering (if step 9 has been omitted) to take into account any changes which we predict the competitors will be making. As a result of this analysis, accounts can either stay in their current box, move to the right or move to the left.

Enter a new figure for your *objectives* sales against each key account. A judgement will need to be made as to what is realistic given the analysis of the customer's buying criteria or critical success factors.

It goes without saying that the objectives should reflect the relative positions on the matrix. It is simply not realistic to state that we will make dramatic improvements in every single key account – and yet the authors often see plans which claim that this will occur. Needless to say, the competitors' plans say the same thing! The benefit of the portfolio analysis is that it enables us to look for the greatest gains in the most attractive accounts, and within these to focus on the criteria which really matter to the customer.

Step 11: Outline objectives and strategies for each key account

Finally, a strategic plan for each key account should be produced. It should outline the objectives and strategies for each one.

Table 8.5 sets out more specific guidelines for setting objectives for each of the key accounts in each of the four boxes.

It will be observed that each box has a 'label'. These labels can be changed but should NOT be changed to derogatory names such as 'Gold', 'Silver', 'Bronze', 'A', 'B', 'C', 'D', etc.!

Step 12: Check the financial outcomes from the strategies

Cost out the actions which comprise the stated strategies in all boxes other than the bottom right hand box. There may be circumstances for those in which a strategic plan should be produced for some of them, but generally speaking, forecasts and budgets should be sufficient, as it is unlikely that the supplying company will ever trade on terms other than low prices.

For an explanation, see the mini case study below.

Category	Description
Strategic customers	Very important customers, but the relationship has developed still further, to the level of partnership.
	The relationship is 'win–win'; both sides have recognized the benefits they gain from working together.
	Customers buy not primarily on price but on the added value derived from being in partnership with the supplier.
	The range of contacts is very broad and joint plans for the future are in place.
	Products and services are developed side by side with the customer. Because of their large size and the level of resource which they absorb, only a few customers fall into this category.
Status customers	Very important customers (in terms of value).
	Commit to security of supply and offer products and services which are tailored to the customer's particular needs.
	Price is less important in the customer's choice of supplier.
	Both parties have some goals in common.
	The two organizations have made some form of commitment to each other.
	Invest as necessary in these customers in order to continue the business relationship for mutual advantage, but do not over invest.
Star customers	Price is still a major factor in the decision to buy but security of supply is very important and so is service.
	Spend more time with some of these customers and aim to develop a deeper relationship with them in time.
Streamline customers	These customers usually want a standard product, 'off the shelf'.
	Price is the key factor in their decision to buy.
	The relationship is helpful and professional, but relatively transactional.
	Do not invest large amounts of time in the business relationship at this stage.

Table 8.5: Guidelines for interpreting the key account matrix.

MINI CASE STUDY

Please see again Figure 8.11. Please pay particular attention to large key account circle in the bottom right hand box. The authors were doing some consultancy for a global paper company.

A main board director was bemoaning the fact that one of the world's biggest media companies – hence a massive user of paper – was putting its paper order out to tender and was determined to accept the two lowest price bids. It was then to drop all other suppliers. The authors quickly established that to lose such a big customer would be a blow to profitability, as all its mill fixed costs would remain the same, and would have little chance of being fully utilized without this customer.

So the authors advised the paper company to bid the lowest price in order to win the contract, then to withdraw all support other than that specified in the contract. In this case, clearly, sending a key account manager on regular visits and offering other services would have been a waste of resources, as it was clear that this particular customer didn't want a close relationship

> with any supplier and was obsessed with lowest price, so making it virtually impossible for any supplier to make much profit.
>
> Meanwhile a plan was put together to build other accounts in order to reduce the reliance on this one, so that never again would the company be held to ransom from a customer which it could not afford to lose.

It is accounts such as these, usually in the bottom right hand box, which are unattractive and driven by price alone that do not justify strategic key account plans. Such plans are only justified if the supplying company believes there is a real opportunity to move them to a more favourable position in the portfolios.

Conclusions

To summarize, the sales force is a vital but very expensive element of the marketing mix and as much care should be devoted to its management as to any other area of marketing management. This is most likely to be achieved if intuitive sense, which is associated with experience, can be combined with the kind of logical framework of thinking outlined here.

Key account plans need particular attention. Research at Cranfield and elsewhere has shown that it is those organizations that invest resources in detailed analysis of the needs and processes of their key accounts, select and categorize their key accounts correctly, which fare much better in building long-term profitable relationships. Armed with a detailed knowledge of their customer's business, it is more likely that they can discover ways of helping the customer create advantage in their marketplace and build these findings into a strategic key account plan which will be signed off by both the supplying company and the customer.

CHAPTER 8 REVIEW

What is the role of personal selling?

This provides the face-to-face element of the communications mix. There are things it can achieve that advertising and promotion can't, e.g. salespeople can be flexible in front of the customer and ask for an order. However, personal selling has to be seen in the context of the total communications mix.

Try Exercise 8.1

How important is personal selling?

Traditionally, companies had sales forces long before marketing was in vogue. Many companies still spend more on sales forces than on advertising and promotion combined. Though key parts of the marketing mix, sales departments often act independently of marketing. Thus, in achieving their short-term sales goals, they sometimes fail to achieve the mix of products and markets consistent with the longer-term strategic marketing objectives.

How many salespeople should you have?

Basically salespeople have three activities. They:

* Make calls
* Travel
* Administer.

Their workload should be analysed to establish how many calls it is possible to make in a typical working day. Equally, an assessment of existing and potential customers should be made and the annual total number of calls calculated (bearing in mind that different customer categories need different call rates).

What should they do?

Achieve objectives consistent with the marketing plan in terms of:

* How much to sell (volume)
* What to sell (mix)
* Where to sell (market segments)
* Allowable costs
* Profit margins.

There can be many other types of sub- or enabling objectives, e.g.:

* Number of telephone contacts
* Number of calls made
* Use of sales aids
* Number of reports submitted
* Safety record, etc.

Try Exercise 8.2

How are they managed?

To maximize performance, get the optimal balance between incentives and disincentives. Incentives are:

* Rewards consistent with performance
* Giving praise and recognition where it is due
* Minimal boredom and monotony
* Freedom from fear and worry
* Feeling of belonging
* Sense of doing a useful job.

'There are no bad salespeople, only bad sales managers.'

Try Exercise 8.3

How should key accounts be managed?

A key account is a customer identified by the selling company as of strategic importance. Future potential should therefore be carefully considered in identifying key accounts. Do not have too many key accounts: each will require significant investment.

Key accounts need a key account manager to take overall responsibility for the commercial relationship. Important skills for this role include influencing skills and project management, as a large part of the role involves internal persuasion and coordination across numerous people involved in sales and implementation. Remuneration schemes should reflect the importance of customer satisfaction in development of these key relationships.

Key accounts will need managing in very different ways according to the stage of relationship development. These stages are:

1. Exploratory
2. Basic
3. Cooperative
4. Interdependent
5. Integrated
6. Disintegrating.

A key account portfolio matrix is invaluable in planning for key accounts. Try developing a matrix, following the 12 steps of the section 'Planning for a key account portfolio' above.

Questions raised for the company

1. Q: Should sales or marketing be responsible for the sales plan?
   A: Marketing objectives should be agreed first. Then, if there is a separate sales force, sales managers can devise a tactical plan to meet the objectives.
2. Q: Salespeople are sometimes described as notoriously reactive and optimistic. Can they be expected to conform to a sales plan?
   A: Salespeople such as the ones described here are perhaps the salespeople you don't need. The sales plan is designed to make best use of a scarce and expensive resource, a wholly admirable objective. It must not be undermined.
3. Q: Suppose the sales plan requires salespeople to play a different role. Can old dogs be taught new tricks?
   A: Whenever change is introduced, there are often some casualties. However, with well-designed training and sensitive management, the problem is not insurmountable.
4. Q: We've implemented key account management. That is, we've labelled our major 50 customers as key accounts and retitled some salespeople as key account managers. Is that it?
   A: Well, that's a good way to hand market share to your competitors. Key accounts expect close relationships, proactive identification of customer needs, creative problem solving and going the extra mile to look after the customer's interests. This requires consultative skills and significant investment, which should only be made for very selective customers.

APPLICATION QUESTIONS

1. What are the key functions of salespeople in your organization? How is their work coordinated?
2. How is the sales force deployed: by geographical territory; by product range; by type of customer? Is this deployment optimal? What other patterns of deployment should be considered by your organization?
3. Who is responsible for the sales force in your organization? What is the relationship between this post of responsibility and other marketing responsibilities in the organization? Does this cause any problems? Where problems arise, how could they be solved?

4. Can you make a case to justify the present size and type of sales force used? Could you defend your position if you were requested to cut back the sales force by 30 per cent? How would you make your case? What do you believe would be the consequences of a 30 per cent cutback in the sales force?

5. How is your own organization's sales force used? Is this the best possible use of the sales force? In what ways do activities of the sales force complement other forms of marketing communications used? Identify any other ways in which you feel the activities of the sales force could enhance the total marketing communications effort.

6. Critically appraise your company's sales plan. Does it flow naturally from the company's marketing objectives?

7. Have you identified key accounts taking into account future potential and not just today's revenue?

8. Have you identified key account managers with the requisite influencing and implementation skills?

9. Do you manage key accounts differentially according to their stage of relationship development? Are there any key accounts where you delude yourselves that a close relationship is possible when the customer has every intention of behaving transactionally?

10. Do you allocate resources (such as your best key account managers) to key accounts differentially, taking into account the position of each account in the portfolio?

EXERCISES

While it is quite possible that some companies will not use advertising and sales promotion, very few fail to have some element of face-to-face selling in their marketing mix. Often the sales force was in existence long before the company became concerned about marketing. This sometimes explains why, in many organizations, sales and marketing are regarded as two separate functions.

When the total cost of recruiting, managing and providing salespeople with all the necessary resources and support systems is taken into account, the sales force is likely to be one of the most costly elements of the company's marketing activities. In order to obtain value for money, it will be important to plan how personal selling will be integrated into the 'communications mix', and then organize the logistics to ensure that the right results are achieved.

Exercise 8.1 looks at how the role of the sales force can be established.

Exercise 8.2 tackles the task of how to set quantifiable objectives for the sales force.

Exercise 8.3 examines issues about managing the sales force and, in particular, how to set the right motivational climate.

As a further exercise, try following the step-by-step guide to creating a key account management portfolio in the section within this chapter on 'Planning for a key account portfolio'.

Exercise 8.1 The role of personal communication in the communications mix

Before attempting to produce a sales plan, we must spend a few minutes getting back to basics and examining exactly what information customers will require from the sales force.

For different sorts of businesses, the role of the salesperson can be entirely different. In some they will just be order-takers, in others negotiators, in others demonstrators, and in others perhaps a composite of these and still other roles. Clearly, then, to claim that a salesperson 'just sells' is very much an oversimplification of the role, and sometimes can be downright misleading.

Taking your marketing objectives as the starting point, i.e. which products/services go to which markets or segments, select one of your key markets/segments as a study vehicle and focus on the customers. What sort of information do they require from your sales force?

The next worksheet (overleaf) is designed to help with this task. There are three steps to be tackled:

1. Establish the communication areas that need to be covered.
2. Because of the costs of having a sales force, assess if there are less costly feasible alternatives to personal visits to achieve the same results.
3. List what these alternatives are, together with when and how they will be used.

Thus, on completion of the worksheet you will have a complete breakdown of the personal communications necessary to achieve the company's marketing objectives in your study market segment. In addition, you will have other information to show how personal visits can be a 'backup' to other methods of contact.

Worksheet What information do customers want from sales representatives? (Exercise 8.1)
For study purposes, just consider *one* important market segment. You can repeat the same procedure for others afterwards.

Recognizing that the sales force plays an important part in the company's communications mix, study the list below and then tick those 'demanded' by customers in column A. Now look carefully at the activities you have just ticked, and, taking each in turn, ask yourself if this information/communication could be provided in a more effective way than by a sales visit. For example, knowing the customer usage of a particular product might make it possible to obtain repeat orders by telephone.

Whenever you see the possibility of an alternative approach, place a tick in column B and make a brief note about the alternative.

(Continued)

Customer info. requirement	A	B	Alternative provision of information
About:			
product range			
product performance			
price			
discounts			
special offers			
promotions			
placing order			
after-sales service			
running cost in use			
guarantees			
spares and accessories			
new developments			
competitor products/performance			
assistance with displays			
assistance with merchandising			
training for own staff			
technical services			
quality assurance			
proof that product/service works			
warehousing/storage			
reordering			
load sizes			
leasing agreement			
delivery arrangements			
franchise agreement			
answers to objections			
joint ventures			
demonstration of product			
long-term contracts			
financial arrangements			
Add any other information requirements that are pertinent to your business			

Exercise 8.2 Quantifiable objectives

Having decided what role the sales force is to play in the communications mix to service your chosen market segment, you can now get down to drawing up some quantifiable objectives. These stem quite logically from the marketing objectives and should cover three main areas:

1. How much to sell (value of unit sales volume)
2. What to sell (the mix of product lines)
3. Where to sell (the markets/segments that take the company towards its marketing objectives).

Please note that in Exercise 8.1 you have already chosen one component, 'where to sell', by selecting an important market or segment.

The sales plan is in effect the translation of these 'ball park' figures into individual targets for each sales representative, taking into account special factors such as their territory/sector size, the size of customers within a particular territory/sector, etc. Thus, how much to sell breaks down into individual targets. The mix of the product lines becomes an individual target. Where to sell becomes a specific customer list.

In addition, there can be other quantifiable objectives, typical examples of which are given on the next worksheet. Using this worksheet, you will be able to devise a set of targets appropriate for each of your sales representatives. The entries towards the end of the worksheet show how the basic targeting can be made somewhat more elaborate if it suits your company to make it so.

If you use one sheet per person, the total will become the sales plan for this particular market segment.

Worksheet Individual sales targets (Exercise 8.2)

Market segment _____

Salesperson _____

Territory _____

Period to which these targets apply,
e.g. year, month, week, call cycle, etc. _____

Target	Number	Qualifying notes (assumptions, special local factors, etc.)
Units sales volume		
Product A		
Product B		
Product C		
Product D		
Number of calls planned to be made		
Number of interviews to be secured		
Number of enquiries to be raised		
Number of quotations to be submitted		
Number of orders to be taken		
Call/interview ratio*		
Interview/enquiries ratio*		
Enquiries/quotations ratio*		
Quotations/order ratio*		
Cost per visit		

(Continued)

Calls per day planned		
Average length of call		
Average daily mileage		
Number of new accounts planned		
Number of letters to be written		
Number of reports to be written		
Number of point-of-sale displays to be organized		
Number of meetings to be held, e.g. with trade		
Number of service calls to be made		
Number of customer complaints		
Number of customer training sessions to be run		
Number of competitor activity reports to be submitted		
Number of general market condition reports to be submitted		
Add any others that are relevant to your type of business		

*based on past experience and future expectations.

Exercise 8.3 Managing the sales force

Although some purists might claim this is an oversimplification, the key *management* activities are:

- Setting performance standards (both quantifiable and qualitative)
- Monitoring achievements against these standards
- Helping/training those who are falling behind
- Setting the right motivational climate.

The word 'management' has been emphasized because many sales managers perceive themselves to be 'super' salespeople and continue to put most of their energies into selling rather than managing.

Setting performance standards

Exercise 8.2 concentrated on the quantifiable standard – *what* has to be achieved. Equally important are the more subjective elements of *how* the tasks are achieved: the quality of the actions.

Some companies have quite deliberately set out to create a style to which salespeople are expected to conform. This can cover appearance (of people and their property), the layout of presentations and reports, the way work is planned, the way customers are addressed and various other aspects of the work. You might have to give some consideration to this question of 'the way we do things around here'. But please note that in the examples given above, there is a standard to work against and performance is, therefore, measurable.

Place less emphasis on non-measurable factors, such as creativity, loyalty, interest, enthusiasm – relying on them too heavily is to plant the seeds of discord. Such subjective judgements can easily be misconstrued as favouritism by some and unfairness by others who have been 'scored' lower. Nonetheless, they can be relevant, so we have included a way of 'measuring' these elements in this exercise.

Monitoring performance

What salespeople are doing can be largely measured by reports, sales figures, internal memos and suchlike. *How* they do things can in most cases only be assessed by being with them and observing their actual performance.

Thus, performance will have to be monitored at these two levels, and the frequency for doing so will depend upon the experience of the salesperson, the newness of the operation and the uncertainty of the situation. As a rule of thumb, the higher the uncertainty surrounding the salesperson, the territory/sector, the product range, the customers, etc. the more frequently should performance be monitored. The appraisal summary (Worksheet 1) provided will enable you to monitor and 'measure' all the relevant quantitative and qualitative elements of your sales force.

Helping/training those whose performance is below par

By having measurable standards of performance, it becomes possible to be quite precise about the area and nature of help that salespeople need. After discussing the problem with them, you will be able to decide if it can be best solved by providing the salespeople with:

- More information (about products, prices, etc.)
- More support (report writing, more joint visits, etc.)
- More training (which generally means improving their skills).

Often training, which can be the most costly solution, is rushed into when other actions would serve the purpose more effectively. Should training be required, much of it can be carried out on the job by a suitable skilled instructor, who would follow a process like this:

1. Instruction/demonstration by instructor
2. Practice by the salesperson
3. Feedback by the instructor
4. Further practice with feedback until performance is acceptable.

Setting the right motivational climate

Perhaps little of the above will really work unless the motivation of the sales force is right. While this subject could be the basis of a whole book by itself, it is possible to see a fairly straightforward way of cutting through much of the theoretical undergrowth.

By and large, if you can reduce those factors which tend to demotivate your staff and at the same time accentuate those which motivate them, then the motivational climate must improve. In saying this, it is important to recognize the difference between removing a demotivating factor and accentuating a motivating one. Removing a demotivating factor will not of itself bring about motivation. All it will do is to stop the complaints about the situation. In contrast to this, accentuating or adding to the motivating factors will undoubtedly lead to a higher commitment to the work. Worksheet 2 enables you to establish exactly what these factors will be for your organization.

(Continued)

Worksheet 1 Individual appraisal summary (Exercise 8.3)

SALESPERSON _____

DIVISION _____

TERRITORY _____ YEAR _____

MANAGER _____

Note:
Score between 5 and 1, when 5 represents excellent and 1 represents poor.

Salesmanship	JAN	FEB	MAR	APR	MAY	JUN	JUL	AUG	SEP	OCT	NOV	DEC
Product knowledge												
Pre-planning												
Objectives												
Introduction												
Participation												
Handling objections												
Use of benefits												
Visual aids												
Third-party proof												
Investment merit												
Closing techniques												
Merchandising												
Range selling												
TOTAL												

Organization	JAN	FEB	MAR	APR	MAY	JUN	JUL	AUG	SEP	OCT	NOV	DEC
Territory planning												
Use of time												
Reporting												
Records												
Sales statistics												
New account												
Follow-up												
Care of equipment												
TOTAL												

Attributes	JAN	FEB	MAR	APR	MAY	JUN	JUL	AUG	SEP	OCT	NOV	DEC
Enthusiasm and drive												
Training and self-development												
Appearance												
Punctuality												
Cooperation												
Customer relations												
TOTAL												
GRAND TOTAL												

Worksheet 2 Motivational climate

Get your salespeople to consider the various things, incidents or situations, that have happened to them in their work over the last, say, six months. (You can select the time period.) Then ask them to make brief notes under the headings shown on the form.

Those things I found DISSATISFYING	Those things which gave me SATISFACTION
Find ways to reduce or eliminate as many of these factors as possible	Find ways to build on or add to these factors. These are the real motivators.

REFERENCES

1. Goffin, K., Lemke F. and Szwejczewski, M. (2006) An exploratory study of 'close' supplier–manufacturer relationships. *Journal of Operations Management*, 25, 189-209.
2. Jantan, M.A., Honeycutt, E.D. Jr, Thelen, S.T. and Attia, A.M. (2004) Managerial perceptions of sales training and performance. *Industrial Marketing Management*, 33(7), 667-673.
3. McDonald, M. and Woodburn, D. (2007) *Key Account Management: The Definitive Guide*, 2nd edition. Butterworth-Heinemann, Oxford.
4. Burnett, K. (1992) *Strategic Customer Alliances*. Pitman, London.
5. Yip, G.S. and Madsen, T.L. (1996) Global account management: the new frontier in relationship marketing. *International Marketing Review*, 13(3), 24-42.
6. Buzzell, R.D. (1985) *Citibank: Marketing to Multinational Customers*. Harvard Business School.
7. Ellram, L.E. (1991) Supply chain management. *International Journal of Physical Distribution and Logistics Management*, 21(1), 13-22.
8. Ryals, L. (2005). Making customer relationship management work: the measurement and profitable management of customer relationships. *Journal of Marketing*, 69, 252-261.
9. Millman, A. and Wilson, K. (1996) Developing key account management competences. *Journal of Marketing Practice & Applied Marketing Science*, 2(2), 7-22.
10. McDonald, M., Millman, A. and Rogers, B. (1996) *Key Account Management - Learning from Supplier and Customer Perspectives*. Cranfield School of Management.
11. Davies, I.A. and Ryals, L.J. (2009) A stage model for transitioning to KAM. *Journal of Marketing Management*, 25(9-10), 1027-1048.

Chapter  9

THE PRICING PLAN

SUMMARY

- Cost-plus pricing approaches and their dangers
- Portfolio management, lifecycle analysis, product positioning and pricing implications
- Costs as an input to pricing decisions
- Pricing for channels
- Gaining competitive advantage through value-in-use
- How to prepare a pricing plan
- Exercises to turn the theory into practice

INTRODUCTION

Those readers who believe they already know enough about pricing, channel strategy and CRM, and who are principally concerned with the preparation of a strategic marketing plan, can go straight to Chapter 12.

The first important point to be made about the pricing plan is that very rarely is there a pricing plan in a marketing plan!

The reason is not too hard to find. Promotion, in all its various forms, can be managed and measured as a discrete subset of the marketing mix. So too can marketing channels. But while the product itself, the price charged, service elements and communication strategies are all part of the 'offer' which is made to the customer, price itself is such an integral part of the offer that it is rarely separated out and put into a plan of its own.

It is more common to find objectives for a certain group of products or for a particular group of customers, with a pricing strategy attached to it in whatever detail is necessary to indicate what the pricing policy is expected to do to help the company achieve its marketing objectives.

However, we have chosen to address the issue of pricing as a separate element of the marketing mix because this is the only sensible way that all the complex issues relating to pricing can be discussed. We shall, then, refer throughout to a pricing plan as if the intention were to write a separate pricing plan, although it will be structured in such a way that the elements of pricing can be integrated into the individual product/segment plans as appropriate.

The same could, of course, be said for each of the other elements of the marketing mix discussed in this book. How they are all integrated into a total plan is discussed in detail in Chapter 13.

PRICING AND ACCOUNTANCY

Many people know the story told on pricing courses of the conversation between the restaurateur who decides to put a peanut rack on the side of the bar and his accountant expert. Essentially the plan is to sell peanuts for £1 a bag, the cost price being 30p.

Unfortunately, the accountant insists that the restaurateur must allocate a proportion of overheads into the peanut operation, including rent, heat, light, equipment, depreciation, decorating, salaries, the chef's wages, window washing, soap, and so on. These allocated costs, plus a rent for the vacant amount of counter space, amount to £5,200 a year which, on the basis of a sales level of 50 bags of peanuts a week, amount to £2 per bag, so demonstrating that, at a selling price of £1 per bag the restaurateur would be losing £1.30 on every bag!

Many readers will appreciate the feelings of this imaginary restaurateur and will readily agree that nowhere in an organization are the seeds of potential strife more firmly sown than in the interface between accountants and marketing people, particularly when it comes to pricing issues. Often, however, both parties are equally to blame.

Accountants often fail to understand the essential role that marketing plays in an organization. Many accountants know quite a lot about business in general, but very little about marketing, and what little is known tends to be somewhat jaundiced.

Somehow, marketing is seen as a less worthy activity than the act of producing goods for society. Marketing's more vocal activities, such as television advertising, are not seen in their total perspective, and it is not always easy to understand the complex decisions that have to be made about an activity that is concerned essentially with human behaviour rather than with things than can be conveniently counted. There is, alas, also the issue of marketers who are unprofessional in the way they manage the marketing function. An ongoing research database at Cranfield confirms the low regard in which marketing people are held. So the blame lies just as much on the side of marketers.

For their part, those marketing people who fail to understand both the financial consequences of their decisions and the constraints of money on their decision making have only themselves to blame for the inevitable internecine disputes that arise.

One area where it all bubbles to the surface is pricing. Our intention here is to explain pricing from a marketing point of view, while still recognizing the financial constraints and implications which accountants face. For one thing is certain – any team comprising a financially alert marketer and a marketing-orientated accountant will make formidable opposition in any market. 'Demand exists only at a price', so price is an important determinant of how much of a certain product will sell, although it is obviously not the only factor involved. Given its importance, both as an element in the overall marketing mix, and as a major factor in determining profitability, it is somewhat surprising to find just how haphazard the pricing policy of so many companies is. More sophistication might be expected.

The pricing decision is important for two main reasons: price not only affects the margin through its impact on revenue; it also affects the quantity sold through its influence on demand.

In short, price has an interactive effect on the other elements of the marketing mix, so it is essential that it is part of a conscious marketing scheme, with objectives which have been clearly defined.

Although in some areas of the economy pricing may be determined by forces which are largely outside the control of corporate decision makers, prices in the marketplace are normally the result of decisions made by company managements. What should the decision be, however, when on the one hand the accountant wants to increase the price of a product in order to maximize profitability, while the marketer wants to hold or even reduce the net selling price in order to increase market share? The answer would appear to be simple. Get the calculator out and see which proposal results in the biggest 'profit'.

But there are some nagging doubts about the delightful simplicity of this approach.

> One thing is certain. Any team comprising a financially alert marketer and a marketing-orientated accountant will make formidable opposition in the marketplace.

In order to introduce a structured consideration of such doubts, let us first quote in full the Boston Consulting Group on the issue of the almost defunct British motorcycle industry:

> The fundamental feature is its emphasis on model-by-model profits made. It is seen as essential that throughout the life cycle, each model, in each market where it is sold, should yield a margin of profit over the costs incurred in bringing it to the market. With this as the primary goal, a number of subsidiary policies follow:
>
> 1. Products should be up-rated or withdrawn whenever the accounting system shows they are unprofitable. Unfortunately, the accounting system will be based on existing methods of production and channels of distribution, not on cost levels that could be achieved under new systems and with different volumes.
> 2. Prices are set at levels necessary to achieve profitability and will be raised higher if possible.
> 3. The cost of an effective marketing system is only acceptable in markets where the British are already established and hence profitable. New markets will only be opened up to the extent that their development will not mean significant front end expense investment in establishing sales and distribution systems ahead of sales.
> 4. Plans and objectives are primarily orientated towards earning a profit on this existing business and facilities of the company, rather than on the development of a long-term position of strength in the industry.
>
> These are the policies that led to the British industry's low and falling share of world markets, to its progressive concentration on higher and higher displacement models. What is more, profitability, the central short-term objective to which these policies have been directed, has in fact deteriorated in the longer term to levels that now call into question the whole viability of the industry.

We now know, of course, that the British motorcycle industry is, to all intents and purposes, dead, and the above viewpoint of the Boston Consulting Group about pricing and profits must be seriously considered at least as a contributing factor. This view is echoed in the National Westminster Bank's *Quarterly Review*, which stated: 'The disastrous commercial performance of the British motorcycle industry has resulted from failure to understand the strategic implications of the relationship between manufacturing volumes and the relative cost position.'

In contrast, the typical Far East manufacturer makes dedicated efforts to increase its market share, and will often achieve this by cutting its prices, despite the possible short-term penalties of doing so. In other words there has tended to be a recognition of the pay-off in the longer term from the sacrifice of short-term profitability.

However, there remain some serious doubts even about this point of view. It is a well-known fact that manufacturers and retailers alike have begun to question the value of price cuts, especially when, against a background of falling profitability, research shows that the average shopper, far from having a precise knowledge of prices, has only a general understanding of and feeling towards value and price.

The idea of a price cut, of course, is to increase the quantity sold, as shown in Figure 9.1. The aim is for area B ($p_2 \times q_2$) to be bigger than area A ($p_1 \times q_1$). Additionally, increased volume should lead in theory to cost reductions through the experience effect (explained in Chapter 5). However, what often happens is that market sales do *not* increase enough to balance revenue and costs, with the result that profitability declines. The result is shown in Figure 9.2, area B being less than area A. In this scenario, revenue has reduced, so given the cut in prices and therefore margins, profitability has reduced even more. It is expressed in another way in Figure 9.3.

This brings into focus the question of *time*, for the shape of demand curves changes over time, depending on a number of factors. There can be little merit in accepting profit reductions in the *long* as well as the *short* term.

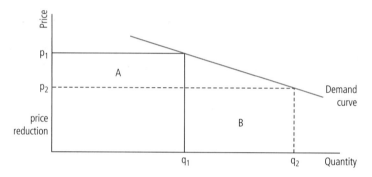

Figure 9.1: The intended effect of a price cut – greater revenue.

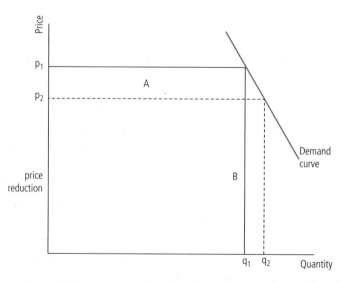

Figure 9.2: The common effect of a price cut – reduced revenue.

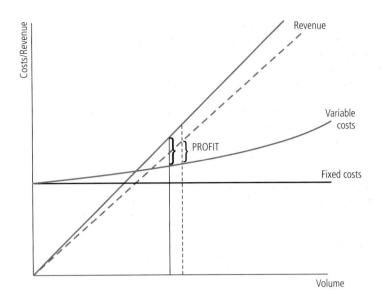

Figure 9.3: How a small reduction in margins can drastically reduce profit.

It is appropriate, then, to begin to introduce those factors that should be taken into account when trying to resolve the question raised earlier of whether the objective for pricing should be to increase profitability or to increase market share. These factors are:

- Objectives (corporate and marketing) and the product portfolio
- The product lifecycle
- The product's position in the market
- Competitors
- Potential competitors
- Costs (own and competitors')
- Channels of distribution.

OBJECTIVES AND THE PRODUCT PORTFOLIO

Unfortunately, many arguments within firms about pricing take place in the sort of vacuum created when no one has bothered to specify the *objectives* to which pricing is supposed to be contributing.

We know now that it is important that a company should have a well-defined hierarchy of objectives to which all its activities and actions, including pricing, can be related. For example, corporate objectives may well dictate that the generation of short-term profits is a requirement. (This may well be due to a particular business unit's position in a matrix *vis-à-vis* other units in the same corporation. For example, a group decision may have been taken to invest heavily in one business unit's growth and to fund this growth from one of their 'cash cow' units elsewhere in their portfolio.)

Conversely, it may well be that a product is a 'star' which the company has chosen to invest in. This might result in a strategy to grow market share today in order to take profits tomorrow, and the pricing strategy would seek to achieve this.

The setting of marketing objectives for any particular product, then, is without doubt the starting point in any consideration of pricing.

PRODUCT LIFECYCLE

The importance of the product lifecycle in determining marketing objectives has already been stressed. For example, for a product estimated to be in the maturity stage of a lifecycle, with only a short time to run, it would probably be unwise to set market share growth as a marketing objective. Profit contribution would probably be a more appropriate goal, providing of course market share did not slip to a point below which it would jeopardize the company's ability to introduce a new or replacement product.

> The role of pricing will change over a product's lifecycle.

It will be remembered that when the market reaches saturation level, we could well have a very profitable 'cash cow' on our hands for many years to come.

It is also important to stress that the role of pricing will change over a product's lifecycle. For example, during the high growth phase in the product lifecycle, price tends not to be the customer's primary consideration, since demand is growing at such a rapid rate and it is still relatively new. Here there are plenty of profit opportunities, which have to be carefully balanced against market share considerations.

It is important, then, not to write one's pricing policy on 'tablets of stone'.

On the other hand, if there is estimated to be plenty of life left in the product, it can often make a lot of sense to reduce the price in order to maintain market share.

MARKETING INSIGHT

There was a period when the policy of Woolworths of Australia was to enter a market later in the product's lifecycle, to price very low, and to promote heavily. However, lifecycle analysis indicated to the company that it unwittingly bought some products early in the lifecycle, *to which they applied exactly the same pricing strategy*. They quickly realized that they were giving profits away unnecessarily and from then on began to be more thoughtful about pricing, devising pricing policies that were appropriate to the product's progress through the lifecycle.

PRODUCT POSITIONING

The meaning of the term 'product positioning' was explained in Chapter 4. For pricing, it is a highly relevant concept.

It is clearly foolish, for example, to position a product as a high-quality, exclusive item, and then to price it too low.

Price is one of the clearest signals customers have of the value of the offer that a company is making them, and there has to be a sensible relationship between the two.

Three simple examples will suffice to illustrate this point.

MARKETING INSIGHT

One company launched a new pure juice 'smoothie' product on the market after tests had indicated an overwhelming acceptance by consumers. When sales fell far short of expectations, research indicated that consumers simply did not believe that the claims on the can about the product could be true at such a low price. So the company doubled the price and relaunched it, and it was a resounding success.

MARKETING INSIGHT

Jaguar launched a luxury car in the 1960s and priced it on their standard cost-plus basis. Customers were buying the car and reselling it immediately at a much inflated price. In other words, the *value* of the car to the customer was much greater than the actual price charged.

MARKETING INSIGHT

Likewise, some tertiary educational establishments claim their courses are the best in the world, then charge lower prices than their competitors. Research indicates that for directors and very senior managers in industry, a low price is more likely to be counterproductive because in this particular product field it is considered to be an indicator of quality.

Product positioning, then, is another major consideration in the pricing decision.

COMPETITION AND POTENTIAL COMPETITION

In spite of product positioning, most products have competitors, and it goes without saying that these must be carefully considered.

It is true, of course, that what are referred to derisively as 'pimply little me-too products' cannot in most circumstances be expected to succeed if they are priced higher than competitive products. It is also true, in such circumstances, that if price is a principal determinant of demand, being higher priced is unlikely to be the right strategy.

This brings into sharp focus again the whole question of product positioning and market segmentation. It will be clear that, wherever possible, a company should be seeking to blend the ingredients of the marketing mix in such a way that their 'offer' to the customer cannot be compared directly with anyone else's 'offer'. For, if two offers *can* be directly compared, it is obvious that the one with the lowest price will win most of the time.

Nonetheless, competitive products, in all their forms, clearly have to be taken into account in the pricing decision, as indeed do *potential* competitors.

> If two products are the same, it is obvious that the one with the lowest price will win most of the time.

Some firms launch new products at high prices to recover their investment costs, only to find that they have provided a price 'umbrella' to entice competitors, who then launch similar products at much lower prices, thus moving down the experience curve quicker, often taking the originating company's market away from them in the process. A lower launch price, with possibly a quicker rate of diffusion and hence a greater rate of experience, may make it more difficult for a potential competitor to enter the market profitably.

COSTS

Another key factor for consideration is costs – not just our own costs, but those of our competitors as well. There are many cost concepts, and this is not the right medium to go into any detail. However, the two most common cost concepts are *marginal costing* and *full absorption costing*.

The conventional profit-maximizing model of economists tends to indicate that a price should be set at the point where marginal cost equals marginal revenue, i.e. where the additional cost of producing and marketing an additional unit is equivalent to the additional revenue earned from its sale. The theory is indisputable, but in practice this procedure is difficult, if not impossible, to apply. This is largely because the economists' model assumes that price is the only determinant of demand, whereas in reality this is rarely the case.

In practice, the costs of manufacturing or providing a service provide the basis for most pricing decisions, i.e. a 'cost-plus' method. However, as the example given earlier indicates, the trouble with most such 'cost-orientated' pricing approaches is that they make little attempt to reconcile what the customer is prepared to pay with what it costs the company to be in business and make a fair return on its investment of resources.

An example of the 'cost-orientated' approach is when a company targets for a certain return on costs, i.e. the company will set itself a target level of profits at a certain projected level of sales volume. In fact, this type of approach uses a simple form of 'breakeven' analysis as depicted in Figure 9.4.

In the diagram, fixed costs are shown as a straight line and all other costs are allocated on a cost-per-unit basis to produce an ascending curve. At point A, revenue covers only fixed costs. At point B, all costs are covered and any additional sales will produce net profit. At point X, Y per cent target profit is being achieved. Obviously, the major problem with such an approach to pricing is that it tends to assume that at a given price a given number of products will be sold, whereas, in reality, the quantity sold is bound to be dependent to a certain extent on the price charged. Also, this model assumes a breakeven *point*, whereas in most companies the best that can be said is that there is a breakeven *area* at a given level of production. It is, however, quite useful for helping us to understand the relationship between different kinds of costs.

By far the most common way of setting price is to use the cost-plus approach, arriving at a price which yields margins commensurate with declared profit objectives.

When making a pricing decision, it is wise to consider a number of different costing options, for any one can be misleading on its own, particularly those that allocate fixed costs to all products in the portfolio. Often the basis of allocation is debatable, and an unthinking marketer may well accept the costs as given and easily make the wrong pricing decision.

For example, in difficult economic times, when cost savings are sought, unprofitable products are eliminated from the range. Unprofitable products are identified by the gross or net margins in the last complete trading year, and also by estimates of these margins against estimated future sales. However, because conventional cost accounting allocates the highest costs to high-volume products, they show lower margins, so sometimes these are sacrificed. But product elimination often saves only small amounts of direct costs, so the remaining products have to absorb higher costs, and the next

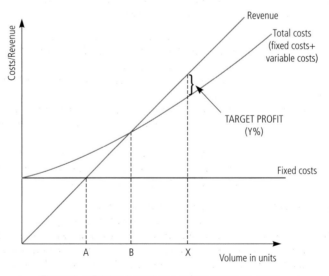

Figure 9.4: Pricing based on a target return on costs.

profitability crisis appears. Product elimination also reduces the scale of operations, as well as reducing the product mix, so there is less incentive to invest and the company is less competitive. This approach may be repeated several times under successive management teams and sometimes leads to the demise of the company.

> Andrew Lorenz, writing in the *Financial Times*, used the expression 'anorexia industrialosa' for this process, which describes an excessive desire to be leaner and fitter, leading to total emaciation and eventually death!

This is not intended to be an attack on any kind of total average costing method. Our intention here is merely to advise caution and a broader perspective when using any kind of costing system as a basis for pricing decisions.

Finally, some account has to be taken of our competitors' costs and to try to understand the basis of their pricing policies. For, clearly, everything that has been said so far about pricing applies as much to them as it does to us.

Whatever your pricing problem, however, you will never go far wrong if you sit alongside your accountant and discuss all these issues.

CHANNELS OF DISTRIBUTION

Conventional pricing theory does not help much in determining one's policy towards margins for distributors and agents. The intermediaries which constitute a particular marketing channel perform a number of functions on behalf of the supplier which enables the exchange transaction between producer and end customer to be fulfilled. In return for their services, these intermediaries seek to be rewarded; this reward is in effect the 'margin' between the price of the goods or service products (such as financial products) ex the factory or its service equivalent, and the price the consumer pays. However, the total channel margin may have to be shared between several intermediaries and still reach the end customer at a competitive price. Intermediaries, therefore, live or die on the economics of their respective operations. The ideal reward structure in the marketing channel is to ensure that an acceptable rate of return on investment is earned at each level; this situation is often not achieved because of the imbalances of bargaining power present.

There are a number of devices available for rewarding channel intermediaries, most of which take the form of discounts against a nominal price list. These are:

Trade discount.	This is discount given against the price list for services made available by the intermediary, e.g. holding inventory, buying in bulk, redistribution, etc.
Quantity discount.	A quantity discount is offered to intermediaries who order in large lots.
Promotional discount.	This is the discount given to distributors to encourage them to share jointly in the promotion of the product(s) involved.
Cash discount.	For example, in order to encourage prompt payments of accounts, a cash discount of around 2.5 per cent for payment within 10 days might be offered.

In the situation where there is a dynamic marketing channel, there will be constant pressure upon suppliers to improve margins. Because of these pressures, the question of margins should be seen at a strategic as well as at a tactical level. This whole area of margin management can be viewed as a series of trade-off type decisions which determine how the total channel margin should be split. The concept of the total channel margin is simple. It is the difference between the level of price at which we wish to position our product in the ultimate marketplace and the cost of our product

at the factory gate, or the internal transfer cost paid for service provision. Who takes what proportion of this difference is what margin management is about. The problem is shown in Figure 9.5.

It will be seen that the firm's channel requirements will only be achieved if it either carries them out itself or goes some way towards meeting the requirements of an intermediary who can perform those functions on its behalf. The objective of the firm in this respect could therefore be expressed in terms of willingness to trade off margin in order to achieve its marketing goals. Such a trade-off need not lead to a loss of profitability; indeed as Figure 9.6 suggests, the margin is only one element in the determination of profitability, profitability being defined as the rate of return on net worth (net worth being share capital and capital reserves plus retained profits).

It can be seen that by improving the utilization of capital assets (capital management) as well as by using a higher gearing, it is possible to operate successfully on lower margins if this means that marketing goals can be achieved more effectively.

From the foregoing, it becomes apparent that the question of margins (both the margin retained by the firm and thus by implication the margin allowed the distributor) cannot be examined without consideration of the wider implications of overall marketing strategy and the financial policy and capital structure of the firm.

As a general rule, however, a firm should not give away its profits to an agent or distributor. Rather, it should give away only the costs it saves by using an intermediary.

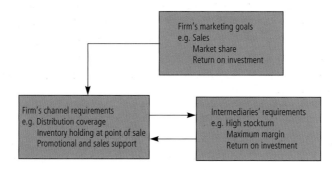

Figure 9.5: The trade-offs affecting channel margins.

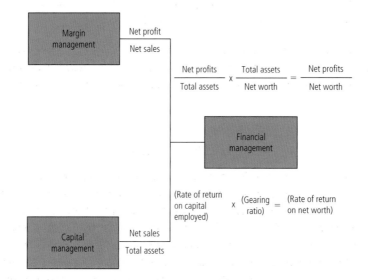

Figure 9.6: Why margins are only one contributor to the return on net work.

GAINING COMPETITIVE ADVANTAGE THROUGH VALUE-IN-USE

The final consideration in pricing relates to the design of the product or service. It stems from the observation that customers do not obtain value at the factory gate, but at the moment when a product is used to achieve the customer's goals – that is, when 'value-in-use' is obtained.[1] Similarly, services such as training do not deliver value at the moment of service delivery, but later when the training is applied in the student's job. If customers achieve higher value-in-use they will be prepared to pay a higher price – even if the core product or service looks similar.

The lesson is that before settling on a pricing strategy, it is worth considering carefully what the customer's goals in using the product or service are, and whether these can be better realized than the competition through such techniques as guarantees, service standards, advice to the customer on their usage processes, and so on. Examples abound; three will make the point.

MARKETING INSIGHT

There are not many more price-sensitive businesses than cleaning of business premises. Poorly-paid staff and the cheapest of supplies are the norm in order to win price-dominated tenders. Yet one company, the memorably named Bugs Burger Bug Killer, found it could commonly charge 100% more than the competitors and still get the business. How? By making a promise not about the service attributes at the moment of service delivery – who would clean the buildings, when, what they would do – but about the value-in-use the customer would get. Here is an extract from their promise to their restaurant and hotel clients for their 'pest extermination' service:

> You don't owe a penny until all the pests on your premises have been eradicated. If you are ever dissatisfied with BBBK's service you will receive a refund for up to 12 months' services, plus fees for another exterminator of your choice for the next year. If a guest spots a pest on your premises, BBBK will pay for the guest's meal or room, send a letter of apology and pay for a future meal or stay. If your facility is closed due to pests, BBBK will pay any fines, as well as all lost profits, plus $5,000.

Customers are prepared to pay considerable sums for a transfer of risk of this sort. Naturally it needs to be carefully costed, but the company was confident that this proposition would only cost a few per cent of revenue based on past records – far outweighed by the extra price premium.

MARKETING INSIGHT

Another business where attention to price is keen is providing automation equipment into factories. There is fierce competition for the equipment purchases themselves, and just as tough a fight to get and keep maintenance, repair and operation (MRO) contracts. One large US-based manufacturer has found that it can gain significantly improved market share and, importantly, build longer-term relationships which can lower costs for both parties, in the face of low-cost Far Eastern competition. It is doing this by focusing not just on its own products and services but on redesigning the customer's factory operations processes. Its aim is not to sell good equipment or efficient service, but to sell more efficient factories. One blue-chip client studied in depth by Cranfield[2] reported that a production line which was previously running at 35 per cent operating efficiency was now running at 85 per cent operating efficiency. Millions of dollars of obsolete stock was taken out of stores through a redesign of the spares ordering process. Factory managers had more time to focus on more strategic issues. And if things did go wrong, they had someone to blame, a genuine benefit as far as these purchasers were concerned! While the supplier found that margins were still modest, it was at least able to protect them from head-on price competition, as competitors were some way away from being able to offer a similar proposition. The firm is achieving growth in revenue, profits and capitalization considerably ahead of its country's stock market average.

MARKETING INSIGHT

If you were the marketing director of a major symphony orchestra, what would you enter in your critical success factor analysis (see Chapter 5) as the buying criteria which customers trade off against price? Many might think of such factors as the quality of the performance and the quality of the food and drink at the venue – product and service attributes. In a major capital city like London, though, with several world-quality orchestras, these are mere hygiene factors. How can an orchestra compete for market share of concert-goers?

With Cranfield's help, a London-based orchestra investigated the customer's true 'goals, purposes or objectives' which constitute value-in-use. Some simple research found that what concert-goers really want is a good night out with friends, a sense of belonging with their fellow concert-goers, a vicarious pride in the performance of 'their' orchestra, and soul-food – the almost spiritual experience which many respondents reported in taking them away from their everyday lives through moving music. This simple insight led to the marketing director and her team brainstorming all sorts of ways in which the orchestra could differentiate itself. Conductors were asked to introduce each piece informally to the audience – against the staid conventions of most classical music, but great for building the kind of vicarious pride and fierce loyalty that is taken for granted in another form of entertainment, team sports. Players were asked to go on a rota to a nominated bar after the performance, which was advertised to the audience, further improving a sense of community. Previously, respondents had complained that within minutes of the performance ending, they felt that they were being swept out by the cleaners! The orchestra now has very high repeat purchase rates, helping it to sustain prices in a crowded market in which discounting is common.

From these and other examples, the 'rules' for gaining competitive advantage through value-in-use can be listed as follows:

1. *Understand the value-in-use required by customers.* This cannot simply be done by satisfaction surveys, which obsess on the boundary between the firm and the customer, not on the customer's end-goal: the quality of the performing, rather than whether the young man had a successful date! Rather, it is necessary to interview some customers in depth, continually asking why they care about a particular feature of a product or service, to establish the 'value-in-use' which they seek. While some specialized market research techniques are available for this, such as repertory grid,[3] some common-sense interviewing can achieve much. Options for recrafting the value proposition to maximize value-in-use then include the following.

2. *Design products and services to reduce lifetime costs.* Customers are often willing to pay a considerably higher initial price for a product with significantly lower post-purchase costs – particularly if the supplier is prepared to contract on the basis of these lifetime costs. Such a transfer of risk should not be undertaken lightly, but if properly costed, the price premium may outweigh the cost implication considerably.

3. *Expand value through functional redesign* – for example:
   - A product that increases the user's production capacity or throughput
   - A product that enables the user to improve the quality of reliability of their end product
   - A product that enhances end-use flexibility
   - A product that adds functions or permits added applications
   - A service with higher post-service value: for example, for a business school, the quality of the alumni network and ongoing career assistance is as important as the teaching during an MBA
   - A service with higher experiential value: a holiday designed with careful attention to end-to-end experience from the moment of booking to the moment of coming back home, so the journey home does not undo all the relaxation of the holiday!

MARKETING INSIGHT

Hotel questionnaires focus on service attributes: the cleanliness of the room, the helpfulness of the staff, food quality. But what is the value-in-use sought by hotel customers? One boutique hotel chain found, with Cranfield's help, that the answer is largely emotional: feeling relaxed, safe and above all, special. The research uncovered all sorts of ways in which feeling special could be enhanced. And this benefit could be promoted, too, making the firm's communications stand out strongly. The chain is growing strongly.

4. *Expand incremental value by developing associated intangibles* – for example, 'prestige', financing, or access to experts.

5. *Expand value-in-use by redesigning the customer's usage processes.* If we take responsibility not just for our products and service delivery but also for the customer's processes, we can expand the creative space for finding differentiation to counteract price pressures. This was evident from the case of the factory equipment manufacturer: a key part of its proposition was to advise its customers on how to organize their own maintenance operation – often with the aid of a full-time employee situated at the customer's site.

MARKETING INSIGHT

It is ever harder to create and patent 'blockbuster drugs' which are so superior to their generic competitors that health customers are willing to pay for them. One of the ways pharmaceutical companies can compete is through service redesign – redesign not of *their* processes but of their *customers*. One company has worked with some pilot hospitals to redesign their treatment processes for outpatients within its therapy area. The effect is a higher throughput of patients, reduced waiting times, better compliance of patients with their treatment regimes and hence better outcomes. Other hospitals are keenly interested to hear from the company's salespeople about these projects – a far cry from the sinking feeling that many medics report when the rep turns up! This approach is helping to maintain a price differential, and gives the company the interesting strategic decision as to whether to start charging for these services separately.

These rules will not, of course, avoid the need for creativity from marketers in how to increase the value perceived by the customer. But we find that for mature marketers with a good knowledge of the target market, simply to ask the question of what the customer's ultimate goals or objectives are will often lead to creative solutions which outflank the competition and lead to price maintenance if not price premiums.

PREPARING THE PRICING PLAN

We have so far considered some of the main issues relevant to the pricing decision. We can now try to pull all of these issues together. However, let us first recapitulate on one of the basic findings which underpin the work of the Boston Consulting Group.

It will be recalled that, under certain circumstances, real costs reduce according to the accumulated experience of producing goods or delivering services. Figure 9.7 describes this effect. One of the implications of this is that unless a firm accumulates experience at the same or at a greater rate than the market as a whole, eventually its costs will become uncompetitive. Figure 9.8 illustrates this point.

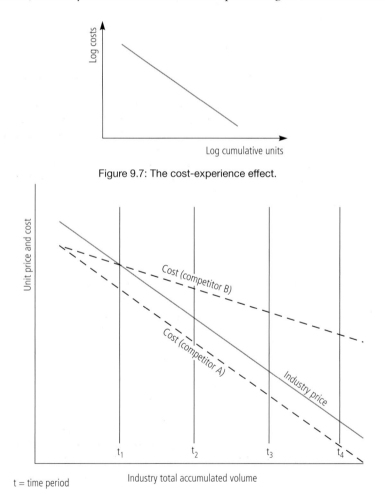

Figure 9.7: The cost-experience effect.

Figure 9.8: How the cost-experience effect impacts on competitiveness.

In the light of this cost-experience effect, two major types of pricing strategy are a *skimming* policy or a *penetration* policy. It is easiest to consider these policies in the context of new product launches.

Essentially, a skimming policy is a high initial price, moving down the experience curve at a slower rate, while a penetration policy is a low initial price, with a much faster rate of product adoption, hence a steeper experience curve.

Both policies are summarized in Figures 9.9a and b.

The circumstances favouring a skimming policy are:

1. Demand is likely to be price inelastic
2. There are likely to be different price-market segments, thereby appealing to those buyers first who have a higher range of acceptable prices
3. Little is known about the costs of producing and marketing the product.

The circumstances favouring a penetration policy are:

1. Demand is likely to be price elastic
2. Competitors are likely to enter the market quickly
3. There are no distinct and separate price-market segments
4. There is the possibility of large savings in production and marketing costs if a large sales volume can be generated (the experience factor).

However, great caution is necessary whatever the circumstances and, apart from these, all the other factors mentioned above should also be considered.

In conclusion, it must be emphasized that the price charged for the product affects and is affected by the other elements of the marketing mix. It is a common mistake to assume either that the lowest price will get the order, or that we can sell enough of our product at a cost-plus price to give us the required rate of return.

The reality is that pricing policy should be determined after account has been taken of all factors which impinge on the pricing decision. These are summarized in Figure 9.10. The first part shows the discretionary pricing range for a company. The second shows those factors we should take account of in reaching a pricing decision.

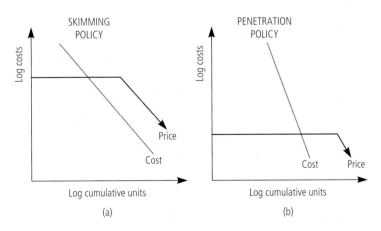

Figure 9.9: Skimming versus penetration pricing.

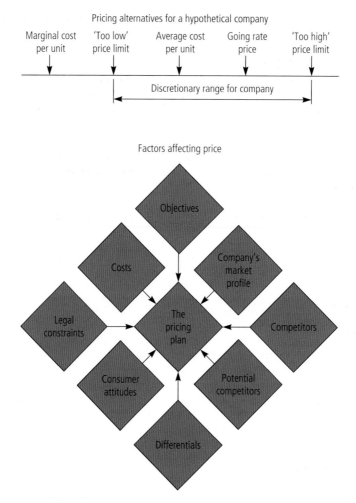

Pricing alternatives for a hypothetical company

| Marginal cost per unit | 'Too low' price limit | Average cost per unit | Going rate price | 'Too high' price limit |

Discretionary range for company

Factors affecting price

Figure 9.10: Factors impinging on the pricing decision.

APPLICATION QUESTIONS

1. When you last introduced a new product or service, how was the price established?
2. Was the pricing decision correct? What additional information could you have used to help you with the pricing decision? What would you do differently given the same circumstances?
3. Describe your pricing strategy for one of your major products. How does it compare with that of your major competitors?
4. Describe how you deal with pricing:
   - in times of high inflation, market stagnation or recession
   - at each phase in the product lifecycle.
5. During the past 10 years, what trends have occurred in margins in your industry? Are these trends acceptable? What policy has your organization got towards these trends?
6. Are trade margins justified? What is your policy towards trade margins?

CHAPTER 9 REVIEW

Reasons for a pricing plan

Pricing is a key part of the marketing mix and needs to be managed intelligently, in the same way as the other parts. Generally, pricing is included as part of product/segment plans and doesn't appear as a separate entity. This can disguise some of the complex issues to be found in pricing.

Cost-plus pricing

Traditionally, pricing has been the remit of accountants. Their concern was mainly about the impact of price on margin and hence revenue. The weaknesses of this approach are:

1. Product can be overpriced because of arbitrary loading of production and other overheads.
2. There is no room for strategic thinking.
3. Products can be eliminated from the range, regardless of their synergy with others.

In contrast, marketers look at price in terms of its influence on demand.

Competitive pricing

The possible pricing spectrum is:

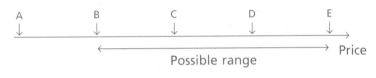

where
A = marginal cost per unit
B = lowest price limit in the market
C = average cost per unit
D = 'going rate' price in the market
E = top end price limit in the market

Try Exercise 9.1

Pricing and the product lifecycle

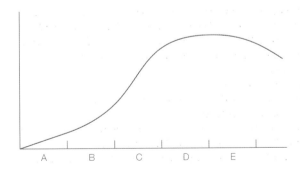

Different positions of the lifecycle call for different pricing strategies:

A Introduction	Either (1) price low to win high market share, or (2) price high in recognition of novelty and prestige.
B Growth	Price competitively to win market share.
C Maturity	As per the growth phase.
D Saturation	Stabilize price; consider raising it.
E Decline	Raise price.

Try Exercise 9.2

Product positioning

Pricing can influence the position of a product in the market, e.g. a high price can convey an image of better quality, design or exclusiveness. Here is one example of product positioning.

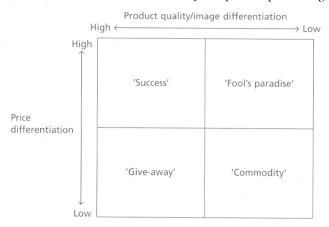

Better positioning beats the competition.

Channel discounts

If there are intermediaries, they have to be rewarded in return for their services, i.e. there has to be a total channel margin allowed for in 'price to customer' calculations. Discounts against nominal price lists can be in the form of:

1. Trade discounts
2. Quantity discounts
3. Promotional discounts
4. Cash discounts.

How the total margin is sliced for distributors is a matter of 'trade-offs' of costs versus the added value of using distributors.

Try Exercise 9.3

Factors affecting price

Price can be influenced by:

- Marketing objectives
- The cost structure
- Legal constraints

- Consumer attitudes
- Competition (direct)
- Competition (substitutes)
- Company/product image
- Economic situation.

Try Exercises 9.4 and 9.5

Questions raised for the company

1. Q: Is it possible to develop a sound pricing policy if one's costing is suspect?
   A: While 'prices' and 'costs' are separate entities, it is essential that a company has an accurate costing system. Without this there is no point of reference to put pricing into perspective.
2. Q: What is the true price of a product?
   A: Seen by the buyer it is purchase price, cost of introduction and cost of usage of the product or service; this can include training costs, maintenance, energy consumption, disruption costs, consumables, floor space, etc. However, these items can be a source of differential advantage over competing products, which in effect provides a 'better price' in real money terms.
3. Q: Is it better to price high or low?
   A: It depends on a number of factors, such as market share, and so on. It is as well to remember, however, that if you try to have the lowest price, someone will usually try to go even lower. This is a difficult battle to win.

EXERCISES

Clearly, pricing is a marketing 'tool' just as much as advertising, promotions and the use of the sales force. Moreover, it is generally easier and quicker to change a price than it is to alter an advertising campaign, revamp a sales promotion, or to deploy the sales force in a different manner.

Pricing decisions not only affect the revenue the company can earn, but also they influence demand, thereby making an impact on the quantities sold. Yet for all this, few companies have a pricing plan. Indeed, rather than a positive strategy, the very topic often becomes a battleground in a war of apparently conflicting interests between marketers and accountants.

Exercise 9.1 looks at how to set a competitive price for a product or service, taking into account a number of different factors which can have a bearing on the pricing decision.

Exercise 9.2 is concerned with selecting the price.

Exercise 9.3 provides some insights into the real impact of price discounts.

Exercise 9.4 is a self-scoring questionnaire which gives you some assessment about your readiness to get involved in aggressive pricing situations.

Exercise 9.5 poses a number of awkward questions about pricing and gives you the opportunity to test out your expertise.

Exercise 9.1 Setting a competitive price

This exercise will enable you to use pricing in a creative way, one which will support your marketing plan. It will use information from your marketing audit and a few new pieces of data to help you to arrive at a sensible pricing plan for your products or services.

(Continued)

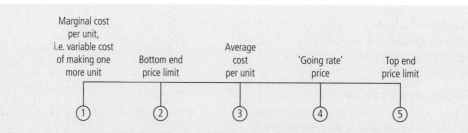

Figure 9.11: Some key positions or the costing/pricing continuum.

It goes without saying that unless the company has an accurate costing system, one that realistically reflects its internal situation, then it will be impossible to establish anything like a sensible pricing policy. The reason for this will become self-evident as you provide the information requested below.

Figure 9.11 shows some key positions on the costing/pricing continuum. Taking just *one* of your company's major products or services, enter on the worksheet the actual figures that correspond to the numbers 1 to 5, in the positions marked in Figure 9.11, i.e. the actual marginal cost, bottom end price limit, etc.

When considering the average cost please remember that costing systems that allocate fixed costs to all products in the range, while being popular, can produce some very misleading results, especially if the basis of cost allocation is somewhat arbitrary. Some products can never survive the cost load they have to carry. Knowing what the customer is prepared to pay for your chosen product/service (the going rate price), consider different costing options, with the objective of getting the average cost per unit as low as possible, thereby providing you with a wider range of pricing options.

Consider other products and services and repeat this process for them. The worksheet is useful in order to establish the range of discretion open to you, but the more important task will be to identify where exactly on this scale to select your price position.

Worksheet Cost price continuum (Exercise 9.1)

PRODUCT/SERVICE	1 Marginal cost per unit	2 Bottom end price limit per unit	3 Average cost per unit	4 Going rate price per unit	5 Top end price limit per unit
Example	£6.50	£8.50	£10	£13	£20

Exercise 9.2: Selecting the price

It can be shown that there are a number of factors that can influence your ultimate choice of price. These will be considered in turn.

Corporate objectives

If the corporate objectives dictate that it will be important to generate short-term profits for your chosen product/service, it would be reasonable to select a high price, somewhere between 4 and 5 on the scale established in Figure 9.11. Alternatively, if the aim is to extend market share, then a position between 3 and 4 would be more suitable.

You can see from this example that whatever the nature of the corporate or marketing objectives for your chosen product or service, it is possible to select a position somewhere on the scale which appears to be most appropriate. Select a position for your chosen product and record the price on the worksheet where indicated.

Worksheet Factors affecting price (Exercise 9.2)

	Example (based on example on preceding worksheet)	Prod. 1	Prod. 2	Prod. 3	Prod. 4
1 Corporate objectives	£18.00				
2 Portfolio matrix	£16.00				
3 Life-cycle analysis	£16.00				
4 Product position	£10.00				
5 Current competition	£12.00				
6 Potential competition	£10.00				
7 Channels of distribution	Not applic.				
8 Differential benefits	£9.00				
9 Consumer attitudes	£9.00				
Total score	£100.00				
Number of factors	8				
Suggested price average	£12.50				

Portfolio matrix

It has been shown that a different marketing strategy would be required according to which quadrant 'housed' your chosen product. Generally speaking, this would mean that prices should be selected as follows:

1. '*Question mark*' – price competitively to get market share.
2. '*Star*' – price to maintain/increase market share.
3. '*Cash cow*' – stabilize or even raise price.
4. '*Dog*' – raise price.

(Continued)

With these guidelines in mind, select a position on the 1–5 scale for your product/service and again record the price on the worksheet.

Lifecycle

Your chosen product's position on its lifecycle will also be significant when calculating its price:

1. *Introduction stage* – either price low to capture market share or, if there is genuine novelty or innovation associated with the product, price high in recognition of its prestige value.
2. *Growth stage* – price low to get market share.
3. *Maturity* – as for growth stage.
4. *Saturation* – stabilize price, consider raising it.
5. *Decline* – raise price.

Using these suggestions, select a position for your chosen product on the 1–5 scale and, again, note the price on the worksheet.

Product position

Your price will have to take into account the marketing profile you are trying to establish for your chosen product. If yours is the biggest, the best, the most technologically advanced product, then your price ought to echo the fact. Similarly, if your target is just high-income customers, your price should reflect that exclusivity. The converse will be true for down-market economy models, where a lower price would be more consistent with the product position.

Carefully consider your product position and use your judgement to 'score' a position on the 1–5 scale. Record your choice of price on the worksheet.

Current competition

Analyse the prices charged by your competitors for their versions of your product or service. Will these influence your ultimate choice of price?

Where does this information suggest you position the price on the 1–5 scale? Enter your answer on the worksheet.

Potential competition

Another consideration you will have to take into account will be the extent to which your chosen price might either attract or repel competitors. Clearly, if you can get away with charging high prices and making correspondingly high margins, then it will not be long before others become interested in your sphere of business.

Estimate the price you can charge using the 1–5 scale as a reference. Note the selected price on the worksheet.

Channels of distribution

If your business is one where you need to use intermediaries to reach your customers, then, in return for their services, they will expect a reward in the shape of a 'mark-up' or margin on the goods. Thus the price you charge at the factory gate has to be profitable for you, yet still allow the intermediary a fair margin without leading to an excessively high price for the ultimate consumer. What will this mean for your pricing decision?

Choose a position on the 1–5 scale and enter the price on the worksheet.

Differential benefits

If your product or service provides differential customer benefits which your competitors do not provide, then you could justify a higher price and gain the reward from higher revenue. Your option for doing this might be limited by some of the other considerations above. For example, it might be better to use your product advantage to gain a larger market share. Nevertheless, if the benefit analysis you carried out in Chapter 4 suggests any room for manoeuvre on pricing, score the new choice on the 1–5 scale and enter the actual figure on the worksheet.

Consumer attitudes

Consumer attitudes to your particular product/service or to your company, because of its name and reputation, might also influence your ultimate choice of price. To what extent will this be the case? Again select a price position on the 1–5 scale that you believe can be justified as a result of consumer attitudes to your product.

Record the price on the worksheet.

You have now looked at nine different factors that are known to influence pricing. These have been considered in isolation and a notional price position for your product has been calculated against each factor.

The price positions were established by using a cost–price continuum, with key positions numbered 1–5. The actual money value of each of these positions was calculated in the worksheet of Exercise 9.1.

The worksheet in this exercise is a record of the results you have attributed to the various pricing factors. You will now use this information in the following way:

1. Find the average price position for your product by adding up the column of prices and dividing it by the number of factors you used (an example is shown on the worksheet). This average figure would seem to be the 'best fit' when taking all the factors into account, and should therefore be selected as the price for your chosen product, unless, of course, there are other factors known to you which would militate against this decision.
2. Now repeat this process for other products or services.

Critique of example provided on worksheets

This approach to pricing raises many important issues. In the example provided it is quite evident that the corporate objectives are for the product to generate revenue. The positions on the portfolio matrix and lifecycle also appear to support this strategy of pricing high.

(Continued)

But look at some of the other factors. The product position would not appear to justify a high price, there seem to be few differential benefits and consumer attitudes are not very positive. In addition it looks as if the company will have to price below the 'going rate' if it is going to cope with the competition.

Result – a compromise price of £12.50 per unit.

Moral – if the company wants to price high, it must upgrade the product in terms of providing more differential benefits and work to improve customer attitudes.

Alternatively, or in addition, it should carefully re-examine the actual costs and its costing system and by doing so try to improve the margin that would be achievable at £12.50. By these means, it might well obtain results similar to its original objectives of pricing high.

Exercise 9.3: The use of discounts

To give a price reduction, which is really what a discount is, appears on the surface to be a fairly straightforward and easy-to-apply mechanism for stimulating demand. However, it is not always fully appreciated how many extra products have to be sold merely to break even, i.e. to get back to the original situation.

Here is a simple example. Suppose a company had sales of 100 units of a product per week, priced at £10. Thus the total income was £1,000 and this yielded a profit of £200. The marketing director of the company decides that a 10 per cent reduction in price will stimulate a demand in sales. What new level of sales in units would have to be achieved to break even?

• • •

Write your answer here _____

• • •

Probably this was how you calculated your figure:

	Units	Price	Total income	Profit
Original situation	100	£10	£1,000	£200

Since 100 units yielded £200 profit, profit per unit = £2. With price reduced to £9 (10 per cent reduction) new profit per unit = £1.

Therefore new situation becomes:

	Units	Price	Total income	Profit
New situation	200	£9	£1,800	£200

Thus the company would have to double its sale of units to maintain its existing profit level if it sold at the new lower price. Perhaps some questions would have to be asked about the feasibility of this happening.

To avoid having to make tedious calculations each time you contemplate making a price reduction, Table 9.1 provides an easy-to-use reference.

If you cut your price	And your present gross profit is							
	5%	10%	15%	20%	25%	30%	35%	40%
	You need to sell this much more to break even							
	%	%	%	%	%	%	%	%
1%	25.0	11.1	7.1	5.3	4.2	3.4	2.9	2.6
2%	66.6	25.0	15.4	11.1	8.7	7.1	6.1	5.3
3%	150.0	42.0	25.0	17.6	13.6	11.1	9.4	8.1
4%	400.0	66.6	36.4	25.0	19.0	15.4	12.9	11.1
5%	–	100.0	50.0	33.3	25.0	20.0	16.7	14.3
6%	–	150.0	66.7	42.9	31.6	25.0	20.7	17.6
7%	–	233.3	87.5	53.8	38.9	30.4	25.0	21.2
8%	–	400.0	114.3	66.7	47.1	36.4	29.6	25.0
9%	–	1,000.0	150.0	81.8	56.3	42.9	34.6	29.0
10%	–	–	200.0	100.0	66.7	50.0	40.0	33.3
11%	–	–	275.0	122.2	78.6	57.9	45.8	37.9
12%	–	–	400.0	150.0	92.3	66.7	52.2	42.9
13%	–	–	650.0	185.7	108.3	76.5	59.1	48.1
14%	–	–	1,400.0	233.3	127.3	87.5	66.7	53.8
15%	–	–	–	300.0	150.0	100.0	76.8	60.0
16%	–	–	–	400.0	177.8	114.3	84.2	66.7
17%	–	–	–	566.7	212.5	100.8	94.4	73.9
18%	–	–	–	900.0	257.1	150.0	105.9	81.8
19%	–	–	–	1,900.0	316.7	172.7	118.8	90.5
20%	–	–	–	–	400.0	200.0	133.3	100.0
21%	–	–	–	–	525.0	233.3	150.0	110.5
22%	–	–	–	–	733.3	275.0	169.2	122.2
23%	–	–	–	–	1,115.0	328.6	191.7	135.3
24%	–	–	–	–	2,400.0	400.0	218.2	150.0
25%	–	–	–	–	–	500.0	250.0	166.7

Example: Your present gross margin is 25 per cent and you cut your selling price by 10 per cent. Locate 10 per cent in the left-hand column. Now follow across to the column headed 25 per cent. You find you will need to sell 66.7 per cent *more* units.

Table 9.1 Effects of price reductions

(Continued)

Exercise 9.4 Questionnaire

This exercise* is really designed for personal insight, but you won't fail to notice that you could use it equally well to analyse your marketing director or chief executive.

Consider these statements and *quickly* tick the score which most aptly represents your position.

	Very true of me	Usually true of me	No feeling either way	Usually untrue of me	Very untrue of me
1. If a rival company is cheaper, I want to match or beat its price.	5	4	3	2	1
2. I would like to talk to competitors about equalizing prices.	5	4	3	2	1
3. I'm prepared to start a discount battle any time; I believe the first one in wins.	5	4	3	2	1
4. Before quoting a special price I will always ask 'Why?'	1	2	3	4	5
5. I fully expect to lose some deals on price.	1	2	3	4	5
6. I always try to keep it simple if I can! '10 per cent off' is the way to do it	5	4	3	2	1
7. I try not to publish discounts. I prefer to negotiate them individually.	1	2	3	4	5
8. I am always prepared to offer bigger discounts than I allow those working for me to offer.	5	4	3	2	1
9. I believe that most people will jump at a 10 per cent discount.	5	4	3	2	1
10. I believe that people who start savage price wars often live to regret it.	1	2	3	4	5

Now add up the total score for all your ticks and write it here _____.

Scoring and interpretation of Exercise 9.4

The questions are not very subtle and so very good scores are required from this exercise. The lowest score for each question is the best, but an extremely low score, of *12 or less*, while suggesting the right instincts, might show you to be rather inflexible. You might well be used to working in an industry where the quality content of what you offer is very high, with

---

* Exercises 9.4 and 9.5 are based on John Winkler's work on pricing and we are indebted to him for the ideas. Readers are recommended to follow this up by reading his book *Pricing for Results* (Butterworth-Heinemann, 2nd edition 1991).

prices that reflect this. In these circumstances you would tend to avoid price fights as much as you can. But if in your current role your firm does not always have a strongly differentiated offer, you may need to be more discriminating.

A score of *13–16* is a good score – you will hold on and make sensible, profitable deals most of the time. Although you might lose out here and there on high volume, you would rather make the largest profits than the largest sales.

Above 25 – you are a potential warmonger, probably used to working at the bottom end of some very tough markets, with some rapacious buyers. There's one other thing, and you might not like to hear this. These buyers are probably taking you to the cleaners.

Exercise 9.5 Awkward questions on pricing[4]

Here are some hypothetical questions concerning pricing. How would you deal with these situations?

Question 1

You are the marketing director of a pharmaceuticals company in a country where there is no equivalent of a National Health Service, and patients have to pay for the drugs they use. Your company produces a life-support drug. Once patients have been treated with it, they must stay on it continuously to survive. This drug has been outdated by a machine which treats new patients and, as a result, your market is gradually eroding. Should you adopt:

(a) A system based on cost-plus?
(b) A system based on what the market will bear?
(c) A system based on some notion of morality?
(d) A system based on what the competition charges?

Question 2

You have an excess of stock of a poor line to clear. You must shift this stock in order to raise money to invest in better products. What is your view of promotional pricing? Do you:

(a) Actively encourage it all the time?
(b) Offer it only to your best customers?
(c) Refuse to use it at all?
(d) Use it sparingly, outside normal markets?
(e) Use it a little, but create an impression that you use it a lot, through advertising, etc.?

Question 3

You want to price aggressively in order to take over a major part of a total market. What level of price discount should you offer in a normal consumer product market, as a minimum, to make the market turn to you in a meaningful way?

(a) 10 per cent off competitors' prices.
(b) 15 per cent off competitors' prices.
(c) 20 per cent off competitors' prices.
(d) 30 per cent off competitors' prices.
(e) Between 40 and 50 per cent off competitors' prices.

(Continued)

Question 4

If you average out all the prices of consumer products in a given market, you can arrive at an average price. Yours is the biggest selling brand in this market. Together with your two nearest competitors you share 60 per cent of the market. Measured against the average market price, where would you expect your brand leader product to be positioned?

(a) 10 per cent less than the average price.
(b) On, or closely around, the average price.
(c) 20 per cent less than the average price.
(d) 7 per cent above the average price.

Answers to Exercise 9.5

Question 1

(a) Score + 1.
(b) Score – 5. They will pay anything to stay alive, but how can you live with yourself?
(c) Score + 5.
(d) Score + 1.

Question 2

(a) Score 0.
(b) Score + 1. A poor tactic because it will make your best customers look for bargains all the time. It might generate some goodwill.
(c) Score + 1. Too rigid.
(d) Score + 5. Get rid of it altogether if you can, otherwise go for (e).
(e) Score + 4. A technique used by some supermarkets. A few loss leaders in reality, but all of them promoted very heavily. But you will still be attracting price cutting in your market, and you will have to advertise your price cuts as well as give the discounts away. This can be expensive unless the volume sales justify it.

Question 3

(a) Score 0.
(b) Score +1.
(c) Score +2.
(d) Score +3.
(e) Score +4.

Question 4

(a) Score 0.
(b) Score +2.
(c) Score –2.
(d) Score +5.

Interpretation of scores

15 or more	You did very well and/or are very experienced
10–14	Think a bit harder before making decisions
Less than 10	Don't engage in pricing decision making!

REFERENCES

1. Vargo, S.L. and Lusch, R.F. (2004) Evolving to a new dominant logic of marketing. *Journal of Marketing*, 68, 1–17.
2. MacDonald, E.K., Wilson, H.N., Martinez, V. and Toosi, A. (2009) Assessing the value-in-use of integrated product-service offerings: a repertory grid approach. *Frontiers in Service conference*, Hawaii, October.
3. Lemke, F., Clark, M. and Wilson, H. (2010) Customer experience quality: an exploration in business and consumer contexts using repertory grid technique. In press for *Journal of Academy of Marketing Science*.
4. Winkler, J. (1991) *Pricing for Results*, 2nd edition. Butterworth Heinemann, Oxford.

Chapter

THE MULTICHANNEL PLAN: THE ROUTE TO MARKET

SUMMARY

- How channels are combined in the customer journey
- How to select the most appropriate channels
- The several components of the distribution mix
- Customer service and customer experience
- How to prepare a multichannel plan
- Exercises to turn the theory into practice

INTRODUCTION*

For years, Place (route to market) was the dull, neglected P of the famous 4Ps of marketing. Companies' distribution policies were driven by mechanistic cost analysis: shipping and storage configurations, trade-offs between holding cost and the risk of being out of stock, and so on. But by the 1990s, new technology was changing the thinking on channels. Evans and Wurster[1] noted how economic value was being split into physical and virtual (information) streams: the traditional economic trade-offs still held for physical distribution of goods and services, but the virtual stream of information exchange defied these rules. Internet experts advised companies to rethink Place as 'spaces' not 'places'. In the early days of such dot-com thinking, strategy focused on using the new internet channel to disrupt existing business models, and new words such as disintermediation, content aggregation and search entered the strategic lexicon.

New, online channels spawned some significant successes based upon 'pureplay' information-based strategies, such as Amazon, eBay, Google and Facebook. However, the majority of the economy is still dominated by companies that need to integrate new channels into a traditional distribution model. Wal-Mart is not closing all its stores to better leverage new channels, while Apple has come full circle by investing successfully in physical stores to complement its telephone and internet channels.

---

* The authors are grateful to Dr. Stan Maklan, Rod Street, Lindsay Bruce and many other colleagues at Cranfield and IBM, as well as the blue-chip members of the Cranfield Customer Management Forum, for their significant contributions to our thinking in this chapter on the place of channels today and how marketers need to respond. The introduction is based on material by Dr Stan Maklan.

Concurrent with the evolving distribution landscape, customer behaviour has changed, as evidenced by the ever-increasing share of purchasing over the internet, telephone and mobile devices. During the dotcom boom, however, many companies mistakenly segmented their customers into those that buy online versus traditional channels. As Alan Hughes, chief executive of UK bank First Direct at the time, put it:

> Customers are only too delighted to use a low-cost channel when it's right for the job, but there are other times – such as when they have a complaint – when they would be mad not to roll out the cavalry of warm human contact.[2]

It turns out that there are few 'online customers'; rather, most customers want to conduct some of their exchanges with suppliers online. When offered a choice of channel, customers will use multiple channels, each dependent on the job that they wish to get done.

And neither is the challenge of channel design restricted to the issue of online versus offline channels. Equally, the maturing of call centre and CRM technology raises questions for firms such as: Should we replace field-based salespeople by desk-based account managers? Can we divert some of the burgeoning call centre traffic to the web? And how can we ensure that the customer's multichannel experience is joined up across multiple channels, so the salesperson knows about a complaint that was made on the web yesterday?

Channels, then, have far more importance than simply the issue of physical distribution, important though that is in the goods sectors of the economy. Revising multichannel strategy offers a vast opportunity to expand market coverage, save costs or improve customer experience. But it is full of pitfalls, and simply following the crowd is hardly likely to lead to competitive advantage.

In this chapter, we discuss how to form a multichannel strategy. However, those readers who believe they already know enough about channels and CRM, and who are principally concerned with the preparation of a strategic marketing plan, can go straight to Chapter 12, although we do urge readers to read the section in this chapter on customer service and experience.

The multichannel plan involves three main decision areas, each of which will be examined in turn:

1. Through what marketing channels do we reach our customers (or what channels do our customers utilize to acquire our products)?
2. In the case of goods, how is the physical movement of our product organized?
3. What service and experience attributes does our customer require (and how well do we meet this requirement)?

SELECTING MARKETING CHANNELS
Three Common Pitfalls

Before we describe how to choose communication channels, we must first point out three common approaches which do *not* work.

1. Offering all channels to all customers

Some companies misunderstand the importance of channel integration as meaning that we should offer all channels to all customers: face-to-face meetings whenever they want, call centres, an online community, a call-back button on the website, and so on. Needless to say, this is a sure-fire way to go bust! Even large, well-resourced organizations cannot keep adding channels indiscriminately to their overall customer management mix.

Some of the banks adopted this policy in the early 2000s, and soon found themselves unable to compete on price with competitors targeting specific segments with specific channel strategies – online specialists such as Egg, phone-and-web providers such as Direct Line, IFA specialists such as Skandia, and so on. Organizations need to make choices and, as in all other areas of business, allocate scarce resources to competing ends.

2. Allocating high value customers to the most expensive channel

Many companies think that the art of channel management is to identify profitable customers in order to serve them across many channels, while forcing unprofitable customers to change their behaviour in order to make them profitable, or accepting that they will leave and become someone else's unprofitable customers. Many banks, for example, allocate personal relationship managers to customers on the basis of their current balance of funds managed.

There is some logic in this approach, but it is only half right. Just because a customer is currently profitable it does not necessarily follow that offering extensive channel choices is an optimal policy: companies often overservice high revenue customers thus sacrificing profit needlessly and making them vulnerable to new entrants who have a lower cost channel structure. Equally, even seemingly unprofitable customers who do not wish to have a long-term relationship with the company can nevertheless be served profitably, and they can often be nudged gently towards use of lower cost channels without damaging their customer experience. Too many firms leave lower value customers feeling unwanted as they pursue obvious high value customers that all of their competitors target with equal vigour.

3. Allocating customers to single channels

The problem we have just described is actually a subset of a bigger problem in the way firms think about channels. Customers should not be allocated to channels at all, as they will typically use different channels at different stages of their journey with the firm: social networks or industry conferences for initial exploration, the website for further information, phone calls to company experts to check on the fit to the customer's requirements, face-to-face meetings to negotiate, and so on. Yet many companies appoint channel barons and give each a profit target, as if the customer meekly stayed within one channel throughout their journey.

Developing a Multichannel Marketing Plan

Below, then, are some simple steps which the marketer can take to develop a more rational channel strategy. They are based on Cranfield's work over a number of years with IBM and the blue-chip members of the Cranfield Customer Management Forum, such as HSBC, BP and British Gas. For further details of these tools, the reader is referred to the Forum's website at www.cranfield.ac.uk/ccmf or the book *The Multichannel Challenge*.[3]

Step 1. Segment far enough along the market map

Market maps show the full extent of where an organization sits in the market and how the enterprise is connected to its end customers. We discussed market maps in Chapter 4. The map may be redrawn as a result of the multichannel strategy process, but the first step is to understand the current market map. In particular, we need to look far enough along the map towards the end customer when segmenting the market, as we may decide in the channel chain analysis which follows that the indirect channels we are currently selling through will be replaced or complemented by other routes to market. The first web boom was driven by a large swathe of businesses trying to disintermediate existing participants, and even now without a proper base of analysis in this area it is possible to have missed whole segments of the market that might otherwise be profitably addressed.

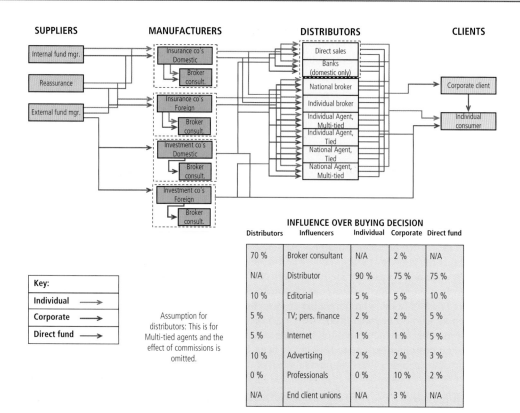

Figure 10.1: Market map – insurance company*.

The end customer is often the consumer, but it may equally be businesses in the case of IT suppliers, telecommunications companies, and so on. For channel strategy purposes, segmentation needs be done at the furthest point in the map towards the end customer where a significant proportion of the buying decision is taken. Generally, this means segmenting at the level of the end customer. This is illustrated in Figure 10.1 for an insurance company. The map shows its route to market for a particular country in mainland Europe. Below the map is a table showing who influences the buying decision, according to estimates by the company on the basis of market research.

In this example, all types of customer are most heavily influenced in their buying decision by the distributor, which may be a broker, agent, bank or direct sales representative. But whether the customer is a consumer or a corporate client, the distributor has a much easier job recommending a particular insurer if the end customer has heard of the insurer and has a positive image of it. So, a proportion of the decision – ranging from 10 per cent for consumers to 25 per cent for businesses – is thought to be made by the customer as a result of other influences – advertising, the internet and so on.

In this situation, segmentation at the level of distributors is certainly relevant for many purposes. But for forming channel strategy, the end customer needed also to be segmented, to evaluate whether their needs could better be served by a different route to market.

Having decided who our customers are, we then need to segment them. The best form of segmentation for forming multichannel strategy is one based on different customer needs or buying criteria: we described how to form a needs-based segmentation in Chapter 4. Once needs-based segments are understood in detail, it may rapidly become intuitively clear what channels or channel combinations will best suit each segment. The insurance company's market for annuity products is segmented as shown in Figure 10.2.

---

*This insurance example, including the channel curve work described under step 4 later in this chapter, comes from the consulting of Professor Elizabeth Daniel and the authors with an anonymous insurance company.

Figure 10.2: Segmentation of market for annuities.

CASE STUDY

The market for annuities is dominated by individuals at the moment of retirement, who have built up a pension pot and wish to convert some or all of it to an annuity which pays a guaranteed amount each year until they die. Consumers vary in their attitudes towards such financial decisions, though, on two key dimensions shown in the figure: their need for advice, from highly independent decision takers to those who prefer to outsource their financial decisions; and their attitude to risk, from those who are very comfortable with risky investments such as shares to those who are risk-averse.

The largest segment is of 'certainty seekers', who wish to convert their pension pot to a guaranteed income with the least possible trouble. This segment typically takes out an annuity with their pension provider. A slightly less risk-averse segment is that seeking 'certainty and growth', representing people who are prepared to take some risk in order to achieve a greater return, for example by investing part of their pension pot in a stock market-based product. 'Wealthy delegators' have a sufficiently large fund that they feel able to take more risk with its investment, and prefer to delegate the fine decisions to an adviser. 'Portfolio managers' may have similar funds but vary in their attitudes from wealthy delegators, preferring to manage their own fund portfolio. Finally, the 'Left it late' segment have little or no pension provision.

Clearly the segments vary not just in what product propositions they want but also in what channel to market will best suit them. Certainty seekers can be efficiently served through a simple 'tick here' form, perhaps backed up by a call centre to answer any questions, so as to keep the process as simple and reassuring as possible. Wealthy delegators need to be reached primarily via advice-providing intermediaries such as independent financial advisers. The 'Left it late' segment are likely to turn to their bank, and perhaps also their accountant or solicitor. 'Portfolio managers', by contrast, want hard information rather than personal reassurance, and so the internet backed

(Continued)

up by skilled telephone-based advisers may combine a low cost of service with immediacy and a sense of control for the customer.

In this case the most actionable insight for the insurer, though, concerned the growing 'certainty and growth' segment. The company decided that, while these customers were unlikely to use an independent financial adviser, they needed some face-to-face contact for help in selecting the right product and to provide reassurance. So distribution via a bank seemed the best option. This led the company to develop a special product variant which was suitable for this channel, and to them working with a high-street bank to distribute it.

By simply asking ourselves what is the right channel strategy for each segment, then, we may improve on an undifferentiated channel strategy which treats all customers equally.

MARKETING INSIGHT

Many IT companies segment purely on the basis of company size or sector. But one major manufacturer applied a needs-based segmentation of its IT director customers to its channel strategy. The 'save my career' segment of IT directors with serious problems to sort out, they decided, needed plenty of face-to-face reassurance from an account manager – and were prepared to pay for it. A 'save my budgets' customer, by contrast, might be perfectly prepared to buy at a distance in order to reduce the cost of sale and thus the price. 'Radical thinkers' needed white papers and seminars with industry opinion leaders plus brainstorming with the firm's thought-leaders. 'Technical idealists' would be visited by company's technical staff while the besuited account managers stayed largely in the background. Overall, channel costs were reduced as the sales force could concentrate on where they were needed, but unlike many channel strategy projects which are driven purely by costs, the customer experience and hence revenue went not down, but up.

Step 2. Develop a channel chain for each segment to show how channels combine

This simple but effective tool helps to work out how channels will best combine by drawing what we call a channel chain diagram.[4] Channel chain analysis was introduced briefly in Chapter 7. In this diagram, the stages of the buying cycle are drawn down the left. (The details of these stages might vary for each case.) Then, against each stage are listed the channels used to accomplish it. The channel used for one stage will often affect which channel is likely to be used at the next stage, so the relevant boxes are joined with a line, hence creating one or more 'channel chains'.

CASE STUDY

A luxury hotel chain used this approach in its market research into how its guests found and booked their room. Three of the seven resulting channel chains are shown in Figure 10.3*.

Around 10 per cent of customers were 'conventionals', initiating their search for a hotel room with a printed guide, and going on to phone the hotel. Some of these 'conventionals' were

---

*This case study is based on the Cranfield Marketing MSc theses of Hrishikesh Mehta, Claudine Epper and Charlene Kosgey.

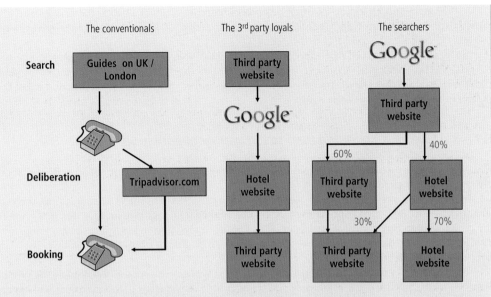

Figure 10.3: Current channel chains – hotel chain.

beginning to complement their search with information from a website such as TripAdvisor which contains consumer reports on their own hotel stays.

A larger proportion of customers were '3rd party loyals', who put their trust in one of the online intermediaries or third parties such as Expedia, due to successful previous experiences. The marketing director was intrigued to note that many of these were looking at the hotel website for further information, but then returning to the third party site to book. This was expensive behaviour for the hotel chain, which had to pay between 10 per cent and 25 per cent of the room rate to the intermediary. As it was based on a pre-existing relationship with the intermediary, though, it was difficult behaviour to change.

More immediately actionable, however, was the third channel chain for the 'searchers'. These customers would start by typing a search term such as 'luxury hotel London' into Google or another search engine. Expedia and its peers were masters at search engine optimization, and would buy paid search entries just to make sure, so the customer would probably end up on one of these intermediary sites. Again, a good proportion (about 40 per cent) of this segment would seek some further information from the hotel's own website. Having a lower loyalty to the intermediary, though, this time some of the customers would 'stick' on the hotel's site and book there, rather than returning to the intermediary. Nevertheless, in total 70 per cent of this segment would book through the intermediary. Even if this booking was with the hotel chain rather than a competitor, this represented an expensive sale.

Fortunately, the research included questions on why customers were making their channel choices and, crucially, why they made these channel switches from one channel to another. To the marketing director's surprise, the main reason for returning to a third party site from the hotel chain's site, even for these customers at the very top end of the market, was price. Consumers wrongly believed that the price would be better on the third party site. With this insight, the marketing director was able to convey some simple messages on the home page to explain that the hotel always offered its best prices directly. Simple search engine optimization also meant that a fair number of these 'searchers' now came straight to the hotel's website, too.

So, an understanding of channel chains led the marketing director to some simple changes at virtually zero cost. By the time she repeated her market research a year later, it was clear that these changes had diverted many customers to buying directly, at considerably lower cost.

A thorough understanding of your customers' current channel chains, then, is essential if these channel chains are to be redesigned to provide added value to the customer, lower costs, or both.

We have seen, however, that the right channel chain will vary both by customer group and by product, presenting the challenge of pulling together the work in each segment or product combination into an integrated strategy which has a reasonably small set of channel chains across the organization. We turn to this issue next.

Step 3. Develop a coverage map to show how channels vary by product and market

The coverage map tool provides a graphical means for thinking through this problem of how channel chains vary across products and across segments.

In its simplest version, shown in Figure 10.4 for a business-to-business telecoms firm, the tool summarizes how different channels are used by different customer groups and for different parts of the product range. The vertical axis plots customer groups, ranging from low value to high value ones. This is based on the observation that we are more likely to be able to afford the use of high cost channels for valuable clients.

The horizontal axis lists the company's products or services in order of the complexity of sale. So a simple product, with few options, which requires little explanation to the customer will appear

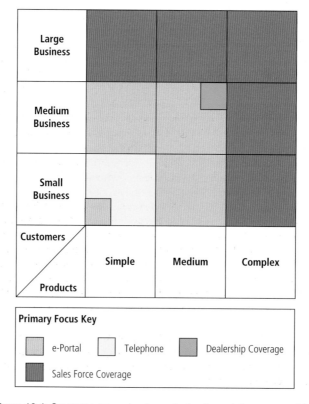

Figure 10.4: Coverage map – business-to-business telecoms provider.

to the left, while a complex product requiring configuration and consultancy and involving price negotiation will be to the right.

This reflects the observation that channels vary in their ability to handle complexity, and customers are well aware of this. An IT company's key accounts or an insurer's high net worth individuals may rightly demand face-to-face meetings with account managers or financial advisers to discuss complex, high risk decisions. But equally they are generally more than happy to use low cost channels such as call centres and the internet for routine, lower value transactions.

A good coverage map will have several features. The simplest is that it will have good coverage: there will be a channel for each area of the map – or at least each area which represents a target segment for the company – and channels will not be competing for the same space on the map. A good map will also use high cost, high bandwidth channels such as the field sales force or face-to-face meetings with a financial adviser only where they are needed, typically in the top right corner of the map, where the customer value justifies the cost and the sales complexity necessitates it. Low cost channels such as the internet will typically dominate the bottom left corner, and in many cases, the whole of the left hand side of the map.

When companies first draw the map to illustrate their current channel model, it often demonstrates the lack of conscious management attention to the design of the channel strategy, by revealing one or more of the following faults:

- overlaps where product/customer combinations are unintentionally served in multiple ways
- holes with insufficient coverage of target customers or parts of the product range
- a resource balance directed to existing rather than potential business
- irrational use of expensive channels, with little differentiation behind the channels used to serve each area of the map.

The company of Figure 10.4, while not wholly dysfunctional, illustrates some of these faults. In particular, there appears to be an unnecessarily heavy use of the sales force. One would want to check out whether the high value customers were happy to conduct simpler transactions remotely instead, and whether the sales force really paid its way for the lowest value customers, or whether this business should be delegated to dealers. Moreover, although the web and dealership channels seem sensibly positioned on the diagram, they are in an immature state. The size of their boxes reflects the proportion of business coming through this channel, so, for example, only about 10 per cent of simple products purchased by small businesses are bought over the web. The telephone channel is also underused: its success with simple products for small businesses could be extended upwards on the diagram to medium-sized businesses, as well as rightwards to medium complexity products.

You may have noticed, however, that this example makes a major simplification. We have described the tool as if each area of the map – that is, each product/segment combination – has one and only one channel serving it. And indeed, that is the way in which the coverage map has generally been described and used in the past.[5] We have seen earlier in this chapter, though, that frequently several channels are needed in the same channel chain to serve a particular product/segment combination. So the tool is far more powerful if each shaded or coloured area on the map is thought of as a channel chain rather than a single channel, even if, for shorthand, the area is labelled by the 'leading' channel in the channel chain, typically that where the order is actually taken. This point will become clearer in the next example.

By developing a current coverage map and brainstorming a future one, major opportunities for improving cost, reach and customer experience often emerge. This is illustrated by a highly successful project within BT, which has been widely credited with helping to turn around the fortunes of the UK's former monopoly telecoms provider.

CASE STUDY

BT GLOBAL SERVICES GOES MULTICHANNEL*

In 2000, BT's Major Customers, a £5 billion turnover division of BT serving the UK's top 1,000 companies (now part of BT Global Services), faced some major challenges in its route to market. All sales were booked by the field sales force – from a £5,000 leased line to a £100 million outsourcing contract. Despite a sales force numbering 2,000 people, BT was unable to serve the market adequately as it compensated for the decline in traditional fixed line telecommunications with growth in ICT products and outsourcing services. Some of these ICT products attracted much lower margins than BT's traditional business, suggesting a lower cost route to market. Conversely, outsourcing contracts required intensive consultancy-led selling. Undifferentiated handling by a single field sales force was no longer sustainable.

To put it another way, the coverage map was entirely populated by one channel – the field sales force – despite the product range displaying a much increased variation in sales complexity. BT began to hypothesize a new coverage map, a simplified version of which is shown in Figure 10.5.

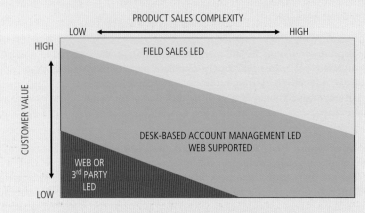

Figure 10.5: Coverage map – BT Major Customers Division.

The field sales force would be needed more than ever for the highly complex deals, such as outsourcing with high value customers. But, BT suspected, a large area in the middle of the chart could be handled effectively by the new channel of desk-based account managers (DBAMs) – fully professional account managers, but working entirely from the office. These staff would have a higher proportion of the day in contact with customers which, combined with savings on supporting staff on the road, would lower costs considerably. It was hoped that customers would also benefit from being able to contact a member of the account team at their convenience. At the bottom left corner of the chart, simpler transactions with lower value customers would be carried out either online or via partners.

A successful pilot with 12 DBAMs found that sales and marketing costs did indeed go down dramatically, from 25 per cent of revenue to 17 per cent, adding 8 per cent of revenue straight to the bottom line. It also actually found increased customer satisfaction, as customers preferred the highly available DBAMs for their simpler needs. As a result, BT had, by 2005, rolled out 400 DBAMs and reduced the field sales force accordingly. They had also introduced desk-based technical specialists to support them. BT estimated that as well as reducing costs – each field sales person costing 2.5 times

*This case study was researched by Dr Stan Maklan and the authors. We are grateful to Ruth Rowan, Olivia Garfield, Lesley Abeny and their colleagues and former colleagues at BT for their collaboration.

as much as a DBAM on a fully allocated cost basis – this was generating over £100 million of additional annual revenue, as the field sales force was able to concentrate on high value opportunities.

The word 'led' against each area of the coverage map is significant, as the named channel is really the name of a channel chain in which the named channel is the likeliest to take the order itself. For example, the web is playing a significant role throughout the sales process in all areas of the map. Dedicated pages for large customers and web conferences help the customer to research BT's offerings, while business rules built into the web solution ensure that customer enquiries and orders are routed to the appropriate person for fulfilling. After sales services allow customers to access basic service and billing information quickly and report faults. This takes pressure off the field and desk-based sales resources: for example, the well-supported web-based customer conferences save field sales over 500 person-days a year.

This closely integrated channel mix required careful attention to reward systems. To break channel silo habits and encourage cooperation early in the change process, BT experimented with what they called 'double bubble': paying both desk and field resources for sales on which they cooperated. Within six months this was deemed too expensive, and a new system was developed that rewarded both field sales people and DBAMs for all sales over their annual targets without paying twice for each sale. The remit of each was clear – DBAMs were responsible for bringing in new business on their accounts, account managers were responsible for the entire account balance. It was in the account manager's interest to help the DBAMs sell aggressively to his or her account; and it was in the interest of the DBAM to help the account manager develop opportunities within the account that the desk could exploit.

BT has developed comprehensive business rules that allocate sales campaigns and leads appropriately, based on the logic of the coverage map. Each of the approximately 65 service and product areas sold by the division is scored on seven aspects of product complexity: product maturity, configurability and integration, commoditization, pricing complexity, the length of time to complete the sale, the need for buyer education, and who in the client organization buys. The scoring is agreed by the most senior people in the division and updated periodically. The score of each product determines which channel will normally sell the product. This preferred channel is embedded in the CRM system so leads are automatically allocated to the right channel, although this automatic allocation can then be overruled by the account teams if their account knowledge suggests it is wrong. Nevertheless, the DBAMs take forward more than 75 per cent of enquiries that reach their desk, and win approximately 64 per cent of these, an achievement that is well above BT's expectations. The DBAMs also perform a critical 'triage' function on leads generated from the web or from marketing campaigns, deciding which opportunities need to be referred to the field sales team for progressing, which need specialist input and which ones they can action alone.

Coverage maps, then, can help to integrate the channel strategy into a coherent design. In particular, they are useful for allocating scarce, expensive channel resource where it is most needed, and making the best use of lower cost channels. It is important to use them in conjunction with channel chain diagrams: each area or colour on the coverage map has a different channel chain. For more examples of coverage maps, channel chains and how they fit together, see Wilson, Street and Bruce, *The Multichannel Challenge*.[6]

Step 4. Develop channel curves to check the advantage to the customer

By this stage in the process, we have numerous ideas for improving our multichannel proposition. How can we validate these ideas before including them in the marketing plan? A useful tool is the channel

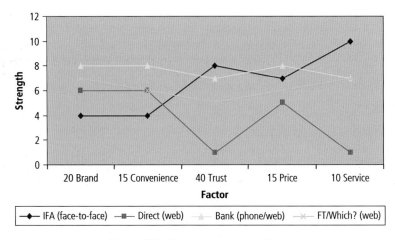

Figure 10.6: Channel curve – pensions.

curve. This tool addresses the question: 'What is the advantage to the customer of our proposed change?' Although we have borne in mind segment characteristics when constructing channel chains, we have only assessed the customer's acceptance of our proposed channel chains intuitively. As this is crucial for estimating the impact of changes on revenue, it is best to do more detailed modelling of the customer perspective before proceeding to piloting. This is the purpose of the channel curve tool.

For example, let us suppose that, on the basis of our coverage map and channel chain work, we would like more customers to use a call centre or web channel in order to lower transaction costs. Clearly we have to look at this issue from the customers' point of view: what is driving their current behaviour, and what would entice them to change? The channel curve analyses this, comparing how different channels (or different channel chains, as we will come on to shortly) rate at meeting the customers' buying criteria. It is illustrated in Figure 10.6 for the insurance company we considered earlier in the chapter, selling pensions to consumers.

First, the main buying factors are listed along the bottom of the chart, with weights indicating their relative importance to the customer's buying decision (out of 100). These represent the key factors taken into account by the customer in deciding where to place their business. The ability of each channel to deliver against each factor is then rated on a 1 to 10 basis: the higher the score, the better this channel meets this buying factor.

This financial services company was currently selling pensions through IFAs, but was contemplating whether it should introduce any further routes to market – direct on the web; selling on the web via a trusted intermediary such as the *Financial Times* or Which?; or selling via integrated call centre and internet banks such as First Direct. This last option represents a call centre/internet channel combination rather than a single 'pureplay' channel. In this situation, such channel combinations can be compared on the channel curve along with any simpler 'pureplay' channel options.

In this particular case, it can be seen that the option of direct sales on the web falls down on the target segment's crucial buying criterion of trust. This reflected the conclusion from market research that, while some customers were willing to do research of possible pension providers online, the great majority would then seek the approval of someone they trusted before they felt confident enough to buy such a high involvement product. The company concluded that a website would be unlikely to deliver this trust – a conclusion which is so far consistent with the available evidence. As the chart suggests, though, they thought it possible that customers would trust a bank with high service standards such as First Direct sufficiently to have such a crucial conversation remotely, suggesting that some trials of this route to market might be worthwhile.

In practice, different segments are best matched to different channels, which would show up clearly if the channel curve was drawn for each segment, since each segment's buying criteria are, by definition, different from those of other segments. In practice, then, this particular manager would need to draw a similar chart for each major target segment.

All this can be used to define a future proposition on the channel curve. This may simply be a question of adding a channel to the mix, or extending its capabilities to handle a wider part of the customer interaction. More often, it will involve improvements to an existing channel offer. In this case, two lines will be needed for the channel in question, one for the current situation and one for the envisaged future situation.

Step 5. Understand channel costs

The channel curve, then, helps us to assess a proposed future channel strategy in terms of what is in it for the customer – and, hence, what is the likely impact on sales. The other main dimension we need to assess in constructing the business case is the impact on costs. This essential step is relatively

CASE STUDY

LOWERING CHANNEL COSTS FOR AN AIRLINE

Figure 10.7 shows the results of an exercise to analyse costs per channel for a major airline for their four major channels: 'Trade', the travel agents; direct sales online; and two categories of call centre. Conventional wisdom in the airline was that e-commerce was by far the cheapest channel, and web sales were priced accordingly with large discounts. The channel director wanted to check out these assumptions in order to work out where to put his future investment.

	Trade	e-Commerce	Call Centre	Contact Centre
Fixed Costs				
Staff & Office	23.8	48.5	248.4	50.7
Investment	0.2	39.4	22.2	0.0
Maintenance	0.2	18.7	7.4	0.0
Communications	0.4	0.0	0.0	0.0
Total	**24.6**	**106.6**	**277.9**	**50.7**
Variable				
Distribution	49.0	11.4	8.9	10.9
Incentives	20.2	55.8	0.0	0.0
Credit Card	6.2	34.6	25.2	22.6
Total	**75.4**	**101.8**	**34.1**	**33.5**
Total	**100.0**	**208.4**	**312.0**	**84.2**

Figure 10.7: Analysing channel costs – an airline.

What he found, after a lot of careful work with the accountants combining information from different sources, came as a surprise. The 'trade' channel (sales through travel agents) had significant commission costs, so the variable costs per sale were far from negligible at 75 currency units per sale. But web sales had an even higher variable cost, for two reasons: credit card charges and the discounts that were being offered online in the mistaken belief that this would save the company money. Furthermore, the fixed costs were much higher for the online channel, due to high costs of IT development and equipment. Higher still were the costs of running call centres.

(Continued)

An analysis purely based on current channel cost might have led to the entirely erroneous conclusion that the direct sales channels should be closed. Indeed, the fact is that some segments wish to deal with travel agents, and this was still the most efficient way to serve customers with more complex requirements. But other segments prefer to buy online, so the challenge was more one of getting the coverage map right and getting costs and prices in line.

So the channel director developed a new coverage map which directed the travel agent channel at the customers where it was needed. In the light of the cost data, he adjusted the online pricing so that only the price-sensitive segment would be discounted, and then only when the plane would otherwise not be full. And he reprioritized investment in website capabilities to reduce the load on the call centres when website users got stuck – an important multichannel effect which was driving up the call centres' overall costs. The whole project resulted in projected savings of several hundred million dollars over five years, a target which the airline is on target to meet at the time of writing.

easy to describe, though often a lot of work in practice. The starting point is to analyse the costs of individual channels.

This example shows how important it is to get a handle on current channel costs. But in the use of call centres by customers who then place the order through another channel, we have also seen how multichannel purchasing can skew this data. The same applies, of course, to other buying combinations such as talking to a travel agent and then buying online. What we really need, therefore, is cost information not per channel but per channel chain.

Step 6. Pilot new channel model

The final step before full implementation of a new channel strategy is to pilot any changes to the route to market. Even with the benefit of channel curve analysis, the customer reaction to new channel models can be difficult to predict with certainty; and there are many examples that show that simply

asking the customers how they will react to a model they have never yet seen is far from reliable! A good pilot is, therefore, critical.

The BT Global Services case we described earlier in this section is a good example. Before rolling out desk-based account managers, the project director conducted a pilot, treating one group of accounts with the new combination of DBAMs and field salespeople, and leaving a 'control' group of similar accounts with the previous, field-based sales model. The metrics which she tracked in this pilot were instructive: revenue and profit in the two groups, of course, but also customer satisfaction and employee satisfaction.

• • •

With the help of this six-step process, which has been refined over a number of years by the blue-chip members of Cranfield's Customer Management Forum, a channel strategy can be defined which reduces costs, improves coverage and enhances customer experience at the same time. In particular, it is the art of combining channels in the same journey, using high touch ones where they are needed and low cost ones where they are appropriate, which opens up the creative space of channel strategy allowing cost reduction and experience improvement to be seen as complementary and not in competition.

This multichannel strategy process applies equally in business-to-business and business-to-consumer contexts, and also to both goods and services. There are, however, some additional considerations in the case of goods which require physical distribution, which we will consider next.

PHYSICAL DISTRIBUTION
The Importance of Distribution

For manufacturers, the physical distribution function of a firm provides the place and time dimensions which constitute the third element of the marketing mix. This is depicted in Figure 10.8, which also shows its relationship to the other utility-producing elements. The figures on the diagram are illustrative only, although they are realistic for some industries.

> If a product is not available when and where the customer wants it, it will surely fail in the market.

To achieve this value-adding function, firms generally have a distributive activity within the corporate organizational structure known variously as physical distribution management (PDM), marketing logistics, or, simply, logistics. Today, it is frequently called 'supply chain management', which also encompasses the supply side of physical flows. A generalized model of the entire manufacturing entity is given in Figure 10.9; this also depicts the position of (finished) product ▶ distribution *vis-à-vis* marketing, production, the procurement system, and the financial/accounting systems.

> Distribution is the movement of all materials, both prior to production and after production. The term 'logistics' is also used in the same way

The movement of all materials, both prior to production (raw materials, subassemblies, etc.) and after production (finished product) constitutes the total logistics flow of the firm. In this chapter, however, we shall confine our attention to the latter, i.e. finished product distribution.

The Distribution Mix

In a typical manufacturing company with a formal distribution structure, the responsibility for distribution-related matters is spread across the other functional departments. For example, production may control warehousing and transportation; marketing may control the channels through which the product moves, the levels of service provided to the customer, and communications; and the finance department may control inventory obsolescence, data processing, and inventory costs.

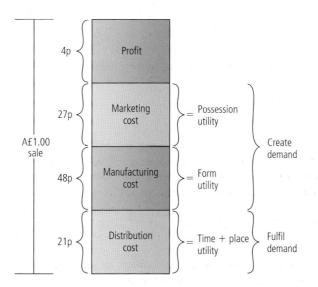

Figure 10.8: The utility producing elements in manufacturing.

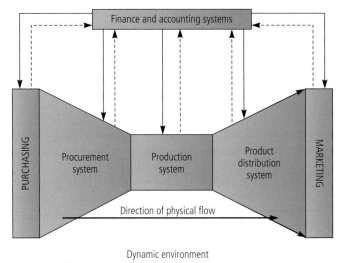

Figure 10.9: Manufacturing flows.

Such a compartmentalized arrangement leads to each department working to its own objectives, attempting to optimize its own particular activity, oblivious of others or of the good of the whole company.

Introducing a more formalized distribution arrangement into the corporate organizational structure, although not completely eliminating interdepartmental friction, does at least ensure that all distribution-related activities are organized under a more centralized control, thereby gaining focus.

This, then, is the basis of the total distribution concept, because it now becomes possible to seek out potential 'trade-offs', i.e. consciously to incur costs in one area in order to achieve an even larger benefit in another. For example, should a series of field warehouses be maintained, or would one suffice, supplemented by an improved trucking operation? Of course, these types of potential 'trade-off' situations place a heavy burden on the cost-reporting systems of a company.

The professional logistics manager, therefore, has several variables to contend with in the search for trade-offs; taken together these constitute the *distribution mix*. Each of these will now be examined briefly.

Facilities

Decisions in this area are concerned with the problem of how many warehouses and plants should be established and where they should be located. Obviously, for the majority of companies it is necessary to take the location of existing plants and warehouses as given in the short term, but the question does arise in the longer term or, indeed, when new plants or warehouses are being considered.

> The principal marketing task here is to forecast the nature, size and geographical spread of demand.

Increasing the number of field locations will result in an increase in trucking costs and a reduction in retail distribution costs. So, another marketing task is to determine the customer service levels that are likely to be required in order to be able to make a decision about this particular trade-off.

Inventory

A major element in any company's total distribution costs is the cost of holding stock, which is often as high as 30 per cent of its value per annum. This is because of items such as interest charges, deterioration, shrinkage, insurance, administration, and so on. Thus, decisions about how much inventory to hold, where to hold it, in what quantities to order, and so on, are vital issues. Inventory levels are also instrumental in determining the level of service that the company offers the customer.

Transport

The important aspects of the transport decision concern such issues as what mode of transport should be used, whether to own vehicles or lease them, how to schedule deliveries, how often to deliver, and so on. Perhaps of the five distribution variables, it is transport that receives the greatest attention within the firm. It is certainly one of the more obvious facets of the distribution task.

Communications

It must always be remembered that distribution not only involves the flow of materials through the distribution channel, but also the flow of information. Here, we are talking about the order processing system, the invoicing system, the demand forecasting system, and so on. Without effective communications support, the distribution system will never be capable of providing satisfactory customer service at an acceptable cost. It is vital that it should be recognized that inefficiency here can lead to a build-up of costs in other areas of the business, such as, for example, in emergency deliveries, as well as a permanent loss of sales through customers turning to alternative sources of supply.

Unitization

The way in which goods are packaged and then subsequently accumulated into larger unit sizes (e.g. a pallet-load) can have a major bearing upon distribution economics. For example, the ability to stack goods on a pallet which then becomes the unit load for movement and storage can lead to considerable cost saving in terms of handling and warehousing. Similarly, the use of containers as the basic unit of movement has revolutionized international transport and, to a certain extent, domestic transport as well. Mobile racking systems and front-end pricing by means of scanners are other unitization innovations that have had a dramatic effect upon the way goods are marketed.

Together, these five areas constitute the total cost of distribution within a company.

Aligning the Interests of the Firm and its Distributors

> The fundamental role of a company's distribution function is to ensure that the 'right product is available at the right time'.

This implies some organization of resources into channels through which the product moves to customers.

> It is necessary to consider both the route of exchange (and its administrative and financial control) and the physical movement route of the product – they may well be different.

Many companies use multiple channels through which to reach their customers, often involving one or even several 'indirect channels' or 'intermediaries'. The role of a distributor is to provide the means of achieving the widest possible market coverage at a lower unit cost. Many such intermediaries hold stock and thereby share some of the financial risk with the principal (or supplier). Figure 10.10 shows that using an intermediary carries benefits for the manufacturer, but it also involves significant 'costs', the most important of which is the loss of control which accompanies such a channel strategy.

THE DISTRIBUTION CHANNEL

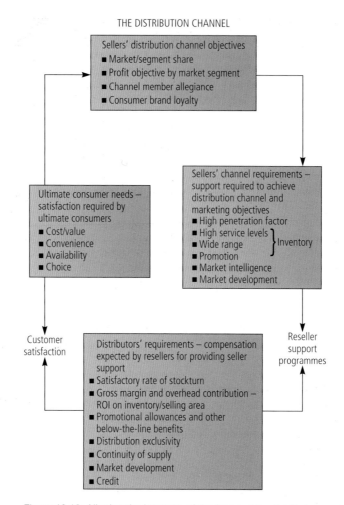

Figure 10.10: Aligning the interests of the firm and its distributors.

Often, too, considerable conflict exists between the respective objectives of suppliers and their distributors; this gives rise to conflict and suspicion in the relationship. Nevertheless, suppliers must evaluate the costs and benefits of each marketing channel potentially open to them and decide on a combination which best suits their type of business and the markets they are engaged in. The alternatives depicted in Figure 10.11 quite obviously have different cost/revenue profiles.

Any cost/benefit appraisal needs to be undertaken in the widest context possible. It needs to consider questions of market strategy, the appropriateness of the channel to the product, and customer requirements, as well as the question of the comparative costs of selling and distribution.

Marketing channel decisions for goods are, therefore, key decisions which involve the choice of an intermediary (or intermediaries) and detailed consideration of the physical distribution implications of all the alternatives, in addition to the other considerations for both goods and service sectors which we discussed earlier in this chapter. The evaluation of distributors is, therefore, of significant importance.

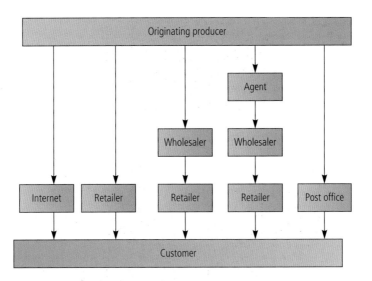

Figure 10.11: Examples of different routes to market.

Evaluation Criteria for Channel Intermediaries

Regardless of the type of intermediary to be used, there are a number of basic evaluation criteria, for example:

- Do they now, or will they, sell to our target market segment?
- Is their sales force large enough and trained well enough to achieve our regional sales forecasts?
- Is their regional location adequate in respect of the retail (and other) outlets serviced?
- Are their promotional policies and budgets adequate?
- Do they satisfy customer after-sales requirements?
- Are their product policies consistent with our own?
- Do they carry competitive lines?
- What are their inventory policies regarding width, depth and cover?
- Are they creditworthy?
- Is distributor management receptive, aggressive, and flexible?

All the above factors, and others, have to be considered when making specific decisions on choice of intermediaries, which in turn is part of the overall channel selection issue.

Developing the Distribution Plan

Figure 10.12 shows the interrelationship between the process described elsewhere in this book and distribution. Here, we see that product, pricing and promotion decisions are separated from distribution.

The first issue is to allocate responsibility for the distribution plan. It is clear that this plan is of necessity cross-functional, so this decision is not trivial. Whoever is responsible for the plan, the aim should be to achieve integrated distribution management. This is an approach to the distribution mission of the firm whereby the multiple functions involved in moving goods from source to user are integrated and viewed as an interrelated system for purposes of planning, implementation and control.

> Integrated distribution management is an approach to the distribution mission of the firm whereby the multiple functions involved in moving goods from source to user are integrated and viewed as an interrelated system for purposes of planning, implementation and control

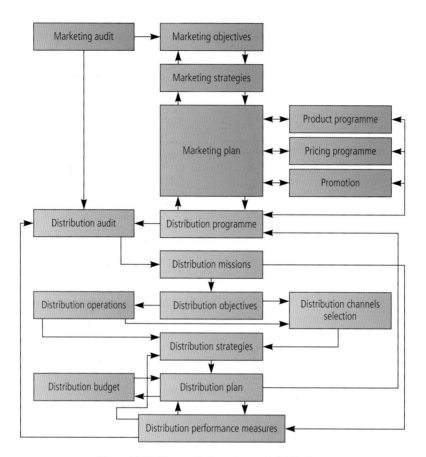

Figure 10.12: The marketing plan and distribution.

Organizationally, it makes a lot of sense to make marketing responsible for distribution, since it is probably in the best position to make the difficult trade-off between very high levels of customer service and the high inventory-carrying costs associated with such levels. On the other hand, labour relations, wage bargaining, the technical aspects, and so on, of distribution also demand specialist attention, and there is a grave danger that such issues may begin to divert too much of the chief marketing officer's attention away from other important marketing areas. The logistics director is one possible answer to this problem. Such a role is to view the whole distribution system in an integrated way.

Whatever the organizational solution, however, all of the above issues are relevant and it is necessary to know where to start.

Where to start?

The distribution audit was referred to in Chapter 2. Like the more general marketing audit referred to there, this is in two major parts – *internal* and *external*. Figures 10.13 and 10.14 illustrate the major components of the distribution audit.

Distribution objectives can be many and varied, but the following are considered basic for marketing purposes:

1. Outlet penetration by type of distribution
2. Inventory range and levels to be held

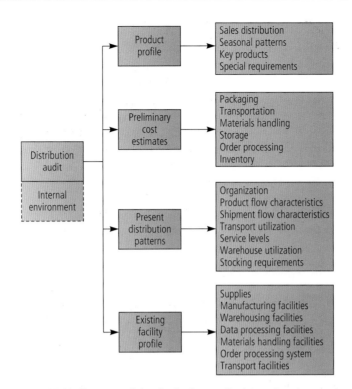

Figure 10.13: Elements of the distribution audit – internal environment.

3. Distributor sales and sales promotion activities
4. Other specific customer development programmes, e.g. incentives for distributors.

When taking an integrated distribution management approach, it is as well to remember that there are several other decisions/trade-offs which need to be specified in the plan. These are depicted in Figure 10.15.

Of course, all of these decisions need not necessarily be located in one plan or be made by one person or department, but clearly they need to be made and written down somewhere in the company's plans.

Finally, the following illustrates a simple iterative approach to distribution planning that should help tighten up what is often a neglected area of marketing management.

Distribution planning approach

1. Determine marketing objectives
2. Evaluate changing conditions in distribution at all levels
3. Determine distribution task within overall marketing strategy
4. Determine distribution policy in terms of type, number and level of outlets to be used
5. Set performance standards for the distribution organization
6. Obtain performance information
7. Compare actual with anticipated performance
8. Adjustment where necessary.

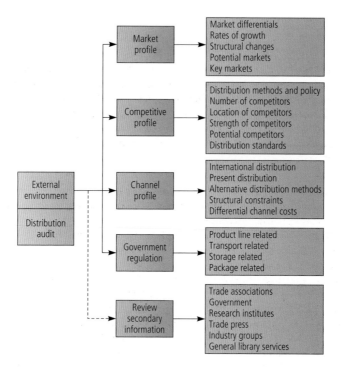

Figure 10.14: Elements of the distribution audit – external environment.

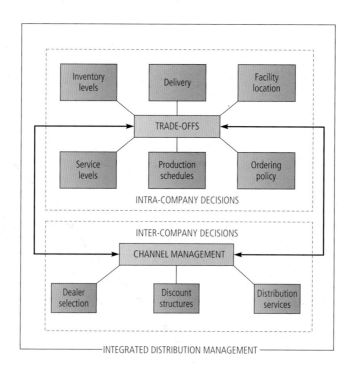

Figure 10.15: Some key distribution decisions.

CUSTOMER SERVICE
Why Service Matters: The Service Profit Chain

As services account for an increasing proportion of gross domestic product in developed economies, it has been argued that goods are becoming commoditized and that differentiation is increasingly obtained through service, although the empirical evidence on this point is mixed. Nonetheless, for many firms, service forms an important part of their differentiation strategy. For these firms, the service-profit chain is important. See Figure 10.16.

The logic of the service profit chain is simple, and evidence for most parts of it has multiplied over the last two decades:

1. Satisfied employees provide better service quality. They stay with the firm longer so that they are more productive and well trained in the firm's processes. They are more committed to the firm and this impacts on how they present themselves.
2. The service quality is noted by customers and they are more satisfied.
3. Satisfied customers are more loyal: they buy more from the firm, they recommend it more, they stay longer.
4. Loyal customers improve profitability because they spend more, they don't leave just on the basis of price, they are familiar with your products and processes so they have lower cost to serve and require lower marketing and promotion budgets versus recruiting new customers. Loyal customers therefore create shareholder value by allowing the firm to improve revenue, reduce cost and reduce risk.
5. There is a positive feedback loop to employees in all of this. Satisfied customers tend to treat service employees better and there is a positive reinforcement between employee and customer satisfaction. This improves employees' job satisfaction and commitment to the firm and its customers.

So what is service quality? It varies by industry, but generally there are five key aspects or 'dimensions' of what customers look for in an excellent service: empathy; tangibility; reliability; responsiveness; and assurance. So if you track these through surveys and make sure you optimize them, you are improving some proven key drivers of customer behaviour. See Figure 10.17.

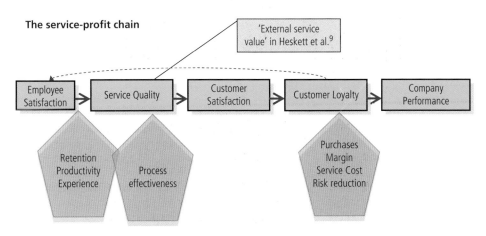

Figure 10.16: The service-profit chain.

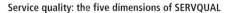

Service quality: the five dimensions of SERVQUAL

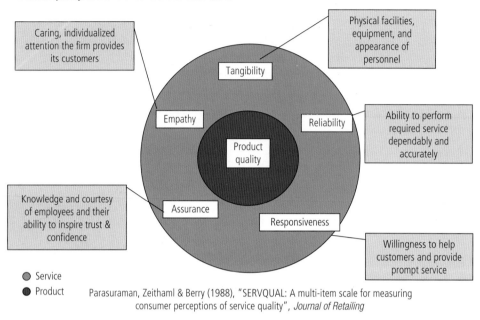

Parasuraman, Zeithaml & Berry (1988), "SERVQUAL: A multi-item scale for measuring consumer perceptions of service quality", *Journal of Retailing*

Figure 10.17: Service quality: the five dimensions of SERVQUAL.

From Service to Experience

If service is becoming increasingly important relative to goods, a further argument states that service, too, is increasingly commoditized, and that the contemporary customer demands more than just competent service, seeking experiences which are 'engaging, robust, compelling and memorable', as Pine and Gilmore put it.[7] This argument, also, is largely conjectural, but increasing attention is being paid by both practitioners and academics as to whether and how the customer experience might go beyond service. Research at Cranfield and elsewhere is showing that experience quality goes beyond service quality in at least five ways:[8]

1. *Usage processes.* The customer's process of using the firm's goods or services is part of customer experience which influences how the customer thinks about the firm. For example, an MBA student's experience of applying knowledge gained during the course will influence their evaluation of Cranfield and the extent to which they recommend Cranfield to others. We discussed how value arises not at the factory gate but in use in Chapter 9.
2. *Peer-to-peer interactions.* In many contexts – an MBA classroom, a holiday, a football match – the interactions we have with other customers are as important in our evaluation of the holistic experience as are the interactions we have with the provider's employees.
3. *Relationship.* Many service quality surveys erroneously focus only on individual customer encounters or transactions. In business-to-business contexts but also many business-to-consumer contexts, we also value the quality of our relationship with firms between and across multiple transactions.
4. *Brand image/communication.* Possessing an iPad may not just be of instrumental value in achieving the owner's tasks; it may also be perceived as valuable due to the statement that it makes about the owner. As with interactions with other customers, the social impact of products or services on non-customers can form part of our customer experience.
5. *Emotions.* Much market research on service quality assumes that the customer is entirely rational. But the emotions we have as we go on a customer journey feed into how we evaluate the firm overall.

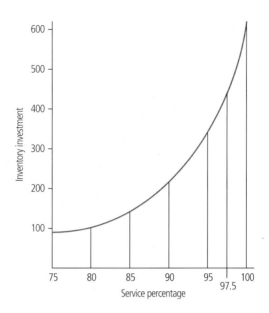

Figure 10.18: The increasing costs of goods availability.

It is therefore essential to ensure, as an important input into the marketing plan, that the customers' needs in each of these areas are well understood.

Customer Service for Goods Firms

The output of a firm's distribution activities is a system organized to provide a continuing link between the first contact with the customer, through to the time the order is received and the goods/services are delivered and used, with the objective of satisfying customer needs continuously. It encompasses every aspect of the relationship.

However, the provision of ▶ customer service in all its various forms is likely to involve the firm in large financial commitments. In fact, it can be demonstrated that once the level of service (defined here as the percentage of occasions the product is available to customers, when and where they want it) increases beyond the 70–80 per cent mark, the associated costs increase exponentially. Figure 10.18 demonstrates the typical relationship between the level of availability and the cost of providing it. From this diagram it will be observed that the cost of increasing the service level by a small amount, say from 95 per cent to 97.5 per cent, results in a sharp increase in inventory costs. The implications of this cost relationship bear closer examination.

Significantly, many companies appear to be unaware of the level of service they are offering, i.e. there is no customer service policy as such. Even where such a policy does exist, the levels are quite often arbitrarily set and are not the result of a careful market analysis.

The question, then, arises: what level of availability should be offered? This question is relatively simple to answer in theory, but very difficult to quantify and achieve in practice, since different product groups in different market segments could well demand different levels of customer service. Readers who did not study the short case history on customer service by segment are referred to the end of Chapter 4.

In theory, at least, it is possible to say that service levels can continue to be improved as long as the marketing advantage that results continues to outrun the additional costs incurred. Conceptually, it is possible to draw an S-shaped curve (see Figure 10.19) which suggests that, at very high levels of customer service, customers are unable to distinguish between small changes in the service offered.

Figure 10.19: The relationship between availability and demand.

When a company is operating in this region, it is quite possibly incurring more costs than are necessary for the level of sales being achieved.

For example, marketing and sales managers who insist on offering maximum service to all customers, no matter what the profitability and location of those customers, are quite probably doing their company a disservice.

By carefully reviewing customer service policy, perhaps even introducing differential service levels for different products or for different customers (at least on a trial-and-error basis), marketing can enhance its contribution to corporate profitability.

> Somewhere between the costs and benefits involved in customer service, a balance has to be found.

Somewhere between the costs and benefits involved in customer service, a balance has to be found. It will be at that point where the additional revenue returns for each increment of service are equal to the extra cost involved in providing that increment. To attempt to ascertain this point of balance, certain information is required, for example:

1. How profitable is the product? What contribution to fixed costs and profits does this product make and what is its sales turnover?
2. What is the nature of the product? Is it a critical item as far as the customer is concerned, where stock-outs at the point of supply would result in a loss of sales? Does the product have characteristics that result in high stockholding costs?
3. What is the nature of the market? Does the company operate in a sellers' or a buyers' market? How frequently is the product purchased? Are there ready substitutes? What are the stockholding practices of the purchasers? Which markets and customers are growing and which are declining?
4. How profitable are the customers constituting each segment?
5. What is the nature of the competition? How many companies are providing an alternative source of supply to our customers? What sort of service levels do they offer?
6. What is the nature of the channel of distribution through which the company sells? Does the company sell direct to the end customer, or through intermediaries? To what extent does the company control the channel and the activities of its members, such as the stock levels and order policies?

This basic information is the raw material of the service level decision. To take an example, the level of service offered is less likely to have an effect on sales if, in fact, the company is the sole supplier of the product, and there are no substitutes. The situation is the case in some industrial markets and from a short-term point of view to offer a higher level of service, say 90 per cent instead of 85 per cent, would probably have the effect of reducing the total profitability of the product.

Developing a customer service package

In general terms, customer service is normally defined as the service provided to the customer from the time an order is placed until the product is delivered. In fact, it is much more than this.

It actually encompasses every aspect of the relationship between manufacturers and their distributors/customers. Under this definition, price, sales representation, after-sales service, product range offering, product availability, etc. are all dimensions of customer service, i.e. the total activity of servicing one's customer.

However, it is more traditional to think of customer service in distribution-related terms. Under this more restricted definition the key elements of customer service are product availability, overall order cycle time, and order cycle time variation. Research has shown that many companies have poor product availability due to a variety of reasons, e.g. poor forecasting, production difficulties, inadequate inventory controls, etc.

Above all else, it is fundamental for suppliers to derive and make operational their concept of customer service from a study of their customers' real needs rather than their own perceptions of such needs. The following list contains the major components of customer service that should be researched.

* Frequency of delivery
* Time from order to delivery
* Reliability of delivery
* Emergency deliveries when required
* Stock availability and continuity of supply
* Orders filled completely
* Advice on non-availability
* Convenience of placing order
* Acknowledgement of order
* Accuracy of invoices
* Quality of sales representation
* Regular calls by sales representatives
* Manufacturer monitoring of retail stock levels
* Credit terms offered
* Customer query handling
* Quality of outer packaging
* Well-stacked pallets
* Easy-to-read use-by dates
* Quality of inner package for in-store handling and display
* Consults on new product/package development
* Reviews product range regularly
* Coordination between production, distribution and marketing.

> It is fundamental for suppliers to derive their concept of customer service from a study of their customers' real needs.

This will almost certainly mean designing different customer service packages for different market groups. At present, very few manufacturers/suppliers bother to do this. Basically, six steps are involved in this process:

1. Define the important service elements (and subelements)
2. Determine customers' viewpoints on these
3. Design a competitive package (and several variations, if necessary)
4. Develop a promotional campaign to 'sell' the service package idea
5. Pilot test a particular package and the promotional campaign being used
6. Establish controls to monitor performance of the various service packages.

Throughout many types of industry, and especially those that are highly competitive, it is increasingly being recognized that, after all the other terms of trade have been tried and exhausted, it will be customer service considerations that will determine who, in the end, gets the order. The distribution function is becoming as important as that.

APPLICATION QUESTIONS

1. Does your company have a problem with:
   (a) channel costs?
   (b) customer experience in individual channels?
   (c) customer experience across channels (multichannel integration)?
   (d) market coverage?
2. If the answer to any of the above is 'yes', are you clear what should be done, or do you need to apply the tools in this chapter to establish a multichannel plan?
3. Is any executive responsible for marketing, sales and service in an integrated way across multiple channels? Or do you have 'channel barons' responsible for different parts of the customer journey? If there is no single person responsible, can a multichannel governance board be set up?
4. What else might prevent you from making the changes you would like to make? Metrics? The investment case? Company culture?
5. Is logistics adequately represented at board or senior management level in your organization? How could improvements be made?
6. What coordination takes place between physical distribution management and marketing management? How can any problems be minimized?
7. How are decisions currently made concerning customer service levels?
8. How do service levels compare with competitors?
9. Can you see any way of making savings in your distribution system without reducing customer service?

CHAPTER 10 REVIEW

Channels for reaching customers

Channels no longer operate alone, but typically are combined within a customer's journey with the firm. Creative combining of channels can result in improvements to one or more of:

- Total channel cost
- Customer experience
- Market coverage.

There is a range of possible channels, for example:

- Direct channels: sales force, call centres, direct mail, branches, retail outlets, transactional website, etc
- Indirect channels: distributors, agents, retailers, specifiers (e.g. architects), influencers (e.g. NICE which makes treatment recommendations to UK doctors), etc.

Which channel or channel combination is best for competitive advantage? There are six steps to forming a multichannel plan:

1. Do a needs-based segmentation as far along the market map as a significant proportion of the buying decision is made.
2. Develop a channel chain for each segment to show how channels combine in the customer journey.

3. Develop a coverage map to show how channels vary by product and by market.
4. Develop channel curves to check the advantage to the customer of a proposed new channel chain.
5. Understand channel costs.
6. Pilot the new channel model, for example using control groups.

Try Exercises 10.1 and 10.2

Physical distribution

For goods companies, physical distribution ensures products get to the right place, on time, and in the right condition. In some businesses, distribution costs can amount to 20 per cent of the selling price. There are five components to manage:

1. *Facilities.* The number, size and geographical location of storage and distribution depots.
2. *Inventory.* The stockholding levels throughout the distribution chain consistent with customers' service expectations.
3. *Transport.* Made up of transport, delivery, schedules, etc.
4. *Communications.* There is also a flow of information, for example order processing, invoicing, forecasting, etc.
5. *Unitization.* The way in which goods are packaged and assembled into large units, e.g. palletization, container loads, etc.

Considerable saving can be made by innovating in this area.

Distribution planning

The approach should follow these steps:

1. Determine marketing objectives
2. Evaluate changing conditions in distribution at all levels
3. Determine the distribution task within marketing strategy
4. Establish a policy in terms of type, number and level of outlets to be used
5. Set performance standards for distributors
6. Obtain performance information
7. Compare actual with anticipated performance
8. Make improvements where necessary.

Try Exercise 10.5

Customer service and experience

Unless a firm has a clear advantage on product design, service will form at least part of the basis of competition. It contributes to customer satisfaction which in turn drives retention, share of wallet, positive word-of-mouth and therefore profits.

While what makes good customer service depends on the context, in general there are five dimensions to get right:

1. *Tangibility.* Physical facilities, equipment and the appearance of personnel
2. *Reliability.* The ability to perform the required service dependably and accurately
3. *Responsiveness:* The willingness to help customers and provide prompt service
4. *Assurance.* The knowledge and courtesy of employees and their ability to inspire trust and confidence
5. *Empathy.* The caring, individualized attention which the firm provides to its customers.

Often, service levels are so patchy that competence on these five dimensions will yield a significant advantage. If, however, service standards are high within your sector, consider differentiating on the wider customer experience. This includes:

1. *The customer's usage processes.* The firm may be able to redesign these to the customer's benefit
2. *Peer-to-peer interactions.* In many sectors, the firm can help customers to gain value from each other
3. *Relationship.* In business-to-business contexts but also many business-to-consumer contexts, it is critical that the firm stays in touch between transactions, proactively suggesting ways it can help and checking that its past sales are indeed leading to the results the customer hoped for
4. *Brand image/communication.* The social impact of product/service ownership on the customer's peer group may be perceived as valuable
5. *Emotions.* How we feel in interacting with the firm or using its goods or services can be as important in our assessment of the firm as the functional benefits we get.

Service considerations for goods companies

Customer expectations about product availability will vary from market to market. In theory, 100 per cent availability should be the norm. In practice, a compromise might have to be found, say 95 per cent, because the additional cost of providing that extra 5 per cent can be prohibitive. In addition, often such high levels of customer service are not necessary. Balance the benefits to the customer with the cost to you.

Factors which impact on customer service include:

- Frequency of delivery
- Time from order to delivery
- Emergency deliveries when required
- Accuracy of paperwork
- Stock availability
- Reliability of deliveries, etc.

Key factors should be identified and researched with a view to improving them.

Try Exercises 10.3 and 10.4

Questions raised for the company

1. Q: How do I know when to review my channel strategy?
   A: If you have no difficulties with customer experience, your channel costs are acceptable, and you have the market coverage you need to achieve your objectives, then you do not need to review your channel strategy. Problems in any of these three areas suggest that you will need to read this chapter with care and go through the exercises.
2. Q: How important is it to have a distribution plan?
   A: It depends on the type of business. In some industries distribution costs amount to 20 per cent or more of sales revenue. Distribution is the Cinderella of marketing, but can often be the area where a competitive edge can be won – through planning.
3. Q: Can services be distributed? After all, they can't be stocked.
   A: No, but services can be franchised. Once a rational decision has been made to use indirect channels, it is the company's responsibility to work at developing a good business relationship based on trust and mutual respect. It is to both parties' mutual advantage.

4. Q: Are there any new developments in distribution?

  A: Franchising is becoming popular. In addition, some transport contractors now also supply warehousing, inventory control and other services, in effect providing the manufacturer with an 'off-the-shelf' distribution facility.

5. Q: I'm not in the entertainment business. Is customer experience relevant?

  A: Yes. The many entertainment examples of highly emotional customer experiences in the popular press are good for opening our minds to the importance of emotion and the *process* of dealing with the firm in all markets. But the specific value that customers require will, of course, be different in each context.

EXERCISES

For many businesses, channels play a small part in their marketing plans. The route to market, whether direct or indirect, tends to be taken for granted – 'the way we do things in this industry'. When channels are considered, the prime concern in the goods sectors seems to be the physical aspects – the logistics of getting goods transported from the company to the customer. In services contexts, the main concern seems to be making use of low-cost channels – indeed a golden opportunity, but cost is only one of several considerations.

The exercises in this section provide a broader view of channels for marketing, sales, service and distribution.

Exercise 10.1 helps you to think through how to make the best use of your most expensive channels with a coverage map.

Exercise 10.2 helps you to decide whether or not intermediaries are required in your type of business.

Exercise 10.3 explains how intermediaries might be selected.

Exercise 10.4 addresses the physical aspects of distribution.

Exercise 10.5 is designed solely to get you to think about your own customer service from the customer's point of view.

Exercise 10.6 looks at the total customer service package and will enable you to check how yours compares with those of your competitors, and, equally importantly, what steps you will have to take to improve your competitiveness.

Exercise 10.1: Developing a coverage map

A coverage map helps you to think through how different channel combinations will be used for different products and markets, in order to lower costs, improve customer experience and/or improve market coverage. This exercise asks you to develop a current and future coverage map as a basis for the multichannel plan.

You should be warned that it is not a quick exercise. To properly follow these steps to developing a multichannel plan will probably take several workshops with key colleagues, and someone will need to collect inputs from customers in between. It may, however,

(Continued)

transform your business! Having said that, even a quick attempt on your own will prove illuminating and demonstrate the value of a more thorough exercise: we recall one business whose performance was vastly improved through a coverage map that one of the authors brainstormed with the marketing director on a short-haul plane journey!

First, review the section 'Selecting marketing channels' earlier in this chapter. Then proceed as follows.

1. List your key needs-based customer segments. If in doubt, see Chapter 4.
2. Draw up channel chains for how each segment currently buys your products and services. *Note*: these may differ for each major group of products/services. See Figure 10.3 for an example of channel chains. You may, of course, need to talk to some customers to complete this step!
3. Now summarize this analysis with a current coverage map, using the worksheet below:
    (a) List products or services along the top, in order of the complexity of the sales process, with simple ones to the left.
    (b) List markets or segments along the side, with highest value segments at the top.
    (c) Choose a name for each major channel chain (see Figure 10.3 for an example). Channel chains may, for example, be named after the 'leading' channel in the chain – for example, see Figures 10.4 and 10.5. Choose a colour for each. Fill in each cell with the requisite colour, and add a key – e.g. see Figure 10.4. Some examples are provided on the worksheet: add or replace these labels as required.
4. Now consider whether this coverage map can be improved. For example:
    (a) Are your most expensive, high touch channels (e.g. sales visits or face-to-face retail outlets) being used where they are most needed – for highly complex sales – and where they are most justified – for highly valuable customers?
    (b) Are you making appropriate use of low cost channels (e.g. internet or call centres) for simple transactions and/or lower value customers?
    (c) Even where high cost channels are needed, are they needed for the whole of the customer journey, or can a channel chain be drawn up that uses lower cost channels for part of it?
    Draw up a revised future coverage map to reflect your conclusions, along with revised channel chains for each area of the map.
5. Optionally, use the channel curve technique to check out how well your proposals will meet customer buying criteria.
6. How might you pilot any changes you recommend?

Worksheet Coverage map (Exercise 10.1)

	Offer A	Offer B	Offer C	Offer D	Offer E	Offer F	Offer G
Segment A							
Segment B							
Segment C							
Segment D							
Segment E							

☐ Face to face sales ☐ Call centre ▨ Online ☐ Distributor ▨ 3rd party integrator ■ Other

Exercise 10.2: Do we need channel intermediaries?

At first sight, the choice of channel is deceptively easy. After all, basically there are only three options from which to choose:

1. To sell direct to the customer/user
2. To sell to customers/users through intermediaries
3. To use a combination of 1 and 2, i.e. dual distribution.

The final choice will always be something of a compromise, with, on the one hand, the desire to keep control of the distribution of one's products or services, and, on the other hand, the practical need to keep channel costs to a bearable level.

The worksheet is designed to help you to make a choice about channels of distribution. This is what you do:

1. Take each product/service in your portfolio in turn and subject them to the algorithm given on the worksheet.
2. Note the decision for each product, i.e. sell direct or use channel intermediaries. Do these seem the best decisions or can you see good reasons for ignoring them?

(Continued)

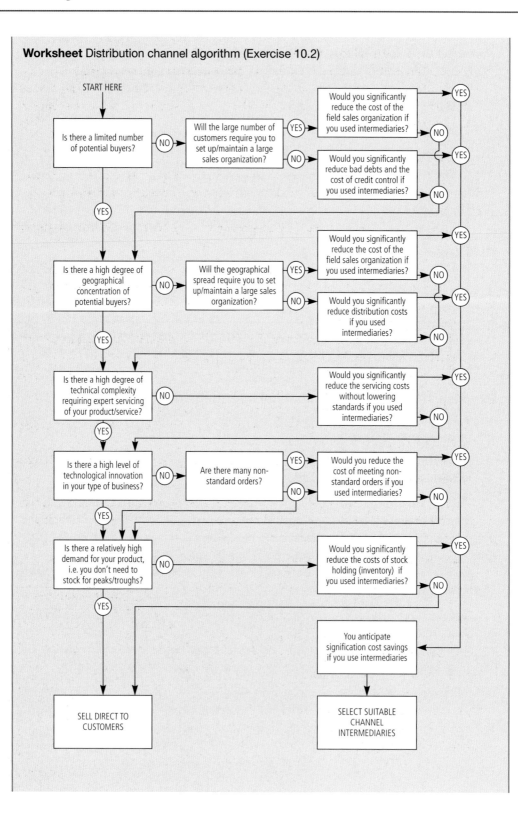

Worksheet Distribution channel algorithm (Exercise 10.2)

3. In working through the algorithm, can you see a case for dual distribution for some products or services? For example, do you sell direct to some customers or regions and sell through intermediaries to others? Remember the major problem associated with dual distribution is determining a fair division of the market between yourself (as the supplier) and the intermediary.

Exercise 10.3 Selecting a suitable intermediary

Exercise 10.2 helped to answer the question of whether or not an intermediary is required. Assuming the answer is affirmative, you are now faced with selecting a suitable candidate to play that role.

The worksheet should help you in your decision making. Here are the instructions for using it:

1. Make a note of organizations that, on the surface, appear to be possible choices as intermediaries. (You will see that the worksheet allows for comparisons between just three prospective intermediaries. You should, of course, draw up your own form to include as many as you like.)
2. Looking at the list of evaluation criteria, take criterion 1 and apply it to all the prospective channel intermediaries. Place scores in columns A, B and C – a number between 0 and 10, depending on whether the intermediary is a very poor fit against this criterion (zero score) or an extremely good fit (10 points).
3. Continue down the list of evaluation criteria, repeating this scoring process.
4. Add any further criteria that are relevant for your business to the bottom of the list and score them likewise.
5. Add up the scores in each column. The highest total represents the most suitable intermediary.

You may decide that some criteria are more important than others on this list. In this case use a points weighting system which takes importance into account. An example of a weighting system is given in Exercise 4.2.

Worksheet Criteria for selecting intermediaries (Exercise 10.3)

	Prospective intermediaries		
Evaluation criteria	A	B	C
1. Currently deals with our target market segment			
2. Is prepared to deal with target market segment			
3. Sales force is sufficiently large			
4. Sales force is well trained			
5. Regional locations well positioned			
6. Promotional policies consistent with ours			
7. Budgets are adequate			

(Continued)

Evaluation criteria	Prospective intermediaries		
	A	B	C
8. Can provide customer after-sales service			
9. Product policies consistent with ours			
10. Does not carry competitor lines			
11. Prepared to carry adequate stocks			
12. Prepared to carry range/cover			
13. Suitable storage facilities			
14. Is creditworthy			
15. Management attitudes compatible with ours			
16. Has suitable reputation (Add others that are relevant)			
17. _____			
18. _____			
19. _____			
20. _____			
21. _____			
22. _____			
23. _____			
24. _____			
25. _____			
26. _____			
27. _____			
28. _____			
29. _____			
30. _____			
TOTAL			

Exercise 10.4 Physical distribution facilities

It has been shown that there are five areas to be considered when it comes to physical distribution, the so-called 'distribution mix'. They are: facilities, inventory, transport, communications, and unitization.

Having established the level of customer service required by each market segment, you must reappraise the location of your own plants and warehouses in order to ensure they are situated in geographically suitable positions *vis-à-vis* the customers. If the nature of demand and the location of major customers are forecast to change dramatically, then relocating manufacturing units and/or warehouses is an option that, in the long term, can lead to savings due to reduced distribution costs.

Such decisions cannot be taken lightly. For most organizations their facilities are taken as fixed, certainly in the short term.

Inventory

The holding of stock, whether by design or accident, is always a costly business. Therefore it is important to know the comparative costs of holding stocks of different products in order to arrive at a sensible stockholding policy.

Worksheet 1 enables you to calculate the various components of inventory cost for each of your major products and thereby produce the necessary cost data. Once in possession of this information, it might become necessary for you to revise the customer service package or indeed earlier deliberations about channel intermediaries.

Transport

This is the area that many people are familiar with, and, as such, has traditionally received most management attention. Worksheet 2 shows a typical way of calculating the merits or demerits of various forms of transporting goods to customers. Try it, using some of your own products as study vehicles.

While cost is an important determinant in the choice of transport, frequency of service and reliability are often just as important. Regular monitoring of transport costs is to be recommended if distribution costs are to be held in check.

Communications

It is often overlooked that accompanying the flow of materials through the distribution channel there is also a flow of information in the form of orders, invoices, demand forecasts, delivery schedules, etc. Each of these 'communications' is likely to be an integral part of your customer service package, and yet, in all probability, they were set up for your own company's administrative convenience.

Look at all your communications associated with distribution and put yourself in the customer's shoes. For example, how sensible does your ordering system seem when viewed from the other end? Get out and speak to some actual customers and seek their views. Anything that can be done to simplify or speed up communications must be to your company's benefit – and it doesn't have to cost you money to improve the situation.

Unitization

Assess whether or not it is possible to make your products more acceptable to users or intermediaries, e.g. for handling or stacking, by packaging them into different sized units such as shrink-wrapped bulk packs, pallet loads, container loads, etc. It is often possible to win substantial cost savings in terms of handling or warehousing by considering this aspect of distribution.

(Continued)

Worksheet 1 Comparative inventory costs (Exercise 10.4)

Area of cost	Product				
	(1)	(2)	(3)	(4)	(5)
Warehouse costs (rent, rates, heat, light, etc.)					
Labour costs					
Losses/shrinkage					
Deterioration/damage					
Insurance					
Interest (on funds tied up in stock)					
Administrative costs					
Other costs relevant to your specific business					
_____					
_____					
_____					
_____					
_____					
_____					
_____					
_____					
_____					

For the purpose of this worksheet take the cost per item, or unit; or you can, if you prefer, just express the costs as a percentage of the book value of the stock.

Worksheet 2 Comparative physical distribution costs (Exercise 10.4)

Method of physical distribution	Product/service				
	(1)	(2)	(3)	(4)	(5)
Use own transport					
Contract hire					
Use carriers					
Other forms of road transport					
_____					
_____					
_____					
Passenger rail train					
Freight train					

Method of physical distribution	Product/service				
	(1)	(2)	(3)	(4)	(5)
Red Star Parcel					
Other forms of rail transport					
_____					
_____					
_____					
Boat on deck					
Boat in hold					
Sea Cat					
Others forms of sea transport					
_____					
_____					
_____					
Air parcel					
Air freight					
Other forms of air transport					
_____					
_____					
_____					
1st class post					
2nd class post					
Parcel post					
Other postal methods					
_____					
_____					
_____					
Other transport methods					
_____					
_____					
_____					
_____					

Exercise 10.5 Customer service audit[*]

Before getting into more detail about customer service, start by completing this customer service audit. If you have 'No' in more than three questions, or if you have difficulty answering

[*] This exercise is based on an audit constructed by Professor Martin Christopher of Cranfield School of Management, and is used with his kind permission.

(Continued)

the open-ended questions, you may have a serious customer service problem in your organization. It is preferable if you can complete this exercise for each segment of the market in which you compete.

1. Do you have a written customer service policy?

   Yes _____

   No _____

2. Is this given a wide circulation within the company?

   Yes _____

   No _____

3. Do customers receive a copy of this policy?

   Yes _____

   No _____

4. What are the three most crucial aspects of customer service as they impinge upon your marketing effectiveness?

   1 _____

   2 _____

   3 _____

5. Is any attempt made to monitor your customer service performance on these three dimensions?

   Yes _____

   No _____

6. Do you monitor competitive customer service offerings?

   Yes _____

   No _____

7. Do you believe that within your company there is adequate knowledge of the true costs of providing customer service

   Yes _____

   No _____

8. Which function(s) has responsibility for customer service management?

   _____

   _____

9. Where does customer service management fit in relation to the marketing function? (Draw an organizational chart if necessary.)

10. Do you have an established method of communications for your customers to contact you about some aspect of their order after the order has been entered?

    Yes _____

    No _____

11. (a) Do you have a single point of contact for customers or (b) do certain departments handle different types of inquiries/complaints?

Yes   (a)   (b)

No   (a)   (b)

12. What do you think are the major areas of weakness in your current approach to customer service management?

_____

_____

_____

_____

_____

Exercise 10.6 The customer service package

Customer service has been defined as the percentage of occasions the product or service is available to the customer *when* and *where* he or she wants it. Obviously, to operate service levels at 100 per cent might, and often does, impose a crippling cost on the supplier, yet to drop below an acceptable level is to surrender one's market share to a competitor.

Research has shown that to improve one's service level by even a small amount when it is already at a high level can become expensive (the law of diminishing returns). Therefore the marketer will have to be certain about the actual levels of customer service provided and to have a greater understanding of customer expectations and needs. It will be highly likely that different market segments will require different levels of customer service.

The ultimate choice of service level for a specific product will be tempered by other influential factors:

1. The contribution to fixed costs, e.g. can it bear the cost of an upgraded service level?
2. The nature of the market, e.g. are there substitute products?
3. The nature of the competition, e.g. do they offer better service levels?
4. The nature of the distribution channel, e.g. do we sell direct or through intermediaries?

The key to marketing success is for your company to develop a customer service package – one that embraces product availability, with attractive order cycle times, and mechanisms for minimizing customer inconvenience arising from order cycle variations.

The worksheet is designed to help you to arrive at a more competitive customer service package or, if this is too expensive, to devise an alternative. The instructions are provided on the worksheet. The space below is for any notes you might wish to make about these issues.

(Continued)

Worksheet Developing a customer service package (Exercise 10.6)

Take one of your market segments and decide what would make the best 'package' by putting a tick against the appropriate items in column 1, i.e. what does your marketing strategy suggest?

In column 2 tick the items that go to make the best competitor package.

In column 3 estimate if the provision of your item is *Better*, *Equal* or *Worse* than the best competitor.

In column 4 indicate the relative cost of improving where you compete unfavourably with the best competitor, i.e. *High*, *Medium* or *Low*.

In column 5 list improvement actions to upgrade the service package to match the best competitor.

In column 6 consider alternative packages, i.e. to fight on different grounds.

Repeat this process for all other market segments.

Components of customer service	(1) Market strategy suggestions	(2) Best comp.	(3) Better, Equal, Worse	(4) Comp. cost H, M, L	(5) Actions to upgrade cust. serv.	(6) Alt. Package
Frequency of delivery						
Time from order to delivery						
Reliability of delivery						
Emergency deliveries when required						
Stock availability						
Continuity of supply						
Advice on non-availability						
Convenience of placing orders						
Acknowledgement of orders						
Accuracy of invoices						
Quality of sales representation						
Regularity of calls by sales reps						
Monitoring of stock levels						
Credit terms offered						

Components of customer service	(1) Market strategy suggestions	(2) Best comp.	(3) Better, Equal, Worse	(4) Comp. cost H, M, L	(5) Actions to upgrade cust. serv.	(6) Alt. Package
Handling of customer queries						
Quality of outer packaging						
Well-stacked pallets						
Easy-to-read use-by dates on outers						
Clear handling instructions on outers						
Quality of inner package for handling						
Quality of inner package for display						
Consultation on new developments, e.g. products or packaging						
Regular review of product range coordination between production, distribution and marketing						
Add others which are relevant for your business						
_____						
_____						
_____						
_____						

REFERENCES

1. Evans, P.B. and Wurster, T.S. (1997) Strategy and the new economics of information. *Harvard Business Review*, Sept–Oct, 71–82.
2. Hughes, A. (2008) Foreword to Wilson, H., Street, R. and Bruce, L. (2008) *The Multichannel Challenge*. Butterworth-Heinemann, Oxford.
3. Wilson, H., Street, R. and Bruce, L. (2008) *The Multichannel Challenge*. Butterworth-Heinemann, Oxford.
4. Wilson, H. and Daniel, E. (2007) The multi-channel challenge: a dynamic capabilities approach. *Industrial Marketing Management*, 36, 10–20.
5. Friedman, L. and Furey, T. (1999). *The Channel Advantage*. Butterworth-Heinemann, Oxford.
6. Wilson, Street and Bruce, op. cit.
7. Gilmore, J.H. and Pine, B.I.I. (2002) Customer experience places: the new offering frontier. *Strategy & Leadership*, 30, 4–11.
8. Lemke, F., Clark, M. and Wilson, H. (2010) Customer experience quality: an exploration in business and consumer contexts using repertory grid technique. In press for *Journal of Academy of Marketing Science*.
9. Heskett, J.L., Jones, T.O., Loveman, G.W., Sasser, W.E.Jr., and Schlesinger, L.A. (1994) Putting the service-profit chain to work. *Harvard Business Review,* Mar–Apr, 164–174.

Chapter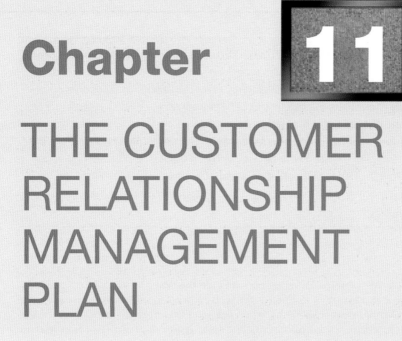

THE CUSTOMER RELATIONSHIP MANAGEMENT PLAN

SUMMARY

- The case for CRM
- A stage model for CRM adoption
- Integration maturity: organizing around the customer
- Interaction maturity: the art of relevant conversation
- Planning for CRM: the benefits dependency network
- Exercises to turn the theory into practice

INTRODUCTION

In the last chapter, we discussed channel strategy: what channel combinations are used for the customer journey across marketing, sales and customer service. Once these channels are in place, we then have the challenge of developing relationships with individual customers through these channels.

We have already discussed how these relationships begin in Chapter 7 on integrated marketing communications. In the great majority of businesses, though, most profits come from repeat purchases or relationships.

This is not easy in a multichannel world. In a single-channel business such as Cranfield's Café Bookshop, the 'CRM' is done in the heads of the staff. Here is what happened when one of the authors walked in on the day of writing this introduction.

Amy (one of the owners) greeted me by name, asked how the book chapter was going, presented me with a double-shot cappuccino without asking, and told me about the lunchtime specials that were likely to appeal to me, including my favourite parsnip and coconut soup. Somewhere within this one-minute masterclass in CRM she asked me to write a sentence of recommendation of the bookshop for new students, and asked me what books she should ensure were in stock for the arrival of the new MSc intake. The colleague I had arranged to meet there said that Amy had guessed who he was, told him that I would be arriving in five minutes or so, and provided him with a coffee on account. Somehow, by the time I left, my wedding anniversary present and card were bought and wrapped as, being a man, I had left them until the last minute . . .

We can all recall similar examples. Entrepreneurs provide this level of service and customer lifetime value management as a matter of instinct: as the well-known Chinese proverb has it, 'A man without a smiling face must not open a shop.' But when one interaction occurs in a call centre, the next online and the next in a bank branch, maintaining the same degree of proactive personalization is significantly harder.

As we have seen in Chapter 8, where the dominant channel is face-to-face sales, the salesperson can similarly do a lot of this job of relationship development through his or her own memory and records. But here, too, coordination among multiple people soon becomes essential.

In this chapter, then, we discuss the mechanisms that all but the simplest businesses need to put in place in order to treat different customers differently. We begin by briefly reviewing the case for long-term relationship development. We summarize the stages of CRM maturity which, our research has found, companies go through as they strive to make the best of every interaction with every customer. We then outline the 10 components of world-class CRM, under the headings of integration maturity and interaction maturity. We describe an invaluable tool for managing cross-functional CRM projects, the benefits dependency network. Finally, the exercises provide a simple diagnostic for assessing your company's current maturity and considering your next steps to include in the marketing plan.

If the reader already knows enough about CRM and wishes to proceed to developing the strategic marketing plan, this chapter can be skipped.

However, we should add a health warning. If the view in the company is that CRM is not the job of marketing but is owned by IT, and if you are not concerned with CRM because an initiative is already in place, it is perhaps worth asking yourself: Do you remember the last time you felt like this? When was it, about the time of business process re-engineering, Total Quality Management, the dotcom boom, the service outsourcing movement? None of these initiatives was inherently a bad idea, but none had a hope if they were not cross-functionally embedded and, in particular, sense-checked against the needs of key target segments in a marketing plan. CRM initiatives which have not a single objective that relates in any way to a customer buying criterion are hardly likely to improve customer relationships.

THE CASE FOR CRM

Acquiring customers can be expensive. Usually it involves certain one-off costs, such as, for example, advertising, promotion, a salesperson's time, commission to intermediaries, and so on. Thus, every customer represents an investment, the level of which will vary from business to business.

If they are treated correctly and remain customers over a long period, there is strong evidence that they will generate more profits for the organization each year they maintain the relationship. Across a wide range of businesses this pattern is the same (Figure 11.1).

> For example, an industrial laundry almost doubled its profits per customer over five years. A car servicing business expects fourth-year customers to generate three times the profit of a first-year customer. A distributor of industrial products found that net sales per account continued to rise even into the nineteenth year of the relationship.

Retaining customers is extremely profitable.

This trend holds true for many sectors. As the relationship extends, the initial 'contact' costs, such as checking creditworthiness, no longer figure on the balance sheet. In addition, the more that is known about the customer as the relationship develops, the more offers can be tailored effectively to meet their needs.

Thus, the customer gets greater value, which in turn encourages more frequent and larger purchases.

It follows, therefore, that when a company lowers its customer defection rate, average customer relationships last longer and profits climb.

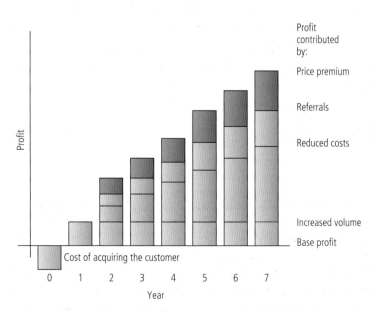

Figure 11.1: Retaining customers pays off.

(*Source*: Based on F.R. Reichheld (1994) Loyalty and the renaissance of marketing. *Marketing Management*, 12(4), 17.)

	Total market	Segment 1	Segment 2	Segment 3	Segment 4	Segment 5	Segment 6
Percentage of market represented by segment	100.0	14.8	9.5	27.1	18.8	18.8	11.0
Percentage of all profits in total market produced by segment	100.0	7.1	4.9	14.7	21.8	28.5	23.0
Ratio of profit produced by segment to weight of segment in total population	1.00	0.48	0.52	0.54	1.16	1.52	2.09
Defection rate	23%	20%	17%	**15%**	28%	30%	**35%**

Figure 11.2: Retaining the right customers – a counter example.

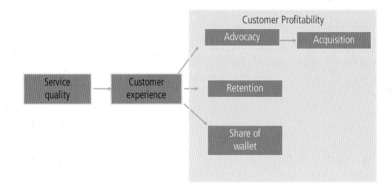

Figure 11.3: The triple benefits of satisfied customers.

There is evidence that few companies bother to measure customer retention on a regular basis, while even fewer measure customer retention by segment. However, as can be seen in the data in Figure 11.2, this particular organization's best performance is in the least profitable segments and its worst performance is in the market's most profitable segments.

High customer retention, then, is highly beneficial to most businesses, not just because of lower acquisition costs, but also because retained customers tend to spend more. Furthermore, satisfied customers who stay with the company are also more likely to praise the company to others, further lowering acquisition costs. This is represented diagrammatically in Figure 11.3.

This figure, which is a simplified version of the service–profit chain we described in the last chapter, shows this triple benefit of high service and experience quality.

You might reasonably ask, though: if retention results from a great customer experience, isn't relationship management just a matter of delivering a great service, with retention automatically following?

Well, yes and no. Certainly a high level of product and service quality at an acceptable price is essential to retention. UK bank First Direct has excellent retention and advocacy rates because its service standards are so high, despite having CRM processes such as cross-sell mailings which are little different from those of its competitors. And without such a high customer satisfaction with existing products, the firm does not have permission from the customer to propose a cross-sell.

And for businesses with intermediaries between them and their end customers, who cannot develop their own individualized relationships, a good customer experience can be the only game in town. FMCG manufacturers have traditionally been in this position – though the maturing of retailers' loyalty cards and social networking both now give them vehicles to begin to build their own one-to-one relationships with consumers.

However, where the firm has access to individual customer data, there are many things the firm can do to develop the relationship with a satisfied customer, by proposing other goods or services which they might find valuable. And if this is done well, it feels like service to the customer and hence enhances retention as well as increasing the share of the customer's wallet in the product/service category. In fact, if the firm does not proactively suggest things that would help the customer, it can feel like being forgotten and neglected.

All too often, though, CRM is not this customer centric. Bombarding our customers with unsolicited, unfocused direct mail, or annoying them with clumsy cross-sell pitches at the end of service calls, may be initiated by a CRM department but it certainly does not represent best practice. Neither does it work very well, even in the short term.

Fortunately, there is now enough evidence about what works in CRM for us to be able to lay out the basic principles of how to get CRM right. First, though, we must define our terms. Here is a selection of definitions of CRM:

> *A continuous performance initiative to increase a company's knowledge of its customers.*
>
> *CRM comprises the organization, processes and systems through which an organization manages its relationships with its customers.*
>
> *Consistent high quality customer support across all communications channels and business functions, based on common information shared by employees, their customers and business partners.*
>
> *A methodology, based on new information technology, that helps companies reach their long-held goals for improved customer satisfaction.*
>
> *An integrated, multiple-delivery channel strategy that allows companies to capture profitable new customers and improve service.*
>
> *ERP is from Mars, CRM is from Venus.*

You will have noted that the IT/systems backbone of CRM keeps peeking through the skin. This is not automatically a bad thing, but we need to recognize CRM, at least as it currently stands, for what it is. Because, on the one hand, in all but the simplest businesses it is impossible to maintain an individualized relationship with the customer across multiple touchpoints and multiple channels without IT support. But on the other hand, the IT will not of itself deliver the benefits we seek. Because as an IT director once told us (and we only exaggerate a little), those annoying people called front-office staff keep on coming between our beautifully crafted IT systems on the one hand and our customers on the other.

So we have all seen 'CRM initiatives' driven out of the IT department which have fallen flat on their face, to vanish without trace a year or two later. IT, then, is a crucial enabler, not the essence of the issue. We suggest that a more appropriate definition of CRM is:

> The management of individual customer relationships across functions, channels and products so as to maximize customer satisfaction and customer lifetime value. In all but the simplest organizations, CRM is underpinned by integrated customer data.

Even this starting point of integrated customer data, though, is far from easy. The fact is that no organizations can become world-class at CRM in one step. We will next turn to the stages through which CRM tends to evolve.

A STAGE MODEL FOR CRM ADOPTION

In a study with CRM software provider Chordiant, we looked at how companies adopt CRM across numerous industry sectors by surveying 600 leading European companies.* The companies fell broadly into four stages, shown in Figure 11.4.

The figure plots these stages on two dimensions:

1. *Integration maturity.* The extent to which the organization has an integrated view of each customer, supported by structures and metrics which encourage the management of customer relationships holistically across products, channels and functions.
2. *Interaction maturity.* The extent to which the organization holds individualized, customer-centric conversations with its customers which the customer perceives as adding value and which optimize customer lifetime value to the firm.

By the beginning of the CRM revolution in the 1990s, many companies had evolved unthinkingly into the situation represented by stage 1. Databases and applications had grown up around the need to take customer orders for different products, each of which often had separate systems. Channel choices were often hardwired into the systems, so in the case of an industrial goods firm, for example, a sales force automation system might take all orders for larger customers, while a call centre for distributors might take the orders for indirect customers. This met immediate operational requirements, but made it very difficult even to know what holdings a customer had across the product range. While naturally individual firms may not be exactly at any of the four stages, many companies today are still closest to stage 1.

Stage 2, 'Information access', represents a common next step. Changing frontline systems can be prohibitively difficult. So often a compromise is reached, where data from different operational systems is dumped (perhaps overnight) into a back-end customer database, or marketing warehouse. This can at least enable some key analytics such as profiling of which segments customers fall into, calculating their propensity to buy products they do not currently hold, and so on. For batch processes like direct mail, this insight can then be actioned in individualized messages. But if the operational systems themselves are not altered, it can be difficult to feed this insight back to frontline staff in field sales, field service, call centres, and so on.

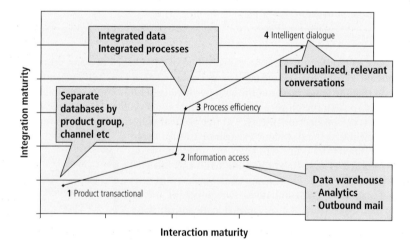

Figure 11.4: A stage model for CRM maturity.

*For details of this study, which one of the authors conducted with CRM expert Aly Moore (then at Chordiant), Dr Aamir Khan of Lahore University Management School and Professor Moira Clark of Henley Management College, see www.cxm-model.com. We are grateful for the assistance of Swati Phadnis with data analysis.

MARKETING INSIGHT

Many loyalty cards run by retailers and travel companies are at stage 2. Nectar is a UK-based loyalty card where the consumer gains points from any of a coalition of retailers from grocer Sainsbury's to petrol retailer BP. Initially, the only information collected by its central database, run by Nectar's coordinators Groupe Aeroplan, was the retailer name and transaction value. This meant that its offers to consumers were somewhat generic, and suffered by comparison with the leading rival Tesco Clubcard, which could offer highly individualized coupons based on basket analysis. Once Nectar began to collect data on individual product purchases, it was able to tailor its offers better, leading to an increase in redemption rates from 13 to 18 per cent in two years. This dialogue helps with retention as well as share of wallet: customers of utility EDF churn 30–50 per cent less if they hold a Nectar card than those that don't.

Some benefits, then, can be gained at stage 2, but it does not make the best use of every touch-point, such as when a customer calls in. And service levels can still suffer if the right hand does not know what the left hand is doing. If the salesperson does not know about a complaint made on the web yesterday, the customer will tend to conclude that the firm does not care.

This, then, is the argument for integrated 'CRM systems': customer databases with applications referring to a central repository of information about the customer. Fortunes have been made by shifting firms to stage 3 where these systems from vendors such as Oracle and SAP replace the previous front-office systems.

Here, there is a significant improvement on the 'integration' axis ... but only a small one on the 'interaction' axis. That is, having an integrated view of the customer will not of itself deliver better conversations with those customers. It will *avoid the disadvantage* that comes from front-office staff not knowing about past interactions, but will not, without further work, *create the advantage* that comes from using this information to increase share of wallet.

> Having an integrated view of the customer will not of itself deliver better conversations with those customers.

For this, we need stage 4, 'Intelligent dialogue'. By this stage – and few companies yet claim to be even near it – each conversation with each customer is individualized and relevant to their needs, irrespective of channel. Some companies are achieving this in specific channels, but few can yet provide truly individualized dialogues irrespective of how the customer contacts them.

MARKETING INSIGHT

UK bank Nationwide has a good reputation for service, meaning its customers are happy to have conversations about buying further products from the bank. Its CRM team develop propensity models which predict the likelihood of a customer buying each product which they do not currently hold. Many banks use this technology to improve the targeting of direct mail, but Nationwide is unusual in being able to deploy it in inbound call centres, on the web and in branches as well. Conversion rates, they find, are higher in these inbound channels, when the customer is calling on their own time when they want to be in conversation with the bank, than in outbound direct mail. They are particularly high when a human agent can help the dialogue, collecting further insight which the systems are not aware of and ensuring that any additional product is right for the customer.

We will now look at what is involved in developing integration maturity in more detail, before taking a similarly close look at interaction maturity.

INTEGRATION MATURITY

Integrated customer data is certainly important, but it is not the only challenge in enabling the firm to focus on maximizing the lifetime value of each customer. We will discuss five key dimensions of integration maturity, which are summarized in Table 11.1.

Data Integration

Mapping out of the customer journey soon reveals many points at which data need to be shared between different touchpoints, if the customer is to feel that the organization knows what it is doing. The most obvious solution is for the applications supporting the first channel – a website, perhaps – to pass the specific information that is needed to the applications supporting the second channel – perhaps a call centre. But this soon results in a spaghetti-like set of connections between systems, with many performance issues and high costs of ownership. Even if it works, the end result is an inflexible system in which it is very hard to evolve the customer journey over time, as is frequently needed, as we saw in the previous chapter in our discussion of multichannel routes to market.

A better solution, therefore, is to have a single central database for key information about the customer – at least, conceptually – with systems reading or writing to the database as required. This has been one of the major drivers of the substantial market for integrated master data and a stronger information architecture, and for the growth of broader, more integrated CRM application suites. Many organizations are working towards a unified view of the customer, so that all aspects of the customer interface can be coordinated.

Task-independent data management

It is not sufficient, though, to have a single repository of customer data – difficult though that is to achieve for many long-standing organizations with complex legacy systems. The customer-facing systems also need to manage customer data independently of the task being performed. For example, if a customer enters their name and address on a website, they do not wish to be asked the same information on the telephone. This requires all tasks to call on a single module which manages this customer data. We call this the principle of task-independent data management.

Data integration	Having a 'single customer view' of each customer across channels, products and business functions
Communications integration	Having a single person responsible for coordinating all inbound and outbound communications with each customer
Process integration	Ensuring that the firm's processes for responding to each customer are joined up through the customer journey, so each step leads seamlessly to the next in the eyes of the customer
Structure integration	Having an organizational structure that encourages all managers and front-office staff to look after the interests of each customer holistically and hence grow their customer value
Metrics integration	Having targets and reward systems which encourage all staff to look after the interests of each customer and grow their value

Table 11.1: Five dimensions of integration maturity

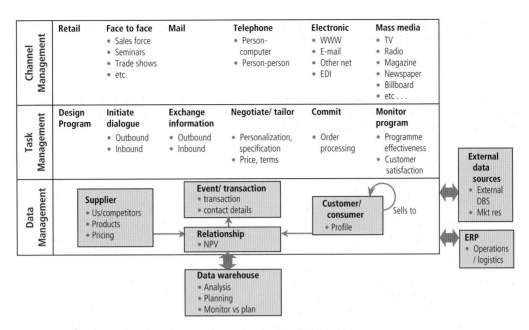

	Retail	Face to face	Mail	Telephone	Electronic	Mass media
Channel Management		• Sales force • Seminars • Trade shows • etc.		• Person-computer • Person-person	• WWW • E-mail • Other net • EDI	• TV • Radio • Magazine • Newspaper • Billboard • etc . . .

	Design Program	Initiate dialogue	Exchange information	Negotiate/ tailor	Commit	Monitor program
Task Management		• Outbound • Inbound	• Outbound • Inbound	• Personalization, specification • Price, terms	• Order processing	• Programme effectiveness • Customer satisfaction

Data Management

Supplier
• Us/competitors
• Products
• Pricing

Event/ transaction
• transaction
• contact details

Relationship
• NPV

Customer/ consumer
• Profile

Sells to

External data sources
• External DBS
• Mkt res

ERP
• Operations / logistics

Data warehouse
• Analysis
• Planning
• Monitor vs plan

Figure 11.5: Towards a flexible CRM architecture.

This point can clearly be seen in Figure 11.5. The 'task management' layer needs to be separate from the 'data management' layer, rather than systems for each task endeavouring to manage parts of the customer data, as is still often the case.

Channel-independent task management

Another point which is clearly illustrated by Figure 11.5 is the importance of channel-independent task management. The 'channel management' layer of managing different channels or media is often bundled in with particular tasks. A 'direct mail system' will be *the* way in which the organization generates leads; an 'order processing system' will assume that orders come in to an order processing clerk (rather than, say, being made by a website); and so on. Such architecture is inherently inflexible. An ideal architecture separates the issue of managing the medium from that of managing the task.

Extending the single customer view to indirect channels

It is widely accepted, then, that maintaining an integrated customer relationship is difficult if not impossible without an integrated customer database linked across channels as well as across products. Leading companies are extending this principle, though, to data held about the customer by intermediaries – indirect channels – as well as the company's own direct channels. The customer holds the supplier responsible for agents, distributors and retailers who provide frontline customer service, so it may be necessary to share customer contact information with them, or even roll out the CRM system to them, too.

The logic for this is clear from our discussion of channel chains in the last chapter. Lines on a channel chain connecting an indirect channel to a direct one will imply the customer passing between two organizations during the same purchase process. So for exactly the same reason that integrated CRM systems are needed within the enterprise, there frequently needs to be data transfer between organizations to make this transition smooth.

The BT Major Customers case study we described in the last chapter is a good example. With a project under the title of *Managed Accounts Through Partners* (MATP), the Major Customers division reduced its number of partners to five, who collectively manage about 1,000 accounts on behalf of BT. These major distributors have access to BT's CRM system and record all their client details and activities on the same system. This allows BT and the partner to put together integrated marketing campaigns as well as provide a seamless service.

MARKETING INSIGHT

General Motors' Dialogue programme, which we describe in detail later, is an example of the same principle of data sharing but with simpler technology. In this CRM initiative, GM collected prospect information through direct channels on such issues as when the prospect intended to buy a new car and which models they were considering. Near to the time of intended purchase, they were therefore able to send local dealerships a list of genuinely interested prospects, along with this information. Information also needed to flow in the other direction if GM was to track the success of the programme.

Details of how this data sharing was achieved varied from country to country. In three cases – Netherlands, Belgium and Italy – an online tool was deployed with dealers to distribute leads and collect feedback. In other countries, leads were simply faxed to dealers and, if necessary, dealers were chased on the end result by outgoing calls from GM's own call centres.

Communications Integration

An integrated relationship with the customer can be undone, though, by communications which are not joined up. All too often one unit is responsible for direct mail, another for e-mail, another for who is invited to seminars, a fourth for the call centre, a fifth for face-to-face interactions. Stories of advertising campaigns leading to a surge in traffic with which the call centre is utterly unable to cope are all too common.

An insurance company rebranded after a takeover, spending hundreds of millions of dollars on launching a new brand name. The market research said that individualized service was needed, so that was the theme of the advertising campaign. Through mass channels. With no individualization. Once customers made contact with the firm, they discovered that inbound channels were no more personalized than outbound ones; 20 per cent of existing customers could not even clear security and get details of their account! The company continued to languish towards the bottom of service quality tables, and in a Web 2.0 age, its customers knew it. Thankfully cynicism doesn't always pay!

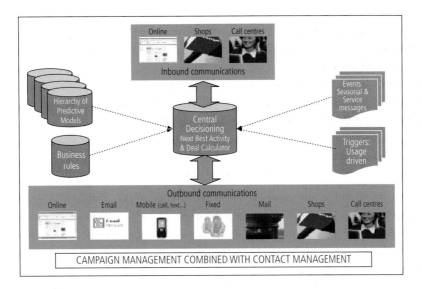

Figure 11.6: Communications integration.

Like all the integration challenges, communications integration is not easy to solve. After all, specialists are needed in managing call centres, websites, and so on. But someone has to be appointed with sufficient authority to ensure that in the eyes of the customer, the experience joins up.

That someone may be a CRM director, or the marketing director, or even a board meeting regularly, though an individual is much the best. The aspiration is shown by Figure 11.6, adapted from a leading telecoms company.

The 'central decisioning' box represents a business process, under the control of an individual and with IT support from CRM technology, which decides what to say to each customer, whether the communication is outbound or inbound. So a mailing about a complex purchase offer with a leaflet providing details might be followed by a conversation the next time the customer calls in or visits a store, while a simpler proposal might be made on the website.

Process Integration

This integration needs to continue through purchase and service interactions. And if the customer is to perceive the journey as easy and joined up, they will expect it to be as straightforward as buying in a coffee shop.

Once we have integrated data, we have some hope of joining up processes across functions, product silos and channel silos. The fact that marketing doesn't talk to sales or service is no excuse for the systems to act as badly as the humans. But this still requires some thinking through of the customer journey.

In the IT trade, this is known as 'workflow management'. And it is indeed vital to map out the firm's flows of work and make sure that a customer contact seamlessly triggers the right response. But it is important to note that the most important workflow to understand and join up is the *customer's* job, be it making a complaint, booking an airline ticket or obtaining advice.

MARKETING INSIGHT

First Direct is famous for its superb telephone service. But 80 per cent of First Direct transactions are now online. This was not achieved by giving away margin through price incentives. Nor by reducing the quality of the existing channel. Nor by insisting that the digital director delivered profits through that single channel. No, the key was attitudinal. When the website was being developed, the chief executive put signs up saying: 'How does it feel to the customer?' Because the answer is positive, customers require no incentive to use the service frequently, freeing up the call centre to concentrate on value-adding matters like new mortgages.

One more story will make the point. This time, it's a counter-example of processes which are not thought through.

A financial services company found that one office had such disastrous service levels that it was thinking of closing it down. Buzz in head office blamed the people. The customer experience director visited with a 'hit squad'. While a few of the staff did indeed seem to have negative attitudes, the great majority were relieved to have some attention. They poured out stories of the process problems that got in the way of serving customers. To take credit card orders, staff had to ask the customer to hang on while they went to a different floor and queued to use the only credit card machine. One agent taking orders in euros would ask the customer to wait while he called his retired father at home, who would look up the latest exchange rates on teletext . . . His father rather enjoyed it, but it was hardly ideal for the customer experience! It wasn't the people that needed fixing but the processes. The office is now frequently visited for the opposite reason – an example to others!

Integrating multichannel processes

One specific integration issue is how to ensure that the customer experience is integrated across the various channels in a channel chain. Scenario analysis is useful for this.

Figure 11.7 shows an example.*

In this example, a bank customer is considering the purchase of an additional product. At the top of the figure, the segment is brought to life by naming and describing a typical member of it. Then a table is drawn up, as shown, describing a walkthrough of the interactions between this named customer and the bank as he conducts the purchase. The walkthrough teases out ways in which the channels need to interact and support each other in order to deliver the ideal experience.

This process of 'walking through' scenarios, stepping into the shoes of the customer to make sure that the movement between the channels is smooth, can benefit from market research to really 'walk through' the customer journey as it is at the moment, in order to work out where the disconnects are and how value can be better created for the customer.

This is illustrated in Figure 11.8 drawn from work in the travel industry looking at the customer highs and lows through their holiday experience. Travelling out to the holiday is often a stressful experience, battering much of the positive anticipation that has built up, to a point where some

---

* We thank IBM for these scenario analysis examples, drawn from their UK channel transformation consulting practice.

Name:	Peter Muller
Job Role:	MD of an IT company in Frankfurt.
Background:	Herr Muller has been a standard current account customer for the last seven years and in that time his interest in investments and his financial sophistication have grown.
Current Portfolio:	Peter now has both a standard current account and flexible fund account. He holds cash, funds and securities in his accounts.
Situation:	He has a good relationship with his broker, but also uses direct channels, especially the Web, for convenience.
Scenario:	Buying Alternative Investment Products (AIP)

Task	Channel	Experience	Implications
Initiate dialogue	Mail	Concise, signed personal note from broker, two weeks before annual review meeting, suggesting that Markus look into AIPs, with leaflet & Web URL	Integration of mail & face-to-face channels
Exchange information	Web	Peter looks up his flexible fund account briefing on AIPs. He models impact on his investment portfolio using what-if facility	Extensions to Web-based portfolio management tool
Negotiate/tailor	Face-to-face	Peter discusses options with his broker. Together they decide on appropriate level of risk	Broker access to personal portfolios in meetings
Etc. . . .	Etc. . . .	Etc. . . .	Etc. . . .

Figure 11.7: Scenario analysis.

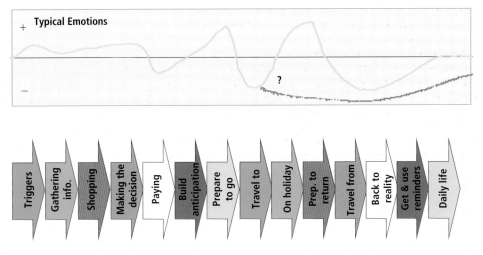

Figure 11.8: Scenario analysis and emotions – a travel company.

really dramatic positive experiences are needed at the start of the holiday itself if the mood is to swing up again rather than continue on a downward path. The journey back is another crucial time: even where this experience cannot be fully improved, the memory of the holiday itself can be reinvigorated by some warm communication soon afterwards.

Structure Integration

One reason why processes are not always integrated is that different parts of the process are the responsibility of different executives. If each business unit head is responsible only for specific product lines or channels, there may be no one motivated to do the most important job of all: maximize the satisfaction and lifetime value of each individual customer.

One of the authors was in a workshop with the operating board of a large European financial services company. Like many such companies, business units were structured primarily on product lines: pensions, mortgages, general insurance, and so on. The director of the protection business unit, selling products which protect the individual against events like redundancy, was bemoaning the fact that when a financial adviser sold, say, a mortgage, they often did not get round to cross-selling the protection product on top of it as, for the adviser, this was a relatively small additional sale. This was a shame, he said, as the margins on protection products were high. He showed the figures and, indeed, they were high. His colleagues, remunerated on the sales of other products, were of course distraught at their fellow director's predicament.

The author asked why the protection product couldn't instead be cross-sold by the service centre when the customer phoned in, as was bound to happen a few times in the early months while setting up the mortgage. The directors looked at him as if he was from Mars. How could one possibly cross-sell from a service centre? It was a cost centre, not a profit centre! And anyway, it belonged to the mortgage business unit – the protection business unit had its own call centre . . .

CASE STUDY[*]

BT Global Services had a similar issue with the channel transformation project we described in the previous chapter. Once some interactions were occurring through desk-based account managers, others through the field sales force and yet others through the web or third parties, how would these channels be motivated to collaborate? The answer was to keep these channel specialists as a minor dimension of the matrix, but to make the major dimension customers. Account directors were responsible for total revenue from a group of customers minus total costs - sales force costs, DBAM costs, costs for tailored web pages, commission for distributors, and so on. This provided the motivation to the account directors to make the best use of each channel. Meanwhile, individual staff were remunerated not on revenue from their channel but on total revenue for the customers with whom they worked. See Figure 11.9.

---

[*] This case study was researched by Dr Stan Maklan and the authors.

Channel Marketing	Account Management			
	Government	**Financial Services**	**Commercial & Brands**	**Corporate Mid-Market**
	Field Sales Govt	Field Sales Fin Ser	Field Sales Comm.	Field Sales MidMkt
Desk Based Resource	DBAM	DBAM	DBAM	DBAM
Bt.com				
Partners				

Figure 11.9: Organizing and rewarding customers: BT Global Services.

Metrics Integration

The BT story illustrates that just as structure needs to encourage a holistic relationship with customers, so do metrics. Important customer-focused metrics include:

- Customer satisfaction
- Customer advocacy, e.g. net promoter score
- Service quality and experience quality (see Chapter 10)
- Customer retention (or its opposite, churn)
- Number of product holdings per customer
- Customer profitability
- Customer lifetime value.

*Measuring multichannel consistency**

Multichannel journeys raise a particular challenge concerning customer satisfaction. Most companies, if they measure channel satisfaction at all, do so in each channel individually. But how about consistency of the experience *across* channels? We have seen that this matters to customers; is it, however, reflected in what is asked in customer satisfaction surveys?

Until now, the value of consistency across channels has been no more than a widely accepted premise. But the case for the importance of consistency has just been strengthened by two pieces of research from the Cranfield Customer Management Forum.

The first involved a blue-chip organization delivering products and services through a number of business-to-business channels. This research confirmed what CRM professionals have long suspected; consistency of information, impression and customer knowledge across different touchpoints (or delivery channels) is critical. In fact, multichannel consistency ranked alongside product satisfaction in terms of its importance in driving customer satisfaction, trust and intention to repurchase (see Table 11.2). We were taken aback by quite how important multichannel consistency is – more so than website satisfaction, or call centre satisfaction, or even sales force satisfaction. It seems that, if the salesperson ploughs blithely on with their sales pitch without mentioning the complaint which the customer made on the web yesterday, customers are as unforgiving as if the product doesn't work.

---

* We acknowledge with thanks the contribution of Rita Madaleno to the research reported in this section, and Lindsay Bruce's contribution to the drafting of this section.

What parts of the experience matter most in driving . . .		
Customer satisfaction	**Trust**	**Intention to repurchase**
1. **Multichannel consistency**	1. Product satisfaction	1. Product satisfaction
2. Value for money	2. **Multichannel consistency**	2. Value for money
3. Product satisfaction		3. **Multichannel consistency**

Table 11.2: The importance of multichannel consistency in a large business to business firm

As an important technical note to those involved in commissioning market research, the results in Table 11.2 were arrived at not by simply asking the customer what drives their customer satisfaction, but by measuring customer satisfaction, separately asking about multichannel consistency, product satisfaction, and so on, and then correlating the two using such techniques as multiple regression. This is a much more reliable way of assessing how customers actually behave.

In the second project, the same approach was applied in a business-to-consumer service organization providing entertainment. Customers were asked the equivalent questions and their answers again revealed the importance of channel consistency. Consistency of information, impression and customer knowledge was the only factor apart from satisfaction with the basic entertainment service that each time appeared among the top three drivers for satisfaction, trust and propensity to recommend.

Interesting it may be, but you might say this discovery is hardly going to rock the marketing world. Marketers have, after all, widely assumed the importance of consistency even without such research-based evidence. The challenge set by this research is not that marketers should *acknowledge* the importance of channel consistency, but that they should *measure* it – to make sure that they actually do something about it.

The billions that have been invested the world over in CRM software systems on the basis that the 'single customer view' would deliver an enhanced customer experience might suggest that organizations recognize the importance of channel consistency. Yet most companies continue to measure customer experience and satisfaction 'silo-fashion', with survey questions related only to certain channels. Better marketers benchmark their performance against competitors. The most innovative not only ask customers how well the company has performed, but also assess the importance of each aspect of experience through techniques such as multiple regression and structural equation modelling, to make sure we do not waste time fixing aspects of the experience that ultimately do not drive repurchasing and advocacy behaviour. But even such relatively sophisticated techniques fail to measure multichannel consistency.

So, how can you be sure that you are delivering a consistent customer experience across different touchpoints? As CRM system vendors will rightly point out, the software is necessary but not sufficient. While the system may deliver a single view of the customer, it does not obviate the need for staff to be adequately trained, equipped and motivated to deliver an appropriate level of service. A bad tempered, discouraged call centre representative is unlikely to deliver good customer service, regardless of whether or not the CRM system has highlighted a cross-selling opportunity. Similarly, the fact that your CRM system identifies the different service quality needs of customers will have little impact on your online sales performance, if your website is unable to differentiate between and meet those service level expectations.

If you want to know that your CRM investment is really paying off, you need to know that customers are receiving a consistent experience across all channels. This, as we have already discovered, is a core driver of customer loyalty and propensity to repurchase or recommend. Equally important, if you haven't yet got it right, is to uncover the source of the inconsistency. In doing so, you avoid being 'blinded' by your CRM system and blaming it when the failure lies in your own processes. Conversely, you also arm yourself with evidence to hold the CRM vendor to account if it is, indeed, the CRM system that has failed to deliver.

In addition to your other customer satisfaction questions, ask your customers to assess their agreement with the following statements on a sliding scale.
I have a consistent impression from [company], regardless of the channel I use.
The information I get from [company] is consistent across all channels.
Regardless of the channel I use, people I deal with are informed about my past interactions with [company].
I can choose among a range of channels while dealing with [company].
Regardless of the sales channel I use to purchase from [company], I can use other channels to get information or help.

Table 11.3: Five killer questions to check multichannel consistency

The solution is twofold. First, you need to include questions in your customer research that investigate whether the customer experience is consistent across your different channels. The five core questions used in our work with the two organizations we have described cover impression, information, choice and staff knowledge (see Table 11.3).

Second, when respondents are matched with their main purchase channel (or channel chain – see Chapter 10), their responses can be broken down to identify where improvement is required. An example of this is shown in the graph in Figure 11.10. From the answers to this question, it is evident that customers in this example who buy mainly from the direct sales force perceive a greater level of consistency than those who most often buy online or through resellers. Further investigation will then reveal the source of this lack of consistency. It may be that the company's sales managers are particularly good at recording information in the CRM system. Or it might be a flaw in the online purchasing system or reseller extranet, where data are poorly recorded or utilized.

When it comes to customer satisfaction, companies are eager to deliver a good customer experience. Traditionally, marketers take a view from their customer insight and measure satisfaction against

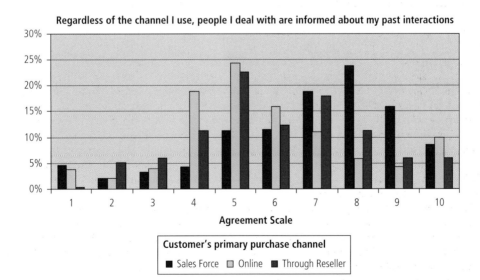

Figure 11.10: Differences in multichannel consistency across customer groups.

factors that they believe are important. But even relatively sophisticated techniques fail to measure how consistent service delivery is across different customer touchpoints.

Consider the cost of investment in CRM software by organizations that fail to measure whether their CRM system actually delivers what it set out to achieve. Is your company one of them? Take a look at how your organization measures customer satisfaction. Multichannel consistency is a crucial driver. With the amount that you invest in CRM, can you afford not to know if it's working?

INTERACTION MATURITY

An integrated view of the customer, and an organization motivated to treat each customer holistically, is half of the CRM challenge. And, indeed, they are hard enough! However, integration maturity is primarily an *enabler* of better conversations, better interactions. We will now look at what makes for powerful, value-creating interactions with customers. The five key factors are listed in Table 11.4.

Individualization	Treating each customer in a way appropriate to everything which is known about them
Customer value orientation	Understanding the customer's overall value to the firm, and taking this into account when determining how to treat the customer (without losing customer centricity)
Customer centricity	Ensuring that every offer to the customer has the customer's best interests at heart, as well as the firm's
Dynamic interaction	Responding to what the customer says or does appropriately and speedily, ideally within the same dialogue
Customization	In categories where this is relevant, tailoring the product or service to the individual customer in accordance with everything that is known about them

Table 11.4: Five dimensions of interaction maturity

CASE STUDY

GM'S DIALOGUE PROGRAMME*

We saw in Chapter 10 that 'channel chains' representing the customer's journey may include indirect channels such as agents, distributors and retailers, as well as the company's own direct channels. Just as these direct channels, such as the web, call centres and the sales force, often complement each other rather work as alternatives, so indirect channels do not necessarily 'own' the whole customer relationship; rather, they may be complemented by the company's direct channels in an integrated channel chain. Maintaining an individualized conversation across both direct and indirect channels is a particular challenge.

An innovative programme termed 'Dialogue' at General Motors Europe provides a good example of the step-change improvements in customer acquisition and retention costs that can result from getting this right. It is worth describing this programme in some detail (Figure 11.11).

The traditional channel chain used for consumer car sales is on the left of the figure. The Original Equipment Manufacturers (OEMs) such as General Motors have traditionally had little

---

*We thank Rob Malyn, then Head of CRM for GM Europe, and his colleagues for their assistance with this case study.

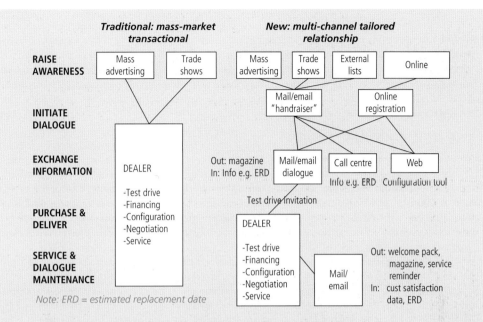

Figure 11.11: Channel chains – General Motors Europe.

one-to-one contact with the motorist, direct consumer sales instead being supported through a network of independent dealers. The manufacturer's communications role has historically been one way. Advertising and product information is communicated to consumers through broadcast media and, to a lesser extent, more targeted channels such as direct mail. The aim is to create awareness of the brand and drive traffic to the dealerships. This model is analogous to that in most consumer packaged goods.

However, this communication approach allows no direct feedback from consumers as to whether they are 'in market' to buy or not, resulting in large amounts of wasted money and effort, especially with infrequent purchase decisions. There is also little opportunity to distinguish between individual potential customers on the basis of model preferences, purchase intentions, and so on.

For the motor industry, the internet opens up real possibilities to move to a two-way communication model. The web offers an inexpensive channel through which consumers could respond to and interact with OEMs, and perhaps even purchase a vehicle online. The prospect of OEMs selling directly via the internet inevitably sets alarm bells ringing among dealers, though, and has forced OEMs to think carefully before upsetting the distribution channel they have been so dependent upon.

The niche for direct online sales is now beginning to be significant, but GM's Dialogue programme, trialled on the new Vectra launches in the early 2000s in seven countries in mainland Europe, sought instead to explore the hybrid solution shown on the right of the figure. The idea was to use the internet to create relationships with customers which might yield valuable information about their purchase intentions and enable higher quality leads to be introduced to dealers during the time window when they were preparing to buy their next vehicle.

Cars are an infrequent purchase, but there is a high incidence of repeat purchase. This suggests there is a compelling case for maintaining contact with existing customers during the years between them buying cars.

(Continued)

In tandem with the arrival of the internet, other developments in hardware and software created the possibility to fully integrate communications with consumers across a range of channels, both online and offline. Advances in database technology meant that it was much easier to 'clean' data held on individual customers so that names could be readily and accurately matched between purchase order systems, acquired lists, those responding to promotions, and so on. CRM software could then enable a complete view of the consumer across channels, enabling a true two-way relationship to be established.

THE NEW CHANNEL CHAIN

In GM's new channel chain, the initial expression of interest could come via any one of a number of sources. In some markets, mailing lists were built through purchasing registration data; where this was not possible lists were purchased through brokers such as Claritas, who offer the possibility to filter those who intend to buy a car in the next 12 months. People who responded to these mailings were termed 'Responders'. A second group, 'Handraisers', consisted of those who initiated the contact by registering on a website, calling a freephone number, or taking a card from a dealership or at a motor show.

In a simple example of giving some channel choice to the consumer, these potential customers were then asked to nominate whether they preferred to receive communications by post or e-mail. Much of the outgoing communication that followed – for example, newsletters and test drive offers – could be sent electronically to those that requested it, although some other pieces, notably the Welcome Pack (provided on car purchase) and the prior-to-test-drive offer (called the Kitchen Table Pack), were delivered only in hard copy.

A further use of the online channel was the development of microsites for each model launch as an interaction and information hub. The potential of these microsites was felt to be so high that targeted mailouts were sent to post-preferring prospective customers as well as those preferring email, to drive traffic to the sites, which was also boosted through point-of-sale material, and so on. The microsites were linked to the main website for Opel, the brand under which the Vectra is sold in most of Europe, providing an opportunity for prospective customers to register.

In certain aspects of the Dialogue programme, then – for example, launch advertising – GM continued to depend largely upon one-way, high volume channels such as TV and print media. But in the subsequent phases, interactive channels were essential to elicit the key information such as the motorist's estimated replacement date (ERD) that would determine where the customer was in the buying process and what products they might be interested in. Subsequent pieces of communication could still be mass produced – for example, a newsletter designed to keep the prospect

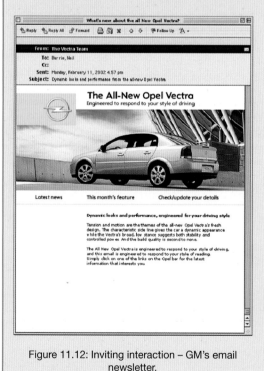

Figure 11.12: Inviting interaction – GM's email newsletter.

informed and interested – but they would only be *sent* to the consumer according to their own individual calendar, which was determined by the ERD. A requalification process gave prospective customers the opportunity to reaffirm their purchase intentions in order to keep these vital data up to date, such as the 'Check/Update your details' prompt in the email newsletter (Figure 11.12). A high proportion of consumers, feeling they were engaged in a relevant conversation, took the trouble to update these details.

A key objective of Dialogue was to supply dealers with well-qualified 'hot' leads at the point of readiness for a test drive, rather than the poor quality leads generated by non-interactive and non-relationship-based marketing campaigns. Ultimately, the programme aimed to better integrate GM's marketing with the work of this indirect sales channel.

GM made successful use of piloting and control groups to measure the effect of the Dialogue programme on sales, and found that the additional cars sold as a result of the programme were equivalent to incremental revenue of over 300 million euros and additional profit of over 50 million euros.

Individualization

The first principle is that each interaction with the customer should be *individualized*. We want to be known as an individual and treated as one. When we are, we respond enthusiastically. Not surprisingly, sales propositions which are individualized are far more effective than generic propositions which are made to every customer.

The simple tailoring of the dialogue with the customer was far from one-to-one, but it was ahead of other manufacturers within this industry which has traditionally left all customer dialogue to the dealers. And it worked in the eyes of the customer. It is proving highly influential as other car manufacturers follow suit.

Customer Value Orientation

Another key aspect of effective CRM is 'customer value orientation'. This means understanding the value of each customer, and taking this into account in the firm's dealings with the customer.

The importance of customer value orientation is illustrated by those few firms that have processes in place to calculate the true profitability of each customer. Where this can be done, it is always insightful. An example is in Figure 11.13.

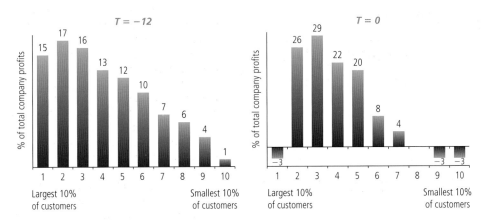

Figure 11.13: Customer profitability of large and small customers.

The chart shows the profits made from each 'decile' of customers, from the largest 10 per cent to the smallest, at two time periods 12 years apart. The trend is alarming: at the end of the 12-year period, the major customers have used their power to negotiate significant discounts simultaneous with improved service levels, so they are actually losing the company money. Channel specialists with low cost models are simultaneously serving the smallest accounts more efficiently, so they are losing money, too!

These data are crucial if the company is to take sensible decisions about how to treat each customer. Recent research by Professor Aamir Khan of Lahore University Management School finds that this customer value orientation or 'customer selectivity' is a strong driver of firm performance – stronger, in fact, than market orientation within some sectors.[1]

Customer Centricity

Customer centricity means that propositions to the customer should have the customer's best interests at heart. In common business parlance, they should be 'win–win' offers.

We have all been on the wrong end of cynical marketing which captures our money for the wrong reasons. Exorbitant charges made by one insurer to customers who wished to cancel their car insurance halfway through the year was one anger-fuelling example, damaging not just the external reputation of the firm but also internal morale. (Call centre agents would get round this restriction by advising customers to say that they were cancelling as they were buying an Aston Martin. At this point the agent would be obliged to say that as they did not cover Aston Martins, the customer would not have to pay a cancellation charge!)

There is no denying that it is possible to run a business with such cynical practices. One of the authors recalls a patisserie near Montmartre that sells beautiful-looking produce which, however, tastes disgusting. The owner has clearly calculated that the cheapest possible cooking oil, rather than butter, will do for the tourist customers who are most unlikely ever to return, however tasty the produce!

Quite apart from the ethics involved, however, the good news for the great majority who wish to go to work and earn an honest pound is that customer centricity pays. Our survey of 600 companies demonstrated that those with more customer centric cross-sell, upsell and retention practices were more profitable relative to competitors. Given the economics of lifetime value, the power of word-of-mouth and the importance of employee motivation, this is not surprising.

Dynamic Interaction

One related feature of good customer conversations is that they should be dynamic. That is, the firm should respond appropriately depending on what the customer says.

Listening, learning and responding are at the heart of normal human relationships, so it is no surprise that it is crucial in commercial encounters. A tailored direct mailing is a form of dialogue, which might be a response to something the customer said to the firm several weeks earlier, but it is hardly as dynamic as a conversation in a store, in a branch, in a sales meeting or on the telephone. Not surprisingly, therefore, these interactive channels at their best have far higher conversion rates than direct mail, which like its cousin e-mail marketing becomes less effective every year.

And yet some companies manage these 'inbound channels' as if they were direct mail encounters, providing agents with predetermined, carefully scripted prompts as to what to offer the customer. A propensity model-driven prompt to an agent is certainly better than having no insight at all, but a prompt calculated in real time during the call – taking into account the reason that the customer called up in the first place – is far more effective.

Customisation

The final feature of mature interactions is appropriate customisation of the core product or service. This is not always relevant, of course, as in some sectors, the product/service cannot be customised. But in many contexts, proactively suggesting appropriate variants of the standard offer to the customer, taking into account everything that the firm knows about them, can deeply impress the customer and differentiate the firm significantly from its peers.

CASE STUDY

O2's VISION SYSTEM

O2's Vision system is a case in point. See Figure 11.14 for the agent's screen. The bars in the top right corner show the three products that the customer is most likely to buy at this moment, based on everything that is known about the customer, including the reason for calling. The agent is not forced to talk about them, but depending on their judgement of the conversation, they are provided the tools to do so if they wish.

Because this interaction is customer centric, dynamic and individualized, it is highly effective. O2 reports conversion rates of consistently above 30%.[2]

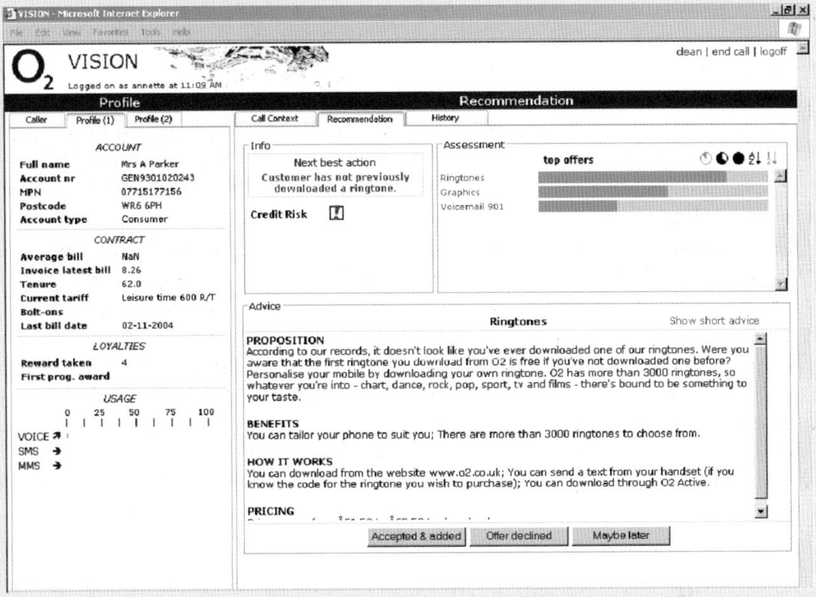

Figure 11.14: O2's vision system.

If you have never had cause to go to a Build-A-Bear Workshop store, borrow a godchild, niece or nephew and make them a tailored teddy bear. Mainly for the sake of the child, but also as an example of adding value through customisation. But keep a tissue to hand, as we challenge anyone to be unmoved by the moment when the bear is given its heart . . .

Customisation can come at a price in a higher cost of manufacture or higher cost to serve, so it is not for every category. But for experiential consumer markets such as this example, mass customisation can still be cost effective.

And in many more relational business contexts, customization is essential. The reader with business-to-business selling experience will need no persuasion on this point, but it is nevertheless insightful to see the *customer* view of the most important factors in their experience of suppliers, see Table 11.5.

While the B2C list is dominated by the customer service factors which we discussed in the previous chapter – helpfulness, valuing the customer's time, customer recognition and so on – the B2B list

B2B	B2C
1. Extent of personal contact	1. Helpfulness
2. Flexibility	2. Value for time
3. Implicit understanding of customer needs	3. Customer recognition
4. Proactivity in eliciting customer's objectives	4. Promise fulfilment
5. Pro-activity in checking that everything is OK	5. Problem solving
6. Promise fulfilment	6. Personalisation
7. Knowledge	7. Competence
	8. Accessibility

Table 11.5 What makes for a great customer experience? Comparing B2B and B2C contexts[3]

has a strong emphasis on understanding the customer's individual needs and flexibly providing a solution which meets those needs. This requires a deep understanding of the customer's business, of course, so knowledgeable staff are paramount. Whatever the contract states, what business customers really value is a supplier who cares about *their* objectives and is prepared to go to whatever lengths are necessary to solve their particular issues. The loyalty that can result from suppliers going the extra mile is incalculable.

PLANNING FOR CRM: THE BENEFITS DEPENDENCY NETWORK

Our CRM stage model demonstrates that it is not possible to move straight to world-class CRM; rather, a series of staged projects is typically needed. Even in steps, achieving CRM maturity is a major undertaking, requiring commitment from the whole organization. This is a far more complex project management task than organizing a marketing campaign. Neither can it be delegated to IT, as we have seen. The reader may be daunted as to how success can be gained.

There is no substitute for high degrees of commitment from experienced executives with consistent backing from the board. Nevertheless, a project management tool which is specifically designed for *IT-enabled* projects which deliver *business benefits* will be a significant help. A tool that many companies have reported is highly beneficial is the *benefits dependency network* (BDN). Developed by John Ward, Elizabeth Daniel and their collaborators at Cranfield and elsewhere[4], this tool works backwards from the project's objectives to ensure that all necessary business changes are made, as well as any necessary IT developments completed. A simplified example from one project the authors advised on, a gift manufacturer's extranet for retailers, is shown in Figure 11.15.

The main elements of the network are as follows:

- First, *drivers* of the project are defined. A driver is a view by top managers as to what is important for the business, such that the business needs to change in response. In this case, the drivers (which are not shown in the figure) included the directors' desire to expand beyond their current profitable but small niche, and their recognition that this would imply reducing the organization's dependence on a small number of large retailers.
- The *investment objectives* are then a clear statement of how the project under consideration will contribute to achieving effective beneficial changes in relation to one or more of the drivers. In this example, the objectives related to turnover, profit, and market share of the small retailer segment.
- In order to achieve these objectives, some *benefits* will need to be delivered to different stakeholders, including customers. These are now explicitly identified and quantified. For the gift manufacturer, these included maximizing the number of 'turns' – how often an item on a retailer's shelf is sold and replenished each year; minimizing the number of returns; and so on.
- In order to achieve the benefits, it is necessary for organizations and people to work in different ways, and it is these changes that are captured in the *business changes* part of the network. In this case, business changes included the need to offer retailers a variety of options for how stocks

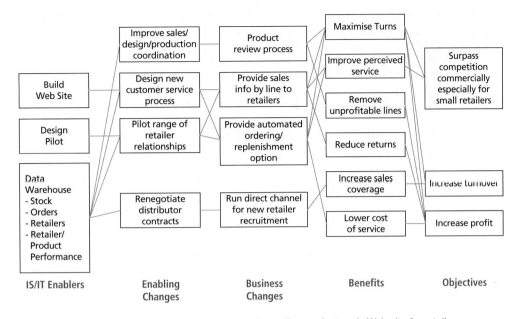

Figure 11.15: Benefits dependency network: a gift manufacturer's Web site for retailers.

would be replenished. At one end of the scale, a retailer could choose to "outsource" much of the selling of gifts to a manufacturer-provided facility on the Web site, which could select and order gifts, keep them replenished, change the gift range according to past and predicted demand, and arrange payment. At the other end of the scale, other retailers could simply choose to use information provided by the Web site to inform their own decisions on what gifts to order, when to replenish and so on. By offering a choice, the retailer was left with the important sense of control.

- Other one-off changes may also be required before the technology can be implemented, for example to define new processes which are needed, and to establish organizational roles and skills sets. These are termed *enabling changes*. Here, these included the renegotiation of contracts for the existing agent network, and a piloting exercise with a handful of retailers.
- It is only when this analysis has been carried out that specific role technology will play in project's objectives can be defined in detail. These technology changes are listed under *IS/IT enablers*. Here, they included extensions to the company's core operational systems, as well as introduction of the Web site itself.

Working with the blue-chip members of the Cranfield Customer Management Forum, we have found that using this technique for CRM projects seems to require an iterative approach. In more traditional IT projects the network is used to ensure that the technology and business changes will deliver benefits required to meet the business drivers. Given the current stage of innovation with many CRM technologies, a further iteration starting with 'what can technology enable us to do?' is needed, to explore the potential changes and consequent benefits that could result. Balancing this more creative use of the BDN with the more outcome-focused, analytical use proved valuable both in uncovering new options and in realistically assessing what could be achieved.

Although time-consuming to apply – a thorough BDN typically taking two half-day workshops – this tool is invaluable for fleshing out the business changes which are needed to make the new use of technology effective if a CRM project is to succeed. This can also lead to more rational decisions on whether to proceed with a project: in one case, a forward-looking BDN brought to light such a scale of business transformation that the company decided it could not currently afford to proceed.

What was the result of the BDN's development in this gift company? It pointed out that many of the business changes relied on the managing director, clarifying the need for a new sales appointment, which was rapidly made. It also made clear that a pilot was needed to flesh out how retailers could best be supported online, as well as how the organization needed to adapt to complement the Web site itself. Most importantly, it convinced senior management that it needed to devote enough time to the relevant business changes and that this was not purely an IT exercise.

The company had experienced considerable difficulties in the past with new computer systems, due not to the system itself as much as the accompanying organizational changes which had not been fully thought through beforehand. The level of rigour demanded by the BDN was not universally popular – salespeople rarely welcome being hauled into meetings of any sort – but the company was left well-placed to avoid a similar expensive mess.

The tool needs, though, to be used at the right point in the planning process. Notice that it is not possible to get as far as listing benefits which will be sufficient to achieve the intended objectives, let alone listing business changes, until the market is well understood and the strategic rationale for the proposed project is clear. That's why we have delayed covering this fine management tool until the end of Chapter 11! However, once a well-thought-through marketing strategy is defined, we believe the BDN to be a real contribution to the crucial issue of implementation. For further examples of applications of the BDN to CRM challenges, see the article "Justifying CRM projects in a business-to-business context: the potential of the Benefits Dependency Network" in the References to this chapter [5].

APPLICATION QUESTIONS

1. Whose responsibility is CRM in your organization? The sales and marketing director? The IT director? Or is it delegated to individual business units, with piecemeal approaches that cannot deliver a joined-up experience to the customer?
2. Most firms do not have an explicit definition of CRM. But what is the implicit definition? A software package for sales automation or outbound direct mail, perhaps? Or a customer database?
3. What stage of CRM maturity are you at? See Figure 11.4. Do your systems and processes support:
   a) Product transactions only (stage 1)?
   b) Access to integrated customer information only for marketers and other back-office staff (stage 2)?
   c) Access to integrated customer information for all front-office staff (stage 3)?
   d) Individualized, relevant conversations with every customer through every channel (stage 4)? For a more detailed diagnostic, see the exercises below.
4. Does your marketing plan include objectives and strategies relating to:
   a) customer retention by segment?
   b) cross-sales to existing customers, by segment (or key account)?
   c) customer profitability or customer lifetime value by segment (or key account)?

CHAPTER 11 REVIEW

The case for CRM

Customer acquisition is expensive. It therefore pays to retain customers for as long as possible. The longer customers stay, the more they spend and the more profit they generate. While a large part of the art of retaining customers is to deliver good products and service, customers also value proactive suggestions from the firm as to other products and services which would add value.

This relationship development in the interests of both parties requires, in all but the simplest organizations, integrated IT systems and cross-functional processes. This is the job of CRM, which we define as:

> The management of individual customer relationships across functions, channels and products so as to maximize customer satisfaction and customer lifetime value. In all but the simplest organizations, CRM is underpinned by integrated customer data.

Four stages of CRM adoption

Achieving world-class CRM is not easy. It requires the organization to develop competencies in two areas:
- *Integration maturity:* The extent to which the organization has an integrated view of each customer, supported by structures and metrics which encourage the management of customer relationships holistically across products, channels and functions.
- *Interaction maturity:* The extent to which the organization holds individualized, customer-centric conversations with its customers which the customer perceives as adding value and which optimise customer lifetime value to the firm.

Most organizations develop these competences in a series of stages – review Figure 11.4:

1. *Product transactional:* The firm has separate systems and processes for selling different products through different channels. This is transactionally adequate, but the firm cannot gain a complete view of the customer. If a firm does not seem to know us as individual customers, we tend to conclude that the firm does not care.
2. *Information access:* At this stage, a marketing database has integrated customer information. This enables analyses such as allocating customers to segments, and can also help to produce more tailored direct mail. But at this stage, front-office staff still do not have a complete view of the customer.
3. *Process efficiency:* At this stage, the firm has implemented an integrated customer database or 'CRM system'. But the promise of the system vendors that relationships would improve has only begun to be realised, because many marketing activities continue to make little use of this individualized insight.
4. *Intelligent dialogue:* At this stage, each conversation with each customer is tailored to everything that is known about the customer. Some firms manage this through one channel – Tesco with its clubcard mailings, Amazon with its online recommendations, O2 with inbound call centre interactions – but none is perfect. This is good news, as differentiation can still be gained from CRM.

Try Exercise 11.1.

Ten criteria for world-class CRM

World-class CRM requires an integrated approach to each customer, and interactions which take full account of everything that is known about the customer. The first 5 criteria for world-class CRM relate to integration:

1. *Data integration:* having a 'single customer view' of each customer across channels, products and business functions
2. *Communications integration:* having a single person responsible for coordinating all inbound and outbound communications with each customer
3. *Process integration:* ensuring that the firm's processes for responding to each customer are joined up through the customer journey, so each step leads seamlessly to the next in the eyes of the customer
4. *Structure integration:* having an organizational structure that encourages all managers and front-office staff to look after the interests of each customer holistically and hence grow their customer value
5. *Metrics integration:* having targets and reward systems which encourage all staff to look after the interests of each customer and grow their value.

The second five criteria for world-class CRM relate to interaction maturity:

6. *Individualization*: treating each customer in a way appropriate to everything which is known about them
7. *Customer value orientation*: understanding the customer's overall value to the firm, and taking this into account when determining how to treat the customer (without losing customer centricity)
8. *Customer centricity*: ensuring that every offer to the customer has the customer's best interests at heart, as well as the firm's
9. *Dynamic interaction*: responding to what the customer says or does appropriately and speedily, ideally within the same dialogue
10. *Customization*: in categories where this is relevant, tailoring the product or service to the individual customer in accordance with everything that is known about them.

Try Exercise 11.1.

Planning for CRM: the benefits dependency network

Sophisticated project management is needed to ensure the CRM projects deliver business benefits. One tool that can help to ensure this is the Benefits Dependency Network.

Try Exercise 11.2.

Questions raised for the company

1. Q: Is CRM relevant for B2B firms?
   A: Yes. Precisely the same principles apply as in B2C contexts. Firms who do not manage each customer relationship holistically, sharing knowledge about the customer across every touchpoint, and crafting individualized propositions for the customer, come across as amateur. In very few firms is client contact exclusively with a single account manager, so systems and processes are needed to share learning and coordinate communications.
2. Q: What should the marketing plan include concerning CRM?
   A: As a minimum, the plan should consider separately objectives and strategies for existing customers, with objectives and strategies for:
   - customer satisfaction and advocacy (positive word-of-mouth)
   - customer retention by segment
   - one of more share of wallet metrics, e.g. number of product holdings or total share of the customer's spend in the relevant product/service category.
   The plan might also include:
   a) Objectives and strategies for customer lifetime value by segment
   b) A project plan for improvements in the firm's CRM capabilities (see Exercise 11.2).
3. Q: How can we calculate customer lifetime value?
   A: Customer lifetime value is the profits from the customer this year and in future years, added up. But future years are 'discounted' to reflect the fact that a dollar today is worth more than a dollar next year. For detailed help, see Managing Customers Profitably by Lynette Ryals[6]. Even to calculate current-year profitability, though, is a great step forward for most companies, who might know the profitability of *products,* but rarely of customers. This requires detailed work with your accountant, but can yield great benefits in targeting resources at the right customers and avoiding over-serving of marginally profitable or loss-making customers.

EXERCISES

Exercise 11.1 profiles your firm's current level of CRM maturity. You can also use this exercise to study a firm you believe to represent best practice within your sector.

Once you have used Exercise 11.1 to determine your firm's next steps for CRM, you can use Exercise 11.2 to develop a plan for making these steps, using the benefits dependency network. This plan can be included, using the BDN diagram as a summary, in your strategic marketing plan.

EXERCISES

Exercise 11.1. Profiling your CRM maturity

Please fill in this form to assess your multichannel CRM maturity. If appropriate choose a business unit to fill it in for you.

Company/Business unit: _____

If you have several different customer groups (boxes on the market map/value network), choose *one* group and fill in the form for this group. For example, a pharmaceutical company could fill in the form for hospital specialists, primary care practitioners (GPs), patients, etc. A financial services company could fill it in for consumers, insurance brokers, company pension schemes, etc.

Customer group: _____

Step 1. Thinking of this customer group, to what extent do you agree with these statements? Please score out of 7, where 7 = 'strongly agree' and 1 = 'strongly disagree'.

Integration maturity

		Score 1–7
Q1	*Data integration:* We have integrated customer data across all products and channels, which gives us all the information we need on a customer	
Q2	*Communications integration:* We have a single person responsible for coordinating all inbound and outbound communications with each customer	
Q3	*Process integration:* Our processes for responding to each customer are joined up through the customer journey, so each step leads seamlessly to the next	
Q4	*Structure integration:* Our organizational structure encourages all staff to look after the interests of each customer holistically and grow their customer value	
Q5	*Metrics integration:* Our targets and reward systems encourage all staff to look after the interests of each customer and grow their customer value	
	Total:	
	Integration score – Divide total by 5:	

(Continued)

Interaction maturity

		Score 1–7
Q6	*Individualization:* Everything we say or write to customers is based on individual-level customer insight	
Q7	*Customer value orientation:* We understand the lifetime value of each customer and take this into account in all our dealings with them	
Q8	*Customer centricity:* We put our customers' interests first when making sales or service propositions to them	
Q9	*Dynamic interaction:* What we say or write to customers depends on what the customer has said to us within the same dialogue	
Q10	*Customization:* We tailor our products and services to customers on the basis of individual customer insight	
	Total:	
	Interaction score—Divide total by 5:	

Step 2. Plot your company/business unit on the grid below. Which stage are you nearest? Of course, all companies vary, so each stage is the centre of a 'cluster' and you may well be between stages, or stronger on integration than interaction or vice versa.

Step 3. The tables below list the aspects or dimensions of multichannel CRM maturity which we were asking about in the questions above. What do you think your company's next

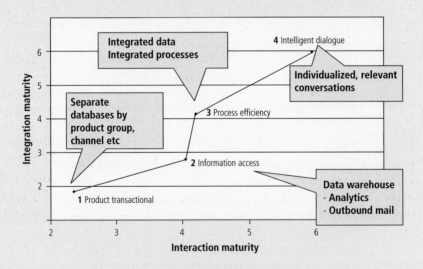

steps could be to improve your multichannel CRM maturity? Choose two or three questions/dimensions where you think you could improve your performance, and write how this might be achieved in the right hand column.

Integration maturity

	Integration dimension	How we might improve
Q1	Data integration	
Q2	Communications integration	
Q3	Process integration	
Q4	Structure integration	
Q5	Metrics integration	

Interaction maturity

	Interaction dimension	How we might improve
Q6	Individualization	
Q7	Customer value orientation	
Q8	Customer centricity	
Q9	Dynamic interaction	
Q10	Customization	

Exercise 11.2. Designing a CRM project

1. Take one or more of your 'next steps' for CRM development which you identified in Exercise 11.1. Develop a Benefits Dependency Network for how you will achieve this greater level of CRM maturity. See the section 'Planning for CRM' for an example. You will need to work in conjunction with colleagues across marketing, sales, customer service and IT in order to develop this key project management tool.
2. Now identify who is responsible for each box on the network. Note that it is not realistic for an IT director to be responsible for business changes which fall outside of the IT function!
3. Now develop measure for success for each box on the network. How will you know when objectives have been reached? When benefits have been delivered?
4. Finally, set up a project team to implement the project. Use the BDN to track not just whether each step in the project plan is achieved on time and to budget, but crucially, whether the intended benefits are being achieved. Only declare project success when this has happened.

REFERENCES

1   Khan, A. (2008) Market orientation, customer selectivity and firm performance. PhD thesis, Cranfield School of Management.

2   Bailey, C., Baines, P., Wilson, H. and Clark, M. (2009) Segmentation and customer insight in contemporary services marketing practice: why grouping customers is no longer enough. *Journal of Marketing Management*, 25(3–4) (July), 227–252.

3   Lemke, F., Clark, M. and Wilson, H. (2010) Customer experience quality: An exploration in business and consumer contexts using repertory grid technique. *Journal of Academy of Marketing Science*.

4   Ward, J. and Daniel, L. (2005) Benefits Management: Delivering value from IS & IT investments. Wiley, Chichester.

5   Wilson, H., Clark, M. and Smith, B. (2007) Justifying CRM projects in a business-to-business context: the potential of the Benefits Dependency Network. *Industrial Marketing Management*, 36(6), 770–783.

6   Ryals, L. (2008) *Managing Customer Profitably*. Wiley, Chichester.

Chapter

IMPLEMENTATION ISSUES IN MARKETING PLANNING

SUMMARY

- The implications of size and diversity on marketing planning
- The role of the chief executive in marketing planning
- The role of the planning department in marketing planning
- Organizing for marketing planning
- The marketing planning cycle
- Marketing planning timescales and horizons
- Barriers to marketing planning and how to overcome them
- Exercises to turn the theory into practice

THE IMPLICATIONS OF SIZE AND DIVERSITY ON MARKETING PLANNING

In Chapter 3, we explained some of the many myths that surround marketing planning and spelled out the conditions that must be satisfied if any company is to have an effective marketing planning system. These are:

1. Any closed-loop marketing planning system (but especially one that is essentially a forecasting and budgeting system) will lead to entropy of marketing and creativity. Therefore, there has to be some mechanism for preventing inertia from setting in through the overbureaucratization of the system.
2. Marketing planning undertaken at the functional level of marketing, in the absence of a means of integration with other functional areas of the business at general management level, will be largely ineffective.
3. The separation of responsibility for operational and strategic marketing planning will lead to a divergence of the short-term thrust of a business at the operational level from the long-term objectives of the enterprise as a whole. This will encourage a preoccupation with short-term results at operational level, which normally makes the firm less effective in the long term.

4. Unless the chief executive understands and takes an active role in marketing planning, it will never be an effective system.
5. A period of up to three years is necessary (especially in large firms) for the successful introduction of an effective marketing planning system.

Some indication of the potential complexity of marketing planning can be seen in Figure 12.1. Even in a generalized model such as this, it can be seen that, in a large diversified group operating in many foreign markets, a complex combination of product, market and functional plans is possible. For example, what is required at regional level will be different from what is required at headquarters level, while it is clear that the total corporate plan has to be built from the individual building blocks.

Furthermore, the function of marketing itself may be further functionalized for the purpose of planning, such as marketing research, advertising, selling, distribution, promotion, and so on, while different customer groups may need to have separate plans drawn up.

Let us be dogmatic about requisite planning levels. First, in a large diversified group, irrespective of such organizational issues, anything other than a systematic approach approximating to a formalized marketing planning system is unlikely to enable the necessary control to be exercised over the corporate identity.

Second, unnecessary planning, or overplanning, could easily result from an inadequate or indiscriminate consideration of the real planning needs at the different levels in the hierarchical chain.

Third, as size and diversity grow, so the degree of formalization of the marketing planning process must also increase. This can be simplified in the form of a matrix (Figure 12.2).

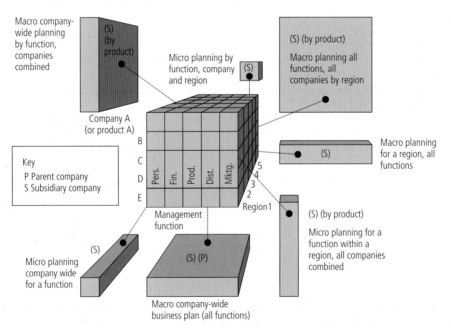

Figure 12.1: The potential complexity of marketing planning.

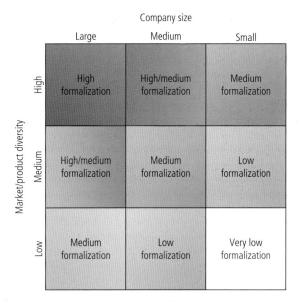

Figure 12.2: Guidelines for formulization of the marketing planning process.

The degree of formalization must increase with the evolving size and diversity of operations. However, while the degree of formalization will change, the need for a complete marketing planning system does not. The problems that companies suffer, then, are a function of either the degree to which they have a requisite marketing planning system or the degree to which the formalization of their system grows with the situational complexities attendant upon the size and diversity of operations.

It has already been stressed that central to the success of any enterprise is the objective-setting process. Connected with this is the question of the design of the planning system and, in particular, the question of who should be involved in what, and how. For example, who should carry out the situation review, state the assumptions, set marketing objectives and strategies, and carry out the scheduling and costing-out programme, and at what level?

These complex issues revolve essentially around two dimensions – the size of the company and the degree of business diversity. There are, of course, many other issues, such as whether a company is operating through subsidiary companies or through intermediaries, but these can only be considered against the background of the two major dimensions of size and diversity.

SIZE

Of these two dimensions, size of operations is, without doubt, the biggest determinant of the type of marketing planning system used.

> Size of operations is, without doubt, the biggest determinant of the type of marketing planning system used.

> In small companies, there is rarely much diversity of products or markets, and top management has an in-depth knowledge of the key determinants of success and failure.

There is usually a high level of knowledge of both the technology and the market. While in such companies the central control mechanism is the sales forecast and budget, top managers are able to explain the rationale lying behind the numbers, have a very clear view of their comparative strengths and weaknesses, and are able to explain the company's marketing strategy without difficulty. This understanding and familiarity with the strategy is shared with key operating subordinates by means of personal, face-to-face dialogue throughout the year. Subordinates are operating within a logical framework of ideas, which they understand. There is a shared understanding between top and middle management of the industry and prevailing business conditions. In such cases, since either the owner or a director is usually also deeply involved in the day-to-day management of the business, the need to rely on informational inputs from subordinates is considerably less than in larger companies. Consequently, there is less need for written procedures about marketing audits, SWOT analyses, assumptions, and marketing objectives and strategies, as these are carried out by top management, often informally at meetings and in face-to-face discussions with subordinates, the results of which are the basis of the forecasts and budgets. Written documents in respect of price, advertising, selling, and so on, are very brief, but those managers responsible for those aspects of the business know what part they are expected to play in achieving the company's objectives.

> Such companies are, therefore, operating according to a set of structured procedures, and complete the several steps in the marketing planning process, but in a relatively informal manner.

On the other hand, many small companies that have a poor understanding of the marketing concept, and in which the top manager leaves their strategy implicit, suffer many serious operational problems.

These operational problems become progressively worse as the size of company increases. As the number and level of management increase, it becomes progressively more difficult for top management to enjoy an in-depth knowledge of industry and business conditions by informal, face-to-face means. In the absence of written procedures and a structured framework, the different levels of operating management become increasingly less able to react in a rational way to day-to-day pressures. Systems of tight budgeting control, without the procedures outlined in this book, are, in the main, only successful in situations of buoyant trading conditions, are often the cause of high levels of management frustration, and are seen to be a major contributory factor in those cases where eventual decline sets in.

In general, the bigger the company, the greater is the incidence of standardized, formalized procedures for the several steps in the marketing planning process.

DIVERSITY OF OPERATIONS

From the point of view of management control, the least complex environment in which to work is an undiversified company. For the purpose of this discussion, 'undiversified' is taken to mean companies with limited product lines or homogeneous customer groups. For example, hydraulic hose could be sold to many diverse markets, or a diverse range of products could be sold into only one market such as, say, the motor industry. Both could be classified as 'undiversified'.

In such cases, the need for institutionalized marketing planning systems increases with the size of the operation, and there is a strong relationship between size and the complexity of the management task, irrespective of any apparent diversity.

MARKETING INSIGHT

For example, an oil company will operate in many diverse markets around the world, through many different kinds of marketing systems, and with varying levels of market growth and market share. In most respects, therefore, the control function for headquarters management is just as difficult and complex as that in a major, diversified conglomerate. The major difference is the greater level of in-depth knowledge which top management has about the key determinants of success and failure underlying the product or market worldwide, because of its homogeneity.

Because of this homogeneity of product or market, it is usually possible for headquarters to impose worldwide policies on operating units in respect of things such as certain aspects of advertising, public relations, packaging, pricing, trade marks, product development, and so on, whereas in the headquarters of a diversified conglomerate, overall policies of this kind tend to be impracticable and meaningless.

The view is often expressed that common planning in companies comprising many heterogeneous units is less helpful and confuses, rather than improves, understanding between operating units and headquarters. However, the truth is that conglomerates often consist of several smaller multinationals, some diversified and some not, and that the actual risk of marketing rests on the lowest level in an organization at which there is general management profit responsibility. Forecasting and budgeting systems by themselves rarely encourage anything but a short-term, parochial view of the business at these levels, and in the absence of the kind of marketing planning procedures described in this book, higher levels of management do not have a sufficiently rational basis on which to set long-term marketing objectives.

Exactly the same principles apply at the several levels of control in a diversified multinational conglomerate, in that, at the highest level of control, there has to be some rational basis on which to make decisions about the portfolio of investments. In our research, the most successful companies were those with standardized marketing planning procedures to aid this process. In such companies, there is a hierarchy of audits, SWOT analyses, assumptions, strategies and programmes, with increasingly more detail required in the procedures at the lowest levels in the organization. The precise details of each step vary according to circumstances, but the eventual output of the process is in a universally consistent form.

The basis on which the whole system rests is the informational input requirements at the highest level of command. Marketing objectives and strategies are frequently synthesized into a multidisciplinary corporate plan at the next general management profit-responsible level until, at the highest level of command, the corporate plan consists largely of financial information and summaries of the major operational activities.

This is an important point, for there is rarely a consolidated operational marketing plan at conglomerate headquarters.

This often exists only at the lowest level of general management profit responsibility, and even here it is sometimes incorporated into the corporate plan, particularly in capital goods companies, where engineering, manufacturing and technical services are major factors in commercial success.

Here, it is necessary to distinguish between short-term operational plans and long-term strategic plans, both products of the same process. Conglomerate headquarters are particularly interested in the progress of, and prospects for, the major areas of operational activities, and while obviously concerned to ensure a satisfactory current level of profitability, are less interested in the detailed short-term scheduling and costing out of the activities necessary to achieve these objectives. This, however, is a major concern at the lowest level of general management profit responsibility.

To summarize, the smaller the company, the more informal and personal the procedures for marketing planning. As company size and diversity increases, so the need for institutionalized procedures increases.

> The really important issue in any system is the degree to which it enables control to be exercised over the key determinants of success and failure.

The really important issue in any system is the degree to which it enables *control* to be exercised over the key determinants of success and failure. To a large extent, the issue, much debated in the literature, of where in an international organization responsibility for setting marketing objectives and strategies should lie, is something of a red herring. Of course, in a diversified multinational conglomerate, detailed marketing objectives and strategies for some remote country cannot be set by someone in London. It is precisely this issue, i.e. finding the right balance between the flexibility of operating units to react to changes in local market conditions and centralized control, that a formally designed system seeks to tackle.

Those companies which conform to the framework outlined here have systems which, through a hierarchy of bottom-up/top-down negotiating procedures, reach a nice balance between the need for detailed control at the lowest level of operations and centralized control. The main role of headquarters is to harness the company's strengths on a worldwide basis and to ensure that lower level decisions do not cause problems in other areas and lead to wasteful duplication.

Figure 12.3 explores four key outcomes that marketing planning can evoke. It can be seen that systems I, III and IV, i.e. where the individual is totally subordinate to a formalized system, or where individuals are allowed to do what they want without any system, or where there is neither system, nor creativity, are less successful than system II, in which the individual is allowed to be entrepreneurial within a total system. System II, then, will be an effective marketing planning system, but one in which the degree of formalization will be a function of company size and diversity.

Creativity cannot flourish in a closed-loop formalized system. There would be little disagreement that in today's abrasive, turbulent, and highly competitive environment, it is those firms that succeed in extracting entrepreneurial ideas and creative marketing programmes from systems that are necessarily yet acceptably formalized that will succeed in the long run. Much innovative flair can so easily get stifled by systems.

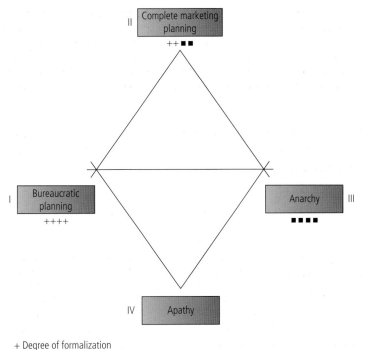

Figure 12.3: Marketing planning effectiveness model.

Certainly there is ample evidence of international companies with highly formalized systems that produce stale and repetitive plans, with little changed from year to year and that fail to point up the really key strategic issues as a result. The scandalous waste this implies is largely due to a *lack of personal intervention by key managers during the early stages of the planning cycle.*

There is clearly a need, therefore, to find a way of perpetually renewing the planning lifecycle each time around. Inertia must never set in. Without some such valve or means of opening up the loop, inertia quickly produces decay.

Such a valve has to be inserted early in the planning cycle during the audit or situation review stage. In companies with effective marketing planning systems, whether such systems are formalized or informal, the critical intervention of senior managers, from the chief executive down through the hierarchical chain, comes at the audit stage. Essentially, what takes place is a personalized presentation of audit findings, together with proposed marketing objectives and strategies and outline budgets for the strategic planning period. These are discussed, amended where necessary, and agreed in various synthesized formats at the hierarchical levels in the organization before any detailed operational planning takes place. It is at such meetings that managers are called upon to justify their views, which tends to force them to be more bold and creative than they would have been had they been allowed merely to send in their proposals. Obviously, however, even here much depends on the degree to which managers take a critical stance, which is much greater when the chief executive takes an active part in the process. *Every hour of time devoted at this stage by the chief executive has a multiplier effect throughout*

> The critical intervention of senior managers, from the chief executive down through the hierarchical chain, comes at the audit stage.

the remainder of the process. And let it be remembered we are not, repeat not, talking about budgets at this juncture in anything other than outline form.

Until recently, it was believed that there may well be fundamental differences in marketing planning approaches, depending on factors such as the type of business-to-business goods and markets involved, company size, the degree of dependence on international sales, and the methods used to market goods abroad. In particular, the much debated role of headquarters management in the marketing planning process is frequently put forward as being a potential cause of great difficulty.

> One of the most encouraging findings to emerge from our research is that the theory of marketing planning is universally applicable, and that such issues are largely irrelevant.

While the planning task is less complicated in small, undiversified companies, and there is less need for formalized procedures than in large, diversified companies, the fact is that exactly the same framework should be used in all circumstances, and that this approach brings similar benefits to all.

In a multinational conglomerate, headquarters management is able to assess major trends in products and markets around the world, and is thus able to develop strategies for investment, expansion, diversification and divestment on a global basis. For their part, subsidiary management can develop appropriate strategies with a sense of locomotion towards the achievement of coherent overall goals.

This is achieved by means of synthesized information flows from the bottom upwards, which facilitates useful comparison of performance around the world, and the diffusion of valuable information, skills, experiences and systems from the top downwards. The particular benefits which accrue to companies using such systems can be classified under the major headings of the marketing mix elements as follows:

- *Marketing information* – there is a transfer of knowledge, a sharing of expertise and an optimization of effort around the world.
- *Product* – control is exercised over the product range. Maximum effectiveness is gained by concentrating on certain products in certain markets, based on experience gained throughout the world.
- *Price* – pricing policies are sufficiently flexible to enable local management to trade effectively, while the damaging effects of interaction are considerably mitigated.
- *Place* – substantial gains are made by rationalization of the supply chain management function.
- *Promotion* – duplication of effort and a multitude of different platforms/company images are ameliorated. Efforts in one part of the world reinforce those in another.

The procedures which facilitate the provision of such information and knowledge transfers also encourage operational management to think strategically about their own areas of responsibility, instead of managing only for the short term.

It is abundantly clear that it is through a marketing planning system and planning skills that such benefits are achieved, and that discussions such as those about the standardization *process* are largely irrelevant. Any standardization that may be possible will become clear only if a company can successfully develop a system for identifying the needs of each market and each segment in which it operates, and for organizing resources to satisfy those needs in such a way that best resource utilization results worldwide.

The Role of the Chief Executive in Marketing Planning

Our research showed that few chief executives have a clear perception of:

- purposes and methods of planning
- proper assignment of planning responsibilities throughout the organization
- proper structures and staffing of the planning department
- the talent and skills required in an effective planning department.

The role of the chief executive is generally agreed as being:

- to define the organizational framework
- to ensure the strategic analysis covers critical factors
- to maintain the balance between short- and long-term results
- to display his or her commitment to planning
- to provide the entrepreneurial dynamic to overcome bureaucracy
- to build this dynamic into the planning operation (motivation).

In respect of planning, the chief executive's principal role is to open up the planning loop by means of personal intervention. The main purpose of this is to act as a catalyst for the entrepreneurial dynamic within the organization, which can so easily decay through bureaucratization. This is not sufficiently recognized in the literature.

When considering this in the context of the reasons for failures of marketing planning systems, it is clear that, for any system to be effective, the chief executive requires to be conversant with planning techniques and approaches, and to be committed to and take part in the marketing planning process.

The Role of the Planning Department in Marketing Planning

This raises the important question of the role of the planning department, which is:

- to provide the planning structure and systems
- to secure rapid data transmission in the form of intelligence
- to act as a catalyst in obtaining inputs from operating divisions
- to forge planning links across organizational divisions, e.g. R and D and marketing
- to evaluate plans against the chief executive's formulated strategy
- to monitor the agreed plans.

The planner is a coordinator who sees that the planning is done – not a formulator of goals and strategies.

The planner's responsibility has three basic dimensions. They are:

1. Directive
2. Supportive
3. Administrative.

In the *directive* role, the planning executive acts on behalf of top management to supervise the planning procedure to promote orderly and disciplined implementation of the planning process. This function can be performed well only when managers have both the *ability* and *willingness* to make it happen. The planning executive is likely to be more effective by acting in a *supportive*, rather than in a *directive*, role.

A *supportive* role brings the planning executive into service as an internal consultant and advisory resource. In this role, the planning executive:

- advises line management on the application of planning principles
- assembles background information to provide insight into the economy, industries, markets, investment alternatives, etc. which are relevant to each business served

- directs or supports forecasting of the economy, industries and end-user markets
- renders assistance in installing progress-monitoring systems and interpreting their output
- renders assistance to line executives in applying advanced methods and procedures
- provides other internal and consulting assistance to line managers in preparing their plans and monitoring their progress.

In their *administrative* role, planners ensure that planning procedures are implemented on schedule and that communications are accurate and rapid. In this role, it is suggested that they have limitations. They can provide coordinating and communicating services, but they cannot enforce them. If line management does not participate willingly, someone else with the appropriate authority must take corrective or disciplinary action.

Again, when this is taken in the context of the failures of marketing planning systems, it is clear that an understanding of the proper role of the planning department is an important determinant of planning success.

The Marketing Planning Cycle

The schedule should call for work on the plan for the next year to begin early enough in the current year to permit adequate time for market research and analysis of key data and market trends. In addition, the plan should provide for the early development of a strategic plan that can be approved or altered in principle.

A key factor in determining the planning cycle is bound to be the degree to which it is practicable to extrapolate from sales and market data, but, generally speaking, successful planning companies start the planning cycle formally somewhere between nine and six months from the beginning of the next fiscal year.

It is not necessary to be constrained to work within the company's fiscal year; it is quite possible to have a separate marketing planning schedule if that is appropriate, and simply organize the aggregation of results at the time required by the corporate financial controller.

Planning Horizons

It is clear that, in the past, one- and five-year planning periods have been by far the most common, although three years has now become the most common period for the strategic plan, largely because of the dramatically increasing rate of environmental change. Lead time for the initiation of major new product innovations, the length of time necessary to recover capital investment costs, the continuing availability of customers and raw materials, and the size and usefulness of existing plant and buildings are the most frequently mentioned reasons for having a five-year planning horizon. Increasingly, however, these five-year plans are taking the form more of 'scenarios' than the detailed strategic plan outlined in this book.

Many companies, however, do not give sufficient thought to what represents a sensible planning horizon for their particular circumstances. First, a five-year time span is clearly too long for some companies, particularly those with highly versatile machinery operating in volatile fashion-conscious markets. The effect of this is to rob strategic plans of reality. A five-year horizon is often chosen largely because of its universality. Second, some small subsidiaries in large conglomerates are often asked to forecast for seven, 10 and, sometimes, 15 years ahead, with the result that they tend to become meaningless exercises. While it might make sense for, say, a glass manufacturer to produce 12-year plans (or scenarios) because of the very long lead time involved in laying down a new furnace, it does not make sense to impose the same planning timescale on small subsidiaries operating in totally different markets, even though they are in the same group. This places unnecessary burdens on operating management and tends to rob the whole strategic planning process of credibility.

The conclusion to be reached is that there is a natural point of focus into the future, beyond which it is pointless to look. This point of focus is a function of the relative size of a company.

Small companies, because of their size and the way they are managed, tend to be comparatively flexible in the way in which they can react to environmental turbulence in the short term. Large companies, on the other hand, need a much longer lead time in which to make changes in direction. Consequently, they tend to need to look further into the future and use formalized systems for this purpose so that managers throughout the organization have a common means of communication.

ORGANIZING FOR MARKETING PLANNING

The purpose of this brief section is not to delve into the complexities of organizational forms, but to put the difficult process of marketing planning into the context of the relevant environment in which it will be taking place. The point is that you start from where you *are*, not from where you would like to be, and it is a fact of business that marketing means different things in different circumstances. It is not our intention here to recommend any one particular organizational form. Rather, it is to point out some of the more obvious organizational issues and their likely effect on the way marketing planning is carried out. As a result of the seemingly permanent debate surrounding organizational forms, one of the authors carried out a research study over a two-year period between 1987 and 1989, taking great care in the process to read the literature on the subject of marketing planning.

The interesting fact to emerge was that most approaches to the subject concentrated almost exclusively on the 'medicine' itself and showed relatively little concern for the 'patient' (if indeed the company can be viewed as being ill and in need of attention).

That this should happen makes about as much sense as a doctor dispensing the same drug to every patient, irrespective of his or her condition. Certainly, the treatment might help a proportion of the clients, but for a vast number it will be at best irrelevant and, at worst, perhaps even dangerous.

In the case of those promoting the 'marketing planning nostrum', it is particularly ironic to observe how the product has somehow become more important than the customer. Whatever happened to all that good advice about focusing on customers and their situations?

What must be recognized is that there has to be a symbiotic relationship between the patient and the cure. It is the two working together which brings success. Similarly, the 'doctor', if the third-party adviser might be described as such, must be more prepared to take a holistic approach to the situation. Instead of writing an instant prescription, the doctor should first find out more about the patient.

Since the research study referred to above set out to consider how marketing planning might be introduced more effectively into organizations, let us remember that, like the good doctor, we are going to try to understand more about our patients.

ORGANIZATIONAL LIFE PHASES

At first sight, every organization appears to be quite different from any other, and, of course, in many ways it is. Its personnel and facilities can never exist in the same form elsewhere. Its products, services, history and folklore also play their part in creating a unique entity.

Yet it is also possible to look at organizations in another way and find that instead of uniqueness, there are also similarities.

What, then, is this commonality all organizations share? As companies grow and mature, it seems that they all experience a number of distinct life phases. Certainly, our research experience has convinced us that, once the phases of corporate life are explained to managers, they can readily position their own company on its lifeline.

The significance of this is that the senior executives can then understand the nature of their company's growing pains and how these might contribute to current operational problems and even to a particular organizational culture.

Moreover, sometimes this culture will be most receptive to marketing planning, at other times less so. Equally, the marketing planning process itself might need to be modified to sit more comfortably within a given corporate culture.

For now, however, let us look at the way companies grow and develop. First, as firms grow in sales, so they tend to go through an organizational evolution. Figure 12.4 shows a firm starting off its existence and growing in turnover over a period of time.

When such a firm starts off, it is often organized totally around the owner who tends to know more about customers and products than anyone else in the company.

This organizational form can be represented as in Figure 12.5, with all decisions and lines of communication revolving around one person. The point here is that formalized marketing planning by means of systems and written procedures will certainly be less relevant than in, say, a diversified multinational.

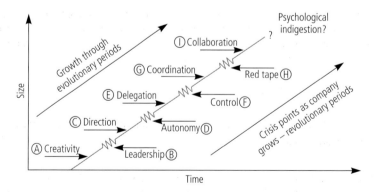

Figure 12.4: Organizational life phases.

(Source: L.E. Greiner (1972) Evolution and revolution as organizations grow. *Harvard Business Review*, July/August.)

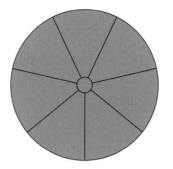

Figure 12.5: Sole owner organizational structure.

Figure 12.6: Functional organizational structure.

The First Crisis and the Solution

However, as this firm grows in size and complexity, as new products and new markets are added, this organizational form begins to break down and the first crisis appears, which is resolved in one of two ways. Either the owner/entrepreneur sells the business and retires or starts up again, or he or she adopts the more traditional organizational form with which most of us are familiar (Figure 12.6) in which certain functional duties are allocated to individuals to manage by means of their own specialized departments. Some aspects of the work will need to be delegated and systems and procedures will have to be developed to replace the ad-hoc arrangements of the initial phase. Above all, organizational loose ends have to be tidied up and a new sense of purpose and direction instilled in the employees.

> Thus, a strong leader is required to bring the company out of the leadership crisis phase and into the next, relatively calm period of directed evolution.

Here, the leader, who may by now no longer be the founder, directs events from a centralized position. He or she presides over a hierarchical organizational structure which is set up to achieve what the leader prescribes. Again, steady growth can accompany this phase of corporate life until another crisis point is reached. This is the so-called 'autonomy crisis'.

The Second Crisis and the Solution

> Eventually the company will reach a certain size or complexity at which the directive leadership is no longer so appropriate.

Individuals working in their particular spheres of activity know more than the central authority. Not only do they resent being told what to do by someone they perceive to be 'out of touch', they actually want to have more personal autonomy to influence company policies and operations. The struggle for power at the 'autonomy crisis' can be accompanied by a tightening of central control, which, in turn, exacerbates the problem, causing poor morale and even, perhaps, high staff turnover.

The crisis is eventually resolved by the company providing a much more delegative style of leadership, which does, in fact, generate more autonomy at lower levels. Again a relatively trouble-free, evolutionary growth period follows from this delegated style.

The Third Crisis and the Solution

However, as growth continues, senior management become increasingly concerned about the high levels of autonomy lower down the organization. They experience feelings of powerlessness and sense the need to regain control.

This control crisis can be another very destabilizing phase of the company's development. Understandable though the feelings of impotence might be for senior management, it seems to be very difficult to turn the clock back to a directive style again. Too much has happened in the intervening years.

The solution to the control crises seems to be to embark upon a programme for establishing better coordination between the various parts of the organization.

This is often achieved by using such mechanisms as formal planning procedures, centralizing some technical functions, but leaving daily operating decisions at the local level, setting up special projects involving lower-level employees, and so on. Thus, another period of relative calm comes with the coordinated evolutionary phase of development.

The Fourth Crisis and the Solution

With continued growth, there is a tendency for the coordinating practices to become institutionalized, thus planning procedures become ritualized, special projects become meaningless chores and too many decisions seem to be governed by company rules and regulations.

A new crisis point has been reached – the 'bureaucracy' or 'red-tape' crisis. Procedures seem to take precedence over problem solving.

The only solution seems to be for the company to strive towards a new phase of collaboration in which, once again, the contributions of individuals and teams are valued as much, if not more, than systems and procedures.

There has to be a concerted effort to re-energize and re-personalize operating procedures. More emphasis has to be put on teamwork, spontaneity and creativity.

If a company can win through to the collaborative phase of evolution then, again, a period of relatively trouble-free growth can be expected as a reward. However, as we have seen, this pattern of evolutionary growth followed by a crisis appears to be ever-repeating.

Each solution to an organizational development problem brings with it the seeds of the next crisis phase.

The Fifth Crisis?

Thus it is that the collaborative evolutionary crisis will probably end when there is a surfeit of integrating mechanisms and, perhaps, employees begin to lose the ability to function independently.

This last point is purely conjecture, because not many companies seem to have moved far enough along their biographical lifeline for this to be an issue. But from the work we have completed in a number of companies, this idea of company life phases has helped us to understand much more about a client's operating problems and how we might more suitably provide help.

Centralization or Decentralization?

Within this second phase of growth, there are basically two kinds of organization, which can be described as either *decentralized* or *centralized*, with several combinations within each extreme.

Looking first at decentralization, it is possible to represent this diagrammatically as in Figure 12.7. The shaded area of the triangle represents the top-level strategic management of the firm. It can be seen from this diagram that the central services, such as market research and public relations, are repeated at the subsidiary company level. It can also be seen that there is a strategic level of management at the subsidiary level, the acid test being whether subsidiary company/unit top management can introduce new products without reference to headquarters.

The point about this kind of decentralized organizational structure is that it leads inevitably to duplication of effort and differentiation of strategies, with all the consequent problems, unless a major effort is made to get some synergy out of the several systems by means of a company-wide planning system.

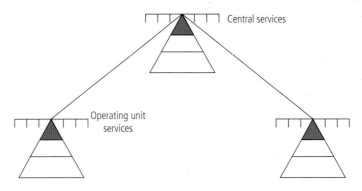

Figure 12.7: Decentralized organization structure.

MARKETING INSIGHT

One telecommunications company had a range of 1,500 products, and one of those products had 1,300 different variations, all of which was the result of a totally decentralized marketing-orientated approach in the subsidiary companies. It was not surprising that any sensible economies of scale in production were virtually impossible, with the result that the company made a substantial loss.

The same problems apply to marketing research, advertising, pricing, distribution, and other business areas. When someone takes the trouble to find out, it is often very salutary to see the reaction of senior managers at headquarters when they are told, for example, that the very same market problem is being researched in many different countries around the world, all at enormous expense.

MARKETING INSIGHT

It is this kind of organizational structure which, above all others, requires strong central coordination by means of some kind of planning system, otherwise everyone wastes enormous amounts of corporate resources striving to maximize their own small part of the business.

If, however, some system can be found of gaining synergy from all the energy expended, then the rewards are great indeed. The point is that marketing in this kind of system means something different from marketing in other kinds of system, and it is as well to recognize this from the outset.

A centrally controlled company tends to look as depicted in Figure 12.8. Here it will be seen that there is no *strategic* level of management in the subsidiary units, particularly in respect of new product introductions. This kind of organizational form tends to lead to standardized strategies, particularly in respect of product management. For example, when a new product is introduced, it tends to be designed at the outset with as many markets as possible in mind, while the benefits from market research in one area are passed on to other areas, and so on.

The problem here, of course, is that unless great care is exercised, subsidiary units can easily become less sensitive to the needs of individual markets, and hence lose flexibility in reacting to competitive moves.

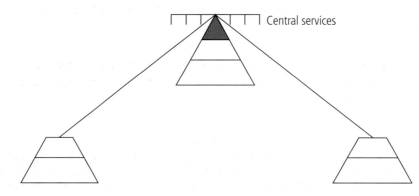

Figure 12.8: A centrally-controlled organization structure.

The point here, again, is that marketing in this kind of system means something different from marketing in the kind of system described above.

There is a difference between financial manipulation and business management in respect of the headquarters role. There is a difference between a corporation and its individual components, and often there is confusion about what kind of planning should be done by managers at varying levels in the organization, such confusion arising because the chief executive has not made it clear what kind of business is being managed.

We have looked briefly at two principal organizational forms, both of which consist essentially of a central office and various decentralized divisions, each with its own unique products, processes and markets which complement the others in the group. In enterprises of this type, planning within the divisions applies to the exploration of markets and improved efficiency within the boundaries laid down by headquarters. The problems and opportunities that this method throws up tend to make the headquarters role one of classifying the boundaries for the enterprise as a whole, in relation to new products and markets that do not appear to fall within the scope of one of the divisions.

In this type of organization, the managers of affiliated companies are normally required to produce the level of profit set by headquarters management within the constraints imposed on them, and such companies need to institutionalize this process by providing a formal structure of ideas and systems so that operating management know what they are expected to do and whether they are doing the essential things.

> The point about these kinds of organization seems to be that some method has to be found of planning and controlling the growth of the business in order to utilize effectively the evolving skills and growing reputation of the firm, and so avoid an uncontrolled dissipation of energy.

It is probably easier to do this in a centrally organized firm, but, as we have pointed out, both organizational forms have their disadvantages.

Finally, the *financial trust* type of organization needs to be mentioned briefly, in which the primary concern of central management is the investment of shareholders' capital in various businesses. The buying and selling of interests in various firms is done for appreciation of capital rather than for building an enterprise with any logic of its own. Planning in this type of operation requires different knowledge and skills, and addresses itself to kinds of problems that are different from those in the two organizational forms described above.

Organizing for Marketing at Board Level

Before going on to describe marketing planning systems, there are two further points worth making briefly about organizing for marketing.

> The first is that where marketing and sales are separated at board level, marketing planning is going to be a very different kind of activity from a situation in which both functions are coordinated at board level.

Figure 12.9 illustrates these two different situations.

In the first of these organizational forms, marketing is very much a staff activity, with the real power vested in the sales organization. While a strong chief executive can ensure that the two activities are sensibly coordinated, unfortunately this rarely happens effectively because he or she is often too busy with production, distribution, personnel, and financial issues to devote enough time to sales

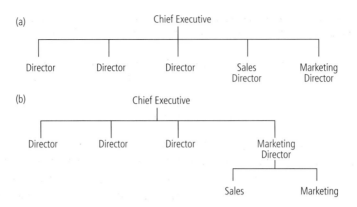

Figure 12.9: Sales and marketing separated and combined.

and marketing. The point here is that a sales force is quite correctly concerned with *today's* products, problems, customers, and so on, while a marketing manager needs to be thinking about the *future*. The sales force is also quite correctly concerned mainly with *individual* products, problems and customers, while a marketing manager needs to be thinking about *groups* of products and customers (portfolio management and market segmentation).

> The two jobs are closely connected, but fundamentally different, and great care is necessary to ensure that what the marketing department is *planning* is the same as what the sales force is actually *doing* in the field. All too often they are not.

The second kind of organizational form tends to make it easier to ensure a sensible coordination between planning and doing.

> The second and final point about marketing organizational forms is that there are a number of issues that all firms have to address.

These are:

* functions (such as advertising, market research, pricing, and so on)
* products
* markets
* geographical locations
* channels.

> Of these, most firms would readily agree that, in most cases, the two main issues are *products* and *markets*, which is why many companies have what are called 'product managers' and/or 'market managers'.

There can be no right or wrong answer to the question of which of these is the better, and common sense will dictate that it is market circumstances alone that will determine which is most appropriate for any one company.

Each has its strengths and weaknesses. A product manager-orientated system will ensure good strong product orientation, but can also easily lead to superficial market knowledge.

MARKETING INSIGHT

Many a company has been caught out by subtle changes in their several markets causing a product to become practically redundant. In consumer goods, for example, many companies are beginning to admit that their rigid product/brand management system has allowed their major customers to take the initiative, and many are now changing belatedly to a system where the focus of marketing activity revolves around major customer/market groups rather than individual products.

On the other hand, a market manager-orientated system can easily result in poor *overall* product development.

Ideally, therefore, whatever organizational form is adopted, the two central issues of products and markets constantly need to be addressed. This conundrum can be summarized in the following brief case study.

Northern Sealants Limited manufactures a range of adhesives that fall into two main categories: seals and sealants. The company supplies these products to a large number of markets. However, the main users come under four industry headings: gas, oil and petrochemical refineries; automative; electrical; and OEM. *Advise how the marketing function should be organized.*

Figure 12.10 illustrates this case diagrammatically in what is often referred to as a matrix organization. Figure 12.11 puts this structure into the context of this particular company. Here, it will be seen that, organizationally, Northern Sealants has both a product management and a market management structure. The basic role of the product manager is to ensure that the aspects of the product are properly managed, while the role of the market manager is to pay particular attention to the needs of the market. Close liaison between the two is obviously necessary and a basic principle of this kind of organization is that ultimate authority for the final decision *must* be vested in either one or the other. Even when this is done, however, communications can still be difficult, and great care is necessary to ensure that vested interests are not allowed to dominate the real product/market issues.

Organizing for Marketing Planning at the Operational Level

In our experience, the very best marketing plans emerge from an *inclusive* process. Fundamentally, marketing planning is simply a process, with a set of underlying tools and techniques, for understanding markets and for quantifying the present and future value required by the different groups of customers within these markets – what marketers refer to as segments. It is a strictly specialist function, just like accountancy or engineering, which is proscribed, researched, developed and examined by professional bodies such as the Chartered Institute of Marketing in Europe and Asia and the American

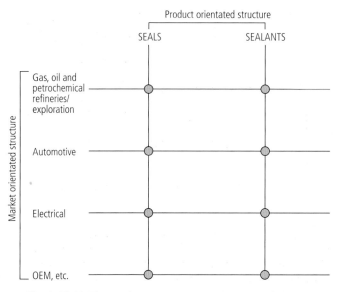

Figure 12.10: The product market range of Northern Sealants

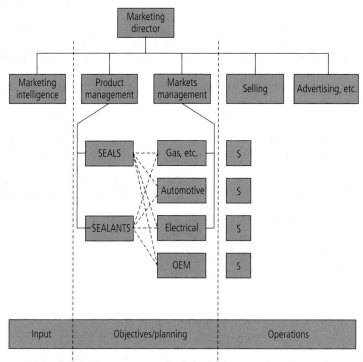

Figure 12.11: The organization structure of Northern Sealants.

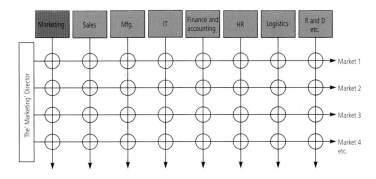

Figure 12.12: Organizing for marketing planning.

Marketing Association in the USA. Sometimes customer-facing activities such as customer service, selling, product development and public relations are controlled by the marketing function, but often they are not, even though many of them are included in the academic marketing curriculum.

In the model in Figure 12.12, representatives from appropriate functions are members of marketing planning teams, with the main body of work being done by the marketing representative who has the professional skills to accomplish the more technical tasks of data and information gathering and market analysis. The team might also include a representative from product development, brand managers, key account managers, and so on, depending on circumstances.

The advantages of this approach are as follows:

1. Any plans emerging are based on a deep understanding of the organization's asset base and capabilities.
2. Members of the team 'own' the plan, thus preventing implementation problems later on.
3. The marketing director, or whoever is responsible to the board for integrating and coordinating all the plans emanating from this process, can be sure that he or she is not foisting unwanted plans onto reluctant functional heads.
4. Any strategic functional plans, such as IT, logistics, purchasing, R and D, and so on, will be genuinely market driven or customer needs driven rather than production driven.
5. Any business or corporate plans that emerge at a higher level will also be market driven.

But this is not how most organizations plan for creating superior value. Too often marketing plans emerge from a marketing 'department' and are developed in isolation and largely ignored by the power brokers.

To summarize, no one particular organizational form can be recommended, common sense and market needs being the final arbiters. However, the following factors *always* need to be considered:

- marketing 'centres of gravity'
- interface areas (e.g. present/future; salespeople/drawing office; etc.)
- authority and responsibility
- ease of communication
- coordination
- flexibility
- human factors.

Wherever practicable, however, it appears to be sensible to try to organize around customer groups, or markets, rather than around products, functions or geography. Increasingly, firms are organizing themselves around customers or around processes, such as product development. Quite a large 'industry', known as Business Process Redesign (BPR), has grown up around this issue. The Cranfield/Chartered Institute of Marketing research study into the future of marketing has clearly demonstrated

> The world's leading companies now organize themselves around customer groups and processes rather than around products.

that the world's leading companies now organize themselves around customer groups and processes rather than around products. Computer firms, such as AT&T for example, organize around end-use markets and appoint multidisciplinary teams to focus their attention on their specific needs. The result is personnel, accounting, production, distribution and sales policies that are tailored specifically to a unique set of market needs.

While this team-building approach has gone a long way towards overcoming this kind of organizational barrier, of much more importance is to get the task of defining strategic business units (SBUs) right. Let us repeat the definition of an SBU:

A strategic business unit:

- will have common segments and competitors for most of its products
- is a competitor in an external market
- is a discrete, separate and identifiable unit
- will have a manager who has control over most of the areas critical to success.

But SBUs are not necessarily the same as operating units, and the definition can, and should, be applied all the way down to a particular product, or customer, or group of products or customers, and it is here that the main marketing planning task lies.

What is certain is that one of the major determinants of the effectiveness of any marketing planning which is attempted within a company will be the way that it organizes for marketing. The purpose of this section has been to point out some of the more obvious facts and pitfalls before attempting to outline a marketing planning system, to which we can turn in the final chapter.

THE MARKETING PLANNING PROCESS AND CORPORATE CULTURE

Assuming that marketing planning is acceptable at something deeper than a cosmetic level, it becomes possible to see how the process aligns with different phases of the company's lifeline.

Creative Evolution Phase

In our research, we did not find a single marketing planner at this stage of development. Most of the companies were still really formulating their business ideas and the senior executive was in close touch with customers and the company's own staff. The organization had a high level of flexibility to respond to changes in customer needs. In our research, many of these companies were showing high growth and to introduce marketing planning did not appear to offer any additional benefits.

It has to be recognized that some companies do not have a sufficiently good product or service to develop very far along their life path. The infant mortality rate for businesses is very high.

However, if the company successfully negotiates this initial phase, eventually it reaches the leadership crisis. As we have seen, a strong leader is required who will provide the drive and direction which will lead to the next evolutionary phase.

Directed Evolution

Companies at this stage of development fall into two camps. Naturally enough, the underlying style behind the marketing planning process was directive in each case, but the impact and effectiveness was significantly different for each type.

The first type we have referred to as 'Directed Marketing Planning Type 1'. Here, the senior executive took responsibility or delegated the task of producing a marketing plan. This person would then spend time analysing data, performing a situational review, and so on, until he or she finished up with a document. Generally, an approving mechanism was built into the process. For example, the board of directors would have to vet the marketing plan before it could be issued, but by and large thereafter the plan acts as a directive for the organization.

The second type – 'Directed Marketing Planning Type 2' – involved the appropriate member of staff being told what information to provide about their areas of work, the form in which the information should be provided, and so on.

Thus, in this case, rather than the plan being directed, the process is spelt out carefully. The resulting information is assembled at a senior level and the resulting planning document is issued as before.

Although in both cases all the creative thinking and control takes place at the top level of the organization, the second method holds a prospect of generating more useful data without sacrificing the directive, power-based culture.

Delegated Evolution

As a solution to the autonomy crisis which can develop when directive leadership becomes inappropriate, more delegation becomes an operational feature of organizations.

What seemed to be a problem for marketing planning in these companies was that people in the 'front line', or operating units, of large companies were expected to produce marketing plans, but without very much guidance.

MARKETING INSIGHT

For example, one company had to send its marketing plans to head office, where they were rigorously examined and then given the corporate thumbs up or down. Only through a process of acceptance or dismissal were the criteria for 'good' plans eventually pieced together.

Our conclusion was that a delegated form of marketing planning can lead to some very high quality inputs and certainly to high levels of commitment on behalf of those involved. Yet, ultimately, the solely bottom-up planning procedures seem to be difficult to integrate and can be demotivating to those involved. Somehow, the sum of the parts is less in stature than it ought to be.

Coordinated Evolution

At this stage, the lessons of the directed and delegated phases seem to have been learned. There is much more emphasis on a plan for planning and a means to incorporate top-down direction and bottom-up quality.

Equally, a coordinated approach enables the company to make best use of its specialized resources and to generate commitment from the staff.

In many ways, the marketing planning processes which are the stuff of textbooks, and so on, appear to be most suited for a company at this stage of its development.

However, as we have seen, it is possible for the planning process to degenerate from essentially a problem-solving process into a fairly meaningless, bureaucratic ritual. It is at this stage that the planning process will become counterproductive.

Collaborative Evolution

Here, the bureaucracy has to make way for genuine problem solving again. At present we do not have very much evidence about what this means in practice. But it is possible to speculate that, as business environments change at an ever-increasing pace, so new marketing planning procedures might need to be developed.

Creativity and expediency would appear to be the passwords to this new phase of development.

CONCLUSIONS

We have shown how the acceptance of marketing planning is largely conditioned by the stage of development of the organization and the corporate culture. Thus it is that different modes of marketing planning become more appropriate at different phases of the company's life.

While the marketing planning process itself remains more or less consistent throughout, *how* that process is managed must be congruent with the current organizational culture. The alternative to this would be to take steps to change the company culture and make it more amenable to a particular planning process.

Since culture tends to act to maintain the existing power structure and the *status quo*, marketing planning interventions in companies must be recognized as having a 'political' dimension and are not purely educational. Not least among the political issues is the question of whether or not a company's management style can adapt sufficiently to enable the marketing planning process to deliver the rewards it promises.

Can managers who have led a company down a particular path suddenly change track? In other words, is it possible for frogs to change into princes?

The iconoclastic books would claim that they can, because this is a much more optimistic message with which to sell copies. However, those who have carried out academic research, or are experienced consultants, would have some reservations.

We remain open-minded about this issue, believing that, if the business pressures on a company are sufficient, intelligent behaviour will win the day. We might be proved wrong, but, in the meantime, this chapter provides some useful messages for both marketing advisers and senior executives of companies.

While we see our research as being an important step along the road to effective marketing planning, we are also realistic enough to recognize that there is still far to travel.

HOW THE MARKETING PLANNING PROCESS WORKS

There is one other major aspect to be considered. It concerns the requisite location of the marketing planning activity in a company. The answer is simple to give.

Marketing planning should take place as near to the marketplace as possible in the first instance, but such plans should then be reviewed at high levels within an organization to see what issues have been overlooked.

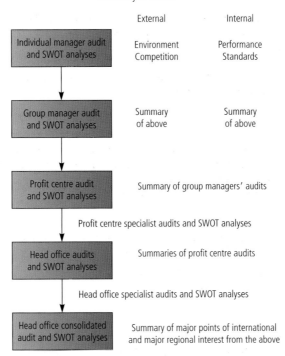

Hierarchy of audits

	External	Internal
Individual manager audit and SWOT analyses	Environment Competition	Performance Standards
Group manager audit and SWOT analyses	Summary of above	Summary of above
Profit centre audit and SWOT analyses	Summary of group managers' audits	
	Profit centre specialist audits and SWOT analyses	
Head office audits and SWOT analyses	Summaries of profit centre audits	
	Head office specialist audits and SWOT analyses	
Head office consolidated audit and SWOT analyses	Summary of major points of international and major regional interest from the above	

Figure 12.13: A hierarchy of audits.

It has been suggested that each manager in the organization should complete an audit and SWOT analysis on their own area of responsibility. The only way that this can work in practice is by means of a *hierarchy* of audits. The principle is simply demonstrated in Figure 12.13.

This illustrates the principle of auditing at different levels within an organization. The marketing audit format will be universally applicable. It is only the detail that varies from level to level and from company to company within the same group. For example, any one single company can specify without too much difficulty the precise headings under which information is being sought.

In the case of an industrial lubricants company, under an assessment of the market environment, information and commentary were required on capital investment schemes, foreign investments, economic growth rates, health and safety regulations (clearly important in this market), inflation rates, tariff protection, etc. together with an assessment of their effect on the lubricants market.

Under the heading 'market', key product groups and key market sectors were defined (in this case the British Standard Industrial Classification System was used). It was left to each subsidiary to specify what the particular key industries were in their particular territories. Data sheets were provided for this purpose.

In the case of the competitive and the internal audit, each operating unit was merely asked to provide, for each major product, its strengths and weaknesses and those of competitive products; likewise for opportunities and threats. To assist with this process, a checklist was provided which included, *inter alia*, international approvals from original equipment manufacturers, compliance with health and safety regulations, and so on. Some data sheets were provided for market share analysis by key industry, pricing against competitive products, etc.

At each operating level, this kind of information can be gathered by means of the hierarchy of audits illustrated in Figure 12.13 with each manager completing an audit for his or her area of account-ability. While the overall format can be universal for a large and diversified group, uniformity is only necessary for units engaged in like activities. The advantages which accrue to the several headquarters levels are substantial in terms of measuring worldwide potential for products and market segments. Without such an information-collecting vehicle, it is difficult to formulate any overall strategic view.

It has to be recognized that information and data are not always readily available in some parts of the world in the sort of format which is required, but given training, resources and understanding between headquarters and units, it is surprising how quickly information links can be forged which are of inestimable value to both sides. The same is also true of agents and distributors, who quickly respond to the give and take of such relationships in respect of audit-type information, which they inevitably find valuable for their own business.

Since, in anything but the smallest of undiversified companies, it is not possible for top manage-ment to set detailed objectives for operating units, it is suggested that at this stage in the planning process, strategic guidelines should be issued. One way of doing this is in the form of a strategic plan-ning letter. Another is by means of a personal briefing by the chief executive at 'kick-off' meetings. As in the case of the audit, these guidelines would proceed from the broad to the specific, and would become more detailed as they progressed through the company towards operating units. Table 12.1 contains a list of the headings under which strategic guidelines could be set.

Under marketing, for example, at the highest level in a large group, top management may ask for particular attention to be paid to issues such as the technical impact of microprocessors on electro-mechanical component equipment, leadership and innovation strategies, vulnerability to attack from the flood of products from countries such as India, China and Korea, and so on. At operating company level, it is possible to be more explicit about target markets, product development, and the like.

It is important to remember that it is top management's responsibility to determine the strategic direction of the company, and to decide such issues as when businesses are to be managed for cash, where to invest heavily in product development or market extension for longer-term gains, and so on. If this is left to operating managers to decide for themselves, they will tend to opt for actions con-cerned principally with today's products and markets, because that is what they are judged on princi-pally. There is also the problem of their inability to appreciate the larger, company-wide position.

Nevertheless, the process just described demonstrates very clearly that there is total inter-dependence between top management and the lowest level of operating management in the objective- and strategy-setting process.

In a very large company without any procedures for managing this process, it is not difficult to see how control can be weakened and how vulnerability to rapid changes in the business environ-ment around the world can be increased. This interdependence between the top-down/bottom-up process is illustrated in Figures 12.14 and 12.15, which show a similar hierarchy in respect of objec-tive and strategy setting to that illustrated in respect of audits.

Having explained carefully the point about *requisite* marketing planning, these figures also illus-trate the principles by which the marketing planning process should be implemented in any com-pany, irrespective of whether it is a small exporting company or a major multinational. In essence, these exhibits show a *hierarchy* of audits, SWOT analyses, objectives, strategies and programmes.

Financial	Operations
Remittances	Land
• dividends	Buildings
• royalities	Plant
Gross margin %	Modifications
Operating profit	Maintenance
Return on capital employed	Systems
Debtors	Raw materials supplies
Creditors	Purchasing
Bank borrowings	Distribution:
Investments	• stock and control
Capital expenditure	• transportation
Cash flow controls	• warehousing
Manpower and organization	*Marketing*
Management	Target markets
Training	Market segments
Industrial relations	Brands
Organization	Volumes
Remuneration and pensions	Market shares
	Pricing
	Image
	Promotion
	Market research
	Quality control
	Customer service

Table 12.1: Chief executive's strategic planning letter (possible areas for which objective and strategies or strategic guidelines will be set)

Figure 12.14: Interdependence of strategic and operational planning.

Figure 12.16 is another way of illustrating the total corporate strategic and planning process. (This was first shown in Chapter 2.) This time, however, a time element is added, and the relationship between strategic planning letters, long-term corporate plans and short-term operational plans is clarified. It is important to note that there are two 'open loop' points on this last diagram. These are the key times in the planning process when a subordinate's views and findings should be subjected to the closest examination by a superior.

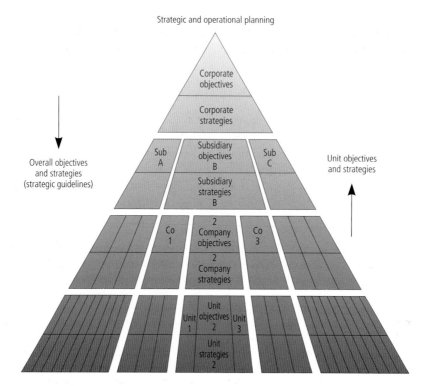

Figure 12.15: The interdependence of top-down/bottom-up planning.

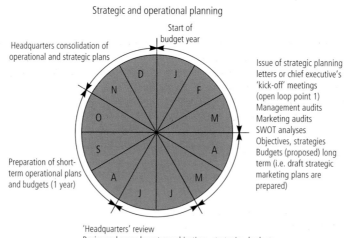

Figure 12.16: A planning timetable.

It is by taking these opportunities that marketing planning can be transformed into the critical and creative process it is supposed to be, rather than the dull, repetitive ritual it so often turns out to be.

These figures should be seen as one group of illustrations showing how the marketing planning process fits into the wider context of corporate planning.

Final Thought

In conclusion, we must stress that there can be no such thing as an off-the-peg marketing planning system.

Nonetheless, both our research and our experience have indicated that marketing planning remains one of the last bastions of management ignorance, largely because of the complexity of the process and its organizational, political and cultural implications.

It is for these reasons, and because so many of the readers of the first edition of this book asked for one, that we added a final chapter which contains both a very brief summary of the main points described in the book and a simple, step-by-step system which can become the basis of your own planning procedures. The system provided has been used successfully in businesses ranging from big international business-to-business companies to small domestic service organizations.

In the end, marketing planning success comes from an endless willingness to learn and to adapt the system to your people and your own circumstances. It also comes from a deep understanding about the nature of marketing planning, which is something that in the final analysis cannot be taught.

Success comes from *experience*. Experience comes from making mistakes. We can minimize these if we combine *common sense* and *sweet reasonableness* with the models provided in this book. But be sure of one thing, above all else. By themselves, the models will not work. However, if you read this book carefully and use the models sensibly, marketing planning becomes one of the most powerful tools available to a business today.

We wish you every success in your endeavours.

TEN BARRIERS TO MARKETING PLANNING

This book has described a number of barriers to effective marketing planning. The 10 principal barriers are:

1. Confusion between marketing tactics and strategy
2. Isolating the marketing function from operations
3. Confusion between the marketing function and the marketing concept
4. Organizational barriers – the tribal mentality, for example the failure to define strategic business units (SBUs) correctly
5. Lack of in-depth analysis

6. Confusion between process and output
7. Lack of knowledge and skills
8. Lack of a systematic approach to marketing planning
9. Failure to prioritize objectives
10. Hostile corporate cultures.

The 'Ten S' Approach to Overcoming these Barriers

Figure 12.17 summarizes the 'Ten S' approach developed by the author to overcome each of these barriers. The sections which follow elaborate briefly on each of the 'Ten Ss'. Ten fundamental principles of marketing planning are provided.

Marketing planning – Principle 1. Strategy before tactics

Develop the strategic marketing plan first. This entails greater emphasis on scanning the external environment, the early identification of forces emanating from it, and developing appropriate strategic responses, involving all levels of management in the process.

A strategic plan should cover a period of between three and five years, and only when this has been developed and agreed should the one-year operational marketing plan be developed.

Never write the one-year plan first and extrapolate it.

Marketing planning – Principle 2. Situate marketing within operations

For the purpose of marketing planning, put marketing as close as possible to the customer. Where practicable, have both marketing and sales report to the same person, who should not normally be the chief executive officer.

Marketing planning – Principle 3. Shared values about marketing

Marketing is a management process whereby the resources of the whole organization are utilized to satisfy the needs of selected customer groups in order to achieve the objectives of both parties. Marketing, then, is first and foremost an attitude of mind rather than a series of functional activities

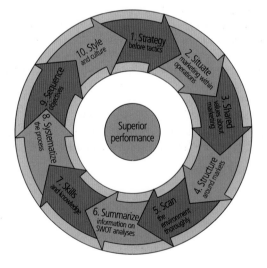

Figure 12.17: Marketing planning for competitive strategy.

confined to the marketing department. However, use the expression 'market-led' or 'customer-driven' to describe the philosophy, *not* 'marketing-driven'.

Marketing planning – Principle 4. Structure around markets

Organize company activities around customer groups if possible rather than around products or functional activities and get marketing planning done in these strategic business units. Without excellent marketing planning in SBUs, corporate marketing planning will be of limited value.

Marketing planning – Principle 5. Scan the environment thoroughly

For an effective marketing audit to take place:

- Checklists of questions customized according to level in the organization should be agreed.
- These should form the basis of the organization's MIS.
- The marketing audit should be a *required* activity.
- Managers should not be allowed to hide behind vague terms like 'poor economic conditions'.
- Managers should be encouraged to incorporate the tools of marketing in their audits, e.g. product lifecycles, portfolios and so on.

Marketing planning – Principle 6. Summarize information in SWOT analyses

Information is the foundation on which a marketing plan is built. From information (internal and external) comes intelligence.

Intelligence describes the *marketing plan*, which is the intellectualization of how managers perceive their own position in their markets relative to their competitors (with competitive advantage accurately defined – e.g. cost leader, differentiation, niche), what objectives they want to achieve over some designated period of time, how they intend to achieve their objectives (strategies), what resources are required, and with what results (budget).

A 'SWOT' should:

- be focused on each specific segment of crucial importance to the organization's future
- be a summary emanating from the marketing audit
- be brief, interesting and concise
- focus on *key* factors only
- list *differential* strengths and weaknesses *vis-à-vis* competitors, focusing on competitive advantage
- list *key* external opportunities and threats only
- identify and pin down the *real* issues – it should not be a list of unrelated points
- enable the reader to grasp instantly the main thrust of the business, even to the point of being able to write marketing objectives
- follow the implied question 'which means that …?' to get the real implications
- not overabbreviate.

Marketing planning – Principle 7. Skills and knowledge

Ensure that all those responsible for marketing in SBUs have the necessary marketing knowledge and skills for the job. In particular, ensure that they understand and know how to use the more important tools of marketing, such as:

1. Information
   - how to get it
   - how to use it
2. Positioning
   - market segmentation
   - Ansoff
   - Porter

3. Product lifecycle analysis
   * gap analysis
4. Portfolio management
   * BCG matrix
   * directional policy matrix
5. Four Ps management
   * product
   * price
   * place
   * promotion.

Additionally, marketing personnel require communications and interpersonal skills.

Marketing planning – Principle 8. Systematize the process

It is essential in complex organizations to have a set of written procedures and a well-argued common format for marketing planning. The purposes of such a system are:

1. To ensure that all key issues are systematically considered
2. To pull together the essential elements of the strategic planning of each SBU in a consistent manner
3. To help corporate management to compare diverse businesses and to understand the overall condition of, and prospects for, the organization.

Marketing planning – Principle 9. Sequence objectives

Ensure that all objectives are prioritized according to their impact on the organization and their urgency and that resources are allocated accordingly.

A suggested method for prioritization is given in Figure 12.18.

Marketing planning – Principle 10. Style and culture

Marketing planning will not be effective without the active support and participation of the culture leaders. But, even with their support, the type of marketing planning has to be appropriate for the phase of the organizational lifeline. This phase should be measured before attempting to introduce marketing planning.

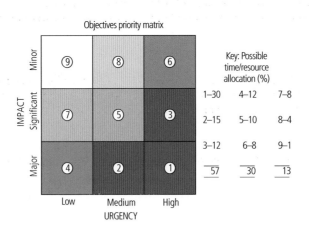

Figure 12.18: Objectives priority matrix.

APPLICATION QUESTIONS

1. Does the principle of hierarchies of audits, SWOTs, objectives, strategies and programmes apply in your company? If not, describe how they are handled.
2. If it does, describe in what ways it differs from the principles outlined here.
3. Design a simple system for your company, or describe in what ways your existing system could be improved.

CHAPTER 12 REVIEW

Conditions that must be satisfied

1. Any closed-loop planning system, especially if it is based just on forecasting and budgeting, will deaden any creative response and will eventually lead to failure.
2. Marketing planning which is not integrated with other functional areas of the business at general management level will be largely ineffective.
3. The separation of operational and strategic marketing planning will lead to divergent plans, with the short-term viewpoint winning because it achieves quick results.
4. The chief executive must take an active role.
5. It can take three years to introduce marketing planning successfully.

Try Exercises 12.1 and 12.2

Ten principles of marketing planning

1. Develop the strategic plan first; the operational plan comes out of this.
2. Put marketing as close as possible to the customer and have marketing and sales under one person.
3. Marketing is an attitude of mind, not a set of procedures.
4. Organize activities around customer groups, not functional activities.
5. A marketing audit must be rigorous. No vague terms should be allowed, and nothing should be hidden. Managers should use tools like portfolio analysis and product lifecycle.
6. SWOT analyses should be focused on segments that are critical to the business; concentrate only on key factors which lead to objectives.
7. People must be educated about the planning process.
8. There has to be a plan for planning.
9. All objectives should be prioritized in terms of their urgency and impact.
10. Marketing planning needs the active support of the chief executive and must be appropriate for the culture.

Planning horizon

There is a natural point of focus in the future beyond which it is pointless to plan for. This can differ from firm to firm, depending on its business. Generally, small firms can use shorter horizons, because they are flexible, to adjust to change. Large firms need longer horizons.

Planning paradox

Companies often set out to achieve the impossible. It is not unknown to see planning objectives which seek to:

* maximize sales
* minimize costs
* increase market share
* maximize profits.

Not only are these incompatible, but they damage the credibility of the managers who subscribe to such commitments.

Organizational barriers

A number of potential barriers exist:
1. *Cognitive* – not knowing enough about marketing planning
2. *Cultural* – the company culture is not sufficiently developed for marketing planning
3. *Political* – the culture carriers feel threatened by marketing
4. *Resources* – not enough resources are allocated to marketing
5. *Structural* – lack of a plan and organization for planning
6. *Lack of an MIS.*

Centralization versus decentralization

For multi-unit/international organizations there are two possibilities.

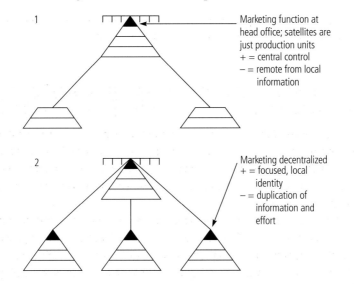

Choose an approach where the advantages outweigh the disadvantages.

Try Exercise 12.4

Questions raised for the company

1. Q: What influences whether research is carried out internally or by external consultants?
   A: There can be a number of factors – speed, timing, cost, nature of the research problem, skill requirements, the need for anonymity or objectivity, access of information, etc. Each decision must be taken on its merits.
2. Q: What criteria should be used to assess external researchers?
   A: Again, there are a number of issues to consider.
      (a) *Reputation* – in general, in the industry, for particular types of research, etc.
      (b) *Capability and experience* – how long established, quality and qualifications of staff, number of staff, repeat business, recommendations and references, etc.
      (c) *Organization* – size, links with sources of information, premises, location, geographical coverage, full-time or part-time interviewers, terms of business, etc.
3. Q: Are there different approaches to marketing planning?
   A: We believe there are. Please see the following diagram.

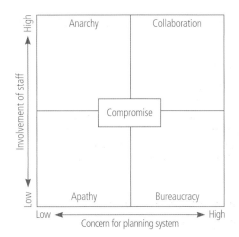

The most successful marketing plans are collaborative. Here, relevant executives take part in the process in a caring way, and at the same time planning is done rigorously.

EXERCISES

As the brief notes have indicated, there are a number of conditions to be met if the marketing planning process is not to become a sterile, closed-loop system. The 10 principles of marketing planning listed in the notes go a considerable way to ensuring that the process does not degenerate into a ritualized 'numbers game'. However, there are still some problematical issues to be addressed.

Exercise 12.1 looks at the theory issue of how formalized the planning process should be, and how to take the correct steps to get close to the ideal system for your company.

Exercise 12.2 examines how to set up a timetable for planning. This is particularly useful in getting all contributors to the marketing plan working in unison, and coming up with the necessary information at the appropriate time.

In these exercises, you will focus on the marketing planning system best suited to your company.

By way of consolidating all of your work through this book, you will design an appropriate planning system and lay down the 'ground rules' for its implementation.

Selecting the appropriate approach
Exercise 12.1 Designing the marketing planning system

Figure 12.19 shows how the degree of formalization of the marketing planning process relates to company size and the diversity of its operations.

1. Select a position on this figure which best describes your company's situation.
2. In the space below, write down a few key words or sentences that would best describe the marketing planning system you would need for your company, e.g. high formalization, etc.

(Continued)

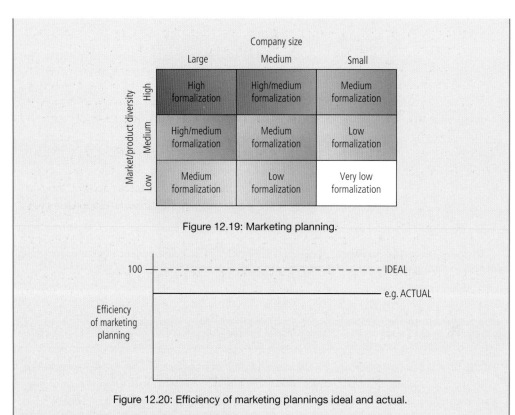

Figure 12.19: Marketing planning.

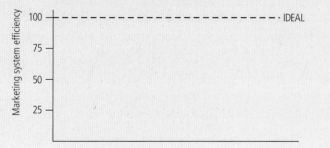

Figure 12.20: Efficiency of marketing plannings ideal and actual.

Identifying the improvement areas

1. Imagine that it is possible to measure the efficiency of a marketing planning system on a scale 0–100, where 100 is equivalent to a 100 per cent efficiency, i.e. the system works well and conforms with your model. How would you rate the current approach to marketing planning in your company? To what extent does it match up with your ideal?
2. Enter your score on Figure 12.20, drawing a horizontal line as shown.

    The difference between your score line and the ideal must represent where there is room for improvement.

    Transfer your score line to the worksheet, the force field diagram, then complete the worksheet by following the instructions given below.

Worksheet Force field diagram (1) (Exercise 12.1)

3. Identify all those factors that have 'pushed' your actual efficiency line below the ideal. Add them to the worksheet, showing them as actual forces pushing down. If you can, represent the biggest forces with longer arrows, as shown in Figure 12.21. You will probably have more than three factors, so list as many as you can. Remember, you should be noting only those that affect the marketing planning system, not the company's general approach to marketing. We will call these downward forces 'restraining forces', because they are acting against improvement.

4. Now ask yourself, why isn't the actual performance line you have drawn lower than it is? The reason is, of course, that there are several parts of the system that work well, or there are other strengths in your company. Identify these positive forces and add them to the worksheet, as shown in Figure 12.22, again relating the arrow size approximately to the influence of each factor.

   Again, the factors shown above are only examples. You will identify many more. We call these 'driving forces' because they are pushing towards improvement.

5. The worksheet should now be complete, showing the two sets of forces lined up against each other. What next? Well, it might have struck you that what you have assembled is

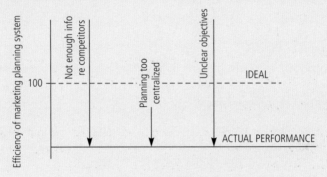

Figure 12.21: Force field diagram (2).

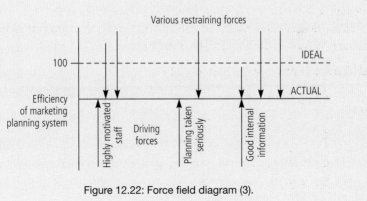

Figure 12.22: Force field diagram (3).

(Continued)

somewhat analogous to a ship at sea. Your ship (the marketing planning system) is wallowing below its ideal level in the water but is prevented from sinking by buoyant forces (driving forces). To restore the ship to its correct level, it would be natural to remove or jettison some of the cargo (the restraining forces), not to try to get out and push from below. As it is for the ship, so it is for your marketing planning system, therefore:

(a) Select the major restraining forces and work out ways that you can reduce their impact, or preferably eliminate them altogether. These will be the source of the greatest improvements, but some remedies might need time to take effect.

(b) So, concurrently, select minor restraining forces and plan to eliminate them also. Although their impact on improvement might be less, you will probably find they respond more quickly to treatment.

(c) Finally, select the smallest driving forces and work out if there are any ways to increase their impact.

6. Assemble your various responses to 5(a), (b) and (c) together into a comprehensive improvement plan, then take steps to get it accepted and acted upon.

Put most of your energy into removing the restraining factors. To focus on the major driving forces, e.g. trying to make highly motivated staff even more motivated, is likely to be counterproductive.

Force field analysis theory

The force field analysis, upon which much of designing a system is based, stems from the work of Kurt Lewin (*Field Theory in Social Science*, Harper, 1951). His reasoning, adapted to the programme situation, operates thus:

1. If a company's marketing system is functioning well, then the company could be said to have no problems. Diagrammatically, the efficiency level could be shown at something approaching 100 per cent. See Figure 12.23.

2. Few companies reach this happy state of affairs. Without resorting to precise measurement (a consensus of views is generally enough), most companies would 'score' their planning system somewhat lower, as shown in Figure 12.24.

3. Wherever the 'actual' line is drawn, it poses two interesting questions upon which the subsequent analysis hinges, namely:

(a) What causes the performance level to be where it is?

(b) Why doesn't it fall any lower?

4. Clearly the answer to 3(a) is that things are going wrong in the system; that there are missing or malfunctioning areas. Until these are put right, there will always be a drag on the efficiency, holding it down. These negative forces are termed *restraining forces*, because they are restraining improvement.

5. Similarly, the reason that efficiency doesn't drop lower than has been shown is that there must be several parts of the planning system that work quite well. There are many strengths in the system. These positive factors are termed *driving forces*, because they are the forces pushing towards better efficiency.

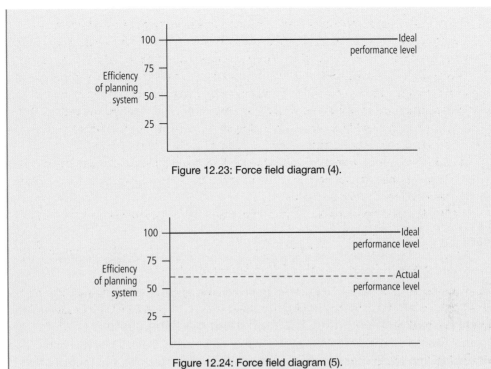

Figure 12.23: Force field diagram (4).

Figure 12.24: Force field diagram (5).

6. In Figure 12.13, for the efficiency of the planning system to be below the ideal level, then the restraining forces must be greater than the driving forces.

7. Let us take a simple illustration. We are driving a car and it is going more slowly than it ought to because the brakes are rubbing (restraining force). If we want to resume driving at normal speed then we have two courses of action open to us:
   (a) We can put our foot down on the accelerator (increase the driving force)
   (b) We can free the brakes (remove the restraining force)
   We can see that by putting our foot down all sorts of troubles are likely to materialize. Unless something is done to free the brakes, then probably they would overheat, perhaps catch fire or jam up completely.

8. A similar overheating could take place in the company's marketing planning system unless it is tackled properly. To get lasting improvements, it will be important to identify all the restraining and driving forces. Indeed, many of the earlier exercises were designed to do just this. Using this information, it will be important *to plan how to reduce or remove the restraining forces and, only when that is done, consider how to plan to boost the driving forces.*

9. Figure 12.25 is an example of how a finished force field diagram might look, although most people will have identified several more factors than shown here. Many of the factors identified by you ought to be unique to your company.

(Continued)

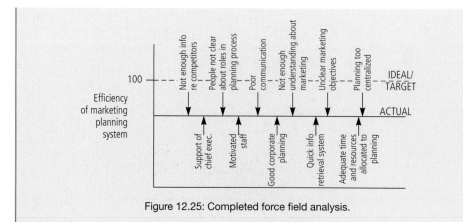

Figure 12.25: Completed force field analysis.

Notes

1. Remember that only factors that affect the marketing planning process ought to appear in the force field diagram.
2. It is possible to draw the force arrows proportional in length to their influence.

Exercise 12.2 Implementing the marketing planning system

Perhaps you will be unable to implement a marketing planning system until your improvement plan from Exercise 12.1 has eliminated the more serious obstacles. Nevertheless, from what you have read in this book, you will know that a successful marketing planning system will have to follow these steps.

1. There will have to be guidance provided by the corporate objectives.
2. A marketing audit must take place.
3. A gap analysis must be completed.
4. A SWOT analysis must be drawn up.
5. Assumptions and contingencies must be considered.
6. Marketing objectives and strategies must be set.
7. Individual marketing programmes must be established.
8. There must be a period of review and measurement.

Because of the work required, all this takes time. Various people might have to participate at different stages. There will certainly have to be several meetings or discussions with other functional departments, either to get information or to ensure collaboration.

Therefore, in order to keep the planning 'train' on the 'rails', it will be in everybody's interest to be clear about the sequencing of these different activities, to have a schedule or timetable.

As the company gets more experienced in planning, then probably the timetable can be tightened up and the whole planning period shortened. However, to get events into perspective, it is often helpful to present a timetable of the planning activities, as shown in Figure 12.26. The circle represents a calendar year and the time periods are merely examples – not to be taken as recommended periods.

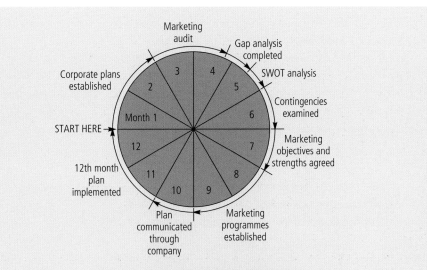

Figure 12.26: Marketing planning timetable.

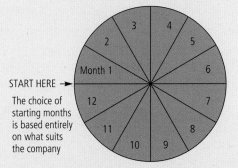

Figure 12.27: Marketing planning timetable template.

In the second planning year, months 11 and 12 could be used to evaluate the first year's plan and thereby prepare information for the next round of corporate planning.

This diagrammatic approach clearly shows how the planning process is a continual undercurrent throughout the year.

Now, as your final task, try drawing up the planning timetable for your company on Figure 12.27.

Exercise 12.3 Organizational structure

Business environments are always changing. Demand patterns change, new technology comes in, new legislation is introduced, there is an economic crisis, and so on.

Since the key to successful marketing is to have a suitable organization structure, one that can adjust and cope with the environment, it is not surprising that much experimentation has taken place with the different types of structure. Perhaps no one has yet found the perfect answer to this complex problem of getting the organization right. Nevertheless, research

(Continued)

studies have shown that, in certain circumstances, some types of structure are going to be more successful than others.

The accompanying worksheet tries to encapsulate these findings in a fairly crude way, showing that structure will to some extent relate to company size and the diversity of its operations. The degree of formality in the marketing planning process will also be related to these factors.

Please answer the following questions:

1. Where would you place your company on the size/complexity of operations continuum?
2. How does your current structure compare with that suggested on the chart?
3. Do the breakdown signals sound familiar?
4. In what ways do you think your structure ought to change?

Worksheet Organizational structure (Exercise 12.3)

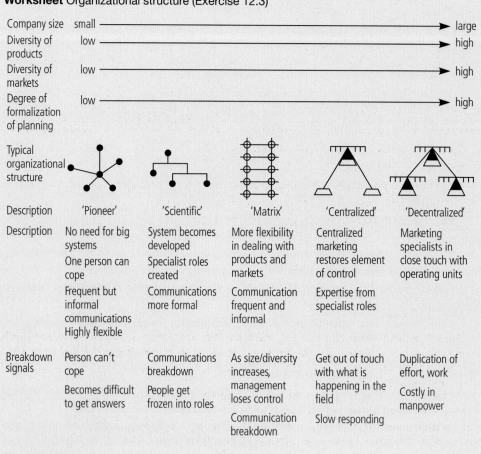

	'Pioneer'	'Scientific'	'Matrix'	'Centralized'	'Decentralized'
Description	No need for big systems	System becomes developed	More flexibility in dealing with products and markets	Centralized marketing restores element of control	Marketing specialists in close touch with operating units
	One person can cope	Specialist roles created			
	Frequent but informal communications	Communications more formal	Communication frequent and informal	Expertise from specialist roles	
	Highly flexible				
Breakdown signals	Person can't cope	Communications breakdown	As size/diversity increases, management loses control	Get out of touch with what is happening in the field	Duplication of effort, work
	Becomes difficult to get answers	People get frozen into roles			Costly in manpower
			Communication breakdown	Slow responding	

Personal notes

Chapter  13

MEASURING THE EFFECTIVENESS OF MARKETING PLANNING

SUMMARY

- An appraisal of marketing investment techniques
- Shareholder value added
- Marketing due diligence and assessing the riskiness of strategic marketing plans
- Linking marketing expenditure to corporate financial objectives
- Measuring promotional expenditure effectiveness.

A THREE-LEVEL MARKETING ACCOUNTABILITY FRAMEWORK

The ultimate test of marketing investment, and indeed any investment, is whether it creates value for shareholders. But few marketing investments are evaluated from this perspective, and many would argue that it is almost impossible to link financial results to any specific marketing activity.

But increasingly, boards of directors and city analysts the world over are dissatisfied with this lack of accountability for what are, very often, huge budgets. Cranfield School of Management has been addressing this problem through its Marketing Value Added Research Club and Marketing Accountability Research Club, formed with a number of blue-chip companies. The club set out to create and test a new framework which shows how marketing systematically contributes to shareholder value, and how its contribution can be measured in an objective and comparable way.

MARKETING INSIGHT

There is an urgent need for such a framework. Not only does marketing need it, to answer the widespread accusations of poor performance,[1] but corporate and financial strategists need it too, to understand how to link marketing activities to the wider corporate agenda. All too often marketing objectives and strategies are not aligned with the organization's overall plans to increase shareholder value.

The purpose of this chapter is to set out the logic of this framework, which is underpinned by two Cranfield PhDs (Wilson, 1996[2] and Smith, 2003[3]).

The chapter starts with a brief justification of the need for a wholly new approach to measuring the effectiveness of marketing.

It then proceeds to set out another accountability framework also developed in the Cranfield Research Clubs.

WHAT COUNTS AS MARKETING EXPENDITURE?

Historically, marketing expenditure has tended to escape rigorous performance appraisal for a number of reasons. First, there has been real confusion as to the true scope and nature of marketing investments. Too often, marketing expenditure has been assumed to be only the budgets put together by the marketing function, and as such, a (major) cost to be controlled rather than a potential driver of value. Second, the causal relationship between expenditure and results has been regarded as too difficult to pin down to any useful level of precision.

Now, because of the demands of increasingly discerning customers and greater competition, marketing investments and marketing processes are under scrutiny as never before. From the process point of view, as a result of insights from management concepts such as the quality movement and re-engineering, marketing is now much more commonly seen as a cross-functional responsibility of the entire organization rather than just the marketing department's problem.

Howard Morganis, past Chairman of Procter and Gamble, said, 'There is no such thing as a marketing skill by itself. For a company to be good at marketing, it must be good at everything else, from R&D to manufacturing, from quality controls to financial controls.' Hugh Davidson[4] in *Offensive Marketing* comments, 'Marketing is an approach to business rather than a specialist discipline. It is no more the exclusive responsibility of the marketing department than profitability is the sole charge of the finance department.'

But there is also a growing awareness that, because of this wider interpretation of marketing, nearly all budgets within the company could be regarded as marketing investments in one way or another. This is especially the case with IT budgets. The exponential increase in computing power has made it possible to track customer perceptions and behaviours on a far greater scale, and with far greater precision than previously. When used correctly, these databases and analytical tools can shed a much greater light on what really happens inside the 'black box'. However, the sums involved in acquiring such technologies are forcing even the most slapdash of companies to apply more rigorous appraisal techniques to their investments in this area.

This wider understanding of what 'marketing' is really all about has had a number of consequences. First, the classic textbook treatment of strategic issues in marketing has finally caught up with reality.

Topics such as market and customer segmentation, product and brand development, databases and customer service and support are now regularly discussed at board level, instead of being left to operational managers or obscure research specialists.

CEOs and MDs are increasingly accepting that they must take on the role of chief marketing officer if they want to create truly customer-led organizations. Sir Clive Thompson commented, 'I am convinced that corporate and marketing strategy are more or less the same things. The chief executive has to be the chief marketer. If you delegate that responsibility, you are not doing your job.'

Second, because of their 'new' mission-critical status, marketing investments are attracting the serious attention of finance professionals. As part of a wider revolution in thinking about what kind of corporate assets are important in today's business environment, intangibles such as knowledge about customers and markets, or the power of brands, have assumed a new importance. The race is on to find robust methods of quantifying and evaluating such assets for the benefit of corporate managements and the wider investment community.

Unfortunately, this new focus on the importance of marketing has not improved the profile of marketing professionals. Instead, the spotlight has merely highlighted their weaknesses and shortcomings. After one 1997 survey on the perceived status of the profession, John Stubbs, CEO of the UK Marketing Council, was forced to comment, 'I was taken aback by just how little reputation marketing actually has among other functions . . . marketing and marketers are not respected by the people in their organisations for their contributions to business strategy, results or internal communication. We often do not know what or who is good or bad at marketing; our measurements are not seen as credible; our highest qualifications are not seen to have compatible status with other professions.'

MARKETING INSIGHT

A survey at Cranfield during a two-year period has revealed that marketers are seen as 'slippery, expensive, unreliable and unaccountable'.[5]

WHAT DOES 'VALUE ADDED' REALLY MEAN?

The term 'value added' is fast becoming the new mantra for the early 21st century business literature, and is often used quite loosely to indicate a business concept that is intended to exceed either customer or investor expectations, or both. However, from the point of view of this chapter, it is important to realize that the term has its origin in a number of different management ideas, and is used in very specific ways by different sets of authors. Most of the ideas come from the USA, and have originated in business school and consultancy research in the mid-1980s.

Value Chain Analysis

First, there is Michael Porter's well-known concept of value-chain analysis.[6] Porter's concept of value added is an incremental one; he focuses on how successive activities change the value of goods and services as they pass through various stages of a value chain. 'The analysis disaggregates a firm into its major activities in order to understand the behaviour of costs and the existing and potential sources of differentiation. It determines how the firm's own

> Value chain analysis is used to identify potential sources of economic advantage.

> SVA is described as 'The process of analysing how decisions affect the net present value of cash to shareholders'

value chain interacts with the value chains of suppliers, customers and competitors. Companies gain competitive advantage by performing some or all of these activities at lower cost or with greater differentiation than competitors.'[6]

Shareholder Value Added (SVA)

Second, there is Alfred Rappaport's[7] equally well-known research on shareholder value added. Rappaport's concept of value added focuses less on processes than Porter's, and acts more as a final gateway in decision making, although it can be used at multiple levels within a firm.

The analysis measures a company's ability to earn more than its total cost of capital . . . Within business units, SVA measures the value the unit has created by analysing cash flows over time.

MARKETING INSIGHT

At the corporate level, SVA provides a framework for evaluating options for improving shareholder value by determining the tradeoffs between reinvesting in existing businesses, investing in new businesses and returning cash to stockholders.

There are a number of different ways of measuring shareholder value added, one of which, *market value added* (MVA), needs further explanation. Market value added is a measure first proposed by consultants Sterne Stewart in 1991, which compares the total shareholder capital of a company (including retained earnings) with the current market value of the company (capitalization and debt). When one is deducted from the other, a positive result means value has been added, and a negative result means investors have lost out. Within the literature, there is much discussion of the merits of this measure versus another approach proposed by Sterne Stewart – EVA (economic value added).

However, from the point of view of *marketing* value added, Walters and Halliday[8] usefully sum up the discussion thus: 'As aggregate measures and as relative performance indicators they have much to offer . . . [but] how can the manager responsible for developing and/or implementing growth objectives [use them] to identify and select from alternative [strategic] options?'

Market value added is one of a number of tools that analysts and the capital markets use to assess the value of a company. Marketing value added as a research topic focuses more directly on the processes of creating that value through effective marketing investments.

Customer Value

A third way of looking at value added is the customer's perception of value. Unfortunately, despite exhaustive research by academics and practitioners around the world, this elusive concept has proved almost impossible to pin down: 'What constitutes [customer] value – even in a single product category – appears to be highly personal and idiosyncratic', concludes Zeithamel,[9] for instance. Nevertheless, the individual customer's perception of the extra value represented by different products and services cannot be easily dismissed: in the guise of measures such as customer satisfaction and customer loyalty, it is known to be the essence of brand success, and the whole basis of a new movement known as relationship marketing.

> Finally, there is the accountant's definition of value added: 'value added = sales revenue – purchases and services'

Accounting Value

Effectively, this is a snapshot picture from the annual accounts of how the revenue from a sales period has been distributed, and how much is left over for reinvestment after meeting all costs, including shareholder dividends. Although this figure will say something about the past viability of a business, in itself it does not provide a guide to future prospects.

One reason that the term 'value added' has come to be used rather carelessly is that all these concepts of value, although different, are not mutually exclusive. Porter's value chain analysis is one of several extremely useful techniques for identifying potential new competitive market strategies. Rappaport's SVA approach can be seen as a powerful tool which enables managers to cost out the long-term financial implications of pursuing one or other of the competitive strategies which have been identified. Customer perceptions are clearly a major driver (or destroyer) of annual audited accounting value in all companies, whatever strategy is pursued.

MARKETING INSIGHT

However, most companies today accept that value added, as defined by their annual accounts, is really only a record of what they achieved in the past, and that financial targets in themselves are insufficient as business objectives. Many companies are now convinced that focusing on more intangible measures of value added such as brand equity, customer loyalty, or customer satisfaction is the new route to achieving financial results.

Unfortunately, research has found that there is no neat, causal link between offering additional customer value and achieving value added on a balance sheet. That is, good ratings from customers about perceived value do not necessarily lead to financial success. Nor do financially successful companies necessarily offer products and services which customers perceive as offering better value than competitors.

In order to explain the link that does exist between customer-orientated strategies and financial results, a far more rigorous approach to forecasting costs and revenues is required than is usual in marketing planning, coupled with a longer-term perspective on the payback period than is possible on an annual balance sheet. This cash-driven perspective is the basis of the SVA approach, and can be used in conjunction with any marketing-strategy formulation process.

MARKETING INSIGHT

However, despite its apparent compatibility with existing planning systems, it is important to stress that adherents of the SVA approach believe that, after all the calculations have been made about the impact of different strategic choices, the final decision about which strategy to pursue should be the one which generates the most value (cash) for shareholders.

This point of view adds a further dimension to the strategic debate, and is by no means universally accepted: there is a vigorous and ongoing debate in the literature as to whether increasing shareholder value should be the ultimate objective of a corporation.

Despite these arguments, there is no denying that during the last 15 years, SVA (or variants on the technique) has become the single most dominating corporate valuation perspective in developed western economies. Its popularity tends to be limited to the boardroom and the stock exchanges, however. Several surveys (e.g. CSF Consulting in 2000, KPMG in 1999) have found that less than 30 per cent of companies were pushing SVA-based management techniques down to an operational level, because of difficulties in translating cash targets into practical, day-to-day management objectives.

This is a pity because, apart from its widespread use at corporate level, the SVA approach particularly merits extensive attention of researchers interested in putting a value on marketing, as it allows marketing investments (or indeed any investments) to be valued over a much longer period of time than the usual one-year budget cycle.

Although common sense might argue that developing strong product or service offerings and building up a loyal, satisfied customer base will usually require a series of 1–2 year investment plans in any business, nevertheless, such is the universal distrust of marketing strategies and forecasts, it is common practice in most companies to write off marketing as a cost within each year's budget. It is rare for such expenditure to be treated as an investment which will deliver results over a number of years, but research shows that companies who are able to do this create a lasting competitive edge.

Meanwhile, as stated earlier, research into marketing accountability continues apace at Cranfield and a three-level model has been developed and tested, and it is to this model that we now turn.

THREE DISTINCT LEVELS FOR MEASURING MARKETING EFFECTIVENESS

When one of the authors was marketing director of a fast-moving consumer goods (fmcg) company 30 years ago, there were many well tried-and-tested models for measuring the effectiveness of marketing promotional expenditure. Indeed, some of these were quite sophisticated and included math-

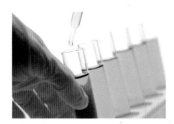

ematical models for promotional campaigns, for advertising threshold and wear-out levels and the like.

Indeed, it would be surprising if marketing as a discipline did not have its own quantitative models for the massive expenditure of fmcg companies. Over time, these models have been transferred to business-to-business and service companies, with the result that, today, any organization spending substantial sums of shareholders' money on promotion should be ashamed of themselves if those responsible could not account for the effectiveness of such expenditure.

MARKETING INSIGHT

Nonetheless, with the advent of different promotional methods and channels, combined with an empowered and more sophisticated consumer, the problems of measuring promotional effectiveness have increased considerably.

Consequently, this remains one of the major challenges facing the marketing community today and, as mentioned above, the research and practice of specialists at Cranfield School of Management continue apace.

But, at this level, accountability can only be measured in terms of the kinds of effects that promotional expenditure can achieve, such as awareness, or attitude change, both of which can be measured quantitatively.

But to assert that such expenditure can be measured directly in terms of sales or profits is intellectually indefensible, when there are so many other variables that affect sales, such as product efficacy, packaging, price, the sales force, competitors and countless other variables that, like advertising, have an intermediate impact on sales and profits. Again, however, there clearly is a cause and effect link, otherwise such expenditure would be pointless. This issue is addressed later in this chapter.

Indeed, this definition of marketing as a function for strategy development as well as for tactical sales delivery, when represented as a map (see Figure 13.1), can be used to clarify the whole problem of how to measure marketing effectiveness.

So, the problem with marketing accountability has never been with how to measure the effectiveness of promotional expenditure, for this we have had for many years. No, the problem occurs because marketing isn't just a promotional activity. As explained in detail in Chapter 1, in world class organizations where the customer is at the centre of the business model, marketing as a discipline is responsible for defining and understanding markets, for segmenting these markets, for developing value propositions to meet the researched needs of the customers in the segments, for getting buy-in from all those in the organization responsible for delivering this value, for playing their own part in delivering this value and for monitoring whether the promised value is being delivered.

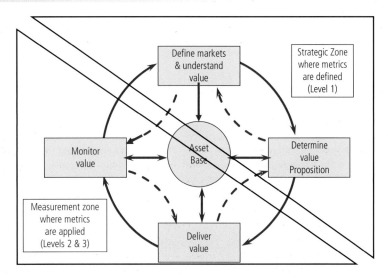

Figure 13.1: Map of the marketing domain and the three-level accountability framework

Level of marketing effectiveness	Areas considered	Outputs
Level 1 Marketing due diligence	The marketing strategy, i.e. the choice of target customers and value proposition	An objective assessment of whether or not the marketing strategy will create or destroy shareholder value, together with the identification of how the strategy may be improved
Level 2 Marketing effectiveness	The marketing tactics (i.e. the full range of products, pricing, promotional and channels), employed for each segment identified and targeted by the marketing strategy	The likelihood of the marketing tactics creating the necessary competitive advantage in each segment
Level 3 Promotional effectiveness	The marketing communications strategy (i.e. advertising, sales team, etc.), employed to communicate with each segment	The effectiveness of the communications activity in achieving marketing communications objectives such as awareness recall, etc.

Level 1: Shareholder Value Added (SVA)

SVA is profit after tax, minus net capital employed multiplied by the cost of capital. There are only three things you can do to affect SVA:

* increase revenue
* decrease costs
* decrease the amount of capital tied up in the business.

All of these are highly influenced by the strategic marketing plan. A very simple example of how SVA can be calculated follows: A has £15,000 invested in the company. The cost of capital is 10 per cent. The company makes a net profit of £2,000. Therefore, the company has created £500 SVA (£15,000 × 10% – £2,000 = +£500).

Level 1 is the most vital of all three, because this is what determines whether or not the marketing strategies for the longer term (usually three to five years) destroy or create shareholder value added. It is justified to use the strategic marketing plan for assessing whether shareholder value is being created or destroyed because, as Sean Kelly[10] agrees:

> The customer is simply the fulcrum of the business and everything from production to supply chain, to finance, risk management, personnel management and product development, all adapt to and converge on the business value proposition that is projected to the customer.

Thus, corporate assets and their associated competences are only relevant if customer markets value them sufficiently highly that they lead to sustainable competitive advantage, or shareholder value added. This is our justification for evaluating the strategic plan for what is to be sold, to whom and with what projected effect on profits as a route to establishing whether shareholder value will be created or destroyed.

MARKETING INSIGHT

A company's share price, the shareholder value created and the cost of capital are all heavily influenced by one factor: risk. Investors constantly seek to estimate the likelihood of a business plan delivering its promises, while the boards try to demonstrate the strength of their strategy.

How much is a company really worth? We spelled out in Chapter 1 the huge discrepancy between the tangible assets and the share price; there are innumerable tools that try to estimate the true value of intangibles and goodwill. However, these mostly come from a cost-accounting perspective. They try

to estimate the cost of recreating the brand, intellectual property or whatever is the basis of intangible assets. Our research into companies that succeed and fail suggests that that approach is flawed, because what matters is not the assets owned, but how they are used. We need to get back to the basics of what determines company value.

We should never be too simplistic about business, but some things are fundamentally simple. We believe that a company's job is to create shareholder value, and the share price reflects how well the investment community thinks that is being done. Whether or not shareholder value is created depends on creating profits greater than investors might get elsewhere at the same level of risk. The business plan makes promises about profits, which investors then discount against their estimate of the chance a company will deliver it. So it all comes down to this. A company says it will achieve $1 billion, investors and analysts think it is more likely to be $0.8 billion. The capital markets revolve around perceptions of risk. What boards and investors both need, therefore, is a strategic management process that gives a rigorous assessment of risk and uses that to assess and improve shareholder value creation. Just such a process has emerged from many years of research at Cranfield, a process we have called, appropriately, 'marketing due diligence'.

There is a whole book dedicated to explaining this process,[11] so we will provide only a brief summary here.

Where Does Risk Come From?

Marketing due diligence begins by looking for the risk associated with a company's strategy. Evaluation of thousands of business plans suggests that the many different ways that companies fail to keep their promises can be grouped into three categories:

- The market wasn't as big as they thought
- They didn't get the market share they hoped for
- They didn't get the profit they hoped for.

Of course, a business can fail by any of these routes or a combination of them. The risk inherent in a plan is the aggregate of these three categories, which we have called, respectively, market risk, strategy risk and implementation risk. The challenge is to accurately assess these risks and their implications for shareholder value creation.

Our research found that most estimates of business risk were unreliable because they grouped lots of different sources of risk under one heading. Since each source of risk is influenced by many different factors, this high-level approach to assessing business risk is too simplistic and inherently inaccurate. A better approach is to subdivide business risk into as many sources as practically possible, estimate those separately and then recombine them. This has two advantages. First, each risk factor is 'cleaner', in that its causes can be assessed more accurately. Second, minor errors in each of the estimations cancel each other out. The result is a much better estimate of overall risk.

How Risky is a Business?

Marketing due diligence makes an initial improvement over high-level risk estimates by assessing market, strategy and implementation risk separately. However, even those three categories are not sufficiently detailed. We need to understand the components of each, which have to be teased out by careful comparison of successful and unsuccessful strategies. Our research indicated that each of the three risk sources could be subdivided further into five risk factors, making 15 in all. These are summarized in Table 13.1.

Armed with this understanding of the components and subcomponents of business risk, we are now half-way to a genuine assessment of our value creation potential. The next step is to accurately assess our own business against each of the 15 criteria and use them to evaluate the probability that our plan will deliver its promises.

This gradation of risk level is not straightforward. It is too simplistic to reduce risk assessment to a tick-box exercise. However, a comparison of a strategy against a large sample of other companies' strategies does provide a relative scale.

MARKETING INSIGHT

By comparing, for instance, the evidence of market size, or the homogeneity of target markets, or the intended sources of profit against this scale, a valid, objective, assessment of the risk associated with business plan can be made.

Overall risk associated with the business plan		
Market risk	**Strategy risk**	**Implementation risk**
Product category risk, which is lower if the product category is well established and higher for a new product category.	Target market risk, which is lower if the target market is defined in terms of homogeneous segments and higher if it is not.	Profit pool risk, which is lower if the targeted profit pool is high and growing and higher if it is static or shrinking.
Segment existence risk, which is lower if the target segment is well established and higher if it is a new segment.	Proposition risk, which is lower if the proposition delivered to each segment is segment specific and higher if all segments are offered the same thing.	Competitor impact risk, which is lower if the profit impact on competitors is small and distributed and higher if it threatens a competitor's survival.
Sales volumes risk, which is lower if the sales volumes are well supported by evidence and higher if they are guessed.	SWOT risk, which is lower if the strengths and weaknesses of the organization are correctly assessed and leveraged by the strategy and higher if the strategy ignores the firm's strengths and weaknesses.	Internal gross margin risk, which is lower if the internal gross margin assumptions are conservative relative to current products and higher if they are optimistic.
Forecast risk, which is lower if the forecast growth is in line with historical trends and higher if it exceeds them significantly.	Uniqueness risk, which is lower if the target segments and propositions are different from that of the major competitors and higher if the strategy goes 'head on'.	Profit sources risk, which is lower if the source profit is growth in the existing profit pool and higher if the profit is planned to come from the market leader.
Pricing risk, which is lower if the pricing assumptions are conservative relative to current pricing levels and higher if they are optimistic.	Future risk, which is lower if the strategy allows for any trends in the market and higher if it fails to address them.	Other costs risk, which is lower if assumptions regarding other costs, including marketing support, are higher than existing costs and higher if they are lower than current costs.

Table 13.1: Factors contributing to risk

What Use is this Knowledge?

Marketing due diligence involves the careful assessment of a business plan and the supporting information behind it. In doing so, it discounts subjective opinions and side-steps the spin of investor relations. At the end of the process the output is a number, a tangible measure of the risk associated with a chosen strategy. This number is then applied in the tried and trusted calculations that are used to work out shareholder value. Now, in place of a subjective guess, we have a research-based and objective answer to the all-important question: 'Does this plan create shareholder value?'

Too often, the answer is no. When risk is allowed for, many business plans create less value than putting the same money in a bank account or index-linked investment. Such plans, of course, actually destroy shareholder value because their return is less than the opportunity cost of the investment. An accurate assessment of value creation would make a huge difference to the valuation of the company. The result of carrying out marketing due diligence is, therefore, of great interest and value to both sides of the capital market.

For the investment community, marketing due diligence allows a much more informed and substantiated investment decision. Portfolio management is made more rational and more transparent. Marketing due diligence provides a standard by which to judge potential investments and a means to see through the vagaries of business plans.

For those seeking to satisfy investors, the value of marketing due diligence lies in two areas. First, it allows a rigorous assessment of the business plan in terms of its potential to create shareholder value. A positive assessment then becomes a substantive piece of evidence in negotiations with investors and other sources of finance. Second, if a strategy is shown to have weaknesses, the process not only pinpoints them but also indicates what corrective action is needed.

For both sides, the growth potential of a company is made more explicit, easier to measure and harder to disguise.

For anyone involved in running a company or investing in one, marketing due diligence has three messages. First, business needs a process that assesses shareholder value creation, and hence the value of a company, in terms of risk rather than the cost of replacing intangible assets. Second, business risk can be dissected, measured and aggregated in a way that is much more accurate than a high-level judgement. Finally, marketing due diligence is a necessary process for both investors and companies.

Eventually, we anticipate that a process of marketing due diligence will become as *de rigueur* for assessing intangible value as financial due diligence is for its tangible counterpart. Until then, early adopters will be able to use it as a source of competitive advantage in the capital market.

Figure 13.2 is a summary of how SVA should be calculated using the marketing due diligence process.

This high-level process for marketing accountability, however, still does not answer the dilemma of finding an approach which is better than the plethora of metrics with which today's marketing directors are bombarded, so Cranfield's Research Club took this issue on board in an attempt to answer the following questions:

* What needs to be measured
* Why it needs to be measured
* How frequently it needs to be measured
* To whom it should be reported
* And the relative importance of each.

Background/Facts

* Risk and return are positively correlated, i.e. as risk increases, investors require a higher return.
* Risk is measured by the volatility in returns, i.e. high risk is the likelihood of either making a very good return or losing all your money. This can be described as the quality of returns.
* All assets are defined as having future value to the organization. Hence assets to be valued include not only tangible assets like plant and machinery, but intangible assets, such as Key Market Segments.
* The present value of future cash flows is the most acceptable method to value assets including key market segments.
* The present value is increased by:
  – increasing the future cash flows
  – making the future cash flows 'happen' earlier
  – reducing the risk in these cash flows, i.e. improving the certainty of these cash flows, and, hence, reducing the required rate of return.

Figure 13.2: Valuing key market segments.

Suggested Approach

- Identify your key market segments. It is helpful if they can be classified on a vertical axis (a kind of thermometer) according to their attractiveness to your company. 'Attractiveness' usually means the potential of each for growth in your profits over a period of between 3 and 5 years. (See the attached matrix)
- Based on your current experience and planning horizon that you are confident with, make a projection of future net free cash in-flows from your segments. It is normal to select a period such as 3 or 5 years.
- These calculations will consist of three parts:
  - revenue forecasts for each year;
  - cost forecasts for each year;
  - net free cash flow for each segment for each year.
- Identify the key factors that are likely to either increase or decrease these future cash flows.
- These factors are likely to be assessed according to the following factors:
  - the riskiness of the product/market segment relative to its position on the ANSOFF matrix;
  - the riskiness of the marketing strategies to achieve the revenue and market share;
  - the riskiness of the forecast profitability (e.g. the cost forecast accuracy).
- Now recalculate the revenues, costs and net free cash flows for each year, having adjusted the figures using the risks (probabilities) from the above.
- Ask your accountant to provide you with the overall SBU cost of capital and capital used in the SBU. This will not consist only of tangible assets. Thus, £1,000,000 capital at a required shareholder rate of return of 10% would give £100,000 as the minimum return necessary.
- Deduct the proportional cost of capital from the free cash flow for each segment for each year.
- An aggregate positive net present value indicates that you are creating shareholder value – i.e. achieving overall returns greater than the weighted average cost of capital, having taken into account the risk associated with future cash flows.

Portfolio analysis – directional policy matrix (DPM)

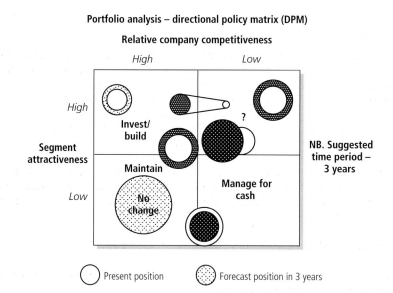

Figure 13.2: Valuing key market segments (*Continued*).

The approach we took to answering these questions was to drive metrics from a company's strategy and the model shown in Figure 13.3 was developed. This clearly shows the link between lead indicators and lag indicators.

This process model is explained in much greater detail in *Marketing Accountability*,[12] so here we will provide a brief summary only.

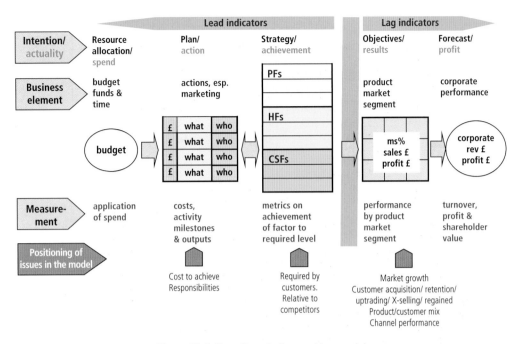

Figure 13.3: Overall marketing metrics model.

Level 2: Linking Activities and Attitudes to Outcomes

Few academics or practitioners have addressed this second level to date, which links marketing actions to outcomes in a more holistic way. We shall describe it briefly here, although it must be stressed that it is central to the issue of marketing metrics and marketing effectiveness.

First, however, let us destroy once and for all one of the great myths of measurement – marketing return on investment. This implies 'return' divided by 'investment' and, for marketing expenditure such as promotional spend, it is an intellectually puerile notion. It's a bit like demanding a financial justification for the wings of an aircraft! Also, as McGovern *et al.*[13] say,

> Measuring marketing performance isn't like measuring factory output – a fact that many non-marketing executives don't grasp. In the controlled environment of a manufacturing plant, it's simple to account for what goes in one end and what comes out the other and then determine productivity.

> But the output of marketing can be measured only long after it has left the plant.

Neither is the budget and all the energy employed in measuring it a proxy for measuring marketing effectiveness, a point we emphasized in great detail in Chapter 1.

In Figure 13.3, reading from right to left, it can be seen that the corporate financial objectives can only be met by selling something to someone – represented in the figure as the Ansoff Matrix (yellow box).

So how do we set about linking our marketing activities to our overall objectives? We will start with the Ansoff Matrix shown in Figure 13.4.

Each of the cells in each box (cells will consist of products for segments) are planning units, in the sense that objectives will be set for each for volume, value and profit for the first year of the strategic plan.

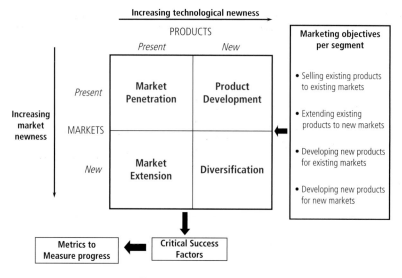

Figure 13.4: Ansoff matrix.

Critical Success Factors	Weighting factor	Your organization	Competitor A	Competitor B	Competitor C
CSF 1					
CSF 2					
CSF 3					
CSF 4					
Total weighted score (score x weight)	100				

• Strategies to improve competitive position/achieve objectives over time (4Ps)
• Metrics (each CSF) to measure performance over time in achieving goals

Figure 13.5: Critical success factors: in each segment, defined by the segment.

For each of the products for segment cells, having set objectives, the task is then to determine strategies for achieving them. The starting point for these strategies is critical success factors (CSFs), the factors critical to success in each product for segment, which will be weighted according to their relative importance to the customers in the segment. See Figure 13.5.

In these terms, a strategy will involve improving one or more CSF scores in one or more product-for-segment cells. It is unlikely, though, that the marketing function will be directly responsible for

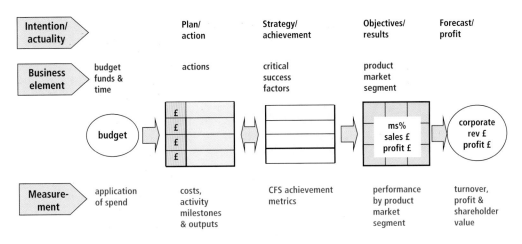

Figure 13.6: Marketing metrics model.

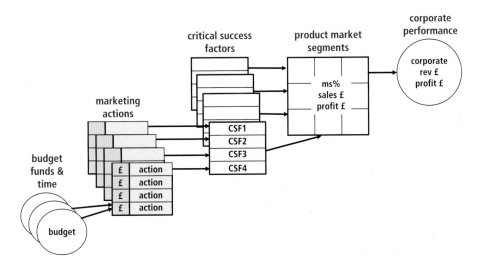

Figure 13.7: Cascading actions from the Ansoff matrix.

what needs to be done to improve a CSF. For example, issues like product efficacy, after-sales service, channel management and sometimes even price and the sales force are often controlled by other functions, so marketing needs to get buy-in from these functions to improve the CSF scores.

It is very rare for this information to be perfectly available to the marketer. While models such as price sensitivity, advertising response or even marketing mix or econometric approaches may help to populate the CSF form, there are generally several other factors where information is less easy to gather. Nevertheless, a CSF analysis indicates where metrics are most needed which can steer the organization towards measuring the right things.

Figure 13.6 shows the actions that have to be taken, by whom and at what cost in order to improve the CSFs.

Figure 13.7 shows how these actions multiply for each box of the Ansoff Matrix.

There are other factors, of course, that influence what is sold and to whom. These may be referred to as 'Hygiene Factors' (HF) – i.e. those standards that must be achieved by any competitor in the

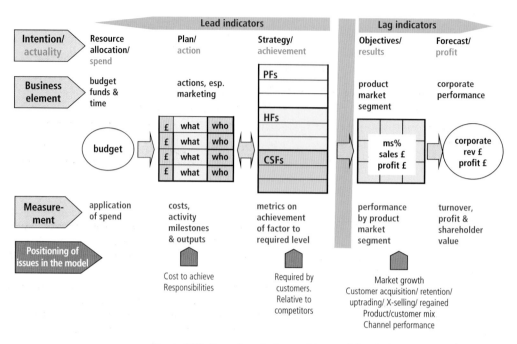

Figure 13.8: Overall marketing metrics model.

market. Other factors may be referred to as 'Productivity Factors' (PF) – i.e. those issues which may impact on an organization's performance unless the required productivity is achieved in its relevant activities.

Thus, it can be seen how the expenditure on marketing and other functional actions to improve CSFs can be linked to marketing objectives and, ultimately, to profitability and it becomes clear exactly what must be measured and why. It also obviates the absurd assumption that a particular marketing action can be linked directly to profitability. It can only be linked to other weighted CSFs which, if improved, should lead to the achievement of volumes, value and, ultimately, profits.

Figure 13.3 is repeated here as Figure 13.8, as it summarizes all of this in one flow chart, which clearly spells out the difference between 'lag indicators' and 'lead indicators'. Lead indicators are the actions taken and the associated expenditure that is incurred. These include, of course, promotional expenditure, which will be addressed later in this chapter. Lag indicators are the *outcomes* of these actions and expenditures and need to be carefully monitored and measured. Thus, retention by segment, loss by segment, new customers, new product sales, channel performance and the like are *outcomes*, but these need to be linked back to the appropriate *inputs*, an issue which is addressed later in this chapter.

There is one other crucial implication to be drawn from this model. Most operating boards on scrutinizing profit and loss accounts typically see only one line for revenue, while costs are covered in considerable detail and it's around costs that most of the discussion takes place. In the view of the authors, there should be at least two sets of figures – one to detail where the sales revenue has come from, as outlined above, another to detail costs. A key task of marketers, rarely carried out, is to link the two documents together. Figure 13.3 goes some way towards this.

We stress, however, that the corporate revenue and profits shown in the right of Figures 13.3, 13.6 and 13.7 are not the same as shareholder value added, which takes account of the risks involved in the strategies, the time value of money and the cost of capital. This brings us to Level 3.

Level 3: Promotional Effectiveness

Level 3 is the fundamental and crucial level of promotional measurement.

> It would be surprising if marketing as a discipline did not have its own quantitative models for the massive expenditure of fmcg companies. Over time, these models have been transferred to business-to-business and service companies, with the result that, today, any organization spending substantial sums of shareholders' money on promotion should be ashamed of themselves if those responsible could not account for the effectiveness of such expenditure.

Nonetheless, with the advent of different promotional methods and channels, combined with an empowered and more sophisticated consumer, the problems of measuring promotional effectiveness have increased considerably. Consequently, this remains one of the major challenges facing the marketing community today.

For example, in fast-moving consumer goods, supermarket buyers expect and demand a threshold level of promotional expenditure in order to be considered for listing. Indeed in most commercial situations, there is a threshold level of expenditure that has to be made in order just to maintain the status quo – i.e. keep up the product or service in consumer consciousness to encourage them to continue buying. The author refers to this as 'maintenance' expenditure.

In most situations, however, not to maintain existing levels of promotion over time results in volume, price and margin pressure, market share losses and a subsequent declining share price.

There is some evidence from the IPA's analysis of almost 900 promotional campaigns, presented in a report.[14] The graph in Figure 13.9 shows that, in one experimental scenario, the promotional budget was cut to zero for a year, then returned to normal, while in another, the budget was cut by 50 per cent. Sales recovery to pre-cut levels took five years and three years respectively, with cumulative negative impacts on net profits of £1.7 million and £0.8 million.

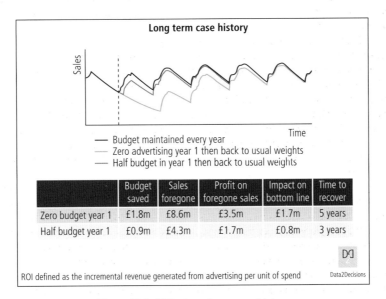

Figure 13.9: ROI – long-term case history.

It is important to make one final point about measuring the effectiveness of promotional expenditure in taking account of 'maintenance' expenditure. This point relates to the tried and tested method of measuring the financial impact of promotional expenditure – net present value.

As can be seen from the following, by not taking account of the expenditure to maintain current sales and by including total promotional expenditure in the NPV calculations, a totally false result ensues. However, by taking account of maintenance expenditure, a much better result emerges.

Present values

Discounting a future stream of revenue into a 'present value' assumes that a rational investor would be indifferent to having a dollar today, or to receiving in some future year a dollar plus the interest that could have been earned by investing that dollar for those years.

Thus it makes sense to assess investments by dividing the money to be received in future years by $(1 + r)$, where r is the discount rate (the annual return from investing that money) and n is the number of years during which the investment could be earning that return.

PV, or NPV or DCF is denoted as:

$$PV = \frac{\sum C_t}{(1+r)^n}$$

where $\sum$ is the sum of the cash flows in years t (1, 2, 3, 4, etc.).

This summation of the cash flows is then divided by $(1 + r)^n$ where r is the discount rate and n is the number of years the investment could be earning that return.

Hence, for a net free cash flow of $2 million a year over four years and a cost of capital of 10 per cent, the net present value is:

$$\frac{2}{(1.1)} + \frac{2}{(1.1)^2} + \frac{2}{(1.1)^3} + \frac{2}{(1.1)^4} = \$6.4 \ million$$

Minus an initial investment of, say, $5 million, the NPV of this investment is $1.4 million.

However, a promotional investment of, say, $7 million, using the above figure, would produce a loss of $0.6 million. If, however, a company needs to spend, say, $6 million just to maintain current sales, the investment is only $1 million and the NPV would then be:

$$-\$1 \ million + \frac{2}{(1.1)} + \frac{2}{(1.1)^2} + \frac{2}{(1.1)^3} + \frac{2}{(1.1)^4} = \$5.4 \ million$$

The research issue facing our community is how to estimate what might be classified as 'maintenance' promotion and what as 'investment' promotion. This is complicated by the different forms of promotion and the many different channels available today, but it is not impossible.

APPLICATION QUESTIONS

Having provided some insights into marketing accountability, it should make it slightly easier to answer the following questions:

* What needs measuring?
* Why?
* When?

- How?
- How frequently?
- By whom?
- Reported to whom?
- At what cost?
- Etc.

It is suggested that the following also need to be explored:

1. What counts as marketing expenditure?
2. What does 'added value' really mean?
   - value chain analysis
   - shareholder value added (SVA)
   - customer value
   - brand value
   - accounting value
   - value-based marketing
3. What are the major 'schools of thought'? What are the strengths and weaknesses of each?
4. Preliminary conclusions from the above with our own recommendations/hypotheses.
5. Some small-scale field work to test findings on world class companies.

The metrics below show a summary of some of the more common metrics that are in use in companies today:

- Brand awareness
- Channel efficiency
- Cost per lead
- Customer satisfaction
- Growth in customers
- Lead conversion rate
- Orders: number average, total value
- Repurchase rate
- Share of customer
- Total marketing cost per order.

Whatever models emerge from the above, it is highly unlikely that any organization will be using them all. There will be examples of excellence along a number of dimensions which will help us to refine and develop the models.

CHAPTER 13 REVIEW

The chapter outlined a number of marketing investment appraisal techniques, starting with a discussion of what counts as marketing expenditure.

It continued by describing three levels of marketing measurement:

1. *Marketing due diligence (MDD)*. MDD assesses the risks associated with the three main components of strategic marketing plans: the market; the marketing strategy; and the profit pool. The forecast net-free cash flows for the planning period are reduced if appropriate by the probability

that they can be achieved. The accountant will then take account of the cost of capital to assess whether these risk-adjusted net-free cash flows will create or destroy shareholder value.

2. *Marketing spend evaluation.* The model provided a framework for linking principal products for market (the Ansoff Matrix) to critical success factors, productivity factors and hygiene factors. These are then translated into actions, with costs and responsibilities associated with each action.

3. *Promotional spend evaluation.* Here, the difference between maintenance and investment expenditure was explained and examples provided which illustrated the very different net present value outcomes based on maintenance and investment expenditure.

Questions raised for the company

Ask the marketing team to attempt to answer the following questions:

1. What needs measuring?
2. Why?
3. When?
4. How?
5. By whom?
6. How frequently?
7. Reported to whom?
8. At what cost?

EXERCISES

For this difficult topic, the authors suggest two main exercises.

The first entails getting a team together and going through the following repeat of Figure 13.2. Just follow the directions and take your time over it.

Background/Facts

- Risk and return are positively correlated, i.e. as risk increases, investors require a higher return.
- Risk is measured by the volatility in returns, i.e. high risk is the likelihood of either making a very good return or losing all your money. This can be described as the quality of returns.
- All assets are defined as having future value to the organization. Hence assets to be valued include not only tangible assets like plant and machinery, but intangible assets, such as Key Market Segments.
- The present value of future cash flows is the most acceptable method to value assets including key market segments.
- The present value is increased by:
  – increasing the future cash flows
  – making the future cash flows 'happen' earlier
  – reducing the risk in these cash flows, i.e. improving the certainty of these cash flows, and, hence, reducing the required rate of return.

Suggested Approach

- Identify your key market segments. It is helpful if they can be classified on a vertical axis (a kind of thermometer) according to their attractiveness to your company. 'Attractiveness' usually means the potential of each for growth in your profits over a period of between 3 and 5 years. (See the attached matrix)
- Based on your current experience and planning horizon that you are confident with, make a projection of future net free cash in-flows from your segments. It is normal to select a period such as 3 or 5 years.
- These calculations will consist of three parts:
  - revenue forecasts for each year;
  - cost forecasts for each year;
  - net free cash flow for each segment for each year.
- Identify the key factors that are likely to either increase or decrease these future cash flows.
- These factors are likely to be assessed according to the following factors:
  - the riskiness of the product/market segment relative to its position on the ANSOFF matrix;
  - the riskiness of the marketing strategies to achieve the revenue and market share;
  - the riskiness of the forecast profitability (e.g. the cost forecast accuracy).
- Now recalculate the revenues, costs and net free cash flows for each year, having adjusted the figures using the risks (probabilities) from the above.
- Ask your accountant to provide you with the overall SBU cost of capital and capital used in the SBU. This will not consist only of tangible assets. Thus, £1,000,000 capital at a required shareholder rate of return of 10% would give £100,000 as the minimum return necessary.
- Deduct the proportional cost of capital from the free cash flow for each segment for each year.
- An aggregate positive net present value indicates that you are creating shareholder value – i.e. achieving overall returns greater than the weighted average cost of capital, having taken into account the risk associated with future cash flows.

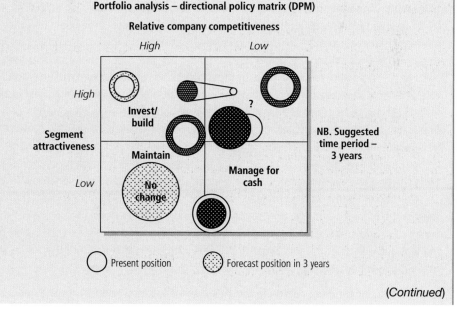

Portfolio analysis – directional policy matrix (DPM)

Relative company competitiveness

NB. Suggested time period – 3 years

○ Present position   ◌ Forecast position in 3 years

(Continued)

The second involves a number of workshops, as follows.

Workshop 1

This workshop has two objectives. The first is to identify those current corporate-level metrics that might be expected to be influenced by marketing activity, and the second is to develop a set of metrics for the key segments in the organization's market.

Corporate metrics

Those likely to be influenced by marketing activity might include measures such as gross sales, market share, gross margin, loyalty (e.g. net promoter score), customer satisfaction, brand equity/image, etc. The reporting might be at total market or by key market segments. These metrics might be included within the customer section of a standard four business perspective balanced scorecard model. The discussion should also lead to possible gaps in the current measures being identified. As the model is designed to help meet medium-term targets, the corporate level goals for the current year and each of the measures over the following three years need to be identified. At this stage in the process, the key objective is simply to list the current metrics and the targets set for them over this three-year period. This list needs to be revisited at the end of the process to see if any other metrics should be recommended at board level, and to ascertain whether the application of the model has identified links between the actions proposed and the corporate measures (the blue arrows in the model).

Market segment metrics

As described earlier, the model process is segment based. As explained in Chapter 4, most markets can be divided into a number of key, differentiated, segments, a process that enables the organization to focus its resources more effectively. However, to apply the model to all segments in one go would be overly complex. Therefore, organizations applying the model are advised to start by focusing on two segments in the initial application in order to gain a detailed, and manageable, understanding of the overall process, and then repeat it for remaining segments over time. In most situations, organizations don't try to cover an entire market. The objective of segmentation is to identify those segments likely to be most attractive when consumer needs/profiles are matched to the capabilities and goals of the organization. This means that once an organization has analysed the market and divided it into segments, using the methodology described in Chapter 4, a few key segments will be the focus of future attention, perhaps at the expense of others that the organization decides are no longer of prime interest. So, the second objective of the first workshop is to focus on two market segments and identify the metrics that are critical first to tracking the segment in the market over time, and second to measuring the performance of the organization against the goals set for each segment. It is recommended that the selected segments for the first application of the model are those likely to be of most value to the future success of the organization. Selected initial segments could be of three types:

- Ones that are currently delivering a high level of value, and forecast to continue to do so
- One that is identified as currently delivering poor returns but is considered as offering high future potential

- One that the organization considers has potential but an appropriate strategy to deliver value has yet to be identified.

Workshop 2

Once the segments have been identified and a full analysis of the two selected segments has been undertaken, the next step is to ensure that the strategies for achieving the goals defined in the marketing plan are appropriate, and that the key metrics necessary to track performance towards achieving these goals have been identified. The focus in the second workshop is on how to use an impact factor analysis to help develop effective strategies for each segment, and identify the metrics necessary to track performance of the strategy.

Workshop 3

Once the strategy for each segment has been confirmed, and the necessary metric set identified using the impact factor analysis framework described earlier in this chapter, the next steps, covered in the third workshop are:

- identify the actions necessary to deliver the strategy. Some of these actions might be under the control of marketing (e.g. develop and implement a specific direct marketing campaign), but others may be within the responsibilities of other departments (e.g. improve customer satisfaction either through changes in the logistics chain or revised call centre goals)
- agree the budgets necessary to fund the agreed actions
- estimate the likely impact of these actions, in financial terms, and identify those actions that are forecast to give a disproportionately high return on investment – that is, those with a high 'gearing'
- identify and agree the appropriate metrics to track the actions, budget funding and impact in achieving goals.

Workshop 4

The objective of the final workshop is to finalize the list of metrics and develop an outline plan for implementing the agreed measurement strategy. For example: Who will be exposed to different metrics? Who will be responsible for collecting the data and producing the metrics? Who is responsible for corrective action if a metric indicates that performance is below target?

The workshop team

The implementation of the model process within the workshops is through a team of appropriate individuals drawn from relevant functions across the organization. Therefore, identifying the key members of this team and whether or not an independent facilitator or appointing one of the team to lead the discussions are vitally important to the success of the process. Having the most appropriate participants is vital to the success of the process. 'Success' is not just in terms of developing a set of metrics, it is also about agreeing an implementation strategy, which in turn relies on the organization having 'bought into' the process and sees

(Continued)

the value to be gained in achieving the organization's goals by implementing the recommendations from the workshops. This is particularly important at board level.

Experience gained in the pilot applications suggests that for the workshops to be effective, this team needs to be kept small – but it is vital that its members are individuals who can play key roles in the marketing, financial and planning processes within the organization. It is also important that the members are sufficiently empowered by senior management to develop a strategy that stands a fair chance of being implemented.

The workshop team should comprise no more than six to eight members. It is suggested that key team members are the:

- market research manager
- corporate planning manager
- corporate finance manager
- customer database manager
- market planning manager
- finance manager (with responsibility for marketing)
- marketing communications/advertising manager
- senior marketing manager (acting as champion of the process)
- customer service (or operations) manager
- brand, product or customer segment manager.

Obviously, good facilitation will be essential to success. What do *we* mean by 'good facilitation'? The main criteria are: all participants are adequately briefed at the outset; the workshops are run objectively; goals are clearly defined; discussions remain focused on the themes and objectives described for each workshop, as described earlier in this chapter; all members are treated as equal participants; evidence provided by members is discussed and approved by the whole team; opinions are challenged; the principles of effective brainstorming are adhered to; the conclusions from each stage are clearly summarized; and actions/tasks are clearly identified at the end of each workshop and allocated to the appropriate members of the team.

In addition to developing a marketing metrics strategy appropriate for the organization, a further key role of the team is to identify responsibility within the strategy for:

- Collecting the data to ensure the metrics can be defined
- Undertaking the measures
- Taking action if the metrics show that performance is not on target.

Team members are also responsible for subsequently reviewing and, if possible, testing the agreed metrics identified in each workshop. This includes identifying whether the data necessary for developing the agreed metrics are currently available, and if not, to assess whether this might be possible in the future.

ACKNOWLEDGEMENTS

The authors are indebted to Professor Robert Shaw of Cass Business School, who worked with them in running Cranfield University School of Management's Value Added Research Club. They are also indebted to Peter Mouncy, who worked with the authors in the School's Marketing Accountability Research Club.

REFERENCES

1. Deloitte (2007) Marketing in 3D. Deloitte and Touche: www.deloitte.co.uk/markting
2. Wilson, H. (1997) PhD Thesis, Cranfield University School of Management.
3. Smith, B.D. (2003) The effectiveness of marketing planning in medical markets. PhD Thesis, Cranfield University School of Management.
4. Davidson, H. (1997) *Offensive Marketing.* Penguin Books.
5. Baker, S. (2000) Defining a marketing paradigm. Unpublished Research Report, Cranfield University School of Management.
6. Porter, M.E. (1980) *Competitive Strategies.* New York, Free Press.
7. Rappaport, A. (1986) *Creating Shareholder Value.* Free Press, Revised Edition 1998.
8. Walters, D. and Halliday, M. (1997) *Marketing and Finance: Working the Interface.* Allen and Unwin.
9. Zeithamel, V.A. (1998) Consumer perceptions of price, quality and value. *Journal of Marketing,* 52, 2–22.
10. Kelly, S. (2005) *The Customer Information Wars.* John Wiley & Sons Ltd.
11. McDonald, M., Smith, B. and Ward, K. (2006) *Marketing Due Diligence – Reconnecting Strategy with Share Price.* Butterworth-Heinemann.
12. McDonald, M. and Mouncey, P. (2009) *Marketing Accountability: How to Measure Marketing Effectiveness.* Kogan Page.
13. McGovern, G., Court, D. and Quelch, J. (2004) *Harvard Business Review,* Nov.
14. Binet, L. and Field, P. (2007) *Marketing in an Age of Accountability.* IPA Datamine.

Chapter

A STEP-BY-STEP MARKETING PLANNING SYSTEM

SUMMARY

PART 1:

■ A summary of the contents of a strategic marketing plan

PART 2:

■ A step-by-step approach to preparing a strategic marketing plan
■ A step-by-step approach to preparing a tactical marketing plan
■ A format for those who have to consolidate many strategic marketing plans
■ Forms and templates are provided to turn the theory into practice

PART 1 MARKETING PLANNING SUMMARY

INTRODUCTION

This chapter contains a step-by-step system for completing:

• a strategic marketing plan
• a tactical marketing plan
• a consolidated multi-SBU strategic marketing plan.

It is, of course, possible to complete the proformas provided without reading this book, but we stress that this is very dangerous and may well lead to a plan without any real substance. Consequently, we refer readers back to the relevant sections of the main text.

THE PURPOSE OF MARKETING PLANNING

The overall purpose of marketing and its principal focus is the identification and creation of competitive advantage.

WHAT IS MARKETING PLANNING?

Marketing planning is simply a logical sequence and a series of activities leading to the setting of marketing objectives and the formulation of plans for achieving them.

Why is Marketing Planning Necessary?

Marketing planning is necessary because of:

- Increasing turbulence, complexity and competitiveness
- The speed of technological change
- The need for *you*
  - to help identify sources of competitive advantage
  - to force an organized approach to developing strategy
  - to ensure consistent relationships
- The need for *superiors*
  - to inform
- The need for *non-marketing functions*
  - to get support
- The need for *subordinates*
  - to get resources
  - to gain commitment
  - to set objectives and strategies.

WHAT SHOULD APPEAR IN THE STRATEGIC MARKETING PLAN?

A summary of what appears in a strategic marketing plan and a list of the principal marketing tools/techniques/structures/frameworks which apply to each step is given in Figure 14.1.

It must be understood from the foregoing that marketing planning never has been just the simple step-by-step approach described so enthusiastically in most prescriptive texts and courses. The moment an organization embarks on the marketing planning path, it can expect to encounter a number of complex organizational, attitudinal, process and cognitive problems, which are likely to block progress (see Chapter 12). By being forewarned about these barriers, there is a good chance of successfully using the step-by-step marketing planning system which follows in Part 2 of this chapter and of doing excellent marketing planning that will bring all the claimed benefits, including a significant impact on the bottom line, through the creation of competitive advantage. If they are ignored, however, marketing planning will remain the Cinderella of business management.

PART 2 A MARKETING PLANNING SYSTEM

INTRODUCTION

This marketing planning system is in three sections. Section A takes you through a step-by-step approach to the preparation of a strategic marketing plan. What actually appears in the strategic marketing plan is given under the heading 'Strategic marketing plan documentation', which appears later in this chapter.

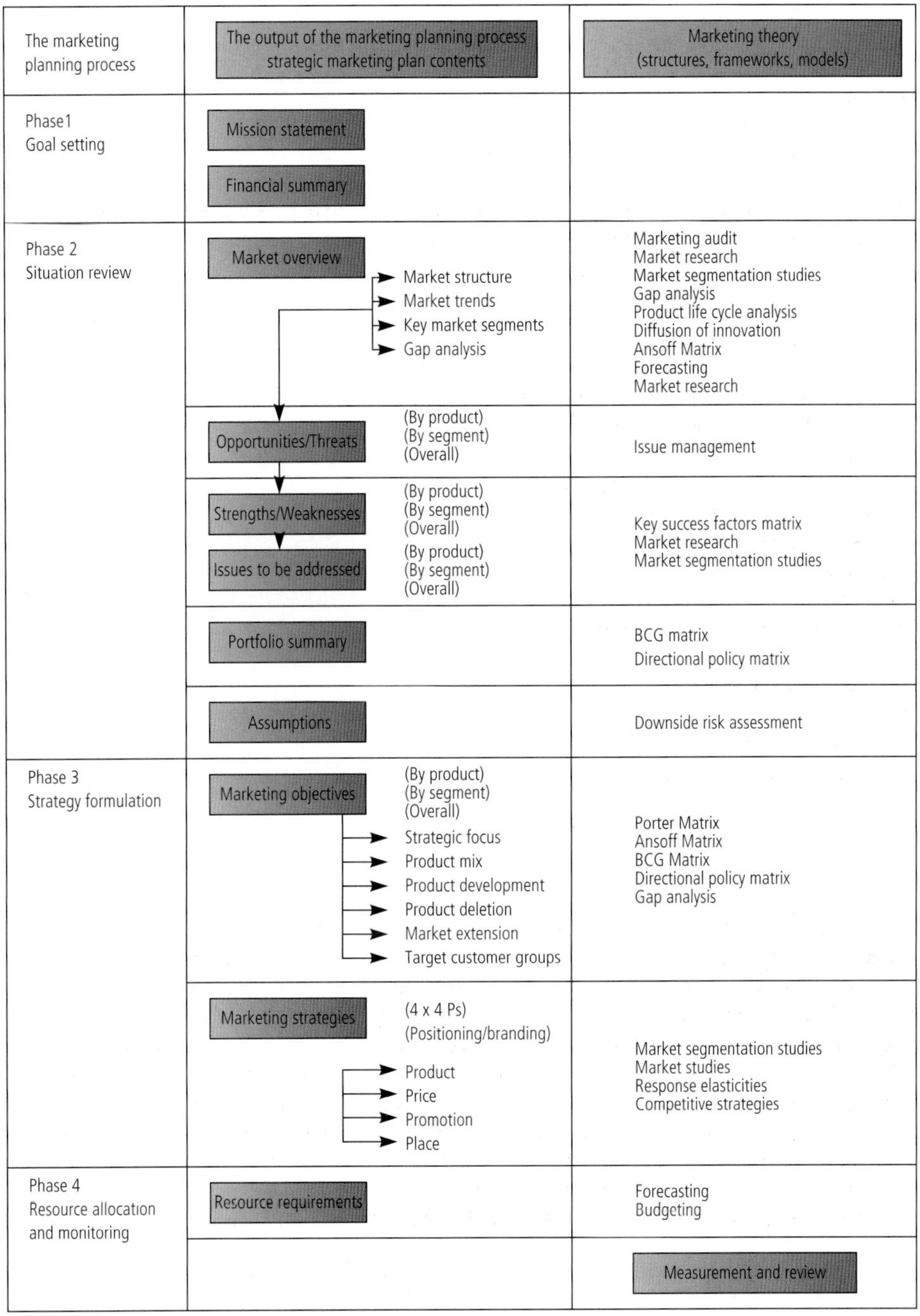

The marketing planning process	The output of the marketing planning process strategic marketing plan contents	Marketing theory (structures, frameworks, models)
Phase 1 Goal setting	Mission statement Financial summary	
Phase 2 Situation review	Market overview → Market structure → Market trends → Key market segments → Gap analysis	Marketing audit Market research Market segmentation studies Gap analysis Product life cycle analysis Diffusion of innovation Ansoff Matrix Forecasting Market research
	Opportunities/Threats (By product) (By segment) (Overall)	Issue management
	Strengths/Weaknesses (By product) (By segment) (Overall) Issues to be addressed (By product) (By segment) (Overall)	Key success factors matrix Market research Market segmentation studies
	Portfolio summary	BCG matrix Directional policy matrix
	Assumptions	Downside risk assessment
Phase 3 Strategy formulation	Marketing objectives (By product) (By segment) (Overall) → Strategic focus → Product mix → Product development → Product deletion → Market extension → Target customer groups	Porter Matrix Ansoff Matrix BCG Matrix Directional policy matrix Gap analysis
	Marketing strategies (4 x 4 Ps) (Positioning/branding) → Product → Price → Promotion → Place	Market segmentation studies Market studies Response elasticities Competitive strategies
Phase 4 Resource allocation and monitoring	Resource requirements	Forecasting Budgeting
		Measurement and review

Figure 14.1: Contents of a strategic marketing plan and associated diagnostic tools.

Section B takes you through the preparation of a one-year marketing plan. What actually appears in a one-year marketing plan is given under the heading 'The one-year marketing plan documentation'. Finally, Section C refers to the need for a headquarters consolidated plan of several SBU strategic marketing plans and provides a suggested format.

SECTION A

Step-by-step approach to the preparation of a strategic marketing plan for a strategic business unit

---

A strategic business unit:

* will have common segments and competitors for most of its products
* will be a competitor in an external market
* will be a discrete and identifiable unit
* will have a manager who has control over most of the areas critical to success

SBUs are not necessarily the same as operating units and the definition can, and should if necessary, be applied all the way down to a particular product or customer or group of products and customers.

The marketing planning process is formally expressed in two marketing plans, the strategic marketing plan and the tactical marketing plan, which should be written in accordance with the format provided in this system. It is designed for strategic business units (SBUs) to be able to take a logical and constructive approach to planning for success.

Two very important introductory points should be made about the marketing plan:

1. The *importance of different sections* – in the final analysis, the strategic marketing plan is a plan for action, and this should be reflected in the finished document. The implementation part of the strategic plan is represented by the subsequent one-year marketing plan.
2. The *length of the analytical section* – to be able to produce an action-focused strategic marketing plan, a considerable amount of background information and statistics needs to be collected, collated and analysed. An analytical framework has been provided in the forms, included in the database section of the 'Strategic marketing plan documentation', which each SBU should complete. However, the commentary given in the strategic marketing plan should provide the main findings of the analysis rather than a mass of raw data. It should compel concentration upon only that which is essential. The analysis section should, therefore, provide only a short background.

BASIS OF THE SYSTEM

Each business unit in the organization will have different levels of opportunity depending on the prevailing business climate. Each business unit, therefore, needs to be managed in a way that is appropriate to its own unique circumstances. At the same time, however, the chief executive officer of the SBU must have every opportunity to see that the ways in which these business units are managed are consistent with the overall strategic aims of the organization.

This system sets out the procedures which, if adhered to, will assist in achieving these aims.

Sections A, B and C set out the three basic marketing planning formats and explain how each of the planning steps should be carried out. They explain simply and clearly what should be presented, and when, in the three-year marketing plan, in the more detailed one-year operational plan and in the headquarters consolidated marketing plan.

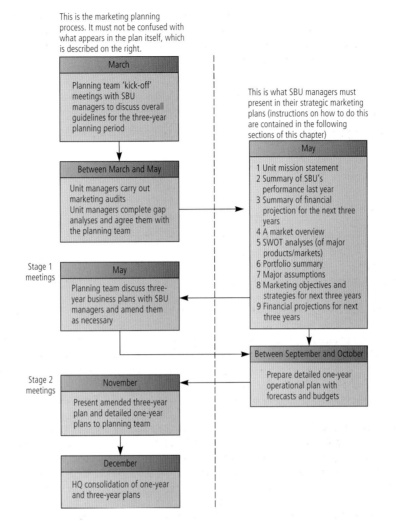

This is the marketing planning process. It must not be confused with what appears in the plan itself, which is described on the right.

March

Planning team 'kick-off' meetings with SBU managers to discuss overall guidelines for the three-year planning period

Between March and May

Unit managers carry out marketing audits
Unit managers complete gap analyses and agree them with the planning team

Stage 1 meetings

May

Planning team discuss three-year business plans with SBU managers and amend them as necessary

Stage 2 meetings

November

Present amended three-year plan and detailed one-year plans to planning team

December

HQ consolidation of one-year and three-year plans

This is what SBU managers must present in their strategic marketing plans (instructions on how to do this are contained in the following sections of this chapter)

May

1 Unit mission statement
2 Summary of SBU's performance last year
3 Summary of financial projection for the next three years
4 A market overview
5 SWOT analyses (of major products/markets)
6 Portfolio summary
7 Major assumptions
8 Marketing objectives and strategies for next three years
9 Financial projections for next three years

Between September and October

Prepare detailed one-year operational plan with forecasts and budgets

Figure 14.2: The marketing planning process and output.

The overall marketing planning format is described in Figure 14.2. (Note that, for the sake of simplicity, it has been assumed that the organization's year runs from January to December.) The following sections explain how each of the steps in the planning process should be completed.

THE MARKETING AUDIT

(For completion between February and May each year)

Note: the marketing audit is not for inclusion in the plan or its presentation

For the purpose of a marketing planning system, it is usual to provide users with an agreed list so that all SBUs using the system use similar nomenclature for products and markets. In this case, we provide an example of such a list in Table 14.1. Please note, more detailed criteria for market segmentation should also be used, where appropriate. For example: geographic location; company organization (centralized or decentralized); purchasing patterns (e.g. price sensitivity, fixed annual budget, local autonomy, etc.); integration level; sales channel preference; support requirements; and so on.

Key industrial market segments	Explanatory notes
Primary metal manufacture	
Transportation equipment manufacture	
General mechanical engineering/fabricated metal products	
Glass and ceramics	Glass, glassware, refractory and ceramic goods
Road passenger and freight transportation (specialists)	
Truck and construction equipment distributors	
Building and construction	
Forestry and timber	
Mining and quarrying	
Food, beverage, tobacco processing and manufacture	
Oil and gas	Extraction and processing of mineral oil and natural gas, excluding off-shore, which is covered in marine
Electricity: power generation and transmission	
Bricks and cement	Manufacture of non-metallic mineral products, excluding glass and ceramics
Textiles	Textile industry and the production of man-made fibres
Leather	
Pulp and paper	
National defence	
Central and local government	Excludes national defence
Aviation	Excludes military aviation and aerospace manufacturing industries
Industrial distributors	Wholesale distribution of industrial machinery, industrial spare parts and tools, etc.
Rubber, chemicals, plastics	Excludes rubber plantations
Cosmetics and pharmaceuticals	

Key marine market segments		
International vessels greater than 4,000 GRT	*Coastal/international vessels less than 4,000 GRT*	*Fishing*
• Oil tankers • LPG and chemical tankers • Containers • General cargo vessels • Bulk carriers • Ferries and roll-on/roll-off vessels • Miscellaneous vessels	• Oil tankers • LPG and chemical tankers • Containers • General cargo vessels • Bulk carriers • Ferries and roll-on/roll-off vessels • Miscellaneous vessels	*Offshore industry* • Drilling rigs • Submersibles • Work units, etc. *Miscellaneous* • Harbour craft • Inland waterways • Dredgers • Military, etc.

Industrial product groups	
Automotive products Engine oils Transmission fluids and gear oils Brake fluids Antifreeze/coolants Greases Miscellaneous 'others'	*Aviation lubricants* Engine oils Transmission oils Hydraulic oils Grease Other
Metalworking products Cutting oils (soluble) Cutting oils (neat) Rolling oils Heat treatment	*Other products* White oils Electrical oils Process oils Textile oils Leather chemicals Laundry and dry cleaning chemicals
Surface treatment products Corrosion preventives (including DWFs) Non-destructive testing materials Industrial cleaning chemicals	Mould releasants Petroleum jelly Defoamers
General industrial lubricants Hydraulic • fire resistant • other	
Gear oils Turbine oils Heat transfer oils Compressor oils (including refrigerator) Grease Circulating oils Other (e.g. wire rope lubricants, Ss)	

Table 14.1: Example of industrial and marine market segments and industrial product groups

All managers carrying out their audit should use internal sales data and the SBU marketing information system to complete their audit. It is helpful at this stage if the various SBU managers can issue to any subordinates involved in the audit a market overview covering major industry and market trends. The audit will inevitably require considerably more data preparation than is required to be reproduced in the marketing plan itself. Therefore, all managers should start a *running reference file* for their area of responsibility during the year, which can also be used as a continual reference source and for verbal presentation of proposals.

It is essential to stress that the audit, which will be based on the running reference file, *is not a marketing plan and under no circumstances should voluminous documents relating to the audit appear in any business plans*.

THE CONTENTS OF A STRATEGIC MARKETING PLAN

The following sections describe what should be presented in strategic marketing plans. These should be completed by the end of May each year.

The actual documentation for the strategic marketing plan is also provided in this section.

STRATEGIC MARKETING PLAN DOCUMENTATION

Form 1 (for details of how to complete this, please refer to Chapter 2, pages 41 to 42)

Form 1

Unit mission statement

This is the first item to appear in the marketing plan.

The purpose of the mission statement is to ensure that the *raison d'être* of the unit is clearly stated. Brief statements should be made which cover the following points:

1. *Role or contribution of the unit*
   e.g. profit generator service department opportunity seeker

2. *Definition of the business*
   e.g. the needs you satisfy or the benefits you provide. Don't be too specific (e.g. 'we sell milking machinery') or too general (e.g. 'we're in the engineering business').

3. *Distinctive competence*
   This should be a brief statement that applies only to your specific unit. A statement that could equally apply to any competitor is unsatisfactory.

4. *Indications for future direction*
   A brief statement of the principal things you would give serious consideration to (e.g. move into a new segment). It helps if these are under the headings

   Things we WILL do
   Things we MIGHT do
   Things we will NEVER do

Form 2

Summary of SBU's performance

This opening section is designed to give a bird's eye view of the SBU's total marketing activities.

In addition to a quantitative summary of performance, as follows, SBU managers should give a summary of reasons for good or bad performance.

Use *constant revenue* in order that comparisons are meaningful.

Make sure you use the same base year values for any projections provided in later sections of this system.

	3 years ago	2 years ago	Last year
Volume/turnover			
Gross profit (%)			
Gross margin (000 ecu)			

Summary of reasons for good or bad performance

Form 3

Summary of financial projections

This is the third item to appear in the marketing plan.

Its purpose is to summarize for the person reading the plan the financial results over the full three-year planning period. It should be presented as a simple diagram along the following lines:

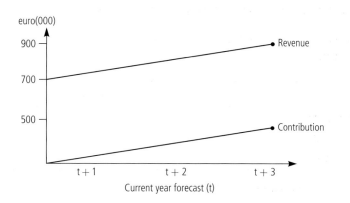

Key (revenue and profit growth)

1. from productivity by product for market for existing products from existing markets
2. from new products in existing markets
3. from existing products in new markets
4. from new products in new markets

This should be accompanied by a brief commentary. For example:

'This three-year business plan shows an increase in revenue from 700,000 euros to 900,000 euros and an increase in contribution from 100,000 euros to 400,000 euros. The purpose of this strategic plan is to show how these increases will be achieved.'

Form 4

Market overview (with 'market map', if appropriate, together with implications for the organization). (Details of how to complete this section are provided in Chapter 4, pages 107 to 108.)

It is also helpful if the principal segments can be described here (see Chapter 4, pages 112 to 117).

- Market definition
- Market map showing vol/rev flows from supplier through to end user, with major decision points highlighted
- Where appropriate, provide a future market map
- Include commentary/conclusions/implications for the company
- At major decision points, include key segments

Form 5

Detailed guidelines for completing SWOT analyses on each market segment are given in in Chapter 6 on pages 247 to 248
Include pictorial representations of the SWOTs, such as bar charts.
Highlight the major conclusions/issues to be addressed

Strategic planning exercise (SWOT analysis)

(Note: This form should be completed for each product/market segment under consideration)

1 SBU description
Here, describe the market for which the SWOT is being done

2 Critical success factors
What are the few key things, from the customer's point of view, that any competitor has to do right to succeed?

1
2
3
4
5

3 Weighting
How important is each of these CSFs? Score out of 100

Total 100

4 Strengths/weaknesses analysis
Score yourself and each of your main competitors out of 10 on each of the CSFs. Then multiply the score by the weight

Comp / CSF	You	Competitor A	Competitor B	Competitor C	Competitor D
1					
2					
3					
4					
5					
Total (score × weight)					

5 Opportunities/threats
What are the few key things outside your direct control that have had, and will continue to have, an impact on your business?

Opportunities

1
2
3
4
5

Threats

6 Key issues that need to be addressed

7 Key assumptions for the planning period

1
2
3
4
5
6
7

8 Key objectives

9 Key strategies

Financial consequences

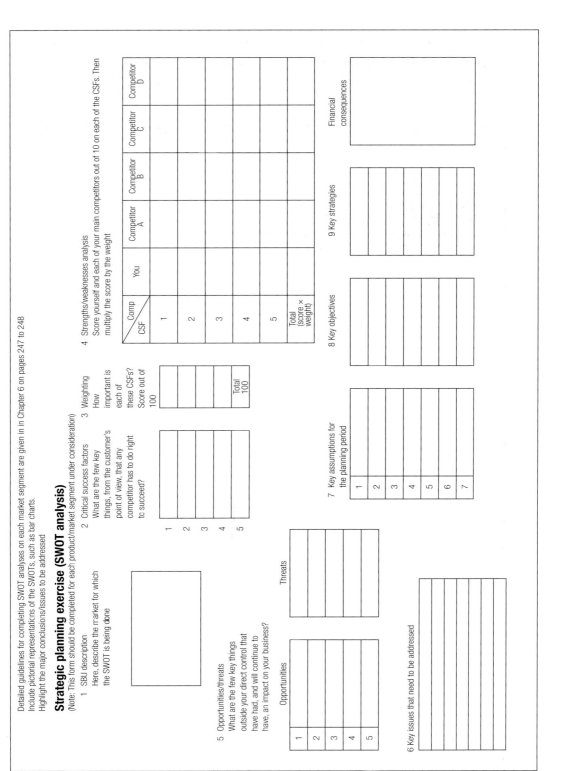

Form 6

Note: **This form should be completed for each product market segment under consideration** (guidelines for completing this section are given in Chapter 6, pages 255 to 258).

Main competitor	Products/markets	Business direction and current objectives and strategies	Strengths	Weaknesses	Competitive position

Form 7

Portfolio summary of the SWOTs

Detailed instructions for how to complete this are given in Chapter 5, pages 177 to 187.

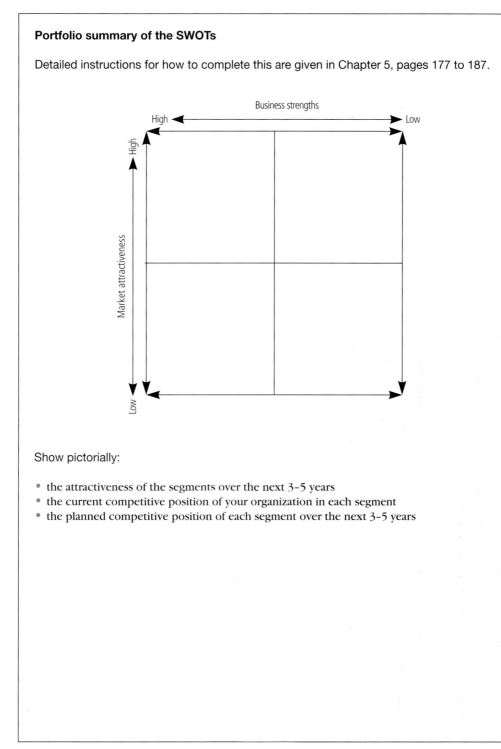

Show pictorially:

- the attractiveness of the segments over the next 3–5 years
- the current competitive position of your organization in each segment
- the planned competitive position of each segment over the next 3–5 years

Form 8

Assumptions

Overall, assumptions should be few in number. If the plan can happen irrespective of the assumption, it should not be included.

Form 9

Marketing objectives and strategies for the next 3–5 years

- Include objectives (volume, value, market share, profit, as appropriate) for the next 3–5 years for each segment as represented by the planned position of each circle on the DPM
  - Include strategies (the 4×Ps) with costs for each objective

Summary of marketing objectives and strategies

Key market segments (list). Summarize remaining market segments as 'OTHER'	Last year (t −1)				Current year (t0)				Planning period (t+3)				Principal marketing strategies (describe)	Cost of marketing strategies
	Vol/ val %	market share %	gross margin		Vol/ val %	market share %	gross margin		Vol/ val %	market share %	gross margin			

Form 10

Summary of marketing objectives and strategies

Principal product groups. Summarize remaining product groups as 'OTHER'	Last year (t −1)				Current year (t0)				Planning period (t+3)				Principal marketing strategies (describe)	Cost of marketing strategies
	Vol/ val %	market share %	gross margin		Vol/ val %	market share %	gross margin		Vol/ val %	market share %	gross margin			

Form 11

Summary (in words and numbers) of main marketing objectives and strategies

Form 12

Consolidated budget for the next 3–5 years

This will be a consolidation of all the revenues, costs and profits for the next 3–5 years and should accord with the financial summary provided earlier

Financial projections for three years

(Financial projections for the full planning period should be provided under all the principal standard revenue and cost headings as specified by your organization)

> **SECTION B**
> The one-year marketing plan

(This should be kept separate from the three-year strategic marketing plan and should not be completed until the planning team has approved the strategic plan in May each year.)

Specific sub-objectives for products and segments, supported by more detailed strategy and action statements, should now be developed. Here, include *budgets* and *forecasts* and a *consolidated budget.* These must reflect the marketing objectives and strategies, and in turn the objectives, strategies and programmes must reflect the agreed budgets and sales forecasts. Their main purpose is to delineate the major steps required in implementation, to assign accountability, to focus on the major decision points, and to specify the required allocation of resources and their timing.

If the procedures in this system are followed, a hierarchy of *objectives* will be built up in such a way that every item of budgeted expenditure can be related directly back to the initial financial objectives (this is known as task-related budgeting). Thus when, say, advertising has been identified as a means of achieving an objective in a particular market (i.e. advertising is a strategy to be used), all advertising expenditure against items appearing in the budget can be related back specifically to a major objective. The essential feature of this is that budgets are set against both the overall marketing objectives and the sub-objectives for each element of the marketing mix. The principal advantage is that this method allows operating units to build up and demonstrate an increasingly clear picture of their markets. This method of budgeting also allows every item of expenditure to be fully accounted for as part of an objective approach. It also ensures that when changes have to be made during the period to which the plan relates, such changes can be made in a way that causes the least damage to the SBU's long-term objectives.

CONTINGENCY PLAN

It is important to include a *contingency plan* in the one-year marketing plan. Notes on this are included below.

GUIDELINES FOR COMPLETION OF A ONE-YEAR MARKETING PLAN

Because of the varying nature of strategic business units, it is impossible to provide a standard format for all SBUs. There is, however, a minimum amount of information which should be provided to accompany the financial documentation between September and October. There is no need to supply market background information, as this should have been completed in the three-year strategic marketing plan.

Suggested Format for a One-Year Marketing Plan

1. (a) *Overall objectives (see Forms 1 and 2 in the one-year marketing plan documentation)* – these should cover the following:

Volume or value	Value last year	Current year estimate	Budget next year
Gross margin	Last year	Current year estimate	Budget next year

Against each there should be a few words of commentary/explanation.

    (b) *Overall strategies* – e.g. new customers, new products, advertising, sales promotion, selling, customer service, pricing. For a list of marketing strategies, see Chapter 6.

2. (a) *Sub-objectives* (see *Form 3 in the one-year marketing plan documentation*) – more detailed objectives should be provided for products, or markets, or segments, or major customers, as appropriate.

    (b) *Strategies* – the means by which sub-objectives will be achieved should be stated.

    (c) *Action/tactics* – the details, timing, responsibility and cost should also be stated.

3. *Summary of marketing activities and costs (see Form 4 in the one-year marketing plan documentation).*

4. *Contingency plan (see Form 5 in the one-year marketing plan documentation)* – it is important to include a contingency plan, which should address the following questions:

    (a) What are the critical assumptions on which the one-year plan is based?

    (b) What would the financial consequences be (i.e. the effect on the operating income) if these assumptions did not come true? For example, if a forecast of revenue is based on the assumption that a decision will be made to buy new plant by a major customer, what would the effect be if that customer did not go ahead?

    (c) How will these assumptions be measured?

    (d) What action will you take to ensure that the adverse financial effects of an unfulfilled assumption are mitigated, so that you end up with the same forecast profit at the end of the year?

To measure the risk, assess the negative or downside, asking what can go wrong with each assumption that would change the outcome. For example, if a market growth rate of 5 per cent is a key assumption, what lower growth rate would have to occur before a substantially different management decision would be taken? For a capital project, this would be the point at which the project would cease to be economical.

5. *Operating result and financial ratios (see Form 6 in the one-year marketing plan documentation).*

Note: This form is provided only as an example, for, clearly, all organizations will have their own formats – this should include:

- Net revenue
- Gross margin
- Adjustments
- Marketing costs
- Administration costs
- Interest
- Operating result
- ROS
  ROI

6. *Key activity planner (see Form 7 in the one-year marketing plan documentation)* – finally, you should summarize the key activities and indicate the start and finish. This should help you considerably with monitoring the progress of your annual plan.

7. *Other* – there may be other information you wish to provide, such as sales call plans.

Form 1

Overall objectives

Product/ market/ segment/ application/ customer	Volume $(t-1)$ $(t0)$ $(t+1)$	Value $(t-1)$ $(t0)$ $(t+1)$	Gross margin $(t-1)$ $(t0)$ $(t+1)$	Commentary

Form 2

Overall strategies

	Strategies	Cost
1		
2		
3		
4		
5		
6		
7		
8		
9		
10		

Comments

Form 3

Sub-objectives, strategies, actions, responsibilities, timing, cost

Product/ market/ segment/ application/ customer	Objective	Strategies	Action	Responsibility	Timing	Cost

Total _____

Form 4

	_t − 1_	_t0_	_t + 1_	_Comments_
Depreciation				
Salaries				
Postage/telephone/ stationery				
Legal and professional				
Training				
Data processing				
Advertising				
Sales promotion				
Travelling and entertainment				
Exhibitions				
Printing				
Meetings/conferences				
Market research				
Internal costs				
Other (specify)				
Total				

Form 5

Suggested downside risk assessment format

Key assumption	Basis of assumption	What event would have to happen to make this strategy unattractive?	Risk of such an event occurring	Impact if event occurs	Trigger point for action	Actual contingency action proposed

Form 6

	(t – 1)	*(t0)*	*(t + 1)*
Net revenue Gross margin Adjustments Marketing costs Administration costs Interest			
Operating result			
Other interest and financial costs			
Result after financial costs			
Net result			

Form 7

Key activity planner

Date/activity	Jan				Feb				March				April				May				June				July				Aug				Sept				Oct				Nov				Dec			
	1	2	3	4	1	2	3	4	1	2	3	4	1	2	3	4	1	2	3	4	1	2	3	4	1	2	3	4	1	2	3	4	1	2	3	4	1	2	3	4	1	2	3	4	1	2	3	4

SECTION C

Headquarters consolidation of several SBU strategic marketing plans

The authors are frequently asked how several SBU strategic marketing plans should be consolidated by senior headquarters marketing personnel. A suggested format for this task is provided below.

DIRECTIONAL STATEMENT

1. *Role/contribution*. This should be a brief statement about the company's role or contribution. Usually, it will specify a minimum growth rate in turnover and profit, but it could also encapsulate roles such as opportunity seeking service and so on.
2. *Definition of the business*. This statement should describe the needs that the company is fulfilling, or the benefits that it is providing for its markets. For example, 'the provision of information to business to facilitate credit decision-making'. Usually, at the corporate level, there will be a number of definitions for its strategic business units. It is important that these statements are not too broad so as to be meaningless (e.g. 'communications' – which could mean satellites or pens) or too narrow (e.g. 'drills' – which could become obsolete if a better method of fulfilling the need for holes is found).
3. *Distinctive competence*. All companies should have a distinctive competence. It does not have to be unique, but it must be substantial and sustainable. Distinctive competence can reside in integrity, specialist skills, technology, distribution strength, international coverage, reputation and so on.
4. *Indications for future direction*. This section should indicate guidelines for future growth. For example, does the company wish to expand internationally, or to acquire new skills and resources? The purpose of this section is to indicate the boundaries of future business activities.

SUMMARY OF THE MAIN FEATURES OF THE PLAN

1. Here, draw a portfolio matrix indicating the current and proposed relative position of each of the strategic business units. Alternatively, this can appear later in the plan.
2. Include a few words summarizing growth in turnover, profit, margins, etc.
3. Draw a graph indicating simply the total long-term plan. At least two lines are necessary – turnover and profit.

FINANCIAL HISTORY (PAST FIVE YEARS)

Include a bar chart showing the relevant financial history, but, at the very least, include turnover and profit for the past five years.

MAJOR CHANGES AND EVENTS SINCE THE PREVIOUS PLAN

Here, describe briefly major changes and events (such as divesting a subsidiary) which occurred during the previous year.

MAJOR ISSUES BY STRATEGIC BUSINESS UNIT

Market Characteristics

Here, it might be considered useful to provide a table listing strategic business units, alongside relevant market characteristics. For example:

	SBU1	SBU2	SBU3	SBU4
Market size				
Market growth				
Competitive intensity				
Relative market share				
etc.				

Competitive Characteristics

Here, it might be considered useful to list the critical success factors by strategic business unit and rate each unit against major competitors. For example:

Critical success factors/competitors	Our company	Competitor 1	Competitor 2
CSF1			
CSF2			
CSF3			
CSF4			
CSF5			

Key Strategic Issues

This is an extremely important section, as its purpose is to list (possibly by strategic business unit), what the key issues are that face the company. In essence, this really consists of stating the major strengths, weaknesses, opportunities and threats and indicating how they will be either built on, or dealt with.

Key strategic issues might consist of technology, regulation, competitive moves, institutional changes, and so on.

Strategic Objectives by Strategic Business Unit and Key Statistics

This is a summary of the objectives of each strategic business unit. It should obviously be tailored to the specific circumstances of each company. However, an example of what might be appropriate follows:

Objectives / Strategic business unit	Market share		Relative market share		Real growth		Key statistics				
							Sales per employee		Contribution per employee		etc.
	Now	+5 years	Now	+5 years	+5 years	p.a.	Now	+5 years	Now	+5 years	
SBU1											
SBU2											
SBU3											
SBU4											
SBU5											

Alternatively, or additionally, put a portfolio matrix indicating the current and proposed relative position of each of the strategic business units.

Financial Goals (next three to five years)

Here, draw a bar chart (or a number of bar charts) showing the relevant financial goals. At the very least, show turnover and profit by strategic business unit for the next five years.

APPENDICES

Include whatever detailed appendices are appropriate. Try not to rob the total plan of focus by including too much detail.

TIMETABLE

The major steps and timing for the annual round of strategic and operational planning is described in the following pages. The planning process is in two separate stages, which are interrelated to provide a review point prior to the detailed quantification of plans. 'Stage One' involves the statement of key and critical objectives for the full three-year planning period, to be reviewed prior to the more detailed quantification of the tactical one-year plan in 'Stage Two' by 30 November, for subsequent consolidation into the company plans.

Planning Team's 'Kick-Off' Meetings (to be completed by 31 March)

At these meetings, the planning team will outline their expectations for the following planning cycle. The purpose of the meetings is to give the planning team the opportunity to explain corporate policy, report progress during the previous planning cycle, and to give a broad indication of what is expected from each SBU during the forthcoming cycle. The planning team's review will include an overall appraisal of performance against plan, as well as a variance analysis. The briefing will give guidance under some of the following headings (as appropriate).

1. *Financial*
    - Gross margins
    - Operating profits
    - Debtors

  - Creditors
  - Cash flow
2. *Manpower and organization*
  - Organization
  - Succession
  - Training
  - Remuneration
3. *Export strategy*
4. *Marketing*
  - Product development
  - Target markets
  - Market segments
  - Volumes
  - Market shares
  - Pricing
  - Promotion
  - Market research
  - Quality control
  - Customer service

This is an essential meeting prior to the mainstream planning activity which SBUs will subsequently engage in. It is the principal means by which it can be ensured that plans do not become stale and repetitive due to over-bureaucratization. Marketing creativity will be the keynote of this meeting.

Top-Down and Bottom-Up Planning

A cornerstone of the marketing planning philosophy is that there should be widespread understanding at all levels in the organization of the key objectives that have to be achieved, and of the key means of achieving them. This way, the actions and decisions that are taken by managers will be disciplined by clear objectives that hang logically together as part of a rational, overall purpose. The only way this will happen is if the planning system is firmly based on market-centred analysis which emanates from the SBUs themselves. Therefore, after the planning team's 'kick-off' meetings, audits should be carried out by all managers in the SBUs down to a level which will be determined by SBU managers. Each manager will also do SWOT analyses and set tentative three-year objectives and strategies, together with proposed budgets for initial consideration by their superior manager. In this way, each superior will be responsible for synthesizing the work of those managers reporting to them.

The major steps in the annual planning cycle are listed below and depicted schematically in Figure 14.3.

Activity	*Deadline*
• Planning team's 'kick-off' meetings with SBU managers to discuss overall guidelines for the three-year planning period	31 March
• Prepare marketing audits, SWOT analyses, proposed marketing objectives, strategies and budgets (cover the full three-year planning horizon)	31 May
• 'Stage One' meetings: presentation to the planning team for review	31 May
• Prepare short-term (one-year) operational plans and budgets, and final three-year SBU managers' consolidated marketing plans	31 October
• 'Stage Two' meetings: presentation to the planning team	30 November
• Final consolidation of the marketing plans	31 December

Figure 14.3: Strategic and operational planning cycle

AND FINALLY, A TEST TO CHECK THE QUALITY OF YOUR STRATEGIC MARKETING PLAN

This test has been developed by Dr Brian Smith, Chief Executive of Pragmedic. It is the result of much in-depth research into the output of the process of strategic marketing planning. It consists of twelve tests. Please answer them honestly, otherwise there is no point in doing them.

  If you get a high score, congratulations. If you get a low score, you have much work to do, but nothing that cannot be accomplished by implementing what has been written in this book.

Test 1

- Our marketing strategy makes it clear what markets or parts of the market we will concentrate our efforts on
    - If your strategy attacks all of your market sector (e.g. retail groceries, superconducting magnets) equally = 0
    - If your strategy is focused by 'descriptor group' (e.g. ABC1s, large firms, SMEs etc.) = 1
    - If your strategy attacks needs-based segments (e.g. efficacy focused customers with high ego needs) = 2
    - If you don't know = −1

Test 2

- Our marketing strategy makes clear what actions fit with the marketing strategy and what does not
    - If your strategy allows complete freedom of action = 0
    - If your strategy allows a high degree of freedom of action = 1
    - If your strategy makes most of your action plan decisions for you = 2
    - If you don't know = −1

Test 3

- Our marketing strategy clearly defines our intended competitive advantage in the target market segments
  - If there is no strong and supported reason why the customer should choose you = 0
  - If there is a reason the customer should buy from you but no strong proof = 1
  - If you can state clearly the reason the customer should buy from you and not the competitor and substantiate that reason = 2
  - If you don't know = −1

Test 4

- Our marketing strategy allows synergy between the activities of the different parts of the organization
  - If the strategy is a compromise of what each department is capable of = 0
  - If the strategy uses the strengths of only one or two departments = 1
  - If the strategy uses the best strengths of all departments = 2
  - If you don't know = −1

Test 5

- Our marketing strategy is significantly different from that of our competitors in our key market segments
  - If you attack the same customers with the same value proposition = 0
  - If you attack the same customers OR use the same value proposition = 1
  - If you attack different customers with a different value proposition = 2
  - If you don't know = −1

Test 6

- Our marketing strategy recognizes and makes full allowance for the needs and wants of our target customers
  - If you only meet the basic functional needs (safety, regulation, efficacy) = 0
  - If you also meet the higher functional needs (efficiency, service, price) = 1
  - If you also meet the emotional and ego needs (brand, confidence) = 2
  - If you don't know = −1

Test 7

- Our marketing strategy recognizes and makes full allowance for the strategies of our competitors
  - If you are ignoring the competitors' strategy = 0
  - If you are allowing for some of the competitors' strategy = 1
  - If you are allowing for all of the competitors' strategy = 2
  - If you don't know = −1

Test 8

- Our marketing strategy recognizes and makes full allowance for changes in the business environment that are beyond our control, such as technological, legislation or social change
  - If your strategy is designed for today's conditions = 0
  - If your strategy allows for one or two changes (e.g. technology or demographics) = 1
  - If your strategy considers the combined effects of all the external factors = 2
  - If you don't know = −1

Test 9

- Our marketing strategy either avoids or compensates for those areas where we are relatively weak compared to the competition
  - If you have taken little or no account of your relative weaknesses = 0
  - If you are trying to fix your relative weaknesses = 1
  - If your strategy means that your relative weaknesses don't matter = 2
  - If you don't know = −1

Test 10

- Our marketing strategy makes full use of those areas where we are relatively strong compared to the competition
  - If you have taken little or no account of your relative strengths = 0
  - If you are trying to use your relative strengths = 1
  - If your strategy means that your relative strengths become more important = 2
  - If you don't know = −1

Test 11

- Our marketing strategy, if successfully implemented, will meet all the objectives of the organization
  - If your strategy, fully and successfully implemented, does not deliver your financial or non-financial objectives = 0
  - If your strategy, fully and successfully implemented, delivers only your financial objectives = 1
  - If your strategy, fully and successfully implemented, delivers your financial and non-financial objectives = 2
  - If you don't know = −1

Test 12

- The resources available to the organization are sufficient to implement the marketing strategy successfully
  - If you have neither the tangible nor the intangible resources to implement the strategy = 0
  - If you have only the tangible or the intangible resources, but not both = 1
  - If you have both the tangible and the intangible resources needed to implement the strategy = 2
  - If you don't know = −1

How Did You Score?

- 18–24 – Well done! (are you sure?)
  - Can I buy some shares?
- 12–17 – You will succeed
  - If your competition is weak!
- 6–11 – You will survive
  - If your competition is weak!
- Less than 6
  - Oh dear, it was nice knowing you.

Index

Compiled by Indexing Specialists (UK) Ltd